ESSAYS IN LEGAL PHILOSOPHY

Essays in Legal Philosophy

EUGENIO BULYGIN

Edited by
CARLOS BERNAL,
CARLA HUERTA,
TECLA MAZZARESE,
JOSÉ JUAN MORESO,
PABLO E. NAVARRO,
and
STANLEY L. PAULSON

OXFORD
UNIVERSITY PRESS

OXFORD
UNIVERSITY PRESS

Great Clarendon Street, Oxford, OX2 6DP,
United Kingdom

Oxford University Press is a department of the University of Oxford.
It furthers the University's objective of excellence in research, scholarship,
and education by publishing worldwide. Oxford is a registered trade mark of
Oxford University Press in the UK and in certain other countries

First Edition published in 2015

Published in the United States of America by Oxford University Press
198 Madison Avenue, New York, NY 10016, United States of America

British Library Cataloguing in Publication Data
Data available

Library of Congress Control Number: 2014958030

ISBN 978–0–19–872936–5

Preface

Legal constructivism, a development traceable to the mid-point of the nineteenth century, wrought a transformation in the academic study of law in Central Europe. The key figures in this development, the *Romanisten* Georg Friedrich Puchta (1798–1846) and Rudolf von Jhering (1818–92), imposed on the law a conceptual scheme reflecting the *Pandektistik* (the method of the *Pandekten* or digests). In private law, it was Jhering who offered the most trenchant statement of legal constructivism. The law appears in two forms, namely, 'as the legal institute, the legal concept, and as legal norms, legal principles'. The latter—'the imperatival, the directly practical form of the command or prohibition'—provides the raw material that is re-formed or *constructed* as the elements of legal institutes or 'juridical bodies' with their own distinct properties. Jhering, with an eye to 'rendering the law scientific' (*die Verwissenschaftlichung des Rechts*), went so far as to set out 'laws of construction'. The key figure in initiating this development in public law was Karl Friedrich von Gerber (1823–91). Although not himself a *Romanist*, Gerber transferred the conceptual scheme of the *Pandektistik* lock, stock, and barrel to public law. As he put it, he was transferring to public law 'something wholly formal, the legal construction'. The impact was profound, with Paul Laband (1838–1918), Georg Jellinek (1851–1911), and Hans Kelsen (1881–1973) following Gerber's lead.

Challenges were posed initially by the later Jhering's 'Damascus *Erlebnis*' and the beginnings of sociological jurisprudence, then by the Free Law Movement, and, in recent years, by the ever greater role accorded to case law. Nevertheless, legal constructivism as an approach to the law is evident in European legal science to the present day. The same is true of the Latin American jurisdictions, which also belong to the civil law tradition. Certainly the number of collaborative efforts between jurists from the civil law countries and their Anglo-American counterparts has grown. Good examples include *Institutionalized Reason. The Jurisprudence of Robert Alexy*, edited by Matthias Klatt, and *The Logic of Legal Requirements. Essays on Defeasibility*, edited by Jordi Ferrer Beltrán and Giovanni Battista Ratti (both books published by the Oxford University Press in 2012). Still, most contemporary work in legal theory and legal philosophy reflects more or less clearly one tradition or the other.

Eugenio Bulygin is the happy exception. On the one hand, he is a distinguished representative of legal science and legal theory as they are known on the European continent—no accident, given the role of the civil law tradition in his home country, Argentina. On the other hand, he has engaged over the past half-century virtually all of the major figures in legal philosophy in the English-speaking countries, including H. L. A. Hart, Joseph Raz, and Ronald Dworkin. In a word, Bulygin is at home in both worlds. He offers a fresh perspective not only in his own highly original contributions to the field but also in hard-headed rejoinders to leading legal philosophers. We, the editors of the present volume, are of one mind in thinking that a selection of Bulygin's papers, including several written together with his close friend and colleague Carlos E. Alchourrón (1931–96), represents a significant contribution to the field.

The papers presented in the volume, selected in close consultation with Professor Bulygin, are set out chronologically, with three exceptions. At the beginning of the volume, the Bulygin–Kelsen–Bulygin exchange counts as the first exception. Certain arguments in Bulygin's paper of 1965, the initial chapter in the volume, were addressed by Hans Kelsen in a paper of 1967, which was not published until 2003. Bulygin's reply to Kelsen, also published in 2003, follows Kelsen's paper in the volume. A second exception to our chronology is Bulygin's paper on 'Permissory Norms and Legal Systems', which appeared initially in 1984 as a joint production by Alchourrón and Bulygin. In 1986, Bulygin published a separate paper on permissory norms, and then, in 2012, he reworked a fair bit of the material from both papers, supplementing it substantially. We felt that 2012 was the correct date for the paper reproduced here, and it appears as the penultimate contribution to the volume. The third exception is the paper 'Von Wright on Deontic Logic and the Philosophy of Law', written by Alchourrón and Bulygin. It was published in 1989, although work on the paper had been completed in 1973. We are treating 1973 as the correct date for our chronology.

An appendix to the volume appears in two parts. Appendix I is a translation of Bulygin's paper, 'Mi visión de la filosofía del derecho', first published in the Spanish journal *DOXA* in 2010. Appendix II is an autobiographical sketch, based on queries put to Professor Bulygin in an effort to fill out his own brief statement on his life.

The development of Argentine legal philosophy is addressed by Manuel Atienza in *La filosofía del derecho argentina actual* (Buenos Aires: Depalma, 1984), as well as in a collection of essays entitled *Argentinische Rechtstheorie und Rechtsphilosophie heute*, edited by Eugenio Bulygin and Ernesto Garzón Valdés (Berlin: Duncker & Humblot, 1987). Regrettably, there is no up-to-date study of the greater field, which would cover the work not only of Alchourrón and Bulygin but also that of Ricardo Caracciolo, Genaro R. Carrió, Ricardo Guibourg, Carlos Santiago Nino, Maria Cristina Redondo, Jorge L. Rodríguez, Hugo Zuleta, and others.

For all of the editors of this selection of Eugenio Bulygin's writings, it has been a pleasure and a privilege to have worked on the project. Many generous people have helped us in countless ways. We should like to thank, in particular, Risto Hilpinen (Miami) for very kindly agreeing to write one of the introductory articles. We also wish to thank Carsten Bäcker (Kiel), Gustavo A. Beade (Buenos Aires), Uta Bindreiter (Lund), Alejandro Daniel Calzetta (Buenos Aires, now Genoa), Pierluigi Chiassoni (Genoa), Luís Duarte d'Almeida (Edinburgh), Pamela F. Finnigan (St Louis, now Denver), Riccardo Guastini (Genoa), Ruben Hartwig (Kiel), Christoph Kallmeyer (Kiel), Carsten Kremer (Frankfurt), Bonnie Litschewski Paulson (Kiel and St Louis), Kathie C. Molyneaux (St Louis), Alejandro Nava Tovar (Mexico City), Giovanni Battista Ratti (Genoa), Alessio Sardo (Genoa), Michael Sherberg

(St Louis), Kevin Toh (San Francisco), María Viana (Sydney), Gesine Voesch (Kiel), and Katharina Will (Kiel, now Berlin). Finally, we thank Natasha Flemming (Oxford), Rashmi Yashwant Bhate, and Barath Rajasekaran (both Chennai, India) for their unflagging, genial support throughout the adventure of publication.

The editors: Carlos Bernal (Sydney),
Carla Huerta (Mexico City),
Tecla Mazzarese (Brescia),
José Juan Moreso (Barcelona),
Pablo E. Navarro (Córdoba in Argentina),
and Stanley L. Paulson (Kiel and St Louis)

Kiel, October 2014

Acknowledgements

Ch. 1	Printed in translation with the permission of the author.
Ch. 2	Printed in translation with the permission of the Hans Kelsen Institute, Vienna.
Ch. 3	Printed in translation with the permission of the author.
Ch. 4	Printed in translation with the permission of the Centro de Estudios Politicos y Constitucionales, Madrid.
Ch. 5	© Carus Publishing Company. Reproduced with permission.
Ch. 6	Printed in translation with the permission of the Centro de Estudios Politicos y Constitucionales, Madrid.
Ch. 7	Printed in translation with the permission of the Centro de Estudios Politicos y Constitucionales, Madrid.
Ch. 8	Printed in translation with the permission of the Centro de Estudios Politicos y Constitucionales, Madrid.
Ch. 9	Reprinted with the permission of Springer Science + Business Media, from *New Studies in Deontic Logic*, ed. Risto Hilpinen, 1981, at 90–124.
Ch. 10	Reprinted with the permission of the author.
Ch. 11	Reprinted with the permission of Springer Science + Business Media, from *Contemporary Philosophy. A New Survey*, vol. 3: *Philosophy of Action*, ed. Guttorm Fløistad, 1982, at 127–52.
Ch. 12	Reprinted with the permission of Springer Science + Business Media, from *Law and Philosophy*, 4 (1985), 145–63.
Ch. 13	Reprinted with the permission of the author.
Ch. 14	Reprinted with the permission of John Wiley & Sons, Ltd, Chichester, UK, from *Ratio Juris*, 3 (1990), 29–45.
Ch. 15	Reprinted with the permission of the author.
Ch. 16	Reprinted with the permission of Springer Science + Business Media, from *Law and Philosophy*, 11 (1992), 201–16.
Ch. 17	Original contribution.
Ch. 18	Reprinted with the permission of the editors of *Analisi e diritto*.
Ch. 19	Reprinted with the permission of the editors of *Analisi e diritto*.
Ch. 20	Printed in translation with the permission of the author.
Ch. 21	Reprinted with the permission of the author.
Ch. 22	Reprinted with the permission of Hart Publishing, Oxford, UK.
Appendix I	Reprinted in translation with the permission of the editor of *DOXA*.

Contents

Table of Abbreviations

Alchourrón and Bulygin, *ALD*	Carlos E. Alchourrón and Eugenio Bulygin, *Análisis lógico y derecho* (Madrid: Centro de Estudios Constitucionales, 1991)
Alchourrón and Bulygin, *NS*	Carlos E. Alchourrón and Eugenio Bulygin, *Normative Systems* (Vienna and New York: Springer, 1971)
ALD	See Alchourrón and Bulygin, *ALD*.
ARSP	*Archiv für Rechts- und Sozialphilosophie*
ARSP Beiheft	*Archiv für Rechts- und Sozialphilosophie*, supplementary volume
Hare, *LM*	Richard M. Hare, *The Language of Morals* (Oxford: Clarendon Press, 1952)
Hart, *CL*, 1st edn., 3rd edn.	H. L. A. Hart, *The Concept of Law* (Oxford: Clarendon Press, 1961). The 2nd edition (Oxford: Clarendon Press, 1992), with a Postscript, ed. Joseph Raz and Penelope Bullock, was published with a new pagination, which was followed in the 3rd edition (Oxford: Clarendon Press, 2012), with an introduction and bibliography of secondary work by Leslie Green.
Hart, *EJP*	H.L.A. Hart, *Essays in Jurisprudence and Philosophy* (Oxford: Clarendon Press, 1983)
Hart, 'Separation'	H.L.A. Hart, 'Positivism and the Separation of Law and Morals', *Harvard Law Review*, 71 (1957/8), 593–629, in Hart, *EJP*, 49–87
HKW 2	*Hans Kelsen Werke*, ed. Matthias Jestaedt, vol. 2 (Tübingen: Mohr Siebeck, 2008), a reprinting of *HP*, with copious notes and index
Jørgensen, 'IL'	Jørgen Jørgensen, 'Imperatives and Logic', *Erkenntnis*, 7 (1937/8), 288–96
Kelsen, *ASL*	Hans Kelsen, *Allgemeine Staatslehre* (Berlin: Springer, 1925) (this text and *GTLS* are different)
Kelsen, *GTLS*	Hans Kelsen, *General Theory of Law and State*, trans. Anders Wedberg (Cambridge, Mass.: Harvard University Press, 1945)
Kelsen, *GTN*	Hans Kelsen, *General Theory of Norms* (first publ. 1979), trans. Michael Hartney (Oxford: Clarendon Press, 1991)
Kelsen, *HP*	Hans Kelsen, *Hauptprobleme der Staatsrechtslehre* (Tübingen: J.C.B. Mohr, 1911), in *HKW 2*
Kelsen, *LT*	Hans Kelsen, *Introduction to the Problems of Legal Theory*, trans. of Kelsen's *RR 1* by Bonnie Litschewski Paulson and Stanley L. Paulson (Oxford: Clarendon Press, 1992)
Kelsen, *PTL*	Hans Kelsen, *The Pure Theory of Law*, trans. of Kelsen's *RR 2* by Max Knight (Berkeley, Cal.: University of California Press, 1967)

Kelsen, *RR 1*	Hans Kelsen, *Reine Rechtslehre*, 1st edn. (Leipzig and Vienna: Franz Deuticke, 1934)
Kelsen, *RR 2*	Hans Kelsen, *Reine Rechtslehre*, 2nd edn. (Vienna: Franz Deuticke, 1960)
N.F.	Neue Folge (new series)
NN	*Normativity and Norms. Critical Perspectives on Kelsenian Themes*, ed. Bonnie Litschewski Paulson and Stanley L. Paulson (Oxford: Clarendon Press, 1998)
ÖZöR	*Österreichische Zeitschrift für öffentliches Recht*
Raz, *AL*	Joseph Raz, *The Authority of Law*, 2nd edn. (Oxford: OUP, 2009) (The 2nd edition contains 'PPT', which is not contained in the 1st edition.)
Raz, 'BN'	Joseph Raz, 'Kelsen's Theory of the Basic Norm', *American Journal of Jurisprudence*, 19 (1974), 94–111, in *AL*, 122–45, in *NN*, 47–67
Raz, *CLS*	Joseph Raz, *The Concept of a Legal System*, 2nd edn. (Oxford: Clarendon Press, 1980)
Raz, 'PPT'	Joseph Raz, 'The Purity of the Pure Theory', *Revue Internationale de Philosophie*, 35 (1981), 441–59, in *AL*, 293–312, in *NN*, 237–52
Raz, *PRN*	Joseph Raz, *Practical Reason and Norms* (London: Hutchinson, 1975), 3rd printing (Oxford: OUP, 1999)
RJBA	*Revista Jurídica de Buenos Aires*
Ross, *DN*	Alf Ross, *Directives and Norms* (London: Routledge & Kegan Paul, 1968)
Ross, 'IL'	Alf Ross, 'Imperatives and Logic', *Theoria*, 7 (1941), 53–71
Ross, *LJ*	Alf Ross, *On Law and Justice*, trans. Margaret Dutton (London: Stevens & Sons, 1958)
Ross, 'Validity'	Alf Ross, 'Validity and the Conflict between Legal Positivism and Natural Law', *RJBA* (1961), 4, 46–93 (bilingual printing), in *NN*, 147–63
von Wright, 'DL'	Georg Henrik von Wright, 'Deontic Logic', *Mind*, 60 (1951), 1–15, in von Wright, *Logical Studies* (London: Routledge & Kegan Paul, 1957), 58–74
von Wright, *NA*	Georg Henrik von Wright, *Norm and Action* (London: Routledge & Kegan Paul, 1963)
WS 1, *WS 2*	*Die Wiener rechtstheoretische Schule*, ed. Hans Klecatsky et al. (Vienna: Europa Verlag, 1968), vol. 1 (1–1201), vol. 2 (1203–2409), a selection of papers by Hans Kelsen, Adolf Julius Merkl, and Alfred Verdross

Introduction I

Normative Systems and Legal Positivism

Eugenio Bulygin and the Philosophy of Law*

Pablo E. Navarro

1. Introduction

Analytical legal philosophy refers to *conceptual* studies about law and legal theory. Unlike other approaches—for example, historical or sociological approaches—analytical studies deal primarily with three types of problem: (i) the characteristic features of judicial reasoning, (ii) the reconstruction of legal concepts, and (iii) the explanation of the systematic nature of law.[1] If such a characterization of analytical legal philosophy is accepted, it is then easy to conclude that Eugenio Bulygin counts as one of the most distinguished writers in contemporary analytical legal philosophy. In a half-century of academic writing he has developed—in part alone, in part together with Carlos E. Alchourrón[2]—a rich conception of law that is well represented in this book. As examples of this analytical persuasion, we present studies on:

- Interpretation and judicial reasoning (chapters 4 and 15)
- Validity and efficacy of law (chapters 1, 3, 10, and 17)
- The concept of a legal system (chapters 7, 13, and 21)
- Legal positivism and legal statements (chapters 6, 8, 11, and 20)
- Completeness and coherence of legal systems (chapters 17 and 22)
- The nature of legal norms (chapters 9, 10, 16, and 21)
- Deontic logic (chapters 5, 9, and 12)

* [*Editors' note*: Pablo Navarro's paper was written as an introduction to the present volume. It has not previously appeared in any form.]

[1] I have drawn this characterization of analytical legal philosophy from Joseph Raz, 'The Institutional Nature of Law', in Raz, *AL*, 103–21, at 103. [*Editors' note*: For this and other abbreviations, see the Table of Abbreviations.]

[2] See e.g. Alchourrón and Bulygin, *NS*, and Alchourrón and Bulygin, *ALD*.

There emerges from this impressive collection a complex variety of strategies for dealing with classical problems of legal philosophy: the normativity of law, the truth-value of legal statements, the systematic nature of law, and so forth. Bulygin's contributions to legal theory have not gone unnoticed, and he has defended his conception in several controversies with some of the most important contemporary authors on legal theory and deontic logic. For example, he exchanged views with Hans Kelsen on validity and effectiveness of law,[3] on deontic logic with Georg Henrik von Wright and Ota Weinberger,[4] on the nature of legal theory with Joseph Raz,[5] on the relation between law and morality with Robert Alexy,[6] and so on.

Analytic philosophy—primarily the writings of von Wright, Alfred Tarski, Rudolf Carnap, Peter Geach, Arthur Norman Prior, and others—has been the major source of Bulygin's philosophical inspiration. He has complemented his analytical conception of legal philosophy with a rather sceptical view regarding ethics and political philosophy. Given this perspective, Bulygin has developed a philosophy of law based on the premiss that law is solely positive law, and he, consequently, has emphatically rejected natural law doctrines.

The study of the logical aspects of legal science (or legal dogmatics) has been one of Bulygin's main interests as a legal philosopher from the beginning. In *Normative Systems*, Alchourrón and Bulygin show that only certain activities taken up by legal dogmatics can be regarded as scientific studies (that is, as a systematization of normative bases). Other activities are to be regarded, by and large, as empirical or normative, for example, interpretation, the elaboration of general principles, the reformulation of normative bases, legal doctrines that purport to solve legal indeterminacies, and so on. Undoubtedly, such activities are an essential part of legal fields of enquiry, but they cannot be justified as scientific knowledge. Along with his interest in the scientific aspects of the study of law, Bulygin's work reflects a firm belief that legal theory must incorporate sophisticated conceptual tools developed in other analytical domains—for example, deontic logic, the philosophy of language, and so on. In particular, he had great confidence in the value of applying

[3] See Bulygin, 'The Concept of Efficacy', in this volume, ch. 1. In 1965, Bulygin criticized Kelsen's reconstruction of efficacy, and that paper, 'Der Begriff der Wirksamkeit', appears here for the first time in an English translation. Kelsen replied in a paper of his own, written presumably in 1967, and it appears here as ch. 2. Bulygin's reply to Kelsen is reproduced here as ch. 3. These two papers also appear here for the first time in English translation. [*Editors' note*: For bibliographical references, see the asterisk footnote at the beginning of each of these three chapters.]

[4] There have been many exchanges between Bulygin and von Wright. See e.g. Alchourrón and Bulygin, 'Von Wright on Deontic Logic and the Philosophy of Law', in this volume, ch. 5. In the volume in which this paper first appeared, von Wright's reply is found at 872–7 [*editors' note*: see the bibliographical reference at the beginning of ch. 5 in this volume]. Alchourrón and Bulygin have debated with Weinberger on the nature of norms and deontic logic. See e.g. Alchourrón and Bulygin, 'The Expressive Conception of Norms', in this volume, ch. 9, and see Ota Weinberger, 'The Expressive Conception of Norms. An Impasse for the Logic of Norms', in *NN*, at 411–32.

[5] See the discussion on the possibility of a theory of law in Joseph Raz, Robert Alexy, and Eugenio Bulygin, *Una discusión sobre la teoría del derecho* (Barcelona: Marcial Pons, 2007).

[6] Robert Alexy and Eugenio Bulygin have debated several times on the relations between law and morality. The most important papers from these exchanges are available in a Spanish edition. See Robert Alexy and Eugenio Bulygin, *La pretensión de corrección del derecho* (Bogotá: Universidad del Externado, 2001).

logical analysis to legal discourse. Thus, in the introduction to *Normative Systems*, Bulygin and Alchourrón write:

The divorce between deontic logic and legal science has had extremely unfortunate effects for the latter. Jurists have not only paid very little attention to the formal investigation of the normative concepts which they use in their disciplines; they have contrived to remain unaffected by the great revival in foundational studies which in the past hundred years has revolutionized the methodology of both formal and empirical sciences... It is true that legal science cannot readily be classified as an empirical science; much less readily can it be classified as a formal one... But this does not preclude the possibility of transferring to the study of law part of the knowledge gained and some of the methods used in the foundational studies of other, more developed, sciences.[7]

It would make little sense to attempt to summarize the contributions to legal philosophy made by Bulygin. It might well be of some interest, however, to offer an analysis of ideas of Bulygin's that mark crucial steps in our understanding of law and legal theory. In the following pages I will focus on four issues: logic and normative systems, validity and applicability of legal norms, the truth-conditions of legal statements, and the problem of legal gaps. Although they bear significant relations to each other, I will make no effort to spell these out. Rather, I will simply provide a sketch of Bulygin's approach to law and legal theory. I briefly indicate the aspects of alternative approaches, thereby providing the context required to follow the development of Bulygin's legal philosophy.

2. Logic and Normative Systems

It is often claimed that a legal norm, to be valid, must be a member of a certain normative system; legal norms cannot exist in isolation from each other. In the middle of the twentieth century, the most important legal philosophers (for example, Kelsen and Hart) developed arguments in which they sought to explain the systematic nature of law. Still, in a paper published in 1968, Hart points out:

there is a good deal of unfinished business for analytical jurisprudence still to tackle, and this unfinished business includes a still much needed clarification of the meaning of the common assertion that laws belong to or constitute a system of laws.[8]

A couple of years after the publication of Hart's paper, analytical studies devoted to the concept of the legal system received a great impetus from two books: *A Theory of a Legal System* by Joseph Raz[9] and *Normative Systems* by Carlos E. Alchourrón and Eugenio Bulygin.[10] Both approaches rejected an old philosophical tradition that had explained the nature of law based on the idea of the *legal norm*. According to the tradition, certain specific features of legal norms (for example, the

[7] Alchourrón and Bulygin, *NS*, 2–3

[8] H. L. A. Hart, 'Kelsen's Doctrine of the Unity of Law', in Hart, *EJP*, 309–42, at 310, in *NN*, 553–81, at 554.

[9] Raz, *CLS*.

[10] Alchourrón and Bulygin, *NS*.

institutionalized nature of legal sanctions) counted as the key to understanding law. Only after clarifying the nature of legal norms did the traditional approach take up the idea of a legal system and its differences from other normative systems—for example, systems of moral norms. Thus, legal systems could only be a set of *legal* norms just as a moral system could only be regarded as a set of *moral* norms.

The traditional view gave rise to many problems. For example, its proponents insisted that every law is a norm. Here Alchourrón and Bulygin assert that '[t]o speak of a normative system (or order) as a set of norms seems to imply that all the sentences composing this system are normative sentences (norms)'.[11] As is clear in the case of legal systems, however, many normative sentences (*laws*) do not establish obligations, prohibitions, or permissions, and it therefore became necessary to regard them as 'legally irrelevant' or as merely fragments of a complete norm. A similar idea had already been stressed by Raz:

> According to Bentham, Austin, Hart, and... according to Kelsen as well, the most important consideration in the individuation of law is to guarantee that every law is a norm. Thereby they make the principles of individuation, and the concept of a law which they define, the only key to the explanation of the normativity of law.[12]

Raz's book on legal systems as well as the book by Alchourrón and Bulygin invert the conceptual priority established by the tradition. According to the new perspective, a norm is a legal norm to the extent that it belongs to a *legal* system. Thus, the main differences between law and other normative systems cannot be found at the level of norms, but rather in the specific characteristics that we predicate of legal systems—for example, coercion and institutionalization. This idea seems to be widely accepted in contemporary legal philosophy. For example, John Gardner writes:

> [W]e should tackle the grandiose question 'What is law', in the first instance, by asking 'What is a legal system?' rather than 'What is a law?' Most of Austin's and Kelsen's major errors were attributable, ultimately, to their failure to see that laws cannot adequately be distinguished from non-laws until legal systems have been distinguished from non-legal systems.[13]

Although both Raz's and Alchourrón and Bulygin's books share a wide philosophical horizon, their studies develop different models of the legal systems that are deeply entrenched in our legal culture. Raz's theory of legal systems might be called 'the institutional model' in so far as it is mainly an approach to the nature of law that attributes a special role to legal authorities in the explanation of the existence, identity, and structure of legal systems. By contrast, Alchourrón and Bulygin's theory—especially as developed in *Normative Systems*—is a 'deductive model' to the extent that it assumes that the content of legal systems includes their logical consequences.

[11] Alchourrón and Bulygin, *NS*, 58. [12] Raz, *CLS*, 169.

[13] John Gardner, 'The Legality of Law', *Associations*, 7 (2003), 89–101, at 91. See also John Gardner, 'The Legality of Law', *Ratio Juris*, 17 (2004), 168–81, at 169 (a longer statement of the same point).

A brief comparison of the two models is useful in coming to an understanding of their respective objectives and main differences.

A. The Institutional Model

In his book, Raz points out that a theory of legal system is actually required by an adequate definition of 'a law', and he underscores the point that 'the existing theories of legal system are unsuccessful in part because they fail to realize this fact'[14]. His criticism is based on two ideas. On the one hand, legal systems contain elements (*laws*) that are not legal *norms* and, on the other, it is not possible to explain the nature of legal norms without taking into account their systematic relations. In this respect, legal systems are more than merely a set of norms, but a theory of legal systems is a part of a general theory of norms.[15] Raz stresses the difference between laws and norms in the following terms:

> 'A law' will be used to designate the basic units into which a legal system is divided, and a 'legal norm' [will designate] a law directing the behaviour of human beings by imposing duties, or conferring powers.[16]

In Raz's approach we find two innovations regarding the traditional theories. On the one hand, the basic units of law are not legal norms but a heterogeneous class of entities: *laws*. This fact does not mean that norms have no special relevance in the analysis of law. On the contrary, Raz explicitly defends the idea that every legal system contains norms and that every other law belonging to a legal system is internally related to norms. Moreover, these laws are relevant only to the extent that they affect the existence and application of legal norms.[17] On the other hand, the structure of a legal system has to be analysed not only in light of the relations between norms but also in the broader context of connections between laws.[18] The *internal* relations between laws determine the *operative* structure of a legal system. For this reason we can say that 'the operative structure of a legal system is based on its punitive and regulative relations',[19] and the proper analysis of this normative structure is necessary for understanding three different things: (i) the organization of legal material from some basic units—that is, the relations between *laws*; (ii) the operative structure of legal systems—that is, the way in which law regulates behaviour; and (iii) the basic characteristics of law—that is, its normative, coactive, and institutionalized nature.

According to Raz, the dynamic nature of law makes it necessary that one distinguish between momentary and non-momentary legal systems. Whereas momentary legal systems are sets of norms that meet the criteria for legal validity at a particular moment, non-momentary legal systems are sequences of momentary legal systems. The normative chain formed by a norm N_1 and another, higher norm N_2, which authorizes the creation of N_1, is a relation of legal validity. This relation determines the *genetic structure* of a non-momentary legal system.[20]

[14] Raz, *CLS*, 2. [15] Raz, *CLS*, 44. [16] Raz, *CLS*, 75. [17] Raz, *CLS*, 169.
[18] Raz, *CLS*, 170. [19] Raz, *CLS*, 185. [20] Raz, *CLS*, 184–5.

B. The Deductive Model

According to Alchourrón and Bulygin, law can be regarded as a *deductive* system. Following Tarski, they say that 'a set of sentences A is a deductive system if and only if all the consequences of A belong to A, that is, if there is no consequence of A which is not included in the set A'.[21] Thus, the structure of legal systems is not completely captured either by genetic relations or by operative relations. Law is more than a set of norms explicitly issued at different times, for it includes implicit norms that can be logically derived from a specific normative basis. The conceptual content of a basis cannot be fully grasped without deriving its logical consequences. Thus, in every legal system we can distinguish between the normative bases of the system and their logical consequences—that is, the logically entailed norms. To make explicit the logical consequences of normative bases is one of the most important tasks performed by legal science in so far as the solution to normative problems is often found not in explicit legal material but rather in the logical consequences of the material.

The incorporation of logical consequences is pertinent to an understanding not only of the *static* aspects of law (that is, how legal norms determine obligations, rights, responsibility), but also of its *dynamic* nature. The analysis of the dynamic nature of legal systems requires that one take into account different sets of norms at different times. In this respect, Bulygin recognizes that one of the great merits of Raz's book was to make explicit the distinction between momentary and non-momentary legal systems, but he goes on to claim that Raz's analysis was not altogether successful.[22] According to Bulygin, the identity of legal systems—as with any other set—is determined by its elements, and no changes in the extension of a certain set can be made without affecting its identity. Thus, the addition of a norm N_1 to a normative set S changes the identity of this set; that is to say, it is replaced by another set S_1. As a result of the act of promulgation, a new set of norms S_1 is added to the sequence of systems belonging to a certain non-momentary legal system. This set S_1 is formed by the explicitly issued norm plus the sum of its logical consequences and the consequences of the other valid norms of the system. The set of norms introduced by the promulgation of a norm is a determined set in the sense that we can decide by the application of logical rules whether or not a norm belongs to this set.

If a given momentary system S were identified with the consequences of a set α of expressly issued norms, it would be tempting to think that the issuance of a new norm or set of norms β would be a new momentary system containing the sum of the logical consequences of α and the logical consequences of β ($Cn(\alpha) + Cn(\beta)$). However, the incorporation of all logical consequences of issued norms offers a more complicated picture, because the new momentary system will be constituted from the consequences of the sum of the logical consequences of α and

[21] Alchourrón and Bulygin, *NS*, 49.

[22] In particular, according to Bulygin, Raz fails to separate different logical relations (e.g. membership and inclusion) in his analysis of both concepts of legal systems. As a result of such confusion, the logical nature of non-momentary legal systems remains unclear.

β ($Cn(\alpha+\beta)$), which may be larger than the set obtained from ($Cn(\alpha) + Cn(\beta)$).[23] For example, let the norm $p \rightarrow Or$ be the unique explicitly issued norm of a certain system S. Certainly, the norm $q \rightarrow Or$ cannot be inferred from this normative basis. If, however, a legal authority validly sets down a definition according to which $q \leftrightarrow p$ is introduced into the new momentary system, one could then obtain $q \rightarrow Or$ as a consequence of the conjunction of $p \rightarrow Or$ and $q \leftrightarrow p$, even if $q \rightarrow Or$ is a consequence neither of $p \rightarrow Or$ alone nor of $q \leftrightarrow p$ alone.

A very important discovery made by Alchourrón and Bulygin is the logical asymmetry between the processes of introducing and derogating legal norms. The traditional view on legal derogation assumed that the elimination of norms, like their issuance, would yield a well-defined set of norms, but in the case of the elimination of logically implicit norms that are entailed by more than one norm that had been explicitly issued, we have no logical criterion that identifies which explicit norm should be dropped in order to eliminate the derived norm.[24] For example, the derogation of a logically entailed norm such as $q \rightarrow Or$ in our previous example requires the elimination of the set $\{p \rightarrow Or, q \leftrightarrow p\}$, and this requirement would be met if one of its members were eliminated. However, we have no criterion for deciding between $p \rightarrow Or$ and $q \leftrightarrow p$. Thus, the remainder of an act of derogation could compel us to choose between open alternatives. In other words, in certain circumstances the elimination of a logical consequence produces a *logical indeterminacy* in the legal system.

It is well to stress the fact that Alchourrón and Bulygin's reconstruction of normative systems takes for granted what is a highly controversial issue: the existence of a genuine logic of norms. Ever since Jørgen Jørgensen formulated his well-known dilemma,[25] scepticism where deontic logic is concerned has been endorsed by prominent philosophers (among others, Hans Kelsen[26]), and its status remains an open question in deontic logic and legal theory.[27] Even if a sound rejoinder to scepticism vis-à-vis deontic logic were at hand, the answer would scarcely be conclusive where another important issue in legal theory is concerned, namely, the legal validity of logically entailed norms. The acceptance of deontic logic gives rise to the question: Are the logical consequences of valid norms also valid in the legal systems? Some philosophers of law (for example, Joseph Raz[28] and Andrei

[23] Alchourrón and Bulygin, 'On the Concept of a Legal Order' (1976), in this volume, ch. 7.

[24] The philosophical significance of this discovery lies in the analogy between derogation and changes in scientific theories. Indeed, this analogy was the starting point in the development of the well-known AGM model—short for 'Alchourrón–Gärdenfors–Makinson model'—which explains rational belief revisions. This model has had a profound impact on different fields such as epistemology and artificial intelligence, and it remains very influential in contemporary logic and analytical philosophy.

[25] See Jørgensen, 'IL'. [26] See Kelsen, *GTN*.

[27] For a general perspective on this issue and its bearing on legal theory, see Pablo E. Navarro and Jorge L. Rodríguez, *Deontic Logic and Legal Systems* (Cambridge: Cambridge University Press, 2014).

[28] See Joseph Raz, 'Authority, Law, and Morality', in Raz, *Ethics in the Public Domain* (Oxford: Oxford University Press, 1994), 210–37, at 210–14.

Marmor[29]) claim that the mere acceptance of deontic logic does not demonstrate the legal validity of logically entailed norms.

The question is still open, and it bears on the main epistemological function of both models with respect to the identification of facts that make legal propositions true. On the one hand, the institutional model helps us to explain the *legal* nature of our rights and duties, as something different from other normative (moral) qualifications, for example, legal positions arising from norms issued by legal authorities. On the other hand, the deductive model shows why it is that some normative propositions can be true even if no explicit decision taken by a legal authority justifies this claim. Thus, the two approaches seem to be in a state of tension, for the first approach emphasizes that some norms are not legally valid because they have not been issued by legal authorities, whereas the second approach emphasizes that some norms are legally valid even though legal authorities have not explicitly issued them.

3. Validity and Applicability of Legal Norms

In legal philosophy, the existence of a legal norm has been traditionally associated with its validity or binding force. Valid legal norms meet certain specific criteria, and in so far as these criteria refer to internal relations between and among norms, they can be considered as the criteria for the identification of a legal system. For this reason, validity is often regarded as membership in a legal system. For example, in the *Pure Theory of Law* Kelsen claims that the existence of a legal norm (its validity) cannot be separated from either its binding force or its membership in a legal system. Bulygin, however, rejects this conclusion:

> In fact, the problem of membership is absolutely independent of any speculation about the binding force of legal norms. It makes perfectly good sense to ask whether a given norm is a member of a certain set of norms, even if we do not regard them as obligatory or binding.[30]

From this conceptual separation of membership and binding force there arises a challenge to a systematic reconstruction of law. If the importance of identifying a legal system does not lie in identifying binding norms, how then is it to be understood?

In offering an answer, Bulygin attempts to take account of both intuitions. He begins with a distinction between several concepts of validity.[31] One concept of validity is normative: to say 'the norm N is valid' is tantamount to prescribing that it ought to be obeyed. Since it is a prescriptive notion it must be set aside in a descriptive discourse about law. 'Validity', however, is also used in two different

[29] See Andrei Marmor, *Positive Law and Objective Values* (Oxford: Oxford University Press, 2001), at 69–70.

[30] Bulygin, 'An Antinomy in Kelsen's Pure Theory of Law' (1990), in this volume, ch. 14, at 247.

[31] See Bulygin, 'Time and Validity' (1982), in this volume, ch. 10, at 171–2.

descriptive senses: membership in a legal system and applicability. Bulygin reserves 'validity' for membership in a momentary legal system, and the idea of binding force is (partially) captured by the concept of *applicability*. The relations between both concepts can be explained as follows:[32] the dynamics of law require that one distinguish between legal systems and legal orders (or non-momentary legal systems). Legal systems are momentary sets of norms whereas legal orders are sequences of legal systems. The identity of a legal system is determined by its elements in the sense that a legal system L_1 is replaced by another system, L_2, each time a new norm is issued (or a valid norm is rescinded) by a competent authority. In this respect, a legal norm exists only as a valid norm, which means that it belongs to a momentary legal system. Its existence can be intermittent, since a legal norm can be issued and rescinded several times.

Applicable norms make a 'practical difference' in that they are not to be ignored in solutions to legal problems. A norm N_j is applicable if and only if another norm N_k, belonging to the legal system, prescribes the application of N_j. Thus, judges have to apply N_j in virtue of the existence of N_k in a particular legal system. Norms such as N_k are the criteria for the applicability of norms in this legal system. Suppose, for example, that a crime C committed at time t_1 is regulated by two different norms (N_1 and N_2) that appear successively. N_1 is valid at the moment of the offence t_1, but at time t_2, N_1 is rescinded and replaced by N_2. According to one of the main criteria for applicability in Argentine criminal law (namely, '*Tempus regit actum*', established in art. 18 of the Constitution), the applicable norm is the norm valid at the moment of the offence.[33] Thus, the applicable norm at the moment of the judgment, t_2, is N_1, not N_2, even if N_1 is no longer part of the legal system.

The set of applicable norms is not necessarily a subset of the valid norms at the moment a particular case is considered or a subset from some other system within this particular legal order. Indeed, the set of applicable norms is normally a selection from various systems of a legal order. Therefore, applicability and systematic validity are logically independent properties. Even if applicable norms are usually a part of the legal system, the validity of a particular norm cannot be regarded as either a necessary or a sufficient condition for its applicability. In order to identify applicable norms, jurists must employ a normative criterion that has to be valid in the legal system. In this way, a systematic reconstruction of law has conceptual priority over the identification of applicable norms.[34]

[32] Other legal philosophers (for example, Joseph Raz, Stephen Munzer, Frederick Schauer) also distinguish between validity and applicability, but they do not recognize in their respective approaches the logical independence of the two properties. See, for example, Raz, 'The Institutional Nature of Law', in Raz, *AL*, 103–21, at 119–21.

[33] Many complexities have been set aside in the situation described, e.g. there could be more than one criterion for applicability. A criterion for applicability can also determine the inapplicability of a certain norm. For example, suppose that a valid norm N is in *vacatio legis*. Even if N is valid in the legal system, neither citizens nor judges are obligated by it until its period of vacancy is completed.

[34] Like validity, the applicability of legal norms is always relative to the existence of a systematic valid norm. Precisely this relativity is responsible for the deep conceptual problems that arise when we analyse the normative basis of a particular legal system. The question 'what is the ground of validity or applicability of these ultimate norms?' is a classical one in legal philosophy, and several answers have

One might well wonder, however, why validity is explained by appeal to membership in a legal system. Would it not be better to claim that a legal norm exists only to the extent that it is applicable? It is worth emphasizing that to identify applicability with existence seems to be misleading rather than illuminating. As Bulygin rightly points out, there is a strong conceptual argument against the view that would render the existence of legal norms a mere function of their applicability:

> the criteria of applicability are to be found in the law, not necessarily in enacted or written law, but in the legal material supplied by the different sources of law. Moreover... they must belong to the system corresponding to the present time (S_p), that is, to the last system of the series of systems pertaining to a legal order. Thus, in order to avoid circularity jurists must be able to identify this system by some independent criterion, which is not one of the criteria of applicability. Therefore, the concept of existence in a system must be independent of the concept of applicability and not a function of it.[35]

4. Normative Propositions and Legal Statements

In *Norm and Action*, the *locus classicus* on agency and deontic logic, Georg Henrik von Wright distinguishes between norms, normative statements, and norm-propositions.[36] Norms are prescriptions, whereas the other notions are descriptive categories. Normative statements indicate the deontic status of certain actions or states of affairs, and their truth-values are conferred by the existence of a norm. The statement that says that a certain norm exists is a 'norm-proposition' (henceforth, 'normative proposition'). According to von Wright, the relation between normative statements and normative propositions can be explained as follows:

> *One* important type of answer to the question: 'Why ought (may, must not) this or that to be done?' is the following: *There is a norm* to the effect that this thing ought (may, must not) be done. The existence of the norm is here the foundation or truth-ground of the normative statement.[37]

Von Wright's distinctions have been influential in legal philosophy. In *Normative Systems*, however, Alchourrón and Bulygin offer a rather different picture. They contend that there is no conceptual difference between legal statements and normative propositions. For the sake of simplicity, I might represent the *descriptive* legal statement 'it is obligatory *p*' as Op. According to Alchourrón and Bulygin, the meaning of 'Op' is the same as the meaning of a normative proposition asserting that the *norm* Op belongs to a certain system (i.e. Op = 'Op' $\in$ Cnα).[38] Thus,

been provided by different theories. It is not necessary to repeat here the merits and shortcomings of these answers.

[35] Bulygin, 'Time and Validity' (n. 31), at 185.

[36] See von Wright, *NA*, at 106.

[37] Georg Henrik von Wright, 'The Foundations of Norms and Normative Statements', in von Wright, *Practical Reason* (Oxford: Basil Blackwell, 1983), 67–82, at 68 (emphasis in original).

[38] See Alchourrón and Bulygin, *NS*, at 121–5.

by contrast with von Wright's tripartite distinction, Alchourrón and Bulygin simply distinguish between norms and normative propositions. In particular, the legal statement 'Op' and the normative proposition ('Op' ∈ Cnα) *mean* the same thing, but the differences between their grammatical forms could give rise to some misunderstandings. Let me invite attention to some of them:

a) There is a well-known ambiguity that infects the language of legal statements because the same statement (that is, the same token) can be used not only to provide information about the deontic status of actions but also to prescribe behaviour, to express acceptance of certain actions, and so forth. In such cases, legal statements do not express propositions, and it is in fact doubtful that they deserve to be called 'statements' at all. From a *descriptive* point of view, however, legal statements are ordinary true or false propositions that inform us about the deontic status of certain actions or states of affairs in the context of a legal system. Thus, normative propositions lack the ambiguity that infects the legal statement. In other words: normative propositions cannot be used to prescribe behaviour.
b) Two legal statements, such as 'Op' and '¬Op', seem to be contradictory. If this were the case, both statements could not be true at the same time, but the corresponding normative propositions ('Op' ∈ Cnα) and ('¬Op' ∈ Cnα) can both be true when the system Cnα is inconsistent. Thus, contrary to what is suggested by the grammatical form of legal statements, no inconsistency stems from a consistent description of an inconsistent normative system.[39]
c) Legal norms correlate cases with deontic solutions, and they are often represented as conditional prescriptions. For this reason, some legal philosophers (including Kelsen) believe that legal statements are also hypothetical or conditional propositions. For example, Kelsen claims that legal propositions (*Rechtssätze*) are hypothetical judgments,[40] and he emphasizes that the proposition describing the validity of a norm of criminal law that prescribes imprisonment for theft 'can only be formulated in this way: If someone steals, he ought to be punished'.[41] Contrary to Kelsen, however, Alchourrón and Bulygin defend the logical form of legal statements in altogether different terms. In so far as legal statements have the same meaning as normative propositions, they are not hypothetical but instead are categorical; that is, they assert that a certain norm belongs to a certain normative system. Moreover, even if many legal statements seem to be *general* propositions (for example, 'all thieves must be punished'), they are indeed *existential* propositions, saying, quite simply, that a certain norm 'exists' in a certain legal system.[42]

39 See Alchourrón and Bulygin, *NS*, at 123.

40 See Kelsen, *RR 2*, § 16 (at 73), *PTL*, at 71.

41 Kelsen, *RR 2*, § 16 (77), *PTL*, 75.

42 See Alchourrón and Bulygin, 'Limits of Logic and Legal Reasoning' (1992), in this volume, ch. 15, at 266.

Legal philosophers often ignore the logical differences between legal statements and normative propositions, overlooking the fact that legal statements have an elliptical form. Rudolf Carnap terms such an elliptical form the *transposed mode of speech*, thereby referring to the notion that 'in order to assert something about an object a, something corresponding is asserted about an object b which stands in a certain relation to the object a'.[43] Thus, according to Bulygin:

> In the expanded form a norm-proposition states that there is (in a given normative system) a norm prohibiting (enjoining, permitting) a certain action. So in order to say that in a given normative system there is a norm (object *a*) prohibiting action *p*, we say that *p* (object *b*) is prohibited.[44]

This reconstruction could be called the 'reductive conception' of legal statements, to wit: in a descriptive discourse about the content of law, these statements can always be replaced by normative propositions. This reductive conception must be clearly differentiated from other well-known reductions, for Alchourrón and Bulygin are not claiming that legal statements are predictive statements or mere descriptions of regularities of behaviour. Rather, they insist that legal statements are only to be understood as, so to speak, elliptically factual propositions. In other words, they are normative propositions that state a fact: A certain norm belongs to a legal system.

It is often claimed, however, that an adequate description of the law requires that one take into account the normativity of legal statements.[45] Many philosophers have developed this idea with the help of a pair of distinctions introduced by Hart in *The Concept of Law*: (i) internal and external statements, and (ii) the internal and external points of view. These distinctions are often interpreted as arguments in favour of the acceptance of legal norms as a requisite for analysing law. According to this claim, law is properly analysed only by a jurist who adopts an internal point of view and describes legal norms by means of internal statements. In other words, no sound description of law can be provided from an external point of view. Bulygin rejects this interpretation. He insists that internal statements are not statements at all (they do not state facts).

To the extent that legal science counts as a *neutral* discourse about law, it is required that one adopt an *external* point of view. It should be pointed out that external statements need not be mere descriptions of external patterns of behaviour. As Hart stresses, although an external observer must understand what it is to adopt the internal point of view, 'this is not to accept the law or share or endorse the insider's internal point of view or in any other way to surrender his descriptive stance'.[46] Therefore, the description of law does not require that one adopt an

[43] Rudolf Carnap, *The Logical Syntax of Language* (London: Kegan Paul, 1955), 80.

[44] Eugenio Bulygin, 'True or False Statements in Normative Discourse', in *In Search of a New Humanism. The Philosophy of Georg Henrik von Wright*, ed. Rosaria Egidi (Dordrecht: Kluwer, 1999), 183–91, at 188.

[45] See e.g. Roger Shiner, *Norm and Nature. The Movements of Legal Thought* (Oxford: Clarendon Press, 1992), at 137.

[46] Hart, *CL*, 3rd edn., 'Postscript', 238–76, at 242.

internal point of view. Indeed, those who use internal statements in recognizing valid rules of the system express their own acceptance of them as guiding rules. Moreover, to grant that a legal theorist must accept the validity (binding force) of a set of norms in order to describe the law is to adopt an ideological position. This point had already been stressed by Alf Ross:

> To me it is astonishing that Hart does not see, or at any rate does not mention, the most obvious use of external language in the mouth of an observer who as such neither accepts nor rejects the rules but solely makes a report about them: The legal writer in so far as his job is to give a true statement of the law actually in force.[47]

Although the distinction between different types of legal statement and legal points of view is necessary for an understanding of the role law plays, legal science might well be limited to registering attitudes toward the acceptance of rules, and this fact does not lend itself to statements expressing any 'normative' character. To summarize: Bulygin and Alchourrón, too, have always stressed that descriptive legal statements lack normativity, and Bulygin has criticized prominent legal philosophers emphatically for ignoring the basic distinction between norms and normative propositions. Indeed, such a distinction would be essential in order to separate description from prescription, information from evaluation, science from politics. Thus, the normativity of both legal statements and legal science is an altogether innocent form of normativity, for these statements convey no 'binding force'; they only refer to the fact that certain norms belong to a certain legal system.

5. Normative Propositions and Legal Positivism

The reconstruction of normative propositions offered by Alchourrón and Bulygin in *Normative Systems* does not take a specific position on the dispute between natural law theories and legal positivism. However, the Argentine professors actually claim that there is a connection between their reductive conception and legal positivism. In their own words:

> [Normative propositions] convey information about the deontic status of certain actions or states of affairs: They say that an action is forbidden, or obligatory, or permitted, and they are true if and only if the referred action has the property of being forbidden, being obligatory, or being permitted. When, however, does an action have the property of being forbidden? This question admits of different answers. Some philosophers believe that being forbidden is an intrinsic (perhaps non-natural) property of the action itself and that its presence can therefore be detected by a close inspection of the action. Other philosophers believe that it is by virtue of God's commands or some eternal principles of natural law that certain actions are forbidden while others are permitted or are obligatory. We are concerned, however, with the positive law and the positivist approach, which is shared by most jurists. The characteristic of this point of view is that an action p is said to be forbidden if and only if there is a norm (of the positive law of the country in question)

[47] Alf Ross, Review: Hart, *The Concept of Law* (Oxford 1961), *Yale Law Journal*, 71 (1961/2), 1185–90, at 1189–90.

that forbids or prohibits that *p*, and not because it is intrinsically bad or disqualified by moral or natural law principles. This amounts to saying that the proposition that *p* is forbidden means the same as the proposition that there is (exists) a legal norm forbidding that *p*.[48]

This connection between normative propositions and legal positivism is somewhat surprising, for other leading figures of legal positivism have endorsed a different position. Three major theses have often been attributed to legal positivism: (i) the reductive semantic thesis (legal statements are not normative; they are factual statements), (ii) the conceptual separation between law and morals (there is no necessary connection between the law as it is and the law as it ought to be), and (iii) the social sources thesis (the identification of the existence and content of law requires no moral argument).[49] The most controversial of these theses is the first in so far as 'simple positivism' is endorsed, for example, by Austin but is rejected by 'sophisticated positivism', for example, by Kelsen, Hart, and Raz.[50] This discrepancy between versions of legal positivism can be perhaps explained in terms of alternative proposals for dealing with the idea that, for example, 'obligation', 'duty', and 'right' are given different meanings in legal and in moral contexts.

Neither version, simple positivism nor sophisticated positivism, is free of difficulties. On the one hand, simple positivism reduces legal statements to mere descriptions of regularities (for example, the probability of sanctions) but, as its critics have remarked, it cannot take account of the fact that law is a social institution with a *normative* aspect. On the other hand, sophisticated positivism claims that legal statements are normative, but this seems to imply that no neutral description of law can be provided and, therefore, that no true *science* of law is possible.

Alchourrón and Bulygin offer an interesting solution to this puzzle. On the one hand, normative propositions are factual propositions but they are not descriptions of regularities of behaviour, and, on the other, norms are only mentioned by normative propositions and, for this reason, normative propositions need not convey any normative force. It would be a mistake, however, to infer from the rejection of the normativity of legal science that legal positivism is conceptually committed to the reductionism favoured by Alchourrón and Bulygin. Other alternatives, developed, for example, by Raz and Hart, are also of interest. It could be said, following Raz, that the relation between legal statements and normative propositions 'is not *identity of meaning* but that between ground and consequence'.[51] This strategy makes clear, as von Wright remarks, that the existence of a norm is the *foundation* of a legal statement. On the contrary, as Alchourrón and Bulygin claim, if legal statements and normative propositions were simply two different formulations of

[48] Alchourrón and Bulygin, 'Von Wright on Deontic Logic and the Philosophy of Law' (1973/89), in this volume, ch. 5, at 103–4.

[49] See Raz, 'PPT', in Raz, *AL*, 293–312, at 295, in *NN*, 237–52, at 239–40.

[50] 'Simple positivism' and 'sophisticated positivism' are terms coined by Roger Shiner. See Shiner, *Norm and Nature* (n. 45, this chapter).

[51] Raz, 'Legal Reasons, Sources and Gaps', in Raz, *AL*, 53–77, at 65 (emphasis added).

the *same proposition*, then it would be rather odd to stress the notion that the existence of a norm is the ground of a legal statement.

Hart also rejects the identity of legal statements and normative propositions. In one of his last published papers, he no longer mentions the distinction between internal and external statements of law. Rather, he offers a new distinction between statements *of the law* and statements *about the law*.[52] His purpose is to vindicate the positivist insight that treats the meaning of legal terms (for example obligation) as different from moral expressions that are similar. According to Hart, theories like the imperative theory developed by Bentham fail to take into account the normativity of legal statements—that is, statements *of the law* or of the legal position of certain individuals. Hart emphasizes that 'to say that a man has a legal obligation to do a certain act is not, though it may imply, a statement *about* the law or a statement that a law exists requiring him to behave in a certain way'.[53] In order to make clear the differences, Hart adds:

> Instead of saying that US male citizens have a legal duty to register for the draft on attaining the age of twenty-one we could with equal truth say that on a given date Congress enacted a law requiring this to be done and providing penalties for non-compliance. This would be a historical proposition *about* the law, not a proposition *of* law, but though both forms of statement are true and are intrinsically connected they do not have the same meaning.[54]

It remains unclear whether this new approach of Hart's—along with recent proposals developed by other legal positivists[55]—is sound, but these alternatives to Alchourrón and Bulygin's reductive proposal show that the relations between legal statements and normative propositions are still deserving of close attention.

6. The Problem of Legal Gaps

The problem of legal gaps has been a major topic in analytical legal philosophy. The problem tends to shroud from view a great variety of issues that must be carefully distinguished. For example, legal philosophers sometimes analyse the problem of legal gaps as a necessary step in elucidating the relations between the application of norms and judicial discretion.[56] On other occasions, jurists disagree about the

[52] H. L. A. Hart, 'Legal Duty and Obligation', in Hart, *Essays on Bentham* (Oxford: Clarendon Press, 1982), 127–61.

[53] Hart, 'Legal Duty and Obligation', in Hart, *Essays on Bentham*, 144.

[54] Hart, 'Legal Duty and Obligation', in Hart, *Essays on Bentham*, 145.

[55] See e.g. Joseph Raz, 'Legal Validity' in Raz, *AL*, 146–59, at 153–7. For criticism, see Luís Duarte d'Almeida, 'Legal Statements and Normative Language', *Law and Philosophy*, 30 (2011), 167–99.

[56] See Fernando Atria, *On Law and Legal Reasoning* (Oxford: Hart Publishing, 2001), at 63–86.

connections between semantic indeterminacies and legal gaps.[57] The most important reason for the persistence of controversies on legal gaps, however, is perhaps the connection of this topic with other, more general philosophical problems, for example, the truth-value of legal propositions. In his well-known paper on the existence of right answers in law, Dworkin has claimed that the *social sources thesis*, a defining tenet of legal positivism, leads to absurd consequences.[58] Dworkin's argument seeks to establish the conceptual relation between a proposition of law 'p' and the statement 'Sp' about the existence of a social source ('Sp' says that there is a legal source that prescribes p). Raz has reconstructed Dworkin's main insight in the following way:[59]

(1)	$p \leftrightarrow Sp$	Sources Thesis
(2)	$-p \leftrightarrow -Sp$	by counterposition in (1)
(3)	$-p \leftrightarrow S\,-p$	by substitution of p with –p in (1)
(4)	$-Sp \leftrightarrow S\,-p$	by transitivity of the biconditional in (2) and (3)

According to Raz, the conclusion establishes that 'whenever *p* has no source…*–p* has a source', but he adds:

> This conclusion is patently false. In England, for example, there is no source for the legal proposition that it is legally prohibited to kill any butterfly, but neither is there a source for its contradiction, i.e. that it is not legally prohibited to kill any butterfly. (1) must be rejected for it entails a false conclusion.[60]

Raz attempts to reject Dworkin's argument, and he shows how vagueness and unresolved conflicts generate legal indeterminacies. Thus, Raz concludes, Dworkin does not offer a refutation of legal positivism but actually ignores it.[61] In his analysis, however, Raz suggests that the principle of bivalence does not apply to legal discourse, that is, in certain circumstances legal statements are neither true nor false. Raz also concludes that there are no genuine legal gaps, for in cases that law does not explicitly regulate there are closure rules that conclusively permit the prima facie non-prohibited action.[62]

By contrast, Bulygin claims that it is not necessary to abandon bivalence in order to refute Dworkin. Bulygin stresses that the impoverished symbolism confers a certain plausibility to Dworkin's argument; in particular, 'p' has no reference to any normative predicate or normative operator. For this reason, it cannot be regarded as a canonical legal statement or normative proposition. If the proposition 'p' were replaced by the corresponding normative proposition, it would then be clear that Dworkin's conclusions can be avoided. Let me then

[57] See Jules Coleman and Brian Leiter, 'Determinacy, Objectivity and Authority', in *Law and Interpretation*, ed. Andrei Marmor (Oxford: Oxford University Press, 1995), 203–78, at 218.

[58] Ronald Dworkin, 'Is There Really No Right Answer in Hard Cases?', in Dworkin, *A Matter of Principle* (Cambridge, Mass.: Harvard University Press, 1985), 119–45.

[59] Raz, 'Legal Reasons, Sources and Gaps' (n. 51, this chapter), 55.

[60] Raz, 'Legal Reasons, Sources and Gaps', 55.

[61] Raz, 'Legal Reasons, Sources and Gaps', 59.

[62] Raz, 'Legal Reasons, Sources and Gaps', 76, and see Joseph Raz, 'Law and Value in Adjudication' in Raz, *AL*, 180–209, at 192.

replace the proposition 'p' with the normative proposition that asserts that the norm 'Op' belongs to a legal system LS. Thus, instead of 'p' we have ('Op' ∈ CnS).[63]

(1)	('Op' ∈ CnS) ↔ (Sp)	Sources Thesis
(2)	–('Op' ∈ CnS) ↔ –(Sp)	by counterposition in (1)
(3)	('O –p' ∈ CnS) ↔ (S –p)	by substitution of p with –p in (1)

Since the expressions (2) –('Op' ∈ CnS) and (3) ('O –p' ∈ CnS) are clearly different, it would be a mistake to conclude (–Sp ↔ S –p). The same result would be obtained if the normative propositions were replaced by their elliptical forms (that is, legal statements).

(1)	(Op) ↔ (Sp)	The Social Thesis
(2)	–(Op) ↔ –(Sp)	by counterposition in (1)
(3)	(O –p) ↔ (S –p)	by substitution of p with –p in (1)

Thus, it is clear that from propositions (2) and (3), the absurd conclusion drawn by Dworkin is no longer derivable. The reason is clear: The absence of a certain norm never serves as a basis for inferring that another (contrary) norm belongs to the legal system.

According to Bulygin, Raz's strategy is not only unnecessary but misleading, too, for Raz grants that analytical rules—such as the principle of prohibition—can serve to close legal systems. Analytical rules say nothing, however, about facts (that is to say, the existence of legal gaps), and, therefore, they are useless for eliminating gaps. Indeed, the lack of a clear distinction between norms and normative propositions is responsible for the mistaken idea that in the absence of any law applying to a dispute, a closure rule is automatically triggered, that is to say, non-prohibited actions are permitted.

Alchourrón and Bulygin provide a complete refutation of this classical point of view, and their analysis is deserving of a brief presentation. According to them, the normative proposition 'the action *p* is obligatory' is true in relation to a system S if and only if the norm 'Op' belongs to the consequences of S (that is, CnS). As already noted, this idea could be represented by the symbols:

$$Op = \text{`}Op\text{'} \in CnS$$

By the same token, the prohibition of an action *p* according to a system S can be represented as follows:

$$Vp = \text{`}Vp\text{'} \in CnS$$

However, the expression 'legally permitted' is ambiguous; it refers to two very different situations—that is, two different facts that render propositions about a legal permission true. On the one hand, one uses the expression 'legally permitted *p*' in

[63] I am following the argument developed in Eugenio Bulygin, *El positivismo jurídico* (Mexico City: Fontamara, 2006), at 84–8.

order to describe the fact that no norm in a system S actually prohibits *p*. On the other hand, 'legally permitted *p*' also means that an explicit or implicit norm in a system S has expressly allowed *p*. To avoid confusion, I will distinguish between 'weak permission' and 'strong permission' respectively.

Weak permission: An action *p* is weakly permitted in the legal system S if and only if *p* is not prohibited in S. In symbols,

$$Pwp = \text{`Vp'} \notin CnS$$

Strong permission: An action *p* is strongly permitted if and only if *p* has been explicitly or implicitly allowed by a legal authority, that is, a norm that permits *p* belongs to the legal system. In symbols, this reads:

$$Psp = \text{`Pp'} \in CnS$$

Therefore, the principle of closure 'non-prohibited actions are permitted' (henceforth PC) admits of two interpretations according to the two meanings of 'permitted'. The weak version says that an action *p* is weakly permitted in S if and only if no norm that prohibits *p* belongs to S, that is:

PC(*w*): 'If *p* is a non-prohibited action in S, then *p* is *weakly* permitted in S'.

In symbols, this interpretation is ('Vp' $\notin$ CnS $\rightarrow$ P*w*p). However, in so far as 'weakly permitted *p*' only means, by definition, that *p* has not been prohibited, such an interpretation expresses a tautology, and its analytical character is evident after the substitution of equivalent expressions:

PC(*w*'): 'If *p* is a non-prohibited action in S, then *p* is a non-prohibited action in S'.

In symbols: ('Vp' $\notin$ CnS $\rightarrow$ 'Vp' $\notin$ CnS). As with any tautology, this analytical truth cannot be denied, but it does not guarantee that a legal system is complete. This true expression only says that non-prohibited actions are not prohibited in a legal system, and this is precisely what happens in cases of legal gaps for the reason that no normative consequences can be derived.

A more promising interpretation of the principle PC arises from the strong meaning of 'permitted'. By definition, 'strongly permitted *p*' means that *p* has been explicitly or implicitly allowed in S, that is, P*s*p = 'Pp' $\in$ CnS. In this respect, PC says:

PC(*s*): 'If *p* is a non-prohibited action in S, then *p* is *strongly* permitted in S'.

In symbols, this strong interpretation is: ('Vp' $\notin$ CnS $\rightarrow$ P*s*p). After substituting the equivalent expression, it follows that ('Vp' $\notin$ CnS $\rightarrow$ 'Pp' $\in$ CnS). Unlike the weak interpretation, the truth of the strong interpretation is not a matter of its meaning but actually depends on the fact that legal authorities have explicitly or implicitly permitted actions that are not prohibited. Suppose, for example, that a legislator decides that fishing is prohibited on Monday and Friday but is permitted the rest of the week. In this case, our authority explicitly allows a certain action, and, according to this norm, it is true that fishing is permitted on these days. There is a contingent legislative fact (that is, the issuance of a norm) that guarantees the truth of our statement about the permission to fish.

Some important differences between the strong and the weak interpretations of PC are captured by the following table:

Weak interpretation	*Strong interpretation*
It is analytically true	Its truth depends on facts
Its negation is necessarily false	Its negation can be true
Its truth is compatible with the existence of legal gaps	Its truth is not compatible with the existence of legal gaps
No normative contradiction stems from the prohibition of a weakly permitted action	The prohibition of a strongly permitted action yields a normative contradiction

Finally, two special cases ought to be mentioned. On the one hand, a legal authority could take a decision in advance on permitting all non-prohibited actions. For example, the legislator could issue a *norm* of closure according to which actions that have not been prohibited are permitted. This norm closes the system, that is, it eliminates normative gaps, but such a norm is contingent and, like any other fact, its existence cannot be proven by logic. The existence of a norm of closure in a legal system sheds light on the truth conditions of the strong version of PC. This principle says that non-prohibited actions are strongly permitted in a certain legal system S. If a norm of closure actually belongs to the system S, then it is also true that there are no normative gaps in this system.

On the other hand, questions can arise about the conceptual relations between strong and weak permissions in relation to the coherence and completeness of legal systems. Three possibilities are worth mentioning. First, in an inconsistent system S, a certain action *p* could be strongly permitted, but from this fact it does not follow that *p* is also weakly permitted in S. Therefore, in a logic of propositions about norms, the formula ($\mathrm{P}sp \rightarrow \mathrm{P}wp$) must be rejected. Second, the formula ($\mathrm{P}wp \rightarrow \mathrm{P}sp$) is not valid in a logic of propositions about norms, for its antecedent is true and its consequence is false in cases of legal gaps. Third, both concepts of permission will overlap only if the normative system is a complete and consistent one. That is, the formula ($\mathrm{P}sp \leftrightarrow \mathrm{P}wp$) is true only if it refers to a complete and consistent normative system.

7. Conclusions

Philosophical problems do not lend themselves to definitive solutions, and it is sometimes claimed that no progress whatever can be achieved in philosophy.[64] Legal philosophy faces a further difficulty: it deals with normative and social

[64] Georg Henrik von Wright, 'Of Human Freedom', in von Wright, *In the Shadow of Descartes. Essays in the Philosophy of Mind* (Dordrecht: Kluwer, 1998), 1–44, at 1.

institutions. Both aspects—the factual and the normative—are necessary to an understanding of the role played by law in our communities, but at the same time they seem to stand in an irreconcilable tension.[65] Finally, legal positivism—as a specific analytical doctrine in philosophy—often faces the charge of futility.[66] What might then be expected from the legal philosophy developed by analytical legal positivists—for example, by Eugenio Bulygin? To a certain extent, it can be said that Bulygin's philosophy reflects an empiricist and naturalistic epistemology along with a denial of moral objectivity. What understanding of legal practice and legal theory can be gained from such a conception? Sometimes even the most distinguished among the analytical legal positivists express scepticism about this philosophical background. For example, Joseph Raz, in a paper published some years ago, contended that Hart's effort to apply certain tools developed by philosophers of language proved to be futile.

> Very little seems to have been gained in all of Hart's forays into philosophy of language. The problems with the explanation of responsibility, legal agents such as corporations, the nature of rights and duties, the relations between law and morality—none of them was solved nor their solution significantly advanced by the ideas borrowed from philosophy of language. Moreover, the reason for that was not that Hart borrowed bad ideas from the philosophy of language, nor that he did not understand properly the ideas he borrowed. Essentially the fault was in the philosophical analysis of the problems which speech-act theory and other ideas from the philosophy of language were meant to solve. Hart's failure on all the points I mentioned resulted from his adherence to naturalism and to empiricist epistemology, and his rejection of evaluative objectivity.[67]

Raz's words do not seem to be addressed to analytical philosophy generally, but only to certain doctrines. In so far as Bulygin endorses the general approach attributed to Hart, it could be said that his legal philosophy, too, is built on a fragile philosophical base. However, Raz's disappointment over such a philosophical foundation need not be endorsed. He provides no detailed argument that would bring to light the limits and shortcomings of the philosophical doctrines mentioned above. In particular, his pessimistic diagnosis of the utility of certain philosophical conceptions might well be regarded as an exaggeration that philosophers like Bulygin would be anxious to reject.

On the contrary, as I have attempted to show, Bulygin—and Alchourrón, too—has made substantial contributions to legal philosophy that cannot easily be separated from the influence of the analytic philosophical doctrines repudiated by Raz. As examples, one might mention the analysis of derogation and the logical indeterminacy of legal systems, the distinction between a logic of norms and a logic

[65] Jeffrey Goldsworthy, 'The Self Destruction of Legal Positivism', *Oxford Journal of Legal Studies*, 10 (1990), 449–86; Pablo E. Navarro, 'On the Self Destruction of Legal Positivism', in *The Legal Ought*, ed. Pierluigi Chiassoni (Turin: Giapichelli, 2001), 83–101.

[66] David Dyzenhaus, 'The Legitimacy of Law: A Response to Critics', *Ratio Iuris*, 7 (1994), 80–94, at 81.

[67] Joseph Raz, 'Two Views of the Nature of the Theory of Law: A Partial Comparison', in Raz, *Between Authority and Interpretation* (Oxford: Oxford University Press, 2009), 47–87, at 52.

of normative propositions, the characterization of legal systems as deductive, the propositional nature of legal science, and so forth. All of these are ideas developed with the tools provided by contemporary logic and the philosophy of language. Their importance is clear not only from their pertinence for understanding law, but also from the fact that they now represent a widely accepted starting point for many conceptual enquiries into logic, epistemology, and the philosophy of law. In this respect, although no definitive conceptual answers could be extracted from Bulygin's contributions to legal philosophy and deontic logic, it is abundantly clear that they are not futile and cannot be ignored.

Finally, although I have mainly focused on Bulygin's legal philosophy, it is well to mention, in concluding this introduction to the present volume, that his contribution cannot be entirely separated from the work he has done together with Carlos Alchourrón. As von Wright writes:

> The achievement and lifelong companionship of Carlos Alchourrón and Eugenio Bulygin are a morally elevating example of how intellectual and temperamental differences between two richly gifted individuals can fuse in a philosophical friendship and result in a fuller synthesis than their endowments, developed in isolation, would perhaps have allowed.[68]

[68] Georg Henrik von Wright, 'Epilogue', in *Normative Systems in Legal and Moral Theory. Festschrift for Carlos E. Alchourrón and Eugenio Bulygin*, ed. Ernesto Garzón Valdés, et al. (Berlin: Duncker & Humblot, 1997), 509–12, at 512.

Introduction II

Aspects of Eugenio Bulygin's Norm Theory*

Risto Hilpinen

1.

In this introductory essay I discuss some of the foundational problems and topics examined by Eugenio Bulygin in his various writings on the theory of norms and deontic logic over the past five decades.[1]

(1) One of the long-standing problems in the theory of normative discourse is the question about the possibility of logical relations among norms and directives. Can there be logical relations among norms? Some authors have maintained that, strictly speaking, a logic of norms is not possible because norms are not the kinds of entity that can stand in logical relations to each other. At best there can be a logic of *norm statements* (normative statements), statements about norms—that is, true or false statements about the existence of norms or the membership of norms in norm systems. Thus, some authors have characterized norms and directives as 'alogical', in contrast to 'logical' statements.[2] In spite of this scepticism about the logic of norms (or normative logic), other authors have developed logical systems for normative discourse, systems of formal deontic logic, and applied them to the study of norm systems.

The possibility of logical relations among norms presumably depends on the ontological character of norms. If norms are understood as complex social entities constituted by intentions, beliefs, and social practices, which begin and cease to exist at certain times in certain environments, it seems hardly plausible to ascribe logical properties to them. However, in so far as norms have intentional content, such norm contents seem capable to standing in logical relations to each other.

(2) The question about the possibility of a logic of norms (deontic logic) is closely related to the question of whether the concepts of truth and deductive

* [*Editors' note*: Risto Hilpinen's paper was written as an introduction to the present volume. It has not previously appeared in any form.]

[1] I wish to thank Professor Eugenio Bulygin and Ms Anneli Hilpinen for comments on an earlier draft of this paper.

[2] See Ross, *LJ*, at 9 n. 4; Kelsen, *GTN*, at chs. 29 and 57. [*Editors' note*: For these and other abbreviations, see the Table of Abbreviations.]

validity are applicable to norms and normative discourse. According to the standard conception of logical consequence, a conclusion follows logically from certain premisses if and only if the conclusion cannot be false if the premisses are true. Thus, it seems essential for logical reasoning that the premisses and the conclusion can be regarded as true or false.[3] The concepts of truth and falsity seem, however, inapplicable to norms and normative discourse, and it therefore seems to follow that norms cannot be justified by logical reasoning. This conclusion is at odds with our discursive practice. We often discuss norms in ways that seem to presuppose the existence of logical relations among them; for example, two norms are said to be mutually inconsistent or one norm is said to follow from another norm.

This problem was discussed in the late 1930s and early 1940s by Jørgen Jørgensen and other philosophers in terms of the question about the possibility of a logic of imperatives, understood as imperative speech acts, as commands.[4] According to a common philosophical view, norms (especially mandatory norms) can be regarded as commands or as analogous to commands.[5] For example, Karl Olivecrona has characterized rules of law as 'independent imperatives', as 'nobody's commands' in the sense that they function independently of any individual person.[6] Thus, the question about the possibility of a logic of imperatives is essentially the same as the question about the possibility of norms. Alf Ross has called this problem 'Jørgensen's dilemma'.[7] David Makinson has called it 'a fundamental problem of deontic logic'; he observes that 'there is a singular tension between the philosophy of norms and the formal work of deontic logicians', because 'the usual presentations of deontic logic... treat norms as if they could bear truth-values', but 'it makes no sense to describe norms as true or false'.[8]

(3) Another problem about norms and norm systems concerns permissory norms. When scholastic philosophers began to study the logic of deontic concepts in the fourteenth century, they took the concepts of obligation, prohibition, and permission to be related to each other in the same way as the concepts of necessity, possibility, and impossibility, and the concept of permission (permissibility) was defined simply as the absence of prohibition (normative 'possibility').[9] In the seventeenth century, Gottfried Wilhelm Leibniz called the deontic categories of the obligatory (*debitum*), the permitted (*licitum*), and the prohibited (*illicitum*) 'modalities of law' (*iuris modalia*), and observed that the basic principles of modal

[3] This is essentially Hans Kelsen's reason for claiming that norms cannot be subject to the principles of 'traditional logic', see Kelsen, *GTN*, at ch. 57. For example, a conflict of norms is, according to Kelsen, not a logical contradiction, 'or anything similar to a logical contradiction', *GTN*, ch. 29.

[4] Jørgensen, 'IL'; Jørgen Jørgensen 'Imperativer og Logik', *Theoria*, 4 (1938), 183–90.

[5] See Alchourrón and Bulygin, 'The Expressive Conception of Norms' (1981), in this volume, ch. 9.

[6] Karl Olivecrona, *Law as Fact* (Copenhagen: Munksgaard, 1939), 43; Olivecrona, *Law as Fact*, 2nd edn. (London: Stevens & Sons, 1971), 130–3.

[7] Ross, 'IL'.

[8] David Makinson, 'On a Fundamental Problem of Deontic Logic', in *Norms, Logic, and Information Systems: New Studies in Deontic Logic and Computer Science*. ed. Paul McNamara and Henry Prakken (Amsterdam: IOS Press, 1999), 29–53.

[9] See Simo Knuuttila, 'The Emergence of Deontic Logic in the Fourteenth Century', in *New Studies in Deontic Logic*, ed. Risto Hilpinen (Dordrecht: D. Reidel, 1981), 225–48, and Simo Knuuttila, *Modalities in Medieval Philosophy* (London and New York: Routledge, 1993).

logic hold for these legal modalities.[10] Consequently the dictum 'what is not prohibited is permitted' becomes a tautology, namely, 'what is not prohibited is not prohibited'. If this dictum is thought to be a more substantive deontic principle, we have to make a distinction between the locutions 'according to the norm system S, an action A is permitted', and 'it is not the case that A is prohibited according to S', and assume that the latter does not necessarily imply the former.

Many philosophers of law have denied the existence of permissory norms, but other authors, including some deontic logicians, have recognized a special category of permissory norms. The latter view has sometimes been explained by means of a distinction between two kinds of permission, 'weak' permissibility, the absence of a prohibition, and 'strong' or 'positive' permission.

(4) A fourth problem is the question about the possibility of legal gaps, the problem of the silence of law. There is a gap in the law if it does not give a complete answer to some legal question; with respect to such questions, the law can be said to be silent. Genuine legal gaps must be distinguished from the indeterminacy resulting from the vagueness of legal concepts and from legal overdetermination—that is, the possibility that the law may give conflicting answers to a given question and thus may be said to speak in many voices. Many authors have denied the possibility of genuine legal gaps, whereas others (including Bulygin) have explained in what sense legal gaps are possible by analysing the circumstances in which they arise. A legal system may be said to have a gap if it does not say anything about the normative status of some action; such actions can be said to be unregulated by the system. If a system contains permissory norms granting 'positive permissions', it may be said to be silent if neither mandatory nor permissory norms support an answer to some question about what an agent ought to do or may do.

(5) In several papers included in this collection, Bulygin examines the concept of legal validity and questions about the existence, efficacy, and applicability of norms. Legal validity is a problematic concept, and different authors have defined it in different ways and put forward different criteria for deciding questions about validity.

2.

In 'The Expressive Conception of Norms', a paper that Bulygin wrote together with Carlos E. Alchourrón, the philosophical disagreements concerning problems (1)–(4) are diagnosed as being partly due to the fact that different authors 'start from two quite different and incompatible conceptions regarding the nature of norms'.[11]

[10] G. W. Leibniz, *Elementa iuris naturalis* (first publ. 1671), in Leibniz, *Sämtliche Schriften und Briefe. Sechste Reihe: Philosophische Schriften*, vol. 1 (Darmstadt: Otto Reichl Verlag, 1930), 431–85.

[11] Alchourrón and Bulygin, 'The Expressive Conception of Norms', in this volume, ch. 9, 147. First published in *New Studies in Deontic Logic*, ed. Risto Hilpinen (Dordrecht: D. Reidel, 1981), 95–124, and reprinted in *NN*, 383–410.

These two views are called the *hyletic* conception and the *expressive* conception.[12] This distinction is also discussed in Bulygin's paper, 'Norms and Logic'.[13]

A norm should be distinguished from a *norm formulation*, the expression of a norm in a language (deontic sentence).[14] The expressive and the hyletic conception represent different views about the semantics and pragmatics of deontic sentences. According to the hyletic interpretation, a norm is the meaning-content of a norm sentence, and it consists of a normative constituent (represented in deontic logic by a deontic operator) and a description of an act or a state of affairs. Alchourrón and Bulygin call such a normative meaning-content a *norm-lekton.*[15] Norm-lekta can be regarded as analogous to the propositional contents of descriptive statements.[16] Unlike descriptive sentences, normative sentences have a prescriptive meaning; for example, that something ought to (or must) be the case or be done. In so far as the norm-lekta resemble propositions, it might be thought possible to apply the concepts of truth and falsity (or some related semantic concept) to them. On the other hand, in their primary use norm-lekta have a normative function, and in normative discourse their 'direction of fit' is from the world to the word (to use J. L. Austin and John Searle's expression),[17] which means that the addressee of a speech act (a norm subject) should or may make the world fit the words, but the concepts of truth and falsity usually have one moving in the other direction; here the speaker is expected to get his words to fit the world.

According to the expressive conception, the normative force of a normative sentence is not due to its prescriptive meaning but rather to the way it is used—its normative (prescriptive) use. A sentence expressing a given proposition can be used in many ways—for example, asserted, presented as a question, commanded, and so on.[18] These speech acts constitute assertions, questions,

[12] See also Carlos E. Alchourrón and Eugenio Bulygin, *Sobre la existencia de las normas jurídicas* (Valencia, Venezuela: Oficina Latinoamericana de Investigaciones Jurídicas y Sociales, Universidad de Carabobo, 1979), at 47–9.

[13] Bulygin, 'Norms and Logic' (1985), in this volume, ch. 12.

[14] Eugenio Bulygin, 'Norms, Normative Propositions, and Legal Statements' (1982), in this volume, ch. 11.

[15] Alchourrón and Bulygin, 'The Expressive Conception of Norms' (1981), in this volume, ch. 9; see also Carlos E. Alchourrón and Eugenio Bulygin, 'On the Logic of Normative Systems', in *Pragmatik: Handbuch pragmatischen Denkens*, vol. 4 of *Sprachphilosophie, Sprachpragmatik und formative Pragmatik*, ed. by Herbert Stachowiak (Hamburg: Felix Meiner, 1993), 273–94, at 274. The term 'lekton' (λεκτόν) was used in Stoic logic to refer to the sense (meaning) of an expression or utterance. Alchourrón and Bulygin's use of 'norm-lekton' for the semantic content of a norm agrees in this respect with the Stoic account of lekta.

[16] In Hector-Neri Castañeda's theory of practical discourse, the concept of *practition* is analogous to Bulygin and Alcourrón's concept of norm-lekton; see Hector-Neri Castañeda, *Thinking and Doing. The Philosophical Foundations of Institutions* (Dordrecht: D. Reidel, 1975), at 43–5.

[17] See J. L. Austin, 'How to Talk: Some Simple Ways' (first publ. 1952), in J. L. Austin, *Philosophical Papers*, 3rd edn., ed. J. O. Urmson and G. J. Warnock (Oxford: Clarendon Press, 1979), 181–200, at 190. See also John Searle, *Expression and Meaning: Studies in the Theory of Speech Acts* (Cambridge: Cambridge University Press, 1979), at 3–4, and G. E. M. Anscombe, *Intention*, 2nd edn. (Oxford: Basil Blackwell, 1963), at 56.

[18] Alchourrón and Bulygin, 'The Expressive Conception of Norms' (1981), in this volume, ch. 9; Bulygin, 'Norms, Normative Propositions, and Legal Statements', in this volume, ch. 11. The distinction between an assertion and other ways of using a proposition (other speech acts) has often been

commands, requirements, permissions, etc. Commands (mandatory norms) and permissory norms have the same kind of propositional content, but not the same illocutionary force. Thus, the distinction between normative and descriptive sentences is a distinction on the level of language use—the pragmatic level rather than the semantic level. We may say that it is a distinction between two kinds of utterances of norm sentences.

The differences between the two conceptions of norms, or two ways of understanding the concept of a norm, help to explain some disagreements concerning questions about the possibility of logical relations among norms and the ontology of norms. In his paper 'Norms and Logic', Bulygin discusses an example of such disagreement. Ota Weinberger, whom Bulygin discusses at length in the paper, adheres to the hyletic conception,[19] but, according to Bulygin, the expressive conception provides a better interpretation of Kelsen's (admittedly somewhat unclear) conception of the nature of norms. Bulygin argues that Weinberger's criticism of Kelsen's view is due in part to the fact that he considers it in the framework of the hyletic conception, which is 'contrary at least to the spirit of Kelsen's theory'.

According to the expressive conception, there cannot, strictly speaking, be any logic of norms or logical relations among norms, for norms, especially legal norms, are usually constituted by normative actions, and norm contents lack a normative component. However, there can be a logic of norm statements (normative statements), statements that give information about the content of a normative (legal) system.[20] Legal and moral philosophers have observed that deontic sentences can be used in two ways: for the purpose of expressing norms, or for making normative statements, that is, statements about norms. For example, the Swedish philosopher Ingemar Hedenius has made a distinction between 'genuine' and 'spurious' legal sentences, and Hans Kelsen has distinguished an 'authentic' interpretation of law by legal organs from a jurisprudential ('nonauthentic') interpretation: only the former can create law.[21] Normative statements have the form 'according to the system S, it is obligatory (permitted, forbidden) that *p*', or 'according to S, it is obligatory (permitted, forbidden) to A', where A is some action type. Such statements are descriptive propositions and give information about some normative

explained in this way ever since the beginnings of the analysis of speech acts in the early twentieth century. For example, in a paper written in 1904, C. S. Peirce wrote:

> One and the same proposition may be affirmed, denied, judged, doubted, inwardly inquired into, put as a question, wished, asked for, effectively commanded, taught, or merely expressed, and does not thereby become a different proposition.

Charles Sanders Peirce, 'New Elements', in *The Essential Peirce*, vol. 2 (1893–1913), ed. Nathan Houser et al. (Bloomington: Indiana University Press, 1998), 300–24.

[19] See Ota Weinberger, 'The Expressive Conception of Norms: An Impasse for the Logic of Norms', *Law and Philosophy*, 4 (1985), 165–98, repr. *NN*, 411–32.

[20] See Bulygin, 'Norms, Normative Propositions, and Legal Statements' (1982), in this volume, ch. 11, and Alchourrón and Bulygin, 'Von Wright on Deontic Logic and the Philosophy of Law' (1973/89), in this volume, ch. 5.

[21] See Ingemar Hedenius, *Om Rätt och Moral* (On Law and Morals) (Stockholm: Tidens Förlag, 1941), at 65–6; Kelsen, *RR 2*, § 46 (at 352), *PTL*, at 355; Kelsen, *GTN*, at 164–5.

system. Their 'truth makers' are various legislative acts, judicial decisions,[22] and (in the case of customary law) legal and normative customs. According to the expressive conception, deontic logic may be regarded as a logic of norm statements, and many philosophers have interpreted the formulas of deontic logic in this way.[23] Some Scandinavian legal realists and moral relativists of the early twentieth century accepted a somewhat similar view about the nature of moral judgments and the science of morality; namely, that moral evaluations are not true or false, and that 'moral philosophy as a science is purely and simply a science of actual moral evaluations in their historical development'.[24]

According to the hyletic conception, the logic of norms can be understood as the logic of norm-lekta, and logical relations among norms (in the sense of norm-lekta) can be based on the notion of logical inconsistency and consistency among them: two norm-lekta are inconsistent if and only if it is logically impossible to perform the actions prescribed by them on one and the same occasion.[25] G. H. von Wright's first (1951) deontic system[26] can be regarded as a logic of norm-lekta, and this interpretation is also possible for the so-called standard system of deontic logic, with the possible exception of the iteration of deontic operators.[27] The hyletic conception makes it possible to distinguish two deontic logics, deontic logic as the logic of norms and as the logic of norm propositions. Many philosophers have assumed that the logic of norms (norm-lekta) can also serve as the logic of norm propositions, but Alchourrón and Bulygin do not accept this assumption of 'some sort of pre-established harmony between logical properties of norms and those of norm propositions'.[28]

Alchourrón and Bulygin note that there seems to be no crucial test that would justify a decision in favour of the expressive or the hyletic conception, but the choice between them may be regarded as a choice between two languages or 'language-forms', and at this point they refer to Rudolf Carnap's principle of tolerance. They also suggest that both views make possible the same conceptual distinctions.[29] Even if there were no logic of norms, strictly speaking, it might be possible

[22] For judicial decisions as sources of law, see Bulygin, 'Judicial Decisions and the Creation of Law' (1966), in this volume, ch. 4.

[23] See Erik Stenius, 'Principles of a Logic of Normative Systems', in *Proceedings of a Colloquium on Modal and Many-Valued Logics* (Helsinki, 23–26 August, 1962), *Acta Philosophica Fennica*, 16 (Helsinki: Societas Philosophica Fennica, 1963), 247–60; Bengt Hansson, 'An Analysis of Some Deontic Logics', *Noûs*, 3 (1969), 373–98, repr. *Deontic Logic: Introductory and Systematic Readings*, ed. Risto Hilpinen (Dordrecht: D. Reidel), 121–47, at 122–3; Dagfinn Føllesdal and Risto Hilpinen, 'Deontic Logic: An Introduction', ibid., 1–35, at 8.

[24] Axel Hägerström, 'On the Truth of Moral Propositions', in Hägerström, *Philosophy and Religion* (New York; Humanities Press, 1964), 78–96. Originally published in Swedish as a monograph, *Om moraliska föreställningars sanning* (Stockholm: Bonniers, 1911). See also Edward Westermarck, *The Origin and Development of Moral Ideas*, vol. 1 (London: MacMillan, 1906), at 18.

[25] Alchourrón and Bulygin, 'On the Logic of Normative Systems' (n. 15, this chapter), 282.

[26] Von Wright, 'DL'.

[27] See Alchourrón and Bulygin, 'On the Logic of Normative Systems' (n. 15, this chapter), at 284.

[28] Alchourrón and Bulygin, 'On the Logic of Normative Systems' (n. 15, this chapter), 285.

[29] See Rudolf Carnap, 'Intellectual Autobiography' in *The Philosophy of Rudolf Carnap*, ed. Paul A. Schilpp (La Salle, Illinois: Open Court, 1963), 3–84, at 54–5.

to apply the logic of action to the analysis of the acts of commanding, permitting, and prohibiting the actions that form the content of norms.

3.

It is interesting to note that some aspects of the distinction between the hyletic and the expressive conception can be found in the discussion of the possibility of a logic of imperatives (commands) in the late 1930s and early 1940s by Jørgen Jørgensen, Alf Ross, and others.[30] Jørgensen proposes two possible ways of solving the problem of logical relations among imperatives (or norms). One possibility is to try to define the concept of logical consequence without resorting to the concept of truth. For example, Alf Ross has argued that logically valid normative reasoning can be understood on the basis of the concept of *norm validity*: 'The logical deduction of [a directive] I_2 from I_1 then means that I_2 has objective validity in case I_1 has objective validity'.[31] Another possibility is to use *norm satisfaction* as a basis for the logic of norms. A norm or directive cannot be said to be true or false, but it can be satisfied or not satisfied; thus, deontic logic can perhaps be understood as 'a logic of norm-satisfaction'.[32] It has also been suggested that it is possible to distinguish two logics of imperatives and norms, the logic of satisfaction and the logic of validity, which are not necessarily the same.[33] Carlos Alchourrón and Antonio Martino have analysed logical reasoning about norms by means of rules of use, that is, Gentzen-type sequent rules for eliminating and introducing formulas with deontic operators in the context of deductive reasoning.[34]

As another way of solving the dilemma posed by Jørgensen, he suggests that our judgments about the logical relations among directives and norms can be regarded as based on the logical relations among certain propositions (statements) related to the norms. According to this approach, every directive (norm) D is related to a certain statement s(D) in such a way that a norm G can be inferred from D if and only if the proposition s(G) associated with G is a logical consequence of s(D). The standard concept of logical consequence based on the concept of truth is applicable to the propositions associated with norms, and thus indirectly to the corresponding norms. What is the statement s(D) associated with a norm D? According to Jørgensen, an imperative (or norm) can be analysed into two parts, the 'imperative factor' and the 'indicative factor'. The former indicates that something is commanded or requested, and the latter describes what is commanded, the content of the command.[35] For example, the indicative factor of the directive

(3.1) Ivan, stay inside!

[30] Jørgensen, 'IL', 290. [31] Ross, 'IL', 59; see also Ross, *DN*, at 175.

[32] Georg Henrik von Wright, 'Norms, Truth, and Logic', in von Wright, *Practical Reason* (Oxford: Blackwell, 1983), 130–209.

[33] Krister Segerberg, 'Validity and Satisfaction in Imperative Logic', *Notre Dame Journal of Formal Logic*, 31 (1990), 203–21.

[34] See Carlos E. Alchourrón and Antonio Martino, 'Logic without Truth', *Ratio Juris*, 3 (1990), 46–67, at 61–4.

[35] Jørgensen, 'IL', 291.

can be taken to be the proposition that Ivan stay inside. To indicate that a proposition is not asserted, it may be expressed in a subjunctive form or by an infinitive clause, 'Ivan to stay inside'.

If the imperative factor (or directive factor) is expressed by the exclamation mark '!', (3.1) has the form

(3.2) !(Ivan to stay inside).[36]

If D = !p, where *p* is a proposition, *p* is the 'indicative' (the proposition or statement) s(D), which determines the logical relations of D to other directives; that is,

(3.3) s(!p) = p.

According to (3.3), imperative reasoning (or reasoning with directives) is reasoning about their propositional contents. Thus 'the imperative factor is so to speak placed outside the brackets much as the assertion-sign in the ordinary logic [logic of statements], and the logical operations are only performed within the brackets'.[37] The logic of imperatives is thus reduced to the logic of statements for which the concept of logical consequence can be defined in the usual way, and 'there seems to be no reason for, and hardly any possibility of, constructing a special "logic of imperatives"'.[38] This account of the semantics of imperatives agrees with the expressive conception, according to which there is no logic of norms qua norms, only a logic of statements about norms.

According to Jørgensen, the logic of imperatives can also be based on another way of transforming imperatives into what he calls 'indicatives'. In this method, imperative sentences are transformed into statements which say that 'the ordered actions are to be performed or the wished state of affairs is to be produced'. This proposal can be understood in different ways. According to Jørgensen, '[s]uch and such action is to be performed' may be regarded as an abbreviation of the sentence form

(3.4) There is a person who is commanding that an action A is to be performed.[39]

For a norm based on a single normative source or norm system S, this can be expressed as

(3.5) According to a norm system S, A is to be performed;

that is,

(3.5)* According to S, doing A is obligatory (required).

Alchourrón and Bulygin call (3.5)* a normative statement, a statement about the content of a certain normative system. Such statements can be true or false, and logical relations among them can be understood in the usual way in terms of the

[36] The distinction between the content (or the topic) and the directive factor of a directive is a special case of the distinction between the illocutionary character and the content of a speech act. R. M. Hare has expressed this distinction by the word 'phrastic' for the content and 'neustic' for the illocutionary character. See Hare, *LM*, at 18; Ross, *DN*, at 18.

[37] Jørgensen, 'IL', 292. [38] Ross, 'IL', 57. [39] Jørgensen, 'IL', 292.

concept of truth. Combined with the view that the normative force of a norm sentence is not due to its prescriptive meaning, but rather to the way it is used, its normative (prescriptive) use, this interpretation of (3.1) leads to the expressive conception of norms. On the other hand, if the expression 'obligatory' in (3.5)* not only indicates the pragmatic function or role of the system S, but is a part of the semantic content of the norm (3.1)—that is, a conceptual component of a norm-lekton—we are led to the hyletic conception of norms. According to this interpretation, the expression 'A is to be performed' expresses the content of a norm.[40]

4.

As mentioned earlier, Ross argues that our conception of logically valid normative reasoning can be based on the 'validity' of norms and directives. He takes the validity of a norm to mean its '"existence" or "being in force"—however these expressions are to be understood'.[41]

Ross distinguishes between different interpretations of the term 'valid' and different ways of using the term, making, for example, the distinction expressed in German by the adjectives *gültig* (valid) and *geltend* (being in force), in Danish, *gyldig* and *gældende*, and in Spanish, *válido* and *vigente*.[42] Ross observes that 'much apparent disagreement between different writers can be attributed to the fact that their works are based on tacitly different assumptions as to the meaning of this term', namely, 'valid law'.[43] Several papers in this volume (chs. 4, 10, 17, and 20) investigate various interpretations, aspects, and criteria of the concept of validity: membership, existence, efficacy, being in force, and applicability.

In 'Valid Law and Law in Force',[44] Bulygin distinguishes between three different concepts related to the validity and existence of norms, *systemic validity, binding force* (normative validity), and *efficacy* (factual validity). These concepts or criteria of normativity do not coincide. For example, the efficacy of norm means that the norm subjects generally behave in accordance with the norm, but a norm may exist in a group of subjects even if it is violated by most members of the group, if most members of the group believe that conformity to the norm is required (accept the norm) and believe that other members of the group generally conform to the norm. Such a norm may possess systemic and normative validity without being efficacious. In this respect norms differ from conventions, whose existence

[40] Bulygin's concept of norm-lekton as the content of a normative utterance is in certain respects analogous to Hector-Neri Castañeda's use of the term 'practition' for the content of various practical attitudes, see Hector-Neri Castañeda, *Thinking and Doing* (Dordrecht: D. Reidel, 1975), at 43–5.

[41] Ross, *DN*, 172.

[42] See Ross, 'Validity', in *NN*, at 158–9; see also Bulygin, 'Valid Law and Law in Force' (1999), in this volume, ch. 17.

[43] Ross, *LJ*, 11. The book is a translation of *Om ret og retfærdighed: En indførelse i den analytiske retsfilosofi* (Copenhagen: Nyt Nordisk Forlag, 1953).

[44] Bulygin, 'Valid Law and Law in Force' (1999), in this volume, ch. 17.

requires general (but not universal) compliance. A perceived failure of efficacy may be regarded as a reason for derogating or revising a norm.

A (legal) norm has systemic validity if it is a member of a legal system (system of norms); thus, systemic validity is a relational concept, a relation between a norm, a system of norms identified by some external criterion, and a point of time. Systemic validity is an abstract notion that acquires empirical content through the criteria used for determining whether a norm belongs to a certain system. One such criterion is the legality of the norm-creating act; if a norm has been created by a competent authority, it is regarded as being part of the resulting normative system. This criterion does not apply to customary norms, which are presumably considered to be valid on the basis of their efficacy.

Normative validity means the binding force or obligatoriness of a norm; in other words, a norm possesses normative validity if the subjects have an obligation to obey it. This criterion of legal validity has been criticized by Alf Ross and other legal positivists who have in effect argued that the obligation to obey a legal norm cannot be distinguished from the obligation prescribed by the norm itself. However, a weak notion of normative validity might be understood as the norm subjects' belief that they and other norm subjects have an obligation to comply with a given norm—that is, the collective acceptance of the norm. Such mutual acceptance may be regarded as a form of weak efficacy, even though it does not entail actual efficacy.

Bulygin, in his paper 'Time and Validity',[45] makes an important distinction between a legal system (normative system) and a legal order (normative order). Normative (legal) systems change over time by acts of issuing and derogating norms, thus forming a temporal sequence of sets of norms. Bulygin uses the expression 'legal system' for a set of legal norms valid according to some criterion of membership at a certain time, and 'legal order' for a sequence of legal systems determined by its original constitution.[46] Joseph Raz has used the expression 'legal system' for what Bulygin calls a legal order, and 'momentary legal system' for the state of a legal order at a certain time.[47] Bulygin's terminology is more convenient, for it agrees with the common use of the term 'belief system' to refer to a set of beliefs accepted at a certain time.

The distinction between a normative order and a normative system helps to clarify various conceptual confusions and puzzles concerning normative change and the existence and applicability of norms. For example, the existence of a norm can be understood in two ways; as existence in a normative system or existence in a normative order. The latter notion can be regarded as meaning existence in some normative system or systems belonging to the normative order in question. As Bulygin points out, a normative (legal) system may require the application of a norm that is no longer valid (that is, does not exist) at the time of the application,

[45] Bulygin, 'Time and Validity' (1982), in this volume, ch. 10.

[46] See ch. 10 this volume, and also Alchourrón and Bulygin, 'On the Concept of a Legal Order' (1976), in this volume, ch. 7.

[47] See Raz, *CLS*, at 34–5.

although it was valid when the incriminating action was performed. Such a situation is not a paradoxical example of applying a non-existent norm, for the norm can be said to exist in the normative order in a cross-temporal sense.[48] This example shows that validity in the sense of membership in a normative system must be distinguished from applicability. In this respect legal systems differ from belief systems: when a proposition has been deleted from a belief system (that is, when the proposition is no longer believed), it is no longer 'applicable', and should have no effect on the agent's actions.

The distinction between a norm system and a normative order and the recognition of the temporary character of normative systems also helps to solve Alf Ross's 'Puzzle of Constitutional Amendment'. Ross has argued that a rule for amending the constitution cannot be amended according to a procedure established by the rule itself, and therefore cannot be amended by any legal procedure.[49] Ross's argument has the following form:

Assume that article 88 of the constitution states that the constitution may be amended by process Q, and only by Q, and let art. 88' state that the constitution may be amended by process R, and only by R:

(4.1) Art. 88: The constitution may be amended by process Q, and only by Q.
(4.2) The constitution is amended by Q by replacing art. 88 with art. 88', according to which the constitution may be amended by process R (different from Q), and only by R.
(4.3) Art. 88' is valid; that is, the constitution may be amended by process R, and only by R.[50]

According to Ross, the reasoning from (4.1) and (4.2) to (4.3) has the form of *modus ponens*, but the conclusion seems to contradict one of the premisses, which he regards as 'a logical absurdity'.[51] As Bulygin points out, some logically valid arguments have this property, but the main error in Ross's reasoning lies elsewhere. The argument is not an instance of *modus ponens*, because the four occurrences of the definite description 'the constitution' in (4.1)–(4.3) do not refer to the same normative system; thus, Ross commits the fallacy of equivocation. As Bulygin notes, the occurrence of 'the constitution' in (4.1) and its first occurrence in (4.2) refer to the constitution before the amendment (call it C), its second occurrence in (4.2) and its occurrence in (4.3) refer to the amended constitution (C'); arts. 88 and 88' never coexist at the same time.[52]

Bulygin's discussion of Ross's example is interesting from the standpoint of the general theory of action, for it shows the logical relevance of temporal distinctions.

[48] See Bulygin, 'Time and Validity' (1982), in this volume, ch. 10.

[49] Ross, *LJ*, 82–3; and see Alf Ross, 'On Self-Reference and a Puzzle in Constitutional Law', *Mind*, 78 (1969), 1–24, at 3–6.

[50] (4.1)–(4.3) have been slightly modified from Bulygin's presentation, see Bulygin, 'Time and Validity' (1982), in this volume, ch. 10.

[51] Ross, 'On Self-Reference and a Puzzle in Constitutional Law' (n. 49, this chapter), 5.

[52] 'Time and Validity' (1982), in this volume, ch. 10. In view of the ambiguity of 'exist' in the present context, 'coexistence' could also be taken to mean 'diachronic' co-existence, existence in the same normative order.

Amending a constitution is an action—in the present case, an action of bringing about that something exists, namely, a new article of the constitution, or an action of replacing an article with a new article. According to von Wright, an action of bringing about that *p* involves a transformation of a state in which it is not the case that *p* into a state in which it is the case that *p*. Thus, an action of this kind involves two 'world states' (or 'occasions'), an *initial state* and an *end state* (or result state).

> When we say that an individual event happens on a certain occasion we may regard this happening of the event as constituted by two successive occasions for the obtaining of certain states of affairs.... Similarly, when we say that an individual act is done on a certain occasion we may regard this occasion for the doing of the act as constituted by the two successive occasions for the corresponding individual event.[53]

In the present example, the validity of the constitutional amendment should be regarded as being evaluated at the initial state in which the original art. 88 is still valid. Thus, an action is in effect regarded as taking place at the initial state transformed by the action. According to the present model, even seemingly instantaneous actions must be analysed in terms of two successive occasions or points of time. If t_1 is the time of the derogation of art. 88, and t_2 is a later moment at which art. 88' has been created, the validity of art. 88' is based on art. 88. Ross's example is an example of a situation in which a derogated norm continues to be applicable to some cases.[54]

5.

One of the controversial topics discussed by Bulygin is the question of permissory norms. As already mentioned, this problem is related to the question about the possibility of legal gaps. In the standard deontic logic, the concept of permission (or permissibility) is defined simply as the absence of prohibition, but this does not mean that the absence of a prohibition from a norm system is the same thing as the presence of a permissory norm in the system. This may be one reason why the P-operator of deontic logic is often expressed by the word 'permissibility' rather than 'permission'. A permission does not necessarily consist only of the fact that a norm system lacks the corresponding prohibition. Normative systems can contain permissory norms in the proper sense; thus, one can make a distinction between a 'weak' and a 'strong' (or 'negative' and 'positive') permission (permissibility).[55] It is

[53] Von Wright, *NA*, 37. See also Georg Henrik von Wright, 'Norms, Truth, and Logic', in von Wright, *Practical Reason. Philosophical Papers* (Oxford: Blackwell, 1983), 130–209, at 174, 195–6, where von Wright notes that an occasion on which a change takes place—for example, a new state of affairs obtains—should be regarded as involving two 'phases', a phase during which this state of affairs is absent and a phase during which it is present.

[54] See 'Time and Validity' (1982), in this volume, ch. 10.

[55] See Bulygin, 'The Silence of the Law' (2002), in this volume, ch. 18.

important to note that the 'weak' permissibility of an action, as defined here, does not entail the existence of permissory norms in a system.

The connection between the problem of permissory norms and legal (normative) gaps can be seen by considering normative propositions, that is, statements about the norms in a given normative system. Let S be a normative system, and let S: OA be the statement that according to S, A is obligatory or required, where A is an action description or a proposition. Thus:

(5.1) S: O ¬A[56]

that is,

(5.2) S: FA

is the proposition that according to S, A is forbidden, or more briefly, that S forbids A. The permissibility of A relative to S might be taken to mean that it is not the case that S forbids A; that is,

(5.3) ¬(S: FA)

If this were then expressed by saying that A is permitted (permissible) according to S, it might seem to be logically equivalent to

(5.4) S: ¬FA

and there would be no logical difference between the 'external' and the 'internal' negation in these deontic statement-forms. If (5.3) is regarded as an expression for negative or weak permissibility and (5.4) represents a 'positive' permission, there would be no difference between the two, and no room for legal gaps. If it is not the case that according to S, A is forbidden, then, according to S, A is permitted. If S is a set of norms, then the assumed equivalence of (5.3) and (5.4) can be expressed as

(5.5) $\neg(FA \in S) \leftrightarrow (PA \in S)$

which (according to the standard deontic logic) is equivalent to

(5.6) $\neg(O\ \neg A \in S) \leftrightarrow \neg O\ \neg A \in S$

Joseph Raz, who denies the possibility of genuine legal gaps, regards this equivalence as a logical truth.[57]

However, as Bulygin points out, there is a conceptual difference between the absence of a prohibition norm from a system and the presence of a permission-granting norm. An action supported by a permissory norm of a norm system can be distinguished from an unregulated action.[58] In other words, the (positive)

[56] If 'A' is an action description, the negation sign ¬ should be reinterpreted as a sign of an omission.

[57] See Bulygin, 'The Silence of the Law' (2002), in this volume, ch. 18; Joseph Raz, 'Legal Reasons, Sources, and Gaps', in Raz, *AL*, 53–77, at 76. Raz uses the expression 'Law conclusively requires (that) A' for $OA \in S$.

[58] Eugenio Bulygin, 'Sobre la equivalencia pragmática entre permiso y no prohibición, *DOXA*, 33 (2010), 283–96.

permission on the right side of (5.5) and (5.6) does not follow from the fact that S does not prohibit A. If A is not prohibited by a system S (that is, A is 'weakly permissible'), adding a permissory norm PA to S changes S and the normative order to which it belongs without derogating any mandatory norm. This can be seen by considering a normative order with several hierarchically ordered authorities. Bulygin gives the following example: consider a situation in which Rex with unlimited legislative competence has appointed a Minister and given the Minister the power to issue norms in the same manner as Rex. Let A be an unregulated action—that is, neither Rex nor the Minister has issued any norm concerning A. However, if Rex then issues a permissory norm concerning A, the Minister will no longer have the competence to prohibit A. We may say that a permissory norm issued by Rex creates an immunity against regulation by the Minister; thus, a permissory norm may change a norm system in a nontrivial way. A search warrant may perhaps serve as an example of a different kind of permissory norm. According to many legal systems, the police may not search a suspect's house without a search warrant, but a court may issue a warrant (a permission to search the house) on the basis of an application by the police. If a judge or a magistrate issues a warrant, he in effect issues a permission for the police to search the house, and the owner of the house lacks the power to prohibit the search. Following Krister Segerberg, such a permission may be called a 'one-time' (or occasional) permission, whereas a permissory norm issued by the legislator (Rex) may be a 'standing' permission.[59] When an agent has taken advantage of (or 'used') a one-time permission, it ceases to exist. In this case no mandatory norm has been derogated; but the concept of permission is built into the law prohibiting an arbitrary search, thus, a one-time permission differs from a mere absence of a prohibition or the derogation of a mandatory norm. These examples illustrate the relativity of permissory norms to a normative order; they involve hierarchically ordered normative systems, with a plurality of norm authorities belonging to different levels.[60] In this respect belief systems are analogous to normative systems; they are not simply sets of beliefs (accepted propositions), but also involve dependence relations among beliefs.

[59] See Krister Segerberg, 'Trying to Meet Ross's Challenge', in *Law and Philosophy in Italy: Some Trends and Perspectives*, ed. Edoardo Ballo and Miriam Franchella (Monza: Polimetrica, 2006), 155–66.

[60] See Eugenio Bulygin, 'Permissory Norms and Normative Systems'(1984/86/2012), in this volume, ch. 21.

1

The Concept of Efficacy (1965)*

Introduction

The concept of efficacy is the focus of this article.[1] The question of greatest interest to me is under what conditions a legal norm is characterized as efficacious or inefficacious. By enquiring into the use of the expressions 'efficacious' and 'inefficacious' in legal discourse, one also arrives at an understanding of their meaning.[2] It is worthwhile noting that I am taking up a purely analytical question here, a question limited to conceptual enquiry. No claim is made of pursuing empirical research into social reality, which must be sharply distinguished from the analytical question. At the same time, however, it must be taken into account that the logical analysis of language not only brings linguistic relations to light but also—as H. L. A. Hart emphasizes[3]—promotes our understanding of the facts. Drawing on a line, slightly modified, of J. L. Austin's: A sharpened awareness of words sharpens our perception of the phenomena.[4]

In the traditional literature in legal philosophy, the question of efficacy is given very little attention. One is often inclined to regard this concept as clear and unproblematic. Even in those relatively rare cases in which efficacy is explicitly considered on its merits, the enquiry yields to the ostensibly far more important problem of validity. For authors in the natural law tradition, this stance is altogether understandable, for if the validity of legal norms is independent of their efficacy, then efficacy will only be of trifling significance. It is less understandable, however, that many legal positivists also neglect efficacy, especially if efficacy is cast

* [*Editors' note*: Eugenio Bulygin's paper was first published as 'Der Begriff der Wirksamkeit', in *Lateinamerikanische Studien zur Rechtsphilosophie*, ed. Ernesto Garzón Valdés (*ARSP Beiheft* 41 [N.F. 4]) (Neuwied am Rhein and Berlin: Hermann Luchterhand, 1965), 39–58. It has been translated for the present volume by Bonnie Litschewski Paulson and Stanley L. Paulson.]

[1] Research made possible by a stipend from the Alexander von Humboldt Foundation, Bonn, is represented in part in this article. I am grateful to the Foundation for its generous support, and to Professor Alf Ross and Professor Ulrich Klug for their invaluable help and stimulating criticism.

[2] See Ludwig Wittgenstein, *Philosophical Investigations* (Oxford: Blackwell, 1953), at § 43: 'The meaning of a word is its use in the language.'

[3] Hart, *CL*, 1st edn., preface, at vii, 3rd edn., at vi. [*Editors' note*: For this and other abbreviations, see the Table of Abbreviations.]

[4] J. L. Austin, 'A Plea for Excuses', *Proceedings of the Aristotelian Society*, 57 (1956/7), 1–30, at 8, repr. Austin, *Philosophical Papers*, 3rd edn., ed. J. O. Urmson and G. J. Warnock (Oxford: Clarendon Press, 1979), 175–204, at 182.

as a necessary and sufficient condition for validity.[5] Only with the emergence of the so-called realist theories of law does the problem of efficacy finally take centre stage. Denying that there is any such thing as validity means that, for legal science, efficacy remains the sole relevant property of legal norms.

Since the concept of efficacy plays a central role in realist theories of law, it will be useful to consider these theories in particular. One of the most important contributions toward clarifying the problem is the book by the Danish legal philosopher Alf Ross, *On Law and Justice*.[6] In his treatise, Ross analyses in detail the concept of valid (*geltend*) or efficacious (*wirksam*) law (for Ross, the two expressions mean the same thing). His unusually instructive exposition will be fundamental to my discussion of the concept of efficacy.

In sections 1 and 2, I point out the difficulties that turn up in Ross's assessment of efficacy, and then I attempt, in section 3, to uncover the reasons for these difficulties. These reasons may well lie, first and foremost, in a view that Ross takes over from Hans Kelsen, namely, that the law consists exclusively of norms addressed to judges. This view conceals the radical difference between compliance with legal norms and their application, a difference clearly expressed only when the application of legal norms is defined as their use in the grounding of legal decisions. The concept of grounding is itself, however, in serious need of clarification, for in the literature of legal science, in this context, logical and psychological questions are very frequently confused. Thus, my discussion of the concept of grounding, in section 4, is given more attention than would be required, strictly speaking, in assessing efficacy. Only if grounding is understood as the logical relation between norm and decision does one arrive at a fully sensible assessment of efficacy. In section 5, I take up the problem of the interpretation of statements about efficacy. Finally, I devote section 6 to the questions of justifying and applying my suggested criterion for efficacy.

1. Criticism of Alf Ross's Theory

To open the discussion of Ross's theory with a brief statement of Kelsen's view of efficacy calls for no special justification. Ross's 'realist legal theory' can be seen in many respects as a product of his critical examination of the Pure Theory of Law.

For Kelsen, a legal norm is efficacious if it is either complied with or applied.[7] Compliance with a norm consists in fulfilling legal obligations, while application of a norm consists in the ordering and execution of coercive acts (sanctions). There is a close connection between the two concepts, for, as is well known, there are

[5] As, for example, in the Pure Theory of Law, where efficacy is a necessary condition, since a norm forfeits its validity if—through *desuetudo*—it becomes inefficacious. See Kelsen, *RR 2*, § 34(g) (at 219–20), *PTL*, at 212–13. However, efficacy is also a sufficient condition for Kelsen in that he recognizes custom as a law-creating source (that cannot be excluded even by the constitution), and customary norms are precisely those norms that derive their validity from their efficacy. On the concepts of necessary and sufficient conditions and the parallel distinction with reference to extensive implication, see Ulrich Klug, *Juristische Logik*, 2nd edn. (Berlin: Springer, 1958), at § 4.

[6] Ross, *LJ*, chs. 1–2.

[7] Kelsen, *RR 2*, § 4(c) (at 11), *PTL*, at 10–11.

in Kelsen's theory no legal obligations without sanctions. That behaviour is prescribed by the legal system—in other words that it counts as the content of a legal obligation—means that a sanction is attached to the opposite behaviour.[8] Thus, a legal norm is characterized as inefficacious if it is not complied with and the corresponding sanction is not applied.

Applying this criterion in a statutory context, say, to the German Civil Code, is difficult, for in a great many of the sections found in the Code, one has no occasion to speak of compliance or noncompliance, for they neither prescribe legal obligations nor contain any sanctions. As an example, consider a norm that prescribes how a testament can be made or a contract can be closed. If the conditions set down in the statute are not fulfilled, the contract in question is null and void, but there is neither a violation of an obligation nor a sanction,[9] neither something illegal nor a consequence of something illegal. How is Kelsen's criterion of efficacy to be applied here? Kelsen's answer would most likely run as follows: These regulations are not independent legal norms, but are, rather, merely norm fragments that have meaning only in connection with proper norms,[10] that is, norms that prescribe sanctions.

I cannot engage here in criticism of Kelsen's definition of the legal norm, a definition based on the presupposition that all legal norms must have the same structure, but the question stands: How can these 'dependent' norms be examined with an eye to their efficacy? It is by no means a matter, here, of exceptional cases, for a significant part of the legal system consists of just such dependent norms.[11]

In Ross's work, there is a refinement of Kelsen's idea that legal norms are directives that order sanctions. Ross does distinguish two types of norm, which he calls 'norms of conduct' and 'norms of competence',[12] but since competence norms are not an independent category and are understood instead as indirectly formulated norms of conduct and therefore as traceable back to norms of conduct, then all legal norms are understood as hypothetical sanction-prescribing regulations (directives) addressed to judges and other legal organs. Judges,[13] then, are the sole addressees of legal norms, and only they can comply with or fail to comply with legal norms. For Ross, the application of legal norms by the judge consists in the judge's compliance with the directives addressed to him, that is to say, in the judge's actions being motivated by these norms. Thus, the application of the legal norm by the courts becomes the sole criterion for efficacy.[14]

8 Kelsen, *RR 2*, § 28(a) (at 120), *PTL*, at 115.

9 Nullity in the sense of the Pure Theory of Law is not a sanction, for there is no coercive act. On the interpretation of nullity as a sanction and for criticism addressed to the notion, see Hart, *CL*, 1st edn., at 33–5, 3rd edn., at 33–5.

10 See Kelsen, *RR 2*, at § 6(e) (55–9), *PTL*, at 54–8.

11 Belonging to this group are all legal norms that confer public or private legal power and that govern the creation, change, and revocation of norms prescribing obligations and sanctions—thus, practically all constitutional and procedural norms, along with a considerable number of the remaining norms of public and private law.

12 Ross, *LJ*, 32–4.

13 The expressions 'judge' and 'court' are used, as in Ross's treatise, in a broad sense, encompassing all the organs that play a role in adjudication and in carrying out sanctions.

14 Whether the populace fulfils its legal obligations (by avoiding sanctions) is, in principle, irrelevant.

At the same time, the concept of application is duly expanded by Ross, for in his work it consists not simply in the ordering or execution of the sanction, as in Kelsen's work. Rather, whenever a judge's action is motivated by a legal norm, one can speak of the application of this legal norm, quite apart from whether the process ends with the acquittal or the conviction of the accused. The limits of Kelsen's concept of application are especially clear in civil proceedings, for these are rarely pursued all the way to the ordering or, indeed, the execution of judgment (the only sanction available in civil proceedings).

Efficacious legal norms are, then, those norms that are in fact applied by the courts, and the question of which norms the courts apply can only be answered by observing the actual behaviour of judges. It is clear, however, that not every instance of a judge's regular behaviour can be regarded as the expression of a legal norm. Judges, too, may well have habits that no norm conditioned or created, but how can a mere habit be distinguished from a legal norm that emerges from a customary practice?

Ross underscores the point that mere observation of a judge's outward behaviour is insufficient for determining which norms the judge applies and which are therefore efficacious.[15] The difference, for Ross, is that in the case of the application of a legal norm, the judge's action is motivated by a normative ideology, that is, by his feeling obligated by the norm.

> The changing behaviour of the judge can only be comprehended and predicted through ideological interpretation, that is, by means of the hypothesis of a certain ideology which animates the judge and motivates his actions. Another way of expressing the same thing is to say that law presupposes, not only regularity in the judge's mode of action, but also his experience of being bound by the rules. In the concept of validity[16] two points are involved: partially the outward observable and regular compliance with a pattern of action, and partly the experience of this pattern of action as being a socially binding norm.[17]

The distinction between a mere habit and an efficacious legal norm lies, then, in the judge's psychological experience (the feeling of being bound by the norm), which turns up as a necessary (even if not a sufficient) condition for efficacy.

For two reasons, this criterion seems unsatisfactory. First, Ross's objections to 'psychological realism'—Knud Illum, Karl Olivecrona—also count directly against his own theory. If the drawback of psychological realism is, as Ross emphasizes, that the concept of efficacious law is bound to psychological facts like the people's

[15] 'What is valid law cannot be ascertained by purely behaviouristic means, that is, by external observation of regularity in the reactions (customs) of the judges... [N]ot every outward and observable regularity in the reactions of the judge is the expression of a valid norm of law.' Ross, *LJ*, 37–8.

[16] 'Validity', the expression used in *On Law and Justice*, the English edition of Ross's treatise, is an unfortunate translation of the corresponding Danish expression, which Ross himself points out. See Ross, 'Validity'. In any case, Ross's 'validity' in this context means the same as 'efficacy'. See the Spanish edition of Ross's treatise, *Sobre el derecho y la justicia*, trans. Genaro R. Carrió (Buenos Aires: Eudeba, 1963).

[17] Ross, *LJ*, 37.

consciousness of law,[18] then scant progress is made by replacing the people's consciousness with the feelings of judges, for this concept also belongs to 'individual psychology'.

Second, Ross's criterion proves to be ill-suited for describing certain legal norms and even leads to express contradiction within Ross's own theory. In most cases, judges doubtlessly feel obligated by the norms they are to apply, but this is a factual, contingent state of affairs that can make no claim of logical necessity. Examples of a different scenario can be found easily enough. Ross himself is ready to help us on this score.

Where an existing actual régime does not receive from those subject to it ideological approval in a formal legal consciousness, but is obeyed solely out of fear, they do not experience it as a 'legal order' but as a dictate of force or violence.... This applies, for example, to the population of an occupied country and their attitude to the régime of force which is supported solely by military strength,...[19]

It is altogether conceivable that the judges of an occupied country also regard the directives of the occupying power as arbitrary and 'illegal' commands and that nonetheless—out of fear or self-interest—they comply with these directives and apply them. According to Ross's own criterion, these directives would not be legal norms since they lack the ideological element of the judge's feeling bound by them, a necessary condition for the existence of efficacious norms. Ross, however, is clearly not applying this criterion when he says:

From a cognitive-descriptive point of view—and this must be the point of view of jurisprudence as a scholarly activity—it is, however, impossible to differentiate between a 'legal order' and a 'régime of violence',... It would, of course, be possible to limit the concept of law by an objective, social psychological characterisation, in such a way that an order is called 'legal' only if it receives ideological approval from the majority of those subject to it. However, I see no advantage in this—it is, in fact, a disadvantage to bind the concept to a criterion which is difficult to work with in practice. Further, the order, whether it receives approval or not, is a fact which needs description and which can be described exactly in the same way as a 'legal order', that is as norms concerning the exercise of force.[20]

This rings true enough to warrant setting aside a characterization of efficacy in terms of psychological experience or feelings.

2. Compliance with, and Use of, Norms

It seems to me that the difficulties that have turned up in analysing Ross's assessments of efficacy have two different sources.

[18] 'The cardinal objection to psychological realism is that the legal consciousness is a concept of individual psychology. By linking the concept of valid law to the individual legal consciousness, this branch of realism converts law into an individual phenomenon on a par with morality.' Ross, *LJ*, 72.

[19] Ross, *LJ*, 55. [20] Ross, *LJ*, 56.

First, the distinction between compliance with and the application of a norm as two fundamentally different procedures has not been made sharply enough. Second, the relation between legal norms and the legal decision has not been clarified; no clear line of separation has been drawn between the logical relation of the judge's grounding a decision and the psychological link of his motivation.

I shall take up the problem of grounding in the next section, turning here to the first issue, the distinction between compliance with and the application of a norm.

In most modern legal theories, the normative (prescriptive or directive) function of legal norms is emphasized, by contrast with the descriptive (or indicative) function of propositions in legal science. Legal norms are, accordingly, imperatives (Kelsen, Karl Engisch)[21] or directives (Ross), that is, sentences that prescribe (or proscribe) certain behaviour and that can therefore be complied with or not complied with by the addressee. The idea that legal norms can only be complied with or not complied with is presupposed, *sub silentio*, by virtually all normative theories of law, while the fact that legal norms can also have other functions is either overlooked or, indeed, not sufficiently appreciated. A norm can not only be complied with, however, it can also be *used*.[22] If a norm is used, for example, to justify or to criticize an action, this is entirely different from compliance with an imperative, and the norm is functioning in an altogether different way. If the judge applies a norm, he is using this norm in order to ground his decision, but it would be misleading to describe this as compliance with the norm. If the judge has to choose between two norms, (a) and (b), and decides to choose (b), surely no one will say that he failed to comply with norm (a). One can criticize the judge for not properly grounding his decision, and the decision may even be overturned owing to a defective grounding, but one has no occasion here to speak of non-compliance or, indeed, of a violation of the judge's obligation. And where there is no non-compliance, there can be no compliance either. In deciding a case, the judge does comply with the norm that obligates him to decide (the norm according to which he is not allowed to forbear from deciding the case), but the norms that he applies are being used by him, not being complied with.[23]

As already established, not all legal norms call for compliance. Legal norms can be complied with only if they prescribe (command or forbid) certain behaviour—that is, they render an action or a forbearance obligatory. Thus, not all sentences characterized in ordinary legal discourse as legal norms are in fact norms if, by 'norm', one understands a regulation or a directive. It seems, then, more reasonable to confine the expression 'legal norm' to directives and to characterize those legal

[21] See Kelsen, *RR 2*, § 16 (at 73), *PTL*, at 71; Karl Engisch, *Einführung in das juristische Denken*, 2nd edn. (Stuttgart: Kohlhammer, 1959), at 21–32, 8th edn. (1983), at 21–32. [*Editors' note*: Still later editions of Engisch's monograph are abridged.]

[22] One need go no further than to simple imperatives (commands) to see clearly the distinction between compliance and use: The father commands that the window be opened; the child opens the window (the child *complies with* the command). To the question 'Why have you opened the window?' the child answers: 'Because my father commanded that I do so' (the child *uses* the command to justify his action).

[23] As Hart notes, legal norms can be used for different purposes, but what is of interest here is an altogether particular use: the grounding of legal decisions.

definitions that are not directives as 'legal rules', similar in terms of function to the rules of a game or the rules of grammar or logic.[24] The expression 'legal rule' would encompass approximately those legal definitions that Hart calls 'secondary rules'.[25] To my knowledge, Hart was the first to claim the distinct character of these rules, holding that they not be reduced to norms ('primary rules' in his terminology). Kelsen and Ross have also seen this difference, but they do regard these rules as norms, albeit not as independent norms but as 'dependent norms' or 'competence norms'. This terminology is not correct, however, for these are not norms at all. That said, it does not follow that they cannot be independent and must necessarily be traceable back to norms, unless one is prepared to maintain at any cost the dogma that the law consists *solely* of legal norms.

However different they may be, rules and norms have something in common: Rules, too, can be used to ground legal decisions. For this reason it is important that Ross regards application and not compliance as the criterion for efficacy, and so his notion of applicability also reaches to legal rules. It seems to me, however, that Ross has not distinguished clearly enough between compliance and use. By interpreting all legal norms[26] as directives addressed to judges, he understands application in such a way that the judge complies with a norm *in that* he grounds his decision with the norm. It turns out, then, that Ross has two different criteria for efficacy that he treats as though they were the same. Having characterized efficacy in terms of a psychological definition (which we have already discussed), he goes on to say:

> Secondly, a more precise definition is required of what it means that the rule is being applied by the courts.... Its 'application' in legal practice... can only mean that in decisions in which its conditioning facts are assumed to exist, it forms an integral part of the reasoning underlying the judgment and has therefore been one of the decisive factors determining the conclusion at which the court has arrived.[27]

This characterization, apparently intended simply as clarification, leads in fact to a completely new concept of application or efficacy. Here, the grounding of the decision by means of a norm is a necessary and sufficient condition for the application of the norm. It is not required that the judge experience the norm as binding or that he have certain feelings; it suffices that he mention the norm in the course of grounding his decision. Even in cases where judges act out of fear or self-interest, this criterion allows one to speak of efficacious legal norms and renders a psychoanalysis of judges unnecessary. In that the reasons for the decision depend upon efficacy and not on the feelings of the judge, the emphasis shifts to what the judge *says* rather than what he *feels*. Accordingly, a norm is efficacious if the judge says that he is applying it, that is, if it is being used by the judge in

[24] Perhaps they are best characterized as definitions.

[25] See Hart, *CL*, 1st edn., at 26–48, 77–9, and 239, 3rd edn., at 26–49, 79–81, and 285.

[26] In what follows, I shall use the expression 'legal norm'—in keeping with ordinary usage—in the broader sense, which also encompasses legal rules.

[27] Ross, *LJ*, 42.

order to ground his decision. The psychological motives that led to his decision are irrelevant.

A mere statement by the judge to the effect that he is applying this or that norm is obviously insufficient if the directive aspect of the decision does not square with its grounding. The decision must be *grounded* by means of the norm. But what is the grounding of a legal decision? Or, to put it another way: What is the relation between the grounding aspect and the directive aspect of a legal decision? Here we arrive at the second source of the difficulties mentioned earlier.[28]

3. The Grounding of the Legal Decision

This problem generates great confusion in traditional legal theory. The wide-ranging opinions reach to two ostensibly opposing and sharply competing theories. One theory emphasizes norms and restricts adjudication to a mechanical operation. We shall designate this the 'syllogism theory'. The other theory emphasizes the creative function of the judge, while largely discounting the significance of norms.

The main theses of the syllogism theory can be summarized in the following statements, which will be referred to as list A.[29]

1. The legal decision is the conclusion of a logical (deductive) argument that is adduced by the judge and has the form of a syllogism.
2. The premisses of this syllogism are given by means of the norms to be applied and the statements describing the facts.
3. The activity of the judge (apart from determining the facts) is purely mechanical; he need only draw out the logical conclusion from the premisses given.
4. The decision is determined by norms, and so knowledge of legal norms (statutes) is the sole purpose of legal science.[30]

As a reaction (in part a very healthy reaction) against the statutory formalism of syllogism theory, there emerged toward the end of the nineteenth century and in the first decades of the twentieth century several movements that rebelled above all against the 'mechanical' view of the judicial function. The new ideas were characteristically expressed in the Free Law Movement and in American Legal Realism. Some of the representatives of these movements have claimed the following theses, which will be referred to as list B.[31]

[28] [*Editors' note*: See the first three paragraphs of section 2 above.]

[29] This theory is given expression in, above all, the exegetical school: Blondeau, Mourlon, Laurent, etc.

[30] Demolombe, *Cours du Code Napoleon*, vol. 1, at 3. The well-known proscriptions of statutory interpretation also belong here: *Constitutio tanta*, § 21 of the Corpus juris; *Corpus juris Fridericiani* of 1747–51; etc.

[31] See e.g. Jerome Frank, *Law and the Modern Mind* (New York: Brentano, 1930), and Hermann Isay, *Rechtsnorm und Entscheidung* (Berlin: Franz Vahlen, 1929).

1. Legal norms are not the sole factor (nor even the most important one) that determines legal decisions.
2. The judge is in fact motivated by a great variety of factors: political deliberations, moral and political ideas, personal values, emotions, etc.
3. The decision is first taken by the judge and then subsequently justified by means of legal norms; the argument found in the grounding aspect of the decision is simply a rationalization of the directive aspect.
4. It follows that knowledge of statutes is of modest significance and must be replaced by the study of the psychological and sociological factors that motivate the judge.

I have intentionally sketched extreme versions of both positions in order to underscore their common error, namely, the confusion between logical and psychological questions. Although these versions of the two positions can scarcely be encountered in so crude a form in current legal theory, still, the two fields, the logical and the psychological, are often not clearly distinguished, and formulations frequently turn up that patently reflect the confusion of the one with the other.[32]

A legal decision is normatively grounded if it can be logically derived from certain norms (along with the statements describing the material facts). The normative grounding is therefore a logical question. The logical relation between the grounding norms and the decision is a relation of logical implication.[33] The norms imply the decision, or—what amounts to the same thing—the decision is deducible from the norms, that is, it can be derived with the help of the laws of logic.[34] That the judge is bound by 'the statute and the law'[35] consists precisely in the requirement that the judge ground his decisions with legal norms. In almost all modern legal systems, judges are expressly obligated to ground their decisions, in other words, *explicitly* to justify them.

This logical relation between the grounding norms and the decision is often confused with the factors motivating the judge. Which motives determine the decision is a psychological question, altogether irrelevant to the grounding of the decision.

[32] For a clear formulation of the distinction between logical and psychological questions (the grounding of a decision versus the means of arriving at the decision), see Engisch, *Einführung in das juristische Denken* (n. 21, this chapter), 2nd edn. at 49, 8th edn. at 49.

[33] Not only can a decision be deductively grounded (as in the normative grounding), it can also be grounded inductively (empirically) when, for example, the judge refers to the probable consequences of his decision. However, even in this case, the grounding consists in a logical relation between the grounding norms and the decision (even though the decision does not represent a logical implication). In no case is this to be confused with the psychological connection that, to be sure, can also exist if the perception of consequences causally determines the judge's decision.

[34] There are no obstacles, in principle, to extending the logical rules of derivation to normative statements. See Hare, *LM*, 17–55; Ulrich Klug, 'Bemerkungen zur logischen Analyse einiger rechtstheoretischer Begriffe und Behauptungen', in *Logik und Logikkalkül*, ed. Max Käsbauer and Franz von Kutschera (Freiburg and Munich: Karl Alber, 1962), 115–25; and Carlos E. Alchourrón, 'Los argumentos jurídicos a fortiori y a pari', in *RJBA* (1961) (issue no. 4), 177–99, in *ALD*, 3–24.

[35] Basic Law (German Constitution of 1949), art. 20.3.

If one keeps in mind this difference between logical and psychological questions, it is clear that the two types of theory sketched above are only ostensibly antagonistic, for they move in different spheres.

Syllogism theory is correct when it claims that the legal decision is the logical conclusion of a deductive argument, where the norms to be applied play the role of premisses (see statements 1 and 2 in list A). Proponents believe, however, that they can then draw conclusions that are admissible only if there is, in addition to the logical relation, also a causal connection between the norms and the decision. That the decision is derivable from the norms in question by no means implies that the judge's activity must be purely mechanical.[36] Mechanical methods of derivation are possible only in strictly formalized languages, and even there only to a limited degree.[37]

The theory of legal realism offers a more or less correct description of the psychological processes of adjudication and causal relations. Statements 1, 2, and 3 in list B are certainly true, but they are scarcely suited to play the role entrusted to them, namely, illustrating the falsity of statements 1 and 2 in list A, for they do not contradict the statements in list A and are indeed altogether compatible with them. The temporal sequence in which the decision is taken and grounded (see statement 3 in list B)—the decision and its grounding qua psychological processes—is irrelevant for the justification of the decision.[38] The same is true of the factors that influence the judge's decision. The grounding of a decision is not diminished because the judge acts out of fear or owing to a bribe. Even a morally bad judge can take well-grounded decisions. And it is indeed very likely that in precisely those cases where his decision is not motivated by the feeling of being bound but by other, less worthy factors, the judge will go to considerable effort to offer a convincing, normative grounding of his decision.

Even the two conclusions—the statements at 4 in both lists, A and B—are not incompatible, although they are often understood as opposing and even contradictory theses. For the practising attorney who seeks to influence the judge and to predict the decision, knowledge of the factors motivating the judge is of the greatest significance. For the judge or the jurist who is to justify or to criticize a decision, however, knowledge of the norms is essential.

When efficacy is determined by designating a norm as efficacious if it is used or invoked to ground the legal decision, what is meant is that the norm enters into

[36] It is a widely held and deeply rooted prejudice of jurists to conflate the logical relation of the grounding of a decision and the doctrine of the mechanical activity of the judge. Proponents as well as critics of the syllogism theory often make the same mistake, for example, when they argue that 'the decision is derivable from the norms, *ergo*, the judge is an automaton.' Or: 'the judge is not an automaton, *ergo*, the decision is not derivable from the norms.' In both cases, the premiss is true and the conclusion is false; and both conclusions are based on the same mistake.

[37] See Ulrich Klug, 'Elektronische Datenverarbeitungsmaschinen im Recht', in *Festschrift Hermann Jahrreiss zu seinem siebzigsten Geburtstag*, ed. Karl Carstens and Hans Peters (Cologne: Carl Heymann, 1964), 189–99.

[38] The confusion is caused, *inter alia*, by the ambiguity of the words 'decision' and 'grounding', for they refer to certain psychological processes (the act of deciding, the act of grounding) as well as to the results of these psychological operations, results that are, however, logical in character.

certain *logical* relations (as explained earlier) with the decision, but not that the norm motivates the judge psychologically and is thereby the cause of the decision. Only by strictly separating the two types of relation can psychologism be avoided in determining efficacy.

Although Ross of course does not endorse either of the extreme theories,[39] he too fails to distinguish clearly between logical and causal relations. Therein may lie another reason for Ross's holding that two altogether different criteria for efficacy are closely related or even 'identical'. For Ross, mentioning a norm in the grounding of a decision appears to come to the same thing as the causal determination of the decision by means of this norm.[40]

4. An Analysis of Claims of Efficacy

My reflections thus far have shown that the proposition 'norm *N* is efficacious' states that *N* is applied by judges, in other words that *N* is used or invoked in the grounding of their decisions. How can this proposition be analysed? What does the ambiguous expression 'is applied' mean? Does the proposition refer to past, present, or future applications of the norm?

The proposition clearly cannot refer to the past, for it is possible that a norm that was applied earlier has lost its efficacy in the meantime, and it clearly cannot be exclusively a matter of a present application, for that would overly restrict the range of application of the word 'efficacious'. Is one compelled here to say that it is a matter of future applications? Ross appears to draw this conclusion, for he claims that the proposition '*N* is efficacious' is a prediction that the norm *N* will be applied by the courts in the future.

This interpretation, however, also gives rise to problems. First, in this interpretation, the meaning of the word 'efficacious' departs sharply from its ordinary use in legal discourse. It does seem altogether reasonable to claim of a norm that it is indeed efficacious at this moment but will very likely no longer be applied in the future (for example, on the assumption that the norm will soon be repealed). Ross would have to reject this statement as contradictory. A second problem is that since the propositions of legal science are, for Ross, statements about the efficacy of legal norms, they must be interpreted as predictions. To what extent is it justified to claim that the propositions found in a textbook on commercial law are in reality predictions? It is hard to dispute the fact that—at least in the preponderance of cases—legal scholars intend not to set out reflections on the future behaviour of judges but, rather, to formulate statements about existing law. What else can

[39] 'I shall not attempt here to assess the merits of these conflicting theories...' Ross, *LJ*, 44.

[40] The application of the norm means 'that in decisions in which its conditioning facts are assumed to exist, it forms an integral part of the reasoning underlying the judgment and has *therefore* been one of the decisive factors determining the conclusion at which the court has arrived.' Ross, *LJ*, 42 (emphasis added). 'A national law system, considered as a valid system of norms, can accordingly be defined as the norms which actually are operative in the mind of the judge, *because* they are felt by him to be socially binding and *therefore* obeyed.' Ross, *LJ*, 35 (emphasis added).

it mean to claim that these statements are 'in reality' predictions if not that one is speaking at best of an ideal science of law and not of legal science as it in fact exists?[41]

It seems to me that these objections can be met if efficacy is interpreted as a disposition.[42] According to this interpretation, the proposition 'norm *N* is efficacious' would refer not to the future but to the present and would therefore not be a prediction. This state of affairs would be similar to that of other dispositional concepts. For example, take the proposition 'sugar is soluble'. Solubility is obviously a present property of sugar. It does not first appear when sugar is put into water, for sugar is soluble even before it is actually dissolved. By comparison to other properties of sugar—for example, colour—solubility manifests peculiar characteristics. It cannot be directly observed, revealing itself only in certain circumstances, namely, when sugar is dissolved. The proposition 'sugar is soluble' is not, however, a prediction of future dissolutions of sugar, for even those sugar cubes that are never touched by liquid and so never dissolve are soluble. Rather, the proposition makes the claim that sugar has the disposition to dissolve when certain conditions obtain.

The function of efficacy could be explained in a similar way, and it seems to me that this interpretation quite faithfully reproduces the colloquial meaning of the word 'efficacious' and its use in legal discourse. Accordingly, the proposition 'norm *N* is efficacious' would not be a prediction of future applications of the norm. Rather, it would be an attributive statement to the effect that the norm has the disposition to be applied when certain conditions obtain—in other words, when the corresponding requirements are met. (In what follows, I shall occasionally replace the somewhat cumbersome expressions 'disposition to be applied' and 'disposition to application' with the more concise expression 'judicially invokable'.) On my interpretation, the proposition 'norm *N* is efficacious' is tantamount to the proposition 'if certain conditions were to obtain (those necessary to the application), then the courts would apply *N*'.[43]

In that I am speaking of the efficacy (or judicial invokability) of legal norms, I follow the ordinary use of language. This form of expression can be misleading, however, if one imagines thereby that, in addition to norms and their application by judges, there is also a new entity, a property by the name of 'efficacy'. This would count as a dangerous hypostatization. One cannot warn often enough against the tendency—encountered very frequently in jurisprudence—to see a substance behind every substantive, a property behind every predicate adjective, and where these are not visible, they are postulated. In particular, there is no special

[41] J. Miedzianagora has already made this objection in 'L'idée de Validité en Droit. A propos du dernier livre d'Alf Ross', *Logique et Analyse*, 4 (1961), 92–121, at 103: 'We see here again that Ross's realism is concerned not with a factual given but with a constructed model of reality; the concept of the doctrine is constructed from the concept of valid law elaborated by Ross in the course of his analysis of the direct content, the "*contenu immédiat*", of norms.'

[42] On the concept of disposition, see Rudolf Carnap, 'Testability and Meaning', *Philosophy of Science*, 3 (1936), 419–71, and 4 (1937), 1–40.

[43] Here it is a matter of a *subjunctive conditional*, not a material implication. The indicative is replaced by the subjunctive precisely to show that there is no prediction here.

property called efficacy. Rather, the proposition '*N* is efficacious' establishes a certain correlation between the norm and its application. One could say instead that 'judges have the disposition to apply norm *N*', just as, instead of saying 'sugar has the disposition to dissolve in water', one can say 'water has the disposition to dissolve sugar' without altering the sense of the expression.[44] Thus, the proposition 'because it is efficacious' would not be a satisfactory answer to the question 'Why is norm *N* applied?' (Only in a concrete case—'Why is norm *N* being applied by judge *X* in case *Y*?'—is it sensible to answer that the norm is efficacious, that is, that it is applied by other judges.) This shows that 'efficacy' does not name a property of norms that is to be seen as the cause of a norm's application.[45]

If the proposition '*N* is efficacious' is analysed as 'if certain conditions were to obtain, then judges would apply *N*', then it is clear why the proposition is not to be interpreted as a prediction. It refers not to the fact of application but to the correlation between the norm and its application, and it claims that this correlation exists, indeed, that it exists in the present. To be sure, on the basis of this determination, the future application of the norm can be predicted, for it is probable that an efficacious norm will be applied in the future as long as no new conditions arise that alter the situation (for example, the abrogation of the norm by lawmakers or a holding of unconstitutionality by the appropriate court). This circumstance can easily lead to interpreting a statement about the (present) efficacy of a norm as a prediction about its future applications. It must be explicitly emphasized, however, that present efficacy does not always permit a prediction of the future application of a norm, just as it does not presuppose the earlier application of the norm. The determination that a norm was applied by a court is certainly a very important element in demonstrating the proposition '*N* is efficacious', but it is not a necessary condition. Even newly issued norms that have not yet been applied can be efficacious. For example, on the basis of our experience that the courts are always prepared to apply constitutionally enacted statutes, a newly enacted statute can be deemed efficacious. If a norm is not applied although all necessary conditions for its application obtain, only then do we consider the non-application of a norm as proof of its inefficacy.

Questioning the meaning of the proposition '*N* is efficacious' must not be confused with questioning its verification, although the issues are related. As an empirical, general statement, this proposition cannot be completely verified, but, rather, can only be confirmed to a certain degree on the basis of experience, where observations of the actual behaviour of judges play a decisive role.

[44] See Charles L. Stevenson, *Ethics and Language* (New Haven: Yale University Press, 1944), at 46–53.

[45] Therefore I have given only a 'definition in use' of the word 'efficacious'. For the reasons why an explicit definition would not be suitable, see H. L. A. Hart, *Definition and Theory in Jurisprudence* (Oxford: Clarendon Press, 1953), repr. *Law Quarterly Review*, 70 (1954), 37–60, and in Hart, *EJP*, 21–48. See also Alf Ross, 'Definition in Legal Language', *Logique et Analyse*, 1 (1958), 139–49.

5. 'Judicial Invokability' as the Criterion for Efficacy

The definition of efficacy as judicial invokability means that only the judicial application of legal norms is seen as relevant. That a legal norm can be judicially invoked serves, then, as a necessary and sufficient condition for efficacy. The question arises of whether it is reasonable to exclude compliance and the non-judicial use of norms (and rules) or whether it might not be advisable to characterize a norm that is generally complied with as efficacious even if it is not applied by the courts.

From this standpoint, Kelsen criticizes Ross's assessment of efficacy, an assessment that coincides on this point with my own.[46] Kelsen argues that a legal norm appears to fulfil its purpose especially well in particular in the case of general compliance. The fact that judges have no occasion to apply the norm should count as the ultimate demonstration of its efficacy. Kelsen remarks, with irony, that to characterize such a norm as 'inefficacious' is especially questionable for a 'realist' legal theory.

If the efficacy of a norm is defined as the norm's being judicially invokable, however, then these objections have no force. According to the criterion introduced here, a norm would be efficacious that is generally complied with and owing to such compliance is not applied (because judges simply have no occasion to decide cases governed by this norm). One imagines a community in which no theft whatever is committed. The corresponding norm in the criminal code, which punishes theft, is *de facto* not applied, but that it can be judicially invoked is claimed with a very high degree of probability. If someone were to steal, he would certainly be punished. Only if there are good reasons to assume that the norm will not be applied even in cases of non-compliance is it considered inefficacious. This position should even be acceptable to Kelsen.

On the other hand—presupposing that the legal system in question has obligatory judicial review—even a norm that is complied with would scarcely be characterized as a *legal norm* if it could not be invoked by the courts. One thinks of the norms that govern the relations between members of a gang. Compliance with these norms, even if it be without exception, is not sufficient to make efficacious legal norms of them.

It is perhaps not superfluous to state expressly that the suggested criterion for efficacy does not have an unlimited range of application. First, I have spoken here solely of legal norms, and the efficacy of other norms was not at issue. Second, the suggested criterion is restricted to legal systems with obligatory judicial review, thereby ruling out international law and primitive systems. Third, the criterion is

[46] Hans Kelsen, 'Eine "Realistische" und die Reine Rechtslehre. Bemerkungen zu Alf Ross: *On Law and Justice*', *ÖZöR*, 10 (1959/60), 1–25, Engl. edn. 'A "Realistic" Theory of Law and the Pure Theory of Law: Remarks on Alf Ross's *On Law and Justice*', trans. Luís Duarte d'Almeida, in *Kelsen Revisited. New Essays on the Pure Theory of Law*, ed. Luís Duarte d'Almeida, et al. (Oxford: Hart Publishing, 2013), 195–221.

applicable only to norms that are used by the courts, so that certain constitutional norms and at least some legal decisions themselves are beyond its scope. In spite of these restrictions, the range of application reaches far enough. Norms (in the narrower sense) as well as rules, general as well as individual legal norms, issued norms as well as norms that have emerged as a matter of custom, all these are germane.

This caveat means that the expression 'efficacious' is ambiguous, that is, in its application to various norms it does not always have the same meaning. This comes as no surprise. If one considers that the word 'norm' is applied to so many, often very different phenomena, it becomes clear that precisely the opposite, unambiguity, would be exceedingly strange. A careful analysis would most likely give rise to even greater differentiation. By contrast, the possibility of one workable definition for all cases seems highly doubtful. Forgoing definitions like this is even less regrettable in that it stems from the insight that expressions like 'law', 'justice', and 'efficacy' do not name essences, and therefore that their meaning—or their meanings—can be clarified only by way of a painstaking analysis of the use of language and not by appeal to a scheme of essences.

2

Validity and Efficacy of the Law (1967/2003)*

Hans Kelsen

1.

To give expression to the idea that a legal norm or a legal system consisting of legal norms exists in a community, one says that this legal norm or this legal system is 'valid' for the members of this community. In this sense, validity is the specific *existence* of the law.

To characterize the specific existence of a legal norm or of a legal system consisting of legal norms as its 'validity' is to give expression to the particular way in which the legal norm or legal system is given, by contrast with the existence of natural facts.

But what does it mean to say that a legal norm or a legal system consisting of legal norms is 'valid'? To answer this question, one must first establish the concept of law that one presupposes in answering.

The law whose concept is presupposed here is a normative, *coercive system* of human behaviour, that is, an aggregate of norms linked to certain circumstances, in particular to certain human behaviour qua condition and to certain coercive acts qua consequence. These coercive acts consist in the deprivation of life, of liberty, of economic, political, or other valuables by coercive means, if necessary by means of physical force, for it is done without the consent—indeed, against the will—of those so deprived. If the coercive act is a reaction to certain human behaviour that is thereby qualified as contrary to law, as illegal, then the act is characterized as a 'sanction'. To be sure, if one uses this word in a broader sense, then one can characterize as sanctions all coercive measures established as the consequence of any circumstance whatsoever.

* [*Editors' note*: Hans Kelsen's paper, presumably written in 1967, was first published as 'Geltung und Wirksamkeit des Rechts', in the volume *Hans Kelsens stete Aktualität*, ed. Robert Walter, Clemens Jabloner, and Klaus Zeleny (Schriftenreihe des Hans Kelsen-Instituts, vol. 25) (Vienna: Manz, 2003), 5–21. It has been translated for the present volume by Bonnie Litschewski Paulson and Stanley L. Paulson.]

2.

The functions of the law are: with respect to certain behaviour to prescribe (or proscribe), to empower, to permit, or with respect to the validity of a legal norm to revoke or to restrict (derogate).

A legal norm *pro*scribes certain behaviour by linking to this behaviour qua condition a sanction qua obligatory consequence, and it thereby *pre*scribes forbearance from this behaviour. A norm of the criminal law establishes: 'If—in the view of the court having jurisdiction—an individual has murdered another individual, then the court, on the motion of a public prosecutor, shall sentence the accused to death.' Another norm of the criminal law establishes: 'If, in the view of the court having jurisdiction, an individual has stolen, then the court, on the motion of the public prosecutor, shall sentence the accused to a prison term.' In this way, the law proscribes murder and theft, which means the same as prescribing forbearance from murder and theft. The law thereby empowers the public prosecutor—that is, confers on him the legal power—to initiate a legal proceeding by way of his motion, and it empowers the court to order a coercive act, the coercive deprivation of life or liberty. A civil law norm establishes: 'If, in the view of the court having jurisdiction, an individual has failed to honour a contract to pay back a loan received, the court, at the behest of the creditor, shall order the debtor to repay the loan and, in case this command is not obeyed, shall order execution of judgment against the debtor's property.' In this way, the law proscribes failure to repay a loan and prescribes its repayment. And the law thereby empowers the creditor—that is, confers on him the legal power—to initiate a legal proceeding with his complaint, and it empowers the court to order a coercive act, the coercive deprivation of the defendant's property.

3.

The empowerment to order a coercive act does not always mean that the human behaviour that is the condition for the empowerment is *proscribed.* A norm of administrative law can establish: 'If an individual who is mentally ill poses a danger to the community, an administrative organ shall order his coercive detention in an asylum.' Another norm of administrative law can establish: 'If it is in the public interest, private property shall be expropriated', that is, the deprivation of property even without the consent—indeed, against the will—of the owner as well as the transfer of this property to the state or to some other public law body are ordered. By means of these legal norms, an organ of the community is empowered coercively to deprive an individual of his liberty or his property, but no behaviour is proscribed by these norms.

4.

Coercively to deprive another of his life, his liberty, or his property is a delict or—as traditionally expressed in the case law—illegal in so far as it is the condition for a sanction established by a legal norm. And it is a sanction in so far as the power to order this deprivation qua consequence is conferred by a legal norm. Where legal norms empower certain individuals—in modern legal systems, organs having particular functions, especially courts—coercively to deprive an individual of life, liberty, or property under certain conditions, these coercive acts are legal. Still, the possibility is not precluded that the order coercively depriving an individual of life, liberty, or property—in particular, the judicial decision containing the order—is challenged and, by means of the decision of a higher court, is overturned. The reason most often given for overturning a decision is that the decision is illegal. This is not correct. If a valid decision and only a valid decision is, until it is overturned, law, then it cannot be illegal. Illegal law is a contradiction in terms. To be sure, unless the judicial decision lies squarely within the discretion of the court, the law does prescribe a certain content for the decision, but it empowers the court not only to take a decision having the prescribed content but also to decide differently. If the court were not also so empowered, there would be no valid, overturnable decision. The law also establishes the possibility, however, in case the court does decide differently, of challenging and overturning the valid decision, which is valid owing to the court's being empowered to decide and is therefore legal.[1]

5.

In the sentences serving here as legal norms, the acts ordering the coercive deprivation of life, of liberty, of economic, political, or other valuables are governed by the 'ought', but this does not mean that they are *prescribed*. An act is legally prescribed, as already noted, if forbearing from the act is the condition for a sanction. The ordering of the coercive acts in the norms introduced here as examples is merely empowered, not prescribed. It is not only legally empowered but also legally prescribed if, in case the order is not carried out or does not proceed according to legally established conditions, a sanction to be directed against the responsible organ is established in a legal norm. The term 'ought' (*sollen*) gives expression to the ways, distinct from 'is' (*sein*), in which the ordering of a coercive act qua consequence is linked to the condition for the order. The sense of the legal norm is not that the ordering of a coercive act in fact proceeds, but, rather, that it is in accordance with the law that the ordering proceed. The legal norm is not a statement about actual events. The term 'ought' frequently means a prescription, that is to say, a prescription is often expressed not only in an imperative but also in an 'ought'-sentence, as in the norms 'you ought not to lie' and 'one ought not to steal'. The term 'ought', however, does not necessarily mean that the behaviour to which it refers is prescribed, as shown in language like 'he ought to be here by noon', which may mean simply that he will *presumably* be here by noon.

[1] See Kelsen, *RR 2*, at § 35(j) (271–80), *PTL*, at 267–76. [*Editors' note*: For these and other abbreviations, see the Table of Abbreviations.]

6.

The law also empowers individuals to regulate their reciprocal private-law relations by means of a declaration of intent, that is, through legal transactions like contracts, testaments, and so on. The law does this by conferring upon individuals the capacity to act to bring about the legal consequences intended by them. This capacity is characterized as the capacity to engage in legal transactions. It, too, is a legal power conferred by the law, for by means of legal transactions, legal norms constituting the rights and obligations of the parties to the legal transaction or even of third parties are created on the basis of the empowering legal norm. Since, however, coercive acts (sanctions) as a reaction to behaviour contrary to a legal transaction proceed only on the basis of the legal norm conferring power to engage in these transactions, the norms created by legal transactions are dependent legal norms.[2]

Even the so-called capacity to commit a delict stems from the legal system, which determines the conditions (age, mental state) that render an individual's behaviour punishable. While the so-called capacity to commit a delict is like the capacity to engage in a legal transaction, it is not usually characterized as a 'legal power' and spoken of as an empowerment to commit delicts—although in so far as 'empowerment' characterizes a function of the positive law, it expresses no moral approval or disapproval.

7.

'To permit' has various meanings. That behaviour is permitted can mean that it is neither prescribed nor proscribed by a norm, that it is 'free' in this sense, like thinking (as when one says 'thoughts are free') or breathing. In this negative sense, with reference to prescribing, permitting is not the function of a norm. There is no 'permission' in this negative sense as the function of a norm, but, rather, only a 'being permitted' as the property of behaviour that is *not* the object of any norm.

That behaviour is permitted can, however, also mean that the validity of a norm proscribing certain behaviour is revoked or restricted by another, derogating norm. Then permission has a positive sense and is the function of a derogating norm. The function of positively permitting is reducible to the function of derogating. Thus, for example, the validity of a legal norm that proscribes, with punishment, entry to certain property is revoked—in accordance with the positive law principle *lex posterior derogat legi priori*—by a legal norm that establishes: 'If someone enters this property, he ought *not* to be punished.' Then one says that entering this property is now legally permitted, that is to say,

[2] See Kelsen, *RR 2*, § 30(a) (at 152), *PTL*, at 148. [*Translators' note*: See also Kelsen, *RR 2*, at § 6(e) (55–9), *PTL*, at 54–8.]

entering this property is no longer legally proscribed. The validity of the legal norm that *proscribes*, with punishment, the creation and manufacture of certain toxic substances can be restricted by a legal norm that excludes from punishment persons—say, pharmacists—who have received an official concession to create and to manufacture such substances for medicinal purposes, that is, this legal norm establishes that such persons ought *not* to be punished. Thus, for these persons, the creation and manufacture of such toxic substances for medicinal purposes is permitted in that, for them, it is not legally proscribed. Behaviour that is permitted by derogating norms is *set* free, not simply 'free' like behaviour that no norm prescribes or proscribes.

8.

Permission is related to prescription and proscription in so far as behaviour that is permitted is not proscribed and behaviour that is merely permitted is not also prescribed. Is, however, behaviour also permitted if it is prescribed? This claim is often made but it is not correct, because permission and prescription are two different normative functions and must therefore be kept separate. The prescription can be complied with or violated, while the permission can be neither complied with nor violated, but only used or not used. If behaviour is permitted, one has two choices, namely, whether to behave or not to behave as one is permitted to do. If behaviour is prescribed, however, one has no choice between behaving or not behaving in accordance with the prescription. If behaviour that is prescribed were also permitted, then one would have both the choice and no choice of behaving as prescribed and—therefore—also as permitted.

With reference to the validity of a system of positive laws, one ordinarily says: 'What is not proscribed is permitted.' This rule, in so far as behaviour that is permitted (in the positive sense) is not proscribed, simply expresses the empty tautology that what is not proscribed is not proscribed. If, however, 'being permitted' (in the negative sense) means neither proscribed nor prescribed, then the rule is not correct, for it is a contradiction to claim that what is not proscribed is neither prescribed nor proscribed. What is not proscribed can be prescribed. Can, however, the following rule be valid: 'What is not permitted is proscribed'? Since permission (in the positive sense of the word) is a normative function in revoking or restricting the validity of a norm that proscribes certain behaviour, the rule in question presupposes a norm of the legislator that proscribes *all* behaviour not permitted by the legislator, that is, the validity of the general proscription of behaviour is not restricted with reference to all possible actions and forbearances that the legislator does not intend to proscribe. This is conceivable in theory, but unworkable in practice.

From time to time it is claimed that the rule 'what is not permitted is proscribed' does not apply in general but does indeed apply with reference to acts of law creation and law application: If such acts are not permitted, they are proscribed. This is incorrect on its face, for these acts are not 'permitted' but stem, rather, from an empowerment, and empowering is a function distinct from permitting. Whoever performs an act without being empowered to do so, where an empowerment is required by prevailing law, does not violate a proscription unless performance of the act is established in a valid legal norm as a condition for directing against him a coercive act (a sanction), which is to say, is proscribed. Acting without being empowered to do so, where empowerment is required, is not, however, necessarily proscribed.[3]

What does it mean to permit illegal behaviour? If permission stems from the legal authority, it is by way of derogation, that is, the revocation or restriction of the validity of a legal norm proscribing certain behaviour and thereby rendering it illegal. If, for example, the validity of the legal norm proscribing, with punishment, the killing of an individual is restricted by a norm that excludes from punishment killing an individual in self-defence, then killing in self-defence is allowed and thereby legal. If permission to behave illegally does not stem from the legal authority, then it is itself illegal behaviour. If, for example, a husband 'allows' the killing of his wife, that is, indicates with the expression 'allow' that he has nothing against the killing of his wife and that he will make no effort either to prevent the killing or to bring legal charges against the murderer, such a 'permission' is a crime, say, incitement to murder.

9.

Legal norms having the functions characterized here are the sense of the acts of will of those individuals who create and apply the law—legislators, judges, administrative officials, and individuals engaged in private-law transactions.[4] These legal norms are the subjective sense of these acts, that is, the sense intended by these actors. To say that this subjective sense is a valid legal norm is to say that it is also interpreted as the objective sense of the act. This is by no means always so in the case of acts that are, like norm-creating acts, directed to the behaviour of others. So, for example, every command-act, even that of a gangster who demands that a businessman pay him a certain sum of money, has the subjective sense of a prescription, but this subjective sense is not—unlike a tax official's command directed to the businessman—interpreted as its objective sense. In other words, the gangster's command is not interpreted as a valid legal norm, although the subjective sense of the gangster's act can be the same as the subjective sense of the tax official's act. If one does not comply with the gangster's command, this behaviour—unlike disobeying the tax official's command—is not interpreted as a 'violation' of a valid legal norm, as 'contrary to law'. *That a legal norm is 'valid' means that it and therefore its functions as characterized here are not only the subjective sense but also the objective sense of the act of will with which—figuratively speaking—this norm is created.* What is the presupposition underlying the interpretation of the subjective sense of an act directed to the behaviour of others also as its

[3] See § 5, this chapter. [*Translators' note*: See also §§ 3, 17–19, and 21.]

[4] That legal norms created by custom are also the sense of acts of will, see Kelsen, *RR 2*, § 4(b) (at 9), *PTL*, at 9.

objective sense? It is the presupposition of the basic norm. Since this presupposition has no further bearing here, I shall confine myself to referring to the exposition found in the second edition of my *Pure Theory of Law*.[5]

10.

The German language has no expression with which to characterize all possible functions of a legal norm.[6] It is in particular not entirely correct to characterize them—as is often done—as 'binding'.[7] The legal norm is 'binding'—that is, binds the addressee of the norm to certain behaviour—only in its prescriptive function, not in its empowering or permissory functions, let alone in its derogating function. That an individual is legally 'bound' to certain conduct means the same as that he is legally obligated to behave in this way.[8] That is not the case, however, if one is merely empowered or permitted to behave in this way, and especially not the case if a norm is valid that revokes or restricts the validity of another norm and imposes no obligation to behave in any particular way at all.[9]

[5] *RR 2*, § 34(a)(b)(c)(d) (196–209), *PTL*, 193–205, and see *RR 2*, second appendix, 402–44, at 443–4 [*translators' note*: the appendices in Kelsen's *Reine Rechtslehre* were not translated in the English edition], where I write: 'The basic norm introduced by the Pure Theory of Law is not law different from the positive law, but, rather, is simply the basis of the validity of the positive law, the logico-transcendental condition for its validity, and has, as such, no ethico-political character but, rather, an epistemic character.' Karl Larenz, *Das Problem der Rechtsgeltung* (Berlin: Junker und Dünnhaupt, 1929), at 17, claims that, with the basic norm, I resort to natural law theory, the very theory that I have challenged. This is not so. I expressly reject this interpretation of the basic norm.

[6] I have tried to come to terms with this difficulty in *RR 2*, § 4(c) (at 10), *PTL*, at 10. There I use the word 'ought' to characterize the various functions of the legal norm as normative functions. I write: 'If we…use the word "ought" in a sense that encompasses all of these meanings (prescription, empowerment, permission), we can give expression to the validity of a norm by saying: Something ought to be or not to be, ought to be done or not to be done.' [*Translators' note*: The parenthetical insertion is Kelsen's addition to his original text.] Although, as already noted, the word 'ought' can have different meanings, it does seem too far removed from ordinary usage to say, of behaviour that is empowered or is permitted, that one 'ought' so to behave.

[7] For example, Ernst Rudolph Bierling, *Zur Kritik der juristischen Grundbegriffe*, first part (Gotha: F.A. Perthes, 1877), 17; Theodor Geiger, *Vorstudien zu einer Soziologie des Rechts* (first publ. 1947) (Neuwied am Rhein and Berlin: Luchterhand, 1964), 167, 169, 205, 207, 212, 213, 257; O.H. Germann, 'Zur Problematik der Rechtsverbindlichkeit und der Rechtsgeltung', *Revue Hellénique de Droit International*, 18 (1965), 1–25. In the second edition of my book *Reine Rechtslehre*, I, too, have occasionally identified 'validity' and 'bindingness'. Thus, I write: 'It is not the case that the subjective sense of every command-act is also interpreted as its objective sense, that is, as a binding norm', and I mean by 'binding' norm a 'valid norm'. Kelsen, *RR 2*, first appendix, 357–401, at 359.

[8] See Hans Welzel, *An den Grenzen des Rechts. Die Frage nach der Rechtsgeltung* (Cologne and Opladen: Westdeutscher Verlag, 1966), at 5, who takes up the question of legal validity as the question of the 'standard that can ultimately turn the *efficacious* directives of the highest state power into *binding* law'.

[9] Alfred Verdross, *Abendländische Rechtsphilosophie* (Vienna: Springer, 1958), at 246, writes: 'In legal theory the expression "validity" is understood in a threefold sense. One can understand thereby either the moral validity of a norm or its efficacy in a certain community, or that the norm of a certain positive legal system was duly created and is therefore binding in this legal system.' Here Verdross

11.

The norm, as stated earlier, is the sense of an act of will, but the existence of a positive law norm, its validity, is different from the existence of the act of will whose objective sense the norm is. The norm can be valid if the act of will whose sense the norm is no longer exists. Indeed, the norm first emerges as valid when the act of will whose sense the norm is ceases to exist. The individual who has created a legal norm with his act intentionally directed to the behaviour of others need not continue to desire this behaviour in order for the norm that is the sense of his act to be valid. When individuals acting as legislators render certain matters normative by enacting a statute and thereby establishing its validity, they then turn, in their enactments, to rendering other matters normative. The statute whose validity they have established can be valid long after these individuals have died and so cannot desire anything at all. It is therefore incorrect to characterize the norm in general and the legal norm in particular as the 'will' of an authority, especially of the legislator or the state, if by 'will' the psychical act of will is understood and this characterization is supposed to mean more than that the norm is *created* through an act of will.

12.

The validity of a legal norm must also be distinguished from its efficacy, although validity is often identified with efficacy.[10] In order to arrive at the concept of efficacy, one must consider the possible relations between actual human behaviour and a legal norm.

If one conceives of the law as a normative, coercive system and therefore understands by a legal norm—that is, the norm of a legal system—a norm establishing

seems to endorse the view that the 'validity' of a legal norm and its 'bindingness' mean the same thing. But he pursues the matter: 'If, for example, a proponent of natural law speaks of the validity of the law, he can only mean its *moral* validity. If, however, a proponent of moderate legal positivism (who reserves the term "law" for the positive law without denying the existence of a higher order of norms) speaks of the validity of a positive legal system, he means its efficacy.' Taking issue here, I should note that 'moral' validity is not legal validity. If a proponent of natural law speaks of a 'moral' validity of the law, he can only mean—correctly—the *basis* of the validity of a legal norm, namely, its correspondence to a norm of morality, in particular the principle of justice. The *basis* of the validity of a legal norm is not, however, its validity. By the 'validity' of a legal norm, one cannot understand its efficacy, for 'validity' and 'efficacy' mean very different things (see § 12, this chapter). Even a proponent of legal positivism cannot mean, by the 'validity' of a legal norm, its efficacy. The Pure Theory of Law, which is a radically positivistic legal theory, emphasizes as strongly as possible the difference between validity and efficacy. With reference to the identity of validity and bindingness, see n. 7, this chapter.

[10] Thus, for example, Rudolf Stammler, *Theorie der Rechtswissenschaft* (Halle an der Saal: Waisenhaus, 1911), at 117, writes: 'The validity of a law is the possibility of its being enforced.' Larenz, *Das Problem der Rechtsgeltung* (n. 5, this chapter), at 14, correctly rejects this identification of validity with efficacy by arguing: 'Legal norms and their claim to validity' are 'logically primary, while actual efficacy in the life of a community presupposes validity…'.

that, under certain conditions, in particular in the case of certain human behaviour, a coercive act as consequence—as a sanction—ought to be ordered, then the possible relation between the actual human behaviour and such a norm is twofold. The behaviour can be compliance with or the application of the norm.[11]

It is *compliance* when it is in relation to a legal norm that proscribes or prescribes certain behaviour. As stated earlier, a legal norm proscribes certain behaviour in that it links to this behaviour, which is thereby qualified as a 'violation' of law, a sanction as obligatory consequence, and a legal norm prescribes certain behaviour in that it links to the opposite behaviour a sanction as obligatory consequence. The individual whose behaviour is the condition for the sanction 'violates' the law with this behaviour, and, with the opposite, sanction-avoiding behaviour, he complies with the law. If the sanction is linked to a positive action as its condition, as in the legal norm 'if someone steals, he ought to be punished with a prison term', then compliance with the legal norm consists in forbearing from theft, that is, forbearing from the behaviour that is linked qua condition to the sanction qua consequence. If the sanction is linked to forbearance from certain behaviour, as in the legal norm 'if someone fails to pay back a loan received, execution of judgment ought to be ordered against his property', then compliance with the legal norm consists in repaying the loan received, that is, it consists in the behaviour whose omission is linked to the sanction.

13.

The assumption is sometimes made that there is an analogy between compliance with a norm and the truth of a statement.[12] It is argued that just as, in the case of contradictory statements, only one can be true, and if the one is true then the other must be false, so, in the case of conflicting norms, only one can be complied with, and if the one is complied with then the other cannot be complied with but must be violated instead. A closer look shows, however, that there are essential differences between compliance with or the violation of a norm and the truth or falsity of a statement. Truth and falsity are properties of the statement. Compliance with and the violation of a norm are properties not of the norm, but, rather, of behaviour that

[11] See Eugenio Bulygin, in 'The Concept of Efficacy' (1965), in this volume, ch. 1. Bulygin claims that, according to my view, 'the law consists exclusively of norms addressed to judges. [Kelsen's] view conceals the radical difference between compliance with legal norms and their application' [Bulygin, in this volume, at 38]. In fact, according to my view, the addressees of legal norms are by no means only judges—legal norms are addressed not only to the courts, but also to administrative officials and, indirectly, to all legal subjects obligated and empowered by these legal norms. This aside, a glance at the index of the second edition of my *Reine Rechtslehre* shows that I do indeed distinguish between 'application' of and 'compliance' with legal norms. The very heading in the book at § 35(f) (239), *PTL*, at 233, reads: 'Law Creation, Law Application, and Compliance with Law'.

[12] See Hans Kelsen, 'Law and Logic', trans. Peter Heath, in Kelsen, *Essays in Legal and Moral Philosophy*, ed. Ota Weinberger (Dordrecht: D. Reidel, 1973), 228–53 (first published as 'Recht und Logik', *Forum. Österreichische Monatsblätter für kulturelle Freiheit*, 12 [1965], 421–5 and 495–500, in *WS 2*, 1469–97).

corresponds or fails to correspond to the norm prescribing or proscribing certain behaviour. Two norms, the one prescribing certain behaviour while the other proscribes this very behaviour, do not represent a logical contradiction, as do two statements, the one affirming something while the other denies this very thing. Setting out the validity of a norm in parallel to the truth of a statement shows that *both* of the conflicting norms can be valid, presenting, then, a norm conflict or a conflict of obligation. Of two contradictory statements, however, only one can be true, and if the one is true then the other must be false. This is established by logic, which thereby resolves the problem of contradiction. But logic cannot establish anything analogous with respect to norm conflicts. A norm conflict can be resolved not by means of logic but only by the authority that issues norms, that is, by means of a norm that revokes the validity of one or both of the conflicting norms.

14.

Of two conflicting general norms, only one can be complied with, and if the one is complied with then the other must be violated. There is, for example, the Old Testament norm, 'you ought to hate your enemies', in conflict with the New Testament norm, 'you ought not to hate your enemies, but to love them'; or there is the norm of a morality that proscribes in all circumstances the killing of an individual, in conflict with the norm of a positive law that prescribes killing individuals in carrying out punishment or in wartime, as enemies. This applies, however, only to the individual's behaviour that serves to comply with the one norm. Only with this behaviour is the other norm necessarily violated. This other norm can be complied with by another individual. Indeed, one and the same individual can comply sometimes with the one norm and sometimes with the other norm, so that one and the same norm can be both complied with and violated. One and the same statement—say, 'all men are mortal'—cannot, however, be true for one individual and false for another or sometimes true and sometimes false for one and the same individual, thus both true and false. If the statement is true, it is always true for everyone. Thus, an analogy cannot be drawn between compliance with a norm and the truth of a statement—or indeed, if at all, only in very narrow measure.

15.

If one understands by 'compliance' with a legal norm actual behaviour that matches the behaviour prescribed in the legal norm, then alongside the norm linking a sanction to certain behaviour—the primary norm—one can assume a secondary norm prescribing the behaviour that avoids the sanction. 'One ought to forbear from theft'—'Whoever steals ought to be punished with a prison term'. 'One ought to repay a loan received'—'If someone fails to pay back a loan received, execution of judgment ought to be ordered against his property'. The secondary norm, however, is frequently not given expression at all in the positive law. Criminal law does not usually establish that 'one ought to forbear from theft' *and* that 'if someone steals, he shall be punished with a prison term'. In civil law, it is not usually established that 'one ought to repay a loan received' *and* that 'if someone fails to pay back a loan received, execution of judgment shall be ordered against his property'. Both criminal and civil law confine themselves to establishing the norm given here in second place. Nonetheless, one assumes that forbearance from theft and the repayment of a loan received are legally prescribed. From this it follows, as already noted, that the law prescribes certain behaviour in that it links to the opposite behaviour obligatory, coercive acts—acts that execute civil judgments or carry out criminal punishment.

16.

If one conceives of the law as a coercive system and takes into account only those norms that establish sanctions, that is, coercive acts as reactions to behaviour thereby qualified as contrary to law, then the law is a reaction to what is contrary to law. And then, as Thomas Aquinas in the *Summa Theologiae I-II* writes, only those who are evil, not the good, are subject to the legal system.

> In the second manner a person subject to the law is said to be constrained by an enforcing principle. Thus, virtuous and just men are not subject to the law, but only wicked men. What is constrained and forced is contrary to will. The will of good men is consonant with the law, whereas the will of wicked men is dissonant, and in this sense the good are not subject to the law, but only the wicked.[13]

If, however, one also takes into account the empowering and permissory functions of the law, then the law is not only a reaction to what is contrary to law and not only are those who are evil subject to the legal system. This is especially true in the case of application of the law by officials of the legal community.

17.

Application of the legal norm is the actual behaviour of one who, in case the condition established in a legal norm obtains, in particular the material fact of illegality specified in the legal norm, carries out the coercive act established in the legal norm as consequence, in particular the act representing criminal punishment or the coercive execution of civil judgments. With reference to the legal norms establishing these coercive acts and so proscribing certain behaviour, it is noteworthy that only those organs having particular functions in technically developed legal

[13] Thomas Aquinas, *Summa Theologiae, I-II*, Question 95, article 5, in: Thomas Aquinas, *Law and Political Theory*, vol. 28 of the *Summa Theologiae* (Questions 90–7), ed. and trans. Thomas Gilby, Blackfriars (London: Eyre & Spottiswoode, 1966), at 134 (trans. amended).

systems, only those individuals specified by the legal system and distinct from the subjects whose legally protected interests have been violated, are to carry out the coercive acts of criminal punishment and the execution of civil judgments. That is, these subjects themselves are not, as in technically primitive legal systems where there is still the principle of self-help, to carry out these coercive acts.

Application—and not compliance in the specific sense of this word—is also the case when a public prosecutor introduces in a judicial proceeding the motion to prosecute an individual for committing, in the view of the public prosecutor, a delict. This motion is brought in the exercise of an *empowerment*, legal power conferred by the legal system on the public prosecutor. The motion counts as compliance with the law only if this act is also prescribed, only if the public prosecutor is obligated by a legal norm to introduce the motion to prosecute, that is, only if forbearance from introducing the motion is the condition for a sanction (disciplinary action) directed against the negligent public prosecutor.

Application of—not compliance with—the law is the case not only when an organ of the state makes use of an empowerment conferred by the legal system, but also when a private individual does so, as, for example, when a creditor brings charges against a dilatory debtor before a court, thereby initiating a legal proceeding.

Just as the law is not 'complied with' when one makes use of an empowerment, so likewise the law is not 'violated' when one does not make use of the empowerment—in so far as the behaviour in the first case is not prescribed and the behaviour in the second case is not proscribed. If someone performs an act without being empowered to do so, where an empowerment is required by prevailing law—if, for example, someone commands that all men over the age of 21 are to marry—this command-act does not have the character of a violation of law, an illegality in the specific sense of these words, for it is not legally proscribed, that is, not the condition for a sanction. The consequence of an individual's performing an act without being empowered to do so is not that a coercive act as sanction ought to be directed against him. Rather, the consequence is that the act lacks the objective sense intended by the individual, that is, this command is not a valid norm. Legally speaking, it does not exist.

It is well to make the terminological distinction between compliance with and application of the law, since the opposite of compliance is characterized as a 'violation' of the law and so behaviour ought to be characterized as 'compliance' with a legal norm only if behaviour can also violate this legal norm. This is true only of those legal norms that prescribe or proscribe certain behaviour, not of legal norms that empower individuals to behave in a certain way.

18.

The situation seems to be somewhat different in the case of a permission (in the positive sense) granted to an individual by the legal system. That is, behaviour is permitted because the validity of a legal norm proscribing, with punishment, certain behaviour—say, entering a certain area—is revoked by another, derogating legal norm, and so entry into this area is permitted. Whoever makes use of this permission and enters the area applies the law granting him this permission, but he neither complies with the law nor violates it if he does not make use of the permission. If the validity of the legal norm proscribing, with punishment, the creation and manufacture of toxic substances is *restricted* by a legal norm excluding from punishment persons who have been granted official permission to create and to manufacture toxic substances for medicinal purposes, then the creation and manufacture of these substances for these purposes is permitted for these persons. Whoever makes use of this permission applies the law but is not complying with it, and whoever makes no use of the permission is not violating the law. Empowerment and permission leave to the individual who is empowered or permitted the choice of whether or not to make use thereof, whereas the prescription and proscription of certain behaviour leave no such choice to the individual addressed by the prescription or proscription. One whose behaviour is characterized as legally 'not permitted', however, violates the law. Here a distinction between empowerment and permission seems to exist, but that is not the case, for to call behaviour 'not permitted' is simply a less than felicitous characterization of *proscribed* behaviour.

19.

If a legal norm links to an individual's behaviour qua condition a sanction qua obligatory consequence (criminal punishment or the execution of civil judgment), then we say that the individual 'violates' the law, 'breaks' the law, that his behaviour is 'il'-legal, 'contrary to' law. These characterizations give expression to the idea of a negation of the law, the notion of something outside the law and against it that threatens, disrupts, or even annihilates the existence of the law. This notion is misleading. It is misleading because one construes as a logical contradiction the relation between a norm that prescribes certain behaviour—a certain action or forbearance from a certain action—and actual behaviour representing forbearance from the prescribed action or the performance of an action whose forbearance is prescribed. But a logical contradiction can only exist between two *statements*, the one saying that something is and the other saying that precisely this something is not. The two statements cannot coexist, for if the one is true, then the other cannot be true and must be false. Between a norm that prescribes certain behaviour and actual behaviour that is the opposite of the behaviour prescribed—behaviour that does not comport with the norm or, as one says, 'violates' the norm, 'breaks' the law—there exists no logical contradiction. To say that a norm is valid that prescribes certain human behaviour and to say that there is actual human behaviour that is the opposite of the behaviour prescribed can both be said without any contradiction. Both can exist side by side, both can be true at the same time. The validity—that is, the specific existence—of a norm that prescribes certain behaviour is not 'broken' by actual behaviour that is the opposite, as a chain that shackles an individual is broken. The chain of the law shackles even the law-'breaking' individual; the norm is not 'violated', not injured as an individual can be injured—that is, deprived of his very existence—by a coercive act directed against him. If a normative system, like the legal system, prescribes certain behaviour precisely by linking a sanction to the opposite behaviour, the essential state of affairs is correctly described by means of a hypothetical judgment stating that, in case of certain behaviour, a certain coercive act ought to be ordered and carried out. In this proposition, illegality appears as a *condition* of the law, not as its negation. What is clear, then, is that illegality is not something outside the law and against it, but is, rather, a material fact within the law, determined by the law. And it is clear that the law, by its very nature, refers precisely and most particularly to illegality. As with everything, so likewise illegality or non-law (*Un-Recht*) can be legally conceived of only as law, that is, only as determined by the law. To speak of 'il'-legal behaviour is to refer to behaviour that is the condition for the coercive act, and to speak of 'legal' behaviour is to refer to the opposite behaviour, namely, that which avoids the coercive act.

20.

The delict, imagined in naïve, pre-scientific thought as negation of the law, as non-law (*Un-Recht*), is reinterpreted by legal science as a condition of the law, reinterpreted in a process similar to that of theology confronting the problem of theodicy, that is, the problem of evil in a world created by a benevolent and omnipotent God. Since everything that exists must be conceived of as willed by God, the question arises: How can evil be conceived of as willed by a benevolent God? The answer of a resolutely monotheistic theology is that evil is interpreted as a necessary condition for the good. If there were no evil, there could be no good either. The assumption that evil is not the work of God, that, rather, it is the work of the devil directed against God, is not compatible with the monotheistic hypothesis, for it includes the notion of a counter-God, a non-God (*Un-Gott*).

21.

It may seem at first that the *efficacy* of norms generally and of legal norms in particular can be asserted only in so far as these norms prescribe or proscribe certain behaviour and so can be complied with or violated. Accordingly, efficacy seems to exist only in being compliant with a prescriptive or proscriptive norm, but the function of norms, as mentioned earlier, is not only to prescribe and to proscribe, but also to empower and to permit. The legal norm that prescribes certain human behaviour by establishing that, in case of the opposite behaviour, a certain individual qua organ of the legal community ought to direct a coercive act qua sanction against the offender, or against an individual related to the offender in a certain way, thereby empowers the first-named individual qua organ to order a coercive act. The constitution empowers a certain organ to issue general legal norms as 'statutes'. If, under certain conditions, a legal norm restricts the validity of a proscription to the advantage of certain subjects, it permits these subjects to do what others are forbidden to do. As stated above, one who makes use of such an empowerment or permission applies the empowering or permissory legal norm just as the judge applies a prescription or proscription when he directs a coercive act as a sanction against the offender and thus renders efficacious the legal norm he applies. If a subject makes use of an empowerment conferred on him by the law—if, as in the examples given earlier, a creditor brings charges against a dilatory debtor, or a public prosecutor introduces in a judicial proceeding the motion to prosecute an individual for committing, in the view of the public prosecutor, a delict, or an administrative organ orders the coercive detention in an asylum of an individual who is mentally ill and poses a danger to the community—then the law is every bit as efficacious as when someone complies with a norm that prescribes certain behaviour. The court, by granting the creditor's charges or convicting the accused, can only render the law efficacious if the creditor has brought charges or the public prosecutor has introduced a motion to prosecute. Thus, the law has already become efficacious through these acts. As mentioned above, however, since the empowerment and the permission leave to the subject granted them the choice of whether or not to make use of them, one cannot properly say that the law is inefficacious where *no* use is made of the empowerment or the permission. To be sure, if one were to assume that a legal norm ought to be characterized as 'efficacious' only if it can also be inefficacious, then the concept of efficacy would have to be restricted to norms that prescribe or proscribe certain behaviour. If one rejects this view, then one can say that the law can be efficacious not only in its prescriptive and proscriptive functions but also in its empowering and permissory functions, even if it cannot be characterized as inefficacious in case no use is made of the empowerment or the permission. The result of this analysis is: The law is efficacious if use is made of the empowerment or the permission granted by the law and the law is thereby applied, or if the proscription established by the law is respected and the law is thereby complied with.[14]

22.

Although 'validity' and 'efficacy' are distinct concepts, as shown earlier, and so the occasional attempt to identify 'validity' with 'efficacy' is emphatically to be

[14] On the concept of efficacy, Bulygin, 'The Concept of Efficacy' (n. 11, this chapter), in this volume, ch. 1, at 48, writes as follows: '[T]he proposition "norm *N* is efficacious" is tantamount to the proposition "if certain conditions were to obtain (those necessary to the application), then the courts would apply *N*".' In reply, it should be noted that the constraint 'if certain conditions were to obtain' is superfluous. For if the conditions specified in the norm—and only these can be considered—do not obtain, then the norm *cannot* be applied. If the court were to claim to apply the norm, the claim would be false. In fact, the efficacy of a legal norm, according to Bulygin, consists in its being applied by the courts or—as he also expresses the point—in its being 'judicially invokable'. Bulygin

rejected,[15] there does nevertheless exist an essential connection between them. *Efficacy is a condition for the validity of a legal norm*, namely, in the sense that a legal norm *forfeits its validity if it does not become efficacious or if it loses its efficacy.* Efficacy must ensue when a legal norm becomes valid, so that the norm not forfeit its validity. A legal norm must become efficacious not to attain validity but to retain validity, for a legal norm is valid before it becomes efficacious. A court that applies, in a concrete case, a statute immediately after it was enacted and therefore before it could become efficacious is applying a valid legal norm. But a legal norm is no longer seen as valid if it remains permanently inefficacious.[16]

writes: '…I am speaking of the efficacy (or judicial invokability) of legal norms…'. This determination of the concept of efficacy, the identification of efficacy with judicial invokability, is untenable because legal norms are applied not only by courts, but—as I have emphasized in the text—also by administrative officials and private persons, and these legal norms can thereby become efficacious. In addition, Bulygin's concept formation, as he himself grants, is not germane at all for the norms of primitive law or of public international law, where no courts are established.

By the 'judicial invokability' of a norm, Bulygin has in mind a norm's being 'used or invoked to ground the legal decision [that is, the judicial decision]' [*translators' note*: Kelsen's insertion]. He means by this that 'the norm enters into certain *logical* relations…with the decision'. According to Bulygin, these logical relations consist in the fact that 'the legal decision is the logical conclusion of a deductive argument, where the norms to be applied play the role of premisses'. That is, the validity of the individual legal norm that represents the judicial decision—say, 'the thief Schulze shall be sent to prison'—is the result of a logical inference from the validity of the general legal norm—'all thieves ought to be sent to prison'—just as the truth of the statement 'the human being Socrates is mortal' is the logical inference from the truth of the statement 'all human beings are mortal'. This view, although widely held in traditional jurisprudence, is mistaken, as I have shown in my article 'Law and Logic' (n. 12, this chapter). The validity of the individual legal norm that represents a judicial decision cannot be the logical inference from the validity of a general legal norm, as the truth of the statement 'the human being Socrates is mortal' is the logical inference from the truth of the statement 'all human beings are mortal'. The validity of a legal norm is conditioned by the act of will whose sense the norm is, while the truth of a statement is not conditioned by an act of thinking whose sense the statement is. The general legal norm 'all thieves ought to be sent to prison' can be valid, and the statement 'Schulze is a thief, for he stole a horse from Maier' can be true, can even be established by the court, but the individual legal norm 'Schulze shall be sent to prison' can nevertheless be *invalid* if this judicial decision, for whatever reason, does not in fact ensue.

[15] See Kelsen, *RR 2*, at § 34(g) (215–21), *PTL*, at 211–14.

[16] See Kelsen, *RR 2*, § 4(c) (at 11), § 34(g) (at 219), *PTL*, at 11 and at 212 respectively. Rupert Schreiber, *Logik des Rechts* (Berlin: Springer, 1962), at 81, claims that the validity of legal norms means the same as their efficacy. He is objecting to my argument supporting the distinction between the validity and the efficacy of a legal norm, the argument, namely, that a legal norm is already valid before it becomes efficacious. '[A] court that applies, in a concrete case, a statute immediately after it was enacted and therefore before it could become efficacious is applying a valid legal norm.' In that the court applies the legal norm, it does provide as well an example of the efficacy of the legal norm. If the norm is valid, it is also already efficacious, even if it is not immediately complied with and applied. If it is applied only later, the consequences of a violation of the statute are also 'extended' to the time immediately following issuance of the legal norm. If, however, a legal norm first becomes efficacious *by being complied with and applied*, then it cannot be efficacious before it is complied with or applied. That the consequences of a violation of the statute are 'extended' to the time immediately following issuance of the legal norm can only mean that one can already say, immediately following the issuance of the legal norm, that certain sanctions ought to be ordered and carried out, not that the competent organs will *actually* order the sanctions and carry them out. Precisely this actual ordering and carrying out of sanctions is, however, efficacy; that the sanctions *ought* to be ordered and carried out is the *validity* of the legal norm. Moreover, if a constitutionally issued legal norm is violated in a concrete case and for whatever reason is in fact not applied and so is not *efficacious* in this case, it does not forfeit its validity thereby.

23.

Eugenio Bulygin claims that, according to the Pure Theory of Law, efficacy is not only the necessary condition for the validity of legal norms, but it is also the sufficient condition for validity. Efficacy is necessary because a legal norm forfeits its validity if it becomes inefficacious through *desuetudo*, and efficacy is sufficient, on Bulygin's reading, in that '[Kelsen] recognizes custom as a law-creating source (that cannot be excluded even by the constitution), and customary norms are precisely those norms that derive their validity from their efficacy'.[17] On the distinction between necessary and sufficient conditions, Bulygin refers to Ulrich Klug.[18]

If efficacy is a sufficient condition for the validity of a legal norm, there exists between the condition and the conditioned, according to Klug, the 'if-so-then-*always*' relation.[19]

Thus, the following sentence must be true: If a legal norm is efficacious, then it is always a valid legal norm. This sentence is indeed true. Efficacy *is* in this sense a sufficient condition for validity, but this is so not because custom is a law-creating material fact and legal norms created by custom derive their validity from efficacy. Efficacy is, as I have expressly established,[20] in no way the basis of the validity of legal norms. The basis of the validity of the norms of a legal system—even those legal norms created by custom—is not the efficacy of these norms, but is, rather, the basic norm that is presupposed when a coercive system, for the most part efficacious, is interpreted as a system of valid legal norms.[21]

According to the Pure Theory of Law, efficacy is indeed the sufficient but not also the necessary condition for the validity of a legal norm. If the efficacy of a legal norm were a necessary condition for its validity, there would exist between the condition and the conditioned what Klug calls the 'if-so-*only*-then' relation.[22] That is, the following sentence would have to be true: If a legal norm is efficacious, only then is it a valid legal norm. This sentence, however, is not true. For as I emphasize in the second edition of my *Pure Theory of Law*, a legal norm is valid before it becomes efficacious, that is, before it is complied with and applied.[23] That a legal norm forfeits its validity if it does not become efficacious or if it loses its efficacy does not mean that efficacy is a necessary condition for its validity.

[17] Bulygin, 'The Concept of Efficacy' (n. 11, this chapter), in this volume, ch. 1, 38 at n. 5.
[18] Ulrich Klug, *Juristische Logik*, 2nd edn. (Berlin: Springer, 1958), 44.
[19] Klug, *Juristische Logik* (n. 18, this chapter), 44.
[20] Kelsen, *RR 2*, § 34(g) (at 219), *PTL*, at 212.
[21] See Kelsen, *RR 2*, § 34(d) (at 208), § 34(g) (at 219), *PTL*, at 204 and at 212 respectively; Robert Walter, 'Wirksamkeit und Geltung', *ÖZöR*, 11 (1961), 531–41.
[22] Klug, *Juristische Logik* (n. 18, this chapter), 44.
[23] [*Translators' note*: See n. 16, this chapter.]

3

Remarks on Kelsen's 'Validity and Efficacy of the Law' (2003)*

Introduction

Early in 2003, I received a most remarkable letter from Professor Robert Walter, the Director of the Hans Kelsen Institute in Vienna, informing me of the existence of an unpublished manuscript of Kelsen's entitled 'Validity and Efficacy of the Law'. In this manuscript, Kelsen responds critically at various points to an article of mine published nearly 40 years ago. Professor Walter invited me to respond briefly to Kelsen's manuscript.

This message had an enormous impact on me. That a theorist of Kelsen's stature had read and responded critically to an article of a young and completely unknown writer in the field (the article was one of my very first publications) is wellnigh unbelievable. For me to learn of this more than 30 years later is regrettable (I assume that Kelsen wrote his manuscript between 1967 and 1970), and it is indeed generous of Professor Walter to offer me the opportunity to respond. That Kelsen can no longer answer my critical reply is to my advantage. For all these reasons I have accepted with pleasure Professor Walter's invitation.

In what follows, I shall confine myself to those statements of Kelsen's that pertain to my article, 'The Concept of Efficacy'.[1] My reply is almost certainly not as brief as Professor Walter may have envisaged, but that is simply because of the great enthusiasm I bring to the project. It is not every day that one has a chance to engage in polemics with Hans Kelsen.

1. Addressees of Legal Norms

Section 12, footnote 11, of Kelsen's text reads:

Bulygin claims that, according to my view, 'the law consists exclusively of norms addressed to judges. [Kelsen's] view conceals the radical difference between compliance with legal

* [*Editors' note*: Eugenio Bulygin's paper was first published as 'Bemerkungen zu Kelsen, Geltung und Wirksamkeit des Rechts', in the volume *Hans Kelsens stete Aktualität*, ed. Robert Walter, Clemens Jabloner, and Klaus Zeleny (Schriftenreihe des Hans Kelsen-Instituts, vol. 25) (Vienna: Manz, 2003), 23–9. It has been translated for the present volume by Bonnie Litschewski Paulson and Stanley L. Paulson.]

[1] Eugenio Bulygin, 'The Concept of Efficacy' (1965), in this volume, ch. 1.

norms and their application.' In fact, according to my view, the addressees of legal norms are by no means only judges—legal norms are addressed not only to the courts, but also to administrative officials and, indirectly, to all legal subjects obligated and empowered by these legal norms. This aside, a glance at the index of the second edition of my *Reine Rechtslehre* shows that I do indeed distinguish between 'application' of and 'compliance' with legal norms. The very heading in the book at § 35(f) (239), *PTL*, at 233, reads: 'Law Creation, Law Application, and Compliance with Law'.[2]

Kelsen is entirely right in saying that he distinguishes between application and compliance, but the sentence that prompts Kelsen's reaction refers not to Kelsen but to Alf Ross, in particular to the 'difficulties that turn up in Ross's assessment of efficacy'.[3] There I claim that Ross had taken over from Kelsen the view that judges are the addressees of legal norms. I still believe today that this is quite correct. If the law is defined as a '*coercive system* of human behaviour' whose norms are 'linked to certain circumstances, in particular to certain human behaviour qua condition and to certain coercive acts qua consequence',[4] then legal norms are addressed to courts (and only exceptionally to administrative officials) because courts alone can order coercive acts. It is true that in Kelsen's late [post-1960] period (especially in the text being discussed here), he also brings into play permissory and empowering norms alongside the norms that order sanctions. The book of Ross's that I criticize, however, appeared in English in 1958[5] (the Danish edition in 1953), and so Ross could not have been influenced by this development in Kelsen's thought.

2. The Definition of Efficacy as Judicial Invokability

In section 21 of Kelsen's text, at footnote 14, he criticizes my definition of efficacy as the disposition of the norm to be applied by the courts if certain conditions obtain, a disposition I characterize as 'judicial invokability' (*Gerichtsfähigkeit*):

> [T]he proposition 'norm *N* is efficacious' is tantamount to the proposition 'if certain conditions were to obtain..., then the courts would apply *N*'.[6]

Here it is a matter not of a prediction of future applications of the norm but—in contrast to Ross[7]—of a dispositional property that, like the solubility of sugar in water, cannot be directly observed. I refer in this connection expressly to Rudolf Carnap's analysis in his article 'Testability and Meaning' (1936–7).

[2] Hans Kelsen, 'Validity and Efficacy of the Law' (1967/2003), in this volume, ch. 2, 60 n. 11; and see Bulygin (n. 1, this chapter), at 38.

[3] Bulygin (n. 1, this chapter), 38.

[4] Kelsen (n. 2, this chapter), 52 (emphasis in original).

[5] Ross, *LJ*. [*Editors' note*: For this and other abbreviations, see the Table of Abbreviations.]

[6] Kelsen (n. 2, this chapter), 66 n. 14; and see Bulygin (n. 1, this chapter), at 48.

[7] It is misleading to use 'valid' as the English translation of the Danish 'gældende' (as distinct from 'gyldig'). The issue here is not normative validity but an empirical concept that should, rather, be translated as 'efficacy'. See Ross, *DN*, 104 at n. 2.

Kelsen has clearly misunderstood me when he writes:

In fact, the efficacy of a legal norm, according to Bulygin, consists in its being applied by the courts...[8]

In my definition, the proposition 'norm *N* is efficacious' is not, by contrast with Ross, a prediction of future applications of the norm.[9] The application of a norm consists in the courts' using this norm as the grounding of their decisions. 'A legal decision is normatively grounded if it can be logically derived from certain norms (along with the statements describing the material facts).'[10]

It is worth noting here that the grounding of judicial decisions turns on logical relations between norms and those decisions, and not on the psychological motivation of the judge.[11]

Kelsen's most important objection to this characterization of application is directed against the definition of efficacy as judicial invokability. The objection consists in Kelsen's sharp rejection of the logical derivation of norms. This question merits a detailed discussion.

3. The Logical Derivation of Legal Norms

In section 21 of Kelsen's text, at footnote 14, he assails my claim that there can be logical relations between norms and, in particular, that an individual norm ('The thief Schulze ought to be punished') can be logically inferred from a general norm ('All thieves ought to be punished'). The validity of a norm, according to Kelsen, always requires an act of will, without which the norm cannot be valid—that is to say, cannot exist.

Here lies the most serious mistake of Kelsen's late period. The idea that behind every norm there must be an act of will, which Kelsen summarizes with the well-known maxim 'no imperative without an imperator', leads to altogether untenable consequences. If there were no logical relations between legal norms and if the derivation of an individual norm from a general norm were impossible, then general norms would be meaningless and legislation—the issuance of general norms—a meaningless undertaking.

This can be shown with a simple example. The teacher issues a general norm, 'all pupils ought to stand up.' No pupil moves, and the teacher asks Franz, sitting in front, 'why aren't you standing up?' Franz, who has thoroughly studied Kelsen's late period, replies, 'you did not order me to stand up, honoured teacher. You said, "all ought to stand up", but I am surely not all, I am Franz.' The teacher receives the same answer from the other pupils. There seems to be no alternative for the

[8] Kelsen (n. 2, this chapter), 66 n. 14; and see Bulygin (n. 1, this chapter), at 48.

[9] For the same reasons, Kelsen is also mistaken when he claims that 'the constraint "if certain conditions were to obtain" is superfluous'. The constraint is not superfluous, because a norm is inefficacious when, under certain conditions, it would not be applied.

[10] Bulygin (n. 1, this chapter), 45.

[11] Bulygin (n. 1, this chapter), 45–7.

teacher other than to turn to every single pupil and to order him to stand up, for, according to Kelsen, from the general norm 'all pupils ought to stand up', no individual norm (say, 'the pupil Franz ought to stand up') can be derived. This is most certainly absurd, but it is exactly what Kelsen claims.

> The general legal norm 'all thieves ought to be sent to prison' can be valid, and the statement 'Schulze is a thief, for he stole a horse from Maier' can be true, can even be established by the court, but the individual legal norm 'Schulze shall be sent to prison' can nevertheless be *invalid* if this judicial decision, for whatever reason, does not in fact ensue.[12]

What can be said here? Of course individual norms can be logically derived from a general norm. Of course the teacher, in that he ordered all pupils to stand up, also ordered every single pupil to stand up. Of course a judicial decision is justified if it arises as a logical inference from a general legal norm figuring as a premiss. Of course the norm 'Schulze, who is a thief, ought to be punished' can be derived from the norm 'all thieves ought to be punished'.

Still, Kelsen's claim that Schulze cannot be sent to prison without a judicial decision does seem to be thoroughly plausible. To send the thief Schulze to prison, a judicial decision is required because the norm in the criminal code is insufficient to the task. Wherein lies Kelsen's mistake then, if indeed there is one? What is the difference between the teacher's order and the norm in the criminal code?

I believe that Kelsen fails to distinguish between two different norms that are in play here. On the one hand, there is the general norm 'all thieves ought to be sent to prison'. To whom is this norm directed and what does it order? Obviously it is directed to the organs of the court and orders judges to sentence thieves to prison. From this general norm, the individual norm 'Judge Nikolussi ought to sentence Schulze to prison' can be logically derived. However, on the other hand, there is a norm that orders administrative officials to imprison thieves only when these thieves have been sentenced by a court having jurisdiction. As long as no decision has been taken, there is the apparent paradox: Both statements, 'Schulze ought to be punished' and 'Schulze ought not to be punished', are true. In fact, there is no contradiction here at all. The two statements are altogether consistent, in that 'Schulze ought to be punished' means that 'judges ought to sentence him', and 'Schulze ought not to be punished' means that 'the appropriate administrative officials ought not to imprison him as long as no decision has been taken'. Because Kelsen does not distinguish between these two norms and treats them as one and the same norm, an apparent contradiction arises. These are two completely different norms, however, whose addressees and content are different. The first norm is directed to courts and orders them to punish thieves (that is, to sentence thieves); the second norm is directed to administrative officials and orders them to imprison only those persons who have been sentenced by courts having jurisdiction. It can of course occur that the first individual norm is valid (Judge Nikolussi, who has jurisdiction, ought to sentence Schulze), while the second norm is not valid (Schulze ought not to be sent to prison). Only after the judge has complied with the first norm by sentencing Schulze does the second norm (Schulze ought now to be imprisoned) acquire validity.

[12] Kelsen (n. 2, this chapter), 66–7 n. 14.

In that Kelsen contests the possibility of logically deriving the individual norm from a general norm, he puts himself in an awkward position, criticized many years ago by Joseph Raz:

> This is quite plainly a wholly unacceptable solution to the problem of practical conflicts. It leads directly to the conclusion that practical reasoning is impossible and practical discourse either equally impossible or at any rate completely pointless. Parliament may legislate that everyone must pay a percentage of his income as a tax. It does not follow according to the new Kelsenian doctrine that I ought to pay tax. Only if and when an official [orders] me to pay tax [will I] have to pay it. But there is no reason why the official should order me to do so. True, there is a law requiring officials to demand payment from defaulters, but by the same mad logic neither this official nor any other official is obliged to demand payment from me.[13]

4. Efficacy as Sufficient and Necessary Condition for Validity

In sections 22 and 23 of his text, Kelsen takes up the problem of the relation between validity and efficacy, emphatically rejecting here my view that, in the Pure Theory of Law, efficacy is a sufficient and at the same time a necessary condition for validity. Kelsen does grant that efficacy is a sufficient condition for validity, but he contests the claim that efficacy can also be considered a necessary condition. His argument is that a legal norm is already valid before it can become efficacious, that is, before it can be complied with and applied. He underscores thereby his view that efficacy can be regarded only as a condition for validity and in no way as its basis, for the basis of validity is the basic norm.

Of course it is correct that, for Kelsen, the basic norm is the basis of validity. The basic norm, however, is not a positive law norm (existing in fact) but, rather, a presupposed norm. The question arises: When and in what circumstances is the basic norm presupposed? The answer is not difficult to find: The basic norm is always presupposed where an efficacious set of norms is at hand.

> For the basic norm states: Coercion ought to be carried out according to the conditions and in the manner specified in the largely efficacious constitution, in the largely efficacious general norms issued in accordance with the constitution, and in the efficacious individual norms. Efficacy is established in the basic norm as a condition for validity.[14]

It is notable here that the presupposition of the basic norm is completely independent of the content of the norms. It follows that efficacy is the sole criterion for presupposing the basic norm and, thus, for validity. Kelsen's ideas can be summarized as follows: There is no validity without efficacy (and so efficacy is a necessary condition for the validity of a legal system), and whenever a system of norms is efficacious, it always has validity (and so efficacy is a sufficient condition for validity).

[13] Joseph Raz, 'Kelsen's General Theory of Norms', *Philosophia*, 6 (1976), 495–504, at 503.
[14] Kelsen, *RR 2*, § 34(e) (212), *PTL*, 208.

Even if the basis of validity is supposed to be the basic norm, that changes nothing in the relation between efficacy and validity.

Kelsen explicitly emphasizes this point. In *General Theory of Law and State* (1945), he offers the following formulation:

> The efficacy of the entire legal order is a necessary condition for the validity of every single norm of the order. A *conditio sine qua non*, but not a *conditio per quam*. The efficacy of the total legal order is a condition, not the reason for the validity of its constituent norms.[15]

In this passage, efficacy appears as a necessary condition for validity. In the article under consideration here, Kelsen recognizes efficacy as a sufficient condition for validity.

> If a legal norm is efficacious, then it is always a valid legal norm. This sentence is indeed true. Efficacy *is* in this sense a sufficient condition for validity.[16]

It follows, then, that efficacy is a necessary and a sufficient condition for validity. QED.

Kelsen states that a newly issued legal norm, which could not yet have been complied with or applied, is nevertheless a valid norm.[17] This cannot count as an objection to my conclusion here, for it is precisely in my definition of efficacy as judicial invokability that a norm can very well be efficacious even if it has not yet been applied. Based on previous experience, the determination can be made that this norm is judicially invokable, that is, that it has the disposition to be applied by the courts in appropriate circumstances. Nothing more is needed to ascertain the efficacy of the norm.

[15] Kelsen, *GTLS*, 119.
[16] Kelsen (n. 2, this chapter), 68.
[17] See Kelsen (n. 2, this chapter), § 22, at 67.

4

Judicial Decisions and the Creation of Law (1966)*

Introduction

Here I seek to examine the structure of judicial decisions along with the role judges play in the creation of law.[1] I will take up two theses that are well known to legal philosophers and that I consider seriously misleading: First, that judicial decisions are individual legal norms and, second, that judges create law when they set forth individual legal norms. In response to these theses, I will defend the following five propositions: (a) Judicial decisions are complex entities that contain both individual and general norms. (b) In an important sense of 'creating', judges do not create individual norms; instead, they create, at least in some instances, general norms. (c) While the general norms created by judges are not binding, they can come into force, and when they do, they become a part of the legal order. (d) An important contribution to the creation of law is the formulation of definitions of legal concepts by judges. Finally, (e) case law is the set of general norms in force that are created by judges and the definitions in force that are formulated by judges.

1. The Constitutive Parts of a Judicial Decision

Here I define 'judicial decision' as a ruling that brings to an end a controversy involving either a conflict of interests (in private law cases) or the appropriate sanction (in criminal law cases). By virtue of a principle explicitly established in modern legislation, judicial decisions *ought to be grounded.* Judges ought to give reasons to support their decisions. Judicial decisions ought to be explicitly justified.

Despite its extraordinary importance, the concept of a normative ground has not been adequately explored in legal philosophy. I will limit myself here to a few observations. Justifying or grounding a decision is a matter of constructing

* [*Editors' note*: Eugenio Bulygin's paper was first published in the Argentine journal *La Ley*, 124 (1966), 1307–15, in *ALD*, 355–76. It was translated for the present volume by Carlos Bernal, Tecla Mazzarese, Michael Sherberg, and María Viana.]

[1] I should like to express my gratitude to Genaro R. Carrió for valuable help with this essay in the form of advice, suggestions, and criticisms.

an inference or a piece of reasoning that is logically valid. Among the premisses of such an inference, there is a general norm, and the conclusion of the inference is the decision taken in the case at hand. The ground of the decision is a *general norm* that is then applied in the decision. The relation between the ground (the general norm) and the decision is logical, not causal. A grounded decision is logically deduced from a general norm (along with empirical propositions and, in some instances, analytic propositions too). The point is not simply that judges find solutions to cases by means of a deductive process that begins with certain general norms. The question of *how* judges arrive at their decisions is psychological in nature and is irrelevant here. What matters here is solely the logical problem concerning the ground of judicial decisions.[2]

The judgment ought not only to be grounded, but it ought, moreover, to be grounded on legal norms along with the concrete circumstances of the case. This means that the general norms that are the normative ground of a judicial decision ought to be—at least in principle—legal norms, and the empirical propositions that are a part of the reasons for the decision ought to correspond to the facts of the case as established in the appropriate way over the course of the judicial proceeding.[3]

Hans Kelsen's theory, according to which the concepts of application and creation of law are correlative (every act of application is also an act of creation and vice-versa, with the exception of the instances at the two extremes, namely, those found at either end of the normative hierarchy), has had considerable influence. Some legal philosophers have concluded that there is no important difference between the legislative and the judicial functions of the state. Nevertheless, the requirement that judges give explicit justification for their decisions confers on the judicial function a peculiar feature that is absent in the legislative function. The difference is to be found in the role played, on the one hand, by the reasons that inform a statute (which are not a part of the statute and are not essential to it) and, on the other, by the reasons that are a constitutive (necessary) part of judicial decisions. A judgment lacking a ground is paradigmatic of an arbitrary decision.[4]

Following familiar legal usage, I shall take 'judicial decision' to refer to the whole that is formed by the *opinion* and the *decision* or *dispositive part of a judgment* (these last two expressions will be used synonymously here). A judicial decision can be conceived as an instance of normative reasoning. The decision is the *conclusion* of this reasoning, whose *premisses* are to be found in the *opinion* (although

[2] Thus, the question of temporal priority is not relevant here; it is possible that in many cases, judges first reach a decision and then attempt to justify it. With respect to the decision, the temporal order has no bearing on the logical priority of the ground.

[3] '...with regard to the case law of this Court, it is a condition of the validity of a ruling that it be a reasonable conclusion derived from the law in force, with specific reference to the proven circumstances of the case'. *La Ley*, 107 (1962), 185.

[4] See Genaro R. Carrió, 'Sentencia arbitraria', *RJBA* (1965) (nos. 1–2), 9–23. [*Editors' note*: For this and other abbreviations, see the Table of Abbreviations.]

not all statements found in the *opinion* are necessarily premisses for inferring the conclusion).

Among the premisses there are three kinds of sentences that I would like especially to highlight: (1) *general normative sentences* that constitute the *normative ground* of the decision; (2) *definitions* in a broad sense, including as well sentences that determine the extension of a concept and sentences concerning meaning postulates; and (3) *empirical sentences* used for the *description of facts*. The decision is an individual norm.

The characterization of the decision as an individual norm is without doubt overly simplistic. As with all procedural acts (and to a considerable degree, legal acts in general), the decision fulfils an important *performative function*,[5] one to which legal philosophers have paid scant attention until now. In some instances this performative function is front and centre, as in the case of a decision rejecting a lawsuit. The difficulties faced by those who, at all costs, try to reduce decisions of this sort to norms serve as a clear indicator of the inadequacy of the conceptual apparatus they are using.[6]

The judicial decision, represented schematically:

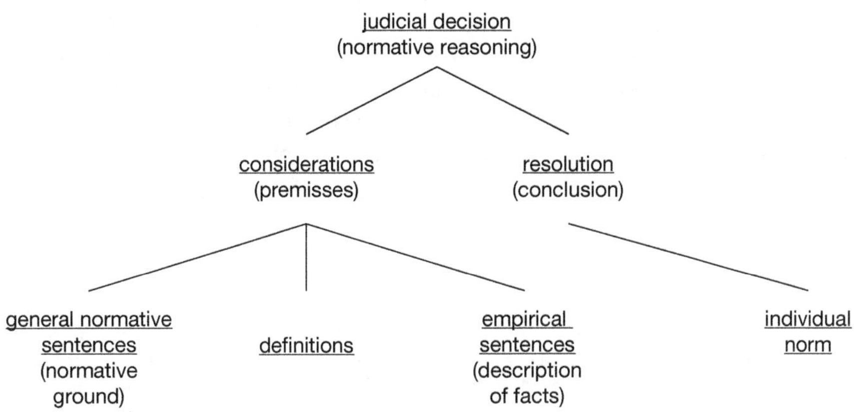

The normative ground and the decision itself are the normative elements of the judicial decision. However, while the normative ground consists of *general* normative sentences, the dispositive part is an individual norm that refers to the behaviour of certain individuals and to specific performance or sanctions.[7] It is

[5] See J. L. Austin, *How to Do Things with Words* (Oxford: Clarendon Press, 1962).

[6] See Carlos Cossio, *Teoría egológica del derecho*, 2nd edn. (Buenos Aires: Abeledo Perrot, 1964), at 181–2.

[7] For a clear distinction between general and individual (particular) norms, see von Wright, *NA*, at 77–81, where the following definitions are found:

> A norm is *individual with respect to the subject* if and only if it refers to the behaviour of one or more specific individuals.

the decision that matters most to the parties in the action, but from the point of view of legal science the decision is of no special interest. What gives the judicial decision its import as precedent and renders it a source of law is not the dispositive part but rather the general norms (and the definitional sentences) on which it is grounded. I shall return to this issue later in the article.

2. What Kind of Norms Do Judges Create?

Given that our topic is limited to the creation of norms, we will leave aside the very important problems raised by the description of facts and their subsumption under legal concepts. These are not purely mechanical tasks. By undertaking them the judge is frequently compelled to evaluate and to take decisions. These decisions concern the meaning and extension of legal terms, and this most certainly does not preclude the possibility that the decisions can in turn have an influence on the normative consequences of the facts.[8] Atypical cases (also called penumbral cases)[9] are of special interest, for they compel judges to make decisions about the inclusion or exclusion of these cases within the field of application of a legal concept. These penumbral cases can arise in connection with any empirical concept (quite apart from the question of how precise the concept may be), and their possibility cannot be eliminated by introducing technical language, for their possibility is a reflection of empirical language generally.[10] It is *always* possible that one may have to decide whether, say, the act in question counts as trade or as robbery, even though 'trade'

A norm is *general with respect to the subject* if and only if it refers to the behaviour of a set of individuals (in other words, *all* individuals who satisfy a certain description).

A norm is *individual with respect to the occasion* if and only if it refers to conduct that should (can or should not) be carried out in a specific situation or on a certain number of occasions.

A norm is *general with respect to the occasion* if and only if it refers to conduct that should (can or should not) be carried out on a limited number of occasions.

A norm is *individual* if it is individual with respect to both subject and occasion.

A norm is *general* if it is general with respect to subject or occasion.

A norm is *eminently general* if it is general with respect to both subject and occasion.

[8] Given that norms are formulated in ordinary language, the words they contain usually have a more or less clear core meaning. For this reason definitions made by judges are not arbitrary, for they serve to delimit the scope of such meanings. Nevertheless, a norm can also be modified through the definition of its concepts. For instance, when after several definitions judges included among the 'objects of indispensable use' the radio and the refrigerator, was not the norm also modified that declares such objects not liable to seizure? The distinction between a definition that specifies the content of a norm and one that modifies it (possibly creating a new norm) is, in fact, blurred. Still, this cannot rule out the conceptual distinction between the two activities.

[9] See Hart, 'Separation', in Hart, *EJP*, and Hart, *CL*, 1st edn., ch. 7, at § 1 (121–32), 3rd edn., ch. 7, at § 1 (124–36); Genaro R. Carrió, *Notas sobre derecho y lenguaje* (Buenos Aires: Abeledo Perrot, 1965), at 44–5.

[10] The issue here is the potential uncertainty or open texture of language. See Friedrich Waismann, 'Verifiability', in *Essays on Logic and Language*, ed. Anthony Flew (Oxford: Basil Blackwell, 1951), 117–44, repr. under the title *Logic and Language. Essays (First Series)* (1955); Carrió, *Notas sobre derecho y lenguaje* (n. 9, this chapter), at 33–4.

and 'robbery' are thought to be terms that give expression to very precise concepts manifesting a finite number of defining characteristics.[11]

Let me return however to the issue of norm creation. What does the vague expression 'to create' a norm mean? Legal philosophers have not made a serious effort to analyse this issue, as if elucidating it did not present problems.

In order to lend some specificity to the concept of the creation of norms, allow me to assume that in order for one to consider a norm formulated by a normative authority to have been *created* by this authority, its content cannot be identical to the content of some other norm belonging to the same legal order, nor can it be a logical (deducible) consequence of other norms. I do not claim here to be giving a definition of 'creating'. Rather, the task is to offer a *necessary condition* for a norm to be deemed 'created' (an explicit definition would raise the difficult problem of the existence of norms, a problem that I would prefer to avoid here).

Let me turn now to the kinds of norm that judges create.

(A) Kelsen and the authors who agree with him on this point argue that when a judge applies a general norm, he creates an individual norm.[12] They base their conclusion on the following premisses: (1) an individual norm is the product of an act of will, not of a simple cognitive act, and (2) in an individual norm, a series of elements that in an applied general norm are only mentioned in the abstract will become concrete. The general norm points to a frame of possibilities. When judges create an individual norm, they choose one of those possibilities and in this way fill in the frame.

Undoubtedly, handing down a decision involves an act of will on the part of the judge. This does not, however, seem to be an adequate criterion for determining whether a norm has been created or not. Every issuance of a norm requires an act of will, so adopting this criterion would give excessive reach to the concept of norm creation.

On the other hand, it is true that the individual norm cannot be deduced from the general norm alone. That is, from the norm 'he who murders another is to be punished by imprisonment for 8 to 25 years', it is not possible deductively to arrive at the norm 'Diaz is to spend 12 years in prison'. Hence, the individual norm seems to satisfy the necessary condition that we have established for the creation of norms. Nevertheless, in a grounded decision, the conclusion is a logical consequence of—it can be deduced from—the premisses, that is, from the applied general norm *and* the description of the facts (plus definitions) taken together. Given the norm 'he who murders another is to be punished by imprisonment of 8 to 25 years' and the descriptive proposition 'Diaz murdered Gonzalez', the individual

[11] Sebastián Soler, in *Interpretación de la ley* (Barcelona: Ariel, 1962), claims that some legal concepts are defined with a precision comparable to that of geometric concepts. However, this does not eliminate the problems that the open texture of language creates, which are also present in applied geometry. It is only in a purely formal (and not empirical) language, such as that of pure geometry, that these problems are not present.

[12] With the exception of certain extraordinary cases, for example, appeals heard by the Supreme Court.

norm 'Diaz is to be punished by imprisonment of 8 to 25 years' can be inferred directly—that is to say, it is logically implied by the premisses.[13]

In this sense, it is possible to claim that the individual norm (the dispositive part of the decision) is not created by the judge but is deduced from the general norm on which it is grounded, from the relevant definitions, and from the facts of the case. It is only in an arbitrary decision, one that is not grounded, that the decision is not a logical consequence of the premisses. In other words, the judge may not create individual norms, since he has the duty to infer them from the general norms and the facts of the case, and to the extent that he does create them, his decisions are arbitrary.

(B) In general, the judge does not create general norms, since he ought to ground his decisions on pre-existing legal (legislated or customary) norms. Nevertheless, unforeseen cases can arise in the legal order, cases in which no general norm is applicable.[14] In these situations the judge may be authorized[15] to create a general norm that allows him to ground his decision. The most common procedure that judges use to create new norms is reasoning by analogy.[16] Given that reasoning by analogy is not logically valid (logical validity would require additional premisses), the norm arrived at by means of analogy is *created* by the judge in the sense we have given to this term.

To illustrate the thesis according to which judges sometimes create general norms, I shall turn to an example of a case that was decided by a civil court in Buenos Aires.[17] The court took up the question of whether a lawyer can represent his mother against his own father in a divorce proceeding. In Argentine law there were no norms in place at the time that explicitly anticipated this situation. The Civil Tribunal decided, in these circumstances, to prohibit this form of representation, basing its decision on the analogous application of a provision in the

[13] [*Editors' note*: Omitted in the reprinted version, see Alchourrón and Bulygin, *ALD*, at 360, is the following text, which appeared between parentheses in the original version of the paper: 'In point of fact, this is not the only possible conclusion; one could also draw other conclusions, such as "Diaz is to spend 20 years in prison", but the fact that it is possible to draw various conclusions from the same premisses does not prevent each of them from being a logical consequence of the premisses', *La Ley*, 124 (1966), 1307–15, at 1310.]

[14] Some authors, such as Kelsen and Cossio, argue that (logical) gaps do not exist, and they appeal in this connection to the principle that 'everything not prohibited is permitted'. This principle could eliminate gaps, however, only if it were a *norm*. In this case it would have to be contingent, unless one were to stipulate the existence of necessary norms, which would be tantamount to accepting natural law. If, instead, this principle is necessary (as maintained by those who deny the possibility of gaps), then it is not a norm. In that case, given that it does not prescribe anything at all, it would also not eliminate legal gaps. See on this problem von Wright, *NA*, at 85–92.

[15] Argentine Civil Code, art. 16: 'If a civil matter cannot be solved either through words or through the spirit of the law, the principles of analogous laws will apply; and, if the matter is still dubious, it will be solved according to the general principles of the law, taking into account the circumstances of each case.'

[16] On the different forms of reasoning by analogy in the law, see Carlos E. Alchourrón, 'Juristische Schlüsse a fortiori und a pari', in *Lateinamerikanische Studien zur Rechtsphilosophie*, ed. Ernesto Garzón Valdés (*ARSP Beiheft* 41 [N.F. 4]) (Neuwied am Rhein and Berlin: Hermann Luchterhand, 1965), 5–26. [*Editors' note*: Spanish text in *RJBA* (1961) (no. 4), 177–99, in Alchourrón and Bulygin, *ALD*, 3–24.]

[17] *La Ley*, 99 (1960), 534.

Argentine Code of Civil Procedure that states: 'Blood relatives or relatives by marriage may not be presented as witnesses against one of the parties to the proceeding, including one's spouse, even if he or she is legally separated.'[18]

The dispositive part of the decision—'the court has decided to declare that the plaintiff's lawyer must be removed from this adjudicative proceeding'—is an individual norm that the court grounded in the following terms:

> By analogy with article 186 of the Code of Civil Procedure, it is not possible for the son of the spouses in a divorce proceeding to represent either one of them as a lawyer, because, either as a witness or as a lawyer for one of the parties involved, the possibility of damaging the principle safeguarded by the law is the same.

It is possible to distinguish two parts of this passage.

(a) The first part consists of the *norm* that justifies the decision ('it is not possible for the son of the spouses in a divorce proceeding to represent either one of them'), which is a *general* norm.[19] This norm was not in place prior to the ruling in question, nor is it a logical consequence of any pre-existing norms, since it cannot be deduced from art. 186, which concerns '*witnesses against* one of the parties to the proceeding', whereas the norm at hand refers to the *lawyer* of one or another of the parties. Consequently, this is a norm created by the court.

(b) The second part of the quoted passage consists of the justification of the reasoning by analogy by means of which the court arrived at such a norm.[20]

The ruling cited is a typical case of the judicial creation of a general norm. It is certainly not an *ex nihilo* creation. The judicial creation of general norms by analogy is a creation on the basis of other norms. In this respect, it differs substantially from legislative creation to the point where it seems wrong to use the same word 'creation' to refer to two such different activities. Thus, it is important to underscore that what judges create—if, indeed, they actually do create something—are not individual norms but general norms.

3. Some Conceptual Distinctions

How can one explain the fact that many legal philosophers still defend the thesis that judicial decisions are individual legal norms?[21] Apparently, these authors are referring to the decision alone. This represents a limitation in the meaning of the

[18] *La Ley*, 99 (1960), 534.

[19] In von Wright's terms it is eminently general, see n. 7, this chapter.

[20] This shows that our framework for justification is too simplistic. A more elaborate analysis should take into account different *levels of justification*.

[21] This is Kelsen's thesis, and it has been defended with particular emphasis by those writing from the standpoint of the 'egological school'. See Kelsen, *RR 2*, § 4(e) (at 20), § 35(g) (at 242–3), *PTL*, at 19 and at 236–7; Kelsen, *GTLS*, at 134–6; Cossio, *Teoría egológica del derecho* (n. 6, this chapter); Julio C. Cueto Rúa, *Fuentes del derecho* (Buenos Aires: Abeledo Perrot, 1961), at 152; José Villanova, 'Acerca de la norma individual', *La Ley*, 67 (1952), at 811.

concept of 'judicial decision', since in ordinary legal language 'judicial decision' refers to the entire complex formed by the opinion and the decision. Taking into account that the aim of legal philosophy is not to attribute new meanings to old terms but instead to elucidate the meanings that these concepts have in legal science, a change in a concept (either broadening or limiting it) is justified only if it contributes to that elucidation (for instance, when it undertakes to eliminate an ambiguity or to elucidate conceptual differences or similarities that are hidden by the ordinary terminology). None of these reasons seems to be relevant to our case. In addition, since the authors do not offer any reasons that would justify the change in the meaning of the term 'judicial decision', the suspicion arises that they did not even notice it.

Nevertheless, even when there are no reasons to justify this change, there may well be motives that could explain it. Those motives are to be found, in my opinion, in the conceptual confusion that these authors have inherited from Kelsen. Every legal norm is necessarily binding in Kelsen's theory since 'binding' is a synonym for 'existence'. The only binding norm that Kelsen finds in a judicial decision is the individual norm, the norm found in the decision. Moving from there to the claim that the judicial decision *is* an individual norm requires but a single step.

Identifying binding force with the existence of a norm (from which it follows that binding force is a necessary property of legal norms) stems from the ambiguity of the term 'validity', which—quite apart from the fact that it plays a major role in the Pure Theory of Law—is used by Kelsen to refer to different things. In particular, Kelsen offers three definitions of 'validity': creation in accordance with a higher-level norm,[22] the specific existence of a norm,[23] and finally, its binding force.[24] The presence of these conceptual distinctions suggests that it would be a good idea to adopt different terms for each of these concepts. Thus, with respect to norms I will distinguish between validity, existence, and binding force. I should like to propose—as a working hypothesis—the following definitions.

Validity: A norm is valid if and only if it has been issued by a competent authority. A normative authority is competent to issue a norm if and only if there is another norm (a higher-level norm) that empowers the authority to issue it. If the act of issuing a norm where there is another norm that empowers that act is termed 'legal', it follows that the validity of a norm is equal to *the legality of the act of issuing the norm.*[25]

Binding force: A norm is binding if and only if the authorities in charge of its application are obligated (prescribed by another norm) to apply it. In particular, a general

[22] 'A legal norm is valid . . . owing to its having been created in a certain way, namely, in a way stipulated in the end by a presupposed basic norm.' Kelsen, *RR 2*, § 34(c) (at 200–1), *PTL*, at 198–9. 'A norm is a valid legal norm by virtue of the fact that it has been created according to a definite rule and [solely] by virtue thereof.' Kelsen, *GTLS*, 113.

[23] '[W]ith the word "validity" we characterize the specific existence of a norm.' Kelsen, *RR 2*, § 4(c) (at 9), *PTL*, at 10.

[24] 'That a norm referring to the behaviour of an individual is "valid" means that it is binding, that the individual ought to behave in the manner specified by the norm.' Kelsen, *RR 2*, § 34(a) (at 196), *PTL*, at 193.

[25] See von Wright, *NA*, at 195.

norm is binding if judges are obligated to apply it—that is to say, have an obligation to use it to ground their decisions.

Existence: As for the concept of existence, I will leave aside the question of its definition because it is not indispensable for the present purposes. It is a *factual* concept, clearly distinguishable from the other two (which are normative concepts), but it is extremely difficult to define.[26] Nevertheless, I consider it important to signal the intimate connection between the existence of a norm and its being in force. For this reason it is advisable to define the term 'being in force', and to distinguish it from 'efficacy', regardless of the fact that both terms are commonly used as synonyms in legal philosophy.[27]

Being in force: A norm is in force if and only if there are good reasons in support of the idea that it will be applied where all conditions for its application are met. Here being in force is understood as a dispositional property.[28]

Efficacy: A norm is efficacious if and only if it is obeyed by the individual or individuals to whom the norm is addressed.

From these distinctions one can draw some interesting conclusions.

a) Both general norms and individual norms can be efficacious, but only general norms can be in force, since only they can serve to justify judicial decisions.[29]

b) Being in force and being efficacious (where efficacy is predicated of general norms) admit of degrees, while validity and binding force do not. In other words, a norm can only be valid or not, binding or not, but it can be more or less in force and more or less efficacious.

c) The application of the concepts of binding force and being in force can be extended to statements that are not norms, in particular, to definitions. A definition can be binding on judges (for instance, a definition issued by the legislator) and can also be in force, namely, when it is in fact used by judges as the grounding for decisions.

d) The concepts of validity, binding force, and being in force designate compatible but independent properties. Given that, in the tradition, the association in legal philosophy of 'validity' with 'binding force' is very widespread, it is particularly important to underscore the point that these concepts are

[26] See von Wright, *NA*, at ch. 7. [*Editors' note*: This footnote was added in the Italian translation, 'Sentenza giudiziaria e creazione di diritto', in *Rivista internazionale di filosofia del diritto*, 44 (1967), 164–80, at 174.]

[27] In ordinary language, however, these two terms do not appear to be synonymous. An individual command is efficacious if it is obeyed, but it would be strange to say that it is in force. A decision in force is one that is not prescribed, and it is efficacious if it is invoked (if it has been fulfilled); a statute is in force when it is applied, and it is efficacious when it fulfils its aim. For instance, the Criminal Code is in force, but if its aim is to eliminate crime, it is not very efficacious. Civil legislation concerning marriage is in force, but because it does not pursue any specific aim, one has no occasion to proclaim it efficacious.

[28] See Eugenio Bulygin, 'The Concept of Efficacy' (1965), in this volume, ch. 1. In that chapter I used the term 'efficacy' for what I term here as 'being in force'.

[29] Sebastián Soler, too, albeit on another basis, defends the idea that only general norms can be in force. See Soler, 'La llamada norma individual', *La Ley*, 66 (1952), 847–58.

independent. The distinction between valid and invalid norms is relevant above all for the problem of the annulment of norms. Invalid norms can not only be derogated, they can also be annulled. Nevertheless, invalid norms are binding if they have not been annulled. Where a norm can only be annulled during a specific period of time, then if that period runs out before the annulment takes place, the question of its invalidity becomes irrelevant. Likewise, an unconstitutional law will not lose its unconstitutionality simply because courts fail to declare it unconstitutional. The validity of a law consists in a logical relation between that law and the constitution; this relation does not turn on what judges might say. Once courts have accepted the law, however, the question of its validity loses its practical interest.

Kelsen has referred to this problem under the rubric of 'conflicts between norms at different levels in the hierarchy'.[30] In a first sense given to 'validity' here (that of conformity with a superior norm—that is to say, legality),[31] an unconstitutional law or an illegal judgment is clearly invalid. Because those norms are binding and because 'binding' for Kelsen means 'validity', they are both valid and invalid at the same time. Still, there is actually no contradiction here, because 'valid' in each of the two contexts has a different meaning. Kelsen, not noticing the ambiguity, felt constrained to fall back on a drastic remedy. In order to eliminate the apparent contradiction he introduced his famous tacit alternative clause. With it, he attributes to every legal institution the competence to create norms with any content whatsoever. In this way, every norm in a positive legal order would, *ex hypothesi*, become valid,[32] and validity would cease to be a contingent feature, becoming instead an *a priori* characteristic.

The converse can also take place—that is, there may be valid norms that are not, however, binding. General norms created by judges have this characteristic, because in cases in which the judge does not ground his decision on a pre-existing norm but on a norm that he has created, this norm is not binding from the standpoint of his colleagues. In order to resolve a similar case, other judges can ground their decisions on a different norm. In this sense, for instance, it would be possible for a court, instead of applying by analogy art. 186 of the Code of Procedure, to create a norm that allows a lawyer to be involved in the situation of our earlier example, based on the lack of an explicit prohibition and on the condition that no one 'shall be... deprived of that which the law does not forbid'.[33] In that case, we would be in the presence of a norm created by a judge by application of general principles of law (another common procedure of the creation of judicial norms).

[30] Kelsen, *RR 2*, § 35(j) (at 271–2), *PTL*, at 267–8; Kelsen, *GTLS*, 153–5.

[31] [*Editors' note*: The phrase 'that is to say, legality' is found in the reprinting of the article, Alchourrón and Bulygin, *ALD*, at 365.]

[32] See Roberto J. Vernengo, 'La función sistemática de la norma fundamental', in *RJBA* (1960) (nos. 1–2), 207–25.

[33] Art.19, Argentine Constitution.

It should be added that these non-binding norms are perfectly valid, for the judge is specifically authorized to make use of analogy or of general principles of law in the case of a gap.[34]

4. Are General Norms Created by Judges Legal Norms?

Is it justified to regard as a 'legal norm' a norm that has been created by a judge in grounding a judicial decision? Do these non-binding norms make up part of the legal order in the same sense as binding norms created by the legislator? Is binding force not perhaps an essential feature of legal norms?

Answering these questions is no easy task. The problem is not merely verbal, for while it is clear that the answers depend on the extension of the concept of legal norm, it is no less clear that we are engaged not in giving a nominal definition but in working up an *explicatum* (in Carnap's sense) of the vague expression 'legal norm'.

In any case, I do not deem it appropriate to consider binding force as the defining characteristic of a legal norm, for in this way norms that are in force but non-binding would be excluded from the legal realm. If legal science has among its aims a description of the law in force,[35] then binding force cannot be the defining criterion.

Thus, it will be useful to divide the general norms created by the judge into two subclasses: (1) those norms that are in force, for which no serious obstacles appear to stand in the way of their acceptance as genuine legal norms; (2) those norms that are not in force. Regarding the latter, serious concerns might well arise. Could a normative statement that is neither binding nor in force be considered an existing legal norm? It seems reasonable to think that being in force is necessary for the existence of a norm. However, even if we insist on classifying these norms as legal, there arises the need to find a criterion that makes it possible to distinguish between these norms and those normative statements that we clearly cannot regard as 'legal norms'—such as, for example, statements made by a lawyer.

One possible criterion to consider is the following: general norms created by judges are not binding but they can be used as the ground for binding and (in most cases, also) efficacious individual norms. The fact that a non-binding general norm constitutes the ground of a binding individual norm allows us to distinguish it not only from 'unofficial' statements (such as the statements of a lawyer or a jurist) but also from general norms formulated in a dissenting opinion in another court.

In any case, I do not think this feature justifies extending the concept of the legal norm to these anomalous norms. Still, no matter how one finally solves the problem of what to call those general norms created by judges that are not in force, it is clear that at this level the question is merely semantic. Legal or not, these are the only norms that judges create. If we take into account the possibility that these

[34] See art. 16, Argentine Civil Code.

[35] See Ross, *LJ*, at chs. 1 and 2.

norms may at some point be in force, in which case their status as legal norms would not be questionable, their relevance to legal science is evident. It is the creation of these general norms (and not the judge's handing down of individual decisions) that makes it possible for us to support the claim that judicial activity is a source of law.

5. Case Law as a Source of Law

I have tried to show the need to revise certain ideas, prevalent in some fields of law, about the judicial creation of legal norms. To conclude, I shall offer a few additional remarks about the role of case law as a source of law, with special reference to three theses. (i) It is a mistake to hold—as is very commonly held—that case law is a set of individual norms (judicial decisions). (ii) Case law is not necessarily a reiteration of rulings. (iii) The contribution of the judge to the creation of law is not restricted to the creation of norms; equally important, and perhaps even more important, are the judge's definitions of legal concepts.

(i) The thesis endorsed in the text according to which case law consists not of individual norms but of general norms on which individual norms are grounded is far less revolutionary than it might appear at first glance. The description of precedent as a product of a 'process of generalization and categorization' made by the judge who applies it[36] is not too far from our thesis. So, what does 'generalizing' an individual norm mean if not finding a general norm of which the former is an instance? In addition, although this general norm *should*, in principle, already be contained in the ruling that serves as precedent, it is also true that its formulation can in fact be deficient, so that it may be difficult to determine with precision the content and scope of the grounding norm. In this sense, it is true that the interpreter or judge must often carry out a complicated task of exegesis in order to separate what common law theory (more elaborate on this point than Roman law) has called the *ratio decidendi* of the case ('grounding' in our terminology), which constitutes the holding, from what are simply *dicta,* that is, statements that are not part of the grounding of the decision.

(ii) Obviously, not every judicial decision that creates a general norm counts as case law. Case law is a set of norms in force that have been created by judges. These norms are in force when they are in fact applied by courts. In order for a norm to be in force, it need not actually be applied in some minimum

[36] Cueto Rúa, *Fuentes del derecho* (n. 21, this chapter), 151. Nevertheless, Cueto Rúa seems to go too far when he maintains that '[w]hen the judgment that is deemed to be a source of law applies not legislative norms but rather judicial norms, as happens in common law, the judge needs to give it a generality that is missing in the judgment and in the original cited source as well' (Rúa, *Fuentes del derecho*, 153), and 'by means of this process, when a judge applies a precedent...he transforms an individual norm into a general one' (Rúa, *Fuentes del derecho*, 155).

number of cases. If there are good reasons to support the idea that the norm could be applied in certain circumstances, this would suffice. In this way, a single judicial decision—if, say, it stems from a court of distinction—could render the created norm as being in force and, consequently, could create case law. Thus, for instance, it would not be excessive to claim that just one ruling from the National Supreme Court—the *Siri* case[37]—constituted case law concerning an appeal to vindicate a constitutionally protected right, a constitutional complaint,[38] despite the fact that the decisions of that court are not binding on other courts of the state.

(iii) Cases in which judges have the opportunity to create a new norm are relatively rare. In most of the cases, what judges create are not norms but definitional statements, in other words, statements that determine the extent of a concept. Just a quick look at any collection of case law is enough to show that summaries of judgments, which extract what is relevant in the ruling, do not contain normative statements. When a judge decides on the meaning of expressions such as 'affluent tenant' or 'usury interest', he is not creating norms but defining concepts. When these definitions come into force—when, in other words, there are good reasons to believe that they will be used by judges—they become part of the legal order. This shows the insufficiency of the traditional definition of a legal order as a set of norms: both norms and definitions are part of the law.[39] Case law is a source of law in the sense that judges contribute to the creation of legal norms and to the definition of legal concepts.

[37] *La Ley*, 89 (1958), 531.

[38] [*Editors' note*: The phrase in question is '*recurso de amparo*', translated as *constitutional complaint* where the jurisdiction expressly provides for it (e.g. the German Constitution, art. 93.4a, the Spanish Constitution, art. 53.2) or as *an appeal on constitutional grounds* (e.g. Argentine Constitution, art. 43). The editors are grateful to Riccardo Guastini, Genoa, for helpful suggestions here.]

[39] Carlos E. Alchourrón has shown the importance of the role that definitions play in law. He underscored this point in his classes at the University of Buenos Aires and in many private discussions in which I was privileged to participate.

5

Von Wright on Deontic Logic and the Philosophy of Law (1973/89)*

Written with Carlos E. Alchourrón

> There are a good many facts in favour of the view that nothing can be part of the law of any community, unless it has either itself been willed by some person or persons, having the necessary authority over that community or can be deduced from something which has been so willed.
>
> G. E. Moore

Although there are only scattered references to specifically legal problems in his writings, it is difficult to exaggerate the importance of Georg Henrik von Wright's work for the philosophy of law. In spite of the fact that he is neither a professional jurist nor a legal philosopher *stricto sensu*, he has already exercised considerable influence on contemporary juristic thinking. This fact is hardly surprising, given his keen interest in such notions as norm, action, and value, which are found at the core of nearly all problems of legal philosophy. One may expect that his influence will increase over time. Still, although the relevance of deontic logic or the theory of action for the philosophy of law is fairly obvious, the application of von Wright's analyses to specifically legal problems often involves considerable difficulties. The highly general character of his writings and the use of logical symbolism make it difficult for many jurists to grasp their full importance and their promise for application to legal issues. Part of the difficulty lies in the fact that many of the concepts introduced by von Wright in the course of his analyses are not entirely suitable for the corresponding legal notions.

* [*Editors' note*: Eugenio Bulygin's paper, written together with Carlos E. Alchourrón, was first published in *The Philosophy of Georg Henrik von Wright*, ed. Paul Arthur Schilpp and Lewis Edwin Hahn (The Library of Living Philosophers, vol. 19) (LaSalle, Ill.: Open Court, 1989), 665–93. Alchourrón and Bulygin's work on the paper was completed in 1973, but publication of the volume was delayed. Spanish version in *ALD*, 69–102.

Accordingly, this article pursues two aims: first, to show the relevance and fruitfulness of von Wright's work for legal philosophy, and, second, to illustrate what sort of transformation or adaptation is needed in order to render his elucidations more suited to legal discourse. We shall concentrate exclusively on problems of the theory of norms and deontic logic; no reference will be made to the general theory of action or axiology, although their importance for the philosophy of law is obvious enough.

In what follows we shall largely be using von Wright's terminology in *Norm and Action*. We shall be concerned only with norms that are prescriptions—that is, no reference will be made to customs or customary norms (although they play an important part in legal life). Moreover, only positive law norms issued by human authorities will be taken into account (this excludes so-called natural law). Accordingly, by a norm we shall understand a prescription to the effect that something ought to or may or must not be done—that is, a prescription issued by one or several human agents (called norm-authorities), addressed to one or several human agents (called norm-subjects), enjoining, prohibiting, or permitting certain actions or states of affairs. Commands (John, take off your hat!) are included in this notion of norm. The verbal formulation (whether by means of a sentence in the imperative mood, a deontic sentence, or a sentence in the indicative) is immaterial; the important thing is the prescriptive use of the words (or other symbols).

1. Existence of Norms

Von Wright offers a detailed discussion of the problem of the existence of a norm or, as he puts it, 'the ontological problem of norms', in *Norm and Action*, chapter 7. It is 'essentially the question what it means to say that there *is* (exists) a norm to such and such effect.'[1] Such questions are often asked by jurists, and our concern here is with the problem of whether and to what extent von Wright's analysis may be regarded as an adequate reconstruction of what jurists understand by the existence of a legal norm (even if von Wright himself had no such purpose in mind when he wrote *Norm and Action*).

In von Wright's account two basic conditions are required for the truth of the statement that a norm is or exists: 1. the giving of the norm by the norm-authority, and 2. the receiving of the norm by the norm-subject. The 'giving-aspect' is the *normative action* performed by the norm-authority. It can be analysed as having two components: 1.1. the *promulgation* of the norm (which is an essentially verbal activity consisting of the use of norm-formulations to enunciate the norm), and 1.2. an effective sanction, that is, an explicit or implicit threat of punishment for disobedience to the norm.[2] For a sanction to be *effective* a special condition must be fulfilled by the person or persons who act as the norm-authority; this is the

[1] Von Wright, *NA*, 107 (emphasis in original). [*Editors' note*: For this and other abbreviations, see the Table of Abbreviations.]

[2] Von Wright, *NA*, 125.

(generic) *ability to command*, which is founded on a 'superior strength of the commander over the commanded'.[3]

However, the giving-aspect alone is not enough; the normative action is successful only if it results in the establishment of a *normative relationship* (or relationship under norm) between the authority and the subject(s). 'When use of prescriptive language leads to or results in the establishment of this relationship between a norm-authority and some norm-subject(s), then the prescription has been given, the normative act successfully performed, and the norm has come into existence.'[4] The 'receiving-aspect' being essential for the norm's existence, the norm-subject must 'receive' the norm. The reception of the norm, however, does not consist of merely becoming aware of the promulgation of the norm; a norm-subject cannot receive a norm 'unless he can do the enjoined or permitted thing'.[5] His ability to act according to the norm is a 'presupposition of norms'.[6] This presupposition connects the notion of existence with the Kantian principle that 'ought entails can'.

According to von Wright, norms have a temporal duration. They come into existence with the establishment of the normative relation, and they cease to exist when this relation dissolves.

> The life-span of a prescription is thus the duration of a relationship between a norm-authority and one or several norm-subjects. As long as this relationship lasts, the prescription is said to be *in force.* The existence of a prescription is not the fact, as such, that it has been given, but the fact that it is in force.[7]

So the existence of a norm depends on the existence of a normative relationship between the norm-authority and the norm-subject.

Before discussing the question of the adequacy of the foregoing analysis for legal norms, we must try to determine von Wright's *explicandum*, the intuitive notion he wishes to clarify.

There are at least three possible *explicanda*, according to three different though related meanings of the term 'norm'. In order to make clear what we mean, we shall consider first the descriptive use of language.

The most common and 'natural' use of descriptive language is to communicate something to somebody else. In a communication at least two persons are involved, the speaker and the hearer (in the case of a written communication the situation is similar). The existence of a communication requires: (i) the utterance of certain words by the speaker, and (ii) the reception of the message by the hearer. There is no effective communication if the hearer does not receive the message.

We may abstract the hearer and concentrate our attention on the speaker alone. Then we have what could conveniently be called an 'assertion'. (We must distinguish, of course, between the act of asserting and the contents of this act, that is, an actual assertion or statement.) An assertion exists even if no one has received it, the only condition for its existence being the performance of the act of

[3] Von Wright, *NA*, 127.
[4] Von Wright, *NA*, 118.
[5] Von Wright, *NA*, 111.
[6] Von Wright, *NA*, 110.
[7] Von Wright, *NA*, 118.

asserting. (A philosopher who is writing a book certainly makes assertions, even if he hides his ideas for fear of being plagiarized.)

At a still higher level of abstraction, we might even dispense with the speaker; in this case we are left with the contents of a possible assertion. This is what logicians usually call a 'proposition'.

Communication, assertion, and proposition are three different concepts, obtained by successive degrees of abstraction. Something analogous happens with prescriptions, although in this field there are no corresponding terminological distinctions, a fact rendering the ambiguity of the term 'norm' and related expressions all the more misleading.

Let us consider first a situation analogous to communication. A typical example would be that of commanding. The communication of the command to the norm-subject seems to be a necessary condition for the existence of a command (at least in normal cases). Hence a command—in order to exist—must not only be given but must also be received by the commandee. This meaning of 'norm' we shall call 'norm-communication'.

The most natural use of prescriptions is to influence other people's behaviour, and the reception of the prescription is most certainly a necessary condition for realizing this aim. We may, however, abstract the receiving-aspect of a prescription and concentrate on its giving-aspect alone. We shall then obtain something analogous to an assertion and call it a 'norm-prescription'. A norm-prescription is the content of an actual act of prescribing. People (and especially jurists) often speak of norms in this second, more abstract sense. All that is needed for the existence of a norm-prescription is its promulgation—that is, the act of prescribing by the corresponding authority. Its reception by the norm-subject is not necessary for its existence. Finally, we may regard a norm as the content of a merely possible act of prescribing. This prescriptive counterpart of a proposition will be called a 'norm-lekton'. Exactly as in the case of assertion and proposition, the concepts of norm-prescription and norm-lekton are obtained by successive abstractions from a common basis (norm-communication).

2. Existence and Promulgation

From von Wright's account of existence, it seems clear that he takes norm-communication as his *explicandum*. As an explication of *this* notion, his analysis is both illuminating and fruitful. Our concern, however, is with legal language, and we are interested in the applicability of von Wright's *explicata* to legal norms. In this sense, the concept of existence as used by von Wright is not entirely adequate, for it may easily be shown that jurists, when they speak of the existence of norms, rarely if ever use the term 'norm' with the meaning of 'norm-communication'. Normally they use the term in the sense of 'norm-prescription'.

As already mentioned, von Wright's concept of existence is particularly suitable for direct commands and permissions (particularly regarding the subject) and even for general norms addressed to a relatively small or at any rate easily identifiable audience (such as military commands). In the case of general norms addressed to a class of persons whose members are not easily identified—as in the case of most legal norms—the situation is different. It is certainly true that the legislator tries to inform the population each time he promulgates a new law by publishing it in the newspapers or at least in some sort of official bulletin (although there are also secret laws). Still, the large number of legal provisions makes it almost impossible for a legal subject to know them all or even those that concern him directly. This fact does not, however, prevent the jurist from speaking of existing legal norms and treating them as such. Legal norms are treated as existent long before they are 'received' by legal subjects. Here the difference between a direct command and a general legal norm is noteworthy.

Let us illustrate the point with an example. Suppose a colonel wants one of his captains to do a certain thing. He gives the order and sends a messenger to the captain. The messenger is killed on his way and is therefore prevented from communicating the command, and, as a consequence, the captain does not do what the command requires of him. Can the captain be charged with and punished for disobedience? Certainly not. If he can prove that he did not receive the command, the question of disobedience does not arise.

The situation differs radically in the case of general legal norms. A legal subject may very well be punished for not complying with a norm—for example, for failing to fulfil a legal obligation—even if he can prove that he was not aware of its existence. Ignorance of the law is not regarded as an excuse, for there is a legal presumption that all laws are known by everybody, and this presumption is *juris et de jure*—that is, it cannot be disproved. This presumption is of course a mere fiction; in fact no one, not even a learned jurist, can know all of a country's laws. However, it shows very clearly that the existence of legal norms is regarded quite independently from the receiving-aspect. A law is said to exist when it has been issued—that is, promulgated by the proper authority.

Moreover, the class of norm-subjects of a legal norm may even (in fact) be vacuous, and yet jurists would not hesitate to treat such a norm as existent. Suppose a law is issued stipulating that all inhabitants of Platina whose income per annum exceeds a certain amount must pay a special tax. Suppose, further, that Platina is a poor part of the country and there is no one whose income reaches that amount. One day, Onassis decides to settle in Platina and this law is applied to him. Would we say that this law did not exist earlier and only came into existence at the moment of Onassis's arrival or of his becoming aware of its promulgation? Jurists would certainly say that the law existed from the time of its promulgation, although it could not be applied then since there was no occasion for doing so.

The foregoing considerations show that in legal language the term 'norm' is ordinarily used in the sense of norm-prescription. It seems reasonable, therefore, to take norm-prescription as the *explicandum*. Accordingly, a norm is the content of an actual act of prescribing, and its existence begins with its promulgation.

The performance of the act of issuing the norm (promulgation) will be the only requirement for its existence. (The concept of promulgation is, of course, in need of clarification. It may be a simple act of uttering or writing down certain words, or it may be the result of a complex process in which the activity of many persons is involved, as, for example, in the enactment of a law by a parliament. However, we shall not take up this problem here.)

According to our argument, any serious act of prescribing gives rise to (the existence of) a norm. Only non-serious utterances of prescriptive sentences are hereby excluded.

The act of issuing a norm—its promulgation—marks the moment at which a norm begins to exist. It ceases to exist when it is derogated. The derogation of a norm may be tacit or explicit. A norm is tacitly derogated when it ceases to exist owing merely to the expiration of a certain period of time; such is the case with particular norms (particular with respect to the occasion) or temporal laws (in which it has been stipulated that they should cease to exist at a certain moment). Such cases are exceptional; usually a legal norm ceases to exist when it is explicitly derogated by the corresponding norm-authority by means of an act of derogation.[8]

The existence of a norm is temporally continuous; a norm is said to be existent from the moment of its promulgation to the moment of its derogation, but the temporal duration of a norm is a mere logical construction. There are no facts (besides the initial fact of promulgation and the final fact of derogation) that would render the statement true that a norm exists for a period of time. There are only certain criteria for the beginning and the termination of norms.

This characterization of the temporal existence of norms—which differs significantly from von Wright's—is in accord with current linguistic usage in the field of law. Jurists often say that there is (there exists) such-and-such a norm, and all they mean is that this norm has been promulgated (perhaps long ago) and has not yet been derogated. It is a noteworthy fact that legal norms very often outlive their authorities. A general legal norm may exist for a long time after the authority that issued it has disappeared. (Laws continue to exist after the death of a king or the dissolution of the parliament that enacted them.) This fact shows that the characterization of the continuous existence of a norm in terms of the continuity of the normative relationship between the norm-authority and the norm-subjects is not suitable for most legal norms.

3. The Ability to Command

As a consequence of having chosen a different *explicandum*, we had to dispense with the receiving-aspect of norms as a criterion for existence. We shall now focus our attention on the giving-aspect.

[8] In von Wright, *NA*, at 191, there is a brief but very interesting discussion of the concept of derogation or cancellation.

According to von Wright, the normative action does not consist of promulgation alone, but requires something else. This second component is the ability to command or, as we prefer to call it, the superiority relation between the norm-authority and the norm-subject. For although von Wright speaks here of a sanction, it is clear that the superiority relation is a more fundamental notion. Indeed, von Wright grants that the threat of punishment—that is, the sanction—may be implicit. In the case of an implicit sanction, how do we know that there is such a thing at all? Obviously because of the 'superior strength of the commander over the commanded'.[9] Only when we know that there is such superiority can we infer that there is an implicit threat of punishment for disobedience.

Still, it does not seem to make much sense to speak of sanctions in the case of a permissory norm. Nonetheless, it seems reasonable to maintain that not everyone can give a permission to someone; the person who gives a permission must be qualified in a certain way, he must have an ability to give that permission. What this ability to permit consists of is not entirely clear, but a possible criterion could be the ability to command. We would then say that a person can give a permission to do a certain thing to another person if and only if he can enjoin or prohibit doing this thing. This would be a reasonable way of extending von Wright's criterion to permissory norms.

What does the superiority relation or the ability to command and give permissions comprise? In von Wright's view, it consists of the possibility of punishing; when the commander can actually punish the norm-subject, he is said to be stronger. This superior strength of the commander constitutes his ability to command.[10]

It certainly seems reasonable that some sort of superiority relation between the norm-authority and the norm-subject be required. We would not normally say that a child who says to an elderly gentleman 'give me your hat!' has given a command, or that Mr Jones, who says to his neighbor 'I allow you to forbear from paying your taxes' has really given him a permission, but the requirement of the actual possibility of punishing is perhaps a bit too strong. The ability to command may be based on a merely moral superiority. When an old but for whatever reason respectable man tells a much younger and stronger man to do a certain thing, it may quite naturally be described as commanding, even if the commander cannot actually punish the commandee, and there is no need for the commandee to believe mistakenly in the superior strength of the commander; he may be aware that there is no physical superiority and yet do the enjoined thing—and his behaviour could well be described as obeying a command. This is why we prefer to speak of the superiority relation without specifying what this superiority comprises.

Von Wright's requirement of the superiority of the norm-authority over the subject as a necessary condition for the existence of a norm is in accordance with an important tradition in legal philosophy, which may be called the

[9] Von Wright, *NA*, 127. [10] See von Wright, *NA*, at 127.

Benthamite–Austinian tradition.[11] Still, there are important reasons that stand in the way of our accepting this requirement, at least in so far as it is defended as a necessary condition for the existence of *all* types of norm. The main reasons are (a) the indetermination of the norm-subjects; as we have already seen, the subjects of a legal norm can be indeterminate and even non-existent, but this does not prevent the norm from existing. (b) The norm-authority may cease to exist whereas the norm is said to remain in existence. It is not clear what the superiority relation between Napoleon and the French citizens of today consists of, but the Civil Code promulgated by Napoleon still exists.

One way of maintaining this requirement is to subscribe to the theory of tacit commands (Austin), according to which every sovereign tacitly commands all that has been commanded by his predecessor. However, this theory is little more than a fiction, elaborated ad hoc.[12]

The result of our discussion may be summed up as follows. In some situations (such as direct commands or permissions), the superiority relation is a necessary condition for the existence of a norm, but there are also contexts in which it is not required. Consequently, if we want to shape a general concept of the existence of norms, applicable to all types of (legal) norm, we must reject the requirement of superiority. The promulgation of the norm is then the only condition for its existence, and this may be regarded as a minimal requirement common to all types of norm.

4. Existence and Validity

An alternative way of interpreting the superiority relation between the norm-authority and the norm-subject is to replace factual (physical) superiority with the normative notion of *competence*. According to this view, a necessary condition for the existence of a norm is the competence of its authority; a norm comes into existence if and only if it is promulgated by a competent authority. An authority is said to be competent to issue a norm if the act of issuing it is permitted by another norm. A norm given by a competent authority is said to be *valid*; the validity of a norm lies in the notion that the act of issuing this norm is permitted (is legal, is lawful).[13]

Hans Kelsen is perhaps the most conspicuous representative of this line of thought, which is shared by many legal philosophers. Von Wright himself presents this view as a possible way of interpreting what he calls the principle of validity:

> It can be taken as saying that validity is a (logical) requirement for the success of the normative act, that a norm cannot come into existence in a system as a result of normative action, unless it is given by a proper, i.e., normatively competent, authority.[14]

[11] Both Bentham and Austin define the law in terms of the commands (the volition) of a sovereign, who is a person or set of persons habitually obeyed by a certain community. See Jeremy Bentham, *Of Laws in General*, ed. H. L. A. Hart (London: Athlone Press, 1970), at 1, 20–30, and John Austin, *The Province of Jurisprudence Determined*, ed. H.L.A. Hart (London: Weidenfeld, 1954), at 194.

[12] For penetrating criticism of this theory see Hart, *CL*, 1st edn., at 62–4, 3rd edn., at 63–6.

[13] See von Wright, *NA*, at 195–7.

[14] Georg Henrik von Wright, *An Essay in Deontic Logic and the General Theory of Action* (Amsterdam: North Holland, 1968) (hereafter, *Essay*), 94.

Kelsen goes so far as to identify existence with validity: 'By "validity" we mean the specific existence of norms.'[15]

The identification of existence with validity is a serious logical mistake, for it leads to an infinite regress.[16] Indeed, on this view a norm requires for its validity (existence) the validity of another norm, namely, the norm that permits the issuing of the first norm. However, the validity of this second norm requires the validity of a third norm, and so forth. Von Wright points out correctly that the validity of a norm cannot be characterized as being relative to the validity of another norm, but only as relative to the *existence* of another norm. This shows that the notion of validity already presupposes the notion of existence, at least in the sense of promulgation, and is not identical with it. Indeed, validity is a relation between two existing norms. The norm that confers competence (legal power) on an authority (permitting it to issue certain types of norms) renders valid the norms issued by that authority, but the validating norm need not be valid, although of course it must exist. It can also be an invalid norm or a sovereign norm.[17] Also, if validity were a necessary condition for the existence of a norm, then neither invalid norms nor sovereign norms could exist. This shows that existence—at least for those who grant the existence of sovereign norms—is independent of validity. (We shall return to this question in section 11 of this chapter.)

It is certainly true that in ordinary legal language the words 'existence' and 'validity' are often used as roughly equivalent. This fact does not prove, however, that the two concepts are identical. The term 'valid', as pointed out by von Wright,[18] is ambiguous; it is sometimes used in the sense of normative validity and sometimes in the sense of existence or being in force. However, the normative notion of validity (as the legality of the norm-creating act) must not be confused with the factual notion of existence. It is true that jurists are usually interested in those norms that exist *and* are valid, but in some contexts they also consider invalid (though existing) norms. The typical case is that of an unconstitutional law, that is, a law issued by the legislator (and so existent), but whose issuance is forbidden by the constitution. Such a law is invalid, but no jurist would claim that it does not exist. It is precisely because it exists that we are interested in its annulment, which may require a complex procedure, but no jurist would bother to annul a norm that does not exist, that is, which has not been promulgated. A non-existent norm is not a norm, but an invalid norm certainly *is* a norm, provided it has been promulgated.

5. Existence and Consistency

We turn now to the last—and perhaps most fundamental—question concerning the existence of norms: the problem of its relation to consistency.

[15] Kelsen, *GTLS*, 30.
[16] See von Wright, *NA*, at 196–7.
[17] See von Wright, *NA*, at 199; von Wright, *Essay* (n. 14, this chapter), at 94–5.
[18] See von Wright, *NA*, at 194–5.

Von Wright regards consistency as a necessary condition for the existence of norms: 'consistent prescriptions are such as *can exist* and inconsistent prescriptions [are] such as cannot exist—as far as logic is concerned'.[19]

What does it mean to say that a norm is (self-)consistent or that two norms are (mutually) consistent? Von Wright seems to use two different though related criteria for consistency. His criterion for the self-consistency of a norm is based on the possibility of performing the prescribed action: a norm is self-consistent if the norm-content is consistent, otherwise it is inconsistent. However, as von Wright points out, 'it is not clear by itself why a prescription should be called consistent if the prescribed action can be performed and inconsistent if it cannot be performed'.[20] Only if it were logically impossible to command and to permit an agent to do and to forbear from doing the same thing on the same occasion would such a prescription be inconsistent. Given von Wright's concept of existence, however, a norm cannot exist unless the norm-subject can do that which is prescribed; consequently, a norm that cannot be obeyed because the prescribed action cannot be performed cannot exist. Hence, it is inconsistent.

What is it for two or more norms to be mutually consistent? Von Wright gives first a *formal criterion* for the consistency (compatibility) of norm-formulations, that is, deontic (O- and P-)expressions. The definition of formal consistency is given in three steps: for sets of O-expressions, for sets of P-expressions, and, finally, for sets of O- and P-expressions (mixed sets). A set of O-expressions (commands) is consistent if and only if 'it is logically possible, under any given condition of application, to obey *all* commands (collectively) which apply on that condition'.[21] A set of P-expressions (permissions) is always consistent. Permissions never contradict each other. This means that although it is perhaps not possible to avail oneself of *all* the permissions at the same time, it is possible to avail oneself of *any one* of them at a given time. A mixed set (of commands and permissions) is consistent 'if, and only if, it is logically possible, under any given condition of application, to obey *all* the commands collectively and avail oneself of *each one* of the permissions individually which apply on that condition'.[22].

This formal criterion for the incompatibility of norm-formulations is, however, *not* von Wright's criterion for the mutual consistency of norms. If it were, then two incompatible norm-formulations could never express norms, for such norms would be inconsistent, and, according to von Wright, inconsistent norms cannot coexist; they 'annihilate one another'.[23] Von Wright, however, believes that two norms expressed by two incompatible norm-formulations can coexist and so are not inconsistent, provided they have been issued by different authorities.[24] Only if both norms stem from the same authority are they inconsistent, for they cannot coexist as expressions of a rational will since one and the same authority's issuing two incompatible norm-formulations shows that its will is not rational. Thus, von Wright's criterion for the inconsistency of norms is based on the irrationality of the will and not on the mere impossibility of performing the prescribed actions.

[19] Von Wright, *NA*, 135.
[20] Von Wright, *NA*, 135.
[21] Von Wright, *NA*, 143.
[22] Von Wright, *NA*, 144.
[23] Von Wright, *NA*, 148.
[24] See von Wright, *NA*, at 148.

(It is equally impossible for a norm-subject to perform the actions prescribed by two incompatible norm-formulations if they have been issued by one and the same authority or by two different authorities.)

It is important to realize that it will *not* do to answer the question why it should be called logically impossible to command and prohibit the same thing by saying that this is impossible because it is logically impossible for one and the same man both to do and forbear one and the same thing at the same time. For if I order a man to do something and you prohibit him to do the same it is also logically impossible that the man should obey both of us, but nevertheless perfectly possible that there should be this command and this prohibition.[25]

Thus, the notion of consistency is confined to norms that stem from the same authority; a set of such norms is called a *corpus*.[26] The consistency or compatibility of norms is therefore the possibility of their coexistence within a corpus.

The rationality of the norm-authority's will takes the place here of the possibility of performing the prescribed actions as the criterion for the consistency of norms. The two criteria are not, however, independent. Indeed, a will is irrational when the authority issues two incompatible norm-formulations (this seems to be the only criterion for irrationality), that is, when it prescribes two actions that cannot both be performed. So the formal criterion for the incompatibility of norm-formulations—restricted by the requirement of identifying the authority—turns out to be the criterion for the inconsistency of norms after all.

The concept of the consistency of norms, as set out by von Wright, gives rise to several difficulties.

1. The logic of norms is thereby restricted to norms issued by one and the same authority. If there can be no incompatibility between norms of different authorities, then there are no logical relations between such norms. However, the notion of a corpus of norms is of little use in the law. There are a great many legal authorities; jurists very often manipulate norms of different authorities, and they would not hesitate to call such a set a normative system.[27] According to von Wright's criterion, there could not be any inconsistency in such a system. Thus, his criterion becomes too restrictive, leaving out the interesting case of what he calls a 'conflict of wills' (that is, two incompatible norms issued by different authorities). This would be the paradigmatic case of what jurists call a contradiction between norms.
2. The requirement that the norm-authority be one and the same is rather problematic. What does it mean to say that the authority must be one and the same? The question is not difficult to answer when the authority is a personal agent, but what of impersonal authorities, which is the usual case in the law? Von Wright's psychologistic conception of norms (as expressions of a will) seems to

[25] Von Wright, *NA*, 148–9 (emphasis in original).

[26] See von Wright, *NA*, at 151.

[27] See Alchourrón and Bulygin, *NS*, at ch. 4 (43–64).

imply that the identity of an impersonal authority is given by the identity of all the individuals who constitute that authority. We would then say that two norms are given by the same law court or by the same parliament if and only if all individual members of the court or the parliament are the same. This would mean—aside from the practical difficulty of establishing the identity of the authority—that two laws enacted by the British Parliament on two successive occasions would count as norms of different authorities and would therefore not be susceptible to inconsistency by virtue of the mere fact that one member of parliament did not attend one of the two parliamentary sessions.

3. It may seem plausible to say of an individual who on a given occasion commands and prohibits one and the same thing that he has behaved irrationally and therefore has issued no norm at all. What of two incompatible norms issued by the same agent on two different occasions? Would we not say in such a case that the agent has changed his mind rather than calling him irrational? Must we then restrict the notion of consistency even further, stipulating that only norms issued by one and the same authority on a given occasion can be inconsistent? This would hardly be a desirable result. We could try to save the theory by saying that there is no inconsistency on the ground that the first norm ceases to exist in the very moment at which the agent changes his mind, but this amounts to requiring the continuous subsistence of the will for the duration of the existence of the norm. Such a requirement is clearly unacceptable, at least for legal norms, which as a rule continue to exist long after the will of the issuing authority has vanished.
4. A surprising consequence of von Wright's criterion is that there cannot be inconsistent norms, either within or outside a corpus. If two incompatible norms 'annihilate one another' when they stem from the same authority, and if they are not inconsistent provided they stem from different authorities, then there are no inconsistent norms. This sounds rather paradoxical. It is like saying that there can be no inconsistent propositions, that no two propositions can ever contradict each other. Of course, if by the existence of a proposition we understand its truth, then we can say that two contradictory propositions cannot coexist, for they cannot both be true. At best, one of them is true. In the case of norms, however, the situation is different. According to von Wright, both norms disappear, for they annihilate one another. (One could perhaps take the view that only one of them must vanish, but it would then be extremely difficult to decide which of the two incompatible norms ought to count as non-existent.)

Von Wright is very emphatic about the serious nature of the problem of contradiction between norms. 'It is serious because, if no two norms can logically contradict one another, then there can be no logic of norms either.'[28] Now, however, it looks as if no two (existing) norms could ever contradict each other.

[28] Von Wright, *NA*, 148.

The situation is perhaps not as dramatic as it appears, for even if, as a consequence of von Wright's conception, there cannot be a logic of norms, there can be a logic of norm-formulations. As a matter of fact, von Wright's logic of norms (prescriptions) is a logic of norm-formulations (deontic expressions).

The source of the difficulties lies in von Wright's decision to have consistency understood as a necessary condition for the existence of a norm, and this is based on his peculiar concept of existence. If we drop this requirement, a satisfactory notion of normative consistency can be elaborated by means of a close analogy to the consistency of propositions. In fact, this notion has already been proposed by von Wright himself as his formal criterion for the compatibility of norm-formulations. What our suggestion amounts to is a rejection of his ontology of norms and an acceptance of his logic, based on a different ontology.

In our discussion of the concept of existence we have argued that at least in legal contexts, von Wright's concept ought to be replaced by that of promulgation. If we do so, then there is no need to relate the concept of consistency to the existence of norms. Von Wright's formal criterion for the compatibility of norm-formulations—that is, the possibility of performing the prescribed action—will then be our criterion for the consistency of norms. This means that we will drop his restriction that norms should have the same authority. What he calls a conflict of wills is, in our account, a genuine contradiction, for we need not deny the possibility of the coexistence of inconsistent norms.

It should be noticed that 'conflict of wills', even in von Wright's view, is just a different name for a formally identical situation: the incompatibility of norm-formulations. This situation is called a 'contradiction' when the incompatible norm-formulations have been issued by the same authority, and a 'conflict of wills' when the authorities are different.

The distinction we have made between norm-prescriptions and norm-lekta (analogous to assertions and propositions) shows that our concept of the consistency of norms is similar to that of the consistency of propositions. A proposition is consistent when the state of affairs that it describes *can obtain*,[29] and it is inconsistent when this state of affairs is logically impossible. Consistency is a property of propositions, but we do not speak of the existence of propositions (except in the sense of truth). On the other hand, assertions can exist, but they can be neither consistent nor inconsistent, unless what we mean is the assertion of an inconsistent proposition, and this certainly can exist. It is perfectly possible to assert a self-inconsistent proposition or several mutually inconsistent propositions. Far from being impossible, this happens very frequently.

A similar distinction can be made in the realm of norms. Consistency is a property of norm-lekta, whereas existence is a property of norm-prescriptions. It seems natural to take as the criterion for the consistency of norms, in the sense of norm-lekta, the possibility of performing the prescribed action, but inconsistent norms can be prescribed in the same way as inconsistent propositions can be

[29] See von Wright, *NA*, at 134.

asserted. This means that according to our criterion inconsistent norms can exist (as norm-prescriptions) and that, for instance, two (existing) commands will be said to be contradictory if and only if the actions prescribed by them cannot be performed (for reasons of logic) by the norm-subject, disregarding the question of whether or not the same authority has issued them.

6. Deontic Logic (DL)

The logic of norms as the logic of the prescriptive normative language (DL) can thus be constructed as a logic of norm-lekta. This would correspond to what von Wright calls the prescriptive interpretation of a deontic calculus.[30] We shall now sketch the main features of such a deontic logic.[31]

The usual expressions of deontic logic will be read as expressions of norms: commands (O*p*), prohibitions (O –*p*), and permissions (P*p*). 'O*p*' will be read as 'it ought to be that *p*' or '*p* ought to be (done)', 'O –*p*' as 'it ought to be that not *p*' or '*p* must not be (done)', and 'P*p*' as 'it may be that *p*' or '*p* may be (done)'.

In ordinary language, a norm prohibiting that *p* may be expressed in different ways, for example, by saying 'you may not do *p*', or 'you ought not to do *p*', or 'you must not do *p*'. This shows that the expressions '–P*p*' and 'O–*p*' have the same prescriptive import. The same is true of 'P*p*' and '–O–*p*'. Thus, we can accept the following as a law of (prescriptive) deontic logic:

$$\text{DL1. } \vdash \text{P}p \equiv -\text{O}-p$$

Following von Wright's criteria for the incompatibility of norm-formulations, we have accepted the notion that a norm commanding that *p* is inconsistent with a norm commanding that not *p*. This means that 'O*p*' and 'O –*p*' are inconsistent. Hence, it follows that one of these norms implies the negation of the other. This leads to accepting, as a criterion for deontic consistency, the following law:

$$\text{DL2. } \vdash \text{O}p \supset -\text{O}-p$$

From DL1 and DL2 follows:

$$\text{DL2.1. } \vdash \text{O}p \supset \text{P}p \text{ (commanding implies permitting)}$$

[30] DL is a case of what Åqvist calls 'atheoretical logic'. See Lennart Åqvist, 'Interpretation of Deontic Logic', *Mind*, 73 (1964), 246–53. Bentham's very interesting discussion of the 'aspects of a law', in Bentham, *Of Laws in General* (n. 11, this chapter), at ch. 10 (93–132), reveals a similar conception of a logic of prescriptive expressions.

[31] For the sake of simplicity we shall deal only with monadic calculi; no reference to dyadic calculi (conditional permission and obligation) will be made, despite their obvious importance for legal matters. For the same reason we will use the symbolism of von Wright's *Essay* (n. 14, this chapter) rather than that of his *NA*.

Furthermore, we must accept the following law of distribution:

$$\text{DL3. } \vdash \mathrm{O}p \cdot \mathrm{O}q \equiv \mathrm{O}(p \cdot q)$$ [32]

When someone prescribes that it ought to be that *p* and that it ought to be that *q*, the prescriptive import of what he has done is the same as if he were prescribing that it ought to be that *p* and *q*.

The corresponding law of distribution for the operator P is:

$$\text{DL3.1. } \vdash \mathrm{P}p \vee \mathrm{P}q \equiv \mathrm{P}(p \vee q)$$

Finally, it seems clear that when someone prescribes that it ought to be that *p*, he also prescribes (implicitly) that the consequences of *p* ought to be. In other words, the consequences of the prescribed situation are also prescribed. This idea can be rendered in a logical calculus in the form of a rule of inference:

$$\text{DLR1. If } \vdash p \supset q, \text{ then } \vdash \mathrm{O}p \supset \mathrm{O}q$$

It may easily be seen that the principles DL1–DL3 together with DLR1 lead to a deontic logic that is very close to von Wright's first system.[33] Thus, his first deontic calculus proves to be an adequate reconstruction of the *prescriptive* notions of permission and obligation.

Two additional comments are perhaps required here. First, if we wish to reconstruct legal prescriptive discourse along lines that are as close as possible to ordinary usage, we must reject as meaningless (ill-formed) those deontic expressions in which a deontic operator is followed by a contradictory or tautological expression, for they do not prescribe (command or permit) any particular state of affairs. Still, such a rejection would lead to a very complicated calculus.[34] It is for such purely formal reasons that most logicians, including von Wright, accept as well-formed formulae (and even as axioms) expressions of the form 'O*t*' or 'P*t*' (where '*t*' stands for a tautology).

Second, we must exclude expressions in which a deontic operator occurs within the scope of another deontic operator. This is so because the content of a norm must be an action, an activity, or a state of affairs that is the result of an action or an activity. Therefore, the expression following a deontic operator must be a *description* of one of these things, but it cannot be a prescription. In other words, deontic operators generate norms from descriptions of a certain kind, but they cannot generate norms from norms. This rules out the iteration of deontic operators. (We shall return to this issue in section 11 of this chapter.)

[32] From the axiomatic point of view, DL3 can be weakened to $\mathrm{O}p \cdot \mathrm{O}q \supset \mathrm{O}(p \cdot q)$, for its converse can be obtained from DLR1.

[33] See von Wright, 'DL'.

[34] See Alchourrón and Bulygin, *NS*, at 43–4.

7. Norms and Norm-Propositions

It is a well-known fact that deontic sentences exhibit in ordinary language a characteristic ambiguity: sometimes they are used prescriptively as norm-formulations, and sometimes they are used descriptively to make normative statements. In the first case they express norms, in the second case, normative propositions.[35]

Although there are important differences between norms and norm-propositions, von Wright has decided not to use a special symbolism for the latter, retaining the ambiguity of the ordinary language in his formal calculus.[36] Thus, in lieu of two symbolisms he has one symbolism with two interpretations—one is prescriptive, the other descriptive. This strategy is based on the idea that there is some sort of logical parallelism or isomorphism between norms and norm-propositions, so that the logical properties of norms are reflected in logical properties of norm-propositions. Thus, although von Wright conceives of his deontic logic as a theory of descriptively interpreted deontic expressions, he, unlike some of his successors in the field, is well aware of the fact that the '"basis" of Deontic Logic is a logical theory of prescriptively interpreted O- and P-expressions'.[37]

It is a major thesis of the present chapter that this belief in some sort of pre-established harmony between the logical properties of norms and those of norm-propositions, a belief widely held by deontic logicians and legal philosophers,[38] is a serious logical mistake, for their respective logical properties are in fact different. In any case, rather than accepting dogmatic presuppositions, the more prudent course is to proceed by enquiring into norms and norm-propositions separately in order to determine whether and under what circumstances they are isomorphic. This is what we propose to do.

In order to distinguish clearly between prescriptive and descriptive deontic sentences we shall stipulate that the usual symbols O and P shall stand for prescriptive operators (with the reading indicated in section 6 earlier in this chapter) and three new symbols, namely '$\mathbb{O}$', '$\mathbb{P}_s$' and '$\mathbb{P}_w$', will be introduced for the descriptive deontic operators. The expression '$\mathbb{O}p$' will be read (descriptively) as 'it is obligatory that *p*', and the expressions '$\mathbb{P}_s p$' and '$\mathbb{P}_w p$' as 'it is permitted that *p*'. (As we shall see presently, the descriptive expression 'it is permitted that *p*' is ambiguous, and this is why we are introducing two symbols for the descriptive permissory operators.)

Norm-propositions convey information about the deontic status of certain actions or states of affairs: They say that an action is forbidden, or obligatory, or permitted, and they are true if and only if this action has the property of being forbidden, being obligatory, or being permitted. When, however, does an action have the property of being forbidden? This question admits of different answers. Some philosophers believe that being forbidden is an intrinsic (perhaps non-natural) property of the action itself and that its presence can therefore be

[35] See von Wright, *NA*, at 104–6. [36] See von Wright, *NA*, at 132.
[37] Von Wright, *NA*, 134. [38] See e.g. Kelsen, *RR 2*, § 16 (at 76–7), *PTL*, at 74–5.

detected by a close inspection of the action. Other philosophers believe that it is by virtue of God's commands or some eternal principles of natural law that certain actions are forbidden while others are permitted or are obligatory. We are concerned, however, with the positive law and the positivist approach, which is shared by most jurists. The characteristic of this point of view is that an action *p* is said to be forbidden if and only if there is a norm (of the positive law of the country in question) that forbids or prohibits that *p*, and not because it is intrinsically bad or disqualified by moral or natural law principles. This amounts to saying that the proposition that *p* is forbidden means the same as the proposition that there is (exists) a legal norm forbidding that *p*. Thus, norm-propositions can be analyzed into propositions about the existence of norms. Now if we accept the idea that the existence of a norm consists in its promulgation by an authority, then to say that an action *p* is forbidden ($\mathbb{O} -p$) is to say that a certain authority has promulgated a norm to the effect that *p* must not be done.

The latter proposition will be represented symbolically as 'N*x*O –*p*', where '*x*' denotes the legislative authority and the operator 'N' denotes the dyadic relation of promulgation: the promulgation of a norm (O –*p*) by an authority (*x*). This leads to the following definition:

$$\text{D1. } \mathbb{O}p = \text{N}x\text{O}p.$$ [39]

The property of being obligatory (or prohibited), as a character of actions, is thus defined in terms of the existence of an obligation-norm. (We need no special symbol for prohibition, for it can obviously be expressed in terms of obligation: $\mathbb{O} -p = \text{N}x\text{O} -p$). By 'obligation-norm' we mean a norm to the effect that *p* ought to be done, but it can also be expressed in terms of P (later we shall see that the formula 'N*x*O*p*' is equivalent to 'N*x* –P –*p*' and 'N*x*O –*p*' to 'N*x* –P*p*').

In a similar way, the property of being permitted can be defined in terms of a permissory norm, but this is only *one* meaning of the term 'permitted' when it occurs in norm-propositions. We shall call it *strong* or *positive permission* ($\mathbb{P}$s).[40]

$$\text{D2. } \mathbb{P}\text{s } p = \text{N}x\text{P}p$$

According to this definition, an action *p* is strongly permitted if and only if there is a legal norm to the effect that *p* may be done (that is, a norm permitting or authorizing *p*). This norm can be expressed in terms of P (N*x*P*p*) or in terms of O (N*x* –O –*p*).

However, the term 'permitted' is also very frequently used in normative propositions with a different meaning. Sometimes what is required for the truth of the

[39] The formula $\mathbb{O}p$ contains an implicit subscript x ($\mathbb{O}_x p$), which remains implicit as long as no confusion arises; otherwise it is made explicit (see n. 18, this chapter).

[40] Following von Wright, in *Normative Systems* we used the terms 'strong' and 'weak'. This terminology may be misleading, for it seems to suggest that the strong form implies the weak form, and this is not the case. Moreover, the terms 'positive' and 'negative' have the advantage of stressing the fact that positive permission requires the existence of a norm-giving act, whereas negative permission means the mere absence of such an act.

proposition 'p is permitted' is not the existence of a norm permitting that p, but the mere absence of a prohibition to do p. When the legislator has not issued any norm to the effect that p ought not be done, the action p is sometimes said to be permitted. This meaning of 'permitted' will be called *weak* or *negative permission* ($\mathbb{P}$w):

$$\text{D3. Pw } p = -\text{N}x\text{O} -p$$

This ambiguity of the term 'permitted', when used in descriptive discourse, has no counterpart in the prescriptive language in which the norms are expressed. (A similar distinction can of course be made regarding obligation, defining weak obligation as mere absence of permission. It is doubtful, however, whether the term 'obligatory' is ever used in such a weak sense.)

We must distinguish carefully between norm-characters expressed by prescriptive operators O and P and action-characters expressed by descriptive operators $\mathbb{O}$, $\mathbb{P}_s$ and $\mathbb{P}_w$. In *Norm and Action*, von Wright makes a clear conceptual and terminological distinction between strong and weak permission,[41] but he does not distinguish between strong permission and the norm-character P.

> Weak permission is not an independent norm-character. Weak permissions are not prescriptions or norms at all. Strong permission only is a norm-character. Whether it is an independent norm-character remains to be discussed.[42]

These phrases seem to imply that strong permissions are norms. It is important, however, to realize that neither positive (strong) nor negative (weak) permissions are norms; both are norm-propositions. The first asserts the existence of a permissory norm; the second asserts the non-existence of a prohibiting norm.

8. Negation in Normative Discourse

The use of 'it is obligatory that p' in the sense of '$\mathbb{O}p$' and of 'it is permitted that p' in the sense of '$\mathbb{P}sp$' or '$\mathbb{P}wp$' is typical for many forms of legal discourse. The main aim of legal science is the description of legal norms and not the prescription of actions. By the same token, legal counsel does not prescribe to his client that this or that is to be done; he only informs the client about the legal status of his actions, saying, for example, that the action p is obligatory ($\mathbb{O}p$) and that the action q is permitted. This last assertion is characteristically ambiguous, for it can mean $\mathbb{P}sq$ or $\mathbb{P}wq$, and which of the descriptive permission-characters is being referred to by 'permitted' is perhaps made clear only from the context.

This ambiguity of 'it is permitted that p', which is very characteristic of descriptive normative discourse, cannot be expressed in the usual symbolism of deontic logic, and it constitutes one reason (but not the only one) for developing a separate symbolism for descriptive normative language.

[41] See von Wright, *NA*, at 86. [42] Von Wright, *NA*, 86–7.

Another reason for the separate symbolism stems from the possibility of two types of negation of the descriptive operators. Consider first the norm-proposition 'it is permitted that *p*' ($\mathbb{P}sp$). Its negation 'it is not permitted that *p*' is ambiguous. It can mean (1) that the norm that permits *p* does not exist, that is, that the legislator did not promulgate the norm '$\mathrm{P}p$'. For this type of negation, called *external negation*, the usual symbol '–' will be used. Thus, on this interpretation '$-\mathbb{P}sp$' means the same as '$-\mathrm{N}x\mathrm{P}p$'. However, the statement 'it is not permitted that *p*' can also mean (2) that there is a norm to the effect that *p* must not be done, that is, that the legislator did promulgate the norm '$\mathrm{O}\,-p$' or (which amounts to the same) '$-\mathrm{P}p$'. This second type of negation of norm-propositions will be called *internal negation*, and it will be symbolized by '¬'. Its definition is:

$$\neg\mathbb{P}sp = \mathrm{N}x\,-\mathrm{P}p\,(= \mathrm{N}x\mathrm{O}\,-p)$$

Taking into account this ambiguity of 'not' when used with norm-propositions, one could expect, given the ambiguity of 'permitted', that the statement 'it is not permitted that *p*' would yield four different interpretations: external and internal negations of strong and of weak permission. In fact this is not the case, for the external negation of a weak permission is equivalent to the internal negation of a strong permission; analogously, the internal negation of a weak permission is equivalent to the external negation of a strong permission. This is shown in the following table:[43]

$$-\mathbb{P}sp = -\mathrm{N}x\mathrm{P}p = -\mathrm{N}x - -\mathrm{P}p = \neg\mathbb{P}wp$$

$$\neg\mathbb{P}sp = \mathrm{N}x\,-\mathrm{P}p = - -\mathrm{N}x\,-\mathrm{P}p = -\mathbb{P}wp$$

Thus, there are only two forms of negation of the statement 'it is permitted that *p*': the assertion that there is no norm permitting that *p* and the assertion that there is a norm prohibiting that *p*.

There are also two forms of negation of the proposition 'it is obligatory that *p*': the assertion that there is no norm commanding that *p* ($-\mathbb{O}p$), and the assertion that there is a norm permitting that not *p* ($\neg\mathbb{O}p = \mathrm{N}x\mathrm{P}\,-p = \mathrm{N}x\,-\mathrm{O}p$).

There is a most interesting discussion of the notion of negation in normative (prescriptive and descriptive) discourse in *Norm and Action.*[44] In order to characterize the notion of negation, von Wright states five conditions that we reproduce here in a substantially equivalent form.

(i) The negation of a given proposition (norm) shall be a proposition (norm).

(ii) Negation shall be unique—that is, there shall be one and only one negation of a given proposition (norm).

[43] For the proof, see the results at § 9 in this chapter.

[44] See von Wright, *NA*, at135–41.

(iii) Negation shall be reciprocal—that is, if a second proposition (norm) is the negation of a first proposition (norm), then the first is the negation of the second.

(iv) A given proposition (norm) and its negation shall be mutually exclusive.

(v) A given proposition (norm) and its negation shall be jointly exhaustive.

Von Wright considers various alternatives for the negation of a norm. In the case of a norm commanding that p, the two possible candidates are: a norm commanding that not p (that is, prohibiting that p), and a norm permitting that not p (permitting the forbearance of p). Of the two, von Wright rejects the first (for reasons that we shall not take up here). Thus, he chooses as the negation norm of the norm commanding that p the norm permitting that not p. In section 6 earlier in this chapter, we have already implicitly accepted this suggestion, taking '$-\mathrm{O}p$' (which on the ground of DL1 is equivalent to '$\mathrm{P} -p$') to be the negation-norm of the norm '$\mathrm{O}p$'.

For the negation of the (descriptively interpreted) norm-proposition '$\mathrm{O}p$', von Wright uses the negation sign '–'. '$-\mathrm{O}p$' means that the norm '$\mathrm{O}p$' does not exist. Thus, the negation expressed by '–' is an operation that leads from the assertion of the existence of a norm to the assertion of the non-existence of the same norm.

Also, according to von Wright, to every norm there corresponds a norm-proposition, that is, a descriptive sentence asserting the existence of this norm. Thus, we can distinguish between the proposition describing (the existence of) a given norm and the proposition describing (the existence of) its negation-norm. The operation that leads from the assertion of the existence of a norm to the assertion of the existence of its negation-norm cannot, however, be expressed in von Wright's symbolic language. All we have done, thus far, is to introduce a new symbol (¬) called internal negation as a name for this operation, and it is important to stress that this particular type of negation is very frequently used in ordinary language (and especially in legal language).

Do the different kinds of negation considered thus far (the two types of 'descriptive' negation—external and internal—and 'prescriptive' negation) meet the requirements (i)–(v)? External negation (–) certainly does. It meets the first three requirements, which is obvious, and it also meets (iv)—exclusiveness—since the propositions '$\mathbb{O}p$' and '$-\mathbb{O}p$' cannot both be true, as well as (v)—exhaustiveness—since one or the other of the two must be true. Indeed, '$\mathbb{O}p \vee -\mathbb{O}p$' is a law of propositional logic. The same is true of $\mathbb{P}$s and $\mathbb{P}$w.

Internal negation satisfies only the first three conditions; it fails to meet the requirements (iv) and (v). $\mathbb{O}p$ and $\neg\mathbb{O}p$ can both be true. They are both true when the system is inconsistent—when, that is to say, the legislator has issued a norm commanding that p and has also issued a norm commanding that not p, that is, prohibiting that p. For the same reason, $\mathbb{P}sp$ and $\neg\mathbb{P}sp$ may both be true. Moreover, they may both be false. This will be the case, for example, when the system is incomplete—that is, when the legislator has not issued any norm at all with respect to p. (We shall return to the problems of completeness and consistency in section

10 of this chapter.) This is an important difference between the two negations, showing that only the external negation is a negation in the full sense.

We must now consider prescriptive negation, that is, the operation that leads from a norm to its negation-norm. That this type of negation meets the first three requirements is clear. The negation-norm is a norm, there is only one negation-norm of a given norm, and they are reciprocal. What, however, can be said about the other two conditions?

In the prescriptive deontic logic sketched in section 6 of this chapter, the norms 'P*p*' and '–P*p*' are mutually exclusive and jointly exhaustive, for the formulae 'P*p* v –P*p*' and '–(P*p* · –P*p*)' are valid. Thus, the prescriptive negation meets both requirements, (iv) and (v). It is important, however, to appreciate what, exactly, this means. To say that 'P*p*' and '–P*p*' are mutually exclusive *does not* mean that the norms 'P*p*' and '–P*p*' cannot coexist in a normative system. It only means that two such norms are inconsistent, for obedience to the second norm cannot coexist with the permission extended by the first norm. Deontic logic as the logic of norm-lekta sets out the criteria for the consistency of possible norms, but it says nothing about the actual existence of norms. This shows the importance of separating the notions of existence and consistency, which was our concern in section 5 earlier in this chapter.

For similar reasons, to say that the norms 'P*p*' and '–P*p*' are jointly exhaustive *does not* mean that in every normative system there must be a norm permitting that *p* or a norm not permitting (that is, prohibiting) that *p*. It only means that any regulation of a given state of affairs *p* necessarily implies the permission of *p* or the prohibition of *p*. This does not mean that every state of affairs is in fact regulated, precisely because deontic logic has nothing to say about the actual facts (the existence of norms).

It is very important to realize that the acceptance of the formulae 'P*p* v –P*p*' and '–(P*p* · –P*p*)' as laws of prescriptive deontic logic does not commit us to the view that all normative systems are in fact complete and consistent.[45] What these formulae do is to state two types of condition: (a) a minimal condition which every norm-formulation must satisfy in order to express a norm (if a sentence neither permits nor prohibits that *p*, then it does not express a norm referring to *p*), and (b) a condition that every norm must satisfy in order to be consistent (if a norm permits and prohibits that *p*, then it is inconsistent regarding *p*).

Von Wright maintains that a norm and its negation-norm do satisfy the requirement (iv) because they cannot coexist within a corpus, but fail to satisfy (v) because both of them can be absent from a corpus.[46] This argument, however, only shows that von Wright cannot draw a clear distinction between the logic of prescriptive norm-formulations (based on the idea of consistency) and the logic of descriptive norm-propositions (based on the idea of the existence of norms), and this is so

[45] This may well be the reason for von Wright's persistent doubts concerning exhaustiveness and completeness. See von Wright, *Essay* (n. 14, this chapter), and Georg Henrik von Wright, 'Deontic Logics', *American Philosophical Quarterly*, 4 (1967), 136–43.

[46] See von Wright, *NA*, at 140, 154–5.

precisely because his criterion for consistency is based on the notion of existence. The separation of the two concepts is a necessary condition for this distinction.

9. The Logic of Norm-Propositions (NL)

The logical features of the action-characters $\mathbb{O}$, $\mathbb{P}$s, and $\mathbb{P}$w are reflected in the descriptive normative logic (NL), which is the logic of norm-propositions in the same sense in which (prescriptive) deontic logic is a logic of norms. It can be construed as an extension of prescriptive deontic logic. To the axioms and rules of inference of DL we must add, in order to characterize the logical properties of the operator N, the two following principles:

$$\text{NL1. } \vdash(\text{N}x\text{A} \cdot \text{N}x\text{B}) \supset \text{N}x(\text{A} \cdot \text{B})$$

(where A and B are well-formed formulae of deontic logic) and

$$\text{NL2. If } \vdash(\text{A} \supset \text{B}), \text{then } \vdash(\text{N}x\text{A} \supset \vdash \text{N}x\text{B})$$

The intuitive justification of these principles is not difficult. NL2 reflects the idea, widely held among jurists, that the logical consequences of a promulgated norm are also regarded as implicitly promulgated. Von Wright calls the norms that are logical consequences of (that is, are entailed by) explicitly promulgated norms *derived norms*.[47]

> The derived norms *are*, necessarily, in the corpus with the original ones. They are there, although they have not been expressly promulgated. Their promulgation is concealed in the promulgation of other prescriptions.[48]

The rationale of NL1 is self-explanatory: if two norms have been promulgated separately by the legislator, then both of them are promulgated. The only problem that may arise in this connection is the notion of legislator. We have thus far supposed, for the sake of simplicity, that there is only one legislative authority, which has been called *x*. However, there may be—and in most legal orders there will in fact be—a great many different authorities. The plurality of norm-creating authorities renders NL1 dubious. It is simply false to claim that if two different authorities (of the same legal order) have promulgated two norms, then there is an authority that has promulgated those two norms. (Such would be the result if we decided to quantify existentially over *x*.) In order to escape from this difficulty, the notion of '*the* legislative authority' can be construed as a (finite) set of norms $x = \{p_1, p_2 \ldots p_n\}$. If X is the conjunction of all the *x*-elements $(p_1 \cdot p_2 \ldots p_n)$, then N$xp$ amounts to $\vdash \text{X} \rightarrow p$, where '→' represents the notion of logical consequence or entailment. Thus, *x* promulgates *p* if and only if *p* is entailed by X. On

[47] See von Wright, *NA*, at 156–8. [48] Von Wright, *NA*, 158 (emphasis in original).

this interpretation, the legislator is a normative system (corresponding to a certain legal order), and it promulgates whatever obtains in the system.[49]

We are now in a position to compare, with the aid of NL1 and NL2, the logical properties of the descriptive operators $\mathbb{O}$, $\mathbb{P}$s, and $\mathbb{P}$w with those of their prescriptive counterparts O and P. Some of the principles of DL have no counterpart in NL; others are valid only for the strong or only for the weak permissory operator. Thus, deontic law DL1 is not valid for $\mathbb{P}$s: neither '$\mathbb{P}sp \supset -\mathbb{O} -p$' nor '$-\mathbb{O} -p \supset \mathbb{P}sp$' is a law of NL. This is the case because '$\mathbb{P}sp \cdot \mathbb{O} -p$' is not inconsistent; it is possible for one and the same state of affairs to be permitted by a certain authority and also to be prohibited by the same or some other authority. This happens when the legislator has promulgated a norm permitting that p and has also promulgated a norm prohibiting that p. Far from being impossible, such a situation occurs often enough, as every lawyer knows from experience. Of course, these two norms are inconsistent, and lawyers will see to it that such an inconsistency is removed, but what they are eager to remove is precisely the *inconsistency* of two norms.

There is in NL a law analogous to DL1, but only for weak permission:

$$\text{NL3. } \mathbb{P}wp \equiv -\mathbb{O} -p$$

There is, however, no counterpart to DL2, for '$\mathbb{O}p \supset -\mathbb{O} -p$' is not valid because '$\mathbb{O}p \cdot \mathbb{O} -p$' is consistent. There are no logical relations between acts or performances; the act of commanding that p is compatible (and can coexist) with the act of prohibiting that p, though, of course, the contents of these two acts (the command Op and the prohibition O $-p$) are incompatible (contradictory). The existence of incompatible norms—as already pointed out—is not, however, impossible.

There is also a law analogous to DL2.1:

$$\text{NL4. } \mathbb{O}p \supset \mathbb{P}sp$$

but the corresponding formula for weak permission ($\mathbb{O}p \supset \mathbb{P}wp$) is not valid. The principle of distribution DL3 is valid in NL:

$$\text{NL5. } \vdash \mathbb{O}p \cdot \mathbb{O}q \supset \mathbb{O}(p \cdot q)$$

but the distributive principle for P (DL3.1) is valid only for $\mathbb{P}$w, not for $\mathbb{P}$s.

$$\text{NL6. } \vdash \mathbb{P}w\left(p \vee q\right) \equiv \mathbb{P}wp \vee \mathbb{P}wq$$

49 See Nicholas Rescher, *Topics in Philosophical Logic* (Dordrecht: D. Reidel, 1968), at 261–2. The whole logic for Nx will be construed in close analogy to Rescher's assertion logic, especially to his system A_0.

The rule of inference of DL holds in NL for $\mathbb{O}$ and for both permissory operators:

NL7. If $\vdash p \supset q$, then $\vdash \mathbb{O}p \supset \mathbb{O}q$

NL8. If $\vdash p \supset q$, then $\vdash \mathbb{P}sp \supset \mathbb{P}sq$

NL9. If $\vdash p \supset q$, then $\vdash \mathbb{P}wp \supset \mathbb{P}wq$

10. Consistency and Completeness

We have seen that the formulae

(1) $\mathbb{P}sp \supset -\mathbb{O} -p$
(2) $-\mathbb{O} -p \supset \mathbb{P}sp$
(3) $\mathbb{O}p \supset -\mathbb{O} -p$

are not valid in NL, for they may be false. The possible falsehood of (1) means that the formula '$\mathbb{P}sp \cdot \mathbb{O} -p$' is consistent, that is, it may be true. It is interesting to enquire into what conditions, exactly, render this last formula true. It is true when the legislator has promulgated incompatible norms concerning *p*, that is, when the legislator has permitted and prohibited that *p*. This suggests the following definition of an inconsistent regulation of a state of affairs (IN(*p*)):

$$\text{IN}(p) = \mathbb{P}sp \cdot \mathbb{O} -p \ (= \mathbb{P}sp \cdot \neg\mathbb{P}sp)$$

The possible falsehood of (3) shows that a state of affairs *p* can be commanded and prohibited. It can be proven that when this is the case, the legislator has promulgated incompatible norms. This is reflected in the following formula:

$$\vdash (\mathbb{O}p \cdot \mathbb{O} -p) \supset \text{IN}(p)$$

(Indeed, given $\vdash$O*p* ⊃ P*p*, (1) can be inferred from (3). If O*p* ⊃ P*p* were not accepted, there would be two different types of inconsistency, one related to (1) and the other to (3).)

If formula (2) is true, we shall say that the legislator has determined a normative status for *p* or that *p* is *normatively determined* (ND(*p*)).

$$\text{ND}(p) = \mathbb{O} -p \text{ v } \mathbb{P}sp$$

(which is to be read: *p* is normatively determined if and only if *p* is prohibited or strongly permitted.)

The idea of normative determination may be used to characterize a concept of completeness for normative systems. The set of norms promulgated by the legislator *x* is complete if and only if every state of affairs is normatively determined by *x*.

The idea of completeness plays an important part in legal thought, for it underlies the famous problem of gaps in law, which has been much discussed by jurists and legal philosophers.[50]

All of this shows that a special symbolism is required for the logic of norm-propositions because certain important properties of normative systems, such as consistency and completeness, cannot be adequately formulated in the traditional (descriptively interpreted) deontic logic.

At the same time, our discussion of the differences between the strong and the weak permissory operator and between external and internal negation has shown that these differences are based on the fact that there may be inconsistent and incomplete systems of norms. For systems that are complete and consistent, there are no such differences. Indeed, it can easily be proven that if we accept $\vdash -\mathrm{IN}(p)$ and $\vdash \mathrm{ND}(p)$ as axiomatic principles (which is tantamount to the assumption that all systems of norms are consistent and complete), then the formulae '$\mathbb{P}sp \equiv -\mathbb{O}\ -p$' and '$\mathbb{O}p \supset -\mathbb{O}\ -p$' become theorems, and the difference between strong and weak permissions and between external and internal negation vanishes. (On this assumption, '$\mathbb{P}sp \equiv \mathbb{P}wp$' and '$-\mathbb{P}sp \equiv \neg\mathbb{P}sp$' are also provable.) Both logics become isomorphic.

Thus, isomorphism may serve as a (partial) explanation of the fact that deontic logicians tend to overlook the difference between prescriptive and descriptive normative logic, especially because they are primarily concerned with ethics. In typical contexts of ethics, it is natural to assume that all actions have some deontic character and that no action can be both obligatory and prohibited. In other words, it is often assumed that ethical systems are always consistent and complete. Still, this fact does not diminish the interest in the distinction in the field of law discussed earlier, where inconsistencies and 'gaps' in the law are familiar though disturbing phenomena, which jurists expend considerable effort toward eliminating.

11. Iteration of Deontic Operators

There is still another reason for developing two separate symbolisms for prescriptive and descriptive deontic expressions, and this reason is related to a very important idea introduced by von Wright.[51] This idea is to use formulae with iterated deontic operators like '$\mathrm{OO}p$' or '$\mathrm{PO}p$' to represent norms of higher order. Such norms play an important part in law, especially in the form of norms of competence. There are several notions widely used in legal theory that are characterized in terms of norms of competence, such as validity, legal order, and authority (organ).

The interpretation of deontic formulae with iterated operators presents certain difficulties that did not escape von Wright's attention. Let us consider, as an example, the iteration of the operator O.

[50] See Alchourrón and Bulygin, *NS*.

[51] See von Wright, *NA*, at ch. 10 (189–207), and von Wright, *Essay* (n. 14, this chapter), at 91–6.

In view of the distinction between prescriptive and descriptive deontic operators, four different cases are to be considered:

(1) $\mathrm{OO}p$

(2) $\mathbb{O}\mathrm{O}p$

(3) $\mathrm{O}\mathbb{O}p$

(4) $\mathbb{O}\mathbb{O}p$

The first formula '$\mathrm{OO}p$' is a norm whose content is another norm ($\mathrm{O}p$). If we accept that only actions or states of affairs resulting from actions can be the content of norms (section 6 in this chapter), then the formula '$\mathrm{OO}p$' must be rejected as meaningless. This result appears to be in accordance with von Wright's opinion that norms cannot be the content of norms.[52]

For similar reasons we have decided to reject formula (2). In its expanded form, it amounts to '$\mathrm{N}x\mathrm{OO}p$'. Part of this formula ($\mathrm{OO}p$) is a meaningless expression, and this is why we prefer to consider the whole formula meaningless.

Formula (3) is a norm whose content is a normative proposition. In its expanded form, it amounts to '$\mathrm{ON}x\mathrm{O}p$', that is, it is a norm to the effect that the authority x ought to issue a norm of the form '$\mathrm{O}p$'. This is exactly what von Wright understands by 'norms of higher order', that is, norms that prescribe (enjoin, permit, or prohibit) the performance of *normative actions*, that is to say, actions consisting of the promulgation (or derogation) of other norms. Thus, an example of a norm of higher order of the form $\mathrm{O}\mathbb{O}p$ may be found among the current prescriptions of a penal code: 'homicide shall be punished with imprisonment from eight to 25 years' can be interpreted as a norm directed to the judge, enjoining him to issue a norm sentencing to a term in prison anyone who has committed homicide.

Perhaps the most important kind of norms of higher order, as von Wright suggests,[53] are the norms of competence. These have the form of $\mathrm{P}\mathbb{O}p$ or $\mathrm{P}\mathbb{P}sp$, that is, they are permissory norms 'to the effect that a certain authority *may* issue norms of a certain content'.[54] Von Wright has some brief but very illuminating remarks about norms of competence,[55] and a careful reading of these remarks can be warmly recommended to legal philosophers. Of special importance, we believe, is his distinction between norms delegating powers (norms of competence), which are essentially permissions, and other norms of higher order, which may also be orders or prohibitions. We shall not take up these issues here.

Finally, the formula $\mathbb{O}\mathbb{O}p$ is a norm-proposition asserting the existence of a norm of higher order, that is, asserting that the authority x has issued a norm to the effect that another authority y should issue a norm of the form $\mathrm{O}p$. Thus, its expanded form is $\mathrm{N}x\mathrm{ON}y\mathrm{O}p$. Here we must distinguish between different

[52] See von Wright, *NA*, at 189; von Wright, *Esssay* (n. 14, this chapter), at 91.

[53] See von Wright, *NA*, at 192.

[54] Von Wright, *NA*, at 192 (emphasis in original).

[55] See von Wright, *NA*, at 192–8.

authorities, for the limiting case of a self-prescription (autonomous norm) where $x = y$ is of little interest for the law. This fact makes it advisable to use subscripts in order to indicate the corresponding authority: '$\mathbb{O}_x\mathbb{O}_y p$' would then correspond to 'N*x*ON*y*O*p*'.

On the basis of these considerations we can establish the following formation rules for expressions with iterated deontic operators.

R1. Prescriptive operators cannot be iterated.

R2. A prescriptive operator cannot occur within the scope of a descriptive operator.

R3. Descriptive operators can be iterated (indefinitely).

R4. Descriptive operators can occur within the scope of a prescriptive operator.

It follows that only descriptive operators can be iterated and that a prescriptive operator can occur only at the beginning of an iterated expression (formula of higher order).

As von Wright shows, *one* important application of expressions of higher order is to characterize the concept of *validity*.[56]

According to von Wright, 'a norm is valid (in a normative system S), if and only if, the normative act of giving this norm is permitted (in that system)'.[57] Here 'permitted' must mean the strong permission, that is, the existence of a permissory norm of higher order. This is clearly stated in *Norm and Action*: 'the validity of a norm means that the norm exists and that, in addition, there exists another norm which permitted the authority of the first norm to issue it'.[58] This shows that validity is a *relation* between two existing norms. To say that a norm N_1 is valid in relation to a norm N_2 means that (1) N_1 has been promulgated by a certain authority (say *y*), and that (2) the norm N_2 has been promulgated by (usually another) authority *x*, and that (3) N_2 permits the issuing of N_1 by *y*.

On the other hand, a norm N_1 is *invalid* in relation to N_2 if and only if both of them exist and N_2 prohibits the issuing of N_1 (by the authority that has in fact issued N_1).[59] Thus, the validity of the norm 'O*p*' implies '$\mathbb{P}$sN*x*O*p*', and the invalidity of 'O*p*' implies '$\mathbb{O}$ –N*x*O*p*'

It follows that a norm can be both valid and invalid in the same system (although in relation to different norms). This occurs when an authority has permitted the issuing of this norm and either the same authority or another has prohibited it. Moreover, it can be the case that a norm is neither valid nor invalid; such a norm is called *sovereign*.[60]

A norm is sovereign if and only if its issuance is neither strongly permitted nor prohibited. Thus, to say that 'O*p*' is sovereign implies '–$\mathbb{P}$sN*x*O*p*' and

[56] See von Wright, *NA*, at 194, and von Wright, *Essay* (n. 14, this chapter), at 94.

[57] Von Wright, *Essay* (n. 14, this chapter), 94.

[58] Von Wright, *NA*, 195.

[59] See von Wright, *NA*, at 197, and von Wright, *Essay* (n. 14, this chapter), at 94.

[60] See von Wright, *NA*, at 199.

'$-\mathbb{O}$ $-\mathrm{N}x\mathrm{O}p$'. It follows that a norm is either sovereign or not sovereign, and it cannot be both sovereign and not sovereign (in the same system).

Von Wright's definitions of validity and invalidity already entail the possibility of sovereign norms (which he, of course, accepts). At the same time, the acceptance of sovereign norms—that is, norms that are neither valid nor invalid—commits us to the view that there are open normative systems, for it is precisely a sovereign norm that provides an example of a *deontically undetermined action*, that is, an action that is neither prohibited nor strongly permitted. It is the normative action of promulgating a sovereign norm.

12. Some Concluding Remarks

We have advanced some reasons in favour of the development of a separate symbolism for the descriptively interpreted deontic expressions in order to identify certain very common uses of the terms 'obligatory', 'permitted', 'prohibited', and so on. These uses are altogether typical for legal discourse. The typically *legal sense* of these and similar terms differs substantially from what we might call their *ethical sense*. It is a noteworthy—although not always noticed—fact that deontic terms are used in quite different senses in moral and legal contexts. *One* important difference is this: no action can be morally permitted and prohibited at the same time. It has been emphasized by G. E. Moore that we cannot say, in any typically ethical sense, that one and the same particular action is at one and the same time both right and wrong.[61] This seems to be a characteristic feature of the ethical use of such words.[62] By contrast, it is perfectly possible for an action to be at the same time both legally permitted and prohibited (as has been argued in section 10).

This difference is closely related to the different nature of moral and legal norms. Legal norms (at least in so far as the positive law is concerned) are in an important sense dependent on human actions; they are essentially man-made norms. Here again we can draw on Moore:

> And... it does seem to be the case that every law, which is the law of any community, is, in a certain sense, *dependent* upon the human will. This is true in the sense that, in the case of every law whatever, there always are *some* men, who, by performing certain acts of will, could make it cease to be the law; and also that, in the case of anything whatever which is *not* the law, there always are *some* men, who, by performing certain acts of will, could make it be the law.... It does seem, therefore, as if laws, in the legal sense, were essentially dependent on the human will.[63]

[61] See G. E. Moore, *Ethics* (London: Oxford University Press, 1912), at 50–82. Like Moore, what we have in mind in speaking of a typically ethical sense is rational (objective) morality, not the (historically changing) positive morality, where the situation is very similar to that of positive law.

[62] Accepting it does not commit us to any form of ethical intuitionism. See Charles L. Stevenson, 'Moore's Arguments against Certain Forms of Ethical Naturalism', in *The Philosophy of G. E. Moore*, ed. Paul A. Schilpp (in The Library of Living Philosophers, vol. 4) (Evanston: Northwestern University Press, 1942), at 71–90.

[63] Moore, *Ethics* (n. 61, this chapter), 92 (emphasis in original).

By contrast, the very idea of moral legislation seems to be absurd. As Hart puts it:

> it is inconsistent with the part played by morality in the lives of individuals that moral rules, princples, or standards should be regarded, as laws are, as things capable of creation or change by deliberate act. Standards of conduct cannot be endowed with, or deprived of, moral status by human *fiat*.[64]

This is why the notion of the existence of a legal norm is quite different from that of a moral norm, and it is why the problems of consistency and completeness have far greater importance in legal discourse than in moral discourse. It is also the reason why most deontic logicians attach little importance to the difference between prescriptive and descriptive normative language. We have seen that this difference is based on the possibility of inconsistency and incompleteness because, for the case of consistent and complete systems, both calculi are isomorphic. Therefore, if it is accepted that a system of moral norms is always consistent and complete, then, as long as we are interested in ethics, there is no need to distinguish between the two logics.

A good many differences of opinion among deontic logicians are due to their (tacit) recourse to different intuitive backgrounds. Some of them, Hector-Neri Castañeda for example, seem to have in mind only moral norms. Von Wright is one of the few who have also taken into account legal language. Even in his work, however, in spite of the sensitivity he shows in connection with legal problems, there is no clear separation between moral and legal senses of deontic terms, and this is perhaps the main source of some of the perplexities.

[64] Hart, *CL*, 1st edn., 171 (emphasis in original), 3rd edn.,176.

6

On the Rule of Recognition (1976)*

1. Two Types of Rule

We can distinguish between two types of rule: rules of conduct (which I will call 'norms') and conceptual rules. These two types of rule are clearly different, even if it is not completely (or always) clear what the exact difference is. I shall not offer here full characterizations of these two types of rule; I will confine myself to pointing out some of their distinguishing traits. (Obviously, it should not be supposed that these two categories are together exhaustive; many kinds of rule are possible, but I am here interested only in these two.)

There are many types of norms or rules of conduct: legal norms, moral norms, norms that we could characterize as purely conventional (such as those that concern the modes of dress), and so on. What all these norms have in common is what I will call their prescriptive or *normative* character: they all require, prohibit, or permit—that is, they all prescribe that a certain action (or class of actions) is obligatory, prohibited, or permitted under given circumstances or cases. The presence of a deontic modality (or normative character) can thus be regarded as a defining (that is, necessary, although probably not sufficient) trait of rules of conduct that we call norms.

There are also several types of conceptual rule: grammar rules, semantic rules, rules of inference (logical rules), the rules of a game (like chess or soccer),[1] and so on. What all these rules have in common is their *definitional* character—that is, they can be seen as definitions of certain concepts.[2]

It seems to me that these two types of rule are mutually exclusive—that is, that no rule can be both normative and conceptual—but in order to avoid the appearance of a dogmatic attitude, I will leave this question open. What I do mean to stress is that even if conceptual rules and norms are not mutually exclusive, it still

* [*Editors' note*: Eugenio Bulygin's paper was first published as 'Sobre la regla de reconocimiento' in *Derecho, filosofía y lenguaje*, ed. Ambrosio L. Gioja (Buenos Aires: Astrea, 1976), 31–9, in *ALD*, 383–91. It was translated for the present volume by Luís Duarte d'Almeida and Kevin Toh.]

1 It should be kept in mind that not all rules of games are conceptual rules. In a game like chess or soccer there are also rules of conduct. For example, the rule defining what should be considered a 'foul' is a conceptual rule, whereas the rule forbidding fouls and imposing penalties on those who commit them is a norm.

2 See Hart, *CL*, 1st edn., at 238–9, 3rd edn., at 284–5; von Wright, *NA*, at 3–7. [*Editors' note*: For these and other abbreviations, see the Table of Abbreviations.]

makes sense to distinguish between the normative and the definitional (conceptual) character of a rule.

In this article I will maintain: 1. that both types of rule are present in law; 2. that Hart's rule of recognition seems to be a conceptual rule far more than a norm, because it has a definitional character while completely lacking any normative character; 3. that, in particular, the rule of recognition does not impose upon judges the duty to apply legal norms; 4. that whenever such an obligation exists—which is a contingent matter—it arises not from the rule of recognition, but from some specific rule of the system that is identified in accordance with the rule of recognition; 5. that Hart's usage of the term 'rule' to refer both to those rules that he calls 'primary rules' (duty-imposing rules) and those that he calls 'secondary rules' (and especially the rule of recognition) is open to criticism; and 6. that this undifferentiated usage is not only terminologically deficient, but is also a symptom of conceptual confusion.

2. The Identification of Valid Law and the Rule of Recognition

In order to see what a rule of recognition is and how it operates, let us introduce a simple model.

Suppose that there is a community of people living in a territory in which an absolute monarch (Rex) has reigned for a long time. Rex governs his people by means of commands and other kinds of rules, which he issues while sitting on his throne. Anything that Rex says while sitting on the throne is considered by the members of the community to be valid law. When sitting on his throne, Rex usually utters sentences of various types, including (a) sentences that express general norms (for example, 'all adult residents have the duty to work without pay for the monarch for three days a month') and (b) sentences that express conceptual rules (for example, 'all residents aged 21 years or older are adults'). Such sentences (or their meanings) are generally considered to be valid law of the country.

Rex also has several ministers, appointed by him, whom he has permitted both to utter sentences expressing rules or norms and to appoint further officers, authorizing (permitting) them in turn to utter certain types of sentence expressing rules or norms. The sentences uttered by the ministers and by these further officers are also considered to be valid law, provided that they belong to the class of sentences whose utterance has been permitted either by Rex or by some higher-ranking officer (which permission may also depend on the adoption of certain formal procedures and be limited to sentences with a certain content). Let us further suppose, to keep things simple, that there is no other type of sentence that is considered to be valid law.

Sometimes Rex utters a sentence derogating a rule issued by him on some prior occasion (and the same happens with the ministers and further officers with respect to the rules that they themselves had issued). In this case, the rule is no longer considered to be valid. However, a minister cannot derogate a rule issued by Rex, nor can a lower-ranking officer derogate either Rex's or a minister's rules. An officer can only derogate rules enacted either by himself or by a lower-ranking officer.

Rex's subjects generally obey his norms, because those who fail to comply with their obligations are severely punished. Thus the population seeks always to obey and to act in accordance with legal norms. Hence their interest in ascertaining the exact content of the law—that is, in knowing what it is that they ought to do according to the law. In such endeavours, legal subjects usually make statements about the law, saying, for example, that (according to the law) action *p* is obligatory under circumstances *q*. Let us call these statements 'legal propositions'. Of course, not only ordinary people but also the officers, the ministers, and Rex himself (whenever he is *not* sitting on his throne) utter legal propositions of this sort.

Legal propositions are either true or false, and they are objective, in the sense that their truth-value is independent of the person who utters the proposition. The proposition 'according to the law, *p* is obligatory in case *q*' is true if and only if there is, among the valid legal sentences, a sentence prescribing that *p* is obligatory in case *q*. The existence of a such a norm is an empirical fact, but the verification of the legal proposition that describes this fact presupposes a criterion for the identification of the sentences that are to be considered valid law. Any (serious) formulation of a legal proposition implies the use of some such criterion, and it can therefore be said that the truth-value of the legal proposition is relative to a criterion for the identification of valid law.

We have said that in the country ruled by Rex everyone uses the same criteria for identification (even if these are seldom made explicit). These criteria can be expressly formulated by means of the following rules:

1. Every sentence uttered by Rex from his throne is valid law.
2. If there is a valid norm that permits a person *x* to utter a sentence *p*, and *x* has uttered *p*, then *p* is valid law.
3. Only those sentences that are valid according to rules 1 and 2 express valid law (and there are no other valid sentences apart from those indicated).

Taken together, these three rules constitute a recursive definition of 'valid law' or 'sentence that expresses valid law' in the sense that it is possible, in a finite number of successive applications of these rules, to determine whether a given sentence is (expresses) valid law, and therefore whether it belongs to the system under consideration. By 'system' we understand here the set of all valid sentences at a moment *t*. It is important to emphasize that the content of a system is relative to a moment in time: a system is in this sense a 'momentary' one.[3]

In order to characterize exhaustively the criteria for validity (including the phenomenon of derogation), we should also introduce alongside the three rules mentioned, which we may conveniently dub 'admission rules', other rules, which may be called 'elimination rules'. The elimination rules would determine that a sentence

[3] See Raz, *CLS*, at 34; Alchourrón and Bulygin, *NS*, at 72–7.

(which is valid according to rules 1 and 2) loses its validity under certain conditions. For the sake of brevity, however, we shall omit this complication.

I believe the criteria for identification just sketched reflect quite accurately the function of what Hart calls the 'rule of recognition'. It seems unquestionable at least that the rule of recognition provides criteria for the identification of the valid rules of the system, and thus that it performs the same function as our criteria for identification (which is not to exclude the possibility that the rule of recognition was intended by Hart to perform other functions as well). We shall in any case adopt Hart's terminology and call the 'rule of recognition' the set of all the criteria for the identification of valid law.

The rule of recognition, being a definition, lacks truth-value. Although one definition may for several reasons prove more convenient than another, it is clear that, in principle, anyone is free to adopt whatever definition he prefers. Among the many possible definitions of 'valid law', however, there is one that deserves special attention: the one effectively used 'either by courts or other officials or private persons or their advisers'.[4]

Moreover, we speak of *one* legal system only when the *same* rule of recognition is generally used by a given social group. We can therefore refer to this definition as the definition 'in use' (keeping in mind, however, that this expression has nothing to do with Russell's 'definitions in use').

The statement that a given criterion or set of criteria is effectively used by the community and by courts is an empirical statement, a statement of fact. Hart describes this situation, somewhat equivocally, as the 'existence' of the rule of recognition.[5] I say 'equivocally' because it is not at all common to speak of the existence of conceptual rules (such as definitions), and it is not quite clear what is meant by it. On the contrary, one speaks frequently of the existence of norms or rules of conduct. Thus Hart's terminology tends to suggest that the rule of recognition is a rule of conduct and not a conceptual one. My thesis, in turn, is that the rule of recognition is a mere definition, and therefore a conceptual rule.

3. The Rule of Recognition and the Obligations of the Judge

We may at this stage, I think, draw the conclusion that the rule of recognition has definitional content in so far as it provides criteria for the identification of valid law. We must now enquire into whether the rule of recognition has some normative content as well.

Hart seems to believe that the rule of recognition not only provides the criteria for the identification of what he calls the 'primary' norms of the system (that is, the duty-imposing norms), but also imposes upon judges the obligation to use and apply the norms identified in accordance with the rule of recognition (that

[4] Hart, *CL*, 1st edn., 98, 3rd edn., 101.

[5] Hart, *CL*, 1st edn., 98, 106–7, 245–6, 3rd edn., 101, 109–10, 292–3.

is, the valid norms of the system). Many quotes could be given in support of this interpretation. Moreover, Joseph Raz, erstwhile student of Hart's and an expert on his work, has explicitly endorsed it in a recent article. 'The rule of recognition', Raz writes, 'imposes an obligation on the law-applying officials to recognize and apply all and only those laws satisfying certain criteria of validity spelt out in the rule'.[6]

In order to see whether the rule of recognition can be interpreted as a duty-imposing rule, we must consider what happens when it is incorrectly applied or set aside. In effect, according to Hart, the main difference between a rule and a mere habit (convergent behaviour) lies in people's reactions in the event of disobedience. It also seems very clear that Hart means to emphasize the fact that the rule of recognition is not a mere habit, but an 'accepted' rule.[7]

I have the impression that Hart is here tacitly assuming that these are the only two possibilities at hand: habit or rule of conduct. Therefore, in order to bring out the fact that the rule of recognition is not a mere habit, he proceeds to show that it is a rule of conduct. If, however, one grants that conceptual rules are distinct from rules of conduct, the 'habit/rule of conduct' dichotomy is discredited.

In the case of conceptual rules there usually are also certain characteristic reactions to those persons who fail to follow or use them, and these reactions allow us to distinguish conceptual rules from mere habits. Such reactions, however, are very different in nature from those that occur in response to departures from norms. It would be inappropriate to say of someone who has made a grammatical error that he has 'disobeyed' the rules of grammar. We would simply say that that person is ignorant (does not know the rules of grammar) or that he speaks another language.

There are certainly situations in which one is obligated to speak correctly—if one is a school teacher, for example. The teacher can be punished if he fails to comply with this obligation: for example, he can be dismissed, but this obligation derives not from the rules of grammar but from a *norm* that imposes the obligation to use the rules of a given grammar.

I would like to suggest that the situation is very similar where the use of the rule of recognition is concerned. In order to show this, I will analyse some typical situations.

Case I. Let us first consider the case of a private citizen. If one does not know how to identify the valid law—which means that one does not know the rule of recognition in use—one may not know what on any given occasion one ought to do according to the law. However, given that legal norms (and the sanctions they stipulate in the event of disobedience) apply to all members of the country's population regardless of their knowledge of such norms (since knowledge of the law is presumed, and the presumption is *juris et de jure*, that is, it admits of no proof to the contrary), one's ignorance of the law is immaterial except when a mistake concerning the law is admitted as an excuse. The same happens when someone who does know how to identify the valid law in accordance with the rule of recognition nonetheless refuses to use it, and treats as valid a rule that is invalid or, vice versa,

6 Raz, 'The Identity of Legal Systems', in Raz, *AL*, at 93.

7 See Hart, *CL*, 1st edn., at 97–107, 3rd edn., at 100–10.

treats as invalid a rule that is valid in accordance with the rule of recognition in use. If such a person fails to comply with the obligations imposed by the valid rules of the system, he will be punished.

This explains why people are especially interested in knowing what the valid norms are, and in order to know this they need to know how to use the rule of recognition (either directly or indirectly through specially trained persons, like lawyers, legal advisers, and so on). Here there is no question of either obeying or disobeying the rule of recognition; the rule can only be correctly or incorrectly used. That is all.

Case II. We should now consider the case of the judge. Before deciding, the judge must determine what legal norms apply to the case at hand. He must therefore formulate a legal proposition of the following form: 'according to the law, *p* is obligatory (prohibited, permitted) under circumstances *q*'. This proposition can be true or false. The fact that it is a judge who utters it has no bearing whatsoever on its truth-value, although it may (and normally will) have some relevance to the legal consequences normally attached to the judicial utterance of propositions of this sort. A judicial decision grounded on a false proposition is usually deemed valid, although it can normally be overturned by a higher court.

II. (*a*) The judge correctly identifies the valid law that is applicable to the case, but refuses to apply the norms that he has identified as valid. Suppose, for example, that there is a valid norm punishing homicide. A man who has killed another is brought before the judge, and the judge says: 'according to the law, I ought to punish this man, but I am not going to do so'. In this situation we should consider separately what the judge says and what the judge does. There is no contradiction in the judge's statement. It may be perfectly reasonable to acknowledge that one ought to do something according to the law and that one ought not to do it, owing, for example, to reasons of morality or religion. As for what the judge does, the situation is also very clear. The judge certainly does not do what he ought legally to do (if he acquits the killer). Therefore he fails to comply with the obligation imposed by the law, but this obligation does not arise from the rule of recognition (which the judge applied correctly), but rather from the norm that he identified by appealing to the rule of recognition. What the judge disobeys is the norm requiring that homicide be punished, not the rule of recognition.

II. (*b*) The judge does not apply the rule of recognition, and what he considers (sincerely or insincerely) to be valid law is not, according to the rule of recognition in use, valid law. Then his statement 'according to the law, *p* is obligatory in circumstances *q*' is false, and if he decides the case based on this proposition, his ruling will be incorrect (even if it may be valid). Such a situation would certainly be very regrettable, but it is very similar to the one we have already considered when speaking of the rules of a language. A judge who does not apply the rule of recognition in use—because of ignorance or for other reasons—is a bad judge, much like one who, owing to his inability

> to apply the rules of grammar correctly, does not know how to speak properly (or at all) the language in question. In neither case, however, can one speak of disobedience.

Of course, judges normally do have the duty (that is, they are under the obligation) to decide cases in accordance with valid laws. In order to comply with this obligation judges must use the rule of recognition. The obligation, however, does not derive from the rule of recognition; it derives from some norm belonging to the system, a norm identified in accordance with the rule of recognition.

Our critical rejoinders to Hart may be summarized as follows:

1. The rule of recognition provides the criteria for the identification of the valid norms of the system, and it is, therefore, a conceptual rule.
2. As a consequence, it is not the case that the rule of recognition imposes an obligation upon judges.
3. Hart's use of the same term, 'rule', to refer both to primary rules of obligation and to the rule of recognition is equivocal, for it glosses over the conceptual distinction between these two types of rule.

7

On the Concept of a Legal Order (1976)*

Written with Carlos E. Alchourrón

Introduction

That legal norms come not singly, but as members of a larger set—a so-called 'legal order'—is widely acknowledged and generally accepted by lawyers.[1] Kelsen articulates the idea very clearly at the beginning of his *General Theory of Law and State*:

> Law is an order of human behavior. An 'order' is a system of rules. Law is not, as it is sometimes said, a rule. It is a set of rules having the kind of unity we understand by a system. It is impossible to grasp the nature of law if we limit our attention to the single isolated rule. The relations which link together the particular rules of a legal order are also essential to the nature of law. Only on the basis of a clear comprehension of those relations constituting the legal order can the nature of law be fully understood.[2]

Consequently, lawyers have made great efforts to clarify the concept of a legal order, which is traditionally regarded as a central topic in jurisprudence. So far, however, these efforts have not met with commensurate success. No resulting definition has managed to clarify the notion of a legal order, which lawyers deploy in its intuitive and rather obscure form. Our goal in this essay is to analyse the concept of a legal order, taking as our starting point the intuitive notion commonly accepted and used.

Two preliminary remarks ought to be made. First, we shall be discussing orders of *norms*, rather than orders of normative propositions—that is, propositions

* [*Editors' note*: Eugenio Bulygin's paper, written together with Carlos E. Alchourrón, was first published as 'Sobre el concepto de orden jurídico', in *Crítica*, 8 (1976), 3–21, in *ALD*, 393–407. The paper was translated for the present volume by Luís Duarte d'Almeida and Kevin Toh. The translators wish to thank Carlos Montemayor and Giovanni Battista Ratti for answering questions about terminology in logic. The editors would like to thank Riccardo Guastini for a number of valuable suggestions on questions about the text.]

[1] The present paper offers in simplified form a summary of some results of the authors' enquiries on the topic of derogation. The main limitation of our discussion is that we discuss here only authoritatively issued norms (that is, *legislated* norms, in a broad sense of the term) and ignore customary norms. If customary norms were taken into account, norms would no longer be classifiable as either 'formulated' or 'derived'—for customary norms, though non-derived, lack canonical formulations—and the scope of the logical indeterminacy stemming from the derogation of derived norms would increase considerably. The main conclusions of the paper, however, would remain sound, perhaps even more dramatically so.

[2] Kelsen, *GTLS*, 3. [*Editors' note*: For this and other abbreviations, see the Table of Abbreviations.]

about norms. The point is worth stressing, for it is one about which many legal minds have been less than fully clear, to put it mildly. When lawyers speak of a positive legal order, such as the French law or the Bolivian law, they are usually thinking about the set of all legal norms that belong to that order. Some philosophers, however, prefer to speak of orders or systems of normative propositions. Perhaps they have noticed that norms, which are prescriptive in meaning, cannot be true or false, and they believe that this prevents norms from entering into the logical relations of deducibility or contradiction that are necessary to distinguish a system (which the law is supposed to be) from a mere aggregate or set of unrelated objects. Other authors speak indiscriminately of systems of norms or normative propositions, believing, or so it seems, that norms and normative propositions are invariably isomorphic.[3] Whether or not they happen to be right in the case of the normative propositions of legal science, our concern in the present paper is to elucidate the concept of a legal order conceived as a set of norms.

Second, a terminological note. When we say that a legal order is a set of 'norms', we do not mean that all of the sentences that make up the order are normative sentences, although some necessarily are.[4] Indeed, we employ here the term 'legal norm' in a broad sense (which matches lawyers' common usage) to refer to any sentence, normative or otherwise, that appears in the texts—constitutions, codes, statutes, etc.—that record the positive law.

1. The Intuitive Notion of a Legal Order

The ideas about a legal order that are widely shared by lawyers could be summed up with the following eight theses.

I. A legal order is the totality of the norms that are valid according to some criterion for validity.

II. A legal order is a set of norms.

III. A legal order is a system of norms.

IV. Legal norms are created and eliminated by voluntary acts.

V. A legal order is dynamic; it is subject to changes across time.

VI. These changes bear on the content of the legal order, but not on its identity. In other words, a legal order can retain its identity over time, even when its content varies from moment to moment.

VII. At any point in time, the content of a legal order is determinate, or at least determinable—that is, at any given moment, it is in principle ascertainable which norms belong to a legal order.

VIII. In every political state there is one, and only one, legal order.

[3] See Roberto J. Vernengo, *Curso de teoría general del derecho* (first publ. 1972), 2nd edn. (Buenos Aires: Cooperadora de Derecho y Ciencias Sociales, 1976), at 293–302.

[4] See Alchourrón and Bulygin, *NS*, at 65–77, where instead of 'norms' we deliberately use the neutral term 'legal sentences'.

Most of these theses are intuitively quite plausible, and all are reflected in the literature. It is not easy, however, to combine all of them in a coherent theory, for the eight theses, acceptable as each may seem when considered on its own, are contradictory in many ways when taken together. Perhaps some of the contradictions could be eliminated by introducing the necessary conceptual distinctions and refinements, but not all are so easily managed. As we shall see, theses III and IV are both incompatible with thesis VII, and perhaps also with thesis VIII.

Thesis I may be regarded as an (incomplete) definition of a legal order, and as such it seems perfectly acceptable. The nature of the validity criterion can be left open. It is unnecessary to settle here whether it is a logico-transcendental basic norm (Kelsen), a rule of recognition (Hart), the positive constitution (Engisch), or a sovereign (Bentham, Austin).

Thesis II, a logical consequence of thesis I, is also intuitively clear. It matters not whether a legal order is taken to consist only of legislated general norms, or to contain customary and judge-made norms as well, or to include all general and particular legal norms. In all these cases, a legal order is conceived as a set (large or small) of legal norms. Thesis II can therefore be interpreted as a definition of an even more general concept of a legal order.

Thesis III is often invoked by lawyers, but what they mean by 'system' is unclear. We will use the term in the following regimented sense: a (deductive) system is a set of sentences that contains all of their consequences.[5] If this definition is applied to a legal order, then a legal system is a set of norms that contains all of their consequences.[6] It follows that we need to distinguish between two classes of norms. One is the class of explicitly *formulated* norms. The other is the class of *derived* norms (as we will call them), norms that follow logically from formulated norms. Such derived norms belong to the system even though they are not explicitly enacted by any legislator.[7]

Thesis IV states an empirical truth that could hardly be disputed, at least in the case of positive law, which is our exclusive concern in this paper. Indeed, legislation is nothing but creation and derogation of positive legal norms. The very possibility of legislation presupposes the truth of thesis IV.

Thesis V follows logically from thesis IV. If we accept thesis IV, we must also accept thesis V.

Thesis VI appears quite plausible, and it is probably accepted by most lawyers. It is, however, incompatible with thesis II. The conception of a legal order as a set of norms clearly implies that the order cannot change without losing its identity. Each time a new norm is created or a norm belonging to the order is derogated, we get a new set, which differs from the prior set. The identity of a set is determined precisely by the identity of its elements. The distinction between an (unchanging) legal order and its (changing) content, a distinction expressed by thesis VI, is incompatible with the conception of a legal order as a set of norms. A legal order

[5] See Alfred Tarski, *Logic, Semantics, Metamathematics*, trans. Joseph H. Woodger (Oxford: Clarendon Press, 1956), at chs. III–V (30–109).

[6] Alchourrón and Bulygin, *NS*, 54–64.

[7] See von Wright, *NA*, at 156–8.

conceived as a set of norms is a *momentary* order—it is of a specific point in time.[8] However, the fact that this is not how lawyers use the term may lead us to suppose that there may be more than just one concept of a legal order. Surely, we may think, there must be a sense of 'legal order' that makes thesis VI true, but thesis II is also difficult to reject. It follows that the only way to maintain both theses would be to recognize two different senses of the term 'legal order', and the same term would then ambiguously express two different concepts.

One way of reconciling theses II and VI is to take 'legal order' to refer not to a set of norms but instead to a *sequence* of sets of norms. The unity of such a sequence, and so the identity of the legal order (in the sense relevant for thesis VI), would then be determined by the identity of the criteria used to identify the normative sets that belong to the sequence.[9] The idea that the application of the same criteria at different moments may lead to different results is expressed by saying that the content of the order is variable. Only a change in the criteria for identification themselves—only their replacement by different criteria (for example, as a consequence of a revolution or a declaration of independence)—will lead to the legal order's losing its identity and being replaced by a new order.

To avoid this ambiguity of 'legal order', we shall henceforth use the term 'system' to refer to sets of norms, and the term 'order' to refer to sequences of such sets. A legal order, then, according to this stipulation, is a sequence of normative systems.

Although thesis VII may appear obvious, it is incompatible, as we shall shortly see, with theses III and IV. If the latter theses are to be maintained, then thesis VII must be rejected.

Thesis VIII follows from thesis VII and cannot, it seems, be endorsed if thesis VII is false.

In order to adjudicate among the foregoing theses, we must scrutinize the logical structure of those acts by which legal norms are created and eliminated. Let us call them 'acts of promulgation' and 'acts of derogation' respectively. We shall address two questions in particular: (1) what exactly happens when a norm is created? and (2) what exactly happens when a norm is derogated?

2. Promulgation

Our first question—what exactly happens when a norm is created?—could be answered by saying that a norm is added to some given set of norms. This answer, however, would clearly be inadequate. An act of promulgation adds many more things to the system besides the promulgated norm.

Let α be a set of formulated norms; the set of all the consequences of α is a normative system. If a new norm n is added to α through an act of promulgation, we obtain a new system corresponding to the combination of the

[8] See Raz, *CLS*, at 34–5. Raz was the first to draw attention to the momentary character of legal systems.

[9] Alchourrón and Bulygin, *NS*, 72–7.

following three sets: (a) the consequences of α, (b) the consequences of $\{n\}$, and (c) the consequences of $\{\alpha + n\}$, which are derivable neither from α alone nor from $\{n\}$ alone.

> Example in section 2:
> Suppose that α consists of the two following norms: 'if *p* is permitted, and *q* is permitted, then *r* is permitted' (in symbols: Pp & $Pq \supset Pr$), and '*p* is obligatory' (Op). Let us suppose in addition that the following new norm is promulgated: '*q* is obligatory' (Oq). Thus, the new system contains not only '*p* is permitted' (Pp), which is a consequence of α, and 'q is permitted' (Pq), which is a consequence of 'Oq', but also '*r* is permitted' (Pr), which can be derived neither from α alone (without 'Oq') nor from 'Oq' alone (without α), but only from the conjunction of the two. These deductive relations are depicted with arrows in Figure 7.1.

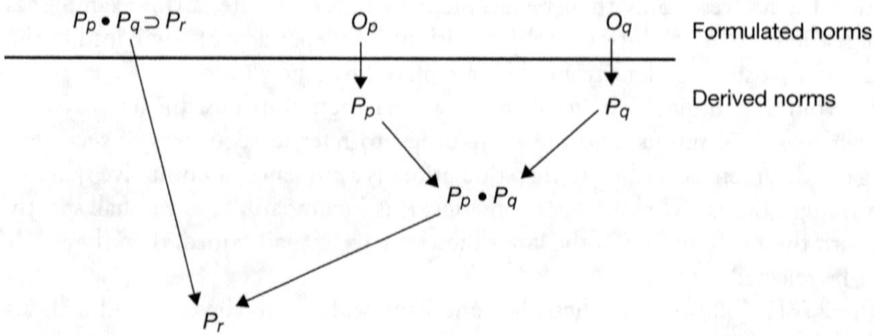

Figure 7.1

Norm-promulgation, however complex, is always univocal in the sense that the result of adding any norm to any given normative system is invariably one determinate normative system.

3. Derogation

Our second question is: What happens when a norm is derogated? The case of derogation is more complex than that of promulgation, and there are several issues to consider. First, derogation of a norm-*formulation* does not necessarily amount to the elimination of any of the system's norms. Second, we will have to distinguish between derogations of formulated norms and derogations of derived norms. Let us consider each issue in turn.

A. Derogation of Norm-Formulations

A normative system is redundant with regard to a given norm if the norm has been formulated more than once—that is, if there are two or more formulations expressing the same norm—or if a derived norm, which by definition is already a part of the system, is explicitly promulgated. The elimination of a redundant norm-formulation leaves the system unchanged. Such an operation is not infrequent in legislative practice and is usually referred to as 'derogation', but it does not amount to a genuine derogation of any norm. Instead, it is a derogation of a mere formulation, the deletion of a linguistic expression from a text. No norm, however, is eliminated from the system. The norm expressed by the derogated text is not itself derogated; it remains in the system, though sometimes only as a derived norm.

> First example in section 3:
> The norms '*p* and *q* are obligatory' (*O* (*p* & *q*)) and '*p* is permitted' (*Pp*) are among the system's formulated norms. If '*Pp*' is derogated, the system remains unchanged, since the consequences of {*O* (*p* & *q*), *Pp*} are the same as the consequences of {*O* (*p* & *q*)}. The only thing that has changed is the way in which the system is presented: '*Pp*' no longer belongs to the system's formulated norms, belonging instead to its derived norms. This kind of derogation is obviously univocal.

B. Derogation of Formulated Norms

This can be said to be the 'standard' case of derogation. Here a given norm is derogated and possibly replaced with a different norm, but the scope of derogation is not restricted to the explicitly derogated norm because all the norms that derive from it and all the norms for the derivation of which the explicitly derogated norm is necessary are derogated as well.

> Second example in section 3:
> The system contains the following formulated norms: '*Pp* & *Pq* ⊃ *Pr*', '*Op*', and '*Oq*'. The authority wants to derogate '*Oq*'. The derogation of '*Oq*' implies the derogation of the derived norms '*Pq*', '*Pp* & *Pq*', and '*Pr*'.

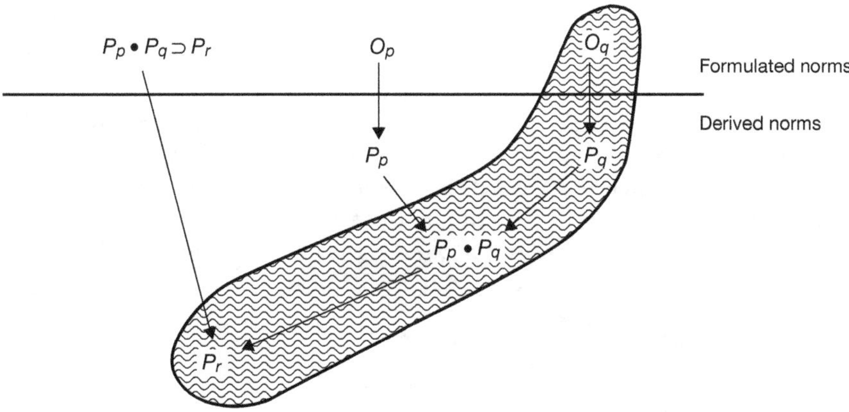

Figure 7.2

The shaded area in Figure 7.2 indicates the scope of the derogation. The norms within that area are all affected by the derogation of '*Oq*', and they are all eliminated from the system in virtue of the same act by which '*Oq*' is derogated. The relevant relation is not a temporal one; it would be a mistake to think that the derogation of the other norms takes place *after* '*Oq*' has been derogated. Rather, the derogation of the other norms is logically implied by the derogation of '*Oq*'. The derogation of the consequences of the derogated norm is part of the content of the act of derogating the explicitly derogated norm.

Again, the derogation here is univocal: the elimination, from a given system, of any given norm leads to another determinate system.

In the first two examples here in section 3, we have two kinds—or rather, two concepts—of derogation. In the first example, a norm-formulation is eliminated, but the system's conceptual content remains unchanged. In the second example, both a norm-formulation and a norm are eliminated, and as a consequence the system changes. After derogation takes place, we have a different system—albeit one that belongs to the same sequence and hence to the same legal order. In the third example in this section, to which we now turn, we deal with the same concept of derogation as in the second example. The only difference is that in the third example, the primary change is to the system's conceptual content, but it is as a consequence of that change that the system's formulation must also be modified.

C. Derogation of Derived Norms

Strange things may happen when a derived norm, rather than a formulated norm, is derogated. We will consider two cases: in one case, the derogation of a derived norm leads to a determinate system, and, in the other, what results is not one determinate system, but a number of alternative systems.

> Third example in section 3:
> In the system containing '$Pp \mathbin{\&} Pq \supset Pr$', '*Op*', and '*Oq*', the norm to be derogated is '*Pq*'. For example, the legislator issues a norm declaring that *q* is not permitted. What norms are affected by this act of derogation?

Clearly, '*Oq*', which entails the derogated norm, must be regarded as derogated as well; otherwise '*Pq*' would not have been derogated, for it would be derivable from '*Oq*'. Also eliminated are those norms—'*Pp* & *Pq*' and '*Pr*'—for the derivation of which '*Pq*' is needed.[10] Hence this act of derogation operates both 'upstream', so to speak (affecting norms that *imply* the derogated norm), and 'downstream' (affecting norms *implied by* the derogated norm). The shaded area in Figure 7.3 represents the scope of the derogation of *Pp*.

[10] In truth this is not always the case, for indeterminacy may extend to derived norms. We shall not, however, analyse this more complex scenario.

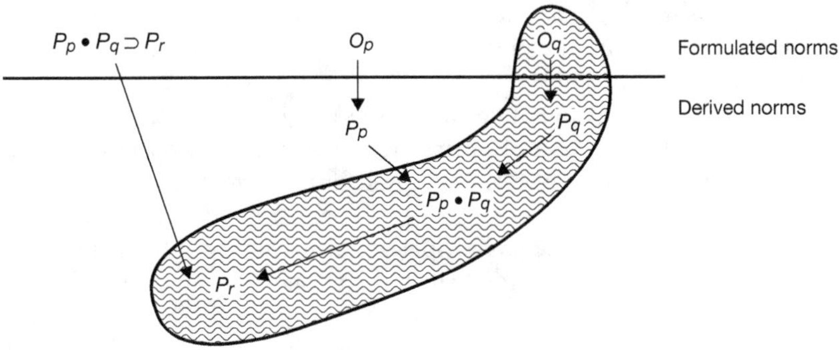

Figure 7.3

Here, then, the derogation of a derived norm—'*Pq*'—is equivalent to the derogation of a formulated norm—'*Oq*'. (Figures 7.2 and 7.3 are accordingly identical.) This is not always the case when derived norms are derogated.

> Fourth example in section 3:
> Suppose now that the norm to be derogated in the last system—that is, the system consisting of '*Pp* & *Pq* ⊃ *Pr*', '*Op*', and '*Oq*'—is the norm '*Pp* & *Pq*'. The derived norm '*Pr*' is thereby also derogated. But what about '*Op*' and '*Oq*'? Evidently at least one of these norms has to disappear, but which one? This question cannot be answered by reference to any logical criteria. As such it would be an insoluble problem. Hence, the outcome of the derogation of '*Pp* & *Pq*' is not one normative system, but instead at least two alternative systems, depicted in Figure 7.4.

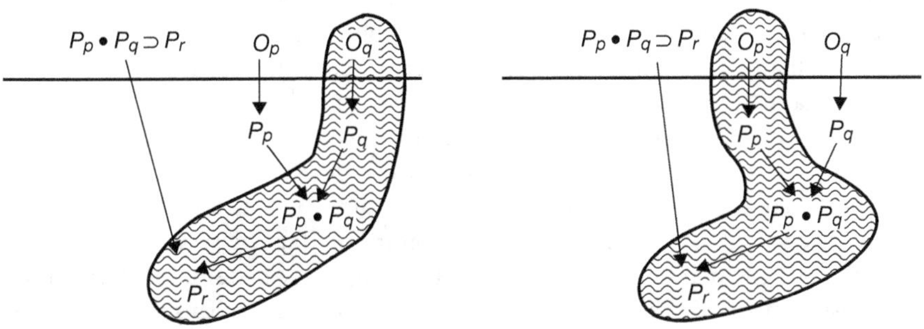

Figure 7.4

This kind of derogation, too, occurs frequently in legislative practice. The standard, most common example is the inclusion in a statute of a provision stating that 'all norms opposed to the present statute are hereby derogated'. Such a provision can destroy the unity of the system, breaking it down into various alternatives. Jurists seem to be oblivious to this disastrous consequence, perhaps because in most cases one of the several alternatives can be chosen on extra-logical grounds. Situations in which the alternatives are not only logically equivalent but also equally reasonable from the point of view of justice or some other practical consideration are relatively rare.[11]

The analysis of the derogation of derived norms offered earlier clearly indicates that the creation and derogation of norms are not symmetrical operations. The creation of a norm will never give rise to any logical indeterminacy of the sort illustrated in the last example.

In what follows we will use the phrase 'logical indeterminacy of the system' as a technical term to refer to a situation in which there is not *one* but several alternative systems.

The possibility of logical indeterminacy shows that the view (widespread among lawyers) that it is always possible to ascertain which norms belong to a legal order at any given moment—the view articulated above as thesis VII—is untenable. The issue is not always decidable, and it is worth stressing that logical indeterminacy is much more frequent than one might initially suppose. Whenever a legislator enacts a general provision derogating *all* norms opposed to some given norm without specifying which norms, exactly, are thereby derogated, logical indeterminacy is the possible (though not necessary) result.

We have already seen that the postulate of the continuous existence of the legal order (thesis VI) can be maintained only if the legal order is conceived as a sequence of legal systems (a sequence, that is, of sets of norms). Legal systems have no continuous existence and are relative to given points in time, but here time has peculiar features: it is discontinuous and discrete, and the temporal moments are those when legislative acts of promulgation and derogation are performed. Every act by which a new norm is created or an existing norm derogated gives rise to a new moment, and with it a new system. (Obviously, there can be legislative acts that do not bring about changes in the system, such as those that either create or derogate redundant norms.)

The postulate of the unity of the legal order (thesis VIII) also now turns out to be problematic. If taken to be about normative systems, the postulate is surely false. It would be thought plausible only if a legal order were conceived as a sequence of normative systems, but the possibility of logical indeterminacy implies that such a sequence is not invariably linear. Sometimes it ramifies. When that happens, the unity of the system can be restored only by reformulating the system—by explicitly designating which norms do and do not belong to the system, in effect choosing one system among the several possible alternative systems. This norm-creating activity should in principle be done by legislators, but it is often carried out by legal science.

[11] Interestingly, the Austrian Foreign Office's 1970 *Guidelines for Legislation* expressly recommends that indeterminate derogation (that is, the blanket derogation of all norms opposed to some given norm) be avoided and that only formal, explicit derogation be used. No reason is given for these recommendations. See *Legistische Richtlinien des Bundeskanzleramtes*, 1970, 43.984-2b/70, guidelines 23 and 24.

4. Gaps, Contradictions, and Logical Indeterminacy

It is well known that a legal system can be substantively defective. It may contain provisions that are unjust, unreasonable, or for some reason inconvenient. Some defects, however, are purely formal or logical. Logical incompleteness, incoherence, and indeterminacy are defects of this latter kind.

The problem of the completeness of a legal system is known in the literature as the problem of legal 'gaps'. When an action is not regulated by a legal system, it is usually said that there is a 'gap', and a system with gaps is an incomplete system.

The problem of legal gaps is one that is complex and equivocal. In fact, several distinct problems have been given this label in the history of legal thought.[12] We will mention here only some aspects of the problem. The concept of a normative gap can be defined in terms of the notion of normative determination. An action *p* (belonging to some given class of actions *H*) is normatively determined in system *S* if and only if *p* is either permitted or prohibited in *S*, that is, if and only if *S* contains either a norm of the form '*Pp*' or a norm of the form '*O* –*p*'.[13] When some action in *H* is not determined in system *S*, there is a gap, and *S* is incomplete relative to *H*. It is only when all actions in *H* are determined that *S* can be said to be complete relative to *H*. The notion of completeness then (and so also the notion of a gap) is a relational notion. This is something that jurists often overlook. Completeness is not an (absolute) property of a normative system but is instead a relation between a normative system and a class of actions. With regard to systems that contain, as legal systems commonly do, conditional (that is, hypothetical) norms, we have a three-place relation among a normative system, a class of actions, and a class of factual circumstances or 'cases'.[14] It follows that questions like 'is legal order *S* (or *the law*, tout court) complete?' or 'does legal order *S* (or *the law*) have gaps?', so often formulated by jurists and legal philosophers, cannot be answered before the values of the three arguments in the relation are specified. The analysis of the logical (syntactical) structure of the concept of completeness—as well as of legal concepts more generally—is one of the important tasks of legal philosophy, a task that can be undertaken only with the tools of modern logic.[15]

It is worth pointing out that jurists frequently conflate cases in which an action is unregulated with cases in which an action is unsatisfactorily regulated (according to some criterion for evaluation).[16] The term 'gap' is used to refer to cases of this second sort as well. Some authors go so far as to opine that only in such cases do

[12] See Alchourrón and Bulygin, *NS*, at 94–116, 144–65.

[13] These norms do not have to be expressly formulated. It would suffice if one of them could be derived in the system.

[14] See Alchourrón and Bulygin, *NS*, at 7–13, 21–34, where 'universe of cases' and 'universe of actions' are used as technical terms.

[15] See Heinz Wagner and Karl Haag, *Die moderne Logik in der Rechtswissenschaft* (Bad Homburg: Gehlen, 1970), at 20–3.

[16] See Alchourrón and Bulygin, *NS*, at 106–16.

we have 'gaps' proper.[17] This unhelpful terminology can only lead to confusion. A deficiently regulated action is nonetheless regulated and should not be confused with an action that is not regulated at all.

A similar confusion results if one uses the term 'gap' to refer to difficulties of subsumption caused by conceptual indeterminacy or vagueness—as, for example, Kantorowicz does, who asserts that there are no fewer gaps than there are words.[18] This is a completely different problem. The process of applying a general norm to a concrete situation may involve difficulties that arise from semantic properties of language such as vagueness or open texture. As Philipp Heck pointed out long ago, concepts do not have clear boundaries. A conceptual core (*Begriffskern*) is surrounded by a halo (*Begriffshof*), and when some given situation falls within this 'halo', one does not know whether the norm applies.[19] We thus have here an epistemological problem. Modern philosophy of language has also scrutinized these issues, although its results are seldom taken into account by jurists.

The elimination of legal gaps is an important practical problem. For this purpose jurists employ several rules, usually cast as rules of inference: arguments *a fortiori, a contrario, a pari* (by analogy), and so on. It is important to keep in mind that none of these rules is a logically valid rule of inference. Instead, their conclusions can be validly drawn only by appealing to additional, suppressed premisses.[20] An incomplete system cannot be made complete by purely logical means.

Contradiction between norms is a problem distinct from that of incompleteness, though with similar practical effects. A gap is an absence of regulation. The system contains too few norms, and the gap can be eliminated only by the addition of a new norm. On the other hand, in the case of a contradiction, there is a surplus of norms. The system contains too many norms, and the problem can be solved only if at least one of the contradictory norms is eliminated. The two situations are nevertheless similar in one respect. In both cases the system fails to perform satisfactorily its most important task—that of regulating human behaviour. In either case, we have a determinate system. We know very well which prescriptions it contains. (In this regard, gaps and contradictions are different from cases of logical indeterminacy.) However, we are unable to adjust our actions in accordance with what the system prescribes because, in the case of a gap, there will be no action that conforms or is contrary to the system, and, in the case of a contradiction, any action will simultaneously conform and be contrary to the system. In both cases the problem is a logical problem, not merely an epistemological one. It is not

[17] See Kelsen, *RR 2*, § 35(g) (at 251–2), *PTL*, at 245–7.

[18] Hermann Kantorowicz (writing under the pseudonym Gnaeus Flavius), *The Battle for Legal Science* (first publ. 1906 under the title *Der Kampf um die Rechtswissenschaft*), trans. Cory Merrill, in *German Law Journal*, 12 (2006), 2005–30. The Spanish counterpart of the term 'gap' (namely *lacuna*) is used in a similar sense in Genaro R. Carrió, *Notas sobre el derecho y lenguaje* (first publ. 1965), 4th edn. (Buenos Aires: Abeledo Perrot, 1985), at 66–89.

[19] Philipp Heck, *Begriffsbildung und Interessenjurisprudenz* (Tübingen: J.C.B. Mohr, 1932), 52–3.

[20] See Carlos E. Alchourrón, 'Los argumentos jurídicos *a fortiori* y *a pari*', *RJBA* (1961) (no. 4), 177–99, in *ALD*, 3–24.

merely that we do not know what the system requires, but, rather, that the system fails to determine it.

The notion of a normative contradiction—the notion, that is, of a formal incompatibility between norms—is not easy to define. It is hard to formulate an intuitively acceptable criterion that is also formally adequate.[21] It seems convenient to define a normative contradiction in terms of the notion of norm-compliance: two norms contradict each other when compliance with one logically excludes compliance with the other. An action that is simultaneously obligatory and forbidden presents an intuitively very clear instance of formal incompatibility thus conceived. According to this criterion, '*Op*' and '*O* –*p*' are contradictory norms.

This criterion, however, does not apply directly to permissory norms, for it makes little sense to speak of complying with or violating permissory norms. One can avail oneself of a permission, but one cannot obey or violate it. It is possible, however, to extend the criterion to permissory norms by characterizing a prohibition (or an obligation) as contradicting a permission whenever it is logically impossible for an agent who avails himself of the permission to comply with the prohibition (or obligation), and vice versa. Accordingly, '*Pp*' and '*O* –*p*' are contradictory. Permissory norms standing together in a pair, on the other hand, are always compatible.

The elimination of contradictions, like the elimination of gaps, is not a logical problem. Logic merely helps us to identify normative conflicts; it cannot eliminate them. The inference rules that jurists employ for that purpose—*lex posterior, lex superior, lex specialis*—however useful they may be in legal practice, are not logically valid. Here, once again, the task is one of (negative) norm-creation, to be carried out primarily by legislators.

The case of logical indeterminacy is quite similar in its practical effects, albeit completely different in origin. Again, there is a failure of the system, for there is no action that can comply with it, not because there are too few norms or too many, but because there are too many systems and no logical criterion for selecting from among the possible alternatives.

The analysis of the logical structure of legislative acts—promulgation and derogation—by prompting us to re-examine the traditional concepts of a legal order and a legal system, and by highlighting for us the clear perils of hasty derogation, illustrates the practical usefulness of the logical analysis of legal concepts.

[21] See von Wright, *NA*, at 134–55; see also Alchourrón and Bulygin, 'Von Wright on Deontic Logic and the Philosophy of Law' (1973/89), in this volume, ch. 5.

8

Legal Statements and Positivism

A Reply to Joseph Raz (1981)*

In his article, 'The Purity of the Pure Theory', Joseph Raz analyses certain doctrines of Hans Kelsen's that stem from his positivist position,[1] and the analysis includes comparisons of Kelsen with H. L. A. Hart. The critical discussion of some ideas of Kelsen and Hart gives Raz an opportunity to make clearer his own thoughts on the role of what he calls 'legal statements', the central axis around which his comparative analysis of the two great contemporary legal philosophers turns.

I disagree, on some crucial points, with Raz's interpretation of Hart and Kelsen, and I have doubts about his analysis of legal statements and about the role he attributes to them. In the pages that follow, I will attempt to articulate my doubts and argue on behalf of my own dissenting view.

1.

Raz rightly shows that the purity of Kelsen's theory—here I am only interested in the purity thesis with respect to morality, not with respect to sociology—is intimately tied to his positivism. Raz characterizes legal positivism by means of the following theses: (i) the reductive semantic thesis, 'which proposes a reductive analysis of legal statements according to which they are non-normative, descriptive statements of one kind or another'; (ii) the contingent connection thesis, 'according to which there is no necessary connection between law and moral values'; and (iii) the sources thesis, 'which claims that the identification of the existence and content of law does not require resort to any moral argument'.[2]

The three theses are independent of each other, but many prominent positivists—among them Jeremy Bentham, John Austin, Oliver Wendell Holmes, and Alf Ross—have held, according to Raz,[3] all three theses. By contrast, Kelsen and Hart, setting themselves apart from the positivist tradition, albeit for different

* [*Editors' note*: Eugenio Bulygin's paper was first published as 'Enunciados jurídicos y positivismo: respuesta a Raz', *Análisis Filosófico*, 1 (1981), 49–59, in *ALD*, 427–38. It was translated for the present volume by Tecla Mazzarese and Michael Sherberg.]

[1] Raz, 'PPT', in Raz, *AL*, 293–312, in *NN*, 237–52. [*Editors' note*: For these and other abbreviations, see the Table of Abbreviations.]

[2] Raz, 'PPT', in Raz, *AL*, 295–6, in *NN*, 239.

[3] See Raz, 'PPT', in Raz, *AL*, at 296, in *NN*, at 239.

reasons, reject the first thesis and accept the other two. The difference from the tradition is due to their differing views on legal statements. Here we confront the central theme of Raz's article: the nature and function of legal statements.

To clarify Kelsen's view, Raz compares it with Hart's view. As is well known, Hart distinguishes two types of legal statement: external and internal. Raz, however, completely ignores the external statements, which is to say that his legal statements correspond in general terms to Hart's internal statements. The only reason Raz gives us for strictly setting aside the external statements is that these are 'statements about people's behaviour and attitudes and need not concern us'.[4] As I will argue later in this chapter, such a reason does not seem to be sufficient. I believe that external statements play a more important role in legal discourse than Raz would grant.

Internal statements, in Raz's opinion, are true or false, but the analysis in terms of truth conditions does not exhaust the meaning of such statements. There is, in addition, their illocutionary and expressive force. The first consists of the typical use of such statements, which is to guide behaviour by 'criticizing, commending, demanding, advising, approving,' and so forth. Expressive force is the 'acceptance by the speaker of standards of behaviour towards conformity with which the statement is used to guide its addressee'.[5] In this way, Hart accounts for the double aspect of the legal statement: its factual (social) aspect and its normative aspect. Due to this normative aspect legal statements 'cannot be reduced to an assertion of any social facts'.[6]

For Kelsen, too, legal statements are normative. Unlike Hart's non-cognitivist interpretation in terms of illocutionary and expressive force, however, Kelsen is a cognitivist: legal statements are normative because they 'express a belief in the existence of a valid norm',[7] and they are normative in the same way in which moral statements are normative.[8] It is this character of legal statements that is tied to Kelsen's rejection of the reductive semantic thesis.

Legal statements that are clearly normative, indistinguishable from moral statements, are, however, but one type of legal statement, which Raz calls *committed statements*. According to Raz, it is possible to distinguish in Kelsen (although he does not do so explicitly) two other types of legal statement. There are *conditional statements*, which affirm what one should do if the basic norm is valid; these are 'morally uncommitted since their normative force depends on the unasserted condition'.[9] And there are *uncommitted* or *detached statements*; these also do not morally commit one who follows them, for they are affirmations from a certain point of view that is not necessarily shared. 'They state what rights and duties there are on the assumption that the basic norm is valid but without commitment to that assumption'.[10]

[4] Raz, 'PPT', in Raz, *AL*, 300, in *NN*, 242–3.
[5] Raz, 'PPT', in Raz, *AL*, 300, in *NN*, 243.
[6] Raz, 'PPT', in Raz, *AL*, 300, in *NN*, 243.
[7] Raz, 'PPT', in Raz, *AL*, 301, see also 307, in *NN*, 243–4, see also 248.
[8] See Raz, 'PPT', in Raz, *AL*, at 299, in *NN*, at 242.
[9] Raz, 'PPT', in Raz, *AL*, 306, in *NN*, 247.
[10] Raz, 'PPT', in Raz, *AL*, 306, in *NN*, 247–8.

Conditional statements are similar to those of legal science, which, when it uses them, can at the same time be pure and describe the law as a normative system. Raz grants the point that this is all that the jurist may need, but he demonstrates that this is not what those who practice law do (lawyers, judges, etc.). They do not confine themselves to speaking about law; rather, they use it to advise their clients, to argue before a judge, to justify a sentence, and so forth. In other words, they do not confine themselves to saying what one ought to do if law is valid. Rather, they assert that law is valid, and jurists do the same.[11] Since Kelsen's analysis, according to Raz, embraces both theoretical and practical discourse, Raz accounts for both species of discourse by introducing non-committed statements. These statements make it possible to describe the law in categorical terms as a system of valid norms, and, at the same time, they do not morally commit those who use them. In this way, legal science describes the law by means of normative statements without thereby implying any moral commitment.

Here Raz compares Kelsen with Hart once again. Hart's internal statements are basically the same as Kelsen's committed statements.[12] Committed statements, however, express moral approval of the law. Since, in Hart's case, it is possible to describe law without expressing any evaluation whatsoever, Hart has to grant that not all legal statements are internal.[13] The question is: what are those legal statements that are not internal? According to Raz, they cannot be external, 'since these are not normative statements but statements about other people's actions and beliefs'.[14] While Hart offers no response here, Kelsen can reply with the doctrine of detached statements. Thus, the comparison of the two great contemporary positivists favours Kelsen (despite the fact that Raz finds defects elsewhere in the Pure Theory of Law that are worked out in Hart).

This will serve as a very brief synthesis of Raz's argument. Let us turn now to criticism.

2.

It would seem proper to distinguish two types of statement in legal discourse: a) theoretical statements about law and b) practical statements that are based upon legal norms and formulate claims, needs, criticism, advice, approbations, and the like.

Statements of the first type assert that these or those norms exist in a legal system; such statements are descriptive or informative. It is a central thesis of legal positivism that such statements are factual, empirical, which is to say that they are about certain social facts, facts that render them true, but these statements express no evaluations whatsoever. This thesis is intimately linked to the thesis concerning legal sources and to the contingent connection thesis—theses that are, for Raz,

[11] See Raz, 'PPT', in Raz, *AL*, at 304, in *NN*, at 246.
[12] See Raz, 'PPT', in Raz, *AL*, at 307, in *NN*, at 248.
[13] See Raz, 'PPT', in Raz, *AL*, at 308, in *NN*, at 249.
[14] Raz, 'PPT', in Raz, *AL*, 308, in *NN*, 249.

defining characteristics of positivism. Moreover, if we name as a weak reductive semantic thesis the claim that theoretical statements about law are descriptive, then this thesis, too, is implied by the positivist position that I have just outlined. This means that the theses of contingent connection and of sources, as well as the weak reductive semantic thesis are—*pace* Raz—not independent. A positivist cannot help but accept all of them. Should he not do so, he ceases to be a positivist. Therefore, the rejection of the weak reductive semantic thesis is incompatible with positivism.

Practical statements are not descriptive of empirical facts. Their function does not consist in asserting that states of affairs are given, but, rather, consists in guiding and evaluating conduct. Thus, these statements pertain to the category of prescriptive language.

Examples of theoretical statements are: 'in Argentine law, divorce does not exist', or 'according to Argentine law, one who commits a robbery will be sentenced to a minimum of one month and up to the maximum of six years in prison'. Examples of practical statements are: 'the defendant owes my client the sum of $1000' (allegation of a lawyer before a court), or 'you ought not to plant trees close to the dividing line of your neighbour's property' (advice given by a lawyer to his client). Utterances concerning rights and obligations such as 'I have a right that John pay me $1000', or 'Henry has an obligation to look after his child' are ambiguous. They can express descriptive statements (theoretical): 'my right (law, contract) confers authority upon me to demand that John pay me $1000', or 'according to law, Henry has an obligation to look after his child', which is either true or false. Or they express prescriptive statements: 'John, pay me $1000!' or 'Henry, look after your child!', in which case they may or may not be obeyed, but they are neither true nor false. The question of knowing what sort of statement is being expressed by an utterance, what sort of linguistic act has been performed, is a complex empirical problem, and there are no established rules for resolving it. Indeed, there are doubtful cases in which not even the speaker really knows what he attempted to do in uttering a certain statement, and it is also possible that an individual is simultaneously performing two different linguistic acts by means of a single utterance. For example. 'I have a right that John pay me $1000', which, expanded, might well mean, 'my right (law, contract) confers authority upon me to demand that John pay me $1000, therefore, John, pay me $1000!' or 'John, pay me $1000! For the law gives me the right to demand this of you'.

This fact has prompted some authors (among them, Raz) to hold that practical statements have truth-values despite the fact that they are prescriptive. This position is, I believe, erroneous, but the problem of assigning truth-values to practical statements does not bear on what follows.

The distinction between theoretical (descriptive) statements and practical (prescriptive or evaluative) statements corresponds exactly to the distinction between external and internal statements in Hart's theory. External statements are descriptive and do not involve evaluation or acceptance of the law. They are statements about the existence of legal rules and about the way the existence of such rules manifests itself, according to Hart, in certain modes of behaviour and in people's attitudes. It can be said, as Raz in fact says, that external statements refer to behaviour and people's attitudes. Certainly such statements are not normative except in the sense that they describe norms, but they do not express norms or evaluations. We find typical examples of such statements in legal science.

In the Anglo-Saxon legal culture, in contrast to the Continental tradition, it would be unusual to draw a clear distinction between the theoretical jurist and the lawyer or practising legal consultant. Perhaps this is the reason Hart does not employ the expression 'legal science'. Still, it is quite clear that, for Hart, a neutral (non-evaluative) description of law is possible. This is implicit in his distinction between law as it is and law as it ought to be, a distinction that constitutes the central idea of his legal positivism (in agreement with Bentham and Austin). Such a description is only possible by means of external statements.[15]

Hart's internal statements are employed by those who accept legal rules in order to formulate claims, needs, criticism, and the like, with an eye to guiding conduct. These are the statements employed quite generally by judges and lawyers when they deal with the law. Such statements are prescriptive or normative. For this reason, it is a mistake to maintain, as Raz does, that internal statements are true with respect to certain social practices and that their meaning can be given, in part, by 'a truth-conditional analysis'.[16]

I have examined this question in detail elsewhere,[17] and there is no need to rehash these matters here. It is appropriate, however, to emphasize that internal statements (a) are used to guide conduct and (b) express the acceptance of legal norms. Raz makes both points explicitly.

As we have seen, Raz characterizes legal positivism by means of three theses: the reductive semantic thesis, the thesis of the contingent connection, and the sources thesis. Hart certainly shares with Kelsen and other great legal positivists the latter two theses, but he rejects, in Raz's opinion, the first thesis. I have my doubts about this point, for I do not grasp what Raz understands by the reductive semantic thesis. If by reductionism one understands that what is in question is what I have termed the weak thesis, according to which theoretical or external statements are descriptive and not normative, then Hart is a reductionist just as Bentham, Austin, Alf Ross, and Kelsen are reductionists (although the situation is less clear in the case of Kelsen). If, however, reductionism is understood as meaning that internal or practical statements are descriptive and not normative (which I will call the strong reductionist thesis), then Hart is not a reductionist—but Bentham, Austin, Alf Ross, and Kelsen are not reductionists either. Thus, neither Hart nor Kelsen departs from the legal positivist tradition on this point, as Raz erroneously

[15] Hart distinguishes three types of external statement, and he criticizes those who only use statements concerning regularities of conduct and typical reactions in the face of deviations. To make the description complete one should keep in mind the fact that people consider certain guidelines as reasons for acting in a deliberate manner. See Hart, *CL*, 1st edn., at 87 and note at 244, 3rd edn., at 89 and note at 291; Eugenio Bulygin, 'Norms, Normative Propositions, and Legal Statements' (1982), in this volume, ch. 11.

[16] Raz, 'PPT', in Raz, *AL*, 300, in *NN*, 243.

[17] See Bulygin, 'Norms, Normative Propositions, and Legal Statements' (1982), in this volume, ch. 11.

claims. No positivist, with the possible exception of some American legal realists, has maintained the strong reductionist thesis. All of the legal positivists are obliged to maintain the weak reductionist thesis; to fail to do so would be incompatible with legal positivism.

3.

Raz's main mistake, which undermines almost everything he does here, consists in his comparison of Hart's internal statements with Kelsen's legal propositions (*Rechtssätze*). By lumping them together under a common label, that of 'legal statement', Raz compares the conceptions of Hart and of Kelsen on the nature of such statements as though it were a matter of two different ways of reconstructing one and the same phenomenon. In fact, the phenomena in question are altogether distinct. In reality, Kelsen's legal propositions correspond to Hart's external statements, and a comparative study of these two conceptions would no doubt be fruitful and illuminating. Kelsen's legal propositions, however, have nothing whatever to do with Hart's internal statements. The two categories of statement are simply not comparable, for they are employed in reconstructing radically different phenomena.

The source of this crucial mistake is found in Raz's idea that Kelsen, with the doctrine of legal propositions, is attempting to reconstruct not only the discourse of legal science but also the discourse of those who practise law, namely lawyers, judges, and others. Raz writes that 'Kelsen does not distinguish between the scholar and the practitioner. His analysis of legal discourse is meant to apply to both.'[18]

I do not know where, in Kelsen's writings, Raz got this idea, which I think is totally mistaken. The reality is quite different. Kelsen distinguishes very well between the scholar and the practitioner, and his analysis of legal propositions is solely a reconstruction of theoretical discourse in legal science.[19] Kelsen never undertook a systematic analysis of the discourse of lawyers and other legal experts (who use the law), something that Hart undertook with his doctrine of internal statements. For Kelsen, such statements would be either individual norms (judicial decisions, private law transactions) or else advice, claims, and criticism. In any case, the main concern here is political, not scientific, but Kelsen's legal propositions are strictly theoretical. They perform no prescriptive function whatsoever, for they are descriptive and presuppose neither the acceptance nor an evaluation of the law they describe. Kelsen is very emphatic on this point, namely, that legal propositions are the statements of legal science. If it is clear that not everything appearing under the title of Continental legal science performs a purely descriptive function—traditional legal dogmatics and, in particular, the dogmatics of criminal law consist largely in formulating norms and recommending solutions—it is

[18] Raz, 'PPT', in Raz, *AL*, 304, in *NN*, 246.

[19] See Kelsen, *RR 2*, § 6(e) (at 59), at § 16 (73–7), § 18 (at 80, 82–6), at § 34(e) (209–12), *PTL*, at 58, 71–5, 76–7, 79–81, 205–8.

no less clear that the principal objective of the Pure Theory of Law is to provide a theoretical foundation for a purely descriptive science of law, a science capable of describing (and this means, for Kelsen, in a non-evaluative form) the phenomenon called law. Such an endeavour, which is in some way ideal, must be able to describe, for Kelsen, Nazi law, communist law, capitalist law, and democratic law in the same neutral terms, without anything in the description that would imply a commitment to one political regime or another.[20] (The characterization of scientific activity as a mere description of law could be criticized as too narrow on the ground that it leaves out of account other activities pursued by legal scholars, work that deserves to be classified as scientific,[21] but this is irrelevant to the present discussion.)

Kelsen repeatedly says that legal propositions, unlike norms, are descriptive, not prescriptive, are true or false but neither valid nor invalid. They do not pretend to guide conduct and can neither be complied with nor applied.[22] Above all, they do not express evaluations (acceptance or approval) of the law. The contrast with Hart's internal statements could not be greater.

4.

Despite the clarity of Kelsen's purposes, his doctrine of legal propositions is not free of serious problems. Although *Rechtssätze* are descriptive, not prescriptive, Kelsen insists on classifying them as normative. They are normative, for they are 'ought'-propositions (*Sollsätze*), not 'is'-propositions (*Seinsätze*), and they are therefore to be distinguished from sociological propositions and from other propositions in the empirical sciences. Neither are they 'fully normative statements', as Raz suggests,[23] for the 'ought' (*sollen*) is purely descriptive, not prescriptive. I must confess that, for me, the category of a 'descriptive "ought"' is incomprehensible. Still, Kelsen emphatically rejected all attempts to interpret his *Rechtssätze* as factual statements.[24]

Kelsen does not explicitly distinguish between normative validity in the sense of binding force and descriptive validity in the sense of membership in a legal order, and he uses the term 'validity' indiscriminately in both senses without noting the ambiguity. This is due, at least in part, to the fact that Kelsen treats the two concepts as co-extensive, which is a mistake.[25] However, as Carlos Santiago Nino convincingly argues,[26] the concept of normative validity (binding force) plays a

[20] See Kelsen, *LT*, at Preface (1–5).

[21] See Alchourron and Bulygin, *NS*, at ch. 5 (65–94).

[22] See Kelsen, *RR 2*, at § 16 (73–7), *PTL*, at 71–5.

[23] Raz, 'PPT', in Raz, *AL*, 297, in *NN*, 240.

[24] See H. L. A. Hart, 'Kelsen Visited', *UCLA Law Review*, 10 (1962/3), 709–28, in Hart, *EJP*, 286–308.

[25] See Carlos Santiago Nino, 'Some Confusions surrounding Kelsen's Concept of Validity', *ARSP*, 64 (1978), 357–77, repr. (in part) in *NN*, 253–61.

[26] See Nino, 'Some Confusions surrounding Kelsen's Concept of Validity' (n. 25, this chapter), 357–77.

fundamental role in Kelsen's thinking. In this sense, when Kelsen asserts that legal norms have objective validity, unlike mere imperatives, which have only the subjective sense of 'ought', what is at issue here is the binding force of legal norms, a notion that stems from the basic norm.[27] If, however, legal norms are objectively valid, then to say that a legal norm is valid is to say that one ought to behave as the norm prescribes. Furthermore, since legal propositions predicate validity of legal norms, they are properly deemed to be normative, not descriptive. This conclusion is clearly incompatible with Kelsen's positivist programme of providing a theoretical foundation for a purely descriptive legal science, unbiased by any evaluation of the law. If one accepts the idea that legal propositions are normative and that legal norms have objective validity, and if one therefore accepts the doctrine of the basic norm, then one is unavoidably driven to the position that Kelsen is not a consistent positivist in the sense of conceptual positivism, characterized by the sources thesis, the contingent connection thesis, and weak reductionism. One cannot help but conclude that Kelsen has betrayed the positivist programme and is, as a result, an ideological positivist in Bobbio's sense[28] or a quasi-positivist in the sense that Alf Ross has lent to this term,[29] namely, a degenerate, morally abhorrent form of natural law. This is Ross's criticism of Kelsen, and it is also Nino's interpretation of the Pure Theory of Law.[30]

Hart also uses the term 'validity' in the sense of binding force, but this concept only appears in his internal statements. A typical example of an internal statement is precisely that which predicates validity of a rule. Such a statement does not limit itself to asserting that the rule in question meets the requirements imposed by the rule of recognition. Rather, it assumes the acceptance both of the rule of recognition and of the rule whose validity is predicated.[31]

I do not know how to reconcile the antagonistic aspects of Kelsen's theory, that is, the descriptive character of legal propositions and the value neutrality of legal science on the one hand and, on the other, the normativity of legal propositions, the objective validity of norms, and the doctrine of the basic norm. Since these two aspects of his theory are flatly contradictory and incompatible, I see no solution other than to sacrifice one aspect or the other. Placed in this critical position,

[27] See Raz, 'BN', in *AL*, 122–45, in *NN*, 47–67.

[28] Bobbio understands by 'ideological positivism' the thesis that every legal order (or system) possesses normative validity, which is to say that its norms are morally obligatory. See Norberto Bobbio, *El problema del positivismo*, trans. Ernesto Garzón Valdés (Buenos Aires: Eudeba, 1965).

[29] See Ross, 'Validity'.

[30] Ross, 'Validity', and see Nino, 'Some Confusions surrounding Kelsen's Concept of Validity' (n. 25, this chapter).

[31] 'The use of unstated rules of recognition, by courts and others, in identifying particular rules of the system is characteristic of the internal point of view. Those who use them in this way thereby manifest their own acceptance of them as guiding rules...The first of these forms of expression we shall call an *internal statement* because it manifests the internal point of view and is naturally used by one who, accepting the rule of recognition and without stating the fact that it is accepted, applies the rule in recognizing some particular rule of the system as valid...[T]he word "valid" is most frequently, though not always, used, in just such internal statements, applying to a particular rule of a legal system, an unstated but accepted rule of recognition.' Hart, *CL*, 1st edn., 99–100 (emphasis in original), 3rd edn., 102–3.

I believe—contrary to Nino—that one must interpret Kelsen with regard to his explicit intentions and reject that part of his theory that is incompatible with these intentions, which clearly mark the path Kelsen has taken in his last publications. As is well known, Kelsen expressly abandons his doctrine of the basic norm,[32] and in doing so he also abandons the objective validity of legal norms and the normativity of legal propositions. It is certainly less than a satisfactory solution to have to eliminate a good part of an author's theory in order to render it coherent, even if the author in question agrees with this solution, but I see here no possibility other than to follow in Kelsen's footsteps.

Raz, by contrast, attempts to explain the double aspect of legal propositions, their normative character on the one hand and their descriptive character on the other. In this connection he resorts to the metaphor of the 'legal man'[33] and to the distinction between committed, conditional, and *detached statements*. The latter are meant to reconcile the normative aspect of the legal statement with its non-evaluative character. Raz's effort, however, cannot be considered successful. In the first place, his detached statements do not represent an independent category, for they are equivalent to conditional statements. In fact, from a conditional statement one can infer a non-committed statement and vice versa, for to assert a conditional 'if *p*, then *q*' is the same as to assert *q* under the condition of *p*. Thus, the two types of statement can only poorly perform their respective roles, for as we have seen, what one does with the one can also be done with the other. Consequently, if the conditional statement 'if the norm *p* is valid, then one ought to do *q*' is not fully normative,[34] then the corresponding non-committed statement is not normative either. The latter is equivalent to the former.

In the second place, the idea of a fully normative statement that is at the same time non-committed does not seem to fare much better than Kelsen's notion of a descriptive 'ought'. They are both hybrid categories that have all the trappings of a contradiction in terms.

5.

My arguments can be summarized in ten propositions.

1) It is essential to distinguish between practical statements, which presuppose the use and therefore the acceptance of norms, and theoretical statements about the existence and content of the law.
2) Practical statements are used to guide and evaluate conduct, which is to say, to express needs, criticism, advice, approval, and the like. They are, therefore, prescriptive or normative statements (in a broad sense).

[32] See Hans Kelsen, 'Die Grundlage der Naturrechtslehre', *ÖZöR*, 13 (1963/4), 1–37, at 2, and 'Diskussionen', 117–62, at 119–20, both repr. in *Das Naturrecht in der politischen Theorie*, ed. Franz-Martin Schmölz (Vienna: Springer, 1963) (same pagination).

[33] See Raz, 'PPT', in Raz, *AL*, at 304, in *NN*, at 246.

[34] See Raz, 'PPT', in Raz, *AL*, at 304–5, in *NN*, at 246–7.

3) Theoretical statements are used to describe norms or the normative status of conduct according to a given legal order. They are, therefore, descriptive statements whose truth or falsity is determined by non-evaluative facts.
4) Practical statements are always committed, for they presuppose that he who uses them accepts the law, although this acceptance need not be based on moral reasons. Theoretical statements are detached (not committed), for they do not express either acceptance or an evaluation of what they describe.
5) Hart's external statements, like Kelsen's legal propositions, attempt to reconstruct theoretical statements. Hart's internal statements are a reconstruction of practical statements.
6) None of the great legal positivists of the nineteenth and twentieth centuries has maintained the strong reductionist thesis, according to which practical or internal statements are descriptive of non-evaluative facts.
7) The acceptance of the weak reductionist thesis, according to which theoretical or external statements are descriptive of non-evaluative facts, along with the thesis of contingent connection and the sources thesis is characteristic of legal positivism.
8) The rejection of the weak reductionist thesis is, therefore, incompatible with conceptual legal positivism and constitutes a clear symptom of ideological positivism or quasi-positivism, which is a form of natural law theory.
9) Some aspects of the Pure Theory of Law—such as the doctrine of the basic norm, the objective validity of legal norms, and the normative character of legal propositions—are incompatible with Kelsen's positivist programme. These doctrines indicate that Kelsen is—his declared intentions aside—a quasi-positivist. Or—the alternative—these doctrines have to be abandoned (a step that Kelsen in fact took late in life).
10) By bringing together under the rubric of legal statements Hart's internal statements and Kelsen's legal propositions, Raz tries to mix vinegar with motor oil. Kelsen's legal propositions represent a reconstruction of the ideals of a purely descriptive legal science, not an attempt to account for practical statements.

9

The Expressive Conception of Norms (1981)*

Written with Carlos E. Alchourrón

1. Two Conceptions of Norms

Questions concerning the ontological status and the logical properties of norms have been much debated in recent years, not only by legal and moral philosophers but also by a steadily increasing number of 'deontic' logicians.[1] In spite of this, a number of very basic problems have apparently not been solved, and they persist.

One such issue is the problem of the possibility of a logic of norms. Some authors think that there are logical relations between norms, and so they favour the development of a specific logic of norms (sometimes called 'deontic logic', although 'normative logic' would perhaps be a more appropriate name).[2] Other writers deny the very possibility of such a logic because in their view there are no logical relations between norms. According to them, deontic logic can only assume the form of a logic of normative propositions—that is, (true or false) propositions about (the existence of) norms.[3]

Another fundamental problem—or perhaps another aspect of the same problem—is the relation of norms to truth, and on this, too, there is no consensus. Whereas some writers readily ascribe truth-values to norms,[4] others emphatically deny that norms could conceivably be true or false. This issue is related to the first

* [*Editors' note*: Eugenio Bulygin's paper, written together with Carlos E. Alchourrón, first appeared in *New Studies in Deontic Logic*, ed. Risto Hilpinen (Dordrecht: Reidel, 1981), 95–124. It was reprinted, with minor refinements made in consultation with Eugenio Bulygin, in *NN*, 383–410. The Spanish version is found in *ALD*, 121–53.]

[1] The authors express gratitude to David Makinson for his helpful remarks and corrections with respect to both style and content.

[2] See Kalinowski's discussion of these terms in Georges Kalinowski, *Lógica de las normas y lógica deóntica* (Valencia, Venezuela: Universidad de Carabobo, 1978, repr. Mexico City: Distribuciones Fontamara, 1993).

[3] See Dagfinn Føllesdal and Risto Hilpinen, 'Deontic Logic: An Introduction', in *Deontic Logic: Introductory and Systematic Readings*, ed. Risto Hilpinen (Dordrecht: Reidel, 1971), 1–35.

[4] See, *inter alia*, Georges Kalinowski, *Le problème de la vérité en morale et en droit* (Lyon: Emmanuel Vitte, 1967), and Jürgen Rödig, *Schriften zur juristischen Logik* (Berlin and Heidelberg: Springer, 1980).

one, but not in a very clear way. Those authors who believe that norms have truth-values will certainly accept the possibility of a logic of norms, but the converse does not hold: *accepting* the idea that there are logical relations among norms does not commit one to the view that norms have truth-values.[5]

A third and apparently unrelated issue is the question concerning permissory norms. A great number of philosophers (especially philosophers of law) deny that there are permissory norms, recognizing only one type of norm (mandatory norms, imperatives, commands). Logicians and lawyers—although probably for different reasons—are less inclined to defend a monistic conception and see no obstacle that would prevent them from speaking of permissory norms (independently of whether or not these are definable in terms of obligations).

To a large extent these discrepancies are due to the fact that authors often start from two quite different and incompatible conceptions regarding the nature of norms, conceptions that are seldom, if ever, made explicit. It may be illuminating to characterize briefly these conceptions in order to see why different writers maintain conflicting and even diametrically opposed views on some very basic features of norms. These two conceptions will be called the *hyletic* and the *expressive* conception of norms.

For the *hyletic conception,* norms are proposition-like entities, that is, the meanings of certain expressions called normative sentences. A normative sentence is the linguistic expression of a norm, and a norm is said to be the meaning of a normative sentence in much the same way as a proposition is regarded as the meaning (sense) of a descriptive sentence. However, normative sentences, unlike descriptive sentences, have *prescriptive meaning:* that something ought to be, ought not to be, or may be the case (or be done).

In this conception, norms are not language-dependent. They can only be expressed by linguistic means,[6] but their existence is independent of any linguistic expression. There are norms that have not yet been formulated in any language and that perhaps will never be formulated. A norm, in this view, is an abstract and purely conceptual entity.

However, norms are not independent of descriptive propositions; they are the result of an operation on such propositions. Thus, in a norm, say '*Op*', we find two components: a descriptive proposition *p* and a normative operator *O*, both belonging to the conceptual import of the norm. In this sense normative operators are similar to modal alethic operators, and a norm is a proposition in much the same sense in which a modal proposition like *Np* is said to be a proposition.

Norms must be distinguished from *normative propositions*, that is, descriptive propositions stating that *p* is obligatory (forbidden or permitted) according to some unspecified norm or set of norms. Normative propositions—which can be

[5] See generally von Wright, *NA*; Ota Weinberger, 'Normenlogik und logische Bereiche', in *Deontische Logik und Semantik*, ed. Amedeo G. Conte, et al. (Wiesbaden: Athenaion, 1977), 176–212. [*Editors' note*: For this and other abbreviations, see the Table of Abbreviations.]

[6] The term 'language' is to be understood in a broad sense; a gesture, a look, a traffic light are in this sense linguistic expressions.

regarded as propositions about sets (systems) of norms—also contain normative terms like 'obligatory', 'prohibited', and so on, but these have a purely descriptive meaning.[7] In what follows the symbols '𝕆' and 'ℙ' will be used to refer to these descriptive deontic operators.

For the *expressive conception*, norms are the result of the *prescriptive use* of language. A sentence expressing one and the same proposition can be used on different occasions to do different things: it can be asserted, questioned, commanded, conjectured, and so on. The result of the performance of these actions will be a statement, a question, a command, or a conjecture. It is only on the pragmatic level of the use of language that the difference between statements, questions, commands, and the like arises; there is no such difference on the semantic level. For instance, the proposition expressed by the sentence 'Peter puts the book on the table' can be used to make an assertion (Peter puts the book on the table.), to ask a question (does Peter put the book on the table?), or to give a command (Peter, put the book on the table!).

The signs '$\vdash$' and '!' will be used to indicate the kind of linguistic act (assertion or command) performed by an (unspecified) speaker. These signs are mere *indicators* of what the speaker does when uttering certain words; they do not contribute to the meaning (that is, the conceptual content) of the words uttered. They show what the speaker is doing, but in doing this or that the speaker is not saying what he is doing; these signs are not a part of what he says or what his words mean. The expression '$\vdash p$' indicates that p is asserted, and '$!p$' indicates that p is commanded, whereas 'Op' expresses a proposition that p ought to be (done). So 'Op' is the symbol for a norm in the hyletic conception, whereas '$!p$' symbolizes a norm in the expressive conception.

It is important to stress the fact that the expressions '$!p$' and '$\vdash p$' do not describe the fact that p has been commanded or asserted. The sentences 'A asserts that p' and 'A commands that p' certainly express propositions that describe certain speech acts, but they do not say what is done with them: they can in turn be asserted, questioned, commanded, and so on. But '$!p$' and '$\vdash p$' do not express any proposition at all, although they are constructed with the help of the proposition p, so they have no truth-value and cannot be negated or combined by means of propositional operators.[8] What a speaker *does* on a certain occasion cannot be said by him (on the same occasion): it can only be shown by a *gesture*, a certain inflexion of the voice, or some special sign. These devices, however, only show the mood in which the sentence is being used; they do not form part of what the sentence says (that is, its conceptual content).

For the expressive conception, norms are essentially *commands*, but they must be carefully distinguished from propositions stating that there is a norm to such-and-such effect or that p is obligatory or prohibited, which are normative propositions. Normative propositions are related to norms in the following way: if p has been

[7] See Alchourrón and Bulygin, 'Von Wright on Deontic Logic and the Philosophy of Law' (1973/89), in this volume, ch. 5.

[8] See Hans Reichenbach, *Elements of Symbolic Logic* (New York: Free Press, 1947), at 336–44.

commanded, then the proposition that *p* is obligatory is true. If –*p* (the omission or forbearance of *p)* has been commanded, then it is true that *p* is prohibited or, what is the same, that –*p* is obligatory.

The two conceptions of norms are radically different and incompatible; there is no room for any eclecticism. If norms are expressions in a certain pragmatic mood, then they are not part of the meaning, and if they are meanings (propositions), they are independent of any use of language or of any pragmatic mood. Yet many authors do not clearly adhere to either of the two conceptions, or they seem rather to adhere to both of them. It is symptomatic of the very intricate nature of the issue that among those who seem to oscillate between the two conceptions are those philosophers who have dug most deeply into these problems. Thus, C. I. Lewis appears to be a clear expressivist when he says that

> the element of assertion in a statement is extraneous to the proposition asserted. The proposition is something assert*able*, the *content* of the assertion; and this same content, signifying the same state of affairs, can also be questioned, denied, or merely supposed, and can be entertained in other moods as well.[9]

Among these moods, Lewis explicitly mentions the 'imperative or hortatory mood', including in his characterization the 'modal statements of possibility and necessity'.[10] In his modal logic, however, he treats the expression 'T*p*' as a proposition, where the modal operator of possibility is part of the content of the proposition.

In Georg Henrik von Wright, too, we find arguments that would permit us to classify him according to either of the two conceptions. On the one hand, he speaks of 'prescriptively interpreted deontic expressions' between which certain logical relations hold,[11] and this seems to locate him among the adherents of the hyletic conception. On the other hand, he states that

> it would be misleading to conceive throughout of the relation between norms and their expressions in language on the pattern of the above two 'semantic dimensions' [sense and reference]. At least norms which are prescriptions must be called neither the reference nor even the sense (meaning) of the corresponding norm-formulations.... The use of words for giving prescriptions is similar to the use of words for giving promises. Both uses can be called *performatory* uses of language.[12]

This seems to suggest expressivism.

What these quotations from the works of the founders of modal and deontic logic show is that both conceptions are plausible, with one perhaps more plausible than the other in some contexts and vice versa, so that it is not easy to take a

[9] Clarence Irving Lewis, *An Analysis of Knowledge and Valuation* (La Salle, Ill.: Open Court, 1946), 48–9 (emphasis in original) (footnote omitted).

[10] Clarence Irving Lewis, *An Analysis of Knowledge and Valuation* (n. 9, this chapter), 49 n. 8.

[11] Von Wright writes: 'The "fully developed" system of Deontic Logic is a theory of descriptively interpreted expressions. But the laws (principles, rules), which are peculiar to this logic, concern logical properties of the *norms* themselves, which are then reflected in logical properties of norm-propositions. Thus, in a sense, the "basis" of Deontic Logic is a logical theory of prescriptively interpreted *O*- and *P*- expressions.' Von Wright, *NA*, 133–4 (emphasis in original).

[12] von Wright, *NA*, 94 (emphasis in original).

decision concerning the two conceptions before exploring the whole range of their implications.

As it stands, however, most legal and moral philosophers as well as deontic logicians share the expressive conception of norms. The most conspicuous and clear cases are those of Jeremy Bentham, John Austin, Hans Kelsen, Alf Ross, Richard Hare, Jørgen Jørgensen, Manfred Moritz, Bengt Hansson, Lennart Åqvist, Joseph Raz, and Franz von Kutschera.[13] Among the far less numerous representatives of the hyletic conception might be mentioned Georges Kalinowski and Ota Weinberger.[14]

It is not surprising that such antagonistic views on the nature of norms should lead to quite different answers to the three problems mentioned at the beginning of this chapter. For the expressive conception, there can be no logic of norms because there are no logical relations among norms. Deontic logic can only assume the form of a logic of normative propositions.[15] For the hyletic conception, there are two logics: a logic of norms and a logic of normative propositions.[16]

Regarding the second issue, the situation is less clear. Adherents of the expressive conception are committed to the view that norms lack truth-values, but among the representatives of the hyletic conception there are two tendencies. Some believe that norms are true or false,[17] others maintain that norms lack truth-values.[18] This question will not be discussed here.

Most expressivists deny that there are permissory norms (which does not amount to denying the existence of permissible states of affairs), because they only accept one kind of normative (prescriptive) action: commanding. This version of

[13] See Jeremy Bentham, *On Law in General*, ed. H. L. A. Hart (London: Athlone Press, 1970); John Austin, *Lectures on Jurisprudence*, 2 vols., 5th edn., ed. Robert Campbell (London: John Murray, 1885); Kelsen, *PTL*; Ross, *LJ*; Hare, *LM*; Jørgensen, 'IL'; Manfred Moritz, 'Permissive Sätze, Erlaubnissätze und deontische Logik', in *Philosophical Essays Dedicated to Gunnar Aspelin on the Occasion of his Sixty-fifth Birthday the 23rd of September 1963*, ed. Helge Bratt, et al. (Lund: C. W. K. Gleerup, 1963), 108–21, and Moritz, 'Kann das (richterliche) Urteil deduziert werden?', in *Festskrift till Per Olof Ekelöf*, ed. Henrik Hessler (Stockholm: P. A. Norstedt & Söner, 1972), 502–18; Bengt Hansson, 'An Analysis of Some Deontic Logics', *Noûs*, 3 (1969), 373–98, repr. *Deontic Logic: Introductory and Systematic Readings* (n. 3, this chapter), 121–47; Lennart Åqvist, 'Interpretations of Deontic Logic', *Mind*, 73 (1964), 246–53; Raz, *CLS*; Raz, *PRN*; Franz von Kutschera, *Einführung in die Logik der Normen, Werte und Entscheidungen* (Freiburg and Munich: Karl Alber, 1973). A less clear case—at least at first glance—is that of Castañeda, but one should not be misled by differences in terminology. What Castañeda calls 'norms' are normative propositions (in our sense). There is, then, a very interesting theory of normative propositions here, but he does not analyse norms, which he refers to as 'regulations', 'ordinances', or 'rules'. See Hector-Neri Castañeda, 'The Role of Science in the Justification of Norms', 16th World Congress of Philosophy, Düsseldorf, plenary session of 29 August 1979. See also Alchourrón's critical note on Castañeda's *Thinking and Doing* (Dordrecht: Reidel, 1975): Carlos E. Alchourrón, 'Prescripciones y normas. La teoría de Castañeda', *Crítica*, 13 (1981), 3–27, in *ALD*, 103–20.

[14] See Kalinowski (nn. 2, 4, this chapter); Weinberger (n. 5, this chapter).

[15] Føllesdal and Hilpinen (n. 3, this chapter), 7–8.

[16] See Carlos E. Alchourrón, 'Logic of Norms and Logic of Normative Propositions', *Logique et analyse*, 12 (1969), 242–68; Alchourrón, 'The Intuitive Background of Normative Legal Discourse and its Formalization', *Journal of Philosophical Logic*, 1 (1972), 447–63.

[17] See Kalinowski (nn. 2, 4, this chapter).

[18] See Weinberger (n. 5, this chapter); von Wright, *NA*, and Georg Henrik von Wright, *An Essay in Deontic Logic and the General Theory of Action* (Amsterdam: North-Holland, 1968); Alchourrón and Bulygin, *NS*.

the expressive conception is the *imperative theory of norms*. There are, however, exceptions even among clear expressivists, some of whom accept a peculiar normative act, that of permitting.[19] We shall consider later whether there are reasons for the expressive conception to accept other types of normative act besides commands and to accept the existence of permissory norms.

No such problems arise for the hyletic conception, and so the authors who share this conception accept at least two kinds of norm: mandatory or *O*-norms and permissory or *P*-norms.

Our purpose here is to examine in some detail the expressive conception. On close inspection, it proves to be far more powerful than might appear on first glance. When duly enriched by some new concepts (compatible with its spirit though usually ignored by its adherents), it is capable of capturing most if not all important features of a normative phenomenon. However, many expressivists, like Horatio, are bound to accept more things than are dreamt of in their philosophy.

In previous publications, especially in *Normative Systems,* we adhered to the hyletic conception. Norms were treated as abstract entities, as propositions with prescriptive meaning, capable of entering into logical relations. Since then, we have come to realize that most writers share the expressive conception; thus, we thought it would be interesting to explore its possibilities in order to uncover its limitations and to show the differences between the two conceptions. This was the impetus for the present paper.

We now have the impression that the same conceptual distinctions appear in both conceptions, although expressed, of course, in different languages. The choice between them is motivated by ontological considerations regarding the nature of norms, but there seems to be no crucial test that would justify a decision in favour of one conception or the other. So, after all, it looks more like a problem of philosophical style and even personal preference than a question of truth. As Rudolf Carnap has it: 'Let us be cautious in making assertions and critical in examining them, but tolerant in permitting linguistic forms.'

2. Norms and Normative Systems

The expressive conception is primarily concerned with norms issued by some agent (norm-authority) and directed to other agents (norm-subjects)—that is, norms that von Wright calls *prescriptions*.[20] We shall take into account only this type of norm, of which many legal norms provide a clear example.[21]

We begin by examining the imperative theory of norms, which accepts only one kind of normative act, the act of commanding, and therefore only one type of

[19] See Manfred Moritz, 'Permissive Sätze, Erlaubnissätze und deontische Logik' (n. 13, this chapter).

[20] See von Wright, *NA,* at 1–10.

[21] The theory can also be adapted to customary norms, however, whose existence is dependent on certain dispositions, which are revealed by certain actions.

norm, mandatory norms. (It is immaterial whether they are conceived of as establishing obligations or prohibitions.)

Commanding is essentially a linguistic activity, a speech act. It consists of formulating certain words (or other symbols) with a certain meaning. A norm is the meaningful sentence in its imperative use ($!p$). The content of the norm is the proposition expressed by 'p'. Thus, the act of commanding can be described as the act of ***promulgating*** a norm. The act of promulgating has temporal but instantaneous existence, yet norms are said to exist continually during a certain period of time (this is clearly so in the case of legal norms). How can this feature of norms be accounted for in the expressive conception?

In order to illustrate it we shall, following H. L. A. Hart, suppose a simplified situation in which a certain population living in a certain country is governed by an absolute monarch called Rex. Rex controls his people by means of general commands requiring them to do various things and to abstain from doing other things. Let us suppose further that Rex is the only legislative authority of this country.

From time to time Rex performs the action of commanding a certain proposition or set of propositions. The propositions that have been commanded by Rex form a set, the *commanded set A*. Each time Rex issues a new command, this set is enlarged by the new proposition commanded by Rex, so that it becomes a new set, A_1. Thus, in the course of time we have not one set but a *sequence* of sets (A_1, A_2, A_3). So far (that is, as long as the imperativist variety of expressivism is accepted), these sets can only be increased by the addition of new propositions, but subtraction does not yet exist.

A proposition becomes a member of some set of the sequence as a result of an act of commanding performed by Rex. Hence, we can say that the norm $!p$ exists from the moment at which p has been commanded and so the proposition p has become a member of the corresponding set. This is, of course, only a mode of speech. In fact, the norm $!p$ has an instantaneous existence, exactly like the act of commanding p. The point, however, is that all the propositions that belong to the set A are regarded as obligatory in A. Since one and the same proposition p can be a member of, for example, successive sets A_2, A_3,...A_n but not of A_1, so p is not obligatory in A_1, but is obligatory in A_2, and so on. As long as the successive sets can only be increased by new commands, p commanded at t_1 belongs to all sets subsequent to the set corresponding to t_1.

Thus, the existence of a norm (= the membership of the norm-content) is dependent on certain empirical facts (acts of promulgation in the case of prescriptions, certain actions revealing dispositions in the case of customary norms). Therefore, since there are no logical relations between facts, there is no room for a logic of norms.

This does not, however, preclude the possibility of a logic of normative propositions. Indeed, as we have already pointed out, the proposition that p is obligatory in A is true if p has been commanded by Rex and so is a member of the commanded set A. Still, this is a sufficient but not a necessary condition for the truth of 'p is obligatory in A'. It may be the case that Rex has never commanded that p, but has commanded, for example, that p & q. This is a different proposition and so, according to our criterion, p would not belong to A. Since, however, p is a consequence of p & q (for it is logically deducible from p & q), it is also true that p is obligatory in A. The obligatoriness of p is a consequence of the obligatoriness of p & q, for p is a consequence of p & q.

We can now define the concept of a normative system as the set of all the propositions that are consequences of the explicitly commanded propositions.[22] (Although we use the traditional expression 'normative system', it must be emphasized that, for the expressive conception, a normative system is not a set of norms but a set of norm-contents, that is, propositions.) This enables us to distinguish between the set A (formed by all the explicitly commanded propositions) as the axiomatic *basis* of the system, and the normative system Cn(A), which is the set of all the consequences of A.

We are now in a position to correct our criterion for the truth of normative propositions. 'It is obligatory that p in A' is true if and only if p is a member of the system Cn(A)—that is, if and only if p belongs to the consequences of A. This means that p is obligatory in A if and only if p has been commanded or is a consequence of the propositions that have been commanded. In this last case we say that $\mathbb{O}_A(p)$ and that p is a *derived obligation.*

The notion of derived obligation is related to the notion of implicit command. This latter concept, in turn, is closely related to that of implicit assertion. Indeed, there are at least two different senses in which a person can be said to have made an assertion. In a psychological sense of 'assertion', what is asserted in an act of assertion is only the sentence uttered, and not even the proposition expressed by that sentence. In this sense of 'assert', if X asserted 'John kissed Mary', he *did not assert* 'Mary was kissed by John' because this is a different sentence, even if both sentences have the same meaning, that is, they express the same proposition. But in another, non-psychological sense of 'asserting', if X asserted 'John kissed Mary', he explicitly asserted the proposition expressed by that sentence, and so he also asserted that Mary was kissed by John. Moreover, he also implicitly asserted all those propositions—such as 'somebody kissed Mary'—that are consequences of the proposition he asserted explicitly. This is a non-psychological sense of assertion, for it is clear that the person in question probably did not think of all such propositions and so had not the slightest intention of asserting them. It may even be the case that q is a consequence of p, and that the person who asserts p not only ignores this fact, but believes q to be false. If he is not prepared to assert q (for example, because he believes it to be false), then we can show that his position is inconsistent by proving that q is a consequence of p. This is a very common way of arguing. We often try to refute our opponent by showing that the propositions he asserts imply some proposition he is not willing to accept. This kind of argument is based on the notion of implicit assertion. In this sense, one asserts all the propositions that are a consequence of the explicitly asserted propositions.

[22] On the notion of consequence, see Alfred Tarski, *Logic, Semantics. Metamathematics*, trans. J. H. Woodger (Oxford: Clarendon Press, 1956), at chs. 3, 5, 12, and 16.

A famous case might be mentioned in this connection. When Bertrand Russell found a contradiction in Gottlob Frege's system, it had an horrendous impact on Frege. Why? Frege certainly did not assert any inconsistent proposition, but Russell showed that the self-contradictory proposition was a theorem (a consequence) of Frege's system. Frege did assert it implicitly by asserting the axioms of his system, and he could not maintain the axioms and reject that theorem.

The same kind of observation can be made regarding the act of commanding. Here, too, we have a non-psychological sense of implicit commanding. If a person commands something, he also commands all the consequences of what he has explicitly commanded (even if he is not aware of them). For instance, if a teacher commands that all his pupils should leave the classroom, he also implicitly commands that John (who is one of his pupils) should leave the classroom, even if he is not aware of the fact that John is there.

These considerations show that there are logical relations between normative propositions. In addition to obligation, we can also define the concepts of prohibition and permission for normative propositions:

> p is prohibited in $A(\mathbb{O}_A(-p))$ = df. the negation of p $(-p)$ is a member of the system $\mathrm{Cn}(A)$
>
> p is permitted in $A(\mathbb{P}_A(p))$ = df. the negation of p $(-p)$ is not a member of $\mathrm{Cn}(A)$

Even if for the imperative theory of norms there are no permissory norms, there are propositions or states of affairs that are permitted. According to the definition, p is permitted if and only if p is not prohibited in A. This shows that permissions have a normative status that differs from that of obligations and prohibitions. The permission that p is given by the absence of certain acts (acts of prohibiting that p or—what is the same—of commanding that $-p$), whereas the prohibition (obligation) requires the existence of certain normative acts.

The analyses of this section show that a careful distinction must be made between (a) the act of promulgation of a norm (commanding), (b) the operation of adding new elements to a system as a result of such acts, and (c) the criteria that govern such an addition of elements. It is important to realize that what is added to the system A as a consequence of an act of promulgating a set of propositions B is not only the set B itself but also all its consequences and, moreover, all those propositions that without being consequences of B or consequences of A are nevertheless consequences of A taken together with B. In other words, if to a set A we add a set B, the resulting system is not $\mathrm{Cn}(A) + \mathrm{Cn}(B)$, but $\mathrm{Cn}(A + B)$. In most cases, this last set will be considerably larger than the first.

3. Rejection

Suppose now that Rex realizes that the state of affairs p that he prohibited some time ago should not be prohibited now (perhaps because he committed a mistake in prohibiting p or because the circumstances that made the prohibition of p appropriate have changed). So he wants to permit p. How can he achieve this?

It is clear that once the act of commanding $-p$ has been performed, nobody can modify this fact. So it will always be true that p is forbidden in A. If Rex wants to permit p, he must change the system into a system where $-p$ does not obtain, but this change is impossible as long as there are only acts of commanding, which alone are accepted by the imperative theory of norms. By commanding, a permitted state of affairs may become prohibited, but not vice versa. The change from a prohibition to a permission requires an operation of *subtraction;* addition alone is clearly not sufficient. Therefore, in order to permit p, Rex must repeal or derogate the norm that prohibits p; more precisely, he has to eliminate $-p$ from the system. For this he must first identify what he wants to eliminate ($-p$) and then perform the operation of subtracting $-p$, so that as a result of this operation, $-p$ will be eliminated from the system. Here again, the act performed by Rex, the *act of rejection*, which is the operation eliminating certain propositions from the system, must be distinguished from the criteria that govern such elimination.[23] We shall begin with an analysis of the act of rejection.

In the same way as there are, among others, these two types of propositional attitude—descriptive and prescriptive (that is, in this context, asserting and commanding)—there are two types of the act of rejection that may refer to the same proposition. We shall call them the descriptive and the prescriptive rejection. The content of both types of act is a proposition, but the two acts reject it in different ways. The first act of rejection is opposed to asserting, the second to commanding. We shall use the signs '⊦' and 'i' to symbolize the two types of rejection.

It is important to realize that rejecting is not the same as negating. When we negate a proposition, we assert another proposition that is the negation of the first. Thus, to negate p is to assert $-p$. Similarly, to negate the command that p can be regarded as commanding that $-p$. In this case, the negation of the command that p would be the prohibition that p. Hence, if Rex, in order to permit that p, were to negate the prohibition that p by commanding that p, the only thing he would achieve is to introduce a contradiction into the system: both p and $-p$ would belong to Cn(A), and both propositions 'p is obligatory in A' and 'p is prohibited in A' would be true, and neither p nor $-p$ would be permitted. This is not what Rex wants to do if he wants to permit that p.

Therefore, rejection is another type of speech act: he who rejects a proposition does not assert any proposition at all. It is the kind of difference that obtains between an atheist and an agnostic. The atheist negates the existence of God; he does this by asserting the proposition that God does not exist. The agnostic rejects the proposition that God exists without asserting the proposition that God does not exist. Incidentally, this also shows that the position of a sceptic need not be inconsistent. It would be self-refuting if the sceptic were to assert that nothing can

[23] The literature on the concept of derogation is rather meager. See, however, the excellent paper by Thomas Cornides, 'Der Widerruf von Befehlen', *Studium Generale*, 22 (1969), 1215–63. Cornides is a true pioneer in this field. Weinberger's distinction between '*Begrenzungssatz*' and '*Tilgungsoperation* (*Streichung*)' seems to reproduce our distinction between rejection and elimination. See Weinberger (n. 5, this chapter), at 192.

be known, for he would then be claiming at least to know the proposition that nothing can be known. If, however, all he does is to reject all propositions, then he does not assert any proposition at all and his position becomes perfectly consistent.

Similarly, the (prescriptive) rejection of *p* is no prescription at all; in particular, it is not a prohibition of *p*. So the sign 'i' is a mere indicator of a certain speech act and does not form part of the conceptual content of this act ('i*p*' like '!*p*' does not express a proposition but only indicates what is done with the proposition *p*).[24]

When lawyers speak of derogation, there is rejection of a norm-content. No act of rejecting is required when what is derogated is not a norm-content but a mere formulation of a norm (a sentence). When the legislator becomes aware that there are two or more redundant formulations—that is, one and the same norm-content is expressed, for example, by different paragraphs of a statute—then he may be willing to derogate the redundant formulations without eliminating the norm-content. In this case what he wants to do is to 'efface' the redundant formulations, leaving only one of them. No rejection of the norm-content is required to achieve this aim. Removing a norm-formulation, however, should not be confused with the elimination of a norm-content. In this latter case, what the authority wants to eliminate from the system is a certain conceptual content (a proposition), and in order to achieve this, the performance of an act of rejection is necessary.

Thus, expressivism must accept, along with commanding, another type of normative act, that of rejecting. The imperative theory of norms cannot account for the phenomenon of derogation, but expressivism is not bound to stand or to fall with it. The acceptance of various types of normative act, in particular acts of rejection, is perfectly compatible with the expressive conception.

If as a result of a rejection, a norm-content is eliminated from the system, the norm ceases to exist. Two important conclusions may be drawn from this fact: (1) norms not only begin to exist at a given time, they also cease to exist at a certain moment; (2) normative sets not only can be extended by the addition of new elements, they also can be restricted by the subtraction of elements.

Conclusion (1) is in need of some clarifying remarks. As we have already seen, the temporal existence of norms is simply a metaphor. What really happens is the performance of two types of act (commanding and rejecting). These are the only empirical facts relevant for the existence of a norm. There is no need for any further fact to render true the proposition that a norm exists.[25] On the other hand, the assertion that a given norm ceases to exist at a certain moment is misleading. All there is is a sequence of different sets of propositions, and a given proposition *p* may be a member of some of these sets and not

[24] Hare describes the difference between negation and rejection when he says that in a negation the term 'not' is part of the phrastic, but it can also occur in neustics: they then become 'not-yes' and 'not-please'. This seems to correspond to what we call rejection. Thus, Hare's 'not-yes' is our descriptive rejection and 'not-please' is the prescriptive rejection. See Hare, *LM*, at 20–1.

[25] See Carlos E. Alchourrón and Eugenio Bulygin, *Sobre la existencia de las normas jurídicas* (Valencia, Venezuela: Universidad de Carabobo, 1979, repr. Mexico City: Distribuciones Fontamara, 1997); for a different view, see von Wright, *NA*, at ch. 7.

of others. If it belongs to a certain set, it never ceases to belong to it, although it may occur that it does not belong to the next set. What we do is to take at different times different sets as points of reference for our assertions that certain propositions or states of affairs are obligatory, prohibited, or permitted. This gives the illusion of a temporal change. In fact, however, normative propositions are timeless, for they always refer to some definite system. Hence, the proposition 'p is obligatory in A_1' is either true or false, but if true it is always true, even after the derogation of p. For if p is eliminated, we obtain a new system, A_2. The proposition 'p is obligatory in A_2' is, in this hypothesis, false, but it is a different proposition. The first proposition ('p is obligatory in A_1') continues to be true, although one is perhaps no longer interested in it. In this sense, normative systems are instantaneous.[26] When jurists speak of a legal system as persisting through time (as for instance the system of French law), what they mean is not one system, but a sequence of systems.

4. Conflicts of Promulgation and Rejection

If X asserts that p and Y asserts that $-p$, the two assertions are said to be incompatible, not in the sense that they could not coexist, but in the sense that the two propositions asserted by X and Y are contradictory, that is, they cannot both be true (or false). The fact that two persons assert two contradictory propositions is certainly possible (and moreover extremely common); it is even possible for one and the same person to assert two contradictory propositions, but such assertions conflict. If we want to integrate them into a coherent whole, we must first resolve the conflict.

Analogously, the command that p and the command that $-p$ conflict because the norm-contents p and $-p$ are contradictory. This is the 'classic' notion of *normative inconsistency*. The concept of contradiction between propositions is extended to commands (norms), based not on the criterion for truth (commands lack truth-values) but on the notion of fulfilment (it is logically impossible to fulfil or to obey both commands $!p$ and $!-p$). Nevertheless, it is surely possible for two persons or even for one person to issue two conflicting commands. As long as they belong to different systems, there is no difficulty; the need to resolve the conflict arises when they are members of the same system. It is the unity of the system that determines this need. A normative system that contains both p and $-p$ is *inconsistent*, and this is regarded as a serious defect of the system, for relative to it the propositions that p is obligatory and that p is prohibited are both true.

Consider now the kind of conflict that would arise not between a theist and an atheist (who assert two contradictory propositions, 'God exists' and 'God does not exist'), but between a theist and an agnostic. An agnostic rejects the proposition that God exists without affirming its negation. Here there is no inconsistency

[26] See Raz, *CLS*, at 34–5, who drew our attention to this fact. See Alchourrón and Bulygin, 'On the Concept of a Legal Order' (1976), in this volume, ch. 7.

between two propositions, but a conflict between two propositional attitudes, assertion and rejection, referring to the same proposition. In a certain sense, assertion and (descriptive) rejection are incompatible.

In a similar way, promulgation of a norm and rejection of the same norm-content are incompatible: there is a kind of conflict between commanding that *p* and rejecting *p*. This conflict is different from that of commanding *p* and –*p*. In the latter case we have an agreement in attitude but a disagreement in content; we call it *normative contradiction* or inconsistency. In the former case we have a disagreement in attitude and an agreement in content; this kind of conflict will be called, following Carnap, *ambivalence.*[27]

The need to resolve the conflict of ambivalence arises when the same proposition is (directly or indirectly) commanded and rejected by the same authority or by different authorities in the same system.

In order to resolve conflicts of ambivalence, certain criteria are used, which will be called *criteria or rules of preference.*[28] The rules of preference are designed to resolve conflicts between acts of promulgation and acts of rejection referring (directly or indirectly) to the same norm-content. They stipulate which of the acts prevails over the other. That the act of rejection of *p* prevails over the act of commanding *p* means that the set that does not contain *p* is to be preferred to the set that contains *p* as the point of reference for normative judgments of the form $\mathbb{O}_A(P)$ or $\mathbb{P}_A(p)$, and vice versa.

The rules of preference are seldom if ever explicitly stated, but they are in fact used by lawyers and by all those who have to manipulate normative systems. Three such rules are commonly used in legal practice; we shall call them rules *auctoritas superior, auctoritas posterior*, and *auctoritas specialis.* These names are an adaptation of certain other analogous but different rules that lawyers explicitly use for resolving contradictions between norms *(lex superior,* and so on), to which we shall return in section 6.

The rule *auctoritas superior* stipulates that an act (be it promulgation or rejection) performed by an authority at a higher hierarchical level prevails over an act performed by an authority at a lower level. This means that when a higher authority (for example, a legislature) has issued a norm, it cannot be repealed by a lower authority (for example, by the executive). Even if it is rejected, the system does not change. On the other hand, when a higher authority rejects a norm-content, this act derogates it (that is, leads to its elimination from the system) if it was issued earlier by a lower authority and prevents its addition to the system by a later act of promulgation by a lower authority. This last case is especially interesting, for it shows that rejection need not be temporally posterior to the act of promulgation.

If we distinguish between the *operation of eliminating* norm-content that has been rejected and the act of *rejecting* (which is frequently also called

[27] Rudolf Carnap, *Introduction to Semantics* (Cambridge, Mass.: Harvard University Press, 1942), 187.

[28] Here the term 'rule' does not mean a norm (command or commanded content) but a purely conceptual criterion.

'derogation'), then we become aware that it makes perfectly good sense to reject the norm-content *p*, even if *p* is not a member of the system. Although such rejection does not lead to the elimination of any norm-content, it may produce the important result of preventing the addition of *p* if *p* is issued later by an authority at a lower level. This is what happens with constitutional rights and guarantees. The constitution rejects in advance certain norm-content (that would affect basic rights), preventing the legislature from promulgating this norm-content, because if the legislature promulgates such norm-content, it can be declared unconstitutional by the courts and will not be added to the system.

The other two rules operate in a similar way. The rule *auctoritas posterior* stipulates that a temporally later act prevails over an earlier act, whether it be promulgation or rejection. Obviously, this rule only applies to acts performed by authorities of equal hierarchy; thus, it is supplementary to the first rule.

Finally, the rule *auctoritas specialis* stipulates that an act of promulgating (rejecting) norm-content that is less general prevails over an act of rejecting (promulgating) norm-content that is more general.

It is important to stress the fact that these rules do not resolve all the possible conflicts between acts of promulgation and rejection. The same authority or two authorities at the same level in the hierarchy may simultaneously perform the acts of promulgating and rejecting the same norm-content. In such a case, clearly none of the three rules is applicable; such cases, though rare, sometimes do occur in legal practice. If such conflicts are to be resolved, further criteria for preference must be introduced, but it would be a mistake to regard the rules of preference (traditional or not) as *logical* rules.

5. Implicit Rejection and Derogation

When Rex rejects a norm-content (or a set of norm-contents), this act identifies what he wants to eliminate (subtract) from the system. The set of the explicitly rejected propositions will be called, accordingly, the *derogandum.*

If the derogandum alone is subtracted from the system, Rex may well fail to achieve his purpose. Indeed, suppose that *p* has been rejected, but the system contains not only *p* but also *p* & *q*. Then to eliminate only *p* simply will not do, for as long as *p* & *q* is a member of the system, so is *p*. What the rejection of *p* would achieve in such a case is at most a change in the status of *p*; if it was explicitly commanded and so a member of the basis, it will now be one of the consequences of the basis but remain a member of the system. Hence, *p* has not been derogated at all.

This argument makes it clear that the derogation of *p* requires not only the explicit rejection of *p* itself but also the rejection of all those propositions of which *p* is a consequence. We shall say that these propositions are implicitly rejected by the act of rejecting *p*. Moreover, it may occur that two or more propositions (taken together) imply a rejected proposition, although none of them (taken alone) does so. Suppose, for example, that $q \supset p$ and q are members of the system and that p is rejected. The set $\{q \supset p, q\}$ implies p, so it must be (implicitly) rejected.

Generalizing from this result, we can state the following *general criterion for implicit rejection*: the rejection of a set of propositions B implicitly rejects all propositions and sets of propositions that imply some of the propositions belonging to B.

It is worth noting that what is rejected by an act of rejection is not a set of propositions, but a *family* of sets. This fact determines an important difference between promulgation and derogation: it is always a *set* of propositions that is promulgated, but it is always a *family* of sets that is rejected. ('Rejected' means here 'explicitly or implicitly rejected'.)

What effects does an act of rejection produce? We must distinguish two cases:

(i) If none of the explicitly rejected propositions is a member of the system Cn(A), then none of the rejected sets is included in A. Here the problem of subtraction does not arise. However, if some of the rejected propositions or sets were promulgated later, this fact would give rise to a conflict of ambivalence. Such a conflict can only be resolved by the application of some rule of preference.

(ii) If some of the explicitly rejected propositions are members of the system Cn(A), then some of the rejected sets are included in A. As the members of Cn(A) are promulgated, we have a conflict of ambivalence and need some rule of preference to resolve it. If it is resolved in favour of promulgation, the rejection produces no effect whatsoever—no derogation takes place, and there is no change in the system. If rejection prevails, however, certain propositions must be eliminated by subtraction from the system. Which are these propositions? What criteria determine the operation of subtraction?

It is clear that neither a rejected proposition nor a rejected set can remain in A, for in that case some of the members of the derogandum (that is, some of the explicitly rejected propositions) would continue to be members of the system Cn(A). In particular, if a set is rejected, at least one explicitly rejected proposition is a consequence of it. Therefore, all rejected sets must be eliminated from A. What does it mean to eliminate a set? If one of its elements is removed from the set, the set as such disappears. What we have in its place is another, less numerous set. On the other hand, as long as all of its members are there, it is the same set. Thus, removing at least one of its elements is a necessary and sufficient condition for the elimination of a set.

Now if—as the hypothesis runs—at least one of the explicitly rejected propositions belongs to the system Cn(A), the set A (that is, the basis of the system) is one of the rejected sets. Hence, it must be eliminated, but if we remove all its elements the whole system collapses. Thus, by derogating one norm-content we would succeed in derogating the whole system. This seems to be a bit too drastic as a method of complying with the requirement that all the rejected sets should be eliminated from A.

This observation suggests the following *adequacy conditions* for the operation of subtraction: (i) no rejected proposition or set of propositions shall remain in the system, and (ii) the set of the subtrahend shall be *minimal*—that is, only those propositions shall be eliminated whose removal is strictly necessary in order to comply with (i). In other words, the remainder of the operation must be the *maximal* subset of *A* consistent with the derogation.

A subset of *A* (that is, the explicitly promulgated propositions) that fulfils the requirements (i) and (ii) will be called a *derogans*. To each non-empty derogandum corresponds at least one derogans.

In order to construct a derogans corresponding to a derogandum, we must take at least one proposition from each of the rejected sets in *A*.[29] Since, however, some of these sets may have several members (none of which is rejected), any of them can be used for the construction of a derogans; so there are several ways of constructing a derogans, and consequently we have not one derogans but several derogantes. Since each derogans is a set of propositions, the set of all derogantes is a family. What we must subtract, however—if we want to satisfy the adequacy conditions—*is only one of them*, for if we remove one derogans, the remainder will contain no rejected set (and therefore no rejected proposition). On the other hand, if more than one derogans is removed, the remainder is no longer a maximal set, and so condition (ii) fails to be fulfilled.

This shows that situations may arise where several derogantes correspond to one derogandum, and therefore there are several different ways of carrying out the subtraction corresponding to the same act of rejection. What makes things even worse, we may have no criteria for preferring one of them. In such situations, there are several possible remainders instead of one; the remainder is not a set but a family of sets. This is what we have elsewhere called the *logical indeterminacy of the system*.[30]

The problem of indeterminacy does not arise if the explicitly rejected propositions (the derogandum) are independent members of *A*. Then it is sufficient to eliminate from *A* the derogandum alone. In general, the derogation is univocal if and only if there is only one derogans and therefore only one remainder.

It may occur that the subtraction of a derogans carries with it the elimination of some other propositions that are a consequence of *A* (that is, they do not belong to *A* but are members of the system Cn(*A*)) and are no longer consequences of *A* minus derogans. Thus, the set of eliminated propositions may, after all, be larger

[29] We say 'at least one' instead of 'only one', for in the case of overlapping sets it is impossible to remove one and only one element from all of them. Consider, for example, the case of the three following sets: (*x*,*y*), (*y*,*z*), and (*x*,*z*): if one element of two of them is removed, both elements of the third are removed as well.

[30] See Alchourrón and Bulygin, 'On the Concept of a Legal Order' (1976), in this volume, ch. 7; Alchourrón and Bulygin, 'Unvollständigkeit, Widersprüchlichkeit und Unbestimmtheit der Normenordnungen', in *Deontische Logic und Semantik* (n. 5, this chapter), 20–32; Alchourrón and Bulygin, *Sobre la existencia de las normas jurídicas* (n. 25, this chapter). This problem has already been seen by Cornides, although he seems not to lend much importance to it, see Cornides (n. 23, this chapter), at 1241.

than the set of subtracted propositions (a derogans). This makes it convenient to distinguish between subtraction and elimination.

To sum up: Derogation, which leads to a new system (the remainder), has been analysed as comprising two components, the act of rejection and the operation of subtraction. The act of rejection identifies a derogandum, and the resulting system is the remainder after subtracting a derogans (corresponding to the derogandum) from the original system. It should be emphasized, finally, that this kind of subtraction is—as our informal analysis shows—a far more complicated operation than the ordinary set-theoretic subtraction.[31]

6. Inconsistency

In section 4, we examined the conflicts of ambivalence that arise between two propositional attitudes: promulgating and rejecting the same norm-content. The two acts are incompatible because they tend to achieve incompatible results, the addition of a norm-content to a system and its subtraction from it. Our purpose now is to analyse the other kind of normative conflict, inconsistency between norm-contents (normative contradiction).

If both a proposition p and its negation $-p$ are members of a normative system, the system is said to be inconsistent. The trouble with an inconsistent system is that it is impossible, for reasons of logic, to obey all of its norms. At the very least, the norms $!p$ and $!-p$ cannot both be complied with. Moreover, if the classic notion of consequence is accepted, the effects of a contradiction are even more disastrous: all propositions belong to an inconsistent system. This is so because according to the classic notion of consequence, from a contradictory pair of propositions any proposition whatsoever can be derived. So all inconsistent systems are equivalent: they contain the same consequences and are equally useless. Everything is obligatory according to such a system, and no one can ever possibly comply with it; thus, it cannot guide any action.

Yet it is extremely important to realize that inconsistent normative systems are perfectly possible, and they frequently occur, at least in certain fields such as law. The reason for this is fairly clear. The selection of the propositions that form the basis of the system (the set A) is based on certain empirical facts: the acts of commanding or promulgating. Now there is nothing extravagant about the idea that an authority commands that p, while another authority (or the same authority, perhaps on a different occasion) commands that $-p$. Even one and the same authority may command that p and that $-p$ at the same time, especially when a great number of norms are issued on the same occasion. This happens when the legislature enacts a very extensive statute, for example, a civil code, which usually contains 4000–6000 dispositions. All of them are regarded as promulgated at the

[31] For a detailed analysis of the concept of derogation, see Carlos E. Alchourrón and David Makinson, 'Hierarchies of Regulations and their Logic', in *New Studies in Deontic Logic*, ed. Risto Hilpinen (Dordrecht: Reidel, 1981), 125–48.

same time, by the same authority, so that it is no wonder that they sometimes contain a certain number of explicit or implicit contradictions.

Nevertheless, many authors are extremely reluctant to accept this relatively simple fact. Some of them (especially deontic logicians and moral philosophers) are perhaps influenced by their (direct or indirect) interest in moral discourse, for it seems hard to accept that the same action may be morally good and bad (obligatory and prohibited) at the same time. There is a grain of truth in this thought. It is probably true of rational morality, but very likely not true of positive morality, and it is plainly false of positive law. Strangely enough, there are also legal philosophers, that is, people whose primary interests concern positive law, who share this antiseptic conception. Kelsen is—or rather was—perhaps its most prominent representative among legal philosophers. In his *Reine Rechtslehre* (1960), he does not deny that legislators can enact contradictory laws, but he firmly maintains that the *system* of law is always consistent. This 'miracle' is achieved, according to Kelsen, by legal science. Jurists eliminate all contradictions, and so 'the chaos becomes a cosmos', that is, 'the multiplicity of general and individual legal norms issued by different legal authorities becomes a unitary and consistent system, a legal order'.[32]

What Kelsen says here sounds perhaps a bit too optimistic, but it is substantially true. Yet far from supporting the contention that legal systems are always consistent, it proves this contention of Kelsen's to be false. Indeed, if contradictions must be eliminated, then there is such a thing as a contradiction that must be eliminated. QED.

This result has even been corroborated by Kelsen himself. Indeed, in his latest publications, 'Derogation' (1962) and 'Law and Logic' (1965),[33] Kelsen changes radically his view concerning normative conflicts, a view that he had maintained in all of his previous writings.

Now, in 'Law and Logic', Kelsen clearly states that conflicts between norms are perfectly possible, where by 'conflicting norms' he understands two norms that prescribe incompatible actions, for example, *p* and *–p*. (So Kelsen's notion of a conflict of norms corresponds exactly to our 'inconsistency between norm-contents'.) According to the new doctrine, such conflicts differ from logical contradiction in so far as two contradictory propositions cannot both be true, whereas two conflicting norms can both be valid, in the sense of their having been issued by competent authorities. Such a conflict can only be resolved—on Kelsen's new view—by explicit or implicit derogation of one (or both) of the two conflicting norms. Thus, Kelsen's new position is in complete agreement with the views put forward in this paper.

It is, of course, a purely terminological matter whether the term 'system' will only be applied to sets of norm-contents once they are purged of their inconsistencies, or whether it will be applied to inconsistent sets as well. The important thing

32 Kelsen, *RR 2*, § 16 (74), *PTL*, 72.

33 Both papers appear in Hans Kelsen, *Essays in Legal and Moral Philosophy*, ed. Ota Weinberger (Dordrecht: D. Reidel, 1973), at 261–75 and 228–53 respectively.

is to identify the inconsistencies and to examine the techniques used to remove them. This is what we propose to do now.

It is interesting to observe that lawyers (not contaminated by philosophy) readily accept the possibility of contradictions in law. This is shown by the fact that there are venerable principles designed to solve such conflicts. The principles *lex posterior*, *lex superior*, and *lex specialis* would have no application at all if there were no inconsistencies in legal dispositions. The very fact that lawyers often resort to such principles shows at least that they believe that normative contradictions are quite possible. This belief is not mistaken.

How are cases of inconsistency treated in legal practice? Two situations are to be distinguished:

(i) When a legislative authority discovers a contradiction in a legal system, it may either derogate one or both of the two conflicting norm-contents or leave things as they are, relying on the ability of judges to resolve the conflict. If the authority chooses to derogate one or both conflicting norm-contents, this resolves the problem. The curious thing about derogation is the fact that a resolution of the conflict can be reached by a rather unexpected procedure (at least if the classic notion of consequence is accepted): by derogating any proposition you wish! This is easy to prove. Suppose that p and $-p$ are members of Cn(A) and that the legislature rejects q; in this case (p, $-p$) is one of the rejected sets (for any proposition, including q, can be derived from a contradiction), and at least one of its members must be eliminated. It is enough that one proposition not be a member of a system for it to be consistent. Hence the derogation of any proposition ensures the consistency of the system. The only problem that may arise in this connection is the indeterminacy of the remaining system.

(ii) The situation of judges seems to be different. Judges are supposed to apply the law, not modify it. They lack competence or power to derogate laws enacted by the legislature (except perhaps in the case of unconstitutional laws). What can judges do when faced with an inconsistent system? What methods do they actually apply to deal with such situations?

We must recall at this point that legal systems are not just sets of norms but are hierarchical structures.[34] There are certain hierarchical relations among legal norms or, as we would say, between norm-contents belonging to a legal system. Such hierarchies may be established by the legislature (that is, by laws themselves) or determined by some general criteria based on the date of promulgation (*lex posterior*), the competence of the promulgating authority (*lex superior*), or the degree of generality of norm-contents (*lex specialis*). They may even be imposed by the judge himself, using his personal criteria for preference.[35]

[34] This is emphasized by most legal philosophers—by Kelsen, Alf Ross, and Hart, for example.

[35] From the logical point of view such an ordering is either a partial ordering (reflexive, transitive, and antisymmetric relation) or a weak ordering (reflexive, connected, and transitive, though not

As in the case of ambivalence, the three well-established traditional principles are not sufficient to resolve all possible contradictions. Sometimes, judges must resort to further criteria—based, for example, on considerations concerning justice or other values involved in the issue.

The hierarchical ordering of the system enables the judge to give preference to some norm-contents or sets of norm-contents over others and so to disregard the hierarchically lower sets. In such cases, lawyers tend to say that the conflict was an apparent one and that there was really no inconsistency at all.

This may be perfectly true, provided that what one understands by 'normative system' is not a set but an *ordered set* of norm-contents, the ordering relations being intrinsic to the concept of a normative system. This shows that lawyers tend to use—at least in some contexts—the term 'normative system' in this special sense.

If by 'normative system' we understand, however, an ordered set of norm-contents, then every modification of the ordering relations modifies *eo ipso* the system itself. The fact that as a result of a new ordering, the system provides different solutions for the same specific cases shows that it is another system, not identical with the original one, *even if it contains the same elements* (norm-contents).

In spite of this, there is a widespread idea that derogation (which removes altogether certain norm-contents) is a far more fundamental operation than simple ordering, and that therefore the judge, although he can impose a new ordering or modify the existing one, cannot derogate legislated norm-contents for the same reasons that he cannot promulgate new norms. The idea is that as long as the system contains the same elements, it remains substantially identical, and so the judge who 'only' orders the elements of the system does not change it and hence does not exceed his powers. Consequently, ordering is regarded as a far more elastic and less permanent operation than derogation.

This idea, however, is mistaken. The impression that removing one or more propositions by derogation is somehow more fundamental and permanent than imposing an ordering on a system proves to be a mere illusion. A modification of the ordering is as fundamental as the removing of elements; indeed, *both procedures are substantially equivalent.*[36] Those norm-contents that are 'set aside' or disregarded by an ordering have as little application (as far as this ordering is concerned) as when they are derogated. As to the alleged permanence of derogation, there is no difference either. A derogation made by a legislature may last for a very short time if the legislature changes its mind and once again promulgates the derogated norm-content. On the other hand, an ordering imposed by a judge may enjoy a very long life if other judges adopt it as well. Thus, the question of temporal duration is quite irrelevant to this issue.

necessarily antisymmetric relation). The first alternative (partial ordering) is thoroughly studied in Alchourrón and Makinson (n. 31, this chapter).

[36] In the sense that to every derogation corresponds a (set of) ordering(s) and to every ordering corresponds a derogation. For a detailed proof, see Alchourrón and Makinson (n. 31, this chapter). They are, however, not quite identical: a partial ordering imposed on a system confers uniqueness upon otherwise indeterminate derogations by means of a process of ranking the various remainders.

The much debated problem of whether judges 'create' law or only apply it can be settled in favour of the first thesis, at least in the sense that they modify the legal system by imposing an ordering on its elements when they have to resolve contradictions, disregarding some of the norm-contents (which amounts to derogating them).

Nevertheless, although these two methods lead to substantially identical results (and this is what justifies calling them equivalent), they are two distinct methods, applied by different kinds of authorities (legislative authority in the case of derogation, judicial authority in the case of ordering). Both are designed to solve the same problem: the inconsistency of a normative system. This shows that inconsistency is indeed treated as a problem that calls for a resolution, and, hence, that there are contradictions as well as inconsistent systems.

7. Permission

For the imperative theory of norms (which is the most popular version of the expressive conception), there is only one type of normative act (commanding). Thus, there are only mandatory norms, prescribing acts and omissions and so giving rise to obligations and prohibitions. Permission appears to be a purely negative notion; it is the absence of prohibition. So there may be permitted states of affairs, but thus far there are neither permissory acts (that is, acts granting permission) nor permissory norms.

How can this theory explain acts granting permission or authorization? When Rex says 'I hereby allow (permit) that *p*', how is this speech act to be analysed?

There seem to be two possible ways out of this difficulty. (i) One way is to describe this act as the act of lifting a prohibition, that is, as the derogation of the prohibition of *p*. (ii) An alternative way is to accept a new kind of normative act, the act of giving or granting permission (in short, the act of permitting). If this is accepted, then it must also be accepted that there are two kinds of norm, mandatory norms and permissory norms (in the sense in which an expressivist uses the term 'norm'). A permissory norm—like a mandatory norm—is a meaningful sentence in its peculiar, that is, *permissory* use. Thus, the act of granting permission can be described as the act of issuing a permissory norm.[37]

These two proposals will be examined separately.

(i) The second analysis entails the explicit acceptance of a new kind of normative act, which is probably the reason it is less popular among expressivists who feel some affinity with Ockham. As has been argued in section 3, however, the first analysis also leads implicitly to the acceptance of a new normative act: the act of rejection. Since philosophers and logicians have so far paid comparatively little attention to the concept

[37] There are relatively few expressivists who accept this second interpretation. See Moritz, 'Permissive Sätze, Erlaubnissätze und deontische Logik' (n. 13, this chapter), who is one of the few.

of derogation, no full analysis of the act of rejection has been elaborated thus far.[38] This is a serious shortcoming of current expressive theories, for it is only with the recognition of the act of rejection as a fundamental, independent normative act that the expressive conception can give an account of such important concepts as derogation and permission. Once this is done, there are two different concepts of permission: *negative permission* (absence of prohibition) and *positive permission* (derogation of a prohibition).

Positive permission is linked to a positive act, the act of rejection, and so to a conflict of ambivalence. This conflict may be actual or merely potential if p has not been thus far prohibited. Once this conflict is resolved by giving priority to the rejection, the prohibition is eliminated (by subtraction), and p is permitted in the positive sense.

The main difference between negative and positive permission (apart from their different origins) appears to be that if p is negatively permitted, then, if an authority prohibits p, there is no conflict because $-p$ is added to the system, and in the new system it is no longer true that p is permitted. However, if p is positively permitted, any act of prohibiting p gives rise to a conflict of ambivalence that calls for a resolution. It will be true that p is prohibited (in the new system) only if this conflict is resolved in favour of the act of prohibiting.[39]

(ii) We turn now to the second analysis of sentences granting permission. For this analysis, there are two different acts: commanding and permitting, the promulgation of a mandatory norm and the promulgation of a permissory norm. Consequently, there are also two kinds of permission: the above-mentioned negative or weak permission (absence of prohibition) and the *strong permission,* granted by a permissory norm. Strong permission, like positive permission, is incompatible with prohibition, but here the conflict seems to be not of ambivalence but of a contradiction between two norms. Yet it must be observed that this contradiction is not the classic contradiction where p and $-p$ are both members of the commanded set. In our hypothesis $-p$ has been commanded, so $-p$ belongs to the commanded set, but p has not been commanded; it has been permitted. What happens with p as a result of its being permitted? It certainly cannot belong to the commanded set, for in that case it would be true that p is obligatory. In other words, how are we to construct the system, once

[38] There are, however, some valuable remarks on the subject. For example, Hare writes: 'Modal sentences containing the word "may" could, it seems, be represented by negating the neustic; thus "You may shut the door" (permissive) might be written "I don't tell you not to shut the door" and this in turn might be rendered "Your not shutting the door in the immediate future, not-please"'; Hare, *LM*, 20–1. If the negation of the neustic is taken to be a rejection—as was suggested in n. 24, this chapter—then Hare's proposal amounts to analysing the act of permitting in terms of rejection.

[39] Some authors interpret permissions as exceptions in a prohibitive norm. Thus, to permit would mean to introduce an exception into a prohibition. This can be explained as a partial derogation of the norm-content—that is, as a derogation of some of the consequences of the prohibitive norm.

we accept two kinds of promulgation? We cannot put together all the promulgated norm-contents, for we could then not distinguish between obligations and permissions. (For an expressivist, the difference can only lie in the kind of act of promulgating, not in the conceptual content of the act; if there were a difference in the proposition, this would mean the acceptance of the hyletic conception!) The only way out seems to be to form two sets: the set of commanded propositions (the commanded set *A*) and the set of permitted propositions (the permitted set *B*). Then, if we want a nonambivalent system, we must somehow unify both sets. It is clear that subtracting the permitted set from the commanded set will not do. What we want here is not to remove obligations but instead to remove prohibitions. Thus, if *p* is prohibited and hence –*p* is a member of *A*, and *p* is permitted as well and hence a member of *B*, what we must subtract from *A* is not *p* but its negation (–*p*). Therefore, the operation of unification requires subtracting from the commanded set the negations of the propositions that are members of the permitted set.[40] Therefore, if *p* is permitted, –*p* must be subtracted (eliminated from *A*), and vice versa. Thus the permission of *p* gives rise to the same operation as the rejection of –*p*.

At this stage one is tempted to ask: are there really two distinct analyses? What is the difference, if any, between issuing a permission and derogating a prohibition? What is the difference between the act of permitting *p* and the act of rejecting –*p*?

There are indeed very strong analogies between the two concepts.

(1) Commanding a proposition is incompatible with permitting its negation, exactly in the same way as commanding that *p* is incompatible with rejecting that *p*. In both cases we have a conflict of ambivalence (two incompatible attitudes regarding the same proposition).

(2) The set of the negations of permitted norm-contents (which is to be subtracted from the commanded set) is formally identical to the set of rejected propositions, for it is constructed in the same way.

(3) The operation of subtraction is the same: the identity of the subtrahend determines the identity of the remainder.

(4) Strong permission proves to be the same as positive permission.

One has the impression that both analyses are substantially equivalent in the sense that they are two different descriptions of the same situation. If this is so, it is a rather surprising result; it shows the fruitfulness of the concept of derogation and its importance for the theory of norms. The concept of a permissory norm can

[40] It would be pointless to form two sets, a set of permitted propositions and a set of their negations, just as it would be pointless to separate the commanded from the prohibited propositions. In both cases, we have the same attitude regarding two contradictory propositions.

be dispensed with, a fact that justifies the position of those expressivists who only accept mandatory norms, provided they accept the existence of derogation.

8. Conclusions

We are now in a position to draw some conclusions from the preceding analyses. We shall do so by comparing the hyletic and the expressive conceptions of norms (henceforth HC and EC).

(1) HC rests upon a very strong ontological presupposition of Platonic flavour: the assumption that there are prescriptive propositions. No such presupposition is needed for EC.

(2) The price that EC must pay for this advantage is the proliferation of illocutionary acts. It must distinguish between asserting and commanding on the one hand, and between two kinds of rejecting (descriptive and prescriptive rejection) on the other. For HC there are only two types of act, assertion and rejection, since commanding is just asserting an *O*-norm and permitting is just asserting a *P*-norm, and there is only one kind of rejection. What varies is the content of this act. It may be a descriptive proposition or it may be a prescriptive proposition, that is, a norm.

(3) EC can dispense with permissory norms since an account of acts granting permission can be given in terms of derogation (rejection and subtraction). For HC there can be permissory norms on the same level as mandatory norms (*O*-norms).

(4) For EC there are two kinds of incompatibility: conflicts between norm-contents (normative inconsistency, $!p$ and $!{-p}$) and conflicts between acts of promulgation and rejection (ambivalence, $!p$ and ¡p).

For HC there are two kinds of inconsistency between norms: the inconsistency between obligation and prohibition (Op and $O{-p}$) and the inconsistency between prohibition and permission ($O{-p}$ and Pp, or, what is the same, Op and $-Op$). Along with these two kinds of inconsistency between norms, there is the conflict of attitudes between promulgation and rejection (ambivalence). Whether the inconsistency between prohibition and permission is reducible to a conflict of ambivalence (as the analysis of section 7 suggests) may be regarded as an open question.

(5) For HC there are two logics: a logic of norms and a logic of normative propositions (a logic of promulgation and of derogation). The logic of norms is concerned with logical relations of prescriptive propositions (norms); it is a peculiarly normative logic.[41] The logic of normative propositions is concerned with logical relations of descriptive propositions about normative systems. Its aim is the development of a comprehensive logic of normative

[41] See Alchourrón (n. 16, this chapter); see also Alchourrón and Bulygin, *NS*.

systems that may be regarded as a special case of Alfred Tarski's logic of systems. Especially interesting would be a logic capable of rendering the dynamic character of normative systems, that is, their temporal development through acts of promulgation and derogation. (It scarcely need be added that at its present stage, deontic logic is far from having reached this aim.)[42]

(6) For EC there is only one possible logic: the logic of (descriptive) normative propositions in the same sense as for HC. This deontic logic looks very much like von Wright's 'classic' deontic logic,[43] but with two important differences. (i) Normative propositions are always relative to a definite normative system, hence the subscripts in formulae like $\mathbb{O}_A(p)$. (ii) The law of deontic subalternation $\mathbb{O}_A(p) \supset \mathbb{P}_A(p)$—analogous to von Wright's theorem $Op \rightarrow Pp$—does not hold without restrictions.[44] It does not hold for inconsistent systems, and one of the main contentions of this paper is that normative systems can be inconsistent. However, from what has been said in sections 6 and 7 of this paper, it follows that a system is consistent (i) if there is at least one derogated proposition, (ii) if the notion of consequence is restricted by an ordering relation imposed on the system,[45] and (iii) if there is at least one positively permitted proposition. (In fact, the three conditions amount to the same: derogation of at least one norm-content.) Thus, the conditions under which a system is consistent (and the law of deontic subalternation holds good) are extremely weak and easily obtainable.

[42] Some hints in this direction are to be found in Alchourrón and Makinson (n. 31, this chapter).

[43] Von Wright, 'DL'; von Wright, *An Essay in Deontic Logic and the General Theory of Action* (n. 18, this chapter).

[44] See E. J. Lemmon. 'Deontic Logic and the Logic of Imperatives', *Logiqué et Analyse*, 8 (1965), 39–71.

[45] See Alchourrón and Makinson (n. 31, this chapter).

10

Time and Validity (1982)*

1. Concepts of Validity

The term 'validity' as it is used in legal language in general, and by legal philosophers in particular, is ambiguous. With the assertion that a legal norm is valid, it is possible to distinguish several meanings of 'validity'.[1] In this paper I shall be concerned for the most part with two such meanings or, as we might also put it, with two concepts of validity—membership and applicability, as I shall call them. Both play a central role in legal practice and in legal theory.

A norm can be said to be valid in the sense that it belongs to (or is a member of) a legal system. This concept of validity is descriptive, for the sentence 'p is valid' is a descriptive proposition, not a norm.[2] Moreover, it is a relational concept: it is a relation between a norm and a system of norms; one and the same norm may be valid in a system S_1 and not valid in a different system S_2.

To establish the criteria for membership in a given system is an important and difficult task. One criterion is the competence of the authority that has created the norm: a norm is valid if it has been issued (enacted, promulgated) by a competent authority. (I shall not discuss the difficulties involved in the notion of competence here.) Sometimes, however, a norm is also considered as a member of a system if there is a firmly established practice to follow what it prescribes, or if it has been used by the courts to justify their decisions. So it is that different criteria for membership determine the various sources of law: legislation, custom, precedent, and so forth.

A norm is often also said to be valid in the sense that it is obligatory, that it has 'binding force'. This, in turn, may have two different meanings. It may mean a prescription to obey and to apply the norm, or it may mean a descriptive proposition that conveys a piece of information about the norm, namely, that it is obligatory

* [*Editors' note*: Eugenio Bulygin's paper was first published in *Deontic Logic, Computational Linguistics and Legal Information Systems*, ed. Antonio A. Martino (Amsterdam: North-Holland, 1982). Later, Professor Bulygin produced a Spanish version of the paper, which appeared in *ALD*, 195–214.]

[1] See von Wright, *NA*, at 194–202; J. W. Harris, *Law and Legal Science* (Oxford: Clarendon Press, 1979), at ch. 4 (107–31); Carlos Santiago Nino, *Introducción al análisis del derecho* (Buenos Aires: Astrea, 1980), at 132–41. [*Editors' note*: For this and other abbreviations, see the Table of Abbreviations.]

[2] Von Wright, *NA*, at 194–202, employs a different terminology. He uses 'normative validity' for what is referred to in this paper as a descriptive concept of validity, namely, membership.

according to some other norm. In the first case, we have a normative concept of validity. It is a non-relative notion, that is, an absolute notion. In this sense, to say that a norm is valid is to prescribe that it ought to be obeyed and applied. According to this sense, therefore, the sentence 'p is valid' is not a proposition; rather, it is a prescription, that is, a norm.

If there is a norm N_i prescribing that another norm N_j be obeyed and applied to a specific case, then N_j can be said to be valid in the sense that it ought to be obeyed and applied according to N_i. This concept of validity is also *relative*, but it counts as a triadic relation between the norms N_i and N_j, and a case C_3: norm N_i prescribes that norm N_j must be applied in case C_3. It is also a descriptive concept, for to say that a norm is valid in this sense is not to issue a prescription but to state the existence of a prescription according to which the norm in question must be applied to a case. Here the sentence 'p is valid' is again a descriptive proposition, although it makes reference to a norm. I shall use the term 'applicability' to refer to this third concept of validity. So we have at least three different concepts of validity: one is normative and two are descriptive (membership and applicability).

It is not easy to determine how the concepts of membership and applicability are related. Before taking up this question it is necessary to analyse in greater detail the concept of membership.

The characterization of membership just provided—although it reflects a very widespread view among legal philosophers and philosophers interested in norms[3]—is clearly incomplete, for it does not take into account the phenomenon of derogation. It is a well-known fact that legal norms can be cancelled or repealed. What consequences does the derogation of a norm have for its membership? It seems natural to assume that a norm, once derogated, ceases to be a member of the system; the opposite view would mean that all legal systems are full of inconsistencies, for when a legislature enacts a new statute, it is almost always incompatible with certain norms that it derogates. Thus, to regard derogated norms as members of a system seems to lead to disastrous results.[4] Therefore, it appears to be convenient to relativize the concept of a system to a given temporal moment. A legal system at a moment t_1 will be, according to this criterion, the set of all norms that became members of the system at some time before or at t_1 (according to certain criteria for membership) and that have not been derogated before t_1. Thus, a legal system becomes a momentary system.[5]

If a legal system is to be conceived as a set (for example, a set of norms),[6] then it must be a momentary system. However, the expressions 'legal system'

[3] See Kelsen, *GTLS*; Kelsen, *RR 2*; von Wright, *NA*.

[4] In § 5, certain arguments put forward against this view will be discussed in detail.

[5] Joseph Raz, to my knowledge, was the first to call attention to this point. See Raz, *CLS*, at 34–5, for a distinction between legal systems and momentary legal systems that is close to my distinction between 'legal order' and 'legal system' respectively.

[6] In most cases a legal system contains not only norms, but also other kinds of sentences. At this stage we can disregard this complication.

and 'legal order' are often used in a different, broader sense, namely, to refer to a temporal sequence of different sets of norms. In order to avoid this ambiguity I shall introduce the following terminological convention. By 'legal system' I shall understand a set of norms valid at a certain moment in time according to certain criteria for membership, whereas the expression 'legal order' will always be used to refer to a sequence of legal systems. Thus, a legal order is not a set of norms, but a family of such sets. All momentary systems within a given period of time belong to it.[7]

In this paper I shall mainly be concerned with the problem of applicability, which can be formulated by means of the following question: which norms are applicable to a given case, that is, which norms should be applied to it? This question refers to the temporal dimension of norms, so we must focus with greater care on the multiple relations between legal norms and time.

2. External and Internal Time

Whenever a new norm becomes a member of a legal system, we obtain a different system because the set of norms that are members of it is different (unless the new norm is completely redundant—in which case it is not a 'new' norm). Sometimes the temporal point of the introduction of a norm can be located with great precision, as in the case of legislative enactment. On other occasions there is no such definite moment, as in the case of customary norms. Even there, however, it is possible to mark two temporal moments, such that the customary norm did not exist at the first moment and exists at the second moment. Of course there will always be a more or less lengthy interval between the two moments during which a question about the existence of a customary norm cannot be settled either way.

The same is true of the derogation of a norm. Except in cases of purely formal derogation, where what is derogated is only a redundant norm-formulation and not a norm, each act of derogation leads to a new system. If the legislative authority substitutes a new norm for an existing norm, I shall say that two simultaneous acts take place—one of derogation and one of promulgation. In this case, the introduction of a new norm and the elimination of an existent norm occur at the same time. This is what usually happens in legislation.

The interval between the two temporal moments during which some norm is introduced and/or removed will be called the external time of a legal system. To

[7] It is not clear whether, for Raz, a legal order (a legal system, in his terminology) is a class of momentary legal systems or a class of norms, that is, whether the relation between a momentary legal system and a legal order is that of membership or of inclusion. Thus he speaks of a momentary legal system as being a subclass of a legal system, but on the same page he also says that a momentary legal system belongs to a legal system. See Raz, *CLS*, at 35. This is, at any rate, a terminological inconsistency.

each interval of external time there corresponds one legal system.[8] According to the definition of the external time, no two consecutive systems are identical, but the non-consecutive systems need not be different, although in reality they usually are different. Although they are not identical, they may have and usually do have a great many common elements. One and the same norm may belong to many different systems, consecutive or not.

The life span or existence of a norm may be characterized as the sequence of all external moments in time at which this norm is a member of the corresponding legal system. It follows that the existence of a norm need not be continuous: a norm may exist during an interval t_1—t_2, disappear at t_2 and reappear at t_3, and so on. This shows that we can distinguish between the existence of a norm in a system, where 'existence' means the membership of the norm in the system in question, and the existence of a norm in a legal order. Here 'existence' means membership in some system of that order.

The period of time during which a norm exists in an order will be called the external time of a norm. It follows that systems have a far more ephemeral existence than norms.

Norms, however, also make reference to temporal events. The time at which the different events relevant to a case take place is determinant of the applicability of norms to that case. The sequence of all temporal moments at which a norm is applicable to some case may be called the internal time of a norm. The time of a norm is a function of its membership in a system, internal time is a function of its applicability.

The external time and the internal time of a norm do not necessarily coincide. A norm may exist in a system or in several consecutive systems without being applicable, and, vice versa, it may be applicable at a time t_1 without being a member of the system corresponding to t_1. The first case is exemplified by a statute enacted at t_1 that stipulates that it will be in force only from t_2. This is a relatively frequent occurrence. For instance, the Argentine Criminal Code was promulgated on 29 October 1921, but by virtue of its article 303, it only became applicable six months later, on 29 April 1922. During this interval the Code existed—that is, it was a member of the successive systems—but it was not applicable to any case and only became applicable after 29 April 1922. The second case is exemplified by a derogated statute that is still applicable, for example, when a decision concerns an offence committed during the time the statute was in force but the court has to decide the case at a time at which the statute no longer exists, that is to say, is not a member of the system that corresponds to the moment of decision.

[8] It would be more accurate to say 'at least one', for there are situations in which more than one system corresponds to the same point in time. See Carlos E. Alchourrón and Eugenio Bulygin, 'Unvollständigkeit, Widersprüchlichkeit und Unbestimmtheit der Normenordnungen', in *Deontische Logik und Semantik*, ed. Amedeo G. Conte, et al. (Wiesbaden: Athenaion, 1977), 20–32; Carlos E. Alchourrón and Eugenio Bulygin, 'Incompletezza, contraddittorieta e indeterminatezza degli ordinamenti normativi', in *Lógica deóntica e semantica*, ed. Giuliano di Bernardo (Bologna: Il Mulino, 1977), 291–306.

Thus, although there may be a partial or even a total overlapping of the external and internal times of a norm, the two concepts are different and have to be carefully distinguished.

3. Criteria for Applicability

According to a very widespread view, there is, among the various systems of a legal order, one that occupies a privileged position: it is the system corresponding to the present moment (henceforth called S_p), for its norms alone are applicable. From the point of view of a judge, the system S_p is the one that corresponds to the moment of his decision. (It is the last link in the chain of systems, although of course the term 'last' is egocentric and refers to different times on each occasion of its use.)

As we shall see later in the paper, there is a sense in which the present system S_p is indeed a privileged one, but not in the way just suggested. As every judge knows very well from his own experience, it is frequently the case that he must apply a norm that has already been derogated but that still retains its applicability. How, then, is he to decide which of the various and incompatible norms belonging to different systems of the same order are to be applied to the case submitted for his decision? There are certain criteria that vary from one field of law to another, which are usually found in the law itself.

Let us consider an example taken from the field of Argentine Criminal Law. The general principle is the non-retroactivity of criminal law, expressed in the well-known aphorism *nullum crimen sine lege*. This principle—included as article 18 of the Argentine Constitution—admits of different interpretations.[9] As an expression of the non-retroactivity principle, however, it means that a criminal law is not to be applied to offences committed before the enactment of the law creating the offence.

This implies the applicability of the law that was in force at the time of the performance of the action, that is, the so-called 'ultra-activity' of criminal law. It is obligatory that a criminal law be applied to all those offences that were committed during its existence, even if the judgments respecting these offences were handed down after its derogation. Here we have, therefore, a typical case of the applicability of a norm that is no longer valid (that is to say, is non-existent). This result may sound paradoxical if expressed in terms of validity, for then a norm is valid and not valid at the same time, but the air of paradox vanishes once the ambiguity of the term 'validity' is uncovered.

There are, however, other principles that greatly limit the applicability of this general principle. In practice, its applicability is reduced to the hypothesis of an act that did not incur criminal liability at the time it took place but that is considered an offence by a later law or to which a later law attaches a more severe

[9] See Alchourrón and Bulygin, *NS*, at 140–3.

punishment. What happens, however, when the later law establishes a less severe punishment?

According to article 2 of the Argentine Criminal Code, the later norm in such a case is to be preferred, that is, the new norm must be applied even if this means leaving aside the principle of non-retroactivity. Moreover, if in the interval between the time of the offence and the moment of decision there was a norm establishing a lesser penalty, this less severe norm must be applied regardless of the fact that it had been derogated before the decision took place and does not therefore belong to the system S_p.

This is not yet the end of the story. There is an exception to the rule respecting the less severe punishment in the case of temporary laws, that is, laws enacted for a limited period of time that establish a definite date for their own expiration. In such a case, it is considered[10] that offences committed during the period of time in which the temporary law was in force must be punished according to it, even if the decision takes place after its expiration and the validity of ordinary legislation—which is by hypothesis less severe—has been restored. This sounds reasonable, for the temporary law would otherwise have limited application.

Combining the three principles (the constitutional principle *nullum crimen*, article 2 of the Criminal Code, and the principle regarding temporary laws) we obtain the following criteria for the applicability of a criminal law:

a) If at the moment the act took place, it was not an incriminating act, the accused must be absolved of criminal liability.
b) The judge must compare all the laws concerning the incriminating act that belong to the various systems corresponding to all temporal moments of the external time, from the moment of the performance of the act to the moment of the decision.
c) If the law corresponding to the moment of the offence is a temporary law, then it should be preferred to all other norms.
d) If this is not the case, then the norm that attaches a less severe punishment to the offence in question is to be preferred to all others, regardless of whether or not it has already been derogated at the moment of the decision.

The existence of a less severe norm that was derogated before the offence was committed is, of course, irrelevant. This is not so, however, for the promulgation of a less severe norm after the verdict of the judge. In such a case the punishment must be reduced—according to article 2, Criminal Code—by applying the new norm, provided the punishment has not yet been carried out.

Of interest is the fact that even if all the norms that the judge must take into account, save for the last one, have been derogated by the time the decision is taken, this is absolutely irrelevant to the judge's choice. The fact that a norm belongs to S_p is by no means dispositive on the question of applicability, but the criteria for

[10] See Sebastián Soler, *Derecho Penal Argentino* (first publ. 1940), 4th edn., 5 vols. (Buenos Aires: Tipográfica Editora Argentina,1970), vol. 1, at 194–7.

applicability must belong to the system that is in force at the moment the decision is taken, that is, system S_p.

My last assertion requires qualification. The following objection might be raised. It is not enough—hence the objection—that the criteria for applicability are to be members of S_p; they must also be applicable at the moment the decision is taken. This is in part true; some criteria for applicability may exist without being applicable. Take the case of article 2, Criminal Code. According to article 303, the Criminal Code became applicable six months after its promulgation. During this interval, article 2, like the rest of the Code, was a member of the corresponding systems but was not applicable. This suggests that there are criteria of a higher level for the applicability of the criteria for applicability. Indeed, article 303 is a third-level criterion: it is the ultimate criterion for the applicability of the Criminal Code. There is an important difference between article 2 and article 303: the former existed during a period of time without being applicable, but article 303 was applicable from the very moment of its promulgation, for it refers to all articles of the Criminal Code except to itself. Although it does not state this exception, the exception is implicit in its meaning. So it seems that for the ultimate criteria for applicability, such as article 303, there is no difference between external and internal time. Whenever they exist, they are applicable. In each area of law there are some ultimate criteria for applicability, and these ultimate criteria must be members of S_p.

In this sense, but only in this sense, system S_p does indeed occupy a privileged position among all the systems of a legal order. The judge must first identify this particular system and, in particular, its criteria for applicability, although these criteria will often direct him to norms that are no longer valid, that is, norms that do not belong to S_p but that he nevertheless has an obligation to apply.

The criteria for applicability may be of different origins. They may be stated by a statute (as in the case of article 2, Criminal Code) or by a constitution (as in the case of the principle *nullum crimen*), established by judicial practice or even by the *communis opinio* of legal theorists. Whatever their source, they appear in the form of directives given to the court to determine which norms ought to be applied in a given case, so they are norms concerning the applicability of other norms pertaining to different systems of one and the same legal order. In this sense, these directives are norms of a higher level, meta-norms, imposing obligations on judges to apply certain first-level norms. The ultimate criteria for applicability are norms of a still higher level.

To impose obligations on judges is not the only function of the criteria for applicability, although they are usually formulated as directives addressed to the judge. At the same time, they identify the temporal moments to which those systems that must be taken into account correspond. The judge must compare the relevant norms belonging to all these systems in order to establish which of them are to be applied. The selection of norms that are applicable to a case is based on certain hierarchical relations between these norms. These hierarchical relations between norms pertaining to different systems of the same order can be based on the specific content of the norms involved (such as the degree of punishment) or on purely 'formal' properties, such as the date of issuance or the hierarchy of the issuing authority, and so forth. It is well to emphasize that in our example the familiar principle *lex posterior derogat priori*, which gives preference to a more recent law over an older law, has no application (although it is widely used to determine which norms are members of a given system). Nor does the principle *lex superior* retain its usual force. The example shows how some implications of a constitutional rule such as *nullum crimen* are set aside by a statute (article 2, Criminal Code).

As a rule, these hierarchical relations are constituted by the criteria for applicability themselves. They establish certain ordering relations and impose on judges the duty to employ certain hierarchies in preference to others. Thus, at least *two* components may be distinguished in them: (i) a statement of a hierarchical relation, which is not a norm, and (ii) a duty-imposing norm at a higher level that prescribes the choice of a given hierarchy and the application of the norm that is superior according to this hierarchy.

To summarize: criteria for applicability fulfil three functions. (1) By setting the relevant moments in time, they determine which norms must be compared; these are norms belonging to the systems that correspond to those moments. (2) They establish the hierarchical relations between norms belonging to different systems (of the same legal order), relations that are transitive and asymmetric, just as all ordering relations are. (3) They impose on judges the obligation to apply the norm that proves to be superior to the others in accordance with these hierarchical relations.

This shows that the concept of a legal system as a set of norms is too narrow. A legal system contains norms at different levels, and it also contains hierarchical relations between norms of the same system and between norms of different systems of the same order.[11] Norms at the first level (primary rules in Hart's terminology) impose obligations and prohibitions on legal subjects and grant them permissions or authorizations. Norms at higher levels (secondary rules in Hart's terminology) confer powers, both public and private, and impose obligations on judges and other law-applying officials.[12] Third-level norms regulate the applicability of second-level norms.

4. A Controversial Case

In the preceding section, the situation of criminal law in Argentina was offered as an example of the criteria for applicability and the ways in which they operate. In other areas of law the criteria may be different, but the situation—in all relevant aspects—is similar to the one examined. There are criteria that in certain

[11] The ordering relations between norms as well as between sets of norms of the same system are analysed by Carlos E. Alchourrón, 'Normative Order and Derogation', in *Deontic Logic, Computational Linguistics and Legal Information Systems*, ed. Antonio A. Martino (Amsterdam: North-Holland, 1982), 51–63.

[12] There may be, of course, and as a matter of fact there usually are other elements as well (e.g. definitions), so that this enumeration is by no means exhaustive. On definitions in law, see Antonio A. Martino, *Le definizioni legislative* (Turin: G. Giappichelli, 1975).

circumstances give preference to a former (already derogated) norm over the norm pertaining to the system S_p (ultra-activity of a norm). In other circumstances, a norm that exists in S_p must be applied to cases that took place before it became a member of the system (retroactivity of a norm). These relations of preference may be based on different criteria. In the civil law it is often the case that the judge must apply a norm that was valid at the moment a contract was signed or a norm that belonged to some intermediate stage. In Argentine law, in a labour contract where the issue is the legality of an act of dismissal, the norm that must be applied is the norm that was valid at the moment the dismissal took place, not the norm that existed when the contract was signed and not the norm corresponding to S_p either. The criteria for applicability, however, must always belong to the system corresponding to the moment of the decision (S_p).

There is no need to discuss all the different criteria for applicability that can be found in different areas of law, but I should like to examine a much debated and controversial case taken from constitutional law in which the conceptual distinctions outlined in this paper seem to be useful in solving the problem.

It is the problem raised by Alf Ross[13] concerning the possibility of amending the rule of a constitution that contains provisions for amending the constitution. Ross raised the question of whether the amending article can be reformed and, if so, by means of what procedure. It seems that the only procedure for constitutional amendment is the one established by the constitution itself in the article in question. Can this article be amended according to the procedure it regulates?

According to Ross, such a rule of amendment cannot be altered according to the procedure established by itself, and since by hypothesis this is the only procedure, it cannot be amended by any legal procedure at all. Any change of the rule of amendment must be regarded as an original law-creating fact, that is, as a breach of the continuity of a legal order qua revolutionary act. The validity of the new constitution cannot be derived from the former constitution.

Ross gives two independent reasons in support of his thesis. He argues on the one hand that if the rule of amendment were applied to itself, it would be self-referential, and this, according to Ross, is impossible, for it cannot be squared with the 'logical theorem' according to which self-referring sentences are devoid of meaning. He holds, on the other hand, that reform of the rule of amendment in accordance with its own provisions involves a contradiction.

In this paper I shall be concerned only with Ross's second argument. The first one, based on the lack of meaning of self-referring sentences, has been discussed extensively.[14] It should be said that the existence of a general logical theorem that proscribes self-referring sentences is rather doubtful, although there may of

[13] See Ross, *LJ*, at 78–84; Alf Ross, 'On Self-reference and a Puzzle in Constitutional Law', *Mind*, 78 (1969) 1–24.

[14] H. L. A. Hart, 'Self-referring Laws', in *Festskrift tillägnad Professor, Juris Doktor Karl Olivecrona*, ed. Fritjof Lejman, et al. (Stockholm: P. A. Norstedt & Söner, 1964), 307–16, in Hart, *EJP*, at 170–8. See also Karl R. Popper, 'Self Reference and Meaning', *Mind*, 63 (1954), 162–9, at 166; Joseph Raz, 'Professor A. Ross and Some Legal Puzzles', *Mind*, 81 (1972), 415–21; Norbert Hoerster, 'On Alf Ross's Alleged Puzzle in Constitutional Law', *Mind*, 81 (1972), 422–6.

course be such theorems in certain logical systems, but clearly not in all of them. Furthermore, it seems reasonable to accept the idea that at least some self-referring sentences are perfectly meaningful.[15]

In order to prove that the idea of amending the rule of amendment according to itself leads to a contradiction, Ross takes up—using as an example article 88 of the Danish Constitution—the following pattern of legal reasoning (which I render here in a slightly simplified version):

(1) article 88: The constitution may be amended by the procedure Q and only by this procedure;

(2) article 88' (stating that the constitution may be amended by procedure R and only by this procedure) has been created in accordance with procedure Q;

(3) article 88' is valid, that is, the constitution may be amended by a process in accordance with procedure R and only by this procedure.

Ross's comment on this inference is as follows: 'As the meaning of art. 88 is to indicate *the only way* in which the constitution may be amended, this is an inference in which the conclusion contradicts one of the premisses, which is a logical absurdity.'[16]

In order to determine whether there is really a contradiction between (1) and (3) and what is entailed by such a contradiction if it exists, it is important to establish with greater precision the meaning of the crucial terms 'amendment' and 'valid'. As noted earlier, the term 'valid' can express three different concepts: membership, binding force, and applicability.

The constitutional amendment may consist of (i) an elimination of some article of the constitution as a result of an act of repealing or derogating the norm expressed in that article, (ii) an addition of some new article as a result of an act of promulgating a new norm, and (iii) a combination of both, that is, the suppression of certain articles and the addition of others (possibly to replace the derogated norms). This is the most frequent case.

It might be said that a constitutional amendment consists of the derogation of some norm belonging to the constitution and/or the promulgation of some new constitutional norms. Derogation and promulgation of norms have an obvious bearing on the *membership* of those norms to the constitution. It is, however, misleading to speak here of 'the constitution'. If a constitutional norm has been repealed and is therefore no longer a member of the constitution after t_1, is it the *same* constitution both before and after t_1? Or are there two different constitutions? The same question may be raised regarding the promulgation of new constitutional norms: if a new norm has been added to the constitution of t_1, is the resulting constitution the same one that was there before t_1?

If by 'constitution' we understand a set of norms (the set of articles that are part of it, from the first to the last one, for example), then it is clear that every

[15] See Hart, 'Self-referring Laws' (n. 14, this chapter).

[16] Ross, 'On Self-reference and a Puzzle in Constitutional Law' (n. 13, this chapter), 5 (emphasis in original).

elimination and every addition of an article give rise to a change of the constitution; the resulting constitution is *different* from the original one. Suppose, for example, that the constitution containing article 88—henceforth C_1—is amended at t_1 according to the process established in article 88 and that this amendment consists of the substitution of article 88' for article 88. In such a case, the constitution C_1 ceases to exist at t_1 and another constitution C_2 that contains 88' instead of 88 is substituted for it. The fact that the only difference between the two constitutions is that article 88 has been replaced by article 88' (all other articles have by hypothesis remained unchanged) is irrelevant to the criterion for identity we have adopted, which coincides with the one in fact used by jurists, at least for the most part. Two constitutions that contain different provisions (regardless of their number) are two different constitutions; the content of a constitution cannot change without changing its identity.

In our example the amendment consists of the substitution of article 88' for article 88. Therefore, the amending authority has performed two acts, that of derogating article 88 and that of promulgating article 88'. Both acts occurred simultaneously, that is, at t_1. There is no mystery at all regarding the validity of the two norms if by 'validity' we understand their membership in the constitution or, more accurately, in the respective constitutions. Article 88 belongs to the constitution C_1, but C_1 ceases to exist at t_1. Article 88' belongs to C_2, which comes into existence at t_1. All we need for the validity, in the sense of membership, of a norm N_i is that it should be created in accordance with another norm N_j, which is a member of the system at the time of the promulgation of N_i. The fact that N_j is derogated after or even simultaneously with the promulgation of N_i is irrelevant for the membership of N_i.

It seems that Ross is using the term 'valid' in this context in the sense of normative validity. Indeed, referring to the inference pattern 'A norm is valid, when created in accordance with conditions C; the norm N has been created in accordance with conditions C; so the norm N is valid', Ross states explicitly that '[t]he first premise is really a norm prescribing an obligation to obey the norms created in the way indicated, and the conclusion is also a directive.'[17] What is more, only if 'valid' means normative validity is it legitimate to infer, as Ross does, that '"p" is valid, so p' (article 88' is valid, that is, the constitution may be amended in accordance with procedure R and only by means of this procedure). Indeed, normative validity behaves like the concept of truth ('"p" is true, so p' is a valid inference), but the descriptive concepts of validity do not behave in this way. Neither from '"p" is a member of S' nor from '"p" is applicable according to q' does it follow that p.

Ross's argument purports to show that the normative validity of article 88' derives from article 88. The 'directive or deontic' inference, as Ross calls it, seems to be logically valid, but article 88', the conclusion, is incompatible with article 88, the first premiss, and this is the cause of the difficulty mentioned by Ross.

[17] Ross, 'On Self-reference and a Puzzle in Constitutional Law' (n. 13, this chapter), 5.

Let us observe, in the first place, that articles 88 and 88' never coexist at the same time: they do not belong to the same system but are members of two different constitutions. Thus, if there is a contradiction between these two norms, it is not a contradiction within a system but instead a contradiction between two norms pertaining to two different systems. This is a very common case, and there is nothing odd about it. There would be a conflict within a system only if article 88 should continue to exist after the promulgation of article 88'. Ross seems to have had in mind something along these lines when, in his first statement of the puzzle, he says: 'Any such derivation presupposes the *continued existence* of the same…'.[18] Hart rightly objected to this,[19] and Ross, in his paper published in *Mind*, tacitly accepts this criticism. At any rate, he drops the requirement of the continued existence of article 88 and distinguishes thereby between legal and logical contradiction. He grants that 'there is no contradiction *in law*, because article 88' supersedes article 88.'[20] However, he insists that there is a logical contradiction between the conclusion and one of the premisses of a logically valid argument. This he calls an absurdity.

To say that a logically valid inference in which the conclusion contradicts one of the premisses is a logical absurdity is certainly an exaggeration. Far from being absurd, it is a useful and frequently used form of reasoning, called *argumentum ad absurdum*. All it shows is that the premiss in question must be false, and this may be a very important piece of information. However, an argument with a false premiss is not a *sound* argument, and in this sense Ross is right. An unsound argument fails to establish the truth of its conclusion, and even if the conclusion happens to be true, its truth is not derived from its premisses.

In a prescriptive argument, like the one under consideration, neither the first premiss nor the conclusion is a proposition. Rather, they are norms, and as such they lack truth-values. It is natural, however, to assume that validity plays here a role similar to that of truth, and then it would indeed follow that the validity of article 88' is not derived from article 88. Thus, if there were a contradiction between (1) and (3), Ross's contention that article 88 cannot be amended according to its own provisions would hold, because the new article 88' could not be derived—in so far as its normative validity is concerned—from article 88.

I doubt that there is such a contradiction. Ross maintains that (1) and (3) contradict each other because (1) prescribes that the constitution may only be amended by procedure Q and (3) prescribes that the constitution may only be amended by procedure R. However, Ross overlooks the fact that 'the constitution' mentioned in article 88 is not the same constitution as that referred to by article 88'. Indeed, (1) prescribes that the constitution C_1 may only be amended by procedure Q, whereas (3) prescribes that the constitution C_2 may only be amended by procedure R. Thus, articles 88 and 88' refer to two different constitutions, and there is no

[18] Ross, *LJ*, 82 (emphasis added). [19] See Hart, 'Self-referring Laws' (n. 14, this chapter).

[20] See Ross, 'On Self-reference and a Puzzle in Constitutional Law' (n. 13, this chapter), at 21 (emphasis in original).

contradiction at all between them. Once we distinguish explicitly between the two constitutions, the alleged contradiction vanishes.[21]

Finally, there is the question of applicability. Would it be correct to say that article 88 was applicable until the moment t_1 and article 88' after that moment? Certainly not, for as with all other norms, a constitutional norm may very well still be applicable after its derogation. Article 88' is only applicable to a case of amendment if it occurs after t_1 and not before. The legality of an amendment made at t_2 must be judged according to the dispositions of article 88', but an amendment made before t_1 or at t_1 must be judged according to article 88, even if the problem of the legality of the act of amendment is submitted to the courts after t_1. Thus, the general criterion for the applicability of articles 88 and 88' is this: article 88 is applicable to all acts of amendment performed during the existence of C_1 (that is, before t_1 or at t_1), and article 88' is applicable to all acts of amendment that occur after t_1, during the time C_2 is in effect, and this quite apart from the question as to when the problem of applicability is raised, that is, whether before or after the norms have been derogated.

It follows that the courts must give preference to the rule of amendment that existed at the time the amendment was passed, regardless of whether or not this rule had been derogated at the moment the decision was taken. Situations in which derogated norms must be applied are very common in the areas of criminal law and civil law, and are also found in constitutional law. Suppose, for example, that at some moment after t_1 the question of the constitutionality of a statute enacted before t_1 is brought before a court. The norms applicable in answering this question are those of C_1 and not of C_2, even if at the point in time at which the court must take a decision the constitution C_1 has ceased to govern and C_2 is in force.

The new constitution C_2 derives its normative validity from article 88 of constitution C_1, but the applicability of article 88' cannot be derived from C_1 because—as argued in the preceding section—the criteria for applicability that are applied by the judge must be in effect at the time of the decision, even when those criteria refer to derogated norms.

5. Derogation and Existence

The question may be raised as to what effects the derogation of a norm produces where its validity is concerned. It should be clear from our earlier discussion that derogation does not necessarily deprive the norm of its applicability. What about its existence or membership?

Throughout the whole discussion I have proceeded on the assumption that as a consequence of its derogation, a norm ceases to exist in the sense that it is no longer a member of subsequent systems. This assumption leads to a somewhat

[21] This was pointed out by Hoerster, 'On Alf Ross's Alleged Puzzle in Constitutional Law' (n. 14, this chapter).

unexpected result: the applicability of non-existent norms. To say that a judge has an obligation to apply a norm that no longer exists sounds odd. I believe, however, that this result is less paradoxical than it appears; after all, the norm in question does not exist in the system corresponding to the moment of the decision, but it exists within the legal order because it was a member of some earlier system. Yet many jurists would probably feel uneasy about this description of the situation. Could this consequence not be avoided by shaping our concepts in a different way? The very fact that a derogated norm may still retain its applicability might be used as an argument against the thesis of its non-existence.

An alternative explanation of the facts can be presented in the following terms.[22] A norm exists (that is, is a member of a system) so long as it is applicable. Thus, a derogated norm—provided it is still applicable to certain cases—has not been eliminated from the system. It continues to be a member of the system although its applicability has been restricted by derogation to a more limited range of cases; for example, it might no longer be applicable to future cases. Thus, derogation only limits the applicability of a norm but does not deprive it of its existence in a system because it does not remove the norm altogether from the system. Only in a limiting case where the derogated norm has no application whatsoever does it cease to be a member of the system in question. This means that derogated norms coexist with new norms in the same system, and, since they are usually incompatible, possible conflicts are avoided by assigning to them different areas of applicability. The old norm is applicable to a certain range of cases, whereas the new norm must be applied in other cases.

This suggestion amounts to shaping the concept of the existence of a norm (and hence the concept of a system of norms) in such a way that existence becomes a function of applicability: in order to know what norms are members of a given system of law, one must know what norms are applicable. Then, however, we must be prepared to say that the existence of a norm does not begin from the moment of its promulgation but instead from the moment of its applicability. Thus, we are committed to saying that the Argentine Criminal Code did not exist until April 1922 although it was duly passed in October 1921.

Since there seems to be no established usage in legal parlance on this point, this result is not particularly surprising. In other cases, however, the same criterion might well lead to more problematic results. Take the case of a contract signed today by Ticius and Sempronius, according to which Sempronius must perform a certain action *p* tomorrow. Sempronius has no obligation to do *p* today; the contract does not give rise to any obligation until tomorrow. Not until tomorrow is Sempronius obligated to do *p*. Shall we say that the contract does not exist today and will first come into existence tomorrow? This mode of speech sounds rather strange, and it is likely to conflict with widespread linguistic usage. Most lawyers

[22] This explanation was suggested to me by Ricardo A. Guibourg during a discussion of an earlier version of this paper, read at SADAF (Sociedad Argentina de Análisis Filosófico) in September 1980.

would probably describe the situation by saying that the contract already exists today although it will not have any effects until tomorrow. Even more odd would be the case of a will. A will does not produce any effects *until* the testator has died, but it would be extremely misleading to say that a will does not exist, not because the person in question failed to make it, but simply because he is still alive. In any case, even before their respective deaths, there seems to be a rather important difference between Sempronius, who has drawn up a will, and Ticius, who has not. On the assumption that existence is a function of applicability, we cannot describe this difference in terms of the actual existence of Sempronius's will and the non-existence of Ticius's will, which would be the natural way of describing the situation.

It seems that the view I am considering leads to a far greater disagreement with respect to ordinary legal discourse. On the other hand, in order to establish the legality of a will, we must resort to norms that exist in the system at the time the will was made and not at the moment at which it becomes applicable. The same is true of a contract.

Still more important seems to be the following argument against the view that renders existence a function of applicability: the criteria for applicability are to be found in the law, not necessarily in the enacted or written law, but in the legal material supplied by different sources of law. Moreover, as has been argued in section 3, they must belong to the system corresponding to the present time (S_p), that is, to the last system of the series of systems pertaining to a legal order. Thus, in order to avoid circularity, jurists must be able to identify this system by means of some independent criterion that is not one of the criteria for applicability. Therefore, the concept of existence in a system must be independent of the concept of applicability and not a function of it. If this is so, then it must be accepted that the derogation of a norm leads to its removal and that a legal system is the set of all norms that have been hitherto validly created and not derogated.

Finally, even if we accept the contention that a norm exists in a system for as long as it is applicable to some cases, we cannot conclude that it is the same norm that continues to exist after its derogation. If at t_1 there is a norm applicable to a certain type of case (including future cases) and at t_2 this norm has been derogated and is therefore no longer applicable to the same cases (for example, to future cases), is it still the same norm?

I think it would be correct to say that it is not the same norm. The norm N has been replaced by the norm N', which has the same content except that its range of applicability is different, and this is enough to assert that they are different norms. Indeed, two norms with the same content, but with the proviso that there are cases to which one is applicable and the other is not, are certainly not identical. So it cannot be maintained that there is one and the same norm, and we should say instead that there are two similar but not identical norms. Thus, a derogation of a norm removes it from the system after all. The difference between the two descriptions lies in the content of the new system (after derogation). According to the first description, the new system does not contain the derogated norm (which may still be applicable, however, to certain cases), and, if a new norm has been issued to replace the derogated one, then the new system contains this new norm. According to the second description, the derogated norm does not belong to the new system (in this the two descriptions coincide), but the new system contains a new norm similar to the derogated norm and, possibly, two new norms, one of which is incompatible with the derogated norm. It would seem that the second description presupposes a rather cumbersome and artificial construction.

6. Conclusions

The main purpose of this paper was to characterize the set of norms *applicable to a case* and to trace the criteria that govern the applicability of norms. In the course of the analysis it became clear that, contrary to a very popular view (at least among legal philosophers), this set is not necessarily a subset of the set of norms existent at the moment when the case is considered, that is, the set of norms corresponding to this particular moment. Nor is it necessarily a subset of some other system, corresponding to some prior moment. In fact, it may be and often is a *selection* from various systems that correspond to different temporal points of the external time of a legal order. In other words, it is a selection from a family of legal systems.

The law provides criteria for the identification of the temporal points to which the systems that must be taken into account correspond. Of all these points there is one that is particularly important: it is the moment at which the case is considered, because the criteria for applicability must belong to the system corresponding to that moment (system S_p). These criteria may then direct one, however, to other systems corresponding to various relevant moments—for instance, to the moment when the offence was committed, to all intermediate systems in the case of the Argentine Criminal Code, or, as in the civil law, to moments corresponding to different events, such as the making of a contract, its fulfilment by one of the parties, its breach, and so forth.

The identification of the relevant systems is only a first step. The next step consists in taking the norms belonging to all these systems and comparing them. There are certain hierarchical relations between the norms, established by the criteria for applicability. These are ordering relations that indicate which norm in every pair of norms is, in some sense, superior to the other member of the pair, and, by virtue of their transitivity (as ordering relations they are transitive and asymmetric), it is possible to determine which norm is superior to all the others (provided that the relation in question is strong enough).

Finally, there are norms (of a higher level) that rule the selection, prescribing the duty to choose certain hierarchical relations and so to give preference to norms that are hierarchically superior according to that relation.

In this way, the problem of determining the set of norms applicable to a case is yet another instance of the more general problem of selecting a set of norms from a family of sets by means of internal relations.[23] Here we have a case of ordering norms regarding time.

The paper also shows the importance of distinguishing between different concepts that are misleadingly covered by the ambiguous term 'validity'. Problems relating to the applicability of norms require separate treatment and should not be confused with problems regarding membership or the existence of norms in a system and, on the other hand, with problems of normative validity. Lack of clear conceptual distinctions counts as one of the main sources of trouble in legal philosophy.

[23] See Carlos E. Alchourrón and David Makinson, 'Hierarchies of Regulations and their Logic', in *New Studies in Deontic Logic*, ed. Risto Hilpinen (Dordrecht: Reidel, 1981), 125–48.

11

Norms, Normative Propositions, and Legal Statements (1982)*

Introduction

Two major events characterize the development of legal philosophy in the decade 1966–1976: first, the increasing interest on the part of legal theorists in deontic logic, along with later attempts to capitalize on the insights achieved by deontic logicians where the clarification of legal reasoning and the analysis of legal concepts are concerned;[1] second, the powerful attack launched by Ronald Dworkin against the hitherto prevailing trend in legal philosophy, namely, legal positivism.

Both issues are far too complex to be treated summarily in a short article. Instead, I shall select one problem that, as a central topic in legal philosophy, has greatly troubled deontic logicians and also has some bearing on Dworkin's theories. The problem I propose to discuss in this paper is the well-known ambiguity of deontic expressions. Unlike imperatives, which are normally used to issue commands or prohibitions, deontic sentences—that is, sentences in which such deontic terms as 'ought', 'may', 'obligatory', 'forbidden', 'permitted', and so on occur—are typically ambiguous. The same string of words—for example, 'it is obligatory to keep promises' or 'smoking is prohibited here'—can be used to issue a prescription (a command or a prohibition) and can also be used to state that a certain prescription exists or that something is obligatory or forbidden according to a given norm or set of norms. In the first case, the deontic sentence expresses a *norm*, in the second

* [*Editors' note*: Eugenio Bulygin's paper first appeared in *Contemporary Philosophy. A New Survey*, vol. 3: *Philosophy of Action*, ed. Guttorm Fløistad (The Hague: Martinus Nijhoff, 1982), 127–52. Spanish version in *ALD*, 169–93.]

[1] The main works falling into this period, listed chronologically, are Ross, *DN*; Juan Ramón Capella, *El derecho como lenguaje. un análisis lógico* (Barcelona: Ariel, 1968); Ilmar Tammelo, *Outlines of Modern Legal Logic* (Wiesbaden: F. Steiner, 1969); Ota Weinberger, *Rechtslogik* (Vienna: Springer, 1970); Norberto Bobbio, *Studi per una teoría generale del diritto* (Turin: Giappichelli, 1970); Alchourrón and Bulygin, *NS*; Heinz Wagner and Karl Haag, *Die moderne Logik in der Rechtswissenschaft* (Bad Homburg v. d. H.: Gehlen, 1970); Ilmar Tammelo and Helmut Schreiner, *Grundzüge und Grundverfahren der Rechtslogik*, vol. 1 (Pullach bei Munich: Verlag Dokumentation, 1974); Johann Mokre and Ota Weinberger, *Rechtsphilosophie und Gesetzgebung* (Vienna: Springer, 1976). [*Editors' note*: For the abbreviations employed here—Ross, Alchourrón and Bulygin—and for others, see the Table of Abbreviations.]

case, a (descriptive) proposition about norms, which will be termed the *normative proposition.*

Most philosophers are of the opinion that norms lack truth-values: they are neither true nor false but they can be obeyed or satisfied. On the other hand, normative propositions are clearly true or false, but, not being prescriptions at all, they can be neither obeyed nor disobeyed.

Are these categories mutually exclusive? Can one and the same expression share both properties, that is, be prescriptive and descriptive at the same time? If they are mutually exclusive, are they also jointly exhaustive? Is every occurrence of a deontic sentence either an enunciation of a norm or an expression of a normative proposition? As we shall see, the answers to these questions are far from clear.

1. The Discussion about Logic

The revival of deontic logic in modern times and its systematic pursuit by logicians began with the publication of Georg Henrik von Wright's classic paper 'Deontic Logic'.[2] The revival took place at a time when there was a fairly well-established opinion to the effect that norms, being disguised imperatives, lack truth-values and that therefore no logical relations obtain between them.[3] Curiously enough, in the first systems of deontic logic we find no discussion of the problem of how its expressions are to be understood—whether as referring to norms or to normative propositions. Most logicians writing on deontic logic in the 1950s and early 1960s seem not to have been aware of the problem. On the whole, it seems that the idea was to offer a logic of norms, but the formulae were usually treated as expressing propositions that are true or false. This is what happened, in particular, in von Wright's first paper on this subject. In 1957, he refers to the matter in the preface to *Logical Studies*.

> Philosophically, I find this paper very unsatisfactory. For one thing, because it treats of norms as a kind of proposition which may be true or false. This, I think, is a mistake. Deontic logic gets part of its philosophic significance from the fact that norms and valuations, though removed from the realm of truth, yet are subject to logical law. This shows that logic, so to speak, has a wider reach than truth.[4]

It would probably be a mistake to treat norms as a kind of true or false proposition, but this does not preclude the possibility of interpreting deontic expressions as propositions about norms, that is, as normative propositions. Von Wright's remark seems to indicate that he was not aware of this possibility at that stage of his work (probably because he overlooked the above-mentioned ambiguity), and he took

[2] Von Wright, 'DL'.

[3] See Walter Dubislav, 'Zur Unbegründbarkeit der Forderungssätze', *Theoria*, 3 (1937), 330–42; Jørgensen, 'IL'; Ross, 'IL'.

[4] Georg Henrik von Wright, *Logical Studies* (London: Routledge & Kegan Paul, 1957), preface, vii–ix, at vii.

it for granted that deontic logic ought to be a reconstruction of logical relations between norms. Yet his contention that logic has a wider scope than truth certainly requires a justification in light of the fact that such notions as logical consequence and consistency are usually defined in terms of truth.

A detailed discussion of the problem of the ambiguity of deontic expressions is to be found in von Wright's *Norm and Action.*[5] In this book, von Wright makes a clear distinction between norms and normative statements or normative propositions, and he emphasizes the ambiguity of deontic sentences: one and the same sentence can be used to express both norms and normative propositions. Instead of eliminating this ambiguity of ordinary language, however, von Wright decides to retain it in his symbolic language. Thus, he constructs only one symbolism rather than two. Then, however, his calculus permits two interpretations: a prescriptive interpretation, in which deontic expressions are norms, and a descriptive interpretation, where they express propositions.

> The 'fully developed' system of Deontic Logic is a theory of descriptively interpreted expressions. But the laws (principles, rules), which are peculiar to this logic, concern logical properties of the *norms* themselves, which are then reflected in logical properties of norm-propositions. Thus, in a sense, the 'basis' of Deontic Logic is a logical theory of prescriptively interpreted *O*- and *P*-expressions.[6]

Von Wright's statement of the problem is very clear, but his solution is far from being satisfactory. In the first place, he does not say how the two interpretations of deontic logic are related. Thus, it is not clear why the logic of normative propositions ought to reflect the logical properties of norms. In the second place, if there are logical relations between norms, then why not elaborate a logic of norms directly?

Von Wright's idea that there is at least a theoretical possibility of constructing two logics—a logic of norms and a logic of normative propositions—proved to be fruitful. The idea was developed by Carlos E. Alchourrón,[7] who tried to show (i) that von Wright's first system of deontic logic is a substantially correct reconstruction of the logical properties of norms, (ii) that the logic of normative propositions (that is, assertions to the effect that certain states of affairs are prohibited, obligatory, or permitted according to a given set of norms, that is, a normative system) differs from the logic of norms on several important points, and (iii) that the two logics are isomorphic in a very special case, namely, when the normative system in question is complete and consistent, two requirements that cannot be assumed on logical grounds alone. These ideas were then further developed in *Normative Systems.*[8]

[5] Von Wright, *NA*. See also Ota Weinberger, 'Können Sollsätze (Imperative) als wahr bezeichnet werden?', published as an appendix to Weinberger's monograph-length paper, 'Die Sollsatzproblematik in der modernen Logik', *Rozpravy Československé akademic věd*, 68 (no. 9) (Prague: Řada SV, 1958), 145–59.

[6] Von Wright, *NA*, 133–4 (emphasis in original).

[7] Carlos E. Alchourrón, 'Logic of Norms and Logic of Normative Propositions', *Logique et Analyse*, 12 (1969), 242–68; Carlos E. Alchourrón, 'The Intuitive Background of Normative Legal Discourse and its Formalization', *Journal of Philosophical Logic*, 1 (1972), 447–63.

[8] Alchourrón and Bulygin, *NS*.

The thesis that there are logical relations between norms and that therefore the logic of norms is in some sense more basic than or prior to a logic of normative propositions is shared by many distinguished philosophers,[9] but opinions on the foundation of this thesis differ considerably. Some authors tend to think that the interpretation of deontic logic as a logic of norms presents no difficulty, either because they believe that norms are true or false[10] or because they simply substitute another pair of values (valid and invalid) for truth and falsity.[11] Both positions are rather problematic from a philosophical point of view. The idea that norms are true or false is often based on an analogy with Tarski's T-condition.

A norm N is true if n (where N is the name of the sentence expressing the norm n). For instance, the norm 'killing is prohibited' is true if and only if killing is prohibited.

A correspondence theory of truth lies behind this idea. Tarski's explicit intention was to reconstruct this theory, which can be traced back to Aristotle. Now it is clearly not sufficient to point out the analogy; what is needed is to show what sorts of fact make norms true. They cannot be empirical facts, and so one must no doubt postulate the existence of some sort of moral fact or another species of fact that is normative in character. This would lead to a rather complicated ontology. In any case, without a detailed elaboration of a theory capable of giving an account of specific normative facts, the contention that norms have truth-values remains without support. Even less satisfactory is the procedure of substituting validity for truth. It is not a question of replacing one term with another; what is required is a demonstration that the concept of validity behaves in a way that is similar—in all relevant respects—to the concept of truth.

Even if we agree, as most logicians and philosophers do, that norms lack truth-values, the question of whether there are logical relations between norms remains open. There might, after all, be a grain of truth in von Wright's remark[12] that the scope of logic is wider than that of truth.[13] Still, a justification is required that goes beyond a simple mention of certain formal analogies between truth and validity.

In any case, there are many authors who reject the idea of a logic of norms. A paradigmatic case is that of Manfred Moritz,[14] who maintains that deontic logic

[9] See Weinberger, 'Können Sollsätze (Imperative) als wahr bezeichnet werden?' (n. 5, this chapter); Georges Kalinowski, *La logique des normes* (Paris: Presses universitaires de France, 1972).

[10] See Kalinowski (n. 9, this chapter); Jürgen Rödig, 'Über die Notwendigkeit einer besonderen Logik der Normen', in *Rechtstheorie als Grundlagenwissenschaft der Rechtswissenschaft*, ed. Hans Albert, et al. (Düsseldorf: Bertelsmann, 1972), 163–85.

[11] Kalinowski (n. 9, this chapter); Rupert Schreiber, *Logik des Rechts* (Berlin and Heidelberg: Springer, 1962); Ross, *DN*.

[12] See the quotation from von Wright in the text, at n. 4, this chapter.

[13] Lennart Åqvist, 'Interpretations of Deontic Logic', *Mind*, 73 (1964), 246–53, has proposed several interpretations of deontic logic that give rise to various systems of atheoretical logic.

[14] See Manfred Moritz, 'Über konditionale Imperative', in *Festskrift til Alf Ross*, ed. Mogens Blegvad, et al. (Copenhagen: Juristforbundets Forlag, 1969), 351–74; Manfred Moritz, 'Kann das (richterliche) Urteil deduziert werden?', in *Festskrift till Per Olof Ekelöf* (Stockholm: P.A. Norstedt & Söners, 1972), 502–18; Manfred Moritz, 'Das sogenannte Ross'sche Paradox. Interpretation und Kritik', *Insikt och handling* [Insight and Action], 10 (1973), 126–37.

can only be interpreted as a logic of normative propositions. If, however, deontic expressions are normative propositions, why should they differ in any significant way from other propositions? After all, logicians are interested solely in the form of a proposition, not in its content. So deontic logic, interpreted in this way, seems to lack any special interest, being simply an 'ordinary' logic applied to norms. This is the conclusion drawn by Moritz, and even if it is not commonly shared by deontic logicians, it is not easy to see how to escape it.

The main argument against the possibility of a logic of norms is this. Logical analysis is the reconstruction of certain logical or conceptual relations that obtain between propositions, that is, between certain abstract entities that are usually regarded as the meanings of descriptive (true or false) sentences. If there is to be a logic of norms, these must be conceptual, proposition-like entities of some sort, that is, normative sentences must have a specific prescriptive meaning. Now the difference between norms and descriptive sentences seems to lie not in their meaning but in the illocutionary act performed by the speaker. One and the same proposition—for example, expressed by the sentence 'John takes off his hat'—can be used on different occasions to make an assertion ('John takes off his hat.'), to ask a question ('does John take off his hat?'), or to issue a prescription ('John, take off your hat!' or 'John ought to take off his hat.'). The meaning of the sentence is the same in all these examples, but what is *done* while uttering the sentence is in each instance different. Therefore, it is only on the pragmatic level of the use of a language that we can distinguish between norms (prescriptions), assertions (statements), questions, conjectures, and so on.[15] There is no such difference on the semantic level; norms are the result of a certain use, namely, the prescriptive use of language.

It is important to stress that the various linguistic and non-linguistic devices used to indicate what is done with a sentence (a full stop, an exclamation point, a question mark, a certain inflexion of the voice, a characteristic gesture) do not form part of the meaning of the words uttered. They show what the speaker is doing in uttering certain words, but in doing what he does he is not saying what he is doing. So these devices do not contribute to the conceptual content of the words uttered.[16]

If this is so, then it is clear that there can be no logical relations between norms. If one still wants to speak of a logic of norms, then one has to accept the idea that norms are abstract entities, entities that are not language dependent,[17] that is to say, there are sentences with a specific prescriptive meaning. This assumption with its strong platonic flavour is, for many empiricist-minded philosophers, hard to swallow.

[15] See Clarence Irving Lewis, *An Analysis of Knowledge and Valuation* (La Salle, Illinois: Open Court, 1946), at 49; Hans Reichenbach, *Elements of Symbolic Logic* (New York: Macmillan, 1947), at 336–44; von Wright, *NA*, at 94.

[16] See Reichenbach, *Elements of Symbolic Logic* (n. 15, this chapter), and Hare, *LM*, who confines logical relations to phrastics.

[17] See Alchourrón and Bulygin, 'Von Wright on Deontic Logic and the Philosophy of Law' (1973/89), in this volume, ch. 5; there we use the term 'norm-lekton' for this meaning.

Thus we are faced with a difficult dilemma. Either we reject the idea of a logic of norms and maintain that deontic logic can only be conceived of as a logic of normative propositions, or we must make the strong ontological assumption to the effect that norms are abstract conceptual entities, independent of any use of language. On the first horn of the dilemma, we must be prepared to explain the peculiar features of deontic logic (unless we abandon altogether the idea of a deontic logic as a specific branch of logic). On the second, we must offer a plausible justification for such an assumption; that is to say, we must elaborate a theory of meaning that would embrace prescriptive meanings, that is, norms as abstract entities.

The best theory, on the second horn of the dilemma, is that of Castañeda,[18] whose *practitions* are the 'prescriptive' counterpart of propositions. Most writers, however, are inclined to embrace the first horn; even von Wright himself later came to accept the idea that deontic logic is, after all, a logic of normative propositions.[19]

What, then, about the peculiar features of deontic logic? Can a logic of normative propositions be developed on its own merits as an interesting branch of logic?

I shall not try to give a full answer to this difficult question. Rather, I shall confine myself to a few informal remarks that indicate what sort of answer seems to me to be most appropriate.

Normative propositions are usually expressed by elliptical sentences stating that a given state of affairs *p* has a certain normative status (is prohibited, permitted, or obligatory) according to some unspecified normative order. This means that in this order there is a norm to the effect that *p* is prohibited (permitted, obligatory), but what does it mean to say that a norm exists or is a member of a set of norms? There are different kinds of norm, and there are also different answers to this question. A special but very interesting case is that of legal norms. Legal norms have a temporal existence; they begin to exist at a certain point in time, and they cease to exist at some later point in time. The temporal existence of legal norms can be analysed in terms of membership in a given legal order. A legal order is a dynamic order, that is, a temporal sequence of changing sets of norms. To each temporal point (that is, the point at which some norm is introduced into the order or removed from it) there corresponds a certain set of norms. A norm can be a member of different sets, and as long as it is a member of some set, it belongs to or exists in the order. Norms come into existence through acts of issuance by competent authorities (and also as a result of firmly established practices, in which case it is impossible to fix an exact moment of the beginning of its existence), and they cease to exist when they are either explicitly or tacitly derogated (cancelled). A tacit derogation takes place when the norm enters into a conflict with a more important norm. There are many different hierarchical criteria regarding the relative importance of norms. Thus, a norm N_1 may be more important than N_2 because N_1 has been issued by a

[18] Hector-Neri Castañeda, *Thinking and Doing* (Dordrecht: D. Reidel, 1975).

[19] See Georg Henrik von Wright, 'Problems and Prospects of Deontic Logic. A Survey', in *Modern Logic. A Survey*, ed. Evandro Agazzi (Dordrecht: D. Reidel, 1980), 399–423.

higher authority, or because it has been issued at a later point in time, or because it attaches a less severe punishment to the same offence, and so forth.

The introduction of norms into a legal order and their removal from it are governed by certain criteria concerning the rationality of the acts of issuance and derogation, criteria that may be termed, in a broad sense, logical. Thus, a logic of normative propositions can be viewed as a calculus of normative systems or dynamic orders. As such it would be both an autonomous branch of logic and a field of research of great practical interest, at least for legal norms.

While the development of a logic of dynamic systems in the sense sketched above does fall outside the period we are considering here, namely, 1966–76, pioneering work was presented in publications that appeared during those years.[20]

The discussion of the problem of the ambiguity of deontic expressions led to a significant clarification of this rather intricate issue. Most deontic logicians now accept the distinction between norms and normative propositions and acknowledge its theoretical importance. In particular, almost all of them accept the idea that the two categories are mutually exclusive (no deontic sentence can express both a norm and a normative proposition at the same time), and many agree that they are also jointly exhaustive in the sense that every deontic sentence (or, better, every use of a deontic sentence) expresses either a norm or a normative proposition, but not both.

2. The Legal Discussion

The ambiguity of deontic sentences did not pass altogether unnoticed by legal philosophers, but it took a very long time to acquire a clear formulation of the issue. Even now there is no consensus among legal philosophers on the logical status of legal statements.

The first to mark the distinction between norms and normative propositions—as in so many other matters—was Jeremy Bentham.[21] He distinguished the 'authoritative imperative' from the non-authoritative formulations to be found in books 'written not by the legislator but by private individuals', and also between directly imperative expressions (explicit commands) and declarative expressions that are

[20] Thomas Cornides, 'Der Widerruf von Befehlen', *Studium Generale*, 22 (1969), 1215–63; Alchourrón and Bulygin, *NS*; Alchourrón and Bulygin, 'Unvollständigkeit, Widersprüchlichkeit und Unbestimmtheit der Normenordnungen', in *Deontische Logik und Semantik*, ed. Amedeo G. Conte, et al. (Wiesbaden: Athenaion, 1977), 20–32; Ota Weinberger, 'Normenlogik und logische Bereiche', ibid. 176–212; W. H. Hanson, 'A Logic of Commands', *Logique et Analyse*, 9 (1966), 329–43; Leo Reisinger, 'Zur Vollständigkeit normativer Systeme', in *Rechtsphilosophie und Gesetzgebung* (n. 1, this chapter), 97–128. Among the more recent publications, see Carlos E. Alchourrón and Eugenio Bulygin, *Sobre la existencia de las normas jurídicas* (Valencia, Venezuela: Universidad de Carabobo, 1979); Alchourrón and Bulygin, 'The Expressive Conception of Norms' (1981), in this volume, ch. 9; Carlos E. Alchourrón and David Makinson, 'Hierarchies of Regulations and Their Logic', in *New Studies in Deontic Logic*, ed. Risto Hilpinen (Dordrecht: Reidel, 1981), 125–48.

[21] See Jeremy Bentham, *Of Laws in General*, ed. H. L. A. Hart (London: Athlone Press, 1970), ch.14, § 32 (at 179).

only indirectly imperative, such as 'it is not permitted to any man to export corn'. When such expressions occur in a statute, the legislator is 'speaking as it were in the person of another man who is considered as explaining the state which things are in, in consequence of the arrangements taken by the legislator'.[22]

In Hans Kelsen's work, there appears the crucial distinction between *Rechtsnorm* and *Rechtssatz*. The *Rechtsnorm* is issued by the legislative authority; it is neither true nor false, but valid or invalid and efficacious or inefficacious. By contrast, the *Rechtssatz* is formulated by legal science; it is descriptive, not prescriptive, hence it is either true or false, but neither valid nor invalid, and it cannot be obeyed or disobeyed either.[23] Thus far, it seems that Kelsen's distinction reflects exactly the difference between norms and normative propositions. Unfortunately, however, this proves to be an illusion, for Kelsen insists that *Rechtssatz* is an 'ought-sentence' (*Sollsatz*), and this is not merely a grammatical category but an ought-sentence according to its meaning. This idea plays an important role in Kelsen's theory, for the distinction between the factual and the normative sciences rests precisely on this point: the propositions of a normative science are ought-sentences and not 'is-sentences'. Thus, this feature of legal sentences cannot be explained away.

There are two kinds of 'ought' according to Kelsen: the prescriptive ought of norms and the descriptive ought of the propositions of legal science. The contention that there are descriptive ought-sentences is far from being clear. One could think that the descriptive ought is something like Hare's 'inverted commas use',[24] which is a mention and not a use of the term 'ought'. However, Kelsen emphatically rejected all attempts to interpret the relation between a *Rechtssatz* and the corresponding *Rechtsnorm* that it describes in terms of the distinction between mention and use.[25] Hart suggested that Kelsen's distinction between propositions of a normative science of law and legal norms is similar to that of an interpreter of a foreign language and the expressions he has to translate.[26] Suppose a German officer issues a command to some English prisoners of war 'Stehen Sie auf!' and the interpreter translates 'stand up!' In this case it would be equally wrong, according to Hart, to say that the interpreter has given a command (for he has no authority to do so) or to say that he just mentioned the command given by the officer, as if he had said 'the officer has commanded that you stand up'. The interpreter reproduces the command, conserving its prescriptive force, but this prescriptive force stems from the officer, not from him. Hart's analogy is interesting but, as it stands, not very illuminating. According to Kelsen the task of a science of law is to describe the law, not just to reproduce it, and it is not clear how the reproduced command of the interpreter can be said to be descriptive, unless we agree that both translations

[22] Bentham, *Of Laws in General*, ch. 13, §§ 1–7 (152–5) (see n. 21, this chapter).

[23] See Kelsen, *RR 2*, at § 16 (73–7), in *PTL*, at 71–5.

[24] Hare, *LM*.

[25] An interpretation of Kelsen along these lines has been proposed by Martin Golding, 'Kelsen and the Concept of "Legal System"', *ARSP*, 47 (1961), 355–86. See also Eugenio Bulygin, 'Sobre la estructura lógica de las proposiciones de la ciencia del derecho', in *RJBA* (1961), no. 4, 215–33, in Alchourrón and Bulygin, *ALR*, 331–8.

[26] H. L. A. Hart, 'Kelsen Visited', *UCLA Law Review*, 10 (1962/3), 709–28, in Hart, *EJP*, 286–308.

('stand up!' and 'the officer has commanded you to stand up') are equivalent. And this would mean analysing the distinction in terms of mention and use.

Two interesting and rather similar attempts to explain the normative character of legal propositions in Kelsen have been made recently by Raz and Nino,[27] but they fall outside the scope of this survey.

A clear formulation of the distinction was made by certain Scandinavian philosophers. As far back as 1941, Ingemar Hedenius made the distinction between 'genuine' and 'spurious' legal sentences, which corresponds exactly to norms and normative propositions.[28] A few years later the same distinction was carefully elaborated by Alf Ross. Legal norms, he wrote, are directives, 'utterances with no representative meaning but with intent to exert influence',[29] whereas propositions of what Ross calls the doctrinal study of law are assertions, that is, utterances with representative meaning. Hence, norms are neither true nor false, whereas normative propositions have truth-values. What are the normative propositions about? In Ross's analysis they refer to 'hypothetical future decisions (of the courts) under certain conditions'.[30] This predictive analysis of legal propositions is altogether independent of the distinction between the two kinds of sentences, namely, sentences expressing norms and those expressing normative propositions. In practice, however, the rejection of the predictive analysis of legal statements by many legal philosophers who did not share Ross's legal realism obscured the importance of the other distinction. The most influential author in jurisprudence during the period we are considering was H. L. A. Hart. In Hart we find a parallel distinction between legal rules and assertions about law, but these are of two different albeit related kinds: *external* and *internal* statements.

> When a social group has certain rules of conduct, this fact affords an opportunity for many closely related yet different kinds of assertion; for it is possible to be concerned with the rules, either merely as an observer who does not himself accept them, or as a member of the group which accepts and uses them as guides to conduct.[31]

Hart also distinguishes between different types of external statement: (i) statements that merely record the regularities of the behaviour of those who comply with the rules, (ii) statements that, in addition, record the regular, hostile reaction to deviations from the usual pattern of behaviour, and (iii) statements that also record *the fact that* members of the society accept certain rules as standards of behaviour.[32] All three types of external statement are statements of fact, but they differ according to the different kinds of fact that they describe. The first two types describe certain actions, while the third describes a far more complex social fact, namely, the fact that a given rule exists, that is to say, is accepted by a social group. This is exactly what we understand by a normative proposition.

[27] See Raz, 'BN'; Carlos Santiago Nino, 'Some Confusions around Kelsen's Concept of Validity', *ARSP*, 64 (1978), 357–77, repr. (in part) *NN*, 253–61.

[28] Ingemar Hedenius, *Om rätt och moral* (Stockholm: Tidens, 1941).

[29] Ross, *LJ*, 8.

[30] Ross, *LJ*, 41.

[31] Hart, *CL*, 1st edn., 86, 3rd edn., 89.

[32] Hart, *CL*, 1st edn., 87, 3rd edn., 89.

Hart contrasts external statements of fact with *internal statements* made by those who accept and use the rules as guides to conduct, that is, by those who adopt an internal point of view.[33] At first glance, the difference between external and internal statements seems to lie on the pragmatic level: internal statements are made from an internal point of view, that is, by those who accept the rules, and external statements are made from an external point of view by those who do not accept the rules. This last remark requires qualification. Of course, one need not reject the rules in order to be able to make external statements; the acceptance of the rules is irrelevant for the external point of view.[34] However, one cannot make internal statements without accepting the rules of the system. Acceptance of the rules is a necessary feature of the internal point of view and therefore also a necessary condition for making internal statements.

Is there any logical difference between these two kinds of legal statement? External statements are statements of fact. Internal statements are not about any fact at all. What are they about? According to Hart, the typical form of an internal statement is 'It is the law that...', which is analysed in the following terms:

> an *internal statement*... manifests the internal point of view and is naturally used by one who, accepting the rule of recognition and without stating the fact that it is accepted, applies the rule in recognizing some particular rule of the system as valid.[35]

Thus, an internal statement is about the validity of a rule, and to say that a rule is valid is to use a rule of recognition, which implies the acceptance of both the rule declared valid and the rule of recognition. This is so because the rule of recognition is a genuine norm: it not only provides a criterion for the identification of the rules of the system but it also prescribes that these be obligatory.[36]

Hence, to say that a rule is valid (in this normative or prescriptive sense) is tantamount to saying that it is obligatory or binding, that it is obligatory to do what the rule prescribes. The expression 'is valid' is, in this use, semantically redundant, exactly in the same way as the expression 'is true' is redundant. To say that the sentence 'the door is open' is true amounts to saying that the door is open. Similarly, to say that the rule 'one must keep one's promises' is valid involves, at the very least, saying that one must keep one's promises. Thus, it becomes clear that the assertion

[33] Hart writes: 'It is important to distinguish the external statement of fact asserting that members of society accept a given rule from the internal statement of the rule made by one who himself accepts it.' Hart, *CL*, 1st edn., 244, 3rd edn., 291.

[34] '... an *external statement* because it is the natural language of an external observer of the system who, without himself accepting its rule of recognition, states the fact that others accept it'. Hart, *CL*, 1st edn., 99 (emphasis in original), 3rd edn., 103.

[35] Hart, *CL*, 1st edn., 99 (emphasis in original), 3rd edn., 102.

[36] See Raz, *AL*, at 93, who writes: 'The rule of recognition imposes an obligation on the law-applying officials to recognize and apply all and only those laws satisfying certain criteria of validity spelt out in the rule...' See also Hacker, who writes: 'So a rule of recognition is a rule imposing a duty upon judicial officials to exercise their adjudicative powers by applying laws satisfying certain criteria.' P. M. S. Hacker, 'Hart's Philosophy of Law', in *Law, Morality, and Society*, ed. P. M. S. Hacker and Joseph Raz (Oxford: Clarendon Press, 1977), 1–25, at 23.

'this rule is valid' is not a statement of fact but a prescription. Hart is quite explicit on this point.

> The use of unstated rules of recognition, by courts and others, in identifying particular rules of the system is characteristic of the internal point of view. *Those who use them in this way thereby manifest their own acceptance of them as guiding rules*...[37]

If this is so, however, then Hart's terminology is confusing, for internal statements are *not* statements at all; they are disguised prescriptions (applied norms, or claims and requests based on rules). They are, of course, not identical with rules. It is one thing *to give a rule* (for example, when a legal authority issues a command) and quite another *to use a rule already given.* But Hart's internal statements share with rules an important property: both are prescriptive and neither is a statement of fact; therefore, both lack truth-values. One cannot maintain that internal statements are prescriptive or normative and at the same time true or false unless one is prepared to accept the existence of certain peculiar facts that would make them true, namely, moral facts or other normative facts that they are about. Hart would certainly not accept the idea that there are such normative facts, and so his internal statements cannot be true or false.[38]

Of course, in ordinary discourse we often say of a deontic sentence that it is true or false. Since we easily shift from a prescriptive use of such sentences to a descriptive use, the impression may be given that one and the same sentence is both normative and true or false, but this is nothing more than an illusion.

Imagine the following dialogue. A father decides, before leaving his house, to order his child to bed at 9 p.m. and tells the babysitter so, but he forgets to give the corresponding command to the child. At 9 p.m. the babysitter says, 'you ought to go to bed now' and the child replies, 'it is not true'.

If the child takes the babysitter's remark to be a piece of information about his father's command, then the child's answer is perfectly meaningful and, on at least one interpretation, also correct. However, if the babysitter wanted to order the child to go to bed (and chose this particular form of words), then the reply is out of place. If the sentence 'you ought to go to bed' is a prescription, then it is equivalent to the imperative 'go to bed!', which clearly cannot be answered by 'it is not true'. It is possible and, indeed, very likely to be the case that the babysitter wanted to do both things, namely, to remind the child of his father's command and to order the child to go to bed. If this is so, then she performed simultaneously two different speech acts: one of giving information and one of commanding. An appropriate answer in this case might be 'no, it is not true that father ordered me to go to bed at 9 p.m., so I'm not going to obey your order', and the child's reply may just be an elliptical form of this.

What this example shows precisely is the ambiguity of deontic expressions and the practical difficulty of determining which speech act or acts have been

[37] Hart, *CL*, 1st edn., 99 (emphasis added), 3rd edn., 102.

[38] Raz seems to accept normative facts, see Raz, *PRN*.

performed on a given occasion (which is an empirical question). What it certainly does not show is that prescriptive ought-sentences can be true or false.

There are, of course, also statements of validity that are genuine descriptive propositions, as, for example, when someone, in saying that a particular rule is valid—meaning only that it meets certain criteria for validity—is not expressing acceptance of the rule (or the rule of recognition), that is, when, in saying 'this statute is valid', one is simply recording the fact that it has been duly enacted by the legislature, but this would be an external statement of fact. This statement is of the third type, for it states the fact that a given rule meets the criteria for identification provided by the rule of recognition (which is more than merely recording regularities of behaviour), but it implies neither the acceptance of the rule of recognition as a binding rule nor the acceptance of the rule declared valid; it merely records such acceptance by members of the group. On the contrary, the utterance of an internal statement ascribing validity to a particular rule implies such acceptance. As Hart writes: 'a person who seriously asserts the validity of some given rule of law, say, a particular statute, himself makes use of a rule of recognition which he accepts . . . '[39]

It seems, incidentally, that this ambiguity of the term 'valid' and hence of statements of the form 'this rule (statute, contract) is valid' remained unnoticed by Hart. At any rate, he does not mention the possibility of factual validity-statements and always speaks of them as internal statements. However, as I have already pointed out, the internal statements that serve as ascriptions of rules are not statements at all. They are disguised ways of spelling out the rule or of making a claim based on the rule. To say, for example, that this contract is valid (in this normative sense) is tantamount to saying that you must do what this contract stipulates; the statement is to *prescribe* a certain form of conduct, but it does not describe anything at all. If a legal positivist account of the law consists of describing the law as it is and not as it ought to be,[40] and internal statements are not descriptive but prescriptive, it then follows that in a positivist account of the law there is no room for internal statements. A consequent legal positivist can describe the law only by means of external statements. Of course, in describing the law, he must, if his description is to be complete, give an account of the internal aspect of the rules, but this can very well be accomplished by means of external statements provided he uses external statements of the third kind, not restricting himself to recording regularities of behaviour alone. There is no need, however, to utter internal statements in order to give a full account of the internal aspect of rules: the third type of external statement can do this job very well.

Hart does not deny this, and his attack concentrates on the predictive theory of law, which only makes use of the first two types of external statement:

we can if we choose occupy the position of an observer *who does not even refer* in this way to the internal point of view of the group. *Such an observer* is content merely to record the

[39] Hart, *CL*, 1st edn., 105, 3rd edn., 108.

[40] Hart, in 'Separation', holds this to be the characteristic feature of legal positivism that he shares with Bentham and Austin.

regularities of observable behaviour in which conformity with the rules partly consists and those further regularities, in the form of the hostile reaction, reproofs, or punishments, with which deviations from the rules are met... If, however, the observer really keeps austerely to this *extreme* external point of view and does not give any account of the manner in which members of the group who accept the rules view their own regular behaviour, his description of their life cannot be in terms of rules at all, and so not in the terms of the rule-dependent notions of obligation or duty. Instead, it will be in terms of observable regularities of conduct, predictions, probabilities, and signs.[41]

Furthermore, Hart continues:

What the external point of view, which limits itself to the observable regularities of behaviour, cannot reproduce is the way in which the rules function as rules in the lives of those who normally are the majority of society.[42]

These quotations show clearly that Hart's attack concerns *only* the predictive theory based on external statements of the first two types. However, Hart is guilty of an omission: he does not say what happens if the observer is less extreme and uses external statements of the third type. Could he not give a full account of the internal aspect of rules and the use of normative language by those who accept them?

In this way Hart lends the impression, without ever asserting it explicitly, that one must use internal statements in order to give an account of the internal aspect of rules, which would be plainly false. It is interesting to note, however, that some of Hart's Oxford colleagues consider that he is using a normative (and not a purely descriptive) concept of law and that consequently internal statements should play a very important role in the analysis of law.

Raz maintains, for example, that Hart 'insisted on the importance of internal statements to the analysis of law'.[43] This assertion is, of course, ambiguous. If what Raz means is that the analysis of law requires taking into account internal statements used by judges, other officials, and even private citizens, then we can agree. If, on the other hand, he wants to suggest that one must use internal statements in order to analyse the law, then he is radically mistaken. There are some other references to Hart that corroborate the second interpretation. Thus, Raz juxtaposes Hart's theory to the 'reductivist interpretation of legal statements' found in Bentham and Austin, according to which

legal statements are synonymous with statements about what certain people commanded or willed... Professor Hart, while accepting the sources thesis, mounted a most formidable criticism of reductivism. He argued that legal statements are deontic or practical. They are used to demand and justify action and thus function in discourse and argument in ways which no theoretical statement could.[44]

Here Raz seems to equate legal statements with internal statements, as if external statements were not legal at all. We also find here the very ambiguity that has

[41] Hart, *CL*, 1st edn., 87 (emphasis added), 3rd edn., 89.
[42] Hart, *CL*, 1st edn., 88, 3rd edn., 90.
[43] Raz, 'Legal Validity', in *AL*, 146–59, at 154.
[44] Raz, 'Legal Reasons, Sources, and Gaps', in *AL*, 53–77, at 53.

already been noted between the two readings of 'internal statement'—its use by judges and other officials on the one hand, its use in analyses of the law on the other.

I do not think that Bentham and Austin ever pretended to be reducing sentences expressing demands or claims as they are usually used by those who accept the rules of law to statements of fact about what certain people commanded or willed. What they wanted to do was to reduce the theoretical statements of those who wish to describe the law of a given society to factual statements. In addition, in the same way that no theoretical statement can perform the task that practical utterances perform, so no practical utterance can replace a theoretical statement made by those who want neither to express their acceptance of the law nor to make claims based on it, but who want simply to describe—in a neutral fashion—the law as it is and not as it ought to be. In other words, Bentham's concern was with statements of what is called, in the Continental tradition and in strict translation from the German, 'legal science' *(Rechtswissenschaft)* or the doctrinal study of law, and in this respect Hart fully agrees with his great predecessor.

John Finnis seems to share this 'normative' interpretation of Hart's theory.

> Thus Hart gives descriptive explanatory priority to the concerns and evaluations (and consequently to the language) of people with an 'internal point of view', viz. those who do not 'merely record and predict behaviour conforming to rules', or attend to rules 'only from the external point of view as a sign of possible punishment', but rather '*use* the rules as standards for the appraisal of their own and others' behaviour'.[45]

One has the impression that this coincidence is significant and that at least part of the blame for this misinterpretation of Hart's theory must rest with Hart himself.

There are certainly many writers who would call themselves 'legal positivists' and who make use of a normative concept of validity and therefore make internal statements. This is what Norberto Bobbio has called, in a very illuminating article, legal positivism *as ideology*.[46] Ideological positivists claim that every positive law is morally binding. This form of positivism must be sharply distinguished from positivism *as an approach*, whose main contention is that it is possible to describe the law of a country as it is, without making any value judgment about it, that is to say, without stating how it ought to be. This is exactly the point of view of an external observer who, without committing himself to the acceptance of the law, describes it by means of external statements of the third type. This is the positivism of Bentham and Hart.

It was Alf Ross, in a very remarkable but little known paper,[47] who called attention to the fact that many legal philosophers who regard themselves as positivists in this second sense and reject positivism as ideology, nonetheless use the normative concept of validity and therefore not only describe the law but also utter disguised

[45] John Finnis, *Natural Law and Natural Rights* (Oxford: Clarendon Press, 1980), 12, quoting from Hart, *CL*, 1st edn., 95–6 (emphasis in original), 3rd edn., 98.

[46] See Norberto Bobbio, *El problema del positivismo jurídico* (Buenos Aires: Eudeba, 1965).

[47] See Ross, 'Validity'.

prescriptions. To say that a norm is valid (in the normative sense) is to claim that it is morally binding. Ross accused Kelsen of being a quasi-positivist of this kind. The question of whether Kelsen is or is not a quasi-positivist need not trouble us here, but what is absolutely clear is that Hart explicitly rejects positivism as ideology and would only subscribe to positivism as an approach. Now if Hart were to grant, as Raz suggests, that the analysis of law requires the use of internal statements and cannot be conducted in terms of external statements alone, then he certainly would be a quasi-positivist in Ross's sense. This, I think, would be a very unfair interpretation of Hart's ideas.

To sum up our discussion of Hart's theory: the distinction between norms and normative propositions—although it is not explicitly discussed by Hart—lies not only behind the pair of concepts *rules* and *assertions about rules*, but also behind the classification of assertions into internal and external statements. External statements are statements of fact, descriptive of certain social facts and hence true or false regarding them. Internal statements are not factual, but normative; they are disguised prescriptions based on rules and hence neither true nor false. Thus, there are two basic kinds of legal sentence: those expressing norms (rules and internal statements) and those expressing normative propositions (external statements about norms). It follows that a descriptive theory of law (legal positivism) can only consist of external statements. Internal statements are often used by members of the group as well as by judges and other officials, but they would be completely out of place in a purely descriptive, positivist account of the law.

How would Hart answer our two questions regarding norms and normative propositions? Although he does not use this terminology, it is clear that norms (rules and so-called internal statements) and normative propositions (external statements) are mutually exclusive. No statement can be internal and external at the same time. But are they also jointly exhaustive? This is not so clear. In my interpretation they are indeed exhaustive, for internal statements—being prescriptive and neither true nor false—are a kind of norm, but I am not sure that my interpretation correctly reflects Hart's own views. It might be argued that internal statements are *sui generis*—that is, neither norms nor normative propositions—because in spite of being prescriptive they are also true or false. In any case, this seems to be the position of most of Hart's Oxford colleagues. Hart himself neither affirms nor denies that internal statements have truth-values. His terminology (statements) suggests that they are true or false, but his characterization of their function implies that they are neither.

3. The Solution of the Problem

Although Hart's main contribution to legal philosophy, *The Concept of Law*, was published in 1961, that is, before the period we are considering here, I thought it convenient to discuss his ideas at length, not only because Hart was the most influential legal philosopher of that period but also because it is impossible to grasp the full extent and the significance of Dworkin's attack on positivism without a clear understanding of what Hart actually said and what is implied by his theories. This is the case not only because it is Hart's theory, as presented in *The Concept of Law*, that Dworkin regards as a paradigmatic case of a positivistic conception of law and that he chooses as a target for his attacks, but also because Dworkin is far more indebted to Hart (or rather to a misinterpretation of Hart) than is commonly assumed.

Dworkin's ideas about a general theory of law and the role of positivism have been expounded in several papers he published between 1967 and 1977, most of which were reproduced in a volume that appeared in 1977.[48] I am largely concerned here with one of his latest and most brilliant papers, 'No Right Answer?',[49] because here Dworkin takes up the nature of legal statements or propositions of law (his terminology) in greater detail. They play a very prominent role in his argument against legal positivism.

In all of Dworkin's work we find no mention of the distinction between norms and normative propositions. This shows clearly that he does not regard the distinction as being of any importance for the analysis of legal statements. Indeed, his propositions of law are neither norms nor normative propositions, although it is not easy to say what they are. He never gives an explicit definition of propositions of law, but there is sufficient material in his papers, especially in 'No Right Answer?', to identify their main properties. This will be our next task.

Propositions of law play an important role in Dworkin's arguments against legal positivism because they function, according to him, in such a way as to preclude the occurrence of 'gaps' in the law. One of the main contentions of positivism, according to Dworkin, is that there are cases for which there is no right answer in the law and hence judges have discretion to decide these hard cases either way. It is this contention that Dworkin tries to show to be false with an argument based on an account of legal statements.

He gives several examples of propositions of law that contain what he calls dispositive concepts. 'Tom's contract is valid', 'Tim is liable in law for the damage his act has caused', and 'Jim's conduct on such and such occasion constitutes a crime' would all be typical propositions of law. If such a proposition is true, then judges have a duty, at least *prima facie*, to decide the claim one way, and 'if it is false, then they have a duty to decide the same claim in the opposite way'.[50] Already here we find the two main properties of legal statements. On the one hand, they are *normative (prescriptive)*, and, on the other, they are either *true* or *false.*

Propositions of law are normative, for they are a direct source of duties or obligations.

> [I]t is a consequence of the proposition that the contract is valid that a judge has a duty to enforce it, and a consequence of the proposition that the contract is not valid that he has the duty not to enforce it.[51]

[48] Ronald Dworkin, *Taking Rights Seriously* (Cambridge, Mass.: Harvard University Press, 1977).
[49] Ronald Dworkin, 'No Right Answer?', in *Law, Morality, and Society* (n. 36, this chapter), 58–84.
[50] Dworkin, 'No Right Answer?', (n. 49, this chapter), 59.
[51] Dworkin, 'No Right Answer?', (n. 49, this chapter), 63.

In addition, Dworkin writes, they are used

> not simply to report in a neutral way that certain events, comparable to the ball landing in a certain area, have occurred, but as an argument in itself that certain legal consequences, and in particular, official duties, follow from these facts.[52]

In this respect, Dworkin's propositions of law are direct descendants of Hart's internal statements, but they play a far more important role than their ancestors. Internal statements are only one kind of legal assertion, but Dworkin's propositions of law occupy a monopolistic position. There seems to be no room for any other kind of legal statement in Dworkin's thought. In this he is closer to Raz than to Hart.

Like Hart's internal statements, propositions of law are distinguished from legal rules, that is, prescriptions issued by the law-maker, which are neither true nor false. Although propositions of law are true or false, they are not identical to external statements. This is shown clearly by Dworkin's opposition to any suggestion that legal statements be reduced to statements descriptive of certain social facts, such as the issuing of commands by the sovereign[53] in the manner of Bentham and Austin. Moreover, Dworkin does not even mention the possibility of external legal statements.

However, unlike Hart's internal statements and like Raz's legal statements, Dworkin's propositions of law are either true or false, but what are they true of? What are the facts, if any, that make them true?

It is extremely difficult to find an answer to this question in Dworkin's writings. It is clear that propositions of law are not true with respect to any social (empirical) facts, for they would then be external and Dworkin is anxious to show that this is one of the typical mistakes of positivism.[54] Perhaps they are true of certain moral or normative facts? Dworkin contemplates this possibility in the following terms.

> Suppose, for example, there are moral facts, which are not simply physical facts or facts about the thoughts or attitudes of people. In that case a proposition of law might be true in virtue of a moral fact.[55]

He decides, however, not to rely on this argument. 'I shall not, in this essay, try to make plausible the idea that moral facts exist…'[56] Instead, he argues that there are facts other than hard (that is, empirical) facts. In particular, he maintains the existence of facts of normative consistency. Are legal statements then true in virtue of such facts of normative consistency? This seems to be Dworkin's answer to the question.

> A proposition of law, like the proposition that Tom's contract is valid, is true if the best justification that can be provided for the body of propositions of law already shown to be true provides a better case for that proposition than for the contrary proposition that Tom's

[52] Dworkin, 'No Right Answer?', (n. 49, this chapter), 64.
[53] See Dworkin, 'No Right Answer?', (n. 49, this chapter), at 70–7.
[54] See Dworkin, 'No Right Answer?', (n. 49, this chapter), at 70–7.
[55] Dworkin, 'No Right Answer?', (n. 49, this chapter), 77.
[56] Dworkin, 'No Right Answer?', (n. 49, this chapter), 70.

contract is not valid, but is false if that justification provides a better case for that contrary proposition than for it.[57]

This, however, can hardly be considered a satisfactory answer.

Leaving aside the extremely problematic idea that there is always such a thing as *the best* justification for every body of propositions of law, to say that a political theory provides a better case for a proposition than for its contrary amounts to stating that the proposition is compatible with that theory whereas its contrary is not. However, this would be a perfectly normal proposition about compatibility between a political theory and a proposition of law, which would be an external proposition, for there would be nothing normative about it. Moreover, Dworkin's criterion for truth could at best function once there is already a body of propositions of law that is established to be true; but how is the truth of *this* body of propositions established? It cannot be the same criterion, for this already presupposes that there is such a body of true legal statements. In other words, in order to show that a proposition of law is true, we must compare it with 'the political theory that provides the best justification for the settled law'.[58] This obviously presupposes the existence of the settled law, but how is this settled law identified? Certainly not by means of the same criterion, for that would lead to an infinite regress. Whether there is some other criterion for the truth of the propositions that belong to the 'settled law' is a mystery Dworkin prefers not to unveil.

To make things even more difficult, Dworkin suggests that propositions of law are, after all, not true or false in any ordinary sense, *but only assertable as true.*

Law is an enterprise such that propositions of law do not describe the real world in the way ordinary propositions do, but are propositions whose assertion is warranted by ground rules like those in the literary exercise. A proposition of law will be assertable as true, under these ground rules, if a sovereign has issued a command of a certain sort, or if officials have adopted rules of a certain form in a certain way...[59]

In other words, propositions of law will be assertable as true that 'provide a better...fit with the political theory that provides the best justification for propositions of law already established'.[60]

The result of our search for properties of propositions of law is truly puzzling. They are not rules, and they are not external statements either. They are normative (prescriptive), but at the same time they are true or false. They are true or false, but there may be no facts that make them true, not social facts, not moral facts, and not facts of normative consistency either. They are true or false, but at the same time they are not quite true or false but only assertable as true or false. They have properties in common with norms (their normativity) and with normative propositions (truth-values), but they are not identical with either of these two categories.

The fact that Dworkin ignores the distinction between norms and normative propositions leads to a curious result: his propositions of law have properties of

[57] Dworkin, 'No Right Answer?', (n. 49, this chapter), 82.
[58] Dworkin, 'No Right Answer?', (n. 49, this chapter), 83.
[59] Dworkin, 'No Right Answer?', (n. 49, this chapter), 74.
[60] Dworkin, 'No Right Answer?', (n. 49, this chapter), 75.

both, even if these properties are incompatible. Thus, according to Dworkin, the concepts *norms* and *normative propositions* are as a pair neither jointly exhaustive nor even mutually exclusive.

This explains the apparent invulnerability of Dworkin's position. None of his critics has succeeded in refuting his theory, for it is invulnerable to any partial attack. However, the very same fact that makes his theory invulnerable also makes it indefensible. Since his propositions of law have incompatible properties they are unintelligible.

The failure of Dworkin's critics lies in the fact that they have not taken notice of the incompatibility of the properties that he ascribes to his propositions of law, and this has no doubt happened because they paid little attention to the conceptual distinction between norms and normative propositions.

4. Conclusions

It is not easy to trace the conceptual distinction between norms and normative propositions. It took considerable time until logicians concerned with deontic logic came to a clear view on the subject. Once the ambiguity of deontic expressions was detected, however, practically all deontic logicians have made use of this conceptual distinction, however different their views on the nature of norms and on the nature of normative propositions, considered separately, may be.

It seems that in legal philosophy exactly the opposite has occurred. On the one hand, philosophers of law such as Hedenius and Alf Ross arrived, much earlier than the logicians, at a clear formulation of the distinction, no doubt because they were more familiar with deontic sentences. Later, however, this important insight was lost. Although Hart does not discuss this problem explicitly, it is still possible to trace this distinction in his work. His successors, however, have preferred to abandon it altogether. The result—as the case of Dworkin clearly shows—could not be more disastrous. I suspect that legal philosophers will have to rediscover this crucial distinction without which no clear treatment of normative language is possible.

12

Norms and Logic

Hans Kelsen and Ota Weinberger on the Ontology of Norms (1985)*

1.

Hans Kelsen's *Allgemeine Theorie der Normen*[1] is not only a remarkable intellectual achievement for a man of his age (he was still working on the book when he died at 91), but also an unusually stimulating contribution to normative theory. This posthumously published book has generated a fair bit of interest among legal philosophers and deontic logicians; the very fact that a philosopher of Ota Weinberger's distinction dedicated an entire book to Kelsen's last work is noteworthy.[2] The interest in Kelsen's book is mainly due to Kelsen's having changed many of the views that he had defended for over 50 years, and these changes concern some fundamental problems about the nature of norms and their relation to logic.

Weinberger is very critical in his approach to this last stage of Kelsen's philosophy. He maintains that Kelsen's position lacks any philosophical basis, leading to an irrationalism regarding norms (*Normenirrationalismus*) that is incompatible with the main tenets of Kelsen's Pure Theory of Law as an analytical '*Strukturtheorie*'.[3]

Although it is true that there are several obscure and even internally incompatible points in Kelsen's book (hardly surprising in an unfinished work), I do not share Weinberger's views.

I shall argue in this paper that Kelsen's ideas can be given a perfectly coherent interpretation and that, although these ideas differ greatly from those defended by Weinberger, they certainly do not lack a philosophical basis nor do they lead to any sort of irrationalism.

* [*Editors' note*: Eugenio Bulygin's article first appeared in *Law and Philosophy*, 4 (1985), 145–63, Spanish version in *ALD*, 249–65. For the present volume, Bonnie Litschewski Paulson and Stanley L. Paulson have translated a handful of quotations from Ota Weinberger's text that appear in German in Bulygin's original article.]

[1] Kelsen, *GTN*. [*Editors' note*: For this and other abbreviations, see the Table of Abbreviations.]

[2] Ota Weinberger, *Normentheorie als Grundlage der Jurisprudenz und Ethik* (Berlin: Duncker & Humblot, 1981).

[3] Weinberger (n. 2, this chapter), 168.

The main thesis of Kelsen's philosophy in the late period, and consequently the main target of Weinberger's attack, is the contention that norms are not subject to laws of logic, that is, that there are no logical relations between norms. This tenet is supported by two reasons: (i) norms are neither true nor false, and since logical relations of entailment and contradiction are defined in terms of truth, no logical relations obtain between norms; (ii) norms are closely connected to certain actions, namely, those of commanding or, more generally, of prescribing. This connection is so strong that there can be no norm without the corresponding act, and since there are no logical relations between acts, there are no such relations between norms either.

Weinberger accepts the idea that norms lack truth-values, but in his opinion this does not preclude the possibility of logical relations between norms, and he rejects Kelsen's definition of norms in terms of acts. Here, I think, lies the main source of their differences. They start from different ontological presuppositions concerning norms.

In a paper I wrote together with Carlos E. Alchourrón,[4] we maintained that there are two opposing views on the nature of norms and that a great many philosophical disagreements among deontic logicians are due to different ontological assumptions. We christened these two views the hyletic and the expressive conceptions of norms. It seems to me that the controversy between Kelsen and Weinberger fits admirably into these two categories, Weinberger being a typical representative of the hyletic conception, whereas Kelsen can be regarded (as I shall try to show) as a clear expressivist.

2.

Most philosophers agree that norms can be separated into a descriptive and a normative component. Philosophers do not quite agree on how to characterize the descriptive component, although for the most part it is treated as a kind of description of a state of affairs or an action.[5] There is no major controversy about this, despite the use of different names by different authors: phrastic (Richard Hare), norm-content (Georg Henrik von Wright, Weinberger), sentence-radical (Erik Stenius), topic (Alf Ross), modally indifferent substrate (Kelsen), and so on. More serious problems arise as soon as we turn to the normative component, where two conflicting views can be discerned that give rise to two radically different conceptions of norms.

For the *hyletic conception*, the normative component forms part of the conceptual content of the norm; it is an operator that, operating on a descriptive sentence, yields a normative sentence. A norm is the meaning of this new (normative)

[4] Alchourrón and Bulygin, 'The Expressive Conception of Norms' (1981), in this volume, ch. 9.

[5] Rather than as a proposition, the descriptive component has also been interpreted as the name of an action or as a verb phrase, see von Wright, 'DL', and Georg Henrik von Wright, 'Deontic Logic Revisited', *Rechtstheorie*, 4 (1973), 37–46.

sentence in the same sense in which a proposition is regarded as the meaning of a descriptive sentence. The peculiar thing about normative sentences *(Normsätze* in Weinberger's terminology) is that they have a *prescriptive meaning*. They do not say that something is the case, but that something ought to be (or may be) the case.

Many philosophers are reluctant to accept the very notion of prescriptive meaning, tending to regard it as wellnigh a contradiction in terms. Thus, they offer an alternative account of the normative component in terms not of the meanings of linguistic expressions but of illocutionary force[6]—that is, in terms of what is done with an expression. Norms in this *expressive* conception are not meanings of a special kind of sentence but are instead the result of a certain type of action performed by a speaker, namely, the action of prescribing (commanding, prohibiting, or permitting). The difference between an assertion, a question, a command, or a conjecture lies not in the meaning of the sentence used but in the different uses of one and the same sentence. So it is a certain use of language—namely, the so-called prescriptive use—that gives rise to norms. Therefore, the prescriptive component is not an operator, but a mere indicator of the force of an expression, that is, an indicator of the action performed by the agent who uses the expression in question.

Following the convention adopted in Alchourrón-Bulygin,[7] I shall use '*Op*' and '!*p*' as symbolic expressions for norms in the hyletic and the expressive conceptions respectively. It is important to emphasize that '*O*' is a quasi-propositional operator,[8] whereas '!' is an indicator of illocutionary force or, as Hans Reichenbach would put it, a sign 'acting in its pragmatic capacity'.[9]

The expressive conception of norms precludes the very possibility of a logic of norms: If normativity consists in a certain use of language and norms are expressions of illocutionary acts, then there are no logical relations between norms. In other words, the expression '!*p*' cannot be negated, and it cannot enter into logical relations with similar expressions either.[10] This does not, however, necessarily lead to any form of irrationalism. Although there is no logic of norms, there is a logic of norm-propositions, that is, propositions about the normative status of certain actions or states of affairs according to a given normative system.

3.

Weinberger's starting point is the distinction between two types of sentence: the *Aussagesatz*, which is the descriptive or declarative sentence expressing a proposition, and the *Normsatz* (normative sentence), the meaning of which is not a

[6] On the distinction between meaning and force, see J. L. Austin, *How To Do Things With Words* (Oxford: Clarendon Press, 1962).

[7] Alchourrón and Bulygin (n. 4, this chapter).

[8] I call this operator quasi-propositional, because the meaning of '*Op*' is not a descriptive proposition but a prescriptive, proposition-like entity.

[9] Hans Reichenbach, *Elements of Symbolic Logic* (New York: Free Press, 1947), 336–42. Weinberger uses both signs '*O*' and '!' as operators, which is why I substitute '*Op*' for his sign '!*p*', even in quotations.

[10] Reichenbach (n. 9, this chapter), 342.

proposition but a norm. This distinction is a semantic one; the difference lies in the meaning of the sentences, normative sentences being endowed with a specifically normative or prescriptive meaning. So Weinberger's *gnoseologisch* differentiated semantic[11] (the distinction between *Aussagesätze* and *Normsätze*) rests on the assumption that there are prescriptive meanings. No justification for this assumption is offered in his book; Weinberger simply assumes that we can understand normative sentences and that this shows that they have prescriptive meaning. Moreover, he reads into Kelsen the same assumption:

> The norm is understood from linguistic expressions; it is the meaning of acts of will because this meaning is understood from the expression of the act, not from the interpretation of the act as a fact.[12]

As a criticism of Kelsen's insistence on the inseparability of act and norm, Weinberger adds:

> One can understand normative sentences very well even if there is no corresponding act of will... In any case, the meaning-construct of the norm can, without an existing act of will, be made the object of consideration.[13]

Weinberger's interpretation of Kelsen's definition of a norm as 'the meaning (*Sinn*) of acts of will' entails a commitment to the hyletic conception of norms, which is, I think, contrary at least to the spirit of Kelsen's theory. Kelsen's definition is undoubtedly rather obscure and can give rise to various interpretations. However, I am inclined to think, contrary to Weinberger, that the term '*Sinn*' refers in this context not to the meaning of a linguistic expression but to its force, that is, to the illocutionary act performed by the speaker. That the terms 'meaning' and '*Sinn*' are often used in this peculiar sense is well known, as J. L. Austin points out.[14] In exactly which sense Kelsen actually intended to use the term '*Sinn*' is hard to say, but I am not so much interested in determining Kelsen's actual intentions. Rather, my interest lies in giving a coherent interpretation of his main ideas, and *one* way, though perhaps not the only way, of rendering Kelsen coherent is to take '*Sinn*' to refer to force, not to meaning.

In any case, Weinberger's argument that we can understand normative sentences does not show that there is such a thing as prescriptive meaning. The term 'understand' is certainly ambiguous. It can refer not only to meaning but also to force, as when someone says: 'I understand that he wants to command me to do something, but I do not understand what it is, for I do not know his language.' The first occurrence of 'understand' makes reference to illocutionary force (in this sense we can understand what X does without knowing X's language). The second occurrence refers to meaning, and here, knowledge of the language is essential. Thus, even if we can, in some sense, understand that an expression uttered on a certain occasion is a command (or a question), this does not prove that there are prescriptive

[11] [*Editors' note*: 'gnoseologisch' or 'epistemologically' differentiated semantic.]

[12] Weinberger (n. 2, this chapter), 117.

[13] Weinberger (n. 2, this chapter), 117.

[14] Austin (n. 6, this chapter), 100.

meanings and, hence, that there are normative sentences as a semantic category distinct from the ordinary sentences expressing propositions.

On the other hand, it is not enough to postulate prescriptive meanings in order to ensure the possibility of a logic of norms. Certainly, whereas the expressive conception precludes such a possibility, the question remains open for the hyletic conception. It is by no means obvious, however, that the question ought to receive an affirmative answer. There are considerable difficulties inherent in the very notion of prescriptive meaning that need to be overcome first.

One main problem concerns the meaning of logical connectives like negation, disjunction, and so on. They are usually defined in terms of truth (for example, by means of truth tables). Since normative sentences lack truth-values, logical connectives must have a different meaning when used in prescriptive discourse. It is far from clear what the meaning of expressions like '*Op* v *Oq*' or '–*Op*' as normative sentences would be.[15]

Weinberger does not even mention this problem in his book on Kelsen, although he grants elsewhere that the negation of a normative sentence is quite different from ordinary (propositional) negation.[16] Indeed, it is so different that it scarcely deserves to be called negation at all, for it is not an operation that would lead from one norm to another norm: '–*Op*' expresses not a norm but the derogation of a norm.[17]

So it seems that for Weinberger there is, in the realm of norms, no operation of negation analogous to propositional negation, but then it is not clear what the disjunction or conjunction of norms could possibly mean or how they are related. De Morgan's laws would obviously not hold, and many other laws of propositional logic would not hold either. One begins to suspect that a normative logic without negation would look extremely strange.

4.

No less difficult is the problem of how to define the concepts of logical implication (entailment) and logical incompatibility (contradiction) between norms. I shall consider these two problems separately, beginning with the latter.

Weinberger's characterization of logical incompatibility between norms does not seem to me to be entirely convincing. He tries to shape a concept of normative

[15] See the discussion of this problem in Georg Henrik von Wright, 'Problems and Prospects of Deontic Logic', in *Modern Logic. A Survey*, ed. Evandro Agazzi (Dordrecht: D. Reidel, 1980), 339–423, and Georg Henrik von Wright, 'Norms, Truth and Logic', in *Deontic Logic, Computational Linguistics and Legal Information Systems*, ed. Antonio A. Martino (Amsterdam: North-Holland, 1982), vol. II, 3–20.

[16] Ota Weinberger and Christiane Weinberger, *Logik, Semantik, Hermeneutik* (Munich: C. H. Beck, 1979), 121–2.

[17] Weinberger and Weinberger (n. 16, this chapter), 121–2. See also von Wright, *NA*, at 138–9, on the requirements that the concept of negation ought to fulfil.

inconsistency closely analogous to the notion of contradictory or inconsistent propositions.

Two propositions '*p*' and '*–p*' are inconsistent because, for reasons of logic, they cannot both be true (the corresponding facts or states of affairs cannot obtain).[18] It is exactly on this point, however, that there is no analogy to norms. In the first place, the incompatibility of '*Op*' and '*–Op*', which one would feel inclined to take as the analogue of '*p*' and '*–p*', is not even mentioned by Weinberger, probably because this would not be a case of incompatibility of *norms*. As already mentioned, '*–Op*' is not a norm, so the only case of incompatibility discussed by Weinberger is '*Op*' and '*O –p*'. Now in what sense can these two norms be said to be inconsistent? Clearly not in the same sense as '*p*' and '*–p*' are inconsistent, for norms are neither true nor false. Nor, for reasons of logic, would it do to say that these two norms cannot both be obeyed or satisfied (at the same time). This is certainly correct, but the impossibility of satisfaction is due to the fact that the propositions '*p*' and '*–p*' (that is, the contents of the two norms) cannot both be true, so we are faced here with an inconsistency of norm-content and not of norms. This inconsistency of norm-content entails the impossibility of satisfying both norms, but it does not follow then that the norms '*Op*' and '*O –p*' are inconsistent as well. Therefore, if the alleged contradiction between '*Op*' and '*O –p*' were only to mean that the two norms cannot be satisfied for reasons of logic (that is, independently of all experience), this would be just another way of saying that the propositions '*p*' and '*–p*' are contradictory, that is, there would be nothing other than an inconsistency between (descriptive) propositions.

Weinberger seems to agree on this point when he says that 'the incompatibility of ['*Op*' and '*O –p*'] does not follow solely from the impossibility that both states of affairs *(p, –p)* be facts'.[19]

What else could explain the alleged inconsistency of '*Op*' and '*O –p*'? They are not incompatible in the sense that they cannot coexist in one and the same system or code of norms, for there is no such impossibility. As a matter of fact, a legislative authority might issue both norms, and in such a case both would be valid, that is, both would belong to the same system. Weinberger grants this, but such an issuance of norms would lead, in his opinion, to a '*logical* defect of the system'.[20]

No doubt it would be a defect, but why call it a logical defect? Weinberger makes a distinction between factually and logically unsatisfiable norms:

> To establish 'ought'-sentences that are impossible to satisfy factually cannot be purposeful; it is therefore impractical to set as an obligation something that cannot be realized—although this is, to be sure, by no means senseless (logically without sense). However, to set down

[18] Weinberger (n. 2, this chapter), 70.

[19] Weinberger (n. 2, this chapter), 70. Weinberger's own text reads: 'Die Unverträglichkeit von ['*Op*' und '*O –p*'] folgt nicht allein aus der Unmöglichkeit, daß beide Sachverhalte (*p*, *–p*) Tatsachen sind.' [*Editors' note*: A printer's error in the original text is corrected here.]

[20] Weinberger (n. 2, this chapter), 70. Weinberger's own text reads: '. . . die gleichzeitige Geltung beider Sollsätze in ein und demselben Normensystem ist ein *logischer* Mangel des Systems.'

norms that are at one and the same time incompatible is indeed senseless and to be rejected on purely logical grounds.[21]

I see no difference between the two situations from a practical point of view. In both cases, the norms are unsatisfiable and therefore impractical, unless it is the case that what the legislator wants is to create precisely such a predicament for the norm-subject.[22] That unsatisfiability is factual in one case and logical in the other seems to be irrelevant to the practical reasonableness of the two norms.

Yet Weinberger insists that although two incompatible norms, '*Op*' and '*O –p*', may be members of one and the same system, this would be a logical deficiency 'by virtue of a rule'.[23] What is this rule that turns the coexistence of the two norms into a logical defect of the system?

According to Weinberger, it is the prohibition against issuing incompatible norms in one system, which he calls the 'norm-logical principle of non-contradiction' (*normenlogisches Widerspruchsprinzip*) or the 'norm-logical postulate of consistency' (*normenlogisches Konsistenzpostulat*).[24] This prohibition is analogous to the prohibition against asserting contradictory propositions.

Common to both relations of incompatibility—that between statements and that between norms—is only that they are independent of experience and that, in each case, the logical postulate is valid, not to set down both statements or both norms at the same time (not to claim or to issue both within one system).[25]

It is more than doubtful that there is such a rule of logic, even in the case of descriptive sentences. Rules of logic have nothing to do with actual assertions; they refer to the content of possible assertions, that is, to propositions. Thus, a rule to the effect that one ought not to assert inconsistent propositions would be a pragmatic rule governing rational behaviour concerning acts of assertion. The rationale for such a rule would be the rule of logic defining inconsistency. It is because two inconsistent propositions cannot both be true that one ought not to assert them, provided that one wants to assert only true propositions. One could also say that it is a technical rule stating that if one does not want to make false assertions, then one should not assert inconsistent propositions. In any case, we must first define inconsistency, and only then are we in a position to formulate the rule prohibiting the assertion of inconsistent propositions—and not the other way around. It would be very strange indeed to say that two propositions are inconsistent because there is a rule that prohibits us from asserting them, yet this is exactly what Weinberger says in relation to norms: They are inconsistent because there is a

[21] Weinberger (n. 2, this chapter), 70.

[22] See Anscombe's example, discussed in von Wright, 'DL', and in von Wright, 'Deontic Logic Revisited' (n. 5, this chapter).

[23] Weinberger (n. 2, this chapter), 70: '...es geht um eine Regel, die sich speziell auf das Sollen bezieht.'

[24] Weinberger (n. 2, this chapter), 69–70: '...man kann das Verbot, unverträgliche Normsätze in *einem* System zu setzen, als "normenlogisches Widerspruchsprinzip" oder "normenlogisches Konsistenzpostulat" bezeichnen.'

[25] Weinberger (n. 2, this chapter), 71.

rule that prohibits us from issuing them. There seems to be no ground for his 'postulate of consistency' (*Konsistenzpostulat*) other than the fact that these norms are unsatisfiable. Thus, when all is said and done, the unsatisfiability of these norms is the only reason for calling them inconsistent, and this is not an altogether convincing reason, as Weinberger himself admits.

It seems that there is no sufficiently strong analogy between the inconsistency of propositions and the alleged incompatibility of norms. Although the coexistence of '*Op*' an '*O* –*p*' would certainly be undesirable and impractical, this alone does not justify our calling them logically inconsistent.

5.

I will now consider Weinberger's foundation of the relation of deducibility or entailment between norms. The problem considered earlier and the present problem are, of course, related.

The main reason adduced by Kelsen in support of his contention that there are no logical relations between norms is the lack of truth-values. He also explores some other properties of norms that could play an analogous role in the realm of norms and could therefore be used for the foundation of a logic of norms, namely, validity and efficacy. His conclusion is that neither of these properties bears an analogy to truth sufficient to justify the existence of logical relations.

Although Weinberger agrees with Kelsen that norms lack truth-values, he thinks that validity can play a role similar to truth. One of Kelsen's arguments against validity as a possible bearer of logical deducibility is that validity means the same as existence, thus there are no invalid norms. This contention is very dubious. Weinberger points out rightly that if 'validity' means membership in a system of norms and 'existence' is understood as relative to a system, then to say that there are no invalid norms is certainly correct but, at the least, is not very illuminating. If, on the other hand, we understand by 'existence' the performance of an act of prescribing, then the 'existence' of invalid norms is clearly possible. It is the same if, by the 'existence' of a sentence, we mean that this sentence, be it descriptive or normative, is a meaningful element of a language.[26]

According to Weinberger, Kelsen's mistake is to compare validity with truth rather than to compare it with assertion. Here Weinberger believes he has found a concept that is common both to norms and to propositions and that can be used as a basis for logical deducibility. As he writes:

> A parallel between the validity of the norm and the validity of the statement can be constructed by means of the following stipulation: 'The norm *N* is valid (in *NS*)' means '*N* is a component of the system of norms *NS*'; 'The statement *A* is valid' means '*A* is a component of a system of statements *AS* (and *is true*)'. Thus, a generic concept (*Oberbegriff*) can be

[26] Weinberger (n. 2, this chapter), 95–7.

found that warrants the common introduction of premisses having the character of statements and of norms.[27]

I have emphasized the phrase '*is true*', for it shows clearly an asymmetry between norms and assertions even in Weinberger's own formulation. A descriptive sentence, to be valid, must not only be asserted (that is, must be a member of an assertion-system), but must *also be true,* whereas there is no such requirement in the case of norms.

Nevertheless, Weinberger believes that it is possible to give a definition of logical deducibility for norms in terms of validity. Essential for this definition, in his opinion, is the existence of a hereditary property (*Erbeigenschaft*), but this need not be truth:

> The conception of a 'hereditary property' of logical consequence for norm-sentences (norms) or the construction of such a property for both categories of sentence can, likewise, be carried out. On the side of premisses, issuance (presupposition) can mean 'set down as true' for statements and 'set down as valid' for norm-sentences. On the side of conclusions, one can say 'established as true' of statements and 'established as valid' of norm-sentences.[28]

In the first place, it is clear that not every hereditary property with respect to a relation renders this relation logical, and I do not think that Weinberger would subscribe to such a bold contention. Only certain hereditary properties like truth give rise to the logical relation of deducibility. The question is whether validity can play a similar role with respect to normative sentences. I am inclined to think that the answer should be negative if by 'validity' we understand—as Weinberger explicitly does—membership in or belonging to a system. In this sense, 'the norm *N* is valid in the system *NS*' means '*N* belongs to *NS*'. Then, however, we have no criterion for distinguishing between logical and nonlogical or ad-hoc rules of inference, for all of them fulfil Weinberger's requirement. All of them preserve validity, and so validity is hereditary in relation to them. Weinberger quite explicitly rejects certain rules of inference like '*Op,* so *O(p* v *q)*' or '*O(p* & *q),* so *Op*'.[29] What are the grounds for this rejection? These rules certainly preserve validity, yet they are rejected as rules of logical inference; thus, this is not a sufficient condition for being a rule of logic, not even for Weinberger himself. He rejects them by appeal to certain intuitive considerations, but he does not make explicit the criterion he uses, which is not the one he officially states in his book.

Moreover, although Weinberger does not give an explicit definition of 'normative system', he probably has in mind a Tarskian concept of a system as a set of sentences that includes all its consequences. This means that the notion of a system already presupposes a set of rules of inference (which define the notion of consequence). To say, however, that the rules of inference preserve the property of

[27] Weinberger (n. 2, this chapter), 97 (emphasis added).

[28] Weinberger (n. 2, this chapter), 122.

[29] See Ota Weinberger, 'Normenlogik anwendbar im Recht', *Logique et Analyse,* 49–50 (N.S. 13) (1970), 93–106, at 102–6; Weinberger and Weinberger (n. 16, this chapter), at 106.

being valid (that is, being a member of the system) is vacuous because it is analytic with respect to the notions of system and validity. Nothing of the kind is the case regarding truth. To say that rules of inference preserve truth is far from being analytic because truth is defined independently of the notion of a system. Here, too, the analogy between propositions and norms breaks down.

6.

It was not my intention to argue that the hyletic conception of norms—of which Weinberger is perhaps the most conspicuous and lucid representative and which was for a long time also shared by Alchourrón and myself—is wrong and that there is no possibility of constructing a genuine logic of norms.[30] What I wanted to do was to point out certain difficulties in Weinberger's arguments on behalf of the hyletic conception, in order to show that it is by no means as obviously correct as a hurried reader of Weinberger might be led to believe. At the same time, I wanted to show that Kelsen's philosophy during the late period—or, putting the point more cautiously, that the expressive conception of norms—is not as hopeless as Weinberger would have us believe.

There is no doubt that if norms are closely linked to types of act, then no logical relations obtain between them and no logic of norms is possible, but this does not necessarily lead to irrationalism. There are several other ways of constructing a logic related to norms, ways that are compatible with the expressive conception. One such way has been proposed recently by Georg Henrik von Wright. It consists in interpreting deontic logic as a logic of (rational) norm-giving.[31] Another attempt to overcome irrationalism without postulating normative meanings is to construct a logic of normative propositions, that is, propositions to the effect that such and such a state of affairs (or an action) is obligatory, prohibited, or permitted according to a given set of norms.

A normative system, according to this conception, would not be a system of norms, but a system of norm-contents, that is, propositions descriptive of certain states of affairs or actions. A proposition, once commanded, is regarded as obligatory as long as the command is not withdrawn or cancelled. Thus all propositions commanded by a certain authority or set of authorities form the *commanded set.* If all logical consequences of the commanded set are also regarded as obligatory (and this means that they are regarded as implicitly commanded), then we arrive at a normative system that is the set of all consequences of the commanded set.

In order to give an account of the derogation or cancellation of norms, we need to introduce the *act of rejection* as a special illocutionary act, different from commanding or prescribing, that leads to the elimination of certain propositions from

[30] I am, however, becoming increasingly sceptical of the hyletic conception.

[31] Von Wright, 'Norms, Truth and Logic' (n. 15, this chapter).

the commanded set according to certain rules.[32] Then the concept of permission can be defined in terms of derogation, an idea that is also shared by Weinberger.[33]

In this way, an expressivist can give an account of the temporal existence of norms in terms of acts of commanding and acts of rejecting certain propositions (norm-contents).

A logic of norm-propositions would then be a logic of propositions to the effect that certain other propositions belong or do not belong to the commanded set, or (which is the same) that they are obligatory, prohibited, or permitted (in relation to a set of norms). Such propositions are true or false, and so they can enter into logical relations.

I shall not try to develop a logic of this kind here, but there is one point that deserves closer attention. It is the relation between general and individual norms and, in particular, the relation between a general law and a judicial decision.

Kelsen maintains, on the one hand, that no individual norm can be derived by logical means from a general norm and, on the other, that an individual norm—the judge's sentencing the convicted criminal, for example—can be justified by a general norm. In order to account for the latter, he introduces the notion of correspondence (*Entsprechung*). But what does 'correspondence' mean in this context? According to Weinberger, it can only be understood as the logical relation of deducibility: A norm is justified by another norm if and only if it is logically derivable from the second norm. Then, however, there are logical relations between norms after all, and so there appears to be a lack of coherence in Kelsen's theory.

It is true that much of what Kelsen actually says on this topic is rather confused—for instance, his theory of the recognition (*Anerkennung*) of validity, which, as Weinberger rightly points out, is inconsistent with the main tenets of the Pure Theory of Law. However, I think that these inconsistencies are mainly due to the fact that Kelsen did not have enough time to harmonize his new ideas with the old ideas. Thus, the problems are more often verbal in nature than substantive. In particular, I believe it is possible to give a coherent account of the relation between a general law and a judicial sentence in terms of the expressive conception of norms. I would even venture the hypothesis that the difference between the hyletic and expressive conceptions is, on this point, not as radical as Weinberger would have us believe. All or nearly all that he has to say on this topic can also be said, albeit in different language, by an expressivist like Kelsen.

Indeed, Weinberger does not maintain that the judicial decision (as a certain act of the judge) can be logically derived from the general norm. This would be absurd, and Weinberger clearly rejects such an interpretation: 'The norm-logical deduction is not the creation of a norm—and no one understands it in this way'.[34] What can be derived, according to Weinberger, is the content of the act of the judge, and this content is an individual norm.

[32] Alchourrón and Bulygin (n. 4, this chapter).
[33] Weinberger and Weinberger (n. 16, this chapter), 128.
[34] Weinberger (n. 2, this chapter), 109.

For an expressivist the situation is similar. If norms depend on acts of prescribing, then there clearly is no logical entailment between a general and an individual norm (for example, between the act of the lawmaker and the act of the judge). There may, however, be a logical relation of deducibility between the contents of those two acts, with the only difference being that what is meant by 'content' here is a proposition, whereas for the hyletic conception what is meant would be a norm.

I shall illustrate this with an example. Suppose the legislative authority issues a general norm to the effect that all landowners should pay a special tax. The proposition commanded by the lawmaker (that is, the content of this norm) is that all landowners are to pay a special tax, and so it is true that all landowners have an obligation to pay the tax (or, as we might also say, they ought to pay it). Now, from 'all landowners are to pay the tax', it follows that landowner A is to pay the tax, so the proposition 'A is to pay the tax' belongs to the commanded set, and therefore it is true that A has an obligation to pay the tax. This shows that Weinberger is correct in asserting that a general norm by virtue of its very meaning (or rather the meaning of its content) concerns all who happen to be its addressees, in our case landowners, and creates an obligation for all of them. This is not yet the end of the matter.

Being a landowner, A has an obligation to pay the tax, but it may very well be the case that he does not pay the tax in the allotted time and so does not fulfil his obligation. In this case, he can be brought before a court. Now the norm that regulates the activity of the judge does not prescribe that all landowners who fail to pay their taxes be sentenced, that is, all those of whom it is true that they ought to pay their taxes and did not pay in the allotted time. Rather, the norm prescribes that all those of whom it has been *proven in a court of law* that they ought to pay and did not pay be sentenced. ('Proven in a court of law' is an abbreviation for the complex judicial process.) Once it has been proven in court that landowner A did not pay his tax, then it is true that the judge ought (or has an obligation) to sentence him either to a fine or to prison. This is so because the proposition that the judge is to sentence A belongs to the commanded set (being a consequence of the explicitly commanded proposition that landowners of whom it has been proven in court that they ought to pay and did not pay are to be sentenced by the judge). Thus, if the judge issues a norm sentencing A, this norm is justified by the general norm concerning the duties of the judge, and this means that its content (which is a proposition) is logically derivable from the content of a general norm.

The existence of two parallel and related sets of norms, which may be called the primary system and the secondary system,[35] addressed to the population in general (or to a subset of it) and to the courts respectively, is an important feature of legal orders. The two systems are related in the sense that the secondary or the judge's system presupposes the existence of the primary or the subject's system; thus, they are found at different levels. This gives rise to some interesting situations that might

[35] See Alchourrón and Bulygin, *NS*, at 148.

well seem paradoxical. For instance, it may be true that A ought to pay his taxes and did not pay them but that the judge nevertheless ought not to sentence him (if, for example, A's failure to pay has not been proven in court). Vice versa, it may be true that the judge ought to sentence A for not having paid his taxes, although it is not true that A failed to pay. This sounds even more paradoxical in the field of penal law. It may be true that A ought to be sentenced to prison and yet that the judge ought not to sentence him, and, conversely, it may be true that the judge ought to sentence A to prison and at the same time it is true that A ought not to be imprisoned.

The air of paradox vanishes once we distinguish clearly between the primary and the secondary systems and keep in mind that a proposition's being proven in court does not entail its truth. Legal proof is very different from scientific proof, for 'proof in court' means not a complete proof but, rather, a certain finite procedure that tends to establish whether or not the proposition in question is true, a procedure that must come to an end in a given time. The result is a decision based on the existing, often rather scant evidence. It is no wonder that a court sometimes decides that a proposition is true when it is in fact false, and vice versa.

Take the famous case of Dmitri Karamazov. He did not kill his father, and so, according to the penal law, he ought not to be punished. There was a certain amount of evidence against him, however, and the jury decided that he had killed his father. Once this decision had been taken, the judge had an obligation to sentence Karamazov to prison. The judge did so, and his decision was perfectly lawful—that is, it was justified by the law of procedure, although not by the penal law.

One could ask, however, what is the point of saying that according to penal law Dmitri ought not to be sentenced, if the sentence was lawful and he was sent to Siberia? There are at least two important points (although they are perhaps irrelevant to Dmitri's personal fate). First, what has to be proven in court is determined by penal law and not by procedural norms, and, second, that a judge's sentence, although lawful, is not justified by penal law makes it possible for us to say that it was wrong, that a judicial mistake was made in the case of Dmitri Karamazov. To say this would not make sense if there were only norms addressed to the judge and no underlying law. This shows, by the way, that those theories that tend to interpret all legal norms as directives addressed to the courts[36] are deeply mistaken. They lead not only to a distortion of the function of the law but also to a most inconvenient limitation on the expressive capacity of legal language.

I hope that this picture of judicial decisions and the underlying general norms shows that the existence of logical relations between norm-contents averts the perils of irrationalism and makes it possible for an expressivist to give an account of all the relevant facts, albeit in different language. This confirms my impression that there is no crucial test that would allow us to decide between the two conceptions. Weinberger's contention, then, that Kelsen's philosophy in the late period is clearly wrong-headed is, at the very least, an exaggeration.

[36] Ross, *LJ*.

13

Legal Dogmatics and the Systematization of the Law (1986)*

1. Preliminary Remarks

Aulis Aarnio's theory of legal reasoning is one of the most important contributions to legal philosophy in recent years. In successive publications, many of which are unfortunately not yet available outside Finland, Aarnio has developed a comprehensive theory of judicial decision-making and of legal dogmatics. It is with the latter topic that I will be concerned here. I intend to discuss some of Aarnio's views on the task of legal dogmatics and the systematization of legal norms, comparing these views with the ideas presented in *Normative Systems*.[1] Aarnio's account of systematization differs, in important respects, a good deal from the picture outlined in *Normative Systems*, and it may be of interest to compare both theories in order to trace the origin of the differences, which, I hope, will shed some light on different aspects of legal dogmatics and the different tasks performed by those working in the field. At the same time I will take into account the forceful criticism (directed both to Aarnio and to *Normative Systems*) that has been put forth in two highly illuminating papers by another distinguished Finnish scholar, Ilkka Niiniluoto.[2]

2. Legal Dogmatics

Legal dogmatics is a complex activity in which at least three different stages can and should be distinguished: (i) the identification of legal norms, (ii) the

* [*Editors' note*: Eugenio Bulygin's paper was first published in *Vernunft und Erfahrung im Rechtsdenken der Gegenwart*, ed. Torstein Eckhoff, et al. (*ARSP Beiheft* 10) (Berlin: Duncker & Humblot, 1986), 195–210. Spanish version in *ALD*, 465–84.]

[1] Alchourrón and Bulygin, *NS*. [*Editors' note*: For this and other abbreviations, see the Table of Abbreviations.]

[2] Ilkka Niiniluoto, 'On Truth and Argumentation in Legal Dogmatics', in *Methodologie und Erkenntnistheorie der juristischen Argumentation*, ed. Aulis Aarnio, et al. (*Rechtstheorie Beiheft* 2) (Berlin: Duncker & Humblot, 1981), 53–76, hereafter 'Legal Dogmatics'; Ilkka Niiniluoto, 'On the Truth of Norm Propositions', in *Zum Fortschritt von Theorie und Technik in Recht und Ethik*, ed. Ilmar Tammelo and Aulis Aarnio (*Rechtstheorie Beiheft* 3) (Berlin: Duncker & Humblot, 1981), 171–80 [hereafter 'Norm Propositions'].

systematization of legal norms, and (iii) the modification or transformation of legal systems. Not all of these activities are theoretical or cognitive in nature; legal dogmatics also fulfils an important practical function. This is why it is so difficult to classify so-called legal 'science'[3] into any of the well-defined categories of sentences endowed with a definite and constant meaning. Thus, two structurally identical sentences with different meanings—that is, sentences that do not correlate the same cases with the same solutions—would count as two different norms (exactly as for Aarnio and Niiniluoto), and two different sentences with identical meaning would also be two different, though equivalent, norms (whereas for Aarnio and Niiniluoto they would express the same norm).

As for the objection that there are, according to *Normative Systems*, two legal orders in a bilingual country, we must distinguish first between a legal *system* as the set of all logical consequences of a given set of norms and a particular *formulation* of the axiomatic basis or code of a system. I firmly believe that to say that there are in Finland two—and in Switzerland even three—different formulations of (an axiomatic basis of) a system is far from being unrealistic and is the only correct way of describing the situation. Of course, these formulations claim to be different formulations *of the same system,* but whether this claim is justified or not is an empirical question. It is by no means warranted a priori that the two formulations are indeed logically equivalent. If they are, no problem arises, for then we have two formulations of one and the same system. If they are not, two situations must be distinguished. (i) Suppose that only one of them is 'authentic' because, for example, the Finnish parliament follows only the Finnish version in voting, not the Swedish version. Now if the two versions are not equivalent—that is, there are some consequences stemming from the Finnish text that are not derivable from the Swedish text, or vice versa—then jurists would say that the Swedish version is a bad translation and should be amended. (ii) It might also be the case that both versions are authentic because, for example, parliament follows both in its voting. Then there are not only two different formulations, but two different legal systems, which is politically a highly undesirable situation but not a logically impossible one.

Nor is it true that in the case of a shift in interpretation the statutes remain the same. If by 'statutes' we understand certain legal norms—and this in the terminology of *Normative Systems* means sentences correlating cases with solutions—then a shift in interpretation entails a change of such correlations and so a change of statutes, that is, of legal norms. No change would take place only in the case in which statutes are mere norm-formulations without meaning. The fact that jurists sometimes use the term 'norm' in this restricted sense does not warrant Niiniluoto's ascription of this use to us. (As we shall see later, even Aarnio—despite his explicit definition of norm as proposition or meaning—uses the term 'norm' on many occasions as synonymous with norm-formulation, that is, a mere text without any fixed meaning.)

[3] The term 'legal science' is not common in the English-speaking countries. One reason Anglo-American writers are not inclined to use this term in connection with the typical activity of legal scholars is owing to its practical or normative aspect.

Thus, Niiniluoto's objection that our definition of 'norm' does not give a realistic picture of the practice of legal dogmatists seems to have no support. On the other hand, if a norm is a sentence with a definite meaning, then the identification of legal norms (or the interpretation of law texts)[4] consists in the determination of the meaning of norm-formulations, that is, sentences occurring in legal texts. Thus, the process of identification will be described in the same terms or very similar terms by a theory that defines norms as propositions or as meaningful sentences. It is important to bear in mind that no detailed account of this process is actually given in *Normative Systems* for the prosaic reason that the problem of identification lies beyond the scope of the book, whose main concern is with the second task of legal dogmatics (systematization), to wit:

> It is particularly important to draw a sharp distinction between *logical problems,* which arise in the course of the activity of jurists that we call the *systematization* of legal sentences, and *empirical problems*, which arise in the course of the prior activity of identifying these sentences. (This division does not claim to exhaust the whole set of problems of the science of law.)[5]

Summing up thus far: Niiniluoto's proposal to treat norms as propositions can hardly be regarded as an alternative that is more satisfactory than that offered in *Normative Systems*. For many purposes, it is substantially equivalent to the account given in *Normative Systems*, and in some respects it is less advantageous. There are certain problems (posed above all by the phenomenon of *derogation)* that cannot be solved at the level of propositions (that is, at the level of the conceptual content of a system), but that require that a particular formulation of the system be considered (see section 3, this article).

The assertion that problems of identification are empirical is in need of clarification. It is, I think, an overstatement, for these problems are not purely empirical. To a certain extent, however, they are indeed empirical.

In this connection it is important to distinguish between the discovery of an existing meaning and the assignment of a (wholly or partially) new meaning. The first activity is empirical despite the fact that meanings are not empirical entities. The meaning of an expression is given either by *common usage* in ordinary language or legal discourse or by the *intention* of the author of the expression (in our case, the norm-authority). Both can be investigated and eventually determined by empirical methods.[6] This is why, unlike Aarnio, I am sceptical about the need for a special (hermeneutical) method for determining the meaning of legal sentences.

In certain circumstances, however, it may prove impossible to discover the meaning of an expression (for example, if it is very obscure or hopelessly ambiguous). In such cases, it may be necessary to *assign* a meaning to it. Jurists usually do this

[4] By 'law texts' I understand not only statutes, but also judicial decisions, legal drafts, and any other relevant text.

[5] Alchourrón and Bulygin, *NS*, 65–6 (emphasis in original).

[6] See Ross, *LJ*, at 121–3, on subjective and objective interpretation. See also Carlos E. Alchourrón and Eugenio Bulygin, 'Definiciones y normas', in *El lenguaje del derecho. Homenaje a Genaro R. Carrió*, ed. Eugenio Bulygin, et al. (Buenos Aires: Abeledo-Perrot, 1983), 11–42, in *ALD*, 439–63.

by means of stipulative definitions, which play the role of proposals. Once such a stipulative definition is generally accepted by the legal community, it becomes a descriptive definition: it is descriptive of prevailing linguistic usage.[7]

This process of assigning a meaning is not cognitive; it is a matter of decision, which of course may be backed by more or less convincing reasons. Thus, the activity that consists in the identification of legal norms is not entirely cognitive—it is not, to the extent that jurists aim not solely at discovering the meaning of norm-formulations but also, at least in certain cases, at assigning new meanings.

The distinction between the discovery and the assignment of a meaning sheds some light on the relation between norm-propositions and norms. Aarnio is not entirely clear on this topic. He speaks, for example, of the 'creation of norm propositions',[8] of their validity instead of their truth, and he even claims that '[t]here exists nothing to which the norm proposition could directly be compared to determine its validity'.[9] This last claim is true only of those cases in which practitioners of legal dogmatics assign a new meaning to an expression. In such cases the norm-proposition is indeed neither true nor false in the sense of correspondence, and something 'softer' than the correspondence theory of truth is in fact required. It would be a mistake, however, to think that this always occurs; situations in which jurists assign a new meaning to a legal sentence are relatively rare. In many cases, norm-formulations have a more or less precise meaning, and it is perfectly possible to determine what it is by observation either of the prevailing linguistic usage or of the intentions of the norm-authority. Here Niiniluoto's contention that norm-propositions are either true or false and that we need the correspondence theory of truth is correct. To *this* extent, his criticism of Aarnio's conception of truth in legal dogmatics is justified, but I think that he exaggerates when he says that '[t]he only notion of truth which is needed in connection with legal dogmatics is [that of] correspondence'.[10] There is a grain of truth in Aarnio's claim on behalf of a coherence or consensus theory of truth in the field of legal dogmatics.

3. Systematization

The second stage in the typical activity of legal dogmatics is the systematization of legal norms. According to *Normative Systems*, systematization includes two different activities: (a) the solution of generic cases by means of the derivation of the consequences of the set of legal norms, and (b) the reformulation of the legal system.

(a) In order to determine the content of a legal system, the practitioner of legal dogmatics must be able to determine which legal consequences

[7] See Niiniluoto, 'Legal Dogmatics' (n. 2, this chapter), at 66–70.

[8] Aulis Aarnio, *On Legal Reasoning* (Turku: Turun Yliopisto, 1977), 17.

[9] Aarnio, *On Legal Reasoning* (n. 8, this chapter), 16.

[10] Niiniluoto, 'Norm Propositions' (n. 2, this chapter), 172.

(solutions) it correlates with different kinds of situations (generic cases). Thus, he must first determine the range of legal problems that the norms in question are supposed to solve, which involves the identification of all relevant cases (Universe of Cases: *UC*) and of the actions regulated by the norms (Universe of Actions: *UA*), which in its turn gives rise to the solutions (Universe of Solutions: *US*). The next step is purely deductive, for it consists in displaying the logical consequences of the legal norms that function as the axiomatic basis of the system. In this way, certain formal or structural properties of the system, such as completeness, consistency, and independence, come to light. To put it in negative terms: setting out the logical consequences of the system (relative to a certain *UC* and a certain *US*) makes it possible for the practitioner of legal dogmatics to uncover formal mistakes or defects in the system (inconsistency, lack of completeness, that is, normative gaps, and redundancy) that might otherwise remain hidden.

It is important to stress that it is only possible to perform this task *once the problem* of *identification of legal norms has been resolved.* This is explicitly stated in *Normative Systems*: 'No matter what procedure is used to identify the sentences [i.e. the legal norms] of the basis, we cannot speak about a system or systematization unless a set of legal sentences has been delimited and identified.'[11] Thus, the identification of legal norms is a prior and necessary step without which no systematization is possible. This is so because a normative system is a system of norms and not a system of norm-formulations. In other words, a legal system is not a purely formal, non-interpreted system, but a system with a definite interpretation.

(b) Another task of legal dogmatics is the reformulation of the system, which consists in finding a new but equivalent axiomatic basis, that is, a new basis without changing the system itself. This new basis must be—according to the principle of economy—smaller and simpler, that is, more general and independent, but it must at the same time be normatively equivalent to the original basis, that is, its logical consequences must be the same. Niiniluoto calls this operation the conservative extension of the legal order.[12] It looks, however, more like a *conservative contraction* of *the basis* of the system.

The importance of the reformulation of the system is twofold:

(i) Reducing the number of norms pertaining to the basis makes it easier to grasp the structure as a whole and to handle it in practice. This aspect of reformulation has been stressed in *Normative Systems*.

[11] Alchourrón and Bulygin, *NS*, 69. [*Editors' note*: The insertion between square-cornered brackets is Bulygin's.]

[12] Niiniluoto, 'Legal Dogmatics' (n. 2, this chapter), 60.

(ii) A reformulation may improve the formulation of the system, for in an important sense one formulation of a system may be better than another, even if they are normatively equivalent.

This second aspect of reformulation was not considered in *Normative Systems*. As far as I know, it was Erik Stenius who first drew attention to the importance of the formulation of a system.[13] Using the term 'codex' for what is called the 'axiomatic basis' in *Normative Systems*—that is, a finite set of regulations from which all other norms of the system are derivable—Stenius stipulates that a codex is well-formed if it is independent, that is, if it contains no regulation that is a logical consequence of other regulations of the codex. Following Risto Hilpinen,[14] let us call such a well-formed codex a *normative* code of the system.

Hilpinen has convincingly shown that two normatively equivalent codes may, nevertheless, be *essentially different.* The difference comes to light in connection with *derogation.*

It has been shown that in certain circumstances the derogation of a norm or of a set of norms can lead to the so-called logical indeterminacy of the system,[15] that is, derogation does not transform a system into another well-defined system. Hilpinen terms *infelicitous* an act of derogating that leads to this result, which is certainly undesirable. Now it may occur that a derogation of the same norm(s) is felicitous regarding a given code and infelicitous regarding another, normatively equivalent code.

I might illustrate this with an example, adapted from Hilpinen in a slightly simplified form. Consider two normative systems Q and R. The code of Q is formed by the following two norms:

Q_1: John ought to work every day between 10 a.m. and 6 p.m.
Q_2: John ought not to drink while he works.

The following two norms constitute the code of R:

$R_1 = Q_1$
R_2: John ought not to drink between 10 a.m. and 6 p.m.

Although the two codes are different, the systems Q and R are normatively equivalent. They correlate exactly the same solutions with the same cases; in other words, the same actions in the same situations are obligatory or prohibited according to both systems. Nevertheless, the two systems are different. What does this difference consist in?

13 In an unpublished but nevertheless influential paper, 'Ross's Paradox and Well-Formed Codices', which Professor Stenius kindly sent to me.

14 Risto Hilpinen, 'On Normative Change', in *Ethik. Grundlagen, Probleme und Anwendungen*, ed. Edgar Morscher and Rudolf Stranzinger (Proceedings of the 5th International Wittgenstein Symposium) (Vienna: Hölder-Pichler-Tempsky, 1981), 155–64.

15 See Carlos E. Alchourron and Eugenio Bulygin, 'Unvollständigkeit, Widersprüchlichkeit und Unvollständigkeit der Normenordnungen', in *Deontische Logik und Semantik*, ed. Amedeo G. Conte, et al. (Wiesbaden: Athenaion, 1977), 20–32; Carlos E. Alchourrón and Eugenio Bulygin, *Sobre la existencia de las normas juridícas* (Valencia, Venezuela: Universidad de Carabobo, 1979), and Alchourrón and Bulygin, 'The Expressive Conception of Norms' (1981), in this volume, ch. 9.

Suppose the norm-authority (in this case John's employer) decides to lift the prohibition of drinking on Saturdays. He can do so by issuing a permissory norm M: 'John may drink on Saturdays between 10 a.m. and 6 p.m.' Since this permission is incompatible with some of the prohibitions, it is supposed that it derogates (at least partially) those prohibitions. Now if permission M is added to R, the derogation generates another well-defined system R', which differs from R in one respect, namely, the norm R_2 is replaced by the norm R'_2. It reads:

R'_2: John ought not to drink between 10 a.m. and 6 p.m., except on Saturdays.

The exception clause lifts exactly that part of the prohibition established by R_2 that is inconsistent with M. Thus, the new system R' is consistent and the act of derogation is felicitous with respect to the system R. This is so because M is inconsistent with R_2, but consistent with R_1.

However, if the same permission M is added to Q the result will be quite different. For M is consistent with each of the two norms of the code Q, but is inconsistent with the conjunction of Q_1 and Q_2. Thus, *the conjunction* Q_1 & Q_2 must be derogated. This entails that at least one of the two conjuncts (Q_1 or Q_2) must be eliminated from the system, but we have no criterion for deciding which of the two ought to be removed. (Eliminating both would certainly be too much.) Hence, the act of derogation is infelicitous, for it gives rise to two alternative systems:

Q' = (Q_1, John ought not to drink while he works except on Saturdays) and
Q = (Q_2, John ought to work every day except on Saturdays)

and there is no way of deciding which of the two is the 'right' one.

This example shows that the felicity of a derogation is relative not to a normative system or theory but rather to a particular formulation or code of the system.

Hilpinen's example shows that normative codes do not satisfy the so-called principle of intensionality: logically equivalent codes may be essentially different. This shows the importance of the reformulation of a system, for even if this operation preserves the equivalence (being no more than a conservative contraction of the code), it may nevertheless *improve* the system not only from the point of view of practical handling but also in the sense that the new code *represents better or more directly the intentions of the norm-authority or the grounds (values) on which the system is based.*[16] In addition, the new code might not give rise to the infelicity of derogation acts, whereas the old code does.

Suppose that the intention of John's employer was to prohibit John's drinking during the day because it would somehow disturb other people, but not because drinking would impair John's ability to work. In such a case, Q_2 is merely an unintended consequence of R. So the code R represents better the intentions of the norm-authority. This is not an explanation of why the derogation produced by the permission M is felicitous regarding R and infelicitous regarding Q. For in that case the same derogation should be felicitous regarding Q if Q is a better or more direct representation of the norm-authority's intentions. Unfortunately this is not

[16] See Hilpinen, 'On Normative Change' (n. 14, this chapter).

so. Suppose the motivation of John's employer was to prohibit John's drinking during working hours (for example, because it would impair John's ability to work). In this case, Q would better represent his intentions, and R_2 would be a merely unintended consequence of Q. However, the derogation produced by M would still be infelicitous with respect to Q and felicitous with respect to R. In order to render the act of derogation felicitous with respect to Q, one must introduce a hierarchical order between the norms Q_1 and Q_2. If one of them is in some sense more important than the other, then the exception clause would be introduced in the less important norm. As long as both norms are equal, however, we have no criterion for removing one instead of the other.[17]

We might sum up the foregoing discussion:

a) It is convenient to discuss the problem of derogation not in relation to normative systems but instead in relation to a particular formulation of a system, that is, a code.
b) The conservative contraction (reformulation) of the code of a system may lead to important improvements, because
c) a given code may better express the intentions of the legislator or the values on which the system is grounded than another code, even if they are normatively equivalent.

All of this suggests, contrary to Niiniluoto, that it is more convenient to define a norm as a meaningful sentence, that is, as a norm-formulation plus its meaning, rather than simply as meaning alone, for logically equivalent formulations may nevertheless be different in an important respect.

4. Modifications of a Legal System

It is well known that legal systems are dynamic in character, meaning that they are subject to change over the course of time. If a legal system is a set of norms (closed under the operation of logical consequence), then it is clear that any change of a system is a replacement of one system by another. In this sense, a legal order may be conceived of as a temporally ordered sequence of successive systems.[18]

There are three ways in which a normative system can change: (i) by the addition of a set of norms (*expansion*), (ii) by the subtraction of a set of norms (*contraction*), and (iii) by a combination of (i) and (ii), that is, by successive expansions and contractions.

[17] See Carlos E. Alchourrón and David Makinson, 'Hierarchies of Regulations', in *New Studies in Deontic Logic*, ed. Risto Hilpinen (Dordrecht: Reidel, 1981), 125–48.

[18] This terminology has been introduced in Carlos E. Alchourrón and Eugenio Bulygin, 'On the Concept of a Legal Order' (1967), in this volume, ch. 7.

Expansion normally takes place when a new norm or set of norms is generated by the sources of law; contraction is a consequence of derogation. Replacement of a norm by another, different norm can be described as contraction and expansion.

In modern times, legislation is by far the most important source of law (at least in the countries of the Roman law tradition), and it consists of the creation (promulgation) and annihilation (derogation) of norms. Thus, legislation is the main factor in legal change, and it is widely accepted that the proper task of the legislative authorities is to modify legal systems. Moreover, there is a widespread belief among jurists that it is not the task of legal theorists or of legal dogmatics in particular to change the law; legal dogmatics is often conceived of as a purely descriptive science whose function is to describe the existent law, not to modify it.[19]

In spite of this belief, it cannot be denied that legal dogmatics as a matter of fact fulfils an important normative function that goes well beyond mere cognition of the law.[20] Practitioners of legal dogmatics often make proposals for changing the existing system, and when these proposals are accepted by the legal community they produce important changes. Of course, the modifications of law introduced by legal dogmatics are usually more subtle and more restricted than those produced by the legislative authorities. It is important to bear in mind, however, that such modifications are *changes*; they are substitutions of a new system for the old one, and as such they must be sharply distinguished from the operation called systematization, which does not transform a system 'into another' that is not equivalent to the first.

Practitioners of legal dogmatics rarely, if at all, change the law in a straightforward way, as the legislator does; what they do is to *adapt* or *adjust* the system to certain requirements. The most important of these are the *rational requirements* of *completeness and consistency* and the *moral requirement* of *justice*. Moreover, practitioners of legal dogmatics usually do not perform their normative function overtly; they try to disguise it by means of different rhetorical devices. This is a tribute to a political ideology according to which only parliament (as the representative of the people) can change the law. Neither the judge nor, even less, the legal theorist ought to invade the proper sphere of legislation. In actual practice, however, things are different. In order to adapt the system to the requirements of completeness, consistency, and justice, practitioners of legal dogmatics modify the system, presenting their proposals as if they were direct consequences of the system itself.

I call the requirements of completeness and consistency rational, for they do not depend on any moral, political, or ideological commitment; if they are not satisfied the system cannot perform its main task, namely, that of regulating human behaviour. The situation is different with respect to the moral requirement of justice. Here the system can function even if it does not satisfy this requirement, but it would function badly.

[19] See Kelsen, *RR 2*, and Ross, *LJ*.

[20] See Carlos Santiago Nino, *Algunos modelos metodológicos de 'ciencia' jurídica* (first publ. 1979) (Mexico City: Fontamara, 1993), at ch. 6.

Completeness is a relative notion; it means that the system provides a solution for each case of a relevant Universe of Cases.[21] The lack of completeness may stem from two different sources: (i) the system does not correlate a generic case with a solution *(normative gap)*, or (ii) the characterization of a case is so vague that an individual or generic case cannot be subsumed under it (*gap in recognition*). (Niiniluoto rightly points out that in *Normative Systems* we did not pay sufficient attention to the subsuming of generic cases under other generic cases.)[22]

Consistency means that no generic case has two or more incompatible solutions. Two norms that provide incompatible solutions to the same case *stand in conflict.*

It is clear that in cases of a normative gap or a gap in recognition as well as in cases of inconsistency, the system fails to perform its regulative or its evaluative function.

Practitioners of legal dogmatics use different techniques to obviate these deficiencies in a legal system. Sometimes they try to solve these problems at the level of the identification of norms: if there are several possible interpretations of a text, they prefer the one that does not give rise to gaps or normative conflicts. Thus, the ideals of completeness and consistency function as criteria for selecting one of several possible interpretations of a norm-formulation. When this is not possible (for example, because the text does not admit of more than one interpretation or because there is already one accepted interpretation), other techniques are used. Normative gaps are closed by analogical reasoning (*argumenta a pari* and *argumenta a fortiori*),[23] which consists of extending the scope of a norm in order to cover the case in question. However, we should not forget that this means, in exact terms, replacing one norm with another. Only the bare text remains the same; the norm expressed by it has changed!

In cases of inconsistency, a technique often used is the *hierarchical ordering* of norms. A norm that for some reason is regarded as higher or more important thereby prevails over an inferior norm. Things become more difficult when sets of norms are to be compared. Some forms of this technique have been thoroughly studied by Alchourrón and Makinson.[24] An important result of their investigations is the proof that the imposition of an ordering onto a system (or any modification of the existing ordering) is tantamount to a derogation of certain norms (that is, those norms that are discarded as inferior). Thus, ordering and derogation are substantially equivalent (though not quite identical) operations, in the sense that to each ordering there corresponds a derogation and to each derogation there corresponds an ordering.

This shows, it is worth noting, that a normative system is not just a set of norms (closed under deduction)—as defined in *Normative Systems*—but an *ordered* set of

[21] See Alchourrón and Bulygin, *NS*, at chs. 1 and 4.

[22] See Niiniluoto, 'Legal Dogmatics' (n. 2, this chapter), at 61. There are a few remarks on this point in Alchourrón and Bulygin, *NS*, at 60–1.

[23] See Carlos E. Alchourron, 'Juristische Schlüsse a fortiori und a pari', in *Lateinamerikanische Studien zur Rechtsphilosophie*, ed. Ernesto Garzón Valdés (*ARSP Beiheft* 41 [N.F. 4]) (Neuwied am Rhein and Berlin: Hermann Luchterhand, 1965), 5–26, Spanish version in *ALD*, 3–24.

[24] Alchourrón and Makinson, 'Hierarchies of Regulations' (n. 17, this chapter).

norms. Any change of the ordering gives rise to a new system, even if the elements (norms) of the system remain the same, for the correlations of cases with solutions are different. Just as the normative status of an action can change as a result of a different ordering of the same set of norms, so one and the same set (code) can give rise to different systems if it is ordered differently.

Thus, the term 'legal system' is ambiguous. This ambiguity enables practitioners of legal dogmatics to claim that they are not changing the system as long as they do not change the norms, even if they change the hierarchical order of these norms. This claim is far more subtle than the claim that the law does not change because the texts have remained the same, but both claims are based on fallacies of ambiguity: the ambiguity of the term 'norm', whose sense shifts from a meaning expressed by a text to the bare text, or the ambiguity of 'legal system', whose meaning changes from 'ordered set of norms' to 'set of norms' (disregarding the ordering).

The *moral requirement of justice* means that a legal system must satisfy certain minimal criteria or standards of justice. As has been emphasized by Nino,[25] this not only means that jurists try to adjust the system to the standards of justice prevailing *de facto* in a given society, but that as moral agents they should and often in fact do adapt the existing system to the standards of a critical or ideal morality.

It is true that legal dogmatists often do not advocate that a legal regulation ought to be discarded because it fails to satisfy the minimal conditions for justice; this happens only in very exceptional cases. A more usual procedure is to argue that the legislator did not foresee the case in question, for if he had foreseen it, he would have introduced a relevant distinction that would have led to another solution (and this, in many instances, may be true). Consequently, the practitioner of legal dogmatics proceeds to close this 'gap', making the relevant distinction and applying by analogy some norm that provides for a more just solution. This is what we called *axiological gaps*.[26]

5. Concluding Remarks

There are no clear-cut limits in the practice of those engaged in legal dogmatics where the three different activities I have thus far described are concerned. The distinctions between identification, systematization, and transformation are purely conceptual; in practice, the three tasks are often performed at the same time, so that it is extremely difficult to separate them. Conceptual distinctions are,

[25] See Carlos Santiago Nino, 'Legal Ethics: between Metaphysics and Futility', in *Essays in Legal Theory in Honor of Kaarle Makkonen*, ed. Urpo Kangas, *Yearbook of the Finnish Lawyers Society*, 16 (1983), 189–220; Carlos Santiago Nino, *Los límites de la responsabilidad penal* (Buenos Aires: Astrea, 1980).

[26] See Alchourrón and Bulygin, *NS*, at ch. 6.

however, very important. Without them, it would be impossible to outline a clear picture of the complex activity that corresponds to legal dogmatics.

The main charge I can raise against Aarnio and Niiniluoto is that they do not always clearly distinguish between the identification of legal norms, their systematization, and the transformation of a legal system.

Aarnio's main (if not exclusive) interest seems to be directed toward the *problem of the identification* of legal norms or, as he puts it, the 'determination of the content of legal regulations'. Even where he speaks of systematization, he has in mind something utterly different from what is understood under this heading in *Normative Systems*. This comes clearly to light in chapter 4, part III of his book *On Legal Reasoning*, especially in section 4.1, 'The Systematizing Task of Legal Dogmatics'.[27]

The starting point for the systematization, according to Aarnio, is a *basic system* (S_b), which, as Aarnio states explicitly, is a system of valid *norms*.[28] I think it is worthwhile to quote in full what Aarnio says about the systematization (or reformulation) of the basic system.

> When the basic system S_b now is substituted by another system S_l identical with it, the manner of organizing (O_l) must be such that the new system S_l provides every case also covered by the system S_b with a solution similar to that provided by S_b. In other words, the systematization must not change the content of the basic system; also in the new system, every norm belonging to the basic system must have the same content as before. However, here lies a difficult and noteworthy problem.
>
> It has been already established above that *only in a few cases is it possible to give one and only one consistent interpretation of a norm belonging to the basic system.* Usually two or more alternative interpretations may be suggested for a certain norm (N_i). The matter may be expressed also by saying that it *is possible to formulate the basic system S_b in more than one way.* However, this raises the problem, what the identity of the basic system S_b and the system S_l substituting for it means.
>
> Alchourron and Bulygin's way of thinking seems to imply that we know the content of the basic system as though beforehand and independently of the new system S_l. The new system only expresses (more accurately) the things that already are contained in the basic system and/or puts the matter in a more comprehensive form. However, this is the very point that turns out to be problematic. Is it on the whole possible to think that an interpretation of the basic system S_b is given independently of the 'systematization' (the reformulation S_l) by means of which the set of norms is organized?...
>
> In regard to our topic the question naturally concerns the fact whether it is possible to uphold the distinction between systematization (reformulation) and interpretation (formulation) in the way Alchourrón and Bulygin think. That is to say, if *the systematization (e.g. the reformulation S_l) affects the way the basic system is being interpreted, also the identity assumption [is cast in] a new light.* A quite specific content must be given to the latter in order to ascertain its validity in the form sketched above....[29]

The problem for Aarnio is that 'every norm can be endowed with one or more contents ("interpretations")'. Thus. for each norm of the basic system there are

[27] Aarnio, *On Legal Reasoning* (n. 8, this chapter), 266–82.
[28] Aarnio, *On Legal Reasoning* (n. 8, this chapter), 273.
[29] Aarnio, *On Legal Reasoning* (n. 8, this chapter), 275 (emphasis added).

several possible interpretations. Now, if the system S_1 reproduces all the conceivable interpretations, then it will be, in a way, 'empty'. Thus, it must pick up one particular interpretation of S_b, say S_{bi}.

> [H]ere the problem is exactly whether it is possible to determine the content of the system S_{bi} irrespective of the system S_1, or are the interpretation of the basic system (the formulation) and the new system (the reformulation) intertwined in such a way that the difference between systematization and interpretation becomes problematic.[30]

Taken literally this text is utterly inconsistent. If by a norm we understand, as Aarnio does,[31] the *meaning* of a norm formulation—that is, a correlation of a case (legal fact) with a solution (legal consequence)—then it simply does not make sense to talk about the interpretation of *norms.* To say that two interpretations are different entails that the correlations they establish between cases and solutions are different, so they are *different norms,* not just two different interpretations of one and the same norm. Only norm-formulations can be interpreted in different ways; each interpretation associates a different norm with the same norm-formulation. Thus, when Aarnio speaks of the interpretation of a norm, we must understand by 'norm' the norm-formulation and not its meaning. Thus his use of the term 'norm' is inconsistent with his own definition.

One way of making Aarnio's text coherent (which I hope reproduces Aarnio's actual intentions) is to accept that what he calls the basic system S_b is not a system of norms but a set of norm-formulations. Then it makes sense to say that each element of S_b can be endowed with one or more contents or interpretations, but then it becomes clear that Aarnio's concern is not with the systematization or reformulation of a legal system (as it is defined in *Normative Systems*), but with the *identification of the norms* expressed by a certain text (that is, the norm-formulations of S_b). In other words, the step from S_b to S_1 has nothing whatsoever to do with what has been called reformulation; rather, it is a step that takes place prior to identifying the norms to be systematized. Given Aarnio's use of the term 'systematization', the difference between systematization and interpretation is, indeed, not only problematic but simply non-existent.

Thus, Aarnio's criticism of *Normative Systems* is misplaced. Systematization begins in *Normative Systems* with a set of norms that has already been interpreted. It is, then, no wonder that knowledge of the content of these norms is given 'as though beforehand and independently of the new system S_1'. As a matter of fact, systematization (in our sense) does not start with Aarnio's basic system S_b (which is a set of mere norm-formulations), but with the set that Aarnio calls S_1, that is, a set of interpreted norm-formulations, in other words, a set of norms.

Both problems—that of the identification of norms with which Aarnio is concerned and that of the systematization of norms discussed in *Normative Systems*—are important, but we must bear in mind that they are different problems, and they

[30] Aarnio, *On Legal Reasoning* (n. 8, this chapter), 276.
[31] Aarnio, *On Legal Reasoning* (n. 8, this chapter), 12, 274.

should not be confused. In this sense, the results of Aarnio's enquiries, far from being incompatible with the analyses of *Normative Systems*, are complementary.

In a similar way, Niiniluoto's criticism of *Normative Systems* is based to a large extent on the lack of a conceptual distinction between the cognitive function of systematization and the normative ('creative') function of legal dogmatics, namely, the modification of the system. Since *Normative Systems* is primarily concerned with the first of these two different functions of legal dogmatics, much of the criticism put forward by Niiniluoto is also misdirected. This happens with three of the six points of his criticism: (a) *legal induction*, (b) *legal systematization*, and (c) *sources*.

The reconstruction of legal induction as 'decision-making' (or 'choice') with 'judicial utilities',[32] and the closure of gaps by means of some sort of inductive inference belong to the normative function of the transformation of a legal system and not to systematization. By contrast, systematization is by definition conservative; it preserves normative equivalence. It was never our intention to deny that the practitioners of legal dogmatics would perform creative activities as well, but our interest was focused on the purely cognitive aspect of legal dogmatics. Legal theorists do, of course, close all sorts of gaps and remove inconsistencies, but this activity is different from mere systematizing as it is characterized in *Normative Systems*.

Nor do I see why the assumption that the sources of law 'are used only once as *inputs* to the legal order' should be unrealistic. Niiniluoto thinks it 'more appropriate to assume that the various sources can be directly employed at any time to any issue at hand'.[33] Unless there is some misunderstanding on my part, I do not see why the two assumptions should be incompatible. The description of what practitioners of legal dogmatics actually do is one thing (here Niiniluoto's assumption is quite correct: of course, they can employ the sources at any time to any issue). Quite another thing, however, is a rational reconstruction of their activity. Here we must distinguish between different stages of the activity or different operations performed by those engaged in legal dogmatics. The fact that such operations are fused in practice does not entitle us to confuse them in thought.

Niiniluoto also complains that the deductivist view in his Figure 1 (in which he admirably reproduces the main ideas of *Normative Systems* with respect to systematization) is too narrow, for, he argues, the structure of argumentation in legal theory is more complex than is suggested in it. This is altogether correct, but one must bear in mind that *Normative Systems* does not pretend to give a full characterization of legal dogmatics; its concern is with only one aspect of it, namely, systematization, and there deductive reasoning is indeed predominant.

The points (e) *changes in interpretation* and (f) *sentences versus propositions* have already been dealt with in section 2 of this article; here, too, Niiniluoto's criticism is based on a misunderstanding (for which the authors of *Normative Systems* are probably responsible). Thus, only the point (d) *subsuming and generic cases* marks a valid criticism—as has already been acknowledged—of the model developed in

[32] Niiniluoto, 'Legal Dogmatics' (n. 2, this chapter), 60.
[33] Niiniluoto, 'Legal Dogmatics' (n. 2, this chapter), 61.

Normative Systems. This criticism, however, is not sufficient to sustain the claim that the approach—which Niiniluoto for some inscrutable reason calls 'logistic'—is unrealistic and ought to be replaced by a different approach.

Of course, the *formulation* of the ideas put forward in *Normative Systems* is very defective and stands in need of many amendments and clarifications, but the general approach still seems to me to be basically sound.

14

An Antinomy in Kelsen's Pure Theory of Law (1990)*

Introduction

Despite the fact that the idea of validity plays a very central role in Kelsen's Pure Theory of Law, there is no consensus among scholars about the exact meaning of this rather elusive notion. Even among those authors who are of one mind regarding Kelsen's concept of validity, there is widespread disagreement in the appraisal of this concept.

In a lecture delivered at the University of Buenos Aires some 30 years ago, Alf Ross pointed out that Kelsen faces serious difficulties owing to his use of the concept of validity qua binding force, a view that Ross characterized as 'quasi-positivism'.[1] In his treatise on legal validity, Carlos Santiago Nino returns to this issue, maintaining, like Ross, that Kelsen employs a normative concept of validity akin to that found in classical authors of the natural law tradition.[2] Nino's attitude towards this phenomenon, however, is diametrically opposed to Ross's. Whereas Ross maintained that the concept of validity qua binding force should be eliminated from legal theory and, in particular, from Kelsen's Pure Theory of Law, Nino believes that the only correct interpretation of Kelsen is that which stems from acknowledging that his concept of validity is normative and not descriptive. Unless we take this step, Nino argues, we cannot grasp Kelsen's ideas about the nature of law.

In view of such basic disagreement, it seems advisable to re-examine the relevant aspects of Kelsen's Pure Theory of Law with an eye to determining the exact role played in it by what Nino calls the normative concept of validity. This is what I propose to do in the present paper.

* [*Editors' note*: Eugenio Bulygin's paper was first published in *Ratio Juris*, 3 (1990), 29–45, and was reprinted, with minor refinements made in consultation with him, in *NN*, at 297–315.]

[1] Ross, 'Validity'. [*Editors' note*: For this and other abbreviations, see the Table of Abbreviations.]

[2] Carlos Santiago Nino, *La validez del derecho* (Buenos Aires: Astrea, 1985); see also Carlos Santiago Nino, 'Some Confusions surrounding Kelsen's Concept of Validity', *ARSP*, 64 (1978), 357–77, in *NN* (repr. in part), 253–61.

1. The Kantian and the Positivistic Ingredients in the Pure Theory of Law

It is not easy to draw a coherent picture of Kelsen's theory of law, owing mainly to two kinds of difficulties. In the first place, Kelsen's written work ranges over a period of nearly 70 years, a fact that makes it easy to understand that his views on certain central topics in legal philosophy underwent considerable change during his long life. This is why it is almost impossible to speak of *the* Pure Theory of Law; none of Kelsen's books, not even the monumental second edition of the *Reine Rechtslehre* (1960), published when he was nearly 80, can be regarded as his final word on the subject. It is an astonishing fact that the last 12 years of his life (he died in 1973 at the age of 91) are especially rich in new ideas that have far-reaching consequences for his theory of law.

In the second place, and this is a more serious problem, we find in Kelsen's thought two groups of ideas that stem from quite different philosophical traditions. These ideas are not only difficult to reconcile but indeed are radically incompatible as I shall try to show in some detail. Both the Kantian and the positivistic persuasions are vividly present in Kelsen's works, and some of his main tenets can be traced back to these two greatly opposed philosophical traditions. Being incompatible, some of his ideas stemming from one of these traditions must be eliminated in order to render the Pure Theory of Law coherent.

Which of the two traditions is to be preferred is, I think, to a certain degree a matter of taste. Personally, I regard Kelsen's positivistic views as the more important development, and I shall adduce reasons in support of this choice. Kelsen's views here made him, along with Max Weber, one of the founding fathers of the positivistic approach to social sciences and perhaps *the* founder of modern legal positivism. What is more, in the last years of his life Kelsen himself showed an increasing preference for the ideas that I term positivistic, and although he as a matter of fact never explicitly rejected his Kantian heritage, his philosophical evolution exhibits a clear tendency in the direction of the positivistic components of his theory of law.

From a chronological standpoint we can distinguish, roughly speaking, three main periods in Kelsen's thought. In the first period, the Kantian and the positivistic elements coexist more or less harmoniously, and Kelsen seems to be unaware of their antagonism. This period corresponds approximately to the first 30 years of his philosophical production (1911–40); it includes such books as *Hauptprobleme der Staatsrechtslehre* (1911), the *Allgemeine Staatslehre* (1925), and the *Introduction to the Problems of Legal Theory*, which is the first edition of the *Reine Rechtslehre* (1934). (Only works directly concerned with the philosophy of law will be mentioned in this connection.) The second period is a transition stage of about 20 years, from 1940, when Kelsen leaves Europe and settles in the United States, to 1960. The main publications of this period are *General Theory of Law and State* (1945), *Théorie pure du droit* (1953),[3] which is a French-language revision of

[3] Hans Kelsen, *Théorie pure du droit*, trans. Henri Thévenaz (Boudry-Neuchâtel: Éditions de la Baconnière, 1953).

the first edition of the *Reine Rechtslehre* (1934), and the second edition of the *Reine Rechtslehre* (1960).[4] The third period, predominantly positivistic in spirit, includes such important papers as 'Derogation' (1962)[5] and 'Law and Logic' (1965),[6] and also his unfinished work *General Theory of Norms* (first published in 1979).

Kelsen's main ideas of Kantian origin are: (1) the characterization of legal norms as ideal entities belonging to the world of *Sollen* ('ought'), distinct from the world of natural reality or the world of *Sein* ('is'); (2) the conception of validity qua binding force (which, following Nino, I call the normative concept of validity); (3) the normativity of legal science; and (4) Kelsen's well-known doctrine of the basic norm as a transcendental category.

All these theses are closely connected. It is because norms are ideal entities belonging to a world that differs radically from the real world that their existence is not a (natural) fact; the specific existence of norms is their validity, understood as binding force. A norm exists if and only if it is valid or binding, that is, when its addressees ought to behave as the norm prescribes. Legal science is normative not only in the sense that it is concerned with norms. It is normative, above all, because the sentences in which it describes law are normative, and they are normative because they refer not to natural facts but to valid norms, that is, to their obligatoriness or binding force. On the other hand, the idea of validity as a binding force is based—as we shall see in some detail later—on the hypothesis of a basic norm, whose main role is to make the idea of validity compatible with Kelsen's positivistic ideal of *eine wertfreie Rechtswissenschaft* (a non-evaluative legal science).

Kelsen's ideal of a positivistic legal science is related to four fundamental theses: (5) a sharp separation between 'is' and 'ought'; (6) the non-cognitivist conception of norms and value judgments as prescriptions that are neither true nor false; (7) the positivity of law, the thesis that all law is positive, that is to say, it is created and destroyed by human acts, or—putting it more cautiously—legal norms come into and pass from existence as a consequence of certain human acts; and (8) a sharp distinction between description and prescription (or evaluation), between reason and volition, between the cognition of law and the creation of law, between the 'science' of law and legal politics.

The non-cognitivist conception of norms as prescriptions that are neither true nor false (thesis 6) has far-reaching consequences; it means that there are no normative facts that would make norms true, that is, there is no reality corresponding to norms. This is the main difference between norms and propositions. Moreover, Kelsen adopts the same sceptical position regarding values: value judgments, too, lack truth-values, with the result that there are no objective values. Still, although Kelsen had always been a sceptic in matters of values, the characterization of legal

[4] [*Editors' note*: See the Table of Abbreviations for full references to these works.]

[5] Hans Kelsen, 'Derogation', in *Essays in Jurisprudence in Honor of Roscoe Pound*, ed. Ralph A. Newman (Indianapolis: Bobbs-Merrill, 1962), 339–55, in *WS 2*, 1429–43, and in Hans Kelsen, *Essays in Legal and Moral Philosophy*, ed. Ota Weinberger (Dordrecht: D. Reidel, 1973), 261–75.

[6] Hans Kelsen, 'Law and Logic', trans. Peter Heath, in Kelsen, *Essays in Legal and Moral Philosophy* (n. 5, this chapter), 228–53 (first published as 'Recht und Logik', *Forum. Österreichische Monatsblätter für kulturelle Freiheit*, 12 [1965], 421–5 and 495–500, in *WS 2*, 1469–97).

norms as prescriptions appears at a relatively late stage of his philosophical development. In the first period of his thought, norms are characterized as judgments or propositions,[7] and he strongly objects to their characterization as imperatives even as late as the *General Theory of Law and State* (1945). It is only in the second edition of the *Reine Rechtslehre* (1960) that Kelsen explicitly identifies norms and imperatives and at the same time extends the notion of 'ought' (*Sollen*) to all deontic modalities: obligation, prohibition, permission, and empowerment (*Ermächtigung*). Later he adds derogation to this list.

Thesis 7 states that all law is positive law; this means that it is created and destroyed by human acts (which holds for enacted law as well as for customary law). This thesis has two important consequences: first, there is no natural law, and second, legal norms have a temporal dimension—they begin to exist at a certain moment and cease to exist at a later moment, that is to say, they are historical. This thesis was firmly maintained by Kelsen throughout his life.

A sharp distinction between the pairs of concepts, description and prescription, cognition and evaluation, science and politics (thesis 8), can be regarded as the core of the positivistic programme of a value-neutral science, whose champions in the field of the social sciences have been Kelsen and Weber.

The three pairs of concepts are closely related. If norms and value judgments lack truth-values, they are not subject to rational scrutiny. Valuations and norms simply express certain preferences, and there are no objective criteria for settling a conflict between ultimate preferences. The reason for this state of affairs is that there are no evaluative or normative facts. Instead, the descriptive propositions are true or false; their truth is objective in the sense that it depends not on the person who utters the proposition but only on the fact that makes it true. So we must distinguish sharply between the cognition of law, expressed by true descriptive propositions, and the creation of legal norms, which is an expression of certain evaluations. Thus, legal science, which aims at the cognition of law, can only describe it; the task of legal science is not to evaluate law or, still less, to create legal norms. All activities that are aimed at the evaluation of the law and at the creation and the modification of legal norms correspond to legal politics and have nothing to do with science. Thus, thesis 8 leads to an important step in the 'purification' of legal theory: the removal of all evaluative (moral and political) elements.

Kelsen certainly did not ignore the fact that jurists generally, and specialists in various substantive fields of law in particular, often perform activities that are quite different from a mere description of existing law. He was not, however, concerned with describing what jurists actually do; rather, his concern was to shape a model of a legal science that would meet the requirements of this programme of a positivistic science, and to provide methodological foundations and conceptual tools for such an enterprise.

It is my contention that the 'Kantian' theses 1–4, and especially thesis 2, validity qua binding force, are incompatible with the ideal of a positivistic science of the

[7] See generally Kelsen, *HP*, and Kelsen, *ASL*; see also Kelsen, *LT*, § 11(b) (at 23).

sort expressed in theses 6–8. Only thesis 5 is to be found in both traditions and is, therefore, acceptable to both; thesis 5, however, lends itself to two different interpretations. On an ontological interpretation (predominant in Kelsen's early writings), the thesis of a sharp separation between 'is' and 'ought' is related to Kelsen's distinction between two radically different realms or worlds: the world of *Sollen* ('ought') and the world of *Sein* ('is') (thesis 1). Thesis 5, however, can also be given a more sober interpretation that, with due caution, might be termed semantic. On this interpretation, thesis 5 means that prescriptive propositions cannot be inferred from descriptive propositions alone and, conversely, that descriptive propositions do not follow logically from prescriptions alone.[8] In this form thesis 5 is fully acceptable to the most rigorous positivist.

2. The Theory of the Two Worlds

Both the Kantian tradition (as expressed in theses 1–4) and the positivistic programme of a non-evaluative science *(eine wertfreie Wissenschaft)* coexisted in Kelsen's work over a very long time. In spite of his efforts, however, he never succeeded in reconciling the incompatible elements in his theory that stem from these distinct traditions. Towards the end of his life the positivistic tendencies became dominant, and Kelsen came to reject, sometimes implicitly (as in the idea of two worlds and the notion of validity qua binding force) and sometimes explicitly (as in the theory of the basic norm), his main theses of Kantian origin.

The idea of a sharp separation between the 'world of *Sein*' ('is') and the 'world of *Sollen*' ('ought') already appears in *Hauptprobleme der Staatsrechtslehre (1911)*, Kelsen's second book. There he is anxious to isolate the 'proper object' of legal science, which, once determined, was supposed to make it possible for him to distinguish legal science from other sciences. (This approach rests on the assumption that every science must have its proper object. There are a number of reasons that count against this assumption, but I shall not take up the matter here.) Such a 'proper object' is the positive law, understood as a set of legal norms created by human acts. According to Kelsen, when a jurist states, for example, that one who commits murder ought to be punished, he is not interested in whether or not someone has actually committed a murder, and he is also not interested in whether or not the punishment will actually be carried out. He is concerned only with what *ought to be* the case, not with what *is* the case, that is, with the norm and not with any actual behaviour. *Sollen* is a special category of thought *(Denkkategorie)* that is not reducible to *Sein*.[9]

It is easy to show that a sharp separation between the 'world of *Sollen*' ('ought') and the 'world of *Sein*' ('is') cannot exist and, as a matter of fact, does not exist within the framework of the Pure Theory of Law, even in its classical formulation

[8] See Georg Henrik von Wright, 'Is and Ought', in *Man, Law and Modern Forms of Life*, ed. Eugenio Bulygin et al. (Dordrecht: D. Reidel, 1985), 263–81, in *NN*, 365–82.

[9] See Kelsen, *HP*, at 7–8, in *HKW 2*, at 86–7.

(Kelsen's second period). Both worlds are greatly intertwined, and a study of norms necessarily requires taking certain facts into account. Even if it were true that jurists are not interested in the actual behaviour of murderers and the officials who punish them (which is rather doubtful), there are other actions without which there would be no norms.

(i) There is the action of issuing the norm performed by the norm authority. Since all legal norms are positive norms (see thesis 7), the act of the authority issuing the norm is at least a necessary condition for its existence.

(ii) Acts consisting in cancelling or derogating a norm must also be considered, since the derogation of a norm brings its existence to an end (at least in some sense of this term). Thus, even a *very* Pure Theory of Law must take into account the acts of lawmaking and the acts of cancelling norms.

(iii) Another necessary condition for the validity (that is, the existence) of a norm, according to Kelsen, is the *efficacy* of the legal system to which this norm belongs: if a legal system is no longer efficacious, its norms cease to be valid, that is, they cease to exist.[10] Moreover, even a particular norm ceases to be valid if it ceases completely to be efficacious.[11]

This shows clearly that there never was such a distinct separation between the world of facts and the ideal world of norms, as is required by thesis 1. The existence of a positive legal norm (and according to thesis 7 there are only positive legal norms) cannot be ascertained without making reference to certain facts.

In Kelsen's third period this connection between norms and facts becomes far stronger, for he emphasizes that there can be no norm without the corresponding act of prescribing *(kein Imperativ ohne Imperator)*. Other clear signs of his increasing preference for the ideas I call positivistic are:

(i) Acknowledgement of the fact that there are no logical relations between norms, a thesis that Kelsen puts forward in 'Law and Logic' (1965)[12] and in *General Theory of Norms* (1979).[13]

(ii) Acceptance of the possibility of the coexistence of incompatible or contradictory valid norms within the same legal order. Before 1965,[14] Kelsen refused to accept the possibility of normative conflicts, which was reasonable as long as he used the normative concept of validity. Thus, I take this acceptance on Kelsen's part as a sign that he has adopted instead a descriptive concept of validity.

(iii) Rejection of the theory of the basic norm as a mere fiction.[15]

[10] See Kelsen, *RR 2*, § 34(g) (at 219), *PTL*, at 212.

[11] See Kelsen, *RR 2*, § 34(g) (at 220), *PTL*, at 213.

[12] See n. 6, this chapter.

[13] See Kelsen, *GTN*.

[14] See note 6, this chapter.

[15] See e.g. Hans Kelsen, 'Die Grundlage der Naturrechtslehre' and (with others) 'Diskussionen', *ÖZöR*, 13 (1963), 1–37, 117–62, at 119–20, repr. under the title *Das Naturrecht in der politischen Theorie*, ed. Franz Martin Schmölz (Vienna: Springer, 1963) (same pagination); Kelsen's paper 'Die Grundlage der Naturrechtslehre' is also in *WS 1*, 869–912.

All this demonstrates that theses 1 and 2, even if not explicitly rejected, have been implicitly abandoned in favour of doctrines that are incompatible with them.

3. Normativity of Legal Science

Before we proceed to the analysis of the concepts of validity used in the Pure Theory of Law, a few words must be said about the normativity of legal science, that is, thesis 3, in which the Kantian influence is very evident. This thesis played a very important part in Kelsen's thought, enabling him to draw a distinction between factual (causal) and normative social sciences, that is, between sociology on the one hand and Legal science on the other. The difference lies in the kind of proposition that each of these fields employs for the description of its objects. As for legal science, the idea is this: Legal science is normative not only in the sense that it describes norms but also in the sense that its propositions are themselves normative. Clearly, however, they are normative in a different sense from the sense in which norms themselves are said to be normative. It is not at all easy to discover what this sense is. Kelsen's well-known distinction between legal norms *(Rechtsnormen)* and legal propositions *(Rechtssätze)*, a term that is sometimes misleadingly translated as 'rules of law',[16] appears at a relatively late stage of his philosophical development, namely, in the second period.[17] In what I have called the first period, the two terms '*Rechtsnorm*' and '*Rechtssatz*' are used as roughly synonymous, following the terminological tradition of German legal theory in which '*Rechtssatz*' is used to refer to legal norms. This is reflected in the title of the second book written by Kelsen, *Hauptprobleme der Staatsrechtslehre entwickelt aus der Lehre vom Rechtssatz* (1911), where the term '*Rechtssatz*' refers to a legal norm and not to a proposition of legal science. In the *Allgemeine Staatslehre* (1925), he speaks of '*Rechtsnormen*' or '*Rechtssätze*' as the 'objective law'.[18] The same lack of any distinction either terminologically or conceptually where '*Rechtsnorm*' and '*Rechtssatz*' are concerned is found in Kelsen's *Introduction to the Problems of Legal Theory*, the first edition of the *Reine Rechtslehre* (1934). The only exception to this general rule regarding the lack of any distinction between '*Rechtsnorm*' and '*Rechtssatz*' in Kelsen's earlier work is his use of '*Rechtssatz*' at some points to designate the reconstructed or hypothetically formulated legal norm.[19] Many years later, Kelsen granted that he had not distinguished terminologically between norms and propositions; at the same time, he claimed to have always had in mind the distinction between the creative function of legal

[16] See *GTLS,* at 45. [17] Specifically, in *GTLS*, which appeared in 1945.

[18] Kelsen, *ASL*, § 10(a) (at 47).

[19] See Eugenio Bulygin, 'Zur Problem der Anwendbarkeit der Logik auf das Recht', in *Festschrift für Ulrich Klug zum 70. Geburtstag*, ed. Günter Kohlmann, 2 vols. (Cologne: Peter Deubner, 1983), vol. 1, 19–31, at 20; also in Spanish under the title 'Sobre el problema de la aplicabilidad de la lógica al derecho', trans. Jerónimo Betegón, in Hans Kelsen and Ulrich Klug, *Normas jurídicas y análisis lógico* (Madrid: Centro de Estudios Constitucionales, 1988), 9–26, at 11.

authority and the cognitive function of legal science.[20] In view of the quotations I have offered earlier, even this claim appears to be an exaggeration. The distinction does, however, appear more or less clearly stated in *General Theory of Law and State* (1945) and in Kelsen's *Théorie pure du droit* (1953), a statement that is otherwise entirely characteristic of Kelsen's earlier position.

> We can thus state simultaneously that the propositions formulated by legal science are hypothetical judgments and that legal norms constitute the object of this science. Here there is no contradiction. Without question, one can regard the norms created and applied within the framework of a legal system as having the character of legal norms only if they are recognized by legal science. It is the role of this science to attribute to certain acts the objective meaning of legal norms, but this does not prevent us from stating that legal norms are the object of legal science or, what amounts to the same thing, that the law is a system of norms. This definition is in complete harmony with Kant's theory, according to which cognition creates its object, for we are speaking here of an epistemological creation and not a creation of man's handiwork in the sense that one speaks of the legislator creating a law. Similarly, natural phenomena, which are the object of the causal sciences, are created by the causal sciences in a purely epistemological sense.[21]

This quotation highlights one of the central 'Kantian' ideas in Kelsen's thought: the epistemological creation of its object by a science, in our case the 'creation' of legal norms by the science of law. It is only by means of their recognition by legal science that certain acts, like those of the legislator, become law-creating acts and give rise to legal norms. This is why legal science is a normative science.

Already, however, in *General Theory of Law and State* (1945), Kelsen writes that judgments of legal science (that is, 'rules of law')[22] should not be confused with legal norms created by legal authorities. He emphasizes that he uses the term 'rule of law' in a descriptive sense. In later works and especially in the second edition of the *Reine Rechtslehre* (1960), a clear distinction is drawn between *legal norms* issued by legal authorities, which are prescriptive and thus—according to thesis 6—lack truth-values, and *legal propositions* formulated by legal science, which are descriptive of norms and thus either true or false. In this way, Kelsen abandons the idea of the epistemological creation of legal norms and assigns to legal propositions a more modest role, that of describing the norms created by legal authorities. This, together with the concept of the existence of a norm as an empirical fact (a concept already implied in thesis 7 and introduced explicitly in Kelsen's third period), leads to the rejection of thesis 3, a step that Kelsen did not take but that is implicit in his later writings.

Kelsen's shift with respect to thesis 3 explains Hart's perplexities[23] in trying to find a coherent interpretation of the theory, in view of Kelsen's insistence on maintaining thesis 3 and his failure to realize that this thesis rises and falls with the

[20] See Hans Kelsen, 'Professor Stone and the Pure Theory of Law', *Stanford Law Review*, 17 (1964/5), 1128–57, at 1132–5, 1136–7.

[21] Kelsen, *Théorie pure du droit* (n. 3, this chapter), 53–4 (English translation by Anne Collins and Bonnie Litschewski Paulson).

[22] See *GTLS*, at 45.

[23] See H. L. A. Hart, 'Kelsen Visited', *UCLA Law Review*, 10 (1962/3), 709–28, in Hart, *EJP*, 286–308.

Kantian idea of the epistemological creation of legal norms by legal science, a thesis that Kelsen explicitly gave up after 1960. The problem is this. Once the idea that legal propositions are mere descriptions of legal norms is introduced, then the thesis of the normativity of legal science in the special sense that Kelsen gave to it in his earlier work, namely, as the normativity of propositions used by legal scientists, is deprived of all support and is left hanging. Thus, in the period after the publication of the second edition of the *Reine Rechtslehre* (1960), the theory of the normativity of legal propositions became a self-contradictory doctrine. If these propositions are descriptive, they are not normative. The occurrence of the term 'ought' is immaterial; it is the meaning of this term that makes all the difference. In other words, even if the *sentences* formulated by legal science are 'ought'-sentences, the *propositions* these sentences express are descriptive and not normative. Kelsen's attempt to save the doctrine by introducing the distinction borrowed from Christoph Sigwart between the prescriptive and the descriptive 'ought'[24] only reveals his confusion of sentences as linguistic entities with propositions as their meanings.

4. Validity, Membership, and the Existence of Norms

Kelsen says repeatedly that validity is the specific existence of norms. Unfortunately, however, and contrary to what Nino seems to believe,[25] the term 'existence' in Kelsen's use is at least as ambiguous as 'validity'. In order to avoid the frequent ambiguities of legal language, I shall distinguish between four different concepts of existence. (Although the term 'existence' clearly belongs to philosophical parlance, the corresponding conceptual distinctions turn up in ordinary legal discourse.)

(A) *Factual existence.* When we say that a norm to such-and-such an effect exists in a certain social group, we mean that this norm is in fact in force in that group. The concept of factual existence or of being in force is explicated differently by different authors. Kelsen uses for it the term 'efficacy' (*Wirksamkeit*); a norm is efficacious if it is obeyed by legal subjects or applied by legal authorities. Alf Ross, at least in the English translation of *On Law and Justice* (which is not very felicitous), uses the term 'validity'.[26] A norm is valid in this sense when the prediction that it will be used in the future to justify judicial decisions is true.[27]

[24] See Kelsen, *RR 2*, § 16 (at 77n.) (note is not included in *PTL*); Christoph Sigwart, *Logic*, trans. Helen Dendy, 2 vols. (London: Swan Sonnenschein, 1895), vol. I, at 17 n.1.

[25] See Carlos Santiago Nino, *Introducción al análisis del derecho*, 2nd edn. (Buenos Aires: Astrea, 1980), at 132–41.

[26] See Ross, *LJ*, at 72–4. Far better is the Spanish edition, Alf Ross, *Sobre el derecho y la justicia*, trans. G.R. Carrió (Buenos Aires: Eudeba, 1963), in which the distinction between the expressions '*gyldig ret*' and '*gældende ret*' of the original Danish is preserved by means of the terms '*válido*' and '*vigente*'. See also Ross, 'Validity', at §§ V–VII.

[27] See my analysis of this concept in Eugenio Bulygin, 'The Concept of Efficacy' (1965), in this volume, ch. 1.

Perhaps the most illuminating analysis of factual existence is given by Hart in *The Concept of Law* in terms of the acceptance of the norm as a standard of behaviour by the social group; this means that members of the group regard conduct in conformity with the norm and reactions against those who violate the norm as required and justified by the norm.[28] This is to say that they regard the norm as obligatory or binding, a fact altogether characteristic of what Hart calls the *internal* point of view.

This factual concept of existence is descriptive (to say that a norm exists in a certain society is to state a fact), and it admits of different degrees of intensity. A norm can exist or be in force to a greater or lesser degree, depending on the degree of its acceptance. What is more, this concept is relative to a certain social group and to a particular point in time.

> (B) *Membership.* Sometimes a norm is said to exist when it belongs to a certain system of norms. Jurists usually accept a genetic criterion for membership. A norm is regarded as belonging to a given system if it has been created by a competent authority and has not subsequently been derogated by the same authority or some other authority of the system.

This concept is often referred to by means of the term 'validity',[29] and, as we shall see presently, Kelsen uses the term 'valid' in this sense at least some of the time. The concept is also descriptive and relative (one and the same norm can be a member of one system and not of another, and it can belong to a system at one time and not at another).

> (C) *Existence as validity.* This is a *normative* concept: a norm exists or is valid in this sense if and only if it is obligatory or binding. (In order to avoid confusion, I shall use the term 'valid' only in this normative sense, unless otherwise indicated.)

It has been stressed by Nino[30] that the concept of validity as binding force is normative in the sense that to say a norm is valid is not to state a fact but to prescribe an obligation to obey the norm in question. Hence, judgments of validity are themselves normative, that is, they are norms. According to Nino, however, binding force implies not only that one ought to do what the norm prescribes—that is, the norm succeeds in establishing the obligation it purports to establish—but also that the norm is justified. This presupposes a conception of 'justified normativity', which—according to both Nino and Joseph Raz[31]—Kelsen shares with natural law theorists. Moreover, Nino maintains that not only is the use of this normative concept of validity supported by quotations from Kelsen's writings, it is 'understood in the general structure of Kelsen's theory'.[32]

[28] See Hart, *CL,* 1st edn., at 53–6, 86, and esp. 244, 3rd edn., at 54–7, 88–9, and esp. 291.

[29] See von Wright, *NA*, at 194–8.

[30] See Nino, 'Some Confusions' (n. 2, this chapter), at § I; Nino, *La validez del derecho* (n. 2, this chapter), at 8.

[31] See Raz, 'BN'.

[32] Nino, 'Some Confusions' (n. 2, this chapter), § I (C).

This concept of existence differs from the others not only in being normative but also in being an absolute concept.

(D) *Existence as formulation.* Jurists sometimes treat as existent norms those norms that are neither accepted nor efficacious, that neither belong to a system of norms (having not been issued by a competent authority) nor are regarded as binding. Such norms exist (in this broad sense) either if they have been formulated by somebody (who need not be a legal authority) or if they are a logical consequence of formulated norms. A typical case is the draft of a statute that has not yet been promulgated. Its norms do not exist in any of the first three meanings I have distinguished, for they are neither accepted nor binding, nor do they belong to the legal order, and yet it makes perfect sense to say that they are there.

This kind of existence, which for lack of a better term I called 'formal' existence in an earlier version of this paper, is a neglected child of the general theory of law; philosophers of law rarely take note of it, and yet it is very important, for it is in a certain sense a basic notion concerning the existence of norms.[33] Obviously, neither this concept nor the concept of membership (which presupposes the concept of existence as formulation) is applicable to customary norms.

The four concepts of existence distinguished thus far are not, of course, incompatible. A norm can exist in all four senses or only in some of them. Moreover, some of these notions are not independent of each other. I have already remarked that membership presupposes existence as formulation. Kelsen has (sometimes) maintained that validity implies efficacy (that is, factual existence). A norm can be in force in a given society without being formulated (this is the case with customary norms) and without being binding, although in order to be in force, norms must of course be regarded as binding by those who employ them. Thus, we see that some concepts of existence are independent, others are not.

While Kelsen pays little attention to concept (D), the other three can be traced to his writings, although he uses the same term 'validity' to refer to both membership and binding force, and this has given rise to a good bit of confusion. Nino, in his very interesting paper of 1978, has clarified some of these confusions but has at the same time contributed to new ones, which is why his title has an almost ironic ring to it: 'Some Confusions surrounding Kelsen's Concept of Validity.'[34]

Nino has perhaps developed the idea of normative validity further than any other writer. He not only emphasizes its role in Kelsen's theory but assumes it as basic to his own views on law and morality.[35] He exaggerates, however, the importance of this concept for the Pure Theory of Law. The consequences that

[33] See Carlos E. Alchourrón and Eugenio Bulygin, 'On the Logic of Normative Systems', in *Pragmatik. Handbuch pragmatischen Denkens,* 5 vols., *Sprachphilosophie, Sprachpragmatik und formative Pragmatik,* ed. Herbert Stachowiak (Hamburg: Meiner, 1993), vol. 4, 273–94, where this concept of existence is analysed in detail.

[34] See Nino, 'Some Confusions' (n. 2, this chapter).

[35] See Nino, *Introducción al análisis del derecho* (n. 25, this chapter); Carlos Santiago Nino, *Los límites de la responsabilidad penal. Una teoría liberal del delito* (Buenos Aires: Astrea, 1980); Carlos Santiago Nino, *Etica y derechos humanos* (Buenos Aires: Paidos, 1984).

Nino draws from Kelsen's premisses go far beyond Kelsen's own statements and intentions, and show clearly that the concept of binding force is inconsistent with legal positivism and with the task of legal science as envisaged by Kelsen. Kelsen would certainly not subscribe either to the view that 'the only conceivable type of normativity is justified normativity'[36] or to the view that to say of a norm or a system of norms that it is valid is tantamount to asserting its justifiability. Kelsen would also not accept the notion that judgments about the validity of legal norms are of the same logical nature as norms themselves, and he would not agree that he shares a concept of validity with traditional natural law theory. In fact, the concept of existence as binding force is connected to Kelsen's idea that norms are ideal entities belonging to the world of 'ought' (thesis 1). We have already seen that this idea, if not altogether abandoned, was at any rate considerably weakened in the last stage of Kelsen's thought. His late conception of norms does not require either the normative concept of validity or the idea of norms as ideal entities; rather, Kelsen's view is very close to the expressive conception of norms.[37]

Nino's suggestion that some authors, like Hart, Alchourrón, and Bulygin, have assumed 'that Kelsen's notion of validity is equivalent to membership, although they do not offer much by way of discussion on the matter,'[38] is, to say the least, an overstatement. I cannot be sure whether Hart ever made this dogmatic assumption; I do know that the other two authors whom Nino refers to did not. What we intended to do in *Normative Systems* (1971) was to reconstruct the concept of membership—without claiming, as Nino seems to believe, that this is the only concept of validity in Kelsen's theory. Indeed, to identify Kelsen's concept of validity with the notion of binding force would be as mistaken as equating it with membership; behind the term 'validity' two different concepts are hidden. Despite the fact that Kelsen uses two different concepts of validity, one of them—precisely the normative notion of binding force—proves to be incompatible with his positivistic views, as I shall try to argue in the next sections of this paper. Thus, what is really imposed by the general structure of Kelsen's positivistic theory of law is the rejection of the normative concept of validity as binding force, something that had already been proposed by Alf Ross.

5. Membership and the Definition of Legal Order

For Kelsen, there is a close connection between membership and validity.

[36] Carlos Santiago Nino, 'Some Confusions' (n. 2, this chapter), *ARSP,* 64 (1978), 357–77, at 373 [*editors' note*: not included in *NN*].

[37] See Alchourrón and Bulygin, *NS*; Alchourrón and Bulygin, 'The Expressive Conception of Norms' (1981), in this volume, ch. 9; Carlos E. Alchourrón and Eugenio Bulygin, 'Pragmatic Foundations for a Logic of Norms', *Rechtstheorie*, 15 (1984), 453–64; Bulygin, 'Norms and Logic' (1985), in this volume, ch. 12.

[38] Nino, 'Some Confusions' (n. 36, this chapter), 365.

The legal order is a system of norms. The questions then arise: What is it that makes a system out of a multitude of norms? When does a norm belong to a certain system of norms, an order? These questions are closely connected to the question regarding the reason for the validity of a norm.[39]

In fact, Kelsen seems to believe that the concepts of membership and binding force are coextensive, which may well explain why he uses the same term, 'validity', to refer to both of them. This would mean that all norms and only norms that are members of a legal system are binding. I agree with Nino that this is a serious mistake.

According to Nino, one must be careful in distinguishing between two quite different problems: the validity of a norm and its membership in a particular system of norms. When Kelsen says that a norm is valid when it derives its validity from a valid norm of the system, his formulation is misleading. This statement should be broken down into two statements: (a) a norm is a member of a given system when it derives from another norm that belongs to that system, and (b) a norm is valid when it derives from another valid norm.[40]

This, I think, is a sound strategy. Following it, Kelsen's concepts of validity should be analysed in two steps. In the present section, I shall analyse statement (a), Kelsen's criterion for membership, leaving for the next section the analysis of statement (b).

I shall try to show that no basic norm is needed either for the problem of establishing whether or not a given norm belongs to a certain system (the problem of membership) or for the definition of the concept of a legal order.

In fact, the problem of membership is absolutely independent of any speculation about the binding force of legal norms. It makes perfectly good sense to ask whether a given norm is a member of a certain set of norms, even if we do not regard them as obligatory or binding. For instance, one may very well ask whether a certain norm belongs to the Mafia code or to the draft of a statute that has never been promulgated.

A satisfactory characterization of a certain legal order a can be provided by a recursive definition of membership along the following lines:

(i) The set of norms C belongs to (or is a member of) *a*.

(ii) If there is a norm *p* that authorizes or confers power or competence on an authority *x* to issue a norm *q*, and *p* belongs to *a*, and *x* issues *q*, then *q* is a member of *a*, unless it is derogated by a competent authority.

(iii) All norms that are logical consequences of the norms belonging to *a* are members of *a*.[41]

Rules (i), (ii), and (iii) jointly determine the conditions under which a norm belongs to (or is a member of) the system of norms *a*. Rule (i) provides a criterion for the membership of the primitive norms of the system by indicating

[39] Kelsen, *GTLS*, 110. [40] See Nino, 'Some Confusions' (n. 2, this chapter), at § II.

[41] See Alchourrón and Bulygin, *NS*, at 73–6; Carlos E. Alchourrón and Eugenio Bulygin, *Sobre la existencia de las normas jurídicas* (Valencia, Venezuela: Universidad de Carabobo, 1979), at 73–6, repr. (Mexico City: Distribuciones Fontamara, 1997), at 67–70.

which norms are contained in the first constitution (set C).[42] Rule (ii) lays down a criterion for the dynamic derivation of norms, making it possible to incorporate new norms into the system and to eliminate norms that belong to the system. It is by virtue of rule (ii) that legal systems are temporal (that is, they are relative to a certain time).[43] Rule (iii) states that *a* is closed under the notion of logical consequence, which is a general requirement for deductive systems.[44] So rules (i), (ii), and (iii) provide a *criterion for the identification* of the norms of the system *a*.

At the same time, they define this system *a*. It is constituted by a certain (finite) set of primitive norms (the first constitution in Kelsen's sense), together with all those norms that derive either dynamically, see rule (ii), or logically, see rule (iii), from these primitive norms. So every constitution—that is, every set of norms containing at least some power-conferring norms—can give rise to a system of norms or a legal order. The minimal condition that must be met by primitive norms is that they must exist in the sense of merely formal existence (sense (D)), that is, they must be formulated. However, they need not be either accepted or efficacious (though this, of course, is not excluded), nor need they be binding. We will require that primitive norms should have factual existence (sense (A)) only if we are interested in a legal order that is actually in use.

This shows that the question of whether the constitution is a member of the system simply does not arise. It makes no sense to raise this question, for the system is defined in terms of a given constitution. We need not go beyond the constitution, for the chain of dynamic derivation begins with it; it is by definition the first member of this chain. Hence, the problem of membership and the identity of a legal system can be resolved without any recourse to Kelsen's basic norm.

6. The Role of Normative Validity in Kelsen's Theory

I turn now to the problem of normative validity or binding force. It has been observed by von Wright[45] that the validity of a norm in its descriptive sense of membership is relative not to the *validity* of another norm, but to the *existence* of another norm. The situation is different with normative validity. Kelsen rightly says that the reason for the validity of a norm can only be the *validity* of the norm from which it derives its validity.[46] This implies that a norm *p* is valid if *p* has been created by a competent authority, say, *x*. That *x* is competent means

[42] A first constitution, according to Kelsen, is one that has been created not by a competent authority but 'by an individual usurper or a kind of assembly', Kelsen, *GTLS*, 115.

[43] See Bulygin, 'Time and Validity' (1982), in this volume, ch. 10.

[44] See Alfred Tarski, *Logic, Semantics, Metamathematics*, trans. J. H. Woodger (Oxford: Clarendon Press, 1956), at chs. 5, 12.

[45] Von Wright, *NA*, 196.

[46] See Kelsen, *RR 2*, § 34(a) (at 196), *PTL*, at 193.

that there is a norm *q* that confers competence or law-making power on *x*.[47] A competence norm prescribes an obligation to obey the norms issued by the competent (delegated) authority.[48] So *q* prescribes the obligation to obey *p* (which is issued by *x*). Of course, the mere fact that *q* commands that *p* be obeyed does not make *p* valid (binding, justified); *p* will be valid only if *q* is valid. Therefore, *q* must be valid.

Now, if the validity of a norm is relative to the validity of another norm, then the chain of validity must be infinite—unless we assume the existence of a norm that is valid in itself, that is, whose validity is not relative to the validity of another norm but is absolute. This role cannot be played by the constitution, for even though it does not make sense to ask whether a (first) constitution belongs to a legal system, the question of whether a given constitution is binding or justified is perfectly meaningful. Plainly, no norm can be binding by definition. This is the reason for Kelsen's appeal to the basic norm in reply to the question concerning the validity of the first constitution. The first constitution is valid in virtue of the basic norm.

> The validity of this first constitution is the last presupposition, the final postulate, upon which the validity of all the norms of our legal order depends. It is postulated that one ought to behave as the individual, or the individuals, who laid down the first constitution have ordained.... That the first constitution is a binding legal norm is presupposed, and the formulation of the presupposition is the basic norm of this legal order.[49]

Thus the basic norm is the ultimate reason for the validity of all other norms; it fulfils this function by conferring competence on the author of the first constitution.

> The whole function of this basic norm is to confer law-creating power on the act of the first legislator and on all the other acts based on the first act.[50]

Kelsen seems to believe that the mere fact that the basic norm confers law-creating powers on the first legislator and thus establishes an obligation to obey his norms is sufficient to make these norms valid (binding). This conclusion would be correct, however, only if the basic norm itself were valid, for, as I have already emphasized, a valid norm can only derive its validity from another valid norm.

The validity of the basic norm must be absolute and not relative to another norm, but Kelsen does not accept the possibility of absolutely valid norms. In order to be absolutely valid, a norm should be self-evident, but this would imply the idea of practical reason, which is rejected by Kelsen. He claims emphatically that there are no self-evident norms.[51]

[47] See Kelsen, *RR 2*, § 34(a) (at 197), *PTL*, at 194.

[48] Ross, *LJ*, and Thomas Cornides, *Ordinale Deontik. Zusammenhänge zwischen Präferenztheorie, Normlogik und Rechtstheorie* (Vienna: Springer, 1974), share Kelsen's conception of competence norms as indirectly formulated commands or obligation norms. For a criticism of this conception, see Hart, *CL*, at 27–33, 3rd edn., at 27–33. The nature of competence norms is discussed in Bulygin, 'On Norms of Competence' (1992), in this volume, ch. 16.

[49] Kelsen, *GTLS*, 115. [50] Kelsen, *GTLS*, 116.

[51] See Kelsen, *RR 2*, § 34(b) (at 199), *PTL*, at 196.

The basic norm is neither a self-evident norm nor does it justify any legal order[52] because it is merely presupposed to be valid but is not really binding.

> The basic norm is not created in a legal procedure by a law-creating organ. It is not—as a positive legal norm is—valid because it is created in a certain way by a legal act, but it is valid because it is presupposed to be valid; and it is presupposed to be valid because without this presupposition no human act could be interpreted as a legal, especially as a norm-creating, act.[53]

If, however, the basic norm is not a valid norm, it follows that the first constitution is not a valid norm and that none of the norms that can be traced back to the first constitution is valid.

It is because the basic norm is a mere hypothesis of legal science that its acceptance does not commit jurists to a certain moral or political position, for it is compatible with any ideology whatever. Kelsen is very emphatic on this point and stresses that his basic norm has nothing to do with natural law. It validates any legal system, whatever its content may be.[54]

Then, however, one cannot speak seriously about the justifiability or 'obligatoriness' of legal systems. A jurist who asserts the validity of a norm does not say that it is justified and ought therefore to be obeyed. What he says, according to Kelsen, is that *if* the basic norm is accepted, then it is obligatory to do what the norm in question prescribes, without asserting categorically that the basic norm is valid or binding.

It is not surprising that this solution à la Vaihinger did not seem satisfactory to most jurists. In fact, the theory of the basic norm (thesis 4) has always been vigorously resisted by legal philosophers. Even its author recognized towards the end of his life the fictitious character of his basic norm, although he did not draw the unavoidable conclusion that the concept of validity as binding force should play no role at all in the Pure Theory of Law, once the theory is stripped of its purely rhetorical Kantianism.

7. Concluding Remarks

The normative validity of legal norms cannot be based on mere hypothesis and still less on a fiction. This is why those philosophers of law who take the idea of validity as binding force seriously cannot be satisfied with Kelsen's basic norm and must resort to more powerful substitutes. Nino, for instance, maintains that the validity of legal norms is based on absolute and objectively valid moral judgments. This way out is closed to Kelsen, owing to his conception of a positivistic theory of law. He cannot accept the view that there are objectively valid moral principles or true norms, for norms lack truth-values (thesis 6). This means that there is no objectively privileged set of norms. In order to give preference to a certain set, an

[52] See Kelsen, *RR 2*, at § 34(i) (223–6), *PTL*, at 217–19.

[53] Kelsen, *GTLS*, 116.

[54] See Kelsen, *RR 2*, at § 34(i) (223–6), *PTL*, at 217–19.

act of will is required, that is, one must take a political decision. For Kelsen, however, who is determined not to exceed the limits of knowledge, political decisions lie outside the scope of a positivistic theory of law. Hence he attempts to make the idea of validity as binding force compatible with his positivistic conception of legal science by means of the doctrine of the basic norm. As we have seen, these efforts led to failure, a fact acknowledged by Kelsen himself. Therefore, in order to render the Pure Theory of Law consistent, it is necessary that one or the other of the two incompatible ideas be rejected. Either we will want to preserve the idea of normative validity (but then true principles or norms must be substituted for the basic norm, implying the rejection of positivism and the acceptance of some sort of natural law),[55] or else we will choose to be thoroughgoing positivists (but then we must reject the idea of validity as binding force). It is only by choosing the second way that we can preserve a strict dichotomy between, on the one hand, knowledge of law, the description of law, and legal science, and, on the other, the evaluation of law, the creation of legal norms, and legal policy. From Kelsen's positivistic perspective, legal science can establish which norms belong to a given legal order but cannot prescribe the obligation to obey these norms, that is, it cannot assert their validity without trespassing the limits imposed by the positivistic ideal of a value-free legal science.

[55] Contrary to Nino, *Introducción al análisis del derecho* (n. 25, this chapter), at 37–43, both Kelsen and Ross maintain that legal positivism is incompatible with the acceptance of true moral or legal principles. See Kelsen's theses 6 and 7 (at 237, this chapter) and Ross's definition of what he calls the 'kernel of legal positivism': 'First, the thesis that the belief in natural law is erroneous: No such law exists, all law is positive law. This is of course a thesis that pertains to the general field of moral philosophy or ethics, for it denies that ethical (moral, legal) principles or judgments are the expression of truths to be discovered and established objectively by some process of cognition.' Ross, 'Validity', § I, *RJBA*, 50, in *NN*, 148.

15

Limits of Logic and Legal Reasoning (1992)*

Written with Carlos E. Alchourrón

Introduction

In a most illuminating paper, Neil MacCormick analyses the nature of legal reasoning and the possibility of developing legal expert systems.[1] We fully agree with his general approach and the main tenets of his paper, which include:

1. Legal reasoning, which purports to show that a decision (or a claim) is justifiable according to the law in force, is essentially deductive in character or can at any rate be reconstructed as a logical inference, in which, on the basis of two kinds of premisses, normative and factual, a conclusion is reached, stating that certain legal consequences are applicable to a particular case. This inference shows that a decision to apply those consequences to this particular case is legally justifiable.

   This does not mean that a decision can actually be deduced from the premisses; deciding is an act of will and as such is not determined by logic. As MacCormick rightly puts it, 'to decide is not to deduce'; what is entailed by the premisses of a sound argument are the *contents* of a (possible) act of deciding. Thus, this act of deciding, once performed, is said to be justifiable by the premisses of the argument.

* [*Editors' note*: Eugenio Bulygin's paper, which he wrote together with Carlos E. Alchourrón, first appeared in *Expert Systems in Law*, ed. Antonio A. Martino (Amsterdam: Elsevier, 1992), 9–27.]

[1] Neil MacCormick, 'Legal Deduction, Legal Predicates and Expert Systems', *Revue internationale de sémiotique juridique*, 5 (1992), 181–202. [*Editors' note*: In the present text, Alchourrón and Bulygin quote from the manuscript from which Neil MacCormick spoke at the international conference 'Logica–Informatica Diritto', held in Florence in 1989. We have been unable to locate the manuscript as delivered in Florence, but we have located the published version of MacCormick's paper. Happily, as far as we can tell from Alchourrón and Bulygin's references, MacCormick's manuscript and the published version of his paper are virtually the same. To remain faithful to Alchourrón and Bulygin's text, we have followed their references to the manuscript and have then included corresponding references to the published version. Where one text departs from the other, we have added a note to that effect.]

2. Current objections to this thesis purporting to show that legal reasoning is not a deductive inference, on the ground that it involves certain operations that are not logical, are not pertinent. Although it is true that, in order to establish the premisses of the argument, one must sometimes resort to interpretations, decisions, and evaluations, the reasoning—that is, the step that leads from the premisses to the conclusion—is, or rather can be reconstructed as, a deductive inference.
3. In so far as the performance of logical inferences lies within existing computational possibilities, it is in principle not impossible to develop legal expert systems for the justification of legal decisions, even if such expert systems for fact-finding, evaluation, and rule-interpretation are not available.

We do not agree, however, with all of the details of MacCormick's presentation, which is perhaps less clear than it ought to be.

Since the problems addressed by MacCormick are of the utmost importance for the application of artificial intelligence to law, we are more interested in clarifying the greater issue than in criticizing our friend MacCormick. Thus, we shall try to restate some of the problems raised in his paper in—we should like to think—more precise terms. As a result of this reformulation certain disagreements will no doubt come to light. We have the impression that our account differs from MacCormick's on such issues as the characterization of subsumptive reasoning, the role of truth and truth-determining procedures in law, and the character of evaluative and interpretative statements, as well as the nature of the normative premisses involved in legal reasoning and the kind of logic that one needs for its reconstruction.

1. Subsumption

According to MacCormick, legal reasoning is deductive–subsumptive in nature. Legal rules can be 'conceptualised as hypothetical in form, prescribing that, if certain circumstances (certain "operative facts") obtain, then certain normative consequences are to follow'.[2] Legal reasoning consists in establishing facts in a particular case subsumable under the hypothesis of the rule and drawing the logical conclusion for the particular case from the rule along with the facts. Thus, the first step is the subsuming of certain particular facts under the predicates contained in legal rules. Usually legal rules are general in the sense that they do not refer directly to individuals (by means of names or definite descriptions) but do refer indirectly by means of general terms or predicates. Predicates are true of certain individuals (by 'individual' we understand here any particular object, be it a person, an action, or an event). Thus, legal rules are to be applied to individuals or particulars of which the predicates occurring in such rules are true. The process that leads to the statement that a predicate is true of a certain individual, which entails that the property

[2] MacCormick, ms., 2, and 'Legal Deduction', 182 (n. 1, this chapter).

designated by the predicate is instantiated in this individual or that this individual belongs to the class that is the extension of the predicate, is—in legal jargon—traditionally called *subsumption.*

It must be stressed that the problem of subsumption is not a specifically legal problem but one relating to the empirical use of language in general, that is, the application of the general terms of a language to particular objects of the world. In other words, it is quite simply the philosophical problem of the relation of (general) words to things.

Any empirical use of a language involves the existence of certain semantic rules, which specify (a) which particular object is referred to by a name, and (b) which attribute (property or relation) is designated by a general term or predicate. Each property determines a class of objects, namely, the class of all objects that have this property. The predicate is true of all the objects that belong to this class, which is called the extension of the predicate; for example, the predicate 'murderer' is true of all those who have the property of being a murderer (or belong to the class of murderers, that is, fall within the extension of 'murderer'). Thus, the sentence 'John is a murderer' is true if and only if John has committed murder. The truth of this sentence is determined by two elements: (i) certain linguistic conventions (namely, the semantic rules of the language) and (ii) certain facts (namely, the fact that John has committed murder).

Two points should be stressed in this connection. First, we must remember that semantic rules, like all linguistic rules, are in an important sense *conventional*; the relation between words and things or properties is not a natural (causal) relation but an artificial one, that is, a relation qua result of linguistic conventions.

In the second place, semantic rules are metalinguistic; they are used to refer not only to reality (like the expressions of our language) but also to linguistic expressions themselves, stating a certain relation between language and the world (between words and things or properties). Thus, they belong not to the language used to refer to reality but to its metalanguage.

It is a well-known fact that the semantic rules of natural languages are of course seldom, if ever, stated explicitly, but they can and should be made explicit in the metalanguage of a reconstructed (artificial) language, such as that used by logicians or computers.

However, subsumption does not always deal with individuals and their attributes. Sometimes the problem is that of determining the relations that obtain between predicates.

Let us illustrate this point by means of an example drawn from Dworkin.

> Suppose the legislature has passed a statute stipulating that 'sacrilegious contracts shall henceforth be invalid'. The community is divided as to whether a contract signed on Sunday is, for that reason alone, sacrilegious. It is known that very few of the legislators had that question in mind when they voted, and that they are now equally divided on the question of whether it should be so interpreted. Tom and Tim have signed a contract on

Sunday, and Tom now sues Tim to enforce the terms of the contract, whose validity Tim contests.[3]

The judge has to decide whether or not the contract is valid, and in order to do so he must determine whether the sentence 'the contract signed by Tom and Tim is sacrilegious' is true.

It should be observed in the first place that in this example the parties agree on two important points, namely, (1) that what they did on a certain occasion was to sign a contract, and (2) that they did this on Sunday. This means that the judge already knows that the individual action performed by Tom and Tim has two properties: that of being a contract and that of having been signed on Sunday. Thus, all he must find out in order to establish the truth of the sentence 'the contract signed by Tom and Tim is sacrilegious' is whether contracts signed on Sunday have the property of being sacrilegious, that is, whether the extension of the predicate 'sacrilegious' includes that of 'contracts signed on Sunday'. In our example, the predicate 'sacrilegious' is admittedly vague and the case of contracts signed on Sunday falls within its area of penumbra. In this hypothesis the judge is unable to discover whether or not such contracts are sacrilegious, for there is no established linguistic usage concerning the relation between these two expressions. In such cases judges must take a decision either to include contracts signed on Sunday in the extension of 'sacrilegious' or to exclude them. Suppose our judge decides that such contracts are sacrilegious. In doing so, he does not state a true or false proposition; rather, he gives a (partial) definition of the predicate 'sacrilegious'. It is a stipulative definition, and as such it is neither true nor false. Moreover, this sentence belongs not to the language but to the metalanguage. It is about the meaning of certain expressions of the language. Given this stipulation, however, the sentence 'contracts signed on Sunday are sacrilegious' expresses an analytic proposition. It is true by virtue of the meaning of the relevant terms alone. This is a typical interpretative sentence and, it should be stressed, is not factual but is instead analytic. Thus, the judge can now draw a (logically valid) conclusion—namely, that the contract signed by Tom and Tim is invalid according to the rule established by the legislature and ought not to be enforced. This reasoning shows that his decision to reject Tom's claim is legally justifiable.

In order to justify his decision, the judge in this case had to establish a semantic rule for the term 'sacrilegious'. If this term already had a clear meaning—that is, an established linguistic usage according to which contracts signed on Sunday were regarded as sacrilegious—then his decision would be based on an analytic statement, namely, 'contracts signed on Sunday are sacrilegious', but the ground of this statement would not be a stipulative definition, that is, a metalinguistic sentence that is true or false in relation to existing linguistic conventions. The crucial difference between the two cases lies in the fact that the judge in one case discovers an existing semantic rule, whereas in the other case

[3] Ronald Dworkin, 'No Right Answer?', in *Law, Morality, and Society. Essays in Honour of H. L. A. Hart*, ed. P. M. S. Hacker and Joseph Raz (Oxford: Clarendon Press, 1977), 58–84, at 58.

it is he who stipulates the rule. In both cases, however, the judge *uses* a true but vacuous sentence. It is analytically true but vacuous in the sense that it does not say anything about the world.

We have already pointed out that in our example the task of the judge was facilitated by the fact that the parties agreed on two points, namely, that what they did was to sign a contract and that it took place on Sunday. In this way, the judge already knows that the individual action in question has two properties, and all he needs to do is to establish a relation between the predicates 'contract signed on Sunday' and 'sacrilegious'. But the possession of these properties could have been contested; in such a case, the judge would have to discover or to decide whether what the parties did was to sign a contract and whether their action was carried out on Sunday. If Tim denies that what they signed was a contract, then the judge must find out whether the individual action performed by Tom and Tim on a certain occasion includes the property expressed by 'signing a contract'. Here the judge is faced with the problem of determining whether the predicate 'signing a contract' is true of the individual action in question. Usually, in order to determine whether or not it was a contract that Tom and Tim signed on a certain occasion, the judge requires factual information; he must know exactly what happened on that occasion. The same problem may arise if Tom and Tim do not agree on the question of when they signed the contract; the judge must then find out exactly when the contract was signed. For instance, Tim might maintain that although they met Saturday evening to discuss the contract, it was Sunday when they reached an agreement. Here the problem for the judge is the lack of factual knowledge: he needs more information concerning the facts of the case. Elsewhere we have called this kind of problem 'gaps in knowledge'.[4] The difficulty in acquiring information about facts can be mitigated—and is usually mitigated in judicial practice—by means of the device of a legal presumption. Presumptions make it possible for the judge to act as if he knew all the relevant facts of the case. According to the general principle of *onus probandi*,[5] the party who affirms the existence of a fact must prove it, for if the alleged fact has not been duly proven, it is held to be non-existent. Several other presumptions, like good faith, the onerous character of commercial acts, and so on, constitute a set of auxiliary rules for determining the 'legal existence' of facts. Thus, if Tim asserts that the contract was signed on Sunday and is therefore invalid, he must produce the corresponding evidence. Yet it is important to emphasize that the judge's final decision that the contract was or was not signed on Sunday purports to be a true statement of fact, although it may happen that it is not true. (The problem of truth and truth-determination will be discussed in the next section of this paper.)

The discussion of our example shows that the term 'subsumption' is used ambiguously to refer to two different problems, for which we shall coin the terms 'individual' and 'generic' subsumption.

[4] Alchourrón and Bulygin, *NS*, at 31–4. [*Editors' note*: For this and other abbreviations, see the Table of Abbreviations.]

[5] *Onus probandi* or 'burden of proof'.

Individual subsumption is the problem of determining the truth of certain individual contingent (synthetic) sentences of the general form 'Fa', where 'F' stands for a predicate and 'a' is a (proper) name, that is, the name of an individual object. In order to resolve this problem, the judge must determine whether a given individual object has the property designated by the predicate in question.

Generic subsumption is the problem of establishing what logical relation obtains between two predicates (which is also a rather frequent case). In this second hypothesis, what is under discussion is the truth of a metalinguistic sentence about predicates of the form '$F < G$'. The resulting universal sentence of the language '$(x)(Fx \rightarrow Gx)$' is analytic, for its truth is based on the meaning of the predicates 'F' and 'G'. Either the semantic rules determining the meaning of these predicates already exist (if there is an established linguistic usage for these terms), or they must be stipulated by the judge.

The difficulties in resolving the problems of subsumption (both individual and generic) stem from two different sources: lack of factual knowledge (gaps in knowledge) and semantic indeterminacy or vagueness of the predicates involved (gaps in recognition[6] or penumbral cases).[7] It is certainly true that the vagueness of a predicate may call for a decision, but, as MacCormick correctly points out, this does not count as an argument against the deductive nature of legal reasoning. Even if a decision is sometimes involved in the task of establishing the premisses of such reasoning, this does not rule out the possibility that reasoning from premisses to a conclusion can be reconstructed as a deductive inference. The whole issue has nothing to do with law and *legal* reasoning in particular, but is a feature of all applied logic.

2. Truth and Truth-Determination in the Realm of Law

According to MacCormick every application of the concept of truth requires a truth-determining procedure, and

> the legal realm... caters with particular thoroughness for the problem of truth-determination. Where determinations of facts are called for in any authoritative law-applying process, legal systems ordinarily make provision to endow determinate individuals with special fact-determining authority. Whether the fact-determining task be given to a jury, a judge, a minister, or some special tribunal, there are usually some legal dispositions giving some individual or group the power to make conclusive determinations of fact... For certain purposes, that which an authorised fact-determiner determines to be true, or certifies as true, has to be deemed true or accepted as the conclusive truth of the matter. For legal purposes, the value 'true' is ascribed to that which is authoritatively so certified. Except in so far as processes of appeal or review can be utilised to reverse or correct certified truths, the legal system admits of no other truth of the relevant matter,...[8]

[6] See Alchourrón and Bulygin, *NS*, at 31–4.

[7] See Hart, 'Separation'; Genaro R. Carrió, *Notas sobre derecho y lenguaje* (Buenos Aires: Abeledo-Perrot, 1965).

[8] MacCormick, ms., 11, and 'Legal Deduction', 189–90 (n. 1, this chapter). [*Editors' note*: The passages cited here are identical in the two works, save for MacCormick's insertion, in the published

This quotation leaves the impression that in legal contexts factual truth depends on what a judge or other 'truth-determiner' says is true. This is certainly not the case. MacCormick's account would be correct if instead of 'true' he had used the term 'proved', but as it stands it is either conceptually or at least terminologically misleading. The confusion between truth and proof occurs rather frequently, and not only among jurists; this is why it is so important to clarify this point.

The truth of an empirical statement of fact such as 'John killed Alfred' does not depend on what a judge or other officials say. It depends only on the semantic rules of language that are employed and on the facts that are referred to by the statement.

The semantic rules determine to what individuals the names 'John' and 'Alfred' refer and what relation is designated by the predicate 'killed'. The sentence 'John killed Alfred' is true if and only if the individual referred to by 'John' stands in the relation designated by the predicate 'killed' to the individual referred to by 'Alfred'. What a judge says about John's killing Alfred is utterly irrelevant to the truth of this sentence.

Our statement of the problem of empirical truth amounts to an acceptance of the correspondence theory of truth in the tradition of Aristotle and Tarski. It is not a *crude* correspondence theory of truth in MacCormick's sense, but a correspondence theory of truth *tout court*. According to MacCormick's characterization of a crude correspondence theory of truth, which he rejects rather concisely—'There are so many objections to such a theory of truth... that I shall excuse myself from going into them here'—the theory holds that truth-values can be ascribed 'only to such statements as those for which there could be a corresponding state of affairs in the perceptual physical world'.[9] As long as we are dealing with empirical sentences, there is nothing objectionable here, and this does not render any correspondence theory a 'crude' theory. If a sentence is empirical, there must be an empirical fact in order to make it true, but this does not exclude the possibility of sentences whose truth is not a matter of empirical or perceptual fact. (The question of whether there are types of fact other than empirical facts need not concern us here.) In this sense, the concept of truth used in law is exactly the same as the concept used in the empirical sciences.

In any case, no sentence is true independently of linguistic conventions. If MacCormick wants to ascribe truth—flouting Quine—to propositions instead of sentences, we have no objections. The truth of propositions is, of course, independent of linguistic conventions, and this is the case not only with propositions about 'brute facts', as MacCormick seems to believe,[10] but with *all* kinds of proposition. It is only the truth of sentences (that is, linguistic entities) that depends on linguistic conventions.

version, of the clause 'or certifies as true' immediately following the clause 'that which an authorised fact-determiner determines to be true'.]

[9] MacCormick, 'Legal Deduction' (n. 1, this chapter), 195. [*Editors' note*: Alchourrón and Bulygin make no reference to MacCormick's ms. here.]

[10] 'Sometimes the proper interpretation of an utterance will be as uttering a proposition of a kind whose truth or falsity is to be conceived of as depending solely on states of the world absolutely

This is not yet the end of the story, however, for in order to punish John the law requires not only that the sentence 'John killed Alfred' be true but also that it should be proven in court. The problem of proof in a court presents features peculiar to judicial contexts, features that differ on some significant points from proof in science, and it might therefore be useful to compare the role played by this concept in these two domains.

(a) Both in science and in the law there are certain criteria that establish what counts as evidence for the truth of an empirical sentence, but in the law there are limitations as to the kind and amount of evidence that is admissible in a judicial proceeding. For instance, the existence of certain contracts can be proved only by means of a written document; the number of witnesses a party may present is also often subject to restrictions.
(b) Even more important is the temporal limitation. All evidence must be produced within a certain period of time, and the question of proving an empirical statement (such as 'John killed Alfred') must be settled within the temporal limits established by legal rules.
(c) For the law, it is typical that the question of proof must be settled and moreover *authoritatively* settled in a judicial proceeding. The judge is not only entitled but has an obligation to decide whether a certain empirical sentence has been proven, and his decision is final in the sense that it brings an end to the controversy and to the possibility of discussing the truth of the sentence within the proceeding. (Still, bringing to an end the discussion of truth does not render the sentence true!)

No such limitations are to be found in scientific contexts. All kinds of evidence available and conducive to truth-determination are admissible at any time, and no one has the authority to *decide* that a sentence has been proven. This is why the problem of empirical truth is always regarded in science as an essentially open question.

This is the case because science is interested almost exclusively in establishing the truth, whereas the law is primarily interested in solving social conflicts. But—and this is a most important point—social conflicts are solved by means of general rules, and the application of such rules to particular cases often requires determining the truth of factual sentences. Hence, a judicial proceeding often—and in the case of a criminal prosecution nearly always—involves a fact-finding procedure that consists in determining the truth of certain empirical (factual) sentences. The fact that this procedure is subject to restrictions and temporal limitations and ends in a judicial decision that is authoritative and final does not mean that the decision is infallible (even if it stems from the supreme tribunal). A decision based on a false statement of fact is valid; this means that it produces all legal effects and cannot be altered (apart from possibilities of appeal or review by a higher court), but it can

independent of any human convention or act of judgment. That is, it will be properly interpreted as stating a proposition of "brute fact".' MacCormick, ms., 10, and 'Legal Deduction', 189 (n. 1, this chapter).

nevertheless be criticized as mistaken. It makes perfectly good sense to say that the decision of a tribunal (even a supreme tribunal) is wrong, although such criticism is external to the legal process and has no immediate legal effects. Suppose that John, accused of having killed Alfred, did not kill him, so that the sentence 'John killed Alfred' is false. Suppose, too, that the judge decides, on the basis of the evidence produced in court, that this statement has been proven, and he therefore sentences John to life imprisonment. That his decision, if final, means—as already mentioned—that it cannot be challenged within the legal process, it means therefore that John must be sent to prison. Yet it is still true that John did not kill Alfred, and the judge has therefore made a mistake, even if this fact will be of no consequence to John's personal fate. Finality of decision does not imply infallibility of the judge, but if—as MacCormick and many jurists seem to believe—truth were dependent on what a judge authoritatively decides ('truth is what the courts say is true'), then judges would indeed be infallible.

This point has been stressed by Hart in relation to judicial statements about norms. Hart has shown that the finality of the decision of the courts by no means entails their infallibility and provides no support for the idea that '[t]he law (or the constitution) is what the courts say it is'.[11]

The situation regarding statements of fact made by the courts is exactly the same, and Hart's arguments can easily be extended to cover them. Facts are what they are and not what judges say they are. Although the fact-finding procedure is completed by an authoritative decision of the judge, based on evidence produced in a limited period, nevertheless, this procedure purports to determine the truth and the judge has an obligation to search for the truth. A failure in the determination of truth—as long as it is exceptional—does not invalidate the decision of the judge, which is regarded as valid and produces all legal effects. This is the price the law is willing to pay for the sake of social stability and peace, that is, for the ability to settle social conflicts within certain temporal limits. However, if judges were regularly to base their decisions on false statements of fact, the whole system of law would be perverted. It is important to emphasize that the rule of criminal law stipulates the duty to sentence those who have committed murder and not those whom the judge says have committed murder. This rule—as with all legal rules—can be occasionally violated by the judge (as a result of an honest mistake or abuse), but it still remains in force for as long as such violations are exceptional. If, however, the court sentences systematically those who have not committed murder—that is, if the rule were violated regularly—it would then cease to exist altogether. In such a case there would be a new rule stipulating that the judge is entitled to punish all those who in his view deserve punishment, but as long as the rule establishing the judge's duty to punish murderers exists, the judge is not free to depart from the rule, which constitutes the standard of correct and incorrect judging. It always makes sense to say that the

[11] See Hart, *CL*, 1st edn., at 138–44, 3rd edn., at 141–7.

decision of the court is incorrect. This is why the courts are not infallible, despite the fact that their decisions are or may be final.

3. The Role of Evaluations in Judicial Reasoning

Another point worth mentioning is the role played by evaluations in the determination of facts and in the interpretation of legal rules. According to MacCormick:

> Determinations of fact require a capacity for evaluation of evidence, and determinations that certain brute facts count as instances of a rule's operative facts require a capacity for interpretation of rule-formulations in the light of human values.[12]

Moreover, 'it is quite often the case that the law makes some provision which is conditional upon the satisfaction of a certain criterion or standard of value'.[13] In such cases 'the task of determining whether the law's conditions are satisfied requires a double evaluation': on the one hand, the evaluation of evidence, and, on the other, the evaluation required by the application of evaluative terms like 'reasonable', 'fair', 'due care', and so on, although in the common law 'such questions as that of what is reasonable or that of what is fair are classed as "questions of fact"'.[14] So MacCormick believes that 'it would be wrong to delegate' these tasks 'to machines, however "intelligent"', for '[s]uch determinations can only be made by beings with intelligence and will as well as a capacity for evaluation of evidence and understanding of values implicit in rules'.[15]

This appears to be an overstatement. In order to see clearly what is at stake here, we must consider separately (i) what kind of evaluation is required for the determination of facts (which occurs in individual subsumption), (ii) in what sense rule interpretation—that is, the determination of semantic rules concerning predicates of the language in which legal rules (statutes, contracts, precedents) are formulated (which occurs both in individual and in generic subsumption)— requires evaluations, and, finally, (iii) what takes place with the applications of evaluative predicates to particular situations.

(i) In order to decide whether a given fact has been proven, the judge must evaluate the evidence produced during the process, but this evaluation is of the same kind as the evaluation of evidence carried out in the empirical sciences. It is not an ethical evaluation but a special kind of evaluation, which we will call—for lack of a better term—*epistemic* evaluation. In evaluating the evidence we do not formulate genuine value-judgments, and in any case the kinds of value that are at stake in this context have nothing to do with 'human values' embodied in

[12] MacCormick, ms., 13, and 'Legal Deduction', at 191 (n. 1, this chapter).
[13] MacCormick, ms., 13, and 'Legal Deduction', at 191 (n. 1, this chapter).
[14] MacCormick, ms., 14, and 'Legal Deduction', at 192 (n. 1, this chapter).
[15] MacCormick, ms., 13, and 'Legal Deduction', at 191 (n. 1, this chapter).

legal rules; factual evidence is evaluated not as right or wrong, good or bad, just or unjust, convenient or inconvenient, but as conducive (and to what degree) or not conducive to the truth of empirical sentences. Thus, the evaluation of evidence is the problem of determining whether an empirical sentence has been duly proven, a problem that we have already discussed in the preceding section.

(ii) We have already seen that interpretative sentences do not express value judgments even if they are based on stipulative definitions. Ethical evaluations may lie at the bottom of semantic stipulations of the judge, but once his decision is taken, the sentence stating, for example, that 'contracts signed on Sunday are sacrilegious' expresses not a value judgment but an analytic proposition. The acceptance of a semantic rule may be, and usually is, based on genuine value judgments—that is, on ethical evaluations of the consequences of adopting one decision or another—but the application of a semantic rule has nothing to do with evaluations.

(iii) As to evaluative terms that occur in legal rules, it is by no means clear and uncontroversial that their application to particular situations always requires genuine evaluation.

It is important to observe that the logical behaviour of evaluative predicates is rather similar to that of deontic predicates. The primary use of deontic predicates such as 'obligatory', 'prohibited', or 'permissible' is to formulate norms or prescriptions in order to render obligatory, prohibited, or permissible certain actions or states of affairs. This use is prescriptive, but it is a well-known fact that the same predicates can also be used *descriptively* to formulate propositions stating that certain actions or states of affairs are obligatory, prohibited, or permissible according to some norm or set of norms. Such norm-propositions are descriptive; they describe the fact that certain norms exist, and they are therefore true or false. They are true when the set of norms in question contains a norm enjoining, prohibiting, or permitting the action referred to, and they are otherwise false. Since the descriptive use of deontic predicates already presupposes the existence of norms, the descriptive use is in a way parasitic upon the prescriptive use of such terms (which gives rise to the existence of norms). Thus, it is convenient to call it a secondary use.

A similar situation obtains in the case of evaluative predicates like 'good', 'right', 'fair', and so on. The primary use of such terms is to evaluate, that is, to formulate value judgments. Value judgments, whatever their nature, entail some sort of approval or disapproval.[16] However, evaluative terms can also be used descriptively in sentences that do not express evaluations (approval or disapproval) but instead express factual propositions to the effect that the thing in question meets the evaluative standards or criteria of a certain community or social group.[17] This is what we propose to call a secondary use of evaluative terms. Such propositions are factual

[16] This is an important insight of ethical emotivism. See Charles L. Stevenson, *Ethics and Language* (New Haven: Yale University Press, 1944).

[17] See Hare, *LM*, at ch. VI (94–110).

and not evaluative. For instance, by saying that this is a good car, I might express a value judgment (primary use of 'good'), but it is also possible that I am not evaluating the car but merely giving a piece of information, namely, that this car meets the criteria for being regarded as a good car, such as being comfortable, economical, fast, and so on, without committing myself to share these criteria (secondary use of 'good'). The secondary (descriptive) use of evaluative terms does not entail any approval; it is purely factual, for it consists in recording that the thing declared good has certain properties that are used as criteria for goodness. Hence, such sentences express factual, descriptive propositions. By analogy to norm-propositions we can speak of evaluative propositions as distinct from value judgments. If we adopt this terminology, the difference between value judgments and evaluative propositions will be the same as that between norms and norm-propositions.

Therefore, the occurrence of evaluative predicates in legal rules and consequently their use by the judge—as, for example, when he states that certain goods are of *merchantable quality* or that a rent is *fair* or that a certain person failed to take *reasonable care* to prevent a harm—does not by itself imply that the judge must carry out an evaluation in order to determine that such predicates are applicable to a given particular. We are inclined to think that in many cases (though not in all cases) judges do not evaluate but merely record the evaluations of the social group to which they belong. In other words, they formulate not value judgments but evaluative propositions, and such propositions are purely descriptive. Thus, the common law seems not to be mistaken after all in classifying such questions as 'questions of fact'. It is of course true that the evaluative criteria used by a social group—which the judge records—are often rather vague, and their vagueness is probably greater than that of the criteria for the application of non-evaluative predicates such as 'tall' or 'signed on Sunday', but the difference is only one of degree.

These remarks are designed to show that the role played by evaluation in judicial reasoning is considerably more modest than is commonly supposed or is at least supposed by MacCormick. Contrary to his view, the task of determining whether the law's conditions are satisfied in most cases, far from requiring a double evaluation, does not require any genuine evaluation at all, even if the laws are 'cast in terms of what is reasonable or [in] cognate terms'.

As for the question of whether computers are capable of performing actions that fall under the heading of 'evaluations', it is not easy to provide a definite answer. They are certainly not able to make ethical evaluations, which requires understanding the values implicit in the rules. We would prefer, however, to adopt a more cautious attitude regarding the evaluation of factual evidence. In any case, when the evidence admissible in a judicial process is sufficiently codified, there seems to be no a priori objection to the use of computers for fact-determining operations.[18] Also, there is no problem about delegating to machines the task of establishing evaluative criteria, as long as the performance of genuine value judgments is not required.

[18] See Ricardo A. Guibourg, 'An Automatic Decision-Making System', in *Artificial Intelligence and Legal Information Systems*, ed. Constantino Ciampi (Amsterdam: North-Holland, 1982), 301–21.

4. Norms and Truth

MacCormick summarily rejects the objection raised by Vincent Wellman against the deductivist thesis for involving the supposition that rule- or norm-formulations have truth-values,[19] and such a supposition, according to Wellman, is at best contestable and at worst false. He concludes that, from a methodological point of view, basing a theory of legal reasoning on it is unsound.

MacCormick's rejection of this view is based on his belief that 'it is simply false to continue to doubt or deny the possibility of truth in formulations of norms'.[20]

Nonetheless, Wellman's objection is perhaps the most serious objection against the deductivist conception of judicial justification. This objection—which is, of course, not new—amounts to the negation of the possibility of a logic of norms. Many philosophers, among them important thinkers such as Georg Henrik von Wright, the founding father of deontic logic, have entertained serious doubts about the very possibility of developing such a logic and have, accordingly, tried to find a way out of this difficulty, offering some alternative logical theory.[21]

What little MacCormick says about the problem of the truth of norm-formulations shows clearly that he completely overlooks a very basic distinction between norms and norm-propositions and hence between norm-formulations and formulations of norm-propositions.[22] We have already mentioned that in ordinary language the same linguistic expressions (such as 'smoking prohibited' or 'it is obligatory that one pay one's debts') can be used both to issue a prescription or a norm (a command, a prohibition, or a permission) and also to state that a certain action or state of affairs is obligatory, prohibited, or permissible according to some (unspecified) norm or system of norms. In the first case we have a norm-formulation, which is prescriptive and so neither true nor false but susceptible of being obeyed or satisfied; in the second case we are faced with a formulation of a norm-proposition, which is descriptive and hence true or false, but which cannot be obeyed or satisfied.

A norm-proposition stating that an action p is obligatory (prohibited) according to a given normative system α is true if and only if there is (in α or among the consequences of α) a norm to the effect that p ought (or ought not) to be done, that is, a norm that enjoins (prohibits) p.

[19] Vincent Wellman, 'Practical Reasoning and Judicial Justification: Toward an Adequate Theory', *University of Colorado Law Review*, 57 (1985/6), 45–115.

[20] MacCormick, ms., 18, and 'Legal Deduction', at 194 (n. 1, this chapter).

[21] See Georg Henrik von Wright, 'Norms, Truth, and Logic', in *Deontic Logic, Computational Linguistics and Legal Information Systems*, ed. Antonio A. Martino (Amsterdam: North-Holland, 1982), 3–20; Georg Henrik von Wright, 'Norms, Truth, and Logic', in von Wright, *Practical Reason. Philosophical Papers* (Oxford: Basil Blackwell, 1983), 130–209; Georg Henrik von Wright, 'Bedingungsnormen—ein Prüfstein für die Normenlogik', in *Theorie der Normen. Festgabe für Ota Weinberger zum 65. Geburtstag*, ed. Werner Krawietz, et al. (Berlin: Duncker & Humblot, 1984), 447–56. See also the review of sceptical theories in Ota Weinberger, 'Der normenlogische Skeptizismus', *Rechtstheorie*, 17 (1986), 13–81.

[22] See von Wright, *NA*, 104–6; Alchourrón and Bulygin, *NS*, 121 *et passim*; Eugenio Bulygin, 'Norms, Normative Propositions, and Legal Statements' (1982), in this volume, ch. 11.

Historically, the distinction between norms and norm-propositions can be traced back to Bentham.[23] It appears in different forms in such authors as Kelsen, Hedenius, and Alf Ross and has been clearly elaborated in von Wright.[24]

There is no doubt about the truth-value of norm-propositions. The question is whether norms can be true or false, for if they lack truth-values, it is not clear how we can make inferences in which norms appear as premisses or the conclusion of a deductive argument. When stating the problem of the deductive justification of judicial decisions, MacCormick seems to have in mind legal rules or norms, as they appear in statutes or codes. The idea is that the decision of a judge is justifiable if it can be inferred from legal rules plus the particular facts of the case, which must be subsumable under the operative facts of the rule. His description of the matter seems to entail that the normative premiss of the justificatory argument must be a norm and not a norm-proposition. However, when he discusses the problem of the truth of norm-formulations, he seems to have in mind norm-propositions and not norms. He says:

> All that is true, but not to the issue. Observe that acts of legislating were (correctly) said to 'establish' norms. This indicates that the conceptual structure of a legal system is one in which statutes and other kinds of rule can be said to exist over time. As Ota Weinberger and I have said and have shown, their existence is a matter of institutional fact. Hence it is perfectly possible for there to be true statements of the existent normative content of such a system at any given time... [T]he legal states of affairs which result from law-creating and conduct-guiding acts... can be truly (or falsely) stated notwithstanding that the acts which brought them about cannot be...[25]

There can be little doubt that it is possible to describe the contents of a system of norms by means of norm-propositions, which—as with all descriptive propositions—are true or false. What is rather doubtful is the ascription of truth-values to norms, and MacCormick seems to agree that norms lack truth-values. Indeed, he explicitly acknowledges that norms established by acts of commanding or legislating 'are to be understood not as describing the world but as guiding conduct in it'. This sounds like an admission to the effect that norms lack truth-values. His answer to Vincent Wellman's objection is not satisfactory unless he is prepared to maintain that the 'normative premiss' of a justificatory argument is a norm-proposition and not a norm, for only norm-propositions and not norms are bearers of truth.

The main problem with the justification of judicial decisions is that, being normative, they cannot be justified by mere assertions of facts (however complex these facts may be). Indeed, when a judge sentences John to life imprisonment on the ground that he finds John guilty of having killed Alfred, the judge not only states a fact (that John has committed murder) but also issues a prescription, that is, a norm to the effect that John be sent to prison for life. A norm-proposition, in stating

[23] Jeremy Bentham, *Of Laws in General*, ed. H. L. A. Hart (London: Athlone Press, 1970), 152–5.

[24] See von Wright, *NA*, 104–6; Bulygin, 'Norms, Normative Propositions, and Legal Statements' (1982), in this volume, ch. 11.

[25] MacCormick, ms., 18–19, and 'Legal Deduction', 194–5 (n. 1, this chapter).

that according to the system of norms in the country in question the judge has an obligation to sentence those who have committed murder, is not, as a mere statement of fact, sufficient to justify the prescription (norm) issued by the judge. In order to justify it, the judge has to use the norm issued by the legislator, for example, the corresponding article of the penal code. It is from the *norm* prescribing that, for all x, if x has committed a murder x ought to be sentenced to life imprisonment, that the judge infers (by means of a deductive argument) that John—who killed Alfred—ought to be sentenced to life imprisonment. This is the kind of argument that MacCormick rightly regards as deductive, but it is essential for this argument that its major premiss be a norm and not a mere norm-proposition. A factual proposition cannot justify a prescription, and a norm-proposition is factual, although the fact referred to by it is not a fact of the natural world, that is, not a 'brute' fact in MacCormick's sense but an 'institutional fact'.

Another major problem with norm-propositions is that they are not universal but particular, even if they refer to universal norms. Although they explicitly state the obligatoriness of a certain action (in certain circumstances), they are in fact reducible to statements about the existence of norms (as is shown by their truth conditions, as stated earlier). Thus, a norm-proposition is always an existential proposition. The major premiss of a justificatory argument used by a judge, however, must be a universal normative sentence (expressing a norm), formulated in terms such as 'for all x and for all y, if x and y are human beings, and x is of age and in full possession of his mental faculties, and x kills y, then x ought to be sentenced to life imprisonment'.

Thus, we arrive at the conclusion (i) that the normative premiss in judicial reasoning must be a norm and not a norm-proposition, and (ii) that norms are neither true nor false. The decisive question is: in what way does this insight affect the deductivist thesis?

The idea that underlies Vincent Wellman's objection is that deductive reasoning can only operate with sentences that are true or false. It is this tacit premiss of his argument that must now be subject to closer inspection.

In the tradition of logic from Aristotle to the present day, the connection between logic and truth is twofold: (1) the propositional connectives (negation, conjunction, etc.) are defined in terms of truth (for example, by means of truth-tables), and (2) the basic notions of logic such as logical consequence (logical implication) and inconsistency (logical incompatibility or contradiction) are also characterized in terms of truth. Thus, a sentence is logically implied or is a consequence of a given set of sentences if and only if there is no interpretation that renders the sentences of the set (premisses of the argument) true and the sentence implied by this set (conclusion of the argument) false. In other words, a case of logically valid reasoning (in which the premisses logically imply the conclusion) is truth-preserving in the sense that if the premisses are true, then the conclusion must also be true. On the other hand, two sentences are incompatible (contradictory, inconsistent) if and only if the truth of one of them implies the falsity of the other.

The crucial problem is this: is it possible to define these notions without having recourse to the concept of truth, in order to be able to apply them to sentences that lack truth-values?

As far back as 1957, von Wright wrote in the Preface to his book *Logical Studies*:

> Deontic logic gets part of its philosophic significance from the fact that norms and valuations, though removed from the realm of truth, yet are subject to logical law. This shows that logic, so to speak, has a wider reach than truth.[26]

This is an interesting idea but it is not enough simply to announce it. One must justify it, and, in particular, one must offer an alternative characterization of the logical connectives of the notions of logical implication (entailment) and inconsistency. This von Wright had not done, and once he realized it, he turned back to the traditional conception of logic,[27] rejecting, precisely because norms lack truth-values, the idea that deontic logic can be interpreted as a logic of norms.

It is an important preanalytical fact that such terms as 'not', 'and', 'or', and so on are used in connection with prescriptions ('do not go out without an umbrella!', 'go to Marks & Spencer's and buy yourself a shirt or a jumper!' are perfectly 'normal' commands), and we often infer prescriptions from other prescriptions (sometimes in combination with factual statements). This fact does not, however, by itself prove that this use is logically 'legitimate', although it poses the following challenge, first formulated by Jørgensen[28] and known since then in the literature as Jørgensen's dilemma: Either the notion of inference and the propositional connectives are characterized in terms of truth, and so there is no logic of norms and logical connectives cannot operate over norms, or there is a logic of norms, but then the concept of inference and the logical connectives cannot be defined in terms of truth. The use of these notions in ordinary language suggests that we should choose the second horn of the dilemma, but then the problem arises of how to characterize such inferences and the connectives without having recourse to the concept of truth.

Those authors who, like Weinberger,[29] maintain that there is a genuine logic of norms and thus that there are normative inferences offer no adequate reasons for this contention. Weinberger's proposal to use the notion of validity as a kind of substitute for truth seems not to be satisfactory,[30] and he makes no attempt to provide an alternative definition of propositional connectives.

It is in view of these difficulties that some authors, including the present authors, have tried to develop a logic of norm-propositions as a substitute for a logic of

[26] Georg Henrik von Wright, *Logical Studies* (London: Routledge & Kegan Paul, 1957), Preface, vii–ix, at vii.

[27] See Georg Henrik von Wright, 'Problems and Prospects of Deontic Logic. A Survey', in *Modern Logic. A Survey*, ed. Evandro Agazzi (Dordrecht: D. Reidel, 1980), 399–423.

[28] Jørgensen, 'IL'.

[29] Ota Weinberger, *Normentheorie als Grundlage der Jurisprudenz und Ethik* (Berlin: Duncker & Humblot, 1981).

[30] See Bulygin, 'Norms and Logic' (1985), in this volume, ch. 12; Kazimierz Opałek and Jan Woleńskl, 'Is, Ought, and Logic', *ARSP*, 73 (1988), 373–85.

norms.[31] These efforts cannot be regarded as fully satisfactory, however, for reasons given earlier.

In recent publications, von Wright looked for another way. He proposed that deontic logic be interpreted not as a logic of norms or as a logic of norm-propositions but as a kind of logic of 'rational legislation'.[32] Von Wright conceived of its 'laws' as quasi-logical 'principles of rational norm giving'. This solution does not seem to be altogether satisfactory either. Ota Weinberger, in particular, criticized this proposal.[33]

Recently Alchourrón and Martino proposed that the logical connectives be defined and the notion of logical implication or entailment be characterized without resorting to the concept of truth.[34] Following the ideas of Gentzen[35] and Belnap,[36] logical connectives have been defined by means of rules of introduction and elimination in a context of deducibility. On the other hand, the authors maintain that it is possible to characterize the concept of logical implication by means of the abstract notion of consequence (Tarski), which is neither syntactic nor semantic.

This amounts to an attempt to justify von Wright's idea, expressed in 1957,[37] that the scope of logic is wider than that of truth, and this justification certainly does look very promising. We shall not try, in this paper, to argue for the viability of this proposal, but it is clear that if it proves to be sound, then it will be of the utmost importance for the application of artificial intelligence to problems of law. Indeed, if it should prove to be possible to extend the scope of logic beyond the limits of truth, so that normative sentences, which lack truth-values, can occur as premisses and as conclusions of deductive inferences, then it will be possible to build a genuine logic of norms and to construct expert systems capable of justifying legal reasoning.

5. What Kind of Logic?

According to a fairly widespread view among jurists and legal philosophers, no specific logic of norms or deontic logic is required in order to give an account of judicial reasoning. Many authors believe that ordinary first-order predicate logic is perfectly sufficient for that task.[38] More generally, MacCormick advocates an extended form of predicate logic in which four types of predicates are allowed: (i)

[31] See von Wright, *NA*; Manfred Moritz, 'Kann das (richterliche) Urteil deduziert werden?', in *Festskrift till Per Olof Ekelöf* (Stockholm: P.A. Norstedt & Söners, 1972), 502–18; Alchourrón and Bulygin, *NS*; Carlos E. Alchourrón and Eugenio Bulygin, 'Pragmatic Foundations of a Logic of Norms', *Rechtstheorie*, 15 (1984), 453–64.

[32] See von Wright, 'Norms, Truth, and Logic' (1982) (n. 21, this chapter); von Wright, 'Norms, Truth, and Logic' (1983) (n. 21, this chapter).

[33] For criticism of this proposal, see Weinberger, 'Der normenlogische Skeptizismus' (n. 21, this chapter).

[34] Carlos E. Alchourrón and Antonio A. Martino, 'Logic without Truth', *Ratio Juris*, 3 (1990), 46–67.

[35] Gerhard Gentzen, 'Untersuchungen über das logische Schließen', *Mathematische Zeitschrift*, 39 (1934), 176–210, 405–31

[36] Nuel D. Belnap, 'Tonk, Plonk and Plink', *Analysis*, 22 (1962), 130–4, repr. *Philosophical Logic*, ed. P. F. Strawson (Oxford: Oxford University Press, 1967), 132–7.

[37] See n. 26, this chapter.

[38] Francisco Miró Quesada, *Ensayos de filosofía del derecho* (Lima: Universidad de Lima, 1988).

purely descriptive predicates, (ii) descriptive interpretative predicates, (iii) evaluative predicates, and (iv) normative predicates. The introduction of normative predicates, in MacCormick's opinion, is sufficient to cope with the problem of norms without any need to resort to deontic logic. His opinion is based on the institutional theory that MacCormick developed together with Ota Weinberger.[39] The argument is that institutional facts have 'normative impact'.

> Hence it can be true both that there are correctly ascribed predicates which state institutional facts and that these predicates, when categorically (i.e. unconditionally) applied, can be translated without loss or residue into deontic statements. The fact that they are so translatable does not, however, preclude using them in the untranslated form in which they so commonly appear in legislative and adjudicative speech and in legal discourse in all its modes.[40]

The implicit assumption that underlies MacCormick's argument is that sentences ascribing normative predicates (like 'being liable', 'having rights or obligations', 'being entitled', 'having authority', and the like) are true or false but have at the same time normative import. We have already seen that this assumption reflects the failure to distinguish between norms and norm-propositions. Sentences in which normative predicates occur can be used both descriptively (to express norm-propositions) and prescriptively (to express norms), but no sentence can be used to describe and to prescribe at the same time; hence, no sentence can be true or false and have, on the same occasion, normative import. MacCormick's mistake is perhaps owing to the fact that he concentrates his attention on predicates instead of sentences. Different utterances of the same sentences may give rise not only to different speech acts but also to different outcomes of those speech acts. One can use a sentence on a given occasion to issue a norm and one can use the same sentence on a different occasion to state a fact, but one cannot use the same sentence on the same occasion to issue a norm and state a fact.

We have already emphasized that the primary use of normative predicates is to formulate norms. Taking into account the fact that predicate logic in its usual theoretic interpretation operates with sentences that are true or false, its application to norm-formulations (that is, sentences that lack truth-values) becomes problematic. Therefore, the occurrence of normative sentences in legal reasoning (which, as we have argued, is essential for judicial justification) entails not only a substantial change in the interpretation of predicate logic along the lines proposed by Carlos E. Alchourrón and Antonio A. Martino in 1988,[41] but also an extension of the logical apparatus of predicate logic by means of the introduction of specifically normative operators.

This is reluctantly granted even by MacCormick when he says:

[39] See Neil MacCormick and Ota Weinberger, *An Institutional Theory of Law* (Dordrecht: D. Reidel, 1986).

[40] MacCormick, ms., 21, and 'Legal Deduction', 196 (n. 1, this chapter).

[41] Alchourrón and Martino, 'Logic without Truth' (n. 34, this chapter).

On the other hand, it may be the case that the rules of standard predicate logic do not all apply in the case of normative predicates, and thus the innovation of allowing that there can be normative predicates requires reconsidering this extension of predicate logic in the light of deontic logic, which amounts to a partial acceptance of the objection at present in question, and an adjustment of position to meet it.[42]

Still, the occurrence of different kinds of predicates does not necessarily lead to sentences of different kinds, and it is sentences, not predicates, that determine the need to widen the scope of the interpretation of predicate logic.

As already mentioned, predicate logic—in the traditional interpretation—deals with descriptive sentences expressing propositions that are true or false. The first two categories of predicate advocated by MacCormick ('purely descriptive predicates' and 'descriptive interpretative predicates') pose no problems. The 'descriptive interpretative predicates' presumably occur in interpretative sentences. We have already seen that these are of two types: metalinguistic sentences stating semantic rules for the predicates of the object-language and analytic sentences of the latter. Here the standard interpretation of predicate logic does not require any amendment, and there seems to be no need to introduce new kinds of predicate besides the descriptive ones.

Evaluative predicates, like normative predicates, can give rise to sentences of two kinds: (i) those expressing evaluative propositions (in our technical sense), which are descriptive and hence true or false, and (ii) those expressing value judgments, which call for special treatment. The questions of whether value judgments can be regarded as true or false and whether a genuine logic of such judgments is possible will not be discussed in this paper (although we are rather sceptical in this respect). As long as judges use evaluative propositions (and, as we have conjectured in section 4, this is frequently the case), ordinary predicate logic is sufficient to deal with such reasoning. The situation with normative predicates is different. Sentences expressing norm-propositions (which are metalinguistic with regard to the language in which legal rules or norms are expressed) require a logic of norm-propositions, that is, a descriptive deontic logic. Which of the systems of deontic logic developed thus far is best suited to this task may be regarded as an open question. But in order to deal with norms—and, as we have argued, their occurrence in legal reasoning is nearly always essential—we need a genuine normative logic.

It is of course true that in some cases there is no need to resort to more sophisticated branches of logic; ordinary predicate logic and even propositional logic may be adequate to account for a great part of judicial reasoning. However, the construction of expert systems of any practical significance cannot be limited to simple cases and consequently requires more complex logical tools. Descriptive deontic logic and normative logic are such tools, but they are by no means the only ones. An alethic modal logic will probably be needed for the reconstruction of certain arguments. Another point being discussed is the problem of conditional or

[42] MacCormick, ms., 21, and 'Legal Deduction', 196–7 (n. 1, this chapter).

hypothetical norms. It is by no means clear that the conditional that occurs in legal norms is a material conditional, and there are strong reasons in favour of other kinds of conditionals, connected with the idea that legal obligations are *prima facie* or defeasible obligations.[43] In any case, there seem to be no serious reasons in favour of restricting the scope of logical theories applicable in legal expert systems, even if not all of them are necessary for all cases.

Still, we agree with MacCormick that in principle no kind of logic is required in order to cope with the problems of legal justificatory reasoning other than the ordinary (classic) deductive logic. It is not necessary and it is scarcely convenient to go beyond the limits of deductive logic, as has repeatedly been suggested by many authors working in the field of artificial intelligence. A great many systems of the so-called non-monotonic logics have been developed in recent times.[44] Their common aim is to account for some frequently used arguments (including legal contexts) that are invalid from the point of view of deductive logic and may nevertheless be perfectly sound. The proposal is to broaden the notion of logical consequence (by weakening its requirements) in order to be in a position to treat such inferences as valid. However, as has been convincingly shown by David Makinson,[45] many instances of such reasoning lend themselves to ordinary deductive logic by means of the explication of implicit or suppressed premisses. By means of this operation, a non-monotonic inference can be transformed into a monotonic inference. Once such hidden premisses are explicitly stated, the argument becomes deductively valid, so that ordinary (monotonic) deductive logic is perfectly capable of accounting for it. Thus, the reconstruction of judicial justificatory reasoning can be achieved within the limits of deductive logic.

[43] See Carlos E. Alchourrón, 'Conditionality and the Representation of Legal Norms', in *Automated Analysis of Legal Texts*, ed. Antonio A. Martino and F. Socci Natali (Amsterdam: North-Holland, 1986), 175–86.

[44] See David Makinson, 'General Patterns in Nonmonotonic Reasoning', in *Handbook of Logic in Artificial Intelligence and Logic Programming*, ed. Dov M. Gabbay, et al., 5 vols. (Oxford: Clarendon Press, 1994), vol. 3, 35–110.

[45] See David Makinson, 'General Theory of Cumulative Inference', in *Proceedings of the 2nd International Workshop on Nonmonotonic Reasoning*, ed. Michael Reinfrank, et al. (Berlin: Springer, 1989), 1–17.

16

On Norms of Competence (1992)*

1.

In this paper I should like to consider the status of norms or rules that confer legal power or competence.[1] Such norms play a very important role in legal discourse, but it is by no means clear what their nature is or how they operate.[2]

In legal theory, it is common to distinguish between powers in public law and powers in private law, yet it seems that the difference between these two concepts is not as great as many jurists have assumed. Hans Kelsen was the first to draw attention to the essential resemblance of the concepts of power in public law and in private law, and other legal philosophers (for example, Alf Ross and H. L. A. Hart) follow him here, at least up to a point.

Kelsen invites attention to the fact that many distinctions made in traditional legal theory are more terminological than conceptual in character; they serve simply to conceal the fact that terms like 'competence', 'power', 'capacity', 'ability', and the like refer to the same concept or in any case to essentially related concepts. Kelsen sets out four such concepts:[3]

1) *Kompetenz* or *Zuständigkeit*, which is the power to create legal norms. The typical cases are those of a court, a parliament, or an executive.
2) *Rechtsmacht*, which is the participation of legal subjects in the creation of legal norms (either general or individual). Examples include those rights that are private (participation in the creation of individual norms) or political (participation in the creation of general norms).

* [*Editors' note*: Eugenio Bulygin's paper was first published in *Law and Philosophy*, 11 (1992), 201–16. Spanish version in *ALD*, 485–98.]

[1] I would like to express my gratitude to Lars Lindahl, whose critical remarks made it possible for me to correct some mistakes and to clear up some inaccuracies.

[2] What is more, there is no agreement on terminology. Anglo–American legal theorists are inclined to use the terms 'legal power' and 'power-conferring rule'—see Jeremy Bentham, Wesley Newcomb Hohfeld, and H. L. A. Hart—whereas in the countries of the Roman Law tradition it is customary to speak of competence and competence norms. In what follows, the pairs 'norm'–'rule' and 'competence'–'power' will be used more or less synonymously unless otherwise indicated.

[3] See Kelsen, *RR 2*, at § 30 (150–62), *PTL*, at 145–58. [*Editors' note*: For these and other abbreviations, see the Table of Abbreviations.]

3) *Handlungsfähigkeit*, which is the ability to create legal norms that bind the person who creates them or to bring about certain legal effects or consequences by means of certain acts. Typical examples in this category are contracts and wills. This is what German legal theory calls *Geschäftsfähigkeit*, which includes the ability to perform procedural acts (*Prozessfähigkeit*) and the ability to comply with one's legal obligations (*die Fähigkeit, Rechtspflichten zu erfüllen*).
4) *Deliktsfähigkeit*, which is the capacity to commit crimes and other offences.

Kelsen believes that these concepts are closely related; in all four of them a legal norm empowers or, in a very broad sense, 'authorizes'—*ermächtigen* is Kelsen's term—certain conduct and thereby renders it pertinent to the law. Every action that is given expression in a legal norm (either as the antecedent of a sanction-imposing norm or as a sanction itself) is automatically 'authorized' by it, in this very broad sense of 'authorizing', which, as Kelsen stresses, does not imply any commendation of the action in question.

Ross makes a distinction between two related concepts: the power of a public authority and so-called private autonomy. The first is the capacity to create legal rules that bind others, and the second is the capacity to create legal rules that bind oneself. Although Ross agrees with Kelsen that these are not essentially different, he thinks that they do differ in some aspects. Thus, power in public law—or, in Ross's terminology, the competence of a public authority[4]—is qualified (which is to say that it can only be exercised by certain persons holding office), heteronomous (that is, the capacity to create rules that bind others), exercised in the public interest, and non-transferable to successors, whereas private autonomy is unqualified (every normal adult has it), autonomous (it is used to bind the competent person himself or herself), discretionary (it is exercised freely), and transferable to a successor.

According to Ross, competence is a special case of power. 'Power exists when a person is able to bring about, through his acts, desired legal effects.' (Kelsen would add that it is also the ability to bring about unwanted legal effects, as in the case of offences.) Competence is a species of the genus power. As Ross writes: 'Competence is the legally established ability to create legal norms (or legal effects) through and in accordance with enunciations to this effect.'[5]

Norms of competence are those norms that establish this ability by stating the conditions necessary for its exercise. These conditions determine personal, procedural, and substantive competence. The enunciations by means of which competence is exercised are called *actes juridiques* or *acts in the law*, or, in private law, dispositive declarations.

Our concern is with norms that grant competence or confer powers and, therefore, make it possible for a person to become able, by means of *actes juridiques*, to produce certain legal effects.

[4] See Ross, *DN*, at 133. [5] Ross, *DN*, 130.

Hart introduces two species of power-conferring rule: those that confer powers on private individuals and those that confer powers of a public or official nature,[6] but there is no essential difference between the two; both are secondary rules.[7]

2.

There is no agreement among legal philosophers on the nature of competence norms or power-conferring rules. Some regard these rules as genuine norms of conduct, that is to say, norms that prescribe that something ought to be done or may be done. Writers differ, however, on the question of whether the genuine norms of conduct are mandatory norms or permissory norms. Thus, we can distinguish between two types of reductive theory: those that reduce power-conferring rules to norms imposing duties or obligations (commands), and those that regard them as permissory norms. We may regard Kelsen, Ross, and Thomas Cornides[8] as typical representatives of the first line of thought. For each of these authors, norms of competence are indirectly formulated commands. According to Ross, they are reducible to norms of conduct, since both types of norm must 'be interpreted as directives to the courts'.[9] For Kelsen (in his earlier stage), all legal norms are commands directed to the courts and to officials, requiring them to apply coercive sanctions under certain conditions.[10] Competence norms are to be interpreted as fragments of legal norms and not, then, as independent and complete norms. This view has been sharply criticized by Hart.[11] I shall not repeat Hart's arguments here, which I find quite convincing.

Cornides does not develop a general theory of competence norms. He considers solely the delegation of power. If a legal authority A commands B to obey the commands issued by C, A delegates his authority to C. Thus, C acquires competence or power over B. So the norm that gives competence to C is a command—not, however, a command directed to C, but to another person or to several other persons B.[12] This account of the delegation of power seems to be quite plausible, but it is not easily extended to other situations in which jurists speak of competence, such as, for example, Kelsen's *Handlungsfähigkeit*, not to mention his *Deliktsfähigkeit*.

Take the case of a will. Is the norm conferring the power to make wills a command? If it is, to whom is it directed? Since a will need not contain any commands, it is difficult to regard it as a command (to whom is it given?) to obey (whose command?), unless one decides that it is a command given to the courts to treat it as a valid will. However, we then face, once more, the theory of competence norms as fragments of other norms.

[6] See Hart, *CL*, 1st edn., at 27–33, 3rd edn., at 27–33.

[7] See Hart, *CL*, 1st edn., at 77–9, 89–96, 3rd edn., at 79–81, 91–9.

[8] See Kelsen, *GTLS*, at 58–64, Ross, *LJ*, at 33, and Thomas Cornides, *Ordinale Deontik* (Vienna: Springer, 1974), at 152–60.

[9] Ross, *LJ*, 33.

[10] Kelsen, *GTLS*, 58–64.

[11] See Hart, *CL*, 1st edn., at 35–41, 3rd edn., at 35–42.

[12] See Cornides, *Ordinale Deontik* (n. 8, this chapter), at 152–60.

Competence norms as permissions: An alternative to treating competence norms as norms of conduct is to treat them as permissions. Georg Henrik von Wright is a classic representative of this point of view. To some extent this approach seems to be shared by Stig Kanger,[13] by Lars Lindahl,[14] and even by Jeremy Bentham, although Bentham regards both formulations of competence norms—in terms of permissory norms and in terms of commands—as equivalent. As he writes: 'Whichever be the form, it comes exactly to the same thing.'[15]

Von Wright calls norms of *the first order* those norms whose contents are acts other than normative acts. A higher-order norm is a norm whose content consists of normative acts, that is, acts of issuing or cancelling certain norms. The subjects of norms of the higher order—that is, the agents whom those norms address—are themselves authorities of lower-order norms. Competence norms are higher-order norms, and von Wright regards it as essential that they should be permissory norms.[16] These higher-order permissions may, of course, be combined with commands or orders to issue norms about certain types of act. The limits of delegated power are often set by prohibitions; the authority may issue norms of a certain kind, but may not issue norms of certain other kinds. Yet competence norms must be sharply distinguished from such commands.

The idea that competence norms are essentially permissory is difficult to reconcile with legal practice. If competence norms are permissions, then a prohibition to make use of the power conferred by such norms would generate a contradiction, but this is not the way such situations are in fact treated by jurists. Situations in which a person has legal competence to produce certain types of act and is at the same time forbidden to exercise this competence are relatively common and are not seen as generating conflicts. Consider the following example. According to Argentine law, a petition directed to a court must be signed by a practising lawyer in order to be legally valid. Only lawyers have competence here. Now if a lawyer is appointed as a judge (and in Argentina one must be a lawyer in order to be a judge), then he is no longer allowed to act as a practising lawyer, for judges cannot represent parties before a court. Suppose now that the following situation arises. A judge is asked by a friend to sign a petition. The judge is a lawyer, so he has competence to sign the petition. This means that a petition signed by this judge would be a valid petition and treated as such by the courts. Since he is a judge, however, he is forbidden to sign the petition. This means that in doing so he would be violating one of his duties as a judge, resulting in liability. On von Wright's account, this state of affairs would yield a contradiction. One and the same act of a given agent is both permitted and prohibited by the legal system. For if the judge has competence to sign the petition, then he is permitted to sign it, but he is at the same time prohibited from signing it. Thus, for von Wright there could be no

[13] See Stig Kanger, 'New Foundations for Ethical Theory', in *Deontic Logic: Introductory and Systematic Readings*, ed. Risto Hilpinen (Dordrecht: D. Reidel, 1971), 36–58.

[14] See Lars Lindahl, *Position and Change. A Study in Law and Logic* (Dordrecht: D. Reidel, 1977), at 193–211.

[15] Jeremy Bentham, *On Laws in General*, ed. H. L. A. Hart (London: Athlone Press, 1970), 28.

[16] See von Wright, *NA*, at 192.

prohibition to make use of a competence granted by another norm without generating a contradiction. Moreover, von Wright expressly maintains that the limits of competence are often set by prohibitions, which is to say that a prohibition can revoke a competence.

It is clear, however, that no jurist would regard this state of affairs as a contradiction or as an inconsistency in the legal system. Even if a judge is forbidden to sign a petition, he or she is still competent to sign it. The fact that such a petition would be regarded as valid clearly shows that the judge retains competence in spite of the prohibition to exercise it. Moreover, jurists do not regard such situations as anomalous, as has been recognized by legal theorists. In the well-known treatise on civil law by Alois Brinz, we have the following description:

> Legal permission (*Dürfen*) (*licere*) and the legal 'can' (*Können*) (*posse*), although linguistically commingled, are intrinsically different. Permission or license is something found in both kinds of act, in both ordinary acts and acts-in-the-law, while the legal 'can' or legal power is found only in acts-in-the-law, that is—in the broadest sense—only in those acts that are imposed or adopted by the law for achieving its invisible legal effects. Where there is legal power for an act-in-the-law, there is usually also a license for it; yet *sometimes legal power exists where license is lacking.*[17]

The situation we have considered fits Brinz's description very well, namely, the existence of a legal power for an act in the law without the corresponding permission or license to exercise this power.

I conclude that neither attempt to reduce power-conferring rules—to commands on the one hand, to permissions on the other—reflects the most characteristic features of such rules.

3.

I wish now to turn to those legal philosophers who regard power-conferring rules or norms of competence as irreducible, that is, as not lending themselves to any reduction to other types of legal norm. Hart and also Ross in *Directives and Norms* are perhaps the most prominent figures in this group. Both have important insights into the nature of such rules, but I have the impression that they have not drawn out all the relevant conclusions from what they say about the differences between norms of conduct and competence norms.

Hart insists that power-conferring rules cannot be reduced either to the general pattern of orders backed by threats (John Austin) or to norms imposing sanctions (Kelsen) or, even more generally, to rules imposing obligations and prohibitions. As Hart writes:

[17] Alois Brinz, *Lehrbuch der Pandekten*, 2nd edn. (Erlangen: Andreas Deichert, 1873), vol. 1, § 65 (at 211–12) (emphasis added), quoted by Lindahl, *Position and Change* (n. 14, this chapter), at 211. [*Editors' note*: The translation from Brinz, appearing in Lindahl's text and taken over verbatim in Bulygin's text, has been amended.]

Such power-conferring rules are thought of, spoken of, and used in social life differently from rules which impose duties, and they are valued for different reasons. What other tests for difference in character could there be?[18]

Hart draws an interesting parallel between power-conferring rules and the rules of a game. In a game like football or chess, there are of course rules that prohibit, under penalty, certain types of behaviour (showing disrespect to the referee or fouling in football, exceeding the allotted time or touching a piece without moving it in chess). These rules, as Hart points out, are analogous to the rules of criminal law punishing theft or murder, but it is essential for a game that there should be rules defining what is to be understood by this game. To this category belong rules about the movement of rooks and bishops, about checkmate, and so on. These rules resemble the power-conferring rules in the law. This resemblance is shown by the fact that we do not say in either case that such rules are obeyed or disobeyed. When a chess player occupies the original position and plays 1.e2-e4, it would be very strange to say that he obeys the rule stipulating that a pawn in the original position may move two fields in advance. In the same way, we do not say that a parliament obeyed the constitution in voting on a proposed statute.

Legal power-conferring rules, like the rules of a game, do not require that persons act in certain ways, that is, they do not impose duties or obligations. Instead, they define the ways in which valid contracts or wills or marriages are made, and they define the conditions of and limits within which the decision of a legal authority (a court, a legislature) shall be valid. If one fails to comply with such rules, the result is not a sanction or a penalty, for there is no breach or violation of any obligation and there is no offence either. Rather, there is a nullity. Hart stresses that the relationship between the conforming action and the rule is poorly conveyed by the terms 'obey' and 'disobey'. Conformity to the conditions specified by a power-conferring rule is a step like a 'move' in a game. It has consequences that the system enables persons to realize, and these consequences are defined in terms of the rules. Failure to conform to the conditions of the enabling rule makes what is done ineffective and so a nullity for this purpose.

What both types of rule—the rules of a game and power-conferring rules—have in common is the fact that they define certain types of behaviour. Hart does not actually say that power-conferring rules are definitions, but it is remarkable that he repeatedly uses the verb 'to define' in connection with such rules.[19]

Ross seems to have changed his position radically in *Directives and Norms* (1968). He no longer regards rules of competence as indirectly formulated commands addressed to the courts, as he had argued in *On Law and Justice* (1958). Now, in contrast to the earlier work, he distinguishes between *regulative* and *constitutive* rules. Regulative rules are those rules that, like parking rules, prescribe certain types of behaviour; constitutive rules, like the rules of chess, define certain

[18] Hart, *CL*, 1st edn., 41, 3rd edn., 41.

[19] See Hart, *CL*, 1st edn., at 27, 29, 30, 31, 94, 99, 238, 3rd edn., at 27, 29, 31 (two occurrences), 97, 102, 285.

patterns of behaviour that are dependent on the rules. The rules of chess, for example, define the game of chess as an institution and provide the logically necessary conditions for the making of chess moves. They 'endow the actions performed in chess with their specific meaning as "moves"'.[20] Ross stresses the difference between the rules of chess and commands. Since the rules of chess define the game, they cannot, strictly speaking, be violated; if a player makes an irregular move, he is not playing chess. Ross nevertheless speaks of the rules of chess in terms of obedience, for he says that 'they are obeyed essentially neither through fear of sanctions nor through respect for authority'[21] but 'by *common acceptance*, or *mutual agreement*'.[22]

Ross observes that some legal rules 'of great consequence to the life of a community' are constitutive rules, like the rules concerning a promise.

> In legal terminology a promise is called an *acte juridique*, or act-in-the-law, which aptly expresses that the promise is not a natural act but one constituted by legal rules. An act-in-the-law is a declaration which (normally) by virtue of constitutive legal rules produces legal effects according to its content. Other examples are wills, laws, judgments, and administrative acts. *Making a will, legislating, deciding a case, resolving*, are none of them natural acts; they are acts-in-the-law, conceivable only as constituted by legal rules.[23]

This quotation shows clearly that norms of competence are constitutive rules; they belong to the same type of rule as the rules that are constitutive of a game.

The distinction between regulative and constitutive rules has become fashionable owing to the work of John R. Searle. I have the impression that Ross had in mind the very distinction made by Searle. In any case, it is worthwhile to examine Searle's characterization of constitutive rules.

According to Searle, regulative rules regulate antecedently or independently existing forms of behaviour, whereas constitutive rules do not merely regulate, 'they create or define new forms of behavior'.[24] For example, the rules of football or chess 'do not merely regulate playing football or chess, but as it were they create the very possibility of playing such games'. 'Constitutive rules constitute (and also regulate) an activity the existence of which is logically dependent on the rules.'[25] Searle is very emphatic about the difference between commands and constitutive rules. 'If our paradigms of rules are imperative regulative rules, such non-imperative constitutive rules are likely to strike us as extremely curious and hardly even as rules at all.'[26] They are almost tautological in character because, Searle continues,

> what the 'rule' seems to offer is part of a definition of 'checkmate' ... That, for example, a checkmate in chess is achieved in such and such a way can appear now as a rule, now as an analytic truth based on the meaning of 'checkmate in chess'. That such statements can be construed as analytic is a clue to the fact that the rule in question is a constitutive one. The rules for checkmate ... must 'define' *checkmate in chess* ... in the same way that ... the rules of chess define 'chess' ...[27]

[20] Ross, *DN*, 54. [21] Ross, *DN*, 54. [22] Ross, *DN*, 55 (emphasis in original).
[23] Ross, *DN*, 56 (emphasis in original).
[24] John R. Searle, *Speech Acts* (Cambridge: Cambridge University Press, 1969), 33.
[25] Searle, *Speech Acts*, 34. [26] Searle, *Speech Acts*, 34.
[27] Searle, *Speech Acts*, 34 (emphasis in original).

I must confess that Searle's remarks do not strike me as being very illuminating. It is not clear how it is possible that constitutive rules are definitions or analytic statements based on meanings of terms so defined, but are also regulative of the activities defined by them. I do not see how one and the same rule can be constitutive and regulative at the same time. In order to clarify these doubts it will be useful to try to define with greater precision the difference between constitutive rules and regulative rules.

4.

In *Norm and Action*, von Wright makes an effort to classify different types of norm or rule. He distinguishes, *inter alia*, between a) prescriptions or regulations, b) determinative rules, and c) technical norms or directives.[28]

a) *Prescriptions* or *regulations* are what I propose to call *norms of conduct*, that is, commands and permissions. A command requires from its addressee that a certain action be performed or that a certain state of affairs should obtain. A prohibition excludes certain states of affairs or the performance of certain actions. A permission authorizes certain actions or states of affairs. When an action or a state of affairs p is required by a norm N, we say that p is obligatory in relation to N; if p is excluded by N, we say that p is prohibited in relation to N; and, finally, if N authorizes p, we say that p is (positively) permitted in relation to N. There is another, weaker sense of permission called negative permission. Sometimes we say that p is permitted by N if N does not prohibit p. The statements that a given action or state of affairs p is obligatory, prohibited, or permitted are norm-propositions; they are descriptive (and hence are true of false) in contradistinction to norms, which are prescriptive (and as prescriptions are neither true nor false). Norm-propositions are always relative to a norm or a set of norms, that is, a normative system. Parenthetically, it may be noted that it is easy to generalize these definitions in order to make them applicable to normative systems: p is obligatory (prohibited, positively permitted) in relation to a norm system α if and only if a norm to the effect that p is required (excluded, authorized) belongs to the consequences of the set α, and p is negatively permitted by a normative system α if and only if the norm excluding p does not belong to the consequences of α.

It is clear that a great many legal norms belong to the category of norms of conduct—that is, they are commands, prohibitions, or permissions—and it is equally clear that power-conferring rules do not belong to this category. I think that the reasons provided by Hart are conclusive.

[28] See von Wright, *NA*, at 6–11 *et passim*.

Norms of conduct are a paradigm of what Ross and Searle call regulative rules. They regulate human behaviour by requiring, excluding, or authorizing certain actions or activities.

b) *Determinative rules* (in von Wright's sense) are what I propose to call *conceptual rules*. Conceptual rules do not prescribe certain behaviour as obligatory, prohibited, or permitted. What they do is *define* concepts. We could say, according to von Wright, that

> when viewed from the point of view of the game itself, the rules determine which are the *correct* moves, and when viewed from the point of view of the activity of playing, the rules determine which are the *permitted* moves. It is understood that moves which are not correct are *prohibited* to players of the game, and that a move which is the only correct move in a certain situation in the game is *obligatory* when one is playing the game.[29]

It is important to stress, however, that such rules do not *prescribe* or establish obligations or prohibitions. Rules of grammar, rules of a logical or mathematical calculus, and (certain) rules of games all belong to this category. Conceptual rules are *constitutive* in Ross's sense of the term and in Searle's. They are constitutive because they define patterns of behaviour that do not exist outside these rules. This is what Ross means when he contrasts acts constituted by rules with natural acts for the performance of which no rules are required. We find the same idea in Searle when he says that constitutive rules constitute an activity the existence of which is logically dependent on the rules.

Searle's remark that constitutive rules also regulate the activities constituted by them is misleading. One and the same rule cannot be a conceptual rule (a definition) and a norm of conduct (a prescription in von Wright's sense) at the same time. If we speak, however, of the rules of a game, then it is certainly true that in one and the same game there may be not only constitutive rules (defining the game) but also regulative rules. This is so, for among the rules of a game there are different kinds of rules, as Hart has observed.[30] Some of the rules of chess are constitutive of the game; they define the concept of chess. However, there are also rules that regulate the behaviour of the players; such rules impose certain obligations and prohibit certain actions of the players (such as, for example, the rules establishing that one must play with the piece that has been touched, or that a player must make a given number of moves in a given period of time on pain of losing the game). These rules are genuine norms of conduct, and they are very different from the rules defining the way in which different pieces (the King, the Queen, and so on) may move.

c) *Directives* or *technical norms*, according to von Wright, belong to a third category, neither that of norms of conduct nor that of conceptual rules.

[29] Von Wright, *NA*, 6 (emphasis in original).
[30] See Hart, *CL*, 1st edn., at 238–9, 3rd edn., at 285.

> Technical norms are concerned with the means to be used for the sake of attaining a certain end. Their general form is 'if you want to attain *x*, do *p*!' As von Wright correctly emphasizes, however, they should not be confused with conditional prescriptions.
>
> As one sort of example of a group of technical norms, one thinks of the rules of a game that indicate how to play in such a way as to win (say, the tactical and strategic rules of chess). These rules are neither norms of conduct nor conceptual rules.

I think it is important to distinguish sharply between these different types of rule, and I would not hesitate to maintain that these three categories of rule are exclusive in the sense that one and same rule cannot fulfil the functions of a norm of conduct, a conceptual rule, and a technical rule at the same time. I think, therefore, that Searle is mistaken when he says that constitutive rules also regulate certain actions. The two categories are logically disjunctive and though we may find many different types of rule among the rules of a game, no rule can belong to more than one type at the same time.

5.

The distinction between regulative and constitutive rules is related to the well-known distinction between synthetic and analytic propositions. Regulative rules or norms of conduct must be synthetic in order to be able to fulfil their role in guiding behaviour because it is essential that they can be obeyed or disobeyed. Self-contradictory norms like 'close the window and leave it open!' that can never be obeyed and tautological norms like 'close the window or leave it open!' that can never be disobeyed do not play any normative role, for they cannot guide conduct. In this sense, regulative norms must be synthetic, that is, they must refer to contingent states of affairs.

By contrast, conceptual rules in general and definitions in particular always create an impossibility. If 'underage' is defined as a person who is not yet 21 years of age, then it is impossible that somebody who is 22 is underage or, to put it in positive terms, then a person who is not yet 21 years of age is necessarily underage. In this way a definition gives rise to necessary propositions that are analytic because their truth depends only on the meaning of the term defined.[31] Thus, constitutive rules, being definitions, either are analytic or (if they are stipulative definitions) give rise to analytic statements. The importance of definitions lies in their making explicit the conceptual apparatus used, and their role is equally important in science and in the law.

[31] Searle has taken notice of this feature; see the quotation earlier, text at n. 27 (this chapter).

Another distinctive feature has to do with the notion of nullity. Hart argues that nullity cannot be assimilated to the sanction.[32] He maintains that in the case of duty-imposing rules (the rules, for example, of criminal law), we can distinguish between two things—a certain type of conduct, which the rule prohibits, and a sanction intended to discourage that type of conduct. It is logically possible and might well be desirable that there should be such rules even though no punishment or anything else untoward is being used as a threat. We can distinguish clearly the rule prohibiting certain behaviour from the provision for the penalty to be exacted if the rule is broken, and we can imagine the former to exist without the latter. In the case of power-conferring rules, no such distinction can be made; we cannot logically distinguish between the rule requiring compliance with certain conditions (for example, attestation of a valid will) and the nullity. If the failure to comply with the essential conditions did not entail a nullity, the rule itself could not be intelligibly said to exist. The provision for a nullity is part of this type of rule in a way in which the penalty attached to a rule imposing obligations is not.

Hart touches here on a very important point. Sanction and nullity are indeed two radically different notions, and any attempt to assimilate nullity to the sanction is doomed to fail. Moreover, the different ways in which the sanction and nullity operate underscore a radical difference between the two types of rule. It is only with respect to a constitutive rule, which defines a certain concept or an activity such as a game, that it makes sense to speak of nullity. If there is a definition that states the conditions that a norm, an act, or a document must satisfy in order to be valid, then the absence of one or more of these conditions will give rise to the nullity of this norm, act, or document. Without nullity, there would be no such definition; thus, a constitutive rule and nullity cannot be separated. The existence of these two types of institution, sanction and nullity, is one indication of the existence of (at least) two types of rule in law: norms of conduct and conceptual rules, or, to express it in Searle's terms, regulative and constitutive rules.

6.

Lindahl begins his discussion of the concept of legal power or competence by distinguishing three different concepts.[33] The first is explained in terms of 'may' or permission; the second in terms of 'can', interpreted as an expression of practical possibility ('can'^{P}); and the third is an expression of possibility in a special technical legal sense ('can'^{J}). This third concept of legal competence is, in the end, discarded by Lindahl, who suggests that the concept of '*rechtliches Können*', the specifically legal ability, can best be explicated in terms of 'may' or 'can'^{P}.

I think that the distinction between conceptual rules and norms of conduct or, what amounts to the same, between constitutive and regulative rules provides an

[32] See Hart, *CL*, 1st edn., at 33–5, 3rd edn., at 33–5.

[33] See Lindahl, *Position and Change* (n. 14, this chapter), at 194–211.

interesting conceptual tool to deal with the rather obscure concept of '*rechtliches Können*'. Its explication in terms of permission ('may') is rather problematic, for it blurs certain important distinctions I tried to make clear earlier in this paper. A more adequate explication of norms of competence can be provided in terms of conceptual or constitutive rules. On this account, rules that establish the competence of a legislator (in its personal, procedural, and material aspects) define the concept of legislator and make the activity of legislating possible. To put it in Ross's terms, legislating is not a natural activity independent of pre-existing rules, but is a pattern of behaviour that is only possible because there are rules establishing which kinds of conduct count as legislation and who can perform these actions. The same happens with a judge and with an administrative authority. The situation is similar in the case of powers conferred on private persons. Power-conferring rules define what is to be understood by a contract, a will, or a promise, and therefore make it possible to engage in the corresponding activities.

Obviously not everything that a legal official (a judge or a legislator) can do 'legally' is defining of his or her office, for not all legal norms referring to those actions are constitutive (definitional) of the concept of judge or legislator. In addition to norms of competence, there may be and often are other kinds of norms, more specifically norms of conduct, referring to actions of officials. In particular, we often find norms granting permissions, rights, liberties, or privileges,[34] and—in view of the terminological confusion found among jurists—it is by no means easy to determine whether such a norm is a competence norm (which is constitutive or definitional) or a norm of conduct. One criterion for distinguishing between competence norms and norms of conduct (granting permissions, rights, or privileges) might run as follows. If legal power subsists in spite of a prohibition to exercise it (as in the case of a judge who signs a petition), then we are faced with a competence, but if a prohibition has the effect of making the 'legal power' to act in a certain way disappear, then a permission, a liberty, or a privilege has been granted by a norm of conduct, not a conceptual rule. If, for instance, the president of a club is entitled to open the annual ball, the norm that grants this entitlement is not definitional of his or her office as president; it is a mere privilege granted by a permissory norm because a prohibition to open the ball would revoke it. Not so in the case of a judge, who can sign a petition (and this will produce all legal effects) despite the fact that he or she is not allowed to sign the petition. Of course it might be difficult to determine, in particular cases, whether we are in the presence of a competence norm or a norm of conduct granting permissions, liberties, or privileges.

[34] For these distinctions, see Wesley Newcomb Hohfeld, *Fundamental Legal Conceptions*, ed. Walter Wheeler Cook (New Haven: Yale University Press, 1919); Ross, *LJ*; Kanger, 'New Foundations for Ethical Theory' (n. 13, this chapter); Lindahl, *Position and Change* (n. 14, this chapter).

17

Valid Law and Law in Force (1999, unpublished)*

1. Some Misunderstandings

Hans Kelsen, Alf Ross, and H. L. A. Hart—the listing here is chronological—are probably the three most remarkable philosophers of law of the twentieth century. All three made unusually significant contributions to juridico-philosophical thought, but the influence of Ross, especially in the English-speaking countries, has not matched that of his distinguished colleagues. Ross's main book, *On Law and Justice*, which appeared in English in 1958, was overshadowed by Hart's *The Concept of Law*, published just three years later. To a large extent, this was due to a series of misunderstandings prompted by a mistaken interpretation of some of Ross's central ideas, due, in turn, to a deficient translation of two terms in the Danish text—'*gyldig*' (in German '*gültig*') and '*gældende*' ('*geltend*')—that play a central role in *On Law and Justice*. Both terms were misleadingly translated as 'valid'. (Happily, this did not occur in the Spanish translation by Genaro R. Carrió, published in 1963. Carrió used the terms '*válido*' and '*vigente*', which—following Ross's later publications—I have rendered in English as 'valid' and 'in force'.)

Another source of misunderstanding, not unrelated to the first, stems from Hart's sharp criticism of the predictive theory of obligation, found in the fifth chapter of Ross's *On Law and Justice*. Hart assumed that his criticism of legal realism was applicable to Ross, who explicitly defends a predictive theory of validity. However—as we shall see—'validity' is used by Ross with a quite different meaning from Hart's.

Alf Ross is frequently labelled as a 'legal realist', and Hart in his paper 'Scandinavian Realism' uses this label with reference to Ross.[1] If, however, by 'legal realism' one understands a doctrine according to which the law is constituted not by norms or rules but by certain facts—for example, the behaviour of judges and other officials—then Ross is certainly not a realist, for in his view the law is a set of norms, that is, a species of directive. This is why Ross rejects all of the reductive

* [*Editors' note*: Eugenio Bulygin presented this chapter as a paper at the Alf Ross Conference on Legal Philosophy, Copenhagen, 11 June 1999. The proceedings of the conference were not published, and the paper appears in the present volume for the first time.]

[1] H. L. A. Hart, 'Scandinavian Realism', *Cambridge Law Journal*, 17 (1959), 233–40, in Hart, *EJP*, 161–9. [*Editors' note*: For this and other abbreviations, see the Table of Abbreviations.]

interpretations of norms, those that attempt to reduce norms to propositions descriptive of certain facts (for example, predictions of future judicial decisions). This point is of great importance for the appraisal of Hart's criticism of legal realism and for the impact this criticism has had on readers of *On Law and Justice*.

A third factor, too, conspired against a clear understanding of Ross's ideas, namely, the unfortunate fact that one of his most important papers on the concept of validity, 'Validity and the Conflict between Legal Positivism and Natural Law' (1960), was originally published in a little-known journal and therefore remained practically unknown to most scholars until it appeared, only very recently, in an accessible collection of papers.[2]

In what follows I will try to remove these misunderstandings with an eye to underscoring the importance of some of Ross's contributions to the analysis of the main concepts used in legal discourse—in particular, the different concepts of validity.

2. Three Concepts of Validity

It is a well-known fact that the terms 'validity' and 'valid' are used with quite different meanings in the theory and philosophy of law. At least three distinct concepts can be distinguished. For example, Jerzy Wróblewski distinguishes between systemic validity, axiological validity, and factual validity.[3] I will refer to these as *validity, binding force*, and *efficacy*.

The concept of (systemic) *validity* may be defined in terms of membership; a norm is valid in a certain legal system if and only if it belongs to or is a member of that system. This concept is descriptive—to say that a given norm belongs to a certain system is to state a fact—and it is relative, that is, it is a triadic relation between a norm, a legal system, and a moment in time. A norm may be valid in a system S_1 and not valid in the system S_2; it may be valid at time t_1 and not valid at time t_2. Jurists and legal philosophers use different criteria to establish that a given norm belongs to a certain system. One such criterion is the legality of the norm-creating act. An act of issuing a norm is legal if and only if there is another norm authorizing this act; such a norm is usually called a norm of competence. According to this criterion, a norm is valid if it has been issued by a competent authority. Another criterion is the efficacy of the norm; a firmly established customary norm is regarded as 'valid', that is, as belonging to the legal system in question. A third criterion is that of logical consequence; a norm that is a logical consequence of a set of valid norms is regarded, according to this criterion, as valid. This distinction between the *meaning* of the term 'validity' and the *criteria* for validity is of great importance, for if (systemic) validity is defined as the legality of the act of issuing the norm, then customary norms cannot be valid because there is no such thing as an act of issuing a customary norm.

[2] Ross, 'Validity', in *RJBA*, 46–93 (bilingual printing), in *NN*, 147–63.

[3] Jerzy Wróblewski, 'Three Concepts of Validity of Law', in *Särtryck ur Tidskrift, utgiven av Juridiska Föreningen i Finland*, nos. 5–6 (1982), 406–19.

By normative validity, I shall understand the *binding force* or *obligatoriness* of a norm. A norm is binding if its addressees have an obligation to behave in the way prescribed by that norm. Normative validity is not a relative concept. Rather, it is an absolute concept, and it is not descriptive but normative. To say that a norm is valid in this sense is not to state a fact, but is to prescribe an obligation to obey this norm; hence, judgments of validity are directives.

Wróblewski's concept of factual validity is what Kelsen calls *Wirksamkeit* (efficacy). (Although Kelsen's characterization of efficacy is clearly inadequate, I wish to retain his terminology.) This concept is descriptive and relative; it denotes a relation between a norm or a set of norms and the factual behaviour of its addressees or norm-subjects, and it admits of various degrees. A norm can be more or less efficacious. The set of all efficacious legal norms can be said to constitute the *law in force*.

3. Systemic Validity or Membership

All three concepts of validity are present in Ross's writings, but he concentrates his attention mainly on factual validity or efficacy. This can be explained by his empiricist and anti-metaphysical leanings. As we shall see later, he believes there is no room for validity as binding force in a positivistic theory of law. Also, even systemic validity appears to be a neglected child in Ross's theory. He seems to regard this concept as unproblematic and perhaps not very important, yet it is indispensable for the characterization of a legal system, even—as I shall try to show—in Ross's own theory.

In the above-mentioned paper on validity, after pointing out that the term 'valid' is used with three different meanings (which roughly correspond to systemic, normative, and factual validity), Ross goes on to say:

> the term is used in current doctrinal expositions of prevailing law to indicate whether or not a legal act—say, a contract, a last will and testament, or an administrative order—has the desired legal effect. The act is said to be invalid or void if this is not the case. It is an internal function, for to state that an act is valid or invalid is to state something *in accordance with* a given system of norms. The statement is a legal judgment applying legal rules to certain facts.[4]

Here validity seems to be a property solely of legal acts. In *Directives and Norms*, however, Ross extends this notion to legal norms:

> *Legislation*... is the establishment and promulgation of directives by agencies made competent to do so by existing rules. Rules of competence define what are the necessary conditions for creating a new legal norm.[5]

It is common in legal discourse to call such norms valid. This concept plays a far more important role in legal philosophy than the paucity of Ross's remarks would

[4] Ross, 'Validity', in *RJBA*, 76 (emphasis in original), in *NN*, 158.
[5] Ross, *DN*, 96 (emphasis in original).

suggest. In Kelsen's theory, it is the basis for his characterization of the concept of a legal system, which is defined as the set of all norms that are valid according to a basic norm. The concept of systemic validity plays a similar role in Hart's theory; there, a legal system is the set of all rules that are valid according to a rule of recognition.

Ross seems to be inclined to replace the concept of systemic validity by factual validity or being in force, but, as we shall see, he is not entirely successful in this endeavour.

4. Normative Validity as Binding Force

The author who has placed the greatest emphasis on the significance of systemic validity is undoubtedly Kelsen. At the same time, he distinguishes this concept of validity neither terminologically nor conceptually from normative validity or binding force. In fact, he sometimes says that to state that a norm is valid means that it ought to be obeyed. This is a normative concept. To say that a norm is valid in this sense is to prescribe an obligation, the obligation to obey the norm. Validity as binding force is repeatedly declared by Kelsen to be the 'specific existence' of a norm. A norm exists for as long as it is valid, that is, binding. The explanation for Kelsen's use of two quite different concepts of validity as if they were identical is that he regards as binding all and only those norms that have been created by competent authorities. This is why he maintains the curious thesis that one cannot regard as simultaneously valid a legal norm that prescribes a certain action and a moral norm proscribing that very action. However, even if these concepts were co-extensional—and it is easy to show that they are not—they would nevertheless be two different concepts. Co-extensionality is not identity.

Ross sharply rejects the notion of normative validity as binding force. He believes that the doctrine is reminiscent of natural law thinking and therefore has no place in a positivistic theory of law. What does it mean, Ross asks, that you have an obligation to obey the law, that you have an obligation to do what is prescribed by a legal norm? Is this obligation different from the one established by the norm itself?

> How do we obey the law? By fulfilling our legal obligations—for example, by paying our debts. It follows that the obligation to obey the law does not prescribe any behaviour that is not already prescribed by the law itself. And it follows in turn that if the duty to obey the prescriptions of a legal system is to mean something different from the obligation prescribed directly by this system, then the difference cannot consist in the *required behaviour—what* we are bound to do—but must consist exclusively in *how* we are bound. The meaning of the binding force inherent in a legal system is that the legal obligations corresponding to the rules of the system—for example, the obligation to pay a debt—are not merely legal duties deriving from the threat of legal sanctions. They are also *moral duties* in the *a priori* sense of true moral obligations deriving from the natural law principles that endow the legal system with its validity or binding force. The duty to obey the law is a moral duty *toward* the legal system, not a legal duty *conforming* to the system.[6]

[6] Ross, 'Validity', in *RJBA*, 62, 64 (emphasis in original), in *NN*, 153–4.

Since the two concepts, that of systemic validity and that of normative validity, are intimately connected in the Pure Theory of Law, it is plausible to explain Ross's attitude towards systemic validity as a consequence of his rejection of validity as binding force. Hence, his attempt to build the notion of a legal system not on validity but on the notion of law in force, that is, on the factual notion of efficacy.

5. Factual Validity or Efficacy

Kelsen defines this concept in terms of the coincidence between the action required by a norm and the actual behaviour of its addressees. Efficacy may assume two forms: either compliance with the norm by the norm addressee (obedience) or the application of the corresponding sanction by legal authorities. This characterization is clearly not satisfactory; as Hart has stressed, a merely external coincidence does not suffice for the claim of efficacy. In order to be in a position to say that a norm is efficacious, the action of the norm-subjects must somehow be motivated by the norm.

Ross offers an analysis of the concept of the factual validity of a norm, its being in force, in terms of future judicial decisions. This is an important step. The proposition that a norm is in force is, according to Ross, a prediction of future applications of this norm by the courts, which is to say that the courts will use this norm to justify their decisions. In Ross's language:

> Its 'application' in legal practice, therefore, can only mean that in decisions in which its conditioning facts are assumed to exist, it forms an integral part of the reasoning underlying the judgment and has therefore been one of the decisive factors determining the conclusion at which the court has arrived.[7]

In *On Law and Justice*, this is the sense in which Ross speaks of validity.

The interpretation of sentences about law in force as predictions of future judicial decisions has been criticized by various authors. An alternative interpretation of Ross's idea, namely, to treat factual validity as a dispositional property of norms, is something I proposed in 'The Concept of Efficacy'.[8] In this interpretation, a sentence about law in force is not a prediction of future applications of a norm, but is an assertion of an actual *dispositional* property of the norm. A norm is in force when it has the disposition to be applied by the courts, where application means its use for justifying judicial decisions. It is interesting that Ross himself was inclined to accept this interpretation, for in a personal letter to me he wrote:

> It was with great pleasure, now on my summer holiday, that I read your article. I find the construction and writing of it superb, and I am inclined to grant most of the points you make. Please

[7] Ross, *LJ*, 42.

[8] Bulygin, 'The Concept of Efficacy' (1965), in this volume, ch. 1. See Kelsen's criticism of the view I proposed there, in Kelsen, 'Validity and Efficacy of the Law' (1967/2003), in this volume, ch. 2. See also my reply to Kelsen's article, in Bulygin, 'Remarks on Kelsen's "Validity and Efficacy of the Law"' (2003), in this volume, ch. 3.

do note that I am in complete agreement with your analysis of the propositions on efficacy [at 47–9, in this volume] ('if certain conditions...'). Perhaps mistakenly, however, I assumed that such sentences are predictions. My mistake, then, is more a matter of logic than of legal analysis. Also, in that exposition, I was still under the influence of logical empiricism, according to which the meaning of a sentence is determined by the conditions for its verification.[9]

6. Norms and Normative Propositions

An important contribution is Ross's sharp distinction between norms and propositions about norms. It is not easy to discern this distinction, for both norms and propositions about norms (which I will call *normative propositions*) may be and often are expressed in similar and sometimes even identical language. The same sentence or phrase—for example 'no smoking'—may be the expression of a norm, when it is used to prohibit smoking, or it may be a normative proposition, when it is used to state the fact (or to inform someone of the fact) that there is a norm prohibiting smoking. Despite this similarity, it is of the utmost importance that norms and normative propositions be distinguished. Norms are directives that can be obeyed or disobeyed, but as such they do not describe anything and so are neither true nor false (in the usual sense of these terms), whereas normative propositions are descriptive and so have truth-values, but they cannot be obeyed or disobeyed and therefore cannot be either efficacious or inefficacious.

This ambiguity of deontic sentences has not gone unnoticed by legal philosophers. Indeed, it was already pointed out by Jeremy Bentham in his treatise *Of Laws in General*.[10] Since, however, the better part of two centuries passed before the treatise was published, Bentham had no direct followers on the matter. In Kelsen's writings, one finds an analogous distinction, that between legal norms (*Rechtsnormen*) and legal propositions (*Rechtssätze*). Kelsen's criterion for distinguishing them is, however, rather confused. Ross (along with Ingemar Hedenius) was one of the first among legal philosophers to draw clearly this distinction, which despite its importance still awaits general recognition. As Georg Henrik von Wright put it recently:

> It has taken me nearly thirty years to see its full significance. And not all logicians and philosophers have seen it even now.[11]

I said that Kelsen's criterion for distinguishing between legal norms, which are prescriptive and so are valid or invalid but neither true nor false, and legal propositions—that is, propositions employed in legal science for describing the law—which are descriptive and so are true or false but neither valid nor invalid, is

[9] Letter from Alf Ross to Eugenio Bulygin, 10 August 1966. [*Editors' note*: translated from the German by Bonnie Litschewski Paulson and Stanley L. Paulson.]

[10] Jeremy Bentham, *Of Laws in General*, ed. H. L. A. Hart (London: Athlone Press, 1970).

[11] Georg Henrik von Wright, 'Value, Norm, and Action in My Philosophical Writings', in *Actions, Norms, Values. Discussions with Georg Henrik von Wright*, ed. Georg Meggle and Andreas Wojcik (Berlin and New York: de Gruyter, 1999), 11–33, at 20.

rather confused. Even if Kelsen emphasizes that legal propositions are descriptive, he maintains at the same time that they are normative or, more precisely, that they are 'ought'-propositions (*Sollsätze*), not 'is'-propositions (*Seinsätze*). According to Kelsen, the term 'ought' that occurs in such propositions is a descriptive 'ought', not a prescriptive 'ought'. The talk of a descriptive 'ought' sounds like a contradiction. How can this surprising doctrine be explained?

One way of explaining it is to maintain that the term 'ought' is merely mentioned, but not used in legal propositions—as, for instance, the term 'cat' is merely mentioned in the phrase '"cat" has three letters'. This is what Hart tried to do, as he tells us in his paper 'Kelsen Visited'.[12] Kelsen, however, refused to accept the interpretation of the relation between a norm and the corresponding legal proposition in terms of mention and use.

On the other hand, legal propositions state the existence of a norm, and norms—according to Kelsen—are not facts. They have a specific existence, that is, their validity, understood as binding force. To say then that a norm is valid is tantamount to saying that it is binding, which is to say that it is obligatory to do what the norm prescribes. In such a case a legal proposition would certainly be normative, but in the strict sense of this term; it would be prescriptive and not descriptive. This is clearly incompatible with the programme of Kelsenian positivism.

Typical examples of normative propositions are, according to Ross, the propositions of legal science, which are assertions about the existence of legal norms, that is, about law in force. They are true or false but can be neither valid nor efficacious.

This sharp separation between norms and legal propositions is essential for a positivistic programme of a purely descriptive legal science that does not issue prescriptions or value judgments. Such a science presupposes (1) that positive law originates in social sources, (2) that there is no necessary connection between law and morality, (3) that it is possible to determine the existence and the contents of the positive law without recourse to any moral argument, and, therefore, (4) that legal propositions describing positive law do not express any evaluation of it. A jurist who uses such propositions is not bound to accept or to reject the law he describes. Thus, he can describe in purely neutral terms any legal order, be it democratic or autocratic, communist or Nazi, capitalist or socialist, disregarding completely the underlying political ideology.

7. Summary: Law in Force or Valid Law?

We are now in a position to summarize Ross's ideas concerning validity, albeit briefly:

a) Ross eliminates normative validity or binding force as a metaphysical idea.
b) As a consequence of his empiricism, he emphasizes the concept of factual validity (that is, efficacy or being in force).

[12] H. L. A. Hart, 'Kelsen Visited', *UCLA Law Review*, 10 (1962/3), 709–28, in Hart, *EJP*, 286–308.

c) He redefines efficacy as the future application of the norm by the courts for justifying their decisions.
d) The programme of a positivistic legal science requires a sharp distinction between legal norms and normative propositions.
e) In his definition of 'legal norm', efficacy becomes a necessary property, that is, a defining feature of a norm. In other words, all law is by definition law in force.

This last point deserves comment. It seems to me that to define 'legal norm' as a directive to which a certain social reality corresponds[13] is a serious mistake, for it means that only those directives that are efficacious can be regarded as legal norms. However, (systemic) validity is independent of efficacy; it makes perfectly good sense to speak of a valid though not efficacious norm. A typical example is a recently promulgated statute; we do not know at the outset whether it will be applied by the courts, yet no jurist would hesitate to say that it is a valid norm, provided it has been duly enacted.

It is noteworthy that Hart committed a similar mistake in *The Concept of Law*, where he defines legal rules as social practices. Social practices are—*ex definitione*—efficacious. So Hart's assertion that a rule can be valid without being efficacious ('... it is plain that there is no necessary connexion between the validity of any particular rule and *its* efficacy...')[14] is self-contradictory. Hart corrects this mistake in his Postscript, where he grants that not all legal rules are social practices. The validity of enacted law does not depend on its efficacy but on internal relations between rules: the rules of competence constituting an authority (called by Hart 'rules of change') and the rules issued by that authority within the range of its competence. So in Hart's last version, there are two kinds of rule: customary rules, which are social practices, and enacted rules, which are not. Less clear, however, is Hart's general concept of a rule, applicable to both kinds of rule.

We find a similar situation in Ross's theory. Even if Ross seems to attach little importance to the concept of systemic validity, attemptinig to replace it with efficacy or being in force, it can be shown that when speaking of a legal system he actually uses the term 'validity' meaning systemic validity. This is partially hidden by the fact that he uses the same term 'valid', but it is clear from the context what kind of validity is meant. This is especially the case with Ross's well-known paper on self-reference, where he asserts that a norm derives its validity from the norm of competence constituting the authority that issued that norm.[15] It is clear that a norm cannot derive its efficacy from another norm. The validity of a norm derived from another norm can only be either systemic validity or normative validity. Since Ross regards normative validity as an expression of natural law doctrines—he goes so far as to accuse Kelsen of being a 'quasi-positivist'[16]—we are left with only one possibility: validity must be understood in this context as systemic validity.

[13] Ross, *DN*, ch. 4. [14] Hart, *CL*, 1st edn., 100 (emphasis in original), 3rd edn., 103.

[15] Alf Ross, 'On Self-Reference and a Puzzle in Constitutional Law', *Mind*, 78 (1969), 1–24.

[16] See Ross, 'Validity', in *RJBA*, at 68–76, 78–82, in *NN*, at 155–8, 159–61.

Therefore, contrary to some formulations by Ross himself, there are two basic concepts in his theory: *valid law* and *law in force* (based on the idea of efficacy). In addition, there are two types of norm: *customary norms* and *enacted norms.* Since they are different kinds of entity, their existence means quite different things. In order to exist, a customary norm must be efficacious, whereas a sufficient condition for the existence of an enacted norm is its systemic validity, that is, it exists if it has been issued by a competent authority. (Whether this condition is also necessary is another story.) This implies that we must drop Ross's requirement that, in order to be a norm, a directive must bear a certain relation to social facts.

Thus, we have two criteria for membership in a legal system. A norm belongs to a system either because it is issued by a competent authority or because it is in force, that is, it can be used by the courts for justifying their decisions. (This 'or' is inclusive, for an issued norm can of course be in force, but it makes no sense to speak of the issuance of a customary norm; once it is issued, it ceases to be merely customary.)

In this version, Ross's theory turns out to be rather similar to Kelsen's, provided that the Pure Theory of Law is purified of certain contaminants.We find the same concept of systemic validity—although deprived of its connotations of binding force—and a similar concept of efficacy, which is now defined in a more satisfactory manner. Thus we can regard Ross's theory as an improved and more coherent version of a positivistic theory of law. This result would probably be welcomed by Ross himself.

18

The Silence of the Law (2002)*

Introduction

In his well-known paper 'Legal Reasons, Sources, and Gaps',[1] first published in 1979[2] and reprinted in *The Authority of Law*,[3] Joseph Raz distinguishes two types of legal gap. The first type is due to the indeterminacy of the law, which stems either from the vagueness of certain terms or from an unresolved conflict between reasons for action. These gaps (where the law speaks either with an uncertain voice or with many voices) are, according to Raz, unavoidable. The second type of gap arises where the law is silent, and Raz emphatically denies the very possibility of such gaps. In this paper I want to take up this latter thesis in some detail.

The proof of the impossibility of legal gaps of the second kind, in Raz's text, is rather simple.

The starting point is that gaps of the second kind can exist only if it is possible that $(-LR_cx,\varphi)$ & $(-LPer_cx,-\varphi)$: it is not true that there is legally a conclusive reason for x to φ, and it is not true that legally x is conclusively permitted not to φ. Since 'Per_cx,φ' is defined in Raz's paper[4] as '$-R_cx,-\varphi$' this formula is equivalent to

(27) $(-LR_cx,\varphi)$ & $(-L-R_cx,\varphi)$.[5]

But in virtue of

(28) $\vdash -(LR_cx,\varphi) \leftrightarrow (L-R_cx,\varphi)$, which, according to Raz, is a logical truth (for the sake of simplicity I omit the proof given by Raz), it follows that

(29) $(L-R_cx,\varphi)$ & $(-L-R_cx,\varphi)$ which is a contradiction.

* [*Editors' note*: Eugenio Bulygin's paper was first published in English in *Analisi e diritto*, 2002, 21–8, under the title 'On Legal Gaps'. For publication in the present volume, Professor Bulygin indicated a preference for the title used in the original Spanish publication of the paper, 'El silencio del derecho', in *Análisis Filosófico*, 22 (2002), 103–14.]

[1] I am deeply indebted to Pablo E. Navarro for critical remarks and comments that, I hope, have led to improvements in this paper.

[2] Joseph Raz, 'Legal Reasons, Sources, and Gaps', in *Law and the Future of Society*, ed. F. C. Hutley, et al. (*ARSP Beiheft* 48 [N.F. 11]) (Wiesbaden: Franz Steiner, 1979), 197–216. [*Editors' note*: For this and other abbreviations, see the Table of Abbreviations.]

[3] Raz, *AL*, 53–77. References following are to the reprinting in Raz, *AL*.

[4] See Raz, *AL*, at 64.

[5] See Raz, *AL*, at 76. I preserve the original numbering of formulae used by Raz in *AL*.

Hence, Raz writes, '(28) entails the rejection of (27) and with it of the possibility of gaps of the second kind.'[6]

Moreover, (28) is logically equivalent to

$$(31)\ \vdash (-LR_c x,\varphi) \leftrightarrow (LPer_c x,-\varphi),$$

which is 'the familiar closure rule that whatever is not legally prohibited is legally permitted and vice versa.'[7] The conclusion drawn by Raz is that 'contrary to much popular imagining, there are no gaps when the law is silent. In such cases closure rules, which are analytic truths rather than positive legal rules, come into operation and prevent the occurrence of gaps.'[8]

Contrary to Raz, I believe that gaps originating in the silence of law—that is, gaps of the second kind—are not only possible but occur rather frequently, and that the Razian closure rule is absolutely void and does not exclude the existence of gaps.

1. Reason-Sentences and Deontic Sentences

The formula $LR_c x,\varphi$ means that legally there is a conclusive reason for x to φ or that legally φ is conclusively required. Let us first simplify the rather cumbersome symbolism used by Raz. If we stipulate that R always stands for a conclusive reason and that all formulae refer to a given subject x, we can drop the subscript$_c$ [9] and the x. So I will write $LR\varphi$ instead of $LR_c x,\varphi$.

Formulae expressed in terms of reasons for action (R-formulae), standing for reason-sentences, can be translated into equivalent formulae expressed in deontic terms, namely, O-formulae, standing for deontic sentences. I think that this can be done without loss of meaning.

Let us see whether this is possible. Raz writes that 'statements of the form LRx,φ... *mean the same as* "Legally x ought to φ", "It is the law that x ought to φ"'.[10] Thus, statements of legal reasons always entail the existence of a norm, which may stem from a legislative act, from a precedent, or from custom. However, some such social fact is necessary for there to be a *legal* reason for action.[11] This is the core of the sources thesis, firmly maintained by Raz. A conclusive reason is a reason that has not been cancelled and is not overridden by another reason.[12] So we must stipulate that a norm like '$O\varphi$' has not been defeated or otherwise cancelled. Accordingly, reason-statements can be represented as 'ought'-statements of the form

[6] Raz, *AL*, 76. [7] Raz, *AL*, 76. [8] Raz, *AL*, 77.

[9] Except in the case of conclusive permission (Per_c) in order to distinguish between different kinds of permissions.

[10] Raz, *AL*, 65 (emphasis added).

[11] 'The sources thesis, it should be remembered, is a thesis about the law and not about practical reason in general. Theses (25) and (26) are not meant as an assertion that only social facts can be reasons or permissions but that only such facts can be legal reasons and legal permissions.' Raz, *AL*, 66.

[12] Raz, *PRN*, 27; Raz, *AL*, 64.

'$O\varphi$'$\in L$, that is, the norm '$O\varphi$' belongs to L; that is to say, it belongs to the legal system in question.[13]

In this way, the main expressions used by Raz have their equivalent expressed in O-formulae.

(A) $LR\varphi \leftrightarrow$ '$O\varphi$'$\in L$ (Legally there is a conclusive reason to φ if and only if the conclusive norm '$O\varphi$' belongs to L.)
(B) $-LR\varphi \leftrightarrow -($'$O\varphi$'$\in L)$ (It is not the case that legally there is a reason to φ if and only if it is not the case that the norm '$O\varphi$' belongs to L.)
(C) $L{-}R\varphi \leftrightarrow$ '$O\varphi$'$\notin L$ (Legally there is no reason to φ if and only if '$O\varphi$' does not belong to L.)

As Raz himself acknowledges—'[i]ntuitively, the negation of a legal reason is nothing more than the absence of a legal reason',[14] an intuition that is confirmed by his formula (28), which purports to be a logical truth—the formulae (B) and (C) mean exactly the same thing.

(D) $LPer_c\varphi \leftrightarrow$ '$O{-}\varphi$'$\notin L$ (Legally it is conclusively permitted to φ if and only if the norm '$O{-}\varphi$' does not belong to L.)
(E) $LPer_c\varphi \leftrightarrow$ '$O\varphi$'$\notin L$ (Legally it is conclusively permitted not to φ if and only if '$O\varphi$' does not belong to L.)

In this way we obtain two sets of formulae (R-formulae and O-formulae) corresponding to the original formulae of Raz:

R-formulae:	O-formulae:
(27')$-LR\varphi$ & $-L{-}R\varphi$	(27") $-($'$O\varphi$'$\in L)$ & $-($'$O\varphi$'$\notin L)$
(28')$-LR\varphi \leftrightarrow L{-}R\varphi$	(28") $-($'$O\varphi$'$\in L) \leftrightarrow ($'$O\varphi$'$\notin L)$
(29')$L{-}R\varphi$ & $-L{-}R\varphi$	(29") ('$O\varphi$'$\notin L)$ & $-($'$O\varphi$'$\notin L)$
(31')$-LR\varphi \leftrightarrow Per_c{-}\varphi$	(31") $-($'$O\varphi$'$\in L) \leftrightarrow ($'$O\varphi$'$\notin L)$

There is no doubt that (29) is a contradiction (this is clearly shown by 29' and 29"). However, if (29) is a contradiction, then (27) must be a contradiction, for (29) is derived from (27) by means of (28), which, according to Raz, is a logical truth. This means that the characterization of a 'legal gap of the second kind' is already contradictory. Therefore it is not particularly surprising that such gaps cannot exist. This is too easy as a method for defining legal gaps out of existence.

On the other hand, if (28) is an analytic truth, then (31), which is logically equivalent to it, is an analytic truth as well, but what does it amount to? As '$LPer_c{-}\varphi$' is by definition equivalent to '$L{-}R\varphi$', (31) expressed in terms of reasons says exactly the same as (28), that is, $-LR\varphi \leftrightarrow L{-}R\varphi$, and in terms of obligations it says that it is not true that the norm '$O\varphi$' belongs to L if and only if this norm does not belong to L. Thus, Raz's 'familiar closure rule' is not only

[13] By 'legal system' I mean any set of norms, not necessarily all the legal norms of a given community.
[14] Raz, *AL*, 67.

an analytic truth but a very trivial tautology. It says as much about gaps as the statement 'it is not true that it is raining if and only if it is not raining' says about the weather. This closure rule, read from left to right, says that whatever is not legally prohibited is legally permitted.[15] 'Legally permitted', however, means in this context simply not prohibited, for according to (23) 'x has a conclusive permission to φ ($Per_c x,\varphi$) = df. It is false that there is a conclusive reason for x to –φ (that is, $-R_c x,-\varphi$).'[16] Substituting in (31) –φ for φ we obtain $-LR-\varphi \leftrightarrow LPer_c\varphi$, and since the right-hand half of this formula is equivalent to –LR–φ, we have $-LR-\varphi \leftrightarrow -LR-\varphi$, which says 'it is not the case that the law requires the omission of an action if and only if it is not the case that the law requires the omission of that action'. Therefore, the alleged closure rule amounts to 'whatever is not prohibited is not prohibited', which is certainly true but not particularly illuminating.[17]

2. Legal Gaps and Conclusive Permissions

What is wrong in Raz's argument against gaps of the second kind? I think the main mistake lies in his characterization of such gaps. He writes: 'A legal system is legally complete if there is a complete answer to all the legal questions... It contains a legal gap if some legal questions subject to jurisdiction have no complete answer.'[18] He continues: 'A complete answer is provided by pointing to a decision which the law requires.'[19] Thus far we can agree, but a few lines further on Raz states that on the question on whether a person ought to perform a certain action, there are two possible complete answers:

(1) $LR_c x,\varphi$ (the law conclusively requires that action), and
(2) $LPer_c x,-\varphi$ (the law conclusively permits the omission of that action).

(1) means in simplified symbolism LRφ, and in O-terms 'Oφ'∈ L. (2) amounts to L–Rφ or 'Oφ'∉ L.

This shows that the two answers are not independent, for (2) is just the negation of (1); thus, if (1) is true, (2) is not true, and vice versa.[20] Therefore the disjunction of (1) and (2) is analytic, and the conjunction of their negations is a contradiction. This is exactly how Raz defines gaps of the second kind: '"$(-LR_c x,\varphi)$ & $(-LR_c x,-\varphi)$" is true.'[21] Expressed in terms of O-formulae it means that ('Oφ'∈ L) & ('Oφ'∉ L).

[15] Raz, *AL*, 76. [16] Raz, *AL*, 64.

[17] Raz, *AL*, 58, considers the possibility of defining a permission as the negation of a prohibition, but then 'what is not prohibited is permitted' means exactly the same as 'what is not prohibited is not prohibited'.

[18] Raz, *AL*, 70. [19] Raz, *AL*, 71.

[20] On the possibility of working with von Wright's T-Logics, in which there are propositions that are neither true nor false (a possibility that Raz grants *expressis verbis*), see José Juan Moreso, Pablo E. Navarro, and Maria Cristina Redondo, 'Legal Gaps and Conclusive Reasons', *Theoria*, 68 (2002), Part I, 52–66, and 'Sobre la lógica de las lagunas en el derecho', *Crítica*, 33 (2001), 47–73.

[21] Raz, *AL*, 71.

A consequence is that there is always a complete answer, and hence all legal systems are complete. Shakespeare would say that something is rotten in the state of Denmark if one can prove by means of logic that all legal systems are complete.

The main problem lies in the second answer. It can be shown that a conclusive permission for the omission of φ (as it is defined by Raz) is not a complete answer if by a complete answer we understand a sentence that states that the action in question is somehow regulated by the law. The mere fact that an action is not prohibited does not imply that this action is regulated by the law. It is regulated if the law permits this action, and permission for an action is not the same as mere non-prohibition. I will return to this question later.

Let us illustrate this problem with the following example. Let α be a legal system that contains no norm regarding φ. The law is silent. Legally there is no reason to φ, and there is no reason not to φ: L–Rφ and L–R–φ are both true. According to Raz, both φ and –φ are conclusively permitted in α. Then the answer (1) is false because there is no legal reason requiring φ, and the answer (2) is true for the very same reason, that is, there is no legal reason requiring φ. Expressed in O-terms it means that 'Oφ'∉ L and 'O–φ'∉ L; φ is neither obligatory nor prohibited in α.

Let us now add to α the norm 'O–φ'. The resulting system (let us call it β) gives rise to a new reason for action: LR–φ. According to β, φ is prohibited, but it remains false that LRφ (it is not obligatory to φ, for it is true that 'Oφ'∉ L, that is, L–Rφ). What about the second answer? If (l) is false, (2) must be true. Can we say, however, that there is a conclusive permission to omit φ? Raz should feel obliged to say yes, for –φ is not prohibited (what is prohibited in β is φ, but not –φ). I doubt very much that (2), informing us that –φ is not prohibited, can be regarded as a satisfactory, let alone complete answer. A complete answer would be to say that φ is prohibited, and so there is a conclusive reason for the omission of φ and not simply a conclusive permission (in the Razian sense) of –φ. This shows that (2) is not a complete answer, and it is not difficult to discover why. Whereas (1) states a reason for action, (2) states no reason at all, saying only that there is no legal reason to φ (L–Rφ).

Let us now add to α the norm '–Oφ'. We obtain a new system γ, in which it is true that '–Oφ'∈ L. Since '–Oφ' is logically equivalent to 'P–φ', γ contains a norm permitting the omission of φ. With respect to γ the answer (1) is not true because there is no reason requiring φ, and hence the answer (2) must be true. Can we say that the omission of φ (that is, –φ) is permitted? The answer is yes, but it is permitted in a stronger sense than the Razian conclusive permission, for it says not only that φ is not required but also that –φ is permitted by a norm. Unfortunately, this statement cannot be expressed in terms of conclusive permissions, as defined by Raz. You can say that there is no reason to φ and that there is no reason not to φ (LRφ and LR–φ are both false in γ). In Raz's own terms, 'it is false that there is a conclusive reason for the act and false that there is a conclusive reason for its omission', so φ is neither obligatory nor prohibited. Strangely enough, Raz remarks that '[t]his kind of situation involves no unresolved conflict *nor any legal gap*'.[22] I would say

[22] Raz, *AL*, 75 (emphasis added).

that an action that is neither obligatory nor forbidden is a typical case of a gap of the second kind, except when this action is permitted by a norm, as in the system γ. However, this is something one cannot say in terms of conclusive reasons, and it is quite clear why. Conclusive permissions are always sourceless,[23] and this means that they state no reasons. Thus, there is a crucial difference between the systems α and γ, namely, that the omission of φ is regulated by γ and not by α. This difference cannot be expressed in Razian language.

3. Strong and Weak Permissions

Raz says that there are many kinds of permissions,[24] but he analyses only two of them: conclusive and explicit permissions. The distinction between strong and weak permission is not even mentioned in his article, perhaps because his position on the matter has been rather vacillating. In the monograph *Practical Reason and Norms*, he grants that the distinction between a permission entailed by a norm and a permission that is the mere consequence of there being no norms prohibiting the action is 'of great importance',[25] but he criticizes earlier characterizations of it[26] for not making clear the meaning and the relevance of the distinction.[27] Nevertheless, his characterization of strong permissions as exclusionary permissions maintains the difference between permitted acts that are regulated by a normative system and those that are not regulated.

> A normative system regulates all the acts regulated by its norms. This means that a normative system regulates all the acts permitted by norms of the system which grant exclusionary permissions. But a system does not regulate acts which are merely weakly permitted by it, that is, acts permitted merely because of the absence of a norm requiring their omission.[28]

In another paper, included in the volume *The Authority of Law*, one finds a similar distinction:

> A normative system does not, however, regulate behaviour which is merely weakly permitted by it. An act is weakly permitted if the system contains no norm prohibiting it. It is strongly permitted if the system contains a norm permitting it.[29]

The distinction between strong and weak permission does not appear, however, in the article 'Legal Reasons, Sources, and Gaps', which was published later. Here it seems that the notion of a strong permission is being treated under the heading of *explicit permission,* but Raz gives only an informal definition of this concept:

[23] Raz, *AL*, 67. [24] Raz, *AL*, 64. [25] Raz, *PRN*, 86.

[26] Such as the characterizations by Georg Henrik von Wright, who first introduced the distinction in *NA*, at 86, and by Alchourrón and Bulygin, who developed it in *NS*, at 119–25.

[27] For a reply to this criticism, see Carlos E. Alchourrón and Eugenio Bulygin, 'Permission and Permissive Norms', in *Theorie der Normen. Festgabe für Ota Weinberger zum* 65. *Geburtstag*, ed. Werner Krawietz, et al. (Berlin: Duncker & Humblot, 1984), 349–71 [*editors' note*: repr. in part in 'Permissory Norms and Normative Systems' (2012), in this volume, ch. 21].

[28] Raz, *PRN*, 150.

[29] Joseph Raz, 'The Institutional Nature of Law' (first publ. 1975), in Raz, *AL*, 103–21, at 117 n. 4.

(22) x has explicit permission to φ ($Per_e x,\varphi$) = df. There is a fact with some force to cancel reasons for no-φ-ing (–φ-ing).[30]

As a definition, (22) is rather poor. Raz's explanation of this concept, however, is far more satisfactory:

[I]n ordinary discourse 'permission' means some act of granting permission and a person is permitted to act only if he is granted permission to do so. 'Explicit permission' is meant to explicate this notion of granted or obtained permissions.[31]

He adds that 'a permission can be granted not only to cancel an existing reason but also to forestall possible reasons by cancelling them in advance.'[32] Raz correctly remarks that 'though a permission can be inferred from the absence of a prohibition, it can also result from a direct law granting it.'[33] It should be clear now why this is so. Explicit permissions (like strong permissions) are the result of legal regulations;[34] they are reasons, but what Raz calls conclusive permission is the mere absence of a reason. That conclusive permissions are not reasons is recognized by Raz when he says that '[e]xplicit permissions are always source-based, conclusive permissions never are.'[35] If they have no sources, they are not reasons, at least not legal reasons. Therefore it is not easy to understand why Raz calls them '*conclusive*'. A reason is conclusive if it is not cancelled or overridden by another reason,[36] but a conclusive permission, as defined by Raz, states no reason at all. It is the absence of a reason, and I do not understand what is meant by 'conclusiveness' in this connection.

If this is accepted, then it is not easy to explain why Raz uses for the definition of completeness the rather obscure notion of conclusive permission instead of explicit permission. The concept of explicit permission seems to reproduce the main features of what was called strong permission in *Normative Systems*;[37] its formalization is '–Oφ'∈ L. The norm to the effect that φ is not obligatory (that is, it is permitted that –φ) belongs to the legal system. The difference between strong and weak permission emerges clearly if we undertake the following thought experiment. If an action is weakly permitted, as occurs with φ in our system α, and we add to the system a norm prohibiting this action, then the resulting system is consistent (our system β). But if φ is strongly permitted, as in our system γ, and we add a norm prohibiting φ, then we generate a conflict, for the norm '–Oφ' is incompatible with the norm 'O–φ', and the resulting system is inconsistent.

[30] Raz, *AL*, 64. [31] Raz, *AL*, 65.

[32] Raz, *AL*, 65. This resembles the characterization of permissions in terms of rejection, as in Alchourrón and Bulygin, 'The Expressive Conception of Norms' (1981), in this volume, ch. 9.

[33] Raz, *AL*, 67.

[34] This is acknowledged by Raz when he says, 'all explicit legal permissions are cancelling permissions and the ability to grant them is a normative power', Raz, *AL*, 67 n. 15.

[35] Raz, *AL*, 67. [36] See Raz, *AL*, at 64.

[37] See Alchourrón and Bulygin, *NS*, at 121–2. In later publications we use the terms positive and negative permissions instead of strong and weak. The reason for this change is that usually in logic a strong concept entails the weak one, which is not the case here.

The outcome of the preceding discussion is that (2), which states a weak permission, is not a complete answer. A complete answer requires a strong permission, so we must replace (2) with

(2') '–Oφ'∈ L (The non-obligatoriness of φ, that is, permission for the omission of φ, belongs to L.)

If completeness is defined in terms of this concept, then the two complete answers to the question of what the law requires concerning the action will be:

(1) LR φ ('Oφ'∈ L): the law conclusively requires that action, and
(2') '–Oφ' (that is, 'P–φ') ∈ L: the law strongly permits the omission of that action.

There is, then, a gap if both of these answers are false: –('Oφ'∈ L) & –('–Oφ'∈ L), and this, far from being a contradiction, is a contingent statement whose truth depends on the content of the legal system in question.

Nor is the formula –('Oφ'∈ L) → ('–Oφ'∈ L) an analytic closure rule, because from the mere fact that a given norm (Oφ) does not belong to a given legal system, it does not follow that another norm (–Oφ) belongs to this system. So it is a contingent rule, and in order that it be true, the system must be complete, for example, it contains a norm permitting all the actions that have not been prohibited by other norms, like the rule *nullum crimen* in criminal law, which operates as a rule of closure.[38] As José Juan Moreso, Pablo E. Navarro, and Maria Cristina Redondo[39] state, 'logic cannot guarantee its truth' where the fact that a norm's belonging to the law depends on the existence of social facts like an authoritative enactment or a precedent. They suggest the possibility of defending it on the basis of non-positivistic arguments, granting that certain norms may belong to the system without having been issued by legal authorities. It is clear, however, that this way out is not open to Raz as long as he maintains the sources thesis.

4. Conclusions

The following conclusions can be drawn from this discussion:

(1) It is not true that all legal systems are necessarily complete. The problem of completeness is an empirical question, a contingent question, whose truth depends on the content of the system. Thus, legal gaps due to the silence of the law, that is, gaps of the second kind, are perfectly possible.

(2) The notion of a conclusive permission as defined by Raz is inadequate for the characterization of the concepts of completeness and legal gaps. What is

[38] On rules of closure, see Alchourrón and Bulygin, *NS*, at 134–44.

[39] José Juan Moreso, Pablo E. Navarro, and Maria Cristina Redondo, *Conocimiento jurídico y determinación normativa* (Mexico City: Fontamara, 2002).

needed is the concept of strong permission, which roughly corresponds to what Raz calls explicit permission.

(3) The Razian closure rule is a mere tautology and does not close any legal system.

(4) If the concepts of completeness and legal gaps are defined in terms of strong permission, then gaps of the second kind are possible and the closure rule is no longer a logical truth but a contingent rule, which is true only if the system is already complete.

19

The Objectivity of the Law (2004)*

Claims regarding 'objectivity' turn up in legal positivism and invite attention to certain problems. For example, is the positivistic ideal of a non-evaluative legal science possible? Is there a special kind of legal 'ought' or legal authority that can be separated from the moral 'ought' and from moral authority? What difference does it make for legal positivism whether morality is objective or subjective?

It will certainly not be difficult for me to adopt a positivistic point of view on these matters, and in what follows I shall try to develop answers to the first two questions posed.[1] My answer, in both instances, will be affirmative. I think there is room for objectivity in the law; thus, a non-evaluative legal science is entirely possible, and there is a specific legal 'ought' that differs from the moral 'ought'. As for the third question, since I do not believe in the objectivity of values generally, I do not think that an ideal or critical morality is objective. I do not, however, take up this issue here.

1. Legal Positivism

Legal positivism can be characterized by means of two theses: first, the sources thesis and, second, the separability thesis. According to the first, what counts as valid law is a matter of social fact, which can be ascertained without any recourse to moral evaluation. This implies that all law is man-made; law is a human artefact. According to the second thesis, there is no necessary (conceptual or logical) connection between the law and morality. A morally justified norm does not necessarily belong to the law, and, vice versa, a legal norm can be morally unjustified. There is still another contention, which—although it is not shared by all positivists[2]—is important to take into account in this connection. It is, as Carlos Santiago Nino puts it, ethical scepticism. According to this position, moral judgments cannot be true, either because they are all false (John Mackie) or because they lack truth-values altogether (and so are neither true nor false). I find this view sound, but I do not regard it as a part of the definition of legal positivism.

* [*Editors' note*: Eugenio Bulygin's paper was first published as 'The Objectivity of Law in the View of Legal Positivism', in *Analisi e diritto* (2004), 219–27. Professor Bulygin asked that the shorter title here be used for the reprinting of the paper in the present volume.]

[1] My warmest thanks to Pablo E. Navarro and Jorge L. Rodríguez, whose critical comments made it possible for me to avoid several mistakes. Those that remain are due solely to my stubbornness.

[2] Jeremy Bentham, for example, is a clear exception, and there are others.

2. Objectivity

In what sense can positive law be said to be objective? This is a complex and much-debated issue. In order to be in a position to answer this question, several distinctions must be made. What concept of objectivity is at stake, and in regard to what law-related activities is this question pertinent?

Andrei Marmor distinguishes between three concepts of objectivity: semantic objectivity, metaphysical objectivity, and discourse objectivity.[3]

A statement is semantically objective if and only if it is a statement about an object, and it is semantically subjective if it is about some mental state of the speaker. This concept of objectivity is a matter of meaning and is independent of truth.

Metaphysical objectivity is defined in terms of the relation between a statement and an existing object that is described by this statement. A statement is objective in this sense if and only if such objects exist, and it is subjective if no such objects exist. This definition of metaphysical objectivity rests on two presuppositions. First, only descriptive statements can be objective in this sense. Second, it presupposes a correspondence theory of truth. However, as Marmor stresses, metaphysical objectivity should not be confused with realism; realism entails the existence of an objective reality that is ontologically independent of our knowledge of it, whereas metaphysical objectivism raises no such claim. Statements about social or cultural objects may be regarded as objective in the metaphysical sense even if they are not ontologically independent of our knowledge.

Whereas metaphysical objectivity limits the scope of objective statements to descriptive statements, discourse objectivity is more liberal in the sense that it not only requires that a statement be true in order to be objective but that it also allows for the truth of statements that are not descriptive.

Brian Leiter distinguishes between epistemic and metaphysical objectivity.[4] The first is the requirement that our cognitive processes be free of bias and of other factors that distort judgment. The second is related to truth; a statement is objective in this sense if and only if it represents things as they truly are, independently of our beliefs. In substance this is, I think, quite similar to what Marmor terms metaphysical objectivity.

In this paper I will concentrate on metaphysical objectivity. Moreover, I will argue that legal statements, or rather the relevant kind of legal statement, can be (at least sometimes) both descriptive and true. If this is so, then such statements are metaphysically objective.

[3] See Andrei Marmor, *Positive Law and Objective Values* (Oxford: Clarendon Press, 2001), at ch. 6 (112–34).

[4] Brian Leiter, 'Introduction', in *Objectivity in Law and Morals*, ed. Brian Leiter (Cambridge: Cambridge University Press, 2001), 1–11.

3. Norms and Normative Propositions

The law consists mainly but not exclusively of norms, that is to say, of regulations establishing that a certain type of action *p* is obligatory, prohibited, or permissible in certain circumstances *q*. Its function is primarily prescriptive. Following the terminology of *Normative Systems,*[5] I will use the terms 'case' for the circumstances and 'solution' for the expression that prescribes that a certain action ought to, must not, or may be performed. Thus, norms can be defined as expressions correlating cases with solutions.

From a positivistic point of view, norms as prescriptions are neither true nor false, but statements about norms—stating, for example, that such and such a norm exists or is valid or is applicable or is in force in a given society—are true or false. Such statements will be said to express normative propositions. To avoid misunderstandings, it is important to emphasize that normative propositions are descriptive and not normative in the usual sense. They are normative only in the sense that they are about norms.[6]

The distinction between norms and normative propositions is of the utmost importance for the philosophy of law. The distinction is partly blurred by the fact that the same linguistic expression (such as 'smoking forbidden', 'it is obligatory to pay the income tax', or 'you may park your car here') can be and actually often is used to express both norms and normative propositions, but this does not preclude their being completely different in meaning, logical structure, and function. Norms can be valid or invalid, efficacious or inefficacious, followed or obeyed, but as prescriptions they are neither true nor false. Normative propositions, by contrast, are true or false but neither valid nor invalid, efficacious nor inefficacious, and they cannot be followed or obeyed. The facts that make normative propositions true are complex institutional facts that presuppose certain social conventions and empirical facts, such as the practices (customs) or actions of certain persons—for instance, in legislation or in judicial decisions. Although there may be practical difficulties in ascertaining such facts, and in particular difficulties in ascertaining such facts in particular cases, there is in principle no insurmountable theoretical obstacle to determining whether or not a given normative proposition is true.

To the extent that legal science can formulate true normative propositions, the positivistic ideal of a non-evaluative legal science seems to be possible. Thus, I can give an affirmative answer to the first of the questions posed earlier.

[5] Alchourrón and Bulygin, *NS*. [*Editors' note*: For this and other abbreviations, see the Table of Abbreviations.]

[6] The distinction between norms and norm(ative) propositions was, as far as I know, first introduced by Georg Henrik von Wright in *NA* and subsequently developed by Carlos E. Alchourrón in his paper 'Logic of Norms and Logic of Normative Propositions', *Logique et Analyse,* 12 (1969), 242–68, Spanish version in Alchourrón and Bulygin, *ALD*, 25–49, and by Alchourrón and Bulygin in *NS*. Similar distinctions, although cast in different terms, can be found in Jeremy Bentham, Hans Kelsen, Ingemar Hedenius, and Alf Ross.

4. Objectivity of Law

Marmor takes up four questions concerning the objectivity of the law:[7] (1) the identification of law ('can we have objectively right and wrong answers to the question of what the law is on particular issues?'), (2) the merits of law ('is the law objectively right or wrong, good or bad?'), (3) the function of law as adjudicator of disputes and conflicts of interest, and (4) the objectivity of legal theory. I will be concerned only with the first and last of these questions.

Given the characterization of metaphysical objectivity and the aforementioned differences between norms and normative propositions, it should be clear that for legal positivism the problem of the objectivity of the law can be raised only with reference to normative propositions and not with reference to norms. This means that objectivity is primarily concerned with the first and last of Marmor's questions: objectivity in the identification of the law and the objectivity of legal theory. To both questions I offer an affirmative answer.

It can be said that the problem of the objectivity of the law is the problem of the truth conditions for normative propositions. The law is objective in the sense that it gives true answers to legal questions. Typical legal questions are of the form 'is the action *p* obligatory (prohibited, permissible) in circumstances *q*, according to L?' (Here 'L' stands for a legal system, but not necessarily an entire legal system like French law; 'L' can also stand for some subsystem, like the French Civil Code or Italian traffic regulations. As has been argued in *Normative Systems,* any set of legal norms can be regarded as a legal system.)

The answers to legal questions are basically of two kinds: *positive* and *negative.* An answer is positive if and only if the law determines the normative status of the action in question, and otherwise it is negative. A positive answer is: 'according to L, *p* is obligatory in case *q*', or 'according to L, *p* is not obligatory in case *q*'. An answer can also be negative. Negative answers are of two kinds: (A) 'according to L, it is not the case that *p* is obligatory in case *q*, and it is not the case that not-*p* is permissible in case *q*', or (B) 'according to L, *p* is obligatory in case *q*, and not-*p* is permissible in case *q*'.

The answer (A) is true if L contains no norm concerning *p* in *q*. Then *p* has no normative status according to L; it is neither obligatory nor prohibited nor permitted in *q*. In such cases one says that L has a *normative gap.*

If the answer (B) is true, one says that L is *inconsistent,* for it contains at least two contradictory or conflicting solutions.

The possibility of normative gaps and contradictions in the law is disputed by many legal philosophers. This is not particularly surprising in the case of those authors who either subscribe to natural law or, what amounts to nearly the same thing, who believe that there is a necessary connection between the law and morality (for example, Ronald Dworkin). It should be surprising, however, in the case

[7] See Marmor, *Positive Law and Objective Values* (n. 3, this chapter), at ch. 7 (160–83).

of the legal positivist, who maintains the sources thesis and the separability thesis. Indeed, on first glance (but only on first glance), it seems reasonable to think that moral principles, in so far as critical or ideal morality is concerned, must be complete and consistent. It would, however, be very strange to expect such perfection from the positive law, which, as already noted, is a man-made contrivance and, as with all of human creation, is fallible. There is certainly no guarantee that the positive law is always complete and consistent. We must take into account that the contention of completeness and consistency means not only that some particularly wise and careful legislator can produce a legal system that is complete and consistent on a certain topic, but also that all legal systems—that is, all possible sets of legal norms—are necessarily complete and consistent. This has the ring of the fantastic. Nonetheless, important philosophers of law have maintained this strange thesis. Hans Kelsen defended this extravagant thesis for many years,[8] and Joseph Raz, although granting the possibility of inconsistent systems, nevertheless believes that there are no normative gaps and hence that the law is for reasons of logic always complete.[9]

5. True versus Right Answers

For a positivist, who makes a sharp distinction between the description of law and its evaluation, it must seem very surprising that much of the contemporary discussion on the objectivity of the law treats this problem in terms of *right answers* instead of *true answers*. Not only Dworkin in his famous papers on the right answer,[10] but also a good many other authors choose to speak of a right answer and not of a true answer. Leiter, for instance, defines objectivity in the following terms: 'The law is *metaphysically* objective insofar as there exist right answers as a matter of law.'[11]

What is the difference between a right answer and a true answer? I have the impression that this terminological distinction highlights a conflation of descriptive and evaluative issues. A right answer is not merely a true answer, it is a good answer, and it is not difficult to discover when an answer is regarded as good, that is, as right or correct. In order to be right, an answer must inform us about obligations and rights. A merely negative answer (for example, 'the law says nothing about this situation'), even if true, would not be regarded as right.

[8] For a detailed analysis of Kelsen's theories on legal gaps, see Alchourrón and Bulygin, *NS*, at ch. 6. [*Editors' note*: For Bulygin's views on Kelsen's claims regarding completeness and consistency, see Bulygin, 'Kelsen on the Completeness and Consistency of Law' (2013), in this volume, ch. 22.]

[9] See Raz, 'Legal Reasons, Sources, and Gaps', in Raz, *AL*, 53–77, and see my criticism in 'The Silence of the Law' (2002), in this volume, ch. 18.

[10] Ronald Dworkin, 'No Right Answer?', in *Law, Morality, and Society. Essays in Honour of H. L. A. Hart*, ed. P. M. S. Hacker and Joseph Raz (Oxford: Clarendon Press, 1977), 58–84; Ronald Dworkin, 'Is There Really No Right Answer in Hard Cases?', in Ronald Dworkin, *A Matter of Principle* (Cambridge, Mass.: Harvard University Press, 1985), 119–45, 405–6 (notes).

[11] Leiter, 'Introduction' (n. 4, this chapter), 3.

As a consequence of this shift from mere descriptions of the law to its evaluation, objectivity is conceived as synonymous with determinacy. David O. Brink is quite explicit on this point when he speaks of the 'objectivity or determinacy' of the law. The law is regarded as objective if and only if it provides positive answers to legal questions. 'A conception of law can be understood to be objective insofar as it represents the law in actual or hypothetical controversies *as determining a uniquely correct* outcome.'[12] This seems to entail that a legal system containing normative gaps or inconsistencies cannot be regarded as objective, and this is a rather peculiar idea of objectivity.

6. Two Concepts of Determinacy

Here we must distinguish between two different though related questions. One question is that of the objectivity of a legal system, that is, the possibility of true statements about the law. The second question addresses the determinacy of the deontic status of an action according to law. To be objective, a legal system must determine a true answer, which may be positive or negative, but it need not be a *correct* answer if by 'correct' answer we understand a positive answer. A legal system can be objectively incomplete or inconsistent, and in such cases we can make objectively true statements *about* the law. Another matter is the determinacy of the 'outcome', that is, the determinacy of the solution that the law provides for a certain problem. If we are interested in the deontic status of an action p in certain circumstances q, we need a univocal deontic characterization of p in q. A negative answer ('p is not prohibited in q, and not-p is not permitted in q' or 'not-p is both prohibited and permitted in q') does not determine the deontic status of p in q.[13] Thus it is essential to distinguish between statements *about the law* and statements about the legal status of an action *according to law*. The indeterminacy of a statement of this latter kind does not necessarily entail the indeterminacy of a statement of the first kind. A legal system that does not determine the legal status of an action may very well be objective in the sense that we can make true statements about it. In other words, it may be objectively true that the law is incomplete or inconsistent and hence does not determine the legal status of a certain action. This is perfectly compatible with the objectivity of the law.

7. Determinacy and Interpretation

Still another problem is the determinacy of interpretation, a problem Brink seems to have in mind when he speaks about objectivity. '[D]ebates about the law's objectivity can be seen as debates about the extent to which legal interpretation is determinate.'[14]

[12] David O. Brink, 'Legal Interpretation, Objectivity, and Morality', in *Objectivity in Law and Morals* (n. 4, this chapter), 12–65, at 12 (emphasis added).

[13] Strictly speaking, p is not determined only in the case of a normative gap; if the system is inconsistent, it is overdetermined. However, the practical outcome is similar in both cases.

[14] Brink, 'Legal Interpretation, Objectivity, and Morality' (n. 12, this chapter), 13.

The problem of interpretation is a difficult issue that cannot be treated at length in this paper. I shall make only a few remarks.

We must distinguish, in the first place, between norms and norm-formulations. A norm-formulation is a purely linguistic entity, a sentence, whereas a norm is an interpreted sentence, that is, a linguistic entity along with its meaning. To interpret a norm-formulation is to assign a definite meaning to it. So interpretation can be seen as the step from a norm-formulation to a norm. This step is not always successful. It may well happen that a norm-formulation is ambiguous, and in such a case we cannot assign a definite meaning to it. Then we have not one norm but several possible norms, and a decision is required on the part of the interpreter in order to determine which norm is to be regarded as *the* norm corresponding to the norm-formulation in question. In many cases there are no objective criteria to guide this decision. If the interpretation is not determinate, then there is no true answer to the question of how a certain situation is regulated by the law, and in such cases, therefore, the law is not objective. Sometimes the legislator himself takes this decision (by means of a so-called legal definition), but in most cases the task is left to judges. Only after the decision of the judge can we know which norm is expressed by a certain norm-formulation. In this sense, judicial decisions contribute to the determinacy of law, that is, to its objectivity.

Some legal philosophers maintain that, since there are no true meanings, the interpretation is always indeterminate and so the law is never objective. This is the main tenet of the so-called 'sceptical school of Genoa'.[15] I have argued elsewhere that this view is untenable,[16] and I will briefly repeat the argument here.

My thesis is that not all norm-formulations can be ambiguous, for in that case there would be no norms at all. The proof of the thesis is a kind of *reductio ad absurdum*. Let us assume that all norm-formulations are always ambiguous. Suppose the interpreter is confronted with a norm-formulation P_1. According to the hypothesis, P_1 is ambiguous, that is to say, it has several meanings and therefore expresses several possible norms. After a careful examination and evaluation of the alternatives, one of them is selected by the interpreter. Since, however, there is no access to meanings other than through language, the interpreter must produce a new norm-formulation that purports to depict the meaning (that is, the norm) he has chosen. Let us call it P_2. According to our hypothesis, P_2 is, however, also ambiguous and therefore it, too, has several meanings. Thus the interpreter must choose one of them, and this can only be accomplished by means of a third norm-formulation, which will also be ambiguous, and so forth *ad infinitum*. Thus, if there are no univocal norm-formulations, all we have is a plurality of possible norms, but we will never be in the presence of an actual norm. This is not a normative or legal problem, it is a linguistic problem. An essential feature of language

[15] The main representatives of the Genoa school are Giovanni Tarello, Riccardo Guastini, Paolo Comanducci, Tecla Mazzarese, and Pierluigi Chiassoni.

[16] Eugenio Bulygin, 'True and False Statements in Normative Discourse', in *In Search of New Humanism. The Philosophy of Georg Henrik von Wright*, ed. Rosaria Egidi (Dordrecht: Kluwer, 1999), 183–91.

is that at least some of its expressions must be univocal. A language that does not meet this condition is useless as a tool for communication. This does not mean that there must be expressions that are always univocal. Rather, it means that in a given context there must be some univocal expressions so that we can grasp the meaning of at least some expressions.

8. Resolution of Controversies

What is the motivation for a concept of objectivity spelled out in terms of right answers rather than true answers? The main problem lies in the fact that a negative answer does not justify the decision of a judge.[17] Judges have an obligation not only to resolve all of the controversies submitted to them but also to justify their decisions by means of the law. Normally a conflict between a plaintiff and a defendant that leads to adjudication is addressed to an action of the defendant. The plaintiff claims that the defendant had an obligation to perform a certain action (let us call it *p*), which the defendant failed to perform. However, legal systems (statutes, customs, precedents) contain only general norms, which refer to types or classes of action and types or classes of circumstance (generic cases), whereas judges have to resolve individual cases. The judge must decide whether the defendant ought to have performed the action *p*. In order to justify his decision he must subsume the individual case under a generic case determined by the legal system. This operation of subsumption is successful if the legal system provides a 'uniquely correct outcome', that is, if the answer is of the form 'according to law, *p* is obligatory in case *q*' or 'according to law, not-*p* is permissible in case *q*'. If the system has a normative gap or is inconsistent, however, then *p* is not deontically determined in case *q*. Thus the system fails to give a positive answer, and in this case the judge cannot justify his decision by means of legal arguments. (The problem of the indeterminacy of an individual case can also stem from a third source: the penumbra or vagueness of the relevant concepts that characterize the case. This is what Alchourrón and I termed, in *Normative Systems*, a gap of recognition.)

In such situations there seem to be only two ways out. Either we recognize that our legal system can be deficient, which is to say that the judge must decide the case not on *legal* grounds but by choosing other (moral or political) criteria. This is what Hart called *judicial discretion*, and in such cases the judge must create a new norm, that is, he acts as a legislator, although such judicial legislation is of course only interstitial. Or, the other way out, we refuse to grant that a legal system can be indeterminate (Dworkin's position). Then, however, in order to make sure that the law is always complete and consistent, we must introduce moral principles into the law, which are supposed to remove all possible deficiencies of positive law by resolving all contradictions and filling all gaps. Quite apart from the fact that this move

[17] [*Editors' note*: On negative answers, see sections 4–6 of this chapter and what follows in the present section.]

amounts to giving up the positivistic concept of law, there is no guarantee that a system containing both legal and moral rules and principles will be complete and consistent. On the contrary, it seems plausible, as Mackie has argued,[18] that resorting to moral norms would introduce more subjectivity into the law. Leiter is quite explicit on this point: 'If... one thinks that adjudication is "objective", in the sense that there are objectively right answers to legal disputes, then it might seem a bad idea to make right answers in law depend on moral considerations as Dworkin does.'[19] As has been convincingly argued by Russ Shafer-Landau, it is by no means clear that ethical theory can be constructed as 'a coherent set of rules from which one can infer all determinate moral verdicts'.[20]

[18] John Mackie, 'The Third Theory of Law', *Philosophy & Public Affairs*, 7 (1977/8), 3–16, repr. *Ronald Dworkin and Contemporary Jurisprudence,* ed. Marshall Cohen (Totowa, New Jersey: Roman & Allanheld, 1983; London: Duckworth, 1984), 161–70.

[19] Leiter, 'Objectivity, Morality, and Adjudication', in *Objectivity in Law and Morals* (n. 4, this chapter), 66–98, at 66–7.

[20] Russ Shafer-Landau, 'Moral Rules', *Ethics*, 107 (1996/7), 584–611, at 584.

20

The Problem of Legal Validity in Kelsen's Pure Theory of Law (2005)*

Introduction

There is no doubt that Hans Kelsen's Pure Theory of Law aims to be a positivistic and normativistic legal theory. Less clear is whether this plan of Kelsen's can be regarded as a success. Kelsen is aware of the dangers threatening his *pure* legal theory:

> A positivistic legal theory faces the task of finding the correct middle way between two extremes, both of which are untenable. The one extreme is the thesis that there is no connection at all between validity as an 'ought' (*Sollen*) and efficacy as an 'is' (*Sein*), that the validity of the law is completely independent of its efficacy. The other extreme is the thesis that the validity of the law is identical with its efficacy.[1]

The first extreme is represented by natural law theory, the second by 'realist' theories. Kelsen's middle way, in the view of Stanley L. Paulson,[2] is characterized by two theses: the separation thesis and the normativity thesis. The separation thesis says that there is no necessary (that is, conceptual) connection between law and morality, while the normativity thesis claims the separability of law and fact, that is, the law consists of norms, which are not reducible to facts.

In laying claim to these two theses, however, it is doubtful that Kelsen can maintain his middle way between the Scylla of the factual and the Charybdis of natural law without being shipwrecked. In a recent book, Bruno Celano gives voice to the opinion that Kelsen fails on both fronts.[3] Both the separation thesis and the

* [*Editors' note*: Eugenio Bulygin's paper was first published as 'Das Problem der Geltung bei Kelsen' in *Hans Kelsen. Staatsrechtslehrer und Rechtstheoretiker des 20. Jahrhunderts*, ed. Stanley L. Paulson and Michael Stolleis (Tübingen: Mohr Siebeck, 2005), 80–95. It has been translated for the present volume by Bonnie Litschewski Paulson and Stanley L. Paulson.]

[1] Kelsen, *RR 2*, § 34(g) (215), *PTL*, 211 (trans. amended here and in quotations from Kelsen following). [*Editors' note*: For these and other abbreviations, see the Table of Abbreviations.]

[2] Stanley L. Paulson, 'Die unterschiedlichen Formulierungen der "Grundnorm"', in *Rechtsnorm und Rechtswirklichkeit. Festschrift für Werner Krawietz zum 60. Geburtstag*, ed. Aulis Aarnio, et al. (Berlin: Duncker & Humblot, 1993), 53–74.

[3] Bruno Celano, *La teoria del diritto di Hans Kelsen* (Bologna: Il Mulino, 1999).

normativity thesis, Celano says, prove in the end to be untenable for the Pure Theory of Law.

The connection between validity and efficacy threatens the normativity thesis. Kelsen emphasizes repeatedly that efficacy is only a *conditio sine qua non* for validity, not a *conditio per quam*. What Kelsen understands by these expressions is not entirely clear. One might be inclined to think that efficacy is only a necessary condition for validity, not a sufficient condition, but Kelsen's texts make clear that this is not the case. The basic norm is presupposed only if the legal system based on it is efficacious, and it is always presupposed if a legal system is efficacious, altogether independently of the content of this system. Thus, efficacy is a necessary condition for the presupposition of the basic norm (no validity without efficacy) and at the same time a sufficient condition (no efficacious legal system without validity), and, therefore, efficacy is the sole criterion for the validity of a legal system.

If, however, validity is understood as the bindingness of the norm, then to say that a norm is valid is a prescriptive statement, and the valid norm must be complied with.

> That a norm referring to the behaviour of an individual is 'valid' means that it is binding, that the individual ought to behave in the manner determined by the norm.[4]

Legal science, then, is no longer a value-free description of the positive law but a form of political ideology. It becomes a justification of existing law, which includes the obligation to apply existing law and to comply with it.[5] Then every existing legal system is just, and what is factual (efficacy) appears to be the sole criterion for the justice of the legal system. Nothing survives of the two theses mentioned by Paulson.

In this article, I should like to defend Kelsen's Pure Theory of Law against such a pessimistic interpretation, a defence not only against Celano but, above all, against Kelsen himself, for it can scarcely be doubted that many of Kelsen's own formulations are incompatible with his normative legal positivism. The focus of this article, then, is not an interpretation but, rather, a reconstruction of Kelsen's theory.

With this in mind, I should like to consider the following theses of the Pure Theory of Law as fundamental and therefore inviolable. All of Kelsen's claims that are incompatible with these theses (and, as we shall see, there are a significant number of such claims) must be eliminated from the Pure Theory of Law if it is to represent a theory free of contradiction.

(1) *Legal positivism*: All law is positive law, that is, it consists of norms that are issued and revoked by means of human acts.

(2) *Moral scepticism*: No norms are 'true'. Norms generally and moral norms in particular are neither true nor false. There are no normative facts that would correspond to moral norms, and, consequently, there is also no objective cognition of morality.

[4] Kelsen, *RR 2*, § 34(a) (196), *PTL*, 193.
[5] See Celano (n. 3, this chapter), at 383.

(3) *Separation of 'is'* (Sein) *and 'ought'* (Sollen): If something is, it does not follow that it ought to be, and, vice versa, if something ought to be, it does not follow that it is.

(4) *Value-free legal science*: Legal science consists in describing the positive law, not in evaluating it. Evaluating positive legal systems as just or unjust is a matter of politics, not science.

1. Validity as Membership

It is difficult to answer the question of how 'validity' in the Pure Theory of Law is to be understood. Many different formulations are found in Kelsen's writings,[6] and it is not easy to decide which of them are to be regarded as defining the concept of validity or concepts of validity. A distinction can be made, however, between at least two different concepts that are characterized in Kelsen's work with the expression 'validity'. Both play a very important role in the Pure Theory of Law, namely, validity as the bindingness of norms and validity as the membership of a norm in a legal system.

Validity qua bindingness says that it is obligatory for one to behave in accordance with the norm. This is a *normative* concept of validity.

By contrast, the claim that a certain norm belongs to a certain legal system is a descriptive statement that is either true or false depending on whether this system does or does not include the norm in question. Validity understood as membership is therefore a *descriptive* concept of validity. Moreover, this is clearly a *relative* concept, describing a relation or connection between a norm and a certain legal system. Thus, a norm can belong to one system and not to another, or to a system at a certain point in time and not at another point in time.

Kelsen introduces the problem of the membership of a norm in a legal system with the following question: 'What establishes the unity of a plurality of norms, why does a certain norm belong to a certain system?'[7] It is regrettable that Kelsen goes on to say here that 'this question is closely connected to the question: Why is a norm valid, what is the basis of its validity?' Kelsen's immediate answer to this second question shows clearly that a completely different problem is being raised here: 'That a norm referring to the behaviour of an individual is "valid" means that it is binding, that the individual ought to behave in the manner determined by the norm.'[8] The questions of when a norm belongs to a legal system and when a norm is binding ought clearly to be separated from one another, for they address

[6] Along with bindingness and membership, Kelsen speaks of validity as the specific existence of the norm: 'With the word "validity" we designate the specific existence of a norm.' Kelsen, *RR 2*, § 4(c) (at 9), *PTL*, at 10. What this is supposed to mean is anything but clear. See Bruno Celano, 'Validity as Disquotation', *Analisi e diritto* (1999), 35–77, at 36–7; Kelsen, *RR 2*, at § 34(a) (196–7), *PTL*, at 193–5.

[7] Kelsen, *RR 2*, at § 34(a) (196), *PTL*, at 193.

[8] Kelsen, *RR 2*, at § 34(a) (196), *PTL*, at 193.

two very different concepts. In characterizing Kelsen's theory, it is best to avoid the word 'validity' altogether and, instead, to speak directly of membership and of bindingness.

2. Legal Order (*Rechtsordnung*) and Legal System (*Rechtssystem*)

When does a norm belong to a legal system? Kelsen's answer to this question is that a certain norm belongs to a legal system if it has been created by an authority having jurisdiction or competence, and the jurisdiction or competence to create this norm is granted to the authority by a (higher) norm.[9] (As we shall see, this is not the sole criterion for membership.) It is advisable here to distinguish between a legal system and a legal order, a distinction that Kelsen unfortunately does not make. The expression 'legal system' designates a set of norms that refers to a particular point in time, thus, a momentary system in Joseph Raz's sense.[10] By contrast, a legal order is to be understood as a temporally sequenced series of momentary legal systems. The points in time that correspond to momentary legal systems are determined by acts of norm creation and derogation.[11] Every interval between two such acts determines the duration of a momentary legal system. It follows, then, that a legal system, thus understood, is normally of brief duration, for whenever a new norm is added by means of an act of norm creation or whenever a norm belonging to the system is eliminated by derogation or revocation, there arises a new system. The identity of the system is determined by the identity of its elements (norms). By contrast, a legal order can exist over longer periods of time, lasting for many years, even for centuries.

If the validity of a norm (in the sense of membership) is characterized as its existence, then the existence of the norm in a legal system must be distinguished from its existence in a legal order. A norm exists in a legal system if and for as long as it belongs to this system. A norm exists in a legal order if it belongs to some system or another that belongs to this legal order. Thus, the existence of the norm in a legal order need not be continuous.

Each point in time t at which a norm is issued or revoked corresponds to a legal system S_t. The system S_t consists, however, not only of all norms issued at point in time t, but also of all norms, issued by competent legal organs ahead of this point in time, that have not been revoked. A legal system contains, therefore, all norms created in accordance with the law that have not been derogated in any of the preceding systems of a legal order.

[9] 'A norm belongs to a system grounded on…a basic norm because it was created in the way specified by the basic norm—and not because it has a certain content.' Kelsen, *RR 2*, § 34(b) (at 199), *PTL*, at 197.

[10] See Raz, *CLS*, at 34–5.

[11] For the sake of simplicity, I disregard customary norms and only take up issued norms.

A difficulty arises here. To belong to a system, the norm must be created by a competent legal authority, and the competence to create norms depends on empowering norms. A person or group of persons is competent to create a certain norm if this person or group is empowered to do so by norms belonging to the system in question. To characterize membership with the help of competence and to characterize competence with the help of membership appear to lead to an infinite regress. If norm creation by competent organs were the sole criterion for membership, then the definition of the legal system would in fact be circular. There must, then, be norms that belong to the system without having been created by a competent legal authority. Such norms are the *primitive* norms of the system, characterized in Georg Henrik von Wright's work as *sovereign* norms[12] and in Ricardo Caracciolo's work as *independent* norms.[13] It is a logical necessity that there be such norms in every system. The set of primitive norms must contain at least some competence norms that empower certain organs to create new norms. Such a set is what Kelsen calls the (historically first) constitution in the material sense.[14]

With the help of the concept of the constitution in the material sense, a *legal order* can be defined as the set of all legal systems that have the same (historically first) constitution (that is, the same primitive norms). A legal order consists, then, of a temporal series of legal systems. And the unity of legal systems—that is, the identity of a legal order—is determined by the historically first constitution: if one and the same constitution, then one and the same legal order.

The criterion for identifying norms that, at a particular point in time t, belong to the corresponding system (S_t) of the legal order can be formulated with the help of the following three rules:[15]

(i) The set c (constitutional norms) belongs to the legal system S_t.

(ii) If a norm N_1, which belongs to S_t, empowers an authority a to issue norm N_2, and a issues norm N_2 not later than t, and N_2 has not been derogated before t, then N_2 belongs to S_t.

(iii) All norms that are logical consequences of the norms belonging to S_t also belong to S_t.

Rule (i) determines the set of primitive norms, that is, the norms that belong to the (first) material constitution. This determination is extensional. Rule (ii) represents the criterion for the dynamic derivation of norms. It makes possible the introduction of new norms into the legal system by means of acts of norm creation, as well as the exclusion of existing norms by means of acts of derogation.[16]

[12] See von Wright, *NA*, at 199.

[13] See Ricardo A. Caracciolo, *El sistema jurídico. Problemas actuales* (Madrid: Centro de Estudios Constitucionales, 1988).

[14] See Kelsen, *RR 2*, at § 35(a) (228–30), *PTL*, at 221–4.

[15] This is a simplified statement. For a full statement, see Eugenio Bulygin, 'Sobre la regla de reconocimiento', *Doxa*, 9 (1991), 257–79, at 263–6; and Bulygin, 'An Antinomy in Kelsen's Pure Theory of Law' (1990), in this volume, ch. 14.

[16] This is the static principle, according to which norms that are derivable from issued norms also belong to the system. In a legal system, both the static principle and the dynamic principle are operative. See Kelsen, *RR 2*, § 34(b) (at 200), *PTL*, at 197–8.

The three rules represent a recursive definition of a legal system. Through the successive application of these three rules, it can be determined which norms belong to the current system of a legal order.

3. Validity, Efficacy, and the Basic Norm

The distinction between validity as membership and validity as bindingness makes possible a clarification of the problem of the relation between validity and efficacy.

First of all, it is understood that membership of a norm in a legal system (with reference to issued norms) is independent of efficacy. To be sure, it is reasonable to ask whether a certain norm belongs to a legal system if neither this norm nor the legal system as a whole is efficacious. Nevertheless, in Kelsen's legal theory, the membership of a norm rests solely on the empowerment of an authority to create the norm, and efficacy is completely irrelevant, not even being mentioned in the definition. By contrast, the bindingness of a norm is dependent on its efficacy. A completely inefficacious legal order—say, for example, Roman law today—cannot be regarded as binding. Kelsen writes:

> the efficacy of a legal system as a whole and the efficacy of a single legal norm are [in each case] the condition for validity, namely, efficacy qua condition in the sense that a legal system as a whole and a single legal norm can no longer be regarded as valid if they cease to be efficacious. Also, the efficacy of a legal system is no more a basis of its validity than is the fact of its issuance. The basis of validity—this is the question of why the norms of this legal system ought to be complied with and applied—is the presupposed basic norm, according to which one ought to comply with a constitution that has in fact been passed and is by and large efficacious, and ought to comply, therefore, with norms that have in fact been issued in accordance with this constitution and that are by and large efficacious.[17]

It is clear from this quotation that Kelsen, in describing the relation between validity and efficacy, has bindingness in mind, not membership.

For the definition of membership, on the other hand, it turns out that the presupposition of the basic norm is superfluous. All one needs is a criterion for identity like the three rules introduced earlier. To be sure, Kelsen does formulate the question of the basis of the validity of the first constitution, but in doing so he refers to bindingness and not to membership. The question of whether the (first) constitution belongs to a legal order makes no sense, for the legal order is defined with the help of the (first) constitution. The chain of dynamic derivation begins with the constitution, which is, *per definitionem*, the first link in the chain. Therefore, the problem of membership and the problem of the identity of a legal system or of a legal order can be taken up without any need to resort to the presupposition of the Kelsenian basic norm.

Thus far, two important consequences of the distinction between bindingness and membership have been covered.

[17] Kelsen, *RR 2*, § 34(g) (at 218–19), *PTL*, at 211–12.

4. Validity as Bindingness

This analysis shows that the basic norm as well as efficacy are linked to bindingness, not to membership. Confusing these two concepts, for which Kelsen uses the same expression, 'validity', leads to serious problems in interpreting his writings.

In what follows, the concept of bindingness will be considered more closely. Alf Ross has sharply criticized using the concept of validity as bindingness. A norm is binding if one ought to behave in accordance with it, but what does this 'ought' (*Sollen*) mean? What kind of obligation is being imposed by it?

A duty is always a duty to behave in a certain way. In this case, the required behaviour is 'to obey the law'. How do we obey the law? By fulfilling our legal obligations—for example, by paying our debts. It follows that the obligation to obey the law does not prescribe any behaviour that is not already prescribed by the law itself. And it follows in turn that if the duty to obey the prescriptions of a legal system is to mean something different from the obligation prescribed directly by this system, then the difference cannot consist in the *required behaviour*—*what* we are bound to do—but must consist exclusively in *how* we are bound. The meaning of the binding force inherent in a legal system is that the legal obligations corresponding to the rules of the system—for example, the obligation to pay a debt—are not merely legal duties derived from the threat of legal sanctions. They are also *moral duties* in the a priori sense of true moral obligations deriving from the natural law principles that endow the legal system with its validity or binding force. The duty to obey the law is a moral duty *toward* the legal system, not a legal duty *conforming* to the system. The duty toward the system cannot derive from this system itself, but must follow from rules or principles that are outside the system.[18]

Ross claims that a positivistic legal theory like the Pure Theory of Law cannot use *this* concept of validity as bindingness without overstepping the bounds of a value-free legal science. Such a theory would be a type of natural law theory, characterized by Ross as 'quasi-positivism'. Thus we face a dilemma. Either the claim 'legal norms are binding' lacks content—for it is superfluous if, by bindingness, legal obligation is meant, that is, it makes no sense to prescribe that one ought to do what one ought in any case to do. Or, by bindingness, a moral obligation is meant, which cannot be squared with Kelsen's positivism, for if one is morally obligated to comply with legal norms, then every existing legal order is morally correct or just.

A similar interpretation of bindingness in Kelsen's legal theory is found in the work of other authors. Joseph Raz distinguishes two types of normativity, social normativity and justified normativity.[19] He attributes the second type of normativity, justified normativity, to Kelsen:

Kelsen uses only the concept of justified normativity... According to him an individual can consider a legal system as normative only if he endorses it as morally just and good.[20]

[18] Ross, 'Validity', in *RJBA*, 54 (emphasis in original), in *NN*, 153–4.
[19] See Raz, 'BN', in Raz, *AL*, at 134, in *NN*, at 57.
[20] Raz, 'BN', in Raz, *AL*, 134, in *NN*, 58.

[T]o judge the law as normative is to judge it to be just and to admit that it ought to be obeyed.[21]

The same interpretation of validity in Kelsen's legal theory is endorsed by Carlos Santiago Nino:

To predicate validity of a legal system, or of a particular legal rule, is to assert that it has binding force, that its prescriptions constitute conclusive reasons for action.[22]

The judgments of validity (including the basic norm) prescribe that the actions commanded by the norms to which they refer ought to be done.[23]

Ross claims that using the concept of bindingness contravenes Kelsen's principles, since it cannot be squared with legal positivism or Kelsen's notion of a value-free legal science, prompting Ross to characterize Kelsen as a 'quasi-positivist'. Nino and Raz, for their part, assess Kelsen's use of a normative concept of bindingness as something altogether commendable.

I believe that the concept of validity as bindingness, as Kelsen defines it, is incompatible with his positivistic programme. This concept, however, can be given a new interpretation. I want to suggest replacing the concept of bindingness with a new concept, namely, a concept that preserves the normativity of Kelsen's bindingness but is also compatible with his positivism. This concept is the concept of applicability.

5. Applicability

As we have seen, Ross claims that within the framework of a positivistic theory of law, one must dispense with validity as bindingness. In earlier work, I endorsed this opinion.[24] Today, I believe instead that one can interpret the normative concept of validity so that Ross's charge of superfluity as well as the moral colouration of the concept can be avoided.

Normative validity ought to be interpreted as legal obligation, not moral obligation. To avoid confusion, I will use instead the expression 'applicability'.[25] A norm is applicable if the judge is obligated to apply it in a certain case. This obligation is established by positive legal norms, which I characterize as 'application norms'. The concept of applicability, like the concept of bindingness, is normative, but there is, as we are about to see, a great difference between the two concepts.

[21] Raz, 'BN', in Raz, *AL*, 137, in *NN*, 60.

[22] Carlos Santiago Nino, 'Some Confusions surrounding Kelsen's Concept of Validity', *ARSP*, 64 (1978), 357–77, at 358, in *NN* (repr. in part), 253–61, at 254.

[23] Carlos Santiago Nino, *La validez del derecho* (Buenos Aires: Editorial Astrea, 1985), 12.

[24] See Bulygin, 'An Antinomy in Kelsen's Pure Theory of Law' (1990), in this volume, ch. 14.

[25] I introduced the concept of applicability in the essay 'Time and Validity' (1982), in this volume, ch. 10. Later, José Juan Moreso and Pablo E. Navarro worked up a thoroughgoing analysis of the concept. See their paper, 'Applicability and Effectiveness of Legal Norms', *Law and Philosophy*, 16 (1997), 201–19.

Applicability can be elucidated with the help of an example from Argentine criminal law. A generally accepted principle for the applicability of criminal law norms is given expression in the familiar *nullum crimen, nulla poena sine praevia lege penale*. This says that criminal law norms have no retroactive force, that is to say, they cannot be applied to delicts committed before the criminal law norm forbidding them was in force. According to this principle, the court ought to apply the norm that was in force at the time of the delict, even if, in the meantime, this norm was revoked and is no longer in force at the time of the judgment.

There are other basic principles that limit the applicability of the *nullum crimen* principle. According to section 2 of the Argentine Criminal Code, the judge ought always to apply the norm that provides for a milder penalty. That may be a norm issued after the deed and valid during the trial or a norm that has been, in the meantime, derogated. The situation arises in which the judge, in order to apply the norm that provides for the mildest penalty, ought to compare all norms that refer to the circumstance and that belong to some system of the legal order during the interval between the point in time at which the delict was committed and the point in time at which the judge is to take a decision. It is to be emphasized here that all norms that the judge must compare, with the exception of the very latest ones, are derogated norms. Thus, the widely disseminated idea that the judge must always apply prevailing law proves to be mistaken. In fact, the judge frequently has to apply norms that have already been revoked. This shows that derogation has an effect only on membership, not on applicability. A derogated norm does not, indeed, belong to later legal systems, but it can perfectly well retain its applicability.

A norm like section 2 of the Argentine Criminal Code is a typical application norm, obligating the judge to apply a certain norm. It is a norm of the positive law, and the obligation it establishes is a legal obligation, not a moral obligation. Moreover, this obligation is not superfluous in Ross's sense, for it does not coincide with obligations imposed by other norms of the Criminal Code. The Criminal Code obligates the judge to impose a certain sentence on the accused, while application norms determine which of the criminal law norms is to be applied. The judge must choose between and among various norms. For this he needs certain criteria. Application norms provide these criteria.

6. Applicability and Membership

The concept of applicability is to be distinguished sharply from the concept of membership. Two problems are of special interest in this context.

First, the distinction provides clarification of a problem that Kelsen struggled with over his entire lifetime without being able to come to a satisfactory solution. This is the problem of irregular norms, that is, norms that have not been issued by competent organs, perhaps because the established procedure was not followed or because the content of the norm goes beyond the competence of the organ. Unconstitutional statutes or illegal judgments serve as examples. Kelsen addresses this problem under the rubric of conflicts between norms at different levels in the normative hierarchy.

From Kelsen's definition of membership, it follows that a norm not issued by the competent organ does not belong to the legal system. Still, such a norm can be applicable, for as long as it has not been declared unconstitutional or illegal, the norm is regarded as valid and courts have the obligation to apply it. Kelsen sees himself in an awkward position. On the one hand, he cannot deny the validity of such norms, for then they would not exist at all. (Validity is, after all, the specific existence of norms!) On the other hand, such norms have *ex hypothesi* not been created by a competent organ. Thus, Kelsen is compelled to turn to the theory of the well-known alternative clause, which is not logically tenable.[26]

The second problem is that the set of norms applicable to a case need not be—widespread opinion to the contrary notwithstanding—a partial set of norms belonging to a certain legal system. Norms that do not belong to the legal system of the judge can nevertheless be applicable. The norms can belong to other legal orders or they may not be legal norms at all.

The applicability of norms that belong to another legal order comes up so often that there is a specific branch of legal science devoted thereto: private international law. A German court can be rightly obligated by norms of German law to apply norms of another legal order to a certain case. That a German judge applies an Italian legal norm does not transform this norm into a German norm. Private international law is interested in precisely those cases in which foreign law ought to be applied, and that law remains what it is, namely, *foreign* law.

The applicability of norms that do not belong to the legal system of the judge is also something that comes up not infrequently. A variety of different cases can be distinguished. It may be—as with the applicability of derogated norms—that legal norms belong to another system of the same legal order. But it may also be that courts are obligated or empowered to apply moral norms (without a clear determination of which morality is in question). That a court applies a moral norm does not mean that this moral norm belongs to the legal system.

7. Bindingness and Applicability

By contrast with the descriptive concept of validity as membership, both bindingness and applicability are normative concepts. As already discussed, the sentence 'the norm *N* belongs to legal system S_t' is a true or false statement. By contrast, the sentences 'the norm *N* is binding' and 'the norm *N* is applicable to a certain case'

[26] See on this problem Roberto J. Vernengo, 'La función sistemática de la norma fundamental', *RJBA* (1960) (no. 1), 207–25; Nino (n. 23, this chapter); Eugenio Bulygin, 'Cognition and Interpretation of Law', in *Cognition and Interpretation of Law*, ed. Letizia Gianformaggio and Stanley L. Paulson (Turin: G. Giappichelli, 1995), 11–35; also in that volume Carlos Santiago Nino, 'Marshall's "Logic" and Kelsen's "Problem"', 219–30; Sandro Nannini, 'Legal Validity and Conformity to Law', 231–46; Juan Ruiz Manero, 'On the Tacit Alternative Clause', 247–55; Letizia Gianformaggio, 'Pure Theory of Law and Tacit Alternative Clause: A Paradox?', 257–73; and Eugenio Bulygin, 'Some Replies to Critics', 305–13.

are normative, for they give expression to norms that cannot be characterized as either true or false. All three concepts—membership, bindingness, applicability—are often understood, not least of all by Kelsen, in terms of a common rubric, 'validity'. These concepts are nevertheless to be distinguished precisely from one another.

All three concepts are relational concepts, but the relations differ. The concept of membership designates a four-place relation between a legal system, an empowering norm of this system, an act of norm creation, and a norm created by means of this act. This scheme is drawn from rule (ii), introduced above. The relation of bindingness is a two-place relation, defined by Kelsen as a relation between a norm and the validity (bindingness) of another norm. The concept of applicability designates a five-place relation between a legal system, an application norm that belongs to this system, a court, a case, and a norm that is to be applied. A norm is applicable if an application norm of the legal system obligates or empowers the court to apply the norm to a certain case.

The most important difference between the concepts of bindingness and applicability is that the relative concept of bindingness presupposes the absolute concept, which is not the case with the concept of applicability. This is shown in Kelsen's description of the bindingness of a norm as *relative to the bindingness* of another norm: 'The basis of the validity of a norm can only be the validity of another norm.'[27] By contrast, applicability is determined as *relative to the existence* of an application norm. This difference leads to problematic consequences that have been addressed by von Wright.[28] I am following his exposition here.

The concept of validity is understood by some philosophers, among them Kelsen, as a concept analogous to the concept of truth. The relative concept of truth presupposes, however, the absolute concept. That a sentence is true relative to another sentence can only mean that if the second sentence is true, then the first sentence is also true. The truth of the first sentence is relative to the truth of the second sentence. The truth of the second sentence, however, is dependent on the truth of a third sentence, and so on. If this series is not infinite, then it must end in a sentence whose truth is not relative to the truth of another sentence but is, rather, absolute.

Similarly, if the validity (bindingness) of a norm is characterized as relative to the validity (bindingness) of another norm, then the series of binding norms must either be infinite or end in a norm whose bindingness is independent of every other norm, that is, the series must end in a norm that is absolutely binding. Since the existence of positive law norms is dependent on human behaviour (acts of norm creation), the set of these norms cannot be infinite. So there must be—for reasons of logic—absolutely binding norms. In this sense, relative bindingness, as Kelsen defines it, presupposes absolute bindingness.

For Kelsen's legal positivism, however, the idea of absolutely valid norms is unacceptable, for there is absolute validity only in natural law, not in positive law. To escape this dilemma, Kelsen resorts to the theory of the basic norm. The validity of the constitution and thereby of the whole legal system rests on the hypothesis of a mythical basic norm.

[27] Kelsen, *RR 2*, § 34(a) (196), *PTL*, 193.

[28] See von Wright, *NA*, at 194–7.

As von Wright emphasizes, however, the analogy between validity and truth is misleading. Validity can be specified as relative to the existence, not the validity, of a higher norm. This concept of relative validity, for which I use the expression 'applicability', presupposes no absolute concept. In other words, the problem that Kelsen seeks to resolve with the help of his basic norm does not arise in connection with applicability, for the concept of applicability is specified as relative to the existence, not the applicability, of an application norm. A norm is applicable if an application norm obligates or empowers the court to apply it. It is inapplicable if the court is proscribed from applying it. This means that a norm is neither applicable nor inapplicable if there is no corresponding application norm. Trivially, applicability presupposes the existence of application norms. A similar resolution of the problem of validity is found in H. L. A. Hart's theory, for he clearly understands that one can speak of validity only within the framework of a rule of recognition. The rule of recognition itself is neither valid nor invalid. To enquire into the validity of the rule of recognition is meaningless. The situation with the ultimate application norms is comparable.[29]

It follows that the hypothesis of a basic norm is altogether superfluous for the concept of validity as applicability. An application norm is applicable if its application is prescribed by a (higher) application norm, but this chain of application norms cannot proceed infinitely. For reasons of logic, there must be ultimate application norms that are neither applicable nor inapplicable. The question of their applicability is simply meaningless.

For Kelsen, bindingness is closely connected to efficacy. Celano claims with good reason that, in the Pure Theory of Law, efficacy is a necessary and sufficient condition for the bindingness of norms, and he bases his criticism of Kelsen on this point.[30] An interesting question is how efficacy stands in relation to applicability. This question must be broken down into at least two questions. (1) Must a norm be efficacious in order to be applicable to a case? (2) For the applicability of a norm, must its application norm be efficacious?

The answer to the first question is without a doubt in the negative. If the efficacy of a norm consists in its being either complied with or applied,[31] then the applicability of a norm is completely independent of its efficacy, for the norm is applicable before it is applied. The question of whether the appropriate court in fact applies or does not apply a norm that is applicable to a case is altogether irrelevant to the applicability of the norm.

The answer to the second question is likewise in the negative as long as its reference is to issued norms. I have deliberately confined my enquiry here to issued norms. If membership is independent of efficacy, then an application norm belongs to the legal system whether it is efficacious or not. The situation becomes complicated if customary norms are taken into account, since their existence and

[29] See Pablo E. Navarro, Claudina Orunesu, Jorge L. Rodríguez, and German Sucar, 'Applicability of Legal Norms', *Canadian Journal of Law and Jurisprudence*, 17 (2004), 337–59.

[30] See Celano (n. 3, this chapter).

[31] See Kelsen, *RR 2*, § 4(c) (at 10), § 28(a) (at 122), *PTL*, at 10–11, 116.

therefore their membership consist in their efficacy. This problem, however, must be addressed in a separate enquiry.

8. Conclusions

The most important conclusions stemming from this enquiry can be summarized as follows:

(1) The expression 'validity' is ambiguous in Kelsen's writings; at least two altogether different concepts characterized by this expression can be distinguished. They are membership and bindingness.

(2) The concept of membership is a descriptive concept. The sentence 'the norm *N* belongs to legal system *S*' is a true or false statement. Bindingness is a normative concept. The sentence 'the norm *N* is binding' gives expression to a norm that cannot be either true or false.

(3) If membership is interpreted as the existence of the norm, then the legal system is to be distinguished from the legal order. A legal system is a set of norms existing over a span of time (an interval between two points in time). A legal order is a temporally sequenced set of legal systems. Thus, the membership of a norm in a legal system is to be distinguished from the membership of a legal system in a legal order.

(4) Accordingly, the problem of the relation between validity and efficacy is a separate problem. There is no relation between the membership of norms and their efficacy (as long as the enquiry is directed to issued norms, leaving customary norms aside).

(5) In defining the concept of membership, the assumption of a basic norm proves to be altogether superfluous. Kelsen needs a basic norm solely for bindingness.

(6) The concept of bindingness is interpreted by many authors—including Ross, Raz, Nino, and Celano—as a moral obligation, an interpretation that is incompatible with Kelsen's positivism.

(7) Bindingness can also be interpreted, however, as a purely legal obligation. I use for this the expression 'applicability'. A certain norm is applicable if a positive law norm (an application norm) obligates or empowers the judge to apply this particular norm to a case.

(8) The concept of applicability must not be confused with the concept of membership. Judges can be obligated to apply a norm that belongs neither to their legal system nor to their legal order.

(9) The analysis of the formal structure of the concepts of applicability and bindingness shows that applicability is fundamentally different from bindingness as Kelsen understands it. Kelsen's definition of relative bindingness presupposes absolute bindingness, which leads him to the assumption of the basic norm. For applicability, this hypothetical basic norm proves to be superfluous.

21

Permissory Norms and Normative Systems (1984/86/2012)*

Written with Carlos E. Alchourrón

1.

It is a well-known fact that permissory norms are not popular among legal philosophers. A great many legal philosophers, tending to think that permissory norms have no independent status, accept only one type of norm, namely, mandatory norms, norms that establish obligations and prohibitions. The tendency to dismiss permissory norms as being of little importance is at least partially based on the conception of norms as prescriptions or directives for conduct. Indeed, permission to smoke in the classroom, for example, does not seem capable of guiding our behaviour in a straightforward way, for it is compatible with both smoking and not smoking, that is, with both the commission of and forbearance from smoking. Here the difference from mandatory norms is very clear. A mandatory norm excludes certain actions and is therefore incompatible with them. Like mandatory norms, however, permissions usually do refer to actions (or states of affairs that are the result of an action), and their reference seems to be similar to the reference of mandatory norms, though it is not easy to characterize it. In a very loose sense, then, they are also prescriptive, although they do not prescribe any particular action. At any rate, permissory norms are normatively relevant in an indirect way, as we shall argue in this paper. Although they are, in an important sense, parasitic upon mandatory norms, they contribute within the framework of a system of norms to the determination of

* [*Editors' note*: In 1984, Eugenio Bulygin and Carlos E. Alchourrón published the paper 'Permission and Permissive Norms' in *Theorie der Normen. Festgabe für Ota Weinberger zum 65. Geburtstag*, ed. Werner Krawietz, et al. (Berlin: Duncker & Humblot), 349–71. Two years later, Bulygin published the paper 'Permissive Norms and Normative Systems' in *Automated Analysis of Legal Texts. Logic, Informatics, Law*, ed. Antonio A. Martino and Fiorenza Socci Natali (Amsterdam: North-Holland, 1986), 211–18. For publication in the present volume, Bulygin has revised and in part rewritten these papers, and he has also introduced a fair bit of new material.]

the normative status of actions regulated by the system. The aim of this paper is to show the existence of this systemic dependency of permissory norms and to characterize the role played in a normative system by permissory norms and by permissory acts. This thesis implies (i) that there are permissory norms and (ii) that they are not superfluous, that is to say, they play a significant role in legal discourse that could not possibly be performed by mandatory norms alone.

2.

When a norm-authority grants permission to perform a certain action, this can be done in many different ways. One of them, frequently employed, is to utter a linguistic expression permitting the action, such as 'I permit you to smoke', 'you are allowed to smoke', 'you may smoke', 'smoke, if you please', and so on. There is no standard linguistic expression for granting permission (a gesture like a nod or a green traffic light may serve the same purpose). The act of granting permission, performed by a norm-authority, will be called a permissory act and the result of such an act a permissory norm.

We must also keep in mind the well-known distinction between norms and normative propositions, that is, the distinction between a permissory norm and a proposition to the effect that such and such an action is permitted (by a certain norm or by a given normative system).[1] A normative statement is true or false, but norms (including permissory norms) lack truth-values.

Those authors who disregard permissory norms as having no independent or autonomous status accept only one kind of permission, defined as the absence of a prohibition. According to this view, the normative proposition '*p* is permitted in A' (where 'A' denotes a given system of norms) is true if and only if system A contains no norm prohibiting *p*. Therefore, for the permissibility of *p*, no permissory norm is needed; *p* is permissible in virtue of the mere fact that it is not forbidden. From this it follows that in principle all actions are permitted unless they are prohibited by some norm. It seems, therefore, that it would make no sense to issue a permissory norm. To permit an action that is not prohibited would be quite pointless, for such a permission would produce no change in the normative status of this action.

3.

In order to elucidate the view according to which a permission is the mere absence of a prohibition, we shall consider a simplified theoretical model in the form of a game similar to that devised by David Lewis.[2] The game is played by two players

[1] See Bulygin, 'Norms, Normative Propositions, and Legal Statements' (1982), in this volume, ch. 11.

[2] See David Lewis, 'A Problem about Permission', in *Essays in Honour of Jaakko Hintikka*, ed. Esa Saarinen, et al. (Dordrecht: Reidel, 1981), 163–75.

called Rex and Subject. (The existence of more than one subject would make no difference here. The case of a plurality of norm-authorities will be considered later.)

Rex has unlimited competence to regulate Subject's actions by means of norms, that is, he can change the normative status of Subject's actions by performing normative acts like commanding or permitting. At the beginning of the game, all actions of Subject are permissible; he is free to do or to forbear from doing any action that lies within the scope of his (physical) possibilities. If, however, Rex commands that Subject shall do p, then action p turns out to be obligatory and its negation ($-p$) prohibited. Therefore, the actions of Subject can be divided into two classes: the class of permissible actions (the sphere of permissibility) and the class of prohibited actions, which are all those actions whose omission is commanded.

To the class of commanded actions belong not only those actions that have been explicitly commanded by Rex, but also those actions that are a logical consequence of what has been commanded. For example, if Rex has commanded $(p.q)$, then not only the complex action $(p.q)$ is obligatory for Subject, but also the actions p and q taken alone are obligatory. Conversely, if Rex has commanded p and also has commanded q (perhaps on a different occasion), the complex action $(p.q)$ is obligatory. We can generalize this result by saying that if a set of actions B is obligatory, than all those actions that are a logically necessary condition for the performance of B are also obligatory.

Suppose now that Rex has performed two successive normative acts regarding the same action p. If Rex has competence to change the normative status of p, then the normative act performed on a later occasion prevails over the act performed on an earlier occasion. In other words, the norm issued on a later occasion derogates the norm issued on a temporally earlier occasion, according to the well-known rule *lex posterior derogat legi priori*. This rule is conceptually linked to the notion of competence if by 'competence' we understand the faculty of changing the normative status of certain actions. Therefore, the rule *lex posterior* is not a contingent rule. Rather, it is conceptually necessary in so far as there is a norm-authority who is competent to change the deontic qualifications of certain actions.

To be sure, this rule can be subject to restrictions or limitations, but this means only that the competence of the authority is restricted or limited. For example, if the rule *lex posterior* is restricted to certain actions of Subject and does not apply to other actions, it follows that Rex has no competence regarding these other actions. If the norm issued on a later occasion only prevails over the former norm when it is more just or convenient, then the competence of the norm-authority is limited. The norm-authority is only competent to replace a norm by a more just or more convenient norm, but has no competence to issue norms that are less just or less convenient than the existing norms. Without the rule *lex posterior*, however, there would be no competence at all, and then there would be no possibility of normative change emerging from acts of authority.[3]

[3] This is the case in morality. Immunity from deliberate change, according to Hart, is a typical characteristic of moral rules. See Hart, *CL*, 1st edn., at 171–3, 3rd edn., at 175–8. [*Editors' note*: For this and other abbreviations, see the Table of Abbreviations.]

4.

An especially interesting case arises when Rex prohibits *p* (by commanding *–p*) at a time t_1 and then on a later occasion t_2 permits *p*. In such a case we would say, according to the rule *lex posterior*, that *p* is permitted from time t_2, even if it was prohibited during the interval t_1–t_2. The permission granted at t_2 cancels the previously issued prohibition. Thus, even if it seems to be pointless to permit an action that is not prohibited, it is by no means pointless to cancel or to derogate an existing prohibition by granting a permission. This fact already shows that permissory norms play at least one important role, namely, that of cancelling or derogating prohibitions, a task that could not possibly be performed by mandatory norms.[4] (We shall see presently that this is not the only function of permissory norms.)

Moreover, it is interesting to note that the permissibility of *p* from time t_2 on is not owing to the mere absence of a prohibition (or Subject's original 'freedom'), but is the result of a normative act carried out by Rex. Is there any difference between the original, purely negative permissibility (for which no act of the norm-authority is needed) and this supervenient or positive permissibility that stems from certain acts of the authority? It has been argued that the fact that the permissibility of an action is owing to a normative act performed by Rex does not give rise to a different concept of permission. By issuing a permissory norm Rex has derogated or cancelled a prohibition, and the action in question has thereby recovered its original status, that of permissibility. However, the situation is not as simple as that. It is an interesting fact that the role played by permissory norms is not exhausted by the derogation of previous prohibitions. An act permitting an action that has not hitherto been prohibited is not at all pointless, as some who have denied the importance of permissory norms have suggested.

Those authors who object to the very idea of permissory norms as being independent of mandatory norms (those norms establishing obligations or prohibitions) and so object to the distinction between weak and strong permissions deny that there is any practical or pragmatic difference between an action that is permitted and an action that is not prohibited. This objection was raised in a book by Delia Teresa Echave, María Eugenia Urquijo, and Ricardo Guibourg,[5] and since then it has been formulated repeatedly by both Manuel Atienza and Juan Ruiz Manero.[6]

The following story is taken from Echave, Urquijo, and Guibourg.[7] A primitive tribe that has lived from fishing and hunting without any normative restrictions whatever decides one day to appoint (by means of a democratic election) a chief,

[4] As we shall see later, even Alf Ross tacitly acknowledged this role of permissory norms.

[5] Delia Teresa Echave, María Eugenia Urquijo, and Ricardo Guibourg, *Lógica, proposición y norma* (Buenos Aires: Astrea, 1980).

[6] See e.g. Manuel Atienza and Juan Ruiz Manero, *Las piezas del derecho* (Barcelona: Ariel, 1996); Juan Ruiz Manero, 'Algunas concepciónes del derecho y sus lagunas', in *Lagunas en el derecho*, ed. Fernando Atria, et al. (Madrid: Marcial Pons, 2005); Manuel Atienza, 'Dos versións del constitucionalismo', *Doxa*, 34 (2011), 73–88.

[7] See Echave, Urquijo, and Guibourg, *Lógica, proposición y norma* (n. 5, this chapter).

conferring on him legislative powers. Soon after the election the new chief, a gentle and peaceful man, issued his first law, 'it is permitted to hunt on Tuesdays and Fridays.' Asked whether this meant a prohibition to hunt on all other days of the week, the chief replied, 'not at all. I have thus far not prohibited anything, I have only permitted hunting on Tuesdays and Fridays.' 'Does this mean you are promising that you'll not forbid hunting on these two days in the future?' was the next question, posed by a somewhat bewildered member of the tribe. The reply: 'No, I do not like to impose restrictions on my people, but I might change my mind in the future if new circumstances should arise.' It is no wonder that the members of the tribe felt a bit disappointed, for they could scarcely suppress the feeling that the election of a legislative authority had been, thus far, completely useless. They always used to hunt on all the days of the week, and now, after the promulgation of the first law, the situation has remained exactly the same.[8]

The moral of this story is valuable. It shows that purely permissory norms are of little if any practical interest. If a normative order has as its task that of guiding human behaviour, it must necessarily contain norms of obligation. This point has been repeatedly stressed by Weinberger.[9] It is norms of obligation alone that divide possible actions into two categories or spheres: the sphere of prohibited actions and the sphere of permitted actions (that is, those not forbidden) or the sphere of permissibility.

Even if the chief had issued certain norms of obligation, for example, prohibiting hunting on Sundays, the permission to hunt on Tuesdays and Fridays would still be of little use. So it seems that there is no point in distinguishing within the sphere of permissibility between strongly and weakly permitted actions.[10]

This is indeed the case for as long as we restrict our attention to very simple cases where there is only one normative authority, as in the case of our tribe or in Lewis's game. As soon as several hierarchically ordered authorities are introduced, however, the situation changes.

In order to clarify this point, we shall introduce a further complication into our game. Suppose that Rex, tired of governing alone, decides one day to appoint a minister and to confer legislative power on him, that is, competence to regulate Subject's actions. From that day forth, Minister can give orders or commands to Subject in the same way as Rex himself does, and an action commanded by Minister becomes as obligatory as if it had been commanded by Rex. However, Minister has no competence to alter the commands and permissions given by Rex; in other words, he is not competent to derogate the norms issued by Rex. Thus, if Rex has prohibited the action *p* and Minister on a later occasion permits the same action, *p* remains prohibited and the permissory act performed by Minister is without effect. We would say, in this case, that the rule *lex posterior* is overridden by the rule *lex superior*, since the two norm authorities, Rex and Minister, are found at

[8] Echave, Urquijo, and Guibourg, *Lógica, proposición y norma* (n. 5, this chapter), 153–8.

[9] See Ota Weinberger, 'Normenlogik und logische Bereiche', in *Deontische Logik und Semantik*, ed. Amedeo G. Conte, et al. (Wiesbaden: Athenaion, 1977), 176–212.

[10] See Lewis, 'A Problem about Permission' (n. 2, this chapter).

different levels in the hierarchy, and a norm issued by a higher authority prevails over a norm issued by a lower authority even if the second norm has been issued later than the first norm. This simply means that the lower authority lacks competence to change the normative status conferred on an action by a higher authority.[11]

Suppose now that Subject is very fond of hunting and that this activity has not yet been regulated by any norms. Subject is free to hunt or to forbear from hunting as he wishes. If at some point Rex decides to prohibit hunting on Sundays, from that moment on hunting on Sundays would be prohibited, but it would still be permitted on all the other days of the week. Now, being afraid that Minister, who intensely dislikes hunters, will prohibit hunting altogether, Subject asks Rex to permit him to hunt at least once a week, and Rex in a moment of generosity decides to grant the permission to hunt on Saturdays. What effects, if any, does this act of permitting give rise to and in what way can the permission to hunt on Saturdays be said to be different from the permission to hunt on Fridays or Mondays?

The permissibility to hunt on Fridays is what we call a *negative permission*. It is the remainder of Subject's original freedom, that which has not been suppressed by normative regulations issued by Rex or by Minister. This negative kind of permissibility will vanish as soon as the action in question is prohibited by the act of a norm-authority (either by Rex or by Minister). The permissibility to hunt on Saturdays, however, is not a merely negative permission. It is a permission, granted by Rex, that stems from an act of authority. This is what we have called *supervenient* or *positive permission*. This kind of permission does not yield to a prohibition issued by Minister, a lower-level authority who lacks competence to derogate norms issued by Rex. Even if the act permitting hunting on Saturdays does not derogate any norm (there was, *ex hypothesi*, no prohibition to hunt on Saturdays), it is far from being pointless, for it limits Minister's competence. After this permission has been granted, Minister is no longer competent to prohibit hunting on Saturdays, although he was competent to do so before Rex issued this permissory norm and he is still competent to prohibit hunting on the other days of the week.

Thus, as we have already seen, the appointment of a minister changes radically the consequences of acts issuing permissions. There is an important difference between norms issued by Rex and norms issued by Minister, and there is, therefore, an important difference between those actions of Subject that are permitted in the strong sense by Rex and those actions that are merely not prohibited, that is, are weakly permitted. The latter but not the former can be prohibited by Minister.

It is easy to find examples of such situations in legal contexts. One typical case is that of constitutional rights, which limit the competence of an ordinary legislature. Once freedom of the press has been guaranteed by the constitution, parliament is no longer competent to suppress or restrict this freedom.

[11] The rule *lex superior*, like *lex posterior*, is not a contingent rule, but, rather, is conceptually necessary. In the same way as the concept of the competence of a norm-authority implies the rule *lex posterior*, so the concept of a hierarchically ordered plurality of norm-authorities implies the rule *lex superior*.

5.

These considerations show that the normative status of actions regulated by a normative system depends not only on mandatory norms but also on permissory norms. In fact, it is the result of interplay between different kinds of norm: mandatory norms, permissory norms, and norms of competence. This also shows that the act of permitting can be described as a illocutionary act of a peculiar kind. By issuing a permission Rex does not prescribe any action of Subject, but he rejects every prohibition of the permitted action, and this prevents an authority at a lower level in the hierarchy from prohibiting it. In an article that Carlos Alchourrón and I wrote together, the nature of such a normative act is analysed in some detail as an *act of rejection*.[12] According to this analysis, the act of permitting *p* can be interpreted as an act of rejecting the obligation of –*p*, which amounts to the rejection of the prohibition of *p*. Rejection is a peculiar illocutionary act that is opposed, in a certain sense, to commanding. Between rejected and positively permitted norm-content (actions), the same relation holds as between prohibited and commanded norm-content. If *p* is rejected, then –*p* is positively permitted and, vice versa, if *p* is positively permitted, then –*p* is rejected.

This is why an act of permitting *p* is incompatible with an act of prohibiting *p*, and an act of permitting –*p* is incompatible with an act of commanding *p*. It also explains why it makes sense to permit an action *p* that is not prohibited. Although such a permissory act does not derogate any existing norm, it rejects the prohibition of *p* by any authority at a lower level in the hierarchy than Rex himself or a still higher authority (if there be any).

6.

A norm-authority can also withdraw a prohibition without rejecting it, that is, without permitting the hitherto prohibited action. Such an act of withdrawal cancels a norm without replacing it with another norm of an opposite modality. In contradistinction to rejection, such an act of withdrawal only makes sense with respect to an explicitly formulated norm; thus, it can be characterized as the derogation of a norm-formulation rather than as the derogation of a norm.

The concept of abrogation introduced by Carlos Alchourrón and David Makinson[13] is apparently intended as a reconstruction of the same notion. If, however, abrogation is the mere withdrawal or the dropping of a norm-formulation (we may call it D), then it is not true that 'derogation coincides with abrogation just when no element of the set D rejected is implied by the complement A–D',[14]

[12] Alchourrón and Bulygin, 'The Expressive Conception of Norms' (1981), in this volume, ch. 9.

[13] See Carlos E. Alchourrón and David Makinson, 'Hierarchies of Regulations and Their Logic', in *New Studies in Deontic Logic*, ed. Risto Hilpinen (Dordrecht: Reidel, 1981), 125–48, at 130.

[14] Alchourrón and Makinson, 'Hierarchies of Regulations and Their Logic' (n. 13, this chapter), 130.

for in the case of an abrogation nothing is rejected, not even D. The main difference between the derogation of a prohibition (which implies rejection) and the withdrawal or abrogation of the prohibition is that the former transforms a prohibited action into a positively permitted one, whereas in the latter case the action in question becomes negatively permitted. This means that if Rex withdraws his prohibition to hunt on Sundays, there is no longer a restriction of Minister's competence, who can prohibit the very same action on another occasion. This, as we have already seen, would not be possible if Rex issued a permissory norm implying a rejection not only of his own prohibition but of every other prohibition of *p*, thereby preventing future prohibitions by any lower authority (though not by an equal or higher authority).[15]

Similarly, withdrawal of a permission does not entail the prohibition of the action in question, as would the derogation of a permission.

7.

Let us now consider a slightly more complicated case.[16] Suppose that Rex has issued the following norm:

(N_1) It is permitted that Subject may drink on Sundays.

On a later occasion Minister issues two new norms:

(N_2) Subject ought to work seven days a week.
(N_3) Subject ought not to drink while working.

What are Subject's obligations, faced with these three norms? In the first place, it is clear that N_1 is compatible with N_2, and it is also compatible with N_3 taken alone. N_1, however, is clearly incompatible with N_2 and N_3 taken together, for it follows from N_2 and N_3 that Subject is prohibited from drinking on Sundays, which is precisely what N_1 allows him to do. Indeed, if Subject must work on every day of the week, then he must work on Sundays, and if he is prohibited from drinking while he works, then he is prohibited from drinking on Sundays. This last action is explicitly permitted by N_1, and since Minister lacks competence to derogate norms issued by Rex, he cannot prohibit Subject from drinking on Sundays. It follows that Minister is competent to issue each of the two norms he has issued, but he lacks competence to issue both of them. If the permission granted by Rex is to be preserved, one of the two norms issued by Minister must be modified in one way

[15] In practice it is not easy to differentiate between derogation and mere withdrawal, for, as is rightly observed by Alchourrón and Makinson (n. 13, this chapter), in some cases the intention remains unclear. The following criterion might be proposed: if only expressly formulated norms are eliminated, then it is withdrawal (and there is no rejection), and if some items that are rejected but not expressly mentioned are eliminated, then it is derogation.

[16] This is an adaptation of an example discussed by Risto Hilpinen, 'On Normative Change', in *Ethics. Foundations, Problems and Applications*, ed. Edgar Morscher and Rudolf Stranzinger (Proceedings of the 5th International Wittgenstein Symposium) (Vienna: Hölder-Pichler-Tempsky, 1981), 155–64.

or another. Either Subject ought to work every day of the week and ought not to drink while he works, except on Sundays, or he ought not to drink while he works and he ought to work every day of the week, except on Sundays.

It is clear that the permission to drink on Sundays is not the mere absence of a prohibition (negative permission), which would yield to any act of authority, but is a normative or positive permission that stems from an act of Rex whose effects Minister cannot change.

The introduction of an exception into one of the two norms (N_2 or N_3) in order to avoid the indeterminacy of Subject's obligations is, of course, not automatic but requires a decision. The problem cannot be solved by an application of the rule 'Everything that is not prohibited is permitted', for this rule simply cannot be applied. Is it prohibited that Subject work on Sundays? Not necessarily, for if we introduce an exception into N_2, the result is that Subject may not work on Sundays. We also cannot say, however, that it is permitted that Subject not work on Sundays, for if the exception is introduced into N_3, then Subject must work on Sundays, although he may drink while working on Sundays. The trouble with the normative system of our example is that Subject's obligations are not clearly determined, and so the sphere of negative permissibility is not determined either, even if the positive permissions are clearly stated.

To sum up: permissory norms are, in an important sense, system-dependent. It is only from the dynamic perspective of a hierarchically structured normative system (with a plurality of norm-authorities at different levels) that changes over the course of time, as a result of different normative acts, are carried out by norm-authorities. There the concept of a permissory norm becomes truly fruitful. The fact that legal systems belong to the kind of system in question explains why permissory norms play a far more important role in legal contexts than in other contexts, for example, in contexts of morality.

8.

The pair of concepts of *negative* and *positive permission* behave in the same way as the concepts of *weak* and *strong permission*, introduced by von Wright[17] and developed further in a paper by Alchourrón and in a treatise that he and I wrote together.[18] This distinction between two kinds of permission has been criticized by several authors, and it is instructive to analyse some examples that stem from this criticism.

One current objection to the doctrine of strong permission is based on the idea that there are no permissory norms, all norms being norms of obligation (or of prohibition, which is the same thing). Without permissory norms, there cannot be anything termed strong permission; thus, permission is always weak, that is, a mere

[17] Von Wright, *NA*.

[18] Carlos E. Alchourrón, 'Logic of Norms and Logic of Normative Propositions', *Logique et Analyse*, 12 (1969), 242–68; Alchourrón and Bulygin, *NS*.

absence of prohibition. Alf Ross is perhaps the most forceful representative of this line of thought.[19] His argument can be reconstructed as follows:

(1) If there are no permissory norms, then there are no strong permissions.[20]

(2) All permissory norms are reducible to obligation norms.[21]

(3) 'Norms of permission have the normative function only of indicating, within some system, what are the exceptions from the norms of obligation of the system.'[22]

(4) There are no permissory norms.

(5) There are no strong permissions.

(6) All permissions are weak permissions, that is, non-prohibitions.[23]

(1), (2), and (3) are the premisses of the argument. (4) is supposed to follow from (2) and (3). (5) follows from (1) and (4) by *modus ponens*. (6) follows from (5) along with von Wright's thesis[24] that all permissions are either strong or weak permissions.

Premiss (1) can be safely granted, but Ross's conclusion does not follow from it even if one grants the theses (2) and (3). As we shall see presently, these two premisses stand in need of closer examination, but in any case (4) does not follow from either of them. Thus, neither (5) nor (6) is justified by way of Ross's reasoning.

The kernel of Ross's argument is thesis (4), that there are no permissory norms. Let us consider the reasons that Ross offers in support of this thesis. These reasons are the theses (2) and (3).

Thesis (2) states that all permissory norms are reducible to obligation norms. Even if this were true, it would not follow that there are no permissory norms. Ross confuses the problem of the 'analysability' of norms of permission with the contention that there are no permissory norms at all. As Ronald Moore states:

> It might be that *all* 'strong' permissions are in some manner analyzable into norms of obligation; but even if they are, this would not help to support the Reflex Thesis unless it were

[19] See Ross, *DN*, at 116–24.

[20] See Ross's discussion of von Wright's ideas in Ross, *DN*, at 120–4. Ross's contention is that von Wright's 'reasoning is obviously circular', for von Wright '*presupposes* that to permit an act is an independent and irreducible normative decision which is distinct from regulating the act under an obligation, distinct, that is, from either commanding or prohibiting it.' Ross, *DN*, 121–2 (emphasis in original). This is simply not true, for von Wright does not even try to prove the existence of permissory norms. His argument is that given the existence of permissory norms, one must distinguish between strong and weak permission, but he does not use his doctrine of strong permission as a proof for the existence of permissory norms. Von Wright's argument certainly presupposes the existence of permissory norms (although not necessarily *irreducible* permissory norms), but this does not render the argument circular, although it might be open to the objection that there are no permissory norms (Ross's thesis 4).

[21] 'For our hypothesis that "obligation" is the single and irreducible normative category to be maintained, we must show how these and similar formulae [someone is entitled to do something, has permission to do something, may do something, is authorized to act in a certain way, etc.] can be analysed in terms of "obligation".' Ross, *DN*, 118.

[22] Ross, *DN*, 120.

[23] 'As I have defined "permission" in the preceding table, the expression *is* identical with the negation of obligation.' Ross, *DN*, 120–1 (emphasis in original). 'Permission in the weak sense is identical with our concept of permission; it means simply that the act is not forbidden...'. Ross, *DN*, 121.

[24] Von Wright, *NA*.

taken to mean that these permissions aren't permissions at all. And arguing that permissions are not permissions if they can be analyzed into things which are not permissions is just as fallacious as arguing that tables which can be analyzed into atoms are not tables.[25]

Still worse, Ross's thesis (2) is incompatible with his thesis (3), where he gives an interpretation of permissory norms that clearly shows that they are not reducible to obligation norms. Indeed, he maintains that the normative function of permissory norms is to provide exceptions to obligation norms. This means that they lift prohibitions, that is, they cancel or derogate (at least partially) norms of obligation. What could it mean to provide an exception to an obligation or a prohibition if not to derogate part of the original norm? If a doctor, having prohibited his patient from drinking wine, later permits him to drink a cup a week, then certainly the prohibition to drink wine has been partially lifted. Now, a prohibition certainly cannot be lifted by means of another prohibition. In order to cancel or derogate a norm of obligation, we need to perform another kind of normative act, one that is radically different from the act of issuing a prohibition. Permissory norms often (if not always) perform the important normative function of derogating prohibitions, as Ross himself recognizes in his thesis (3). (The idea that strong permission may be the result of a derogation was already suggested by Weinberger.)[26] However, if permissory norms are expressions of acts of derogation or rejection, then they are not reducible to obligation norms. Hence thesis (3) contains a negation of thesis (2), and far from supporting (4), thesis (3) provides an excellent example of permissory norms that are not reducible to obligation norms. So (4) is unwarranted because it does not follow from (2), which—as is shown by (3)— is false, and it does not follow from (3) either. Of course, since (2) and (3) are mutually inconsistent, (4) follows trivially from the conjunction of (2) and (3) according to the principle *ex falso sequitur quodlibet.* This is not, however, a justification of the thesis that there are no permissory norms, and if (4) is not justified, (5) and (6) have no ground and Ross's whole argument collapses.

9.

Joseph Raz, in *Practical Reason and Norms,* entertains serious doubts about the purpose and the very sense of the distinction between strong and weak permission. His main argument is that this distinction depends on the formulation of the norm, which presupposes that norms must be authoritatively formulated. But what about customary norms? Raz maintains that every general norm of the form 'every *x* ought to φ in C' can also be formulated as 'everyone is required to φ in C except one who is not an *x*', or as a pair of sentences, namely, 'all are required to φ

[25] Ronald Moore, 'Legal Permissions', *ARSP*, 59 (1973), 327–46, at 335 (emphasis and quotation marks in original).

[26] Ota Weinberger, 'Der Erlaubnisbegriff und der Aufbau der Normenlogik', *Logique et Analyse*, 16 (1973), 113–42.

in C' and 'everyone who is not an *x* is permitted not to φ in C'. 'How', Raz asks, 'is one to decide whether a permission is a strong one or not?'[27] He continues:

> Why assign such importance to the stylistic inclination of the legislator anyway? Does anything turn on whether an obligation is imposed on people over thirty or on all with an exemption for those under thirty? Are we to say that if the law is formulated in the first way then those under thirty have a weak permission to refrain from the action required of their elders, whereas if it is formulated in the second way they have a strong permission?[28]

Raz is so certain that his ironical questions can only be answered in the negative that he does not go to the trouble of giving reasons for his scepticism. Yet a positive answer is by no means as absurd as he thinks. Let us consider first the alleged equivalence between the following norms:

(1) Every x ought to φ in C.
(2) Everyone is required to φ in C, except one who is not an x.
(3) All are required to φ in C.
(4) Everyone who is not an x is permitted not to φ in C.

Raz maintains that (1), (2), and the conjunction of (3) and (4) are equivalent.

Since it is not easy to handle Raz's symbolism, which is rather unusual, I will try to give examples that, I hope, correspond to his formulae.

(1') All males over 21 ought to report for military service.
(2') Everyone over 21 is required to report for military service, except females.
(3') Everyone over 21 is required to report for military service, and
(4') Females are permitted not to report for military service.

It can be easily shown that (1') and (2') are not equivalent. Take the norm

(5) All females over 21 are required to report for military service.

The conjunction of (1') and (5) is perfectly consistent; there is no incompatibility at all. However, the conjunction of (2') and (5) is clearly inconsistent. According to (2') it is permitted that females over 21 not report for military service, while according to (5) they ought to do so. Thus, (1') and (2') are different norms.

As for the conjunction of (3') and (4'), it is, as it stands, clearly inconsistent unless (4') is understood as an exception to (3'), derogating at least part of (3'). If we call (3") that part of (3') that is not derogated by (4'), then the conjunction of (3") and (4') is indeed equivalent to (2'), but not to (1'). However, the conjunction of (3') and (4') is equivalent neither to (1') nor to (2').

It follows that it is certainly not the same whether an obligation is imposed on people over 30 or on all with an exemption for those under 30. In the first case, nothing is said about those under 30, so the addition of a new norm establishing the same obligation for people under 30 is compatible with the first norm. In the second case, however, such an addition would give rise to an inconsistency. Hence, in the first case, contrary to Raz's view, people under 30 have only a weak

[27] Raz, *PRN*, 87. [28] Raz, *PRN*, 88.

permission, whereas according to (4') they have a strong permission to forbear from the action required of their elders.

Yet there is a genuine problem behind Raz's criticism, although his formulation of it is not satisfactory. The problem—which is not only genuine but important—is how to find out what norm is expressed by a given norm-formulation, which has nothing to do with the distinction between strong and weak permission. To discover the meaning of a given linguistic expression is an empirical question for which no mechanical—let alone infallible—method exists. There may be reasonable doubts about the meaning of certain words or sentences used in a legal text. It may be the case that these doubts cannot be removed by mere cognition and that a decision is required regarding the question of what norm is expressed by the text. Only when we get agreement on the content of a normative system (that is, on the question of what norms belong to it) are we in a position to assert which actions are strongly permitted and which are only weakly permitted by that system. Thus, the empirical problem of identifying the norms of a system is prior to the problem of finding out which actions or states of affairs are strongly permitted and which are not. Both problems should be clearly distinguished and kept apart.

Since there is, at least in legal contexts, always a plurality of normative authorities with different competences according to their place in the hierarchy, the distinction between strong and weak permission proves to be, after all, an important theoretical tool for the description of the dynamics of a legal order.

22

Kelsen on the Completeness and Consistency of Law (2013)*

1. Two Dubious Theses in Kelsen's Theory of Law

My aim in this essay is to discuss two prominent theses of Kelsen's that I find rather dubious.[1] One is the thesis of the necessary completeness of law. This thesis states that every legal system is necessarily complete in the sense that there are no legal questions for which it provides no answer, no legal problems for which it has no solution. As Kelsen puts it: 'The legal order cannot have any gaps.'[2] The second is the thesis of the necessary consistency of law. This thesis states that no two legal norms that belong to the same system can ever contradict each other. In other words, no two contradictory norms can be simultaneously valid. 'It is not possible', Kelsen writes, 'to describe a normative order by asserting the validity of the norms "*a* ought to be" and at the same time "*a* ought not to be".'[3] Together, these theses state that, whatever its content, any given set of legal norms belonging to the same system is necessarily complete and consistent.

Both theses are to be understood as referring to positive (that is, man-made) law. Perhaps the two theses would seem fairly reasonable to anyone who believes that there is a 'natural' law, especially if natural law is believed to be God-made. Kelsen's only concern is positive law. It seems strange, however, that a human artefact like positive law should necessarily possess those two properties, completeness and consistency. It seems, moreover, that neither thesis is true. Trivially, legal systems can be inconsistent. A system is inconsistent if it contains at least two norms, one of which prohibits, and the other permits, the performance of some given action, and, as every lawyer knows, examples of such situations abound. The case

* [*Editors' note*: Eugenio Bulygin's paper was first published in *Kelsen Revisited. New Essays on the Pure Theory of Law*, ed. Luís Duarte d'Almeida, John Gardner, and Leslie Green (Oxford: Hart Publishing, 2013), 225–43.]

[1] For many useful comments and helpful suggestions, which greatly improved this paper, I am grateful to Maria Cristina Redondo, Hernán Bouvier, Jorge L. Rodríguez, Pablo E. Navarro, Paolo Comanducci, and Stanley L. Paulson. I should also like to thank two anonymous reviewers, whose remarks made it possible for me to avoid several mistakes.

[2] Kelsen, *GTLS*, 147. [*Editors' note*: For this and other abbreviations, see the Table of Abbreviations.]

[3] Kelsen, *RR 2*, § 43(a) (329), *PTL*, 328.

against completeness is perhaps less obvious, although many jurists would maintain that a legal system has 'gaps', that is, situations that the law does not regulate at all. In *Normative Systems*, Carlos Alchourrón and I have argued that the completeness thesis is indeed also false.[4] It is the product of a failure to draw two crucial distinctions. One is the distinction between *norms*, which are prescriptive and therefore neither true nor false, and *norm-propositions*, which are truth-apt descriptions of (the existence of) norms. The other is the distinction between *negative* (or 'weak') and *positive* (or 'strong') *permission*. In this essay I shall again take up these distinctions. I will also try to answer a more puzzling question. Why would anyone think that positive law is always and necessarily complete and consistent? Why would Kelsen, in particular, endorse such strange and seemingly false theses?

I have just mentioned that our proposed refutation of the completeness thesis was based in part on the distinction between norms and norm-propositions. Although Kelsen does not use this terminology, which was introduced by Georg Henrik von Wright,[5] he does draw a seemingly analogous contrast between the '*Rechtsnorm*' (the legal norm) and the '*Rechtssatz*' (the legal sentence or proposition). Are the two distinctions really analogous? This is by no means clear. I propose to begin by taking a closer look at these two Kelsenian notions with an eye to determining what he may have meant by them.

2. Kelsen's Distinction between '*Rechtsnorm*' and '*Rechtssatz*' and his Consistency Thesis

Although the *terminological* distinction between '*Rechtsnorm*' and '*Rechtssatz*' is one that Kelsen has always drawn to some extent, the fact is that the *meaning* of these terms undergoes important changes throughout the body of his work, reflecting a radical modification in his conceptions of the law and of the role of legal science.

During the first 'period' of his work (until 1940),[6] the terms were used more or less interchangeably to refer to *legal norms* rather than to sentences or propositions. This was consistent with contemporary usage. In 'traditional German jurisprudence', as Kelsen remarks elsewhere, '*Rechtssatz*' and '*Rechtsnorm*' were employed as synonymous terms.[7] Thus, in his first major work (1911), Kelsen uses the term

[4] See Alchourrón and Bulygin, *NS*, at 116–44.

[5] See von Wright, *NA*, at 106; von Wright's terminology has been widely used in the literature ever since.

[6] On the periodization of Kelsen's work, see Stanley L. Paulson, 'Four Phases in Hans Kelsen's Legal Theory?' *Oxford Journal of Legal Studies*, 18 (1998), 153–66; and Stanley L. Paulson, 'Arriving at a Defensible Periodization of Hans Kelsen's Legal Theory', *Oxford Journal of Legal Studies*, 19 (1999), 351–64.

[7] Kelsen makes this remark in a footnote to the second edition of the *Pure Theory of Law*, a footnote not included in the English translation; see the original text, Kelsen, *RR 2*, § 16 (74, at n.). In the note, Kelsen adds that even Adolf Merkel, whom he characterizes as 'perhaps the most remarkable representative of [traditional] general jurisprudence' (my translation), explicitly identified the concepts of *Rechtsnorm* and *Rechtssatz*. [*Editors' note*: Kelsen's reference is to the German criminal lawyer and legal theorist, Adolf Merkel (1836–96).]

'*Rechtssatz*' almost exclusively.[8] In the 1925 *Allgemeine Staatslehre*, he indistinctly speaks of 'objective law constituted by legal norms (*Rechtsnormen*) or legal propositions (*Rechtssätze*)'.[9] In the first edition of the *Reine Rechtslehre* (1934), the term '*Rechtssatz*' stands for the 'reconstructed legal norm'.[10]

The differentiated use of '*Rechtsnorm*' and '*Rechtssatz*' to refer to two distinct entities occurs for the first time in 1941[11] and features prominently in his 1945 *General Theory of Law and State*. In both cases, however, the distinction is obscured by an unfortunate translation. Although '*Rechtsnorm*' is correctly translated into English as 'legal norm', '*Rechtssatz*' is confusingly rendered as 'rule of law'.[12] What does the term '*Rechtssatz*' mean in Kelsen's work?

We need to keep in mind that in this second, 'Kantian' stage of Kelsen's development, which runs until 1960, a legal norm is not simply a norm issued by legal authorities such as legislatures or judges, it is the product of a reformulation or reconstruction by legal science. Prohibitions and commands issued by legal authorities by means of statutes or judicial decisions constitute only the 'raw material' from which legal science constructs legal norms.[13]

This idea of a science that 'creates' its own object was repeatedly formulated by Kelsen in many of his works. Here is a quotation from the 1953 *Théorie pure du droit*:

> We can thus state simultaneously that the propositions formulated by legal science are hypothetical judgments and that legal norms constitute the object of this science. Here there is no contradiction. Without question, one can regard the norms created and applied within the framework of a legal system as having the character of legal norms only if they are recognized by legal science. It is the role of this science to attribute to certain acts the objective meaning of legal norms, but this does not prevent us from stating that legal norms are the object of legal science or, what amounts to the same thing, that the law is a system of norms. This definition is in complete harmony with Kant's theory, according to which cognition creates its object, for we are speaking here of an epistemological creation and not a creation of man's handiwork in the sense that one speaks of the legislator creating a law. Similarly, natural phenomena, which are the object of the causal sciences, are created by the causal sciences in a purely epistemological sense.[14]

[8] The term already turns up in the title of the book, which can be translated as *Main Problems in the Theory of Public Law, Developed from the Doctrine of the Legal Norm*. See Kelsen, *HP*, title page, in *HKW 2*, at 49.

[9] Kelsen, *ASL*, § 10(a) (47).

[10] See Kelsen, *RR 1*, § 11(b) (at 21–2), Kelsen, *LT*, § 11(b) (at 23), and, in the latter work, the translators' supplementary note 5 (132–4).

[11] Stanley L. Paulson drew my attention to this. See Hans Kelsen, 'The Pure Theory of Law and Analytical Jurisprudence', *Harvard Law Review*, 55 (1941/2), 44–70, at 51, repr. Hans Kelsen, *What is Justice?* (Berkeley: University of California Press, 1957), 266–87, 390 (notes), at 268.

[12] See Kelsen, *GTLS*, at 45, and Kelsen, 'The Pure Theory of Law and Analytical Jurisprudence' (n. 11, this chapter), at 51, repr. at 268.

[13] See Kelsen, *RR 2*, § 16 (at 74–5), *PTL*, at 72.

[14] Hans Kelsen, *Théorie pure du droit*, trans. Henri Thévenaz (Boudry-Neuchâtel: Éditions de la Baconnière, 1953), 53–4 (English translation by Anne Collins and Bonnie Litschewski Paulson).

This forms the basis of Kelsen's views, during this period, on the normativity of legal science. Legal science is normative not merely in the sense that it is concerned with norms, but also, above all, because its propositions are normative; its propositions are *norms*.[15]

A reminder of the same idea can be found even in the second edition of his *Reine Rechtslehre* (1960):

> Just as the chaos of sensual perceptions first becomes a cosmos, that is, nature as a unified system, through the cognition of natural science, so the multitude of general and individual legal norms, created by legal organs, first becomes a unitary system free of contradiction, a legal order, through the science of law. But this 'creation' has a purely epistemological character.[16]

Here, however, it is in connection with the legal 'order' as a unitary and consistent system—and not with the reconstruction of legal norms—that Kelsen speaks of 'epistemological creation'; it is the legal order qua unitary and consistent system that is produced by legal science.

The idea that a legal system *should* be complete and consistent stems from the doctrines of popular sovereignty and the separation of powers; it can be traced back to the Enlightenment, particularly to Montesquieu. The strict divide between, on the one hand, *legislative* power as the political power *par excellence*, to be exercised by a parliament composed of representatives of the people and tasked with enacting general norms and thus creating 'the law', and, on the other hand, a purely technical *judicial* power, to be exercised by professional judges whose role is that of strictly applying general law to particular cases, yields the requirement that for every legal problem there be one and only one legal solution. The law, in other words, must be both complete and consistent, otherwise judges would not be able to perform their task.

Of course, one should not mistake this *ideal* of a complete and consistent legislation—an aspiration that to this day, rightly or wrongly, is shared by many jurists—for a description of how things actually are. French commentators on Napoleon's 1804 *Code Civil*—the first serious attempt to implement the doctrine of the separation of powers—were well aware of this gap. 'In reality, there is no doubt', writes Demolombe, one of the most important commentators on the *Code*, that 'laws can by no means encompass all the various, numerous hypotheses that emerge in practice on a daily basis'.[17] They thus acknowledged the possibility of non-regulated actions or states of affairs, 'gaps' in the law.

This insight, however, was progressively lost. Particularly among German jurists, and even though the German Civil Code came to be enacted only in 1900, the

[15] The thesis of the normativity of legal science played an important role in the development of Kelsen's thought. It enabled him to draw a distinction between causal (factual) and normative social sciences, between sociology and jurisprudence. According to Kelsen, the difference lies in the kind of proposition used by these sciences for the description of their objects. See e.g. Kelsen, *GTLS*, at 163–4.

[16] Kelsen, *RR 2*, § 16 (74), *PTL*, 72 [*editors' note*: translation amended].

[17] 'En réalité, sans doute, les lois ne peuvent pas embrasser toute les hypothèses si variées, si nombreuses, que chaque jour la pratique soulève', Charles Demolombe, *Cours de Code Napoléon*, vol. 1 (Paris: Lahure, 1880), 136.

idea of a complete and consistent codification did not lose steam. The specific idea that legal science 'epistemologically' creates law was partly rooted in the fact that it then fell to jurists—that is, to legal science—to construe and adapt legislation to those requirements of completeness and consistency. Legal norms are understood as being 'created' by legal science in the sense that only legal science can confer 'objective' normative meaning on prescriptive acts performed by legal authorities (namely, the acts of issuing commands and prohibitions), for such acts themselves are seen as having only the 'subjective' meaning of legal norms.[18] Buttressed by Neo-Kantian epistemology, this idea became characteristic of Kelsen's second, 'Kantian' period.

It is this idea of an epistemological 'creation' of legal norms that explains why Kelsen regarded legal systems as being necessarily consistent. If legal norms are 'created' or at any rate 'reconstructed' by legal science, then it is hardly surprising that they should be consistent, for it would be unusual, to say the least, if a science were to formulate contradictory sentences. 'The unity of the object of enquiry', Kelsen writes in 1934, is an 'epistemological postulate', and 'the negative criterion for this unity is non-contradiction, a logical principle that also applies to cognition in the realm of norms.'[19] 'Normative cognition tolerates no contradiction between two norms of the same system.'[20] One finds passages to the same effect in *General Theory of Law and State*. For example:

> All quest for scientific knowledge is motivated by an endeavour to find unity in the apparent multiplicity of phenomena. Thus, it becomes the task of science to describe its object in a system of consistent statements, that is, statements not contradicting each other. That is true also for the sciences of law and morality, sciences whose objects are norms. Contradictions are also banned within the sphere of these sciences. Just as it is logically impossible to assert both 'A is' and 'A is not', so it is logically impossible to assert both 'A ought to be' and 'A ought not to be'... It is one of the main tasks of the jurist to give a consistent presentation of the material with which he deals. Since the material is presented in linguistic expressions, it is *a priori* possible that it may contain contradictions. The specific function of juristic interpretation is to eliminate these contradictions by showing that they are merely sham contradictions. It is by juristic interpretation that the legal material is transformed into a legal system.[21]

Once again, the idea subsists even in the second edition of the *Reine Rechtslehre*:

> To be sure, it is undeniable that legal organs may create conflicting norms—that they perform acts whose subjective meaning is an 'ought' and which may be in conflict with each other if their subjective meaning is interpreted as their objective meaning... But since the cognition of law, like any cognition, seeks to understand its subject as a meaningful whole and to describe it in noncontradictory statements, it starts from the assumption that conflicts of norms within the normative order which is the object of this cognition can and must be solved by interpretation.[22]

[18] See e.g. Kelsen, *LT*, at § 3 (9–10). [19] Kelsen, *LT*, § 50(a) (111–12).
[20] Kelsen, *LT*, § 31(h) (75). [21] Kelsen, *GTLS*, 374–5.
[22] Kelsen, *RR 2*, § 34(e) (209–10), see also at § 43(a)(b) (328–32), *PTL*, 205–6, see also at 328–31.

Yet during this very same period in his work, Kelsen simultaneously—and self-contradictorily—insists that the *Rechtssätze* are not to be confused with the legal norms produced by legal authorities, and indeed that the 'functions' of legal science and legal authority are quite distinct; the former is 'descriptive', the latter 'prescriptive'. In *General Theory of Law and State*, for example, he is already writing that:

It is the task of the science of law to represent the law of a community, i.e. the material produced by the legal authority in the law-making procedure, in the form of statements to the effect that 'if such and such conditions are fulfilled, then such and such a sanction shall follow'. These statements, by means of which the science of law represents law, must not be confused with the norms created by the law-making authorities. It is preferable not to call these statements norms, but legal rules [*Rechtssätze*]. The legal norms enacted by the law-creating authorities are prescriptive; the rules of law formulated by the science of law are descriptive. It is of importance that the term 'legal rule' or 'rule of law' be employed here in a descriptive sense.[23]

It is true that at this stage, namely 1945, there are still vacillations. Having previously insisted that legal norms are 'hypothetical judgments' rather than imperatives,[24] Kelsen, in *General Theory of Law and State*, still resists the characterization of legal norms as imperatives or commands.[25] However, in the second edition of the *Reine Rechtslehre*—even though, as already noted, there are in this book still echoes of the Kantian idea that legal science epistemologically 'creates' its object[26]—the view is far more explicitly stated that the judgments of legal science, *Rechtssätze*, are *not* to be confused with legal norms issued by legal authorities.

The distinction between the legal proposition or sentence (*Rechtssatz*) and the legal norm (*Rechtsnorm*) gives expression to the distinction between the function of legal cognition and the entirely different function of legal authority, represented by the organs of the legal community. The task of legal science is to cognize the law—from the outside, so to speak—and, on the basis of its cognition, to describe the law. Legal organs—as the legal authority—must first create the law so that it can then be cognized and described by legal science.[27]

This step cannot help but lead Kelsen to reject his earlier theses that legal norms are judgments and not imperatives, and that norms are epistemologically 'created' by legal science.

Legal science describes the legal norms created by acts of human behaviour, norms that are to be applied and complied with by means of human acts. It thereby describes the norm-constituted relations between the facts determined by these legal norms. The propositions or sentences (*Sätze*) in which legal science describes these relations must be distinguished, as legal *propositions* (*Rechtssätze*), from the legal *norms* (*Rechtsnormen*) created by legal organs… Legal *propositions* are hypothetical judgments stating that, according to a legally cognized

[23] Kelsen, *GTLS*, 45.
[24] See e.g. Kelsen, *LT*, § 11(b) (at 23).
[25] Kelsen, *GTLS*, 35.
[26] See passage quoted at n. 16, this chapter.
[27] Kelsen, *RR 2*, § 16 (74), *PTL*, 72. [*Editors' note*: Bonnie Litschewski Paulson and Stanley L. Paulson have translated anew the Kelsen quotations at nn. 27 and 28, with an eye to correcting the misleading translation of *Rechtssatz* as 'rule of law', which turns up in this chapter, at 339 and 342, n. 23, with reference to Kelsen's *General Theory of Law and State* (1945). The misleading 'rule of law' also occurs in the translation of the second edition of the *Reine Rechtslehre* (1960), quoted here.]

national or international legal order, certain consequences (determined by this legal order) ought to take place under certain conditions (determined by this legal order). Legal *norms* are not judgments, that is, they are not statements about an object of cognition.[28]

In spite of the odd Kantian passage, then, we can say that with the publication of the second edition of the *Reine Rechtslehre* Kelsen rejects his earlier thesis that legal *norms* are the epistemological 'creation' of legal science. Indeed, he comes to recognize that 'the science of law is just as incompetent to solve by interpretation existing conflicts between norms, or better, to repeal the validity of positive norms, as it is incompetent to issue legal norms'.[29] He should therefore have also expressly rejected the normativity of propositions of legal science, as he now assigns to legal propositions—to *Rechtssätze*—a far more modest role: *Rechtssätze* are descriptive of norms created by legal authorities. Kelsen does not explicitly acknowledge the change and proceeds without modifying his terminology.[30] However, it is very clear that after 1960 he no longer takes legal norms to be created by legal science, and that he takes legal science and its propositions to be strictly descriptive. Not to abandon his early doctrine that the propositions of legal science are normative would therefore have been self-contradictory. If *Rechtssätze* are descriptive, then they are not normative; if they are normative, then they are not descriptive. (Incidentally, this explains Hart's perplexities when he tries to find a coherent interpretation of Kelsen's theory in view of Kelsen's insistence that legal propositions are 'normative'. Hart failed to realize that this claim of Kelsen's rises and falls with the idea of the epistemological creation of norms, and that this was an idea that Kelsen had tacitly given up by 1960.)[31]

In fact, the Kantian aspect of Kelsen's work—to which the thesis of the normativity of legal science belongs—is radically incompatible with its positivistic aspect, which includes the theses that all law is man-made and that there is a sharp distinction between description and prescription, between cognition of law and creation of law. Elsewhere I have explored this antinomy, which lies at the core of the Pure Theory of Law.[32] I have also argued that Kelsen's development of the positivistic aspect is the more important one. For present purposes, however, what matters is

[28] Kelsen, *RR 2*, § 16 (73), *PTL*, 71 (emphasis in original). [*Editors' note*: translation amended, see n. 27, this chapter.]

[29] Hans Kelsen, 'Derogation', *Essays in Jurisprudence in Honor of Roscoe Pound*, ed. Ralph A. Newman (Indianapolis: Bobbs-Merrill, 1962), 339–55, at 355, repr. Hans Kelsen, *Essays in Legal and Moral Philosophy*, ed. Ota Weinberger (Dordrecht: D. Reidel, 1973), 261–75, at 274, and in *WS 2*, 1429–43, at 1443.

[30] Curiously, admitting some years later that in his works there was no clear terminological distinction between the concepts of '*Rechtsnorm*' and '*Rechtssatz*', Kelsen nevertheless claims *always* to have had in mind the difference between the creative function of legal authorities and the cognitive function of legal science. See Hans Kelsen, 'Professor Stone and the Pure Theory of Law', *Stanford Law Review*, 17 (1964/5), 1130–57, at 1136–7. This claim seems not to be warranted.

[31] See H. L. A. Hart, 'Kelsen Visited', *UCLA Law Review*, 10 (1962/3), 709–28, in *EJP*, 286–308. Kelsen's effort to preserve something of his original doctrine by introducing a distinction between a prescriptive and a descriptive '*Sollen*'—a distinction he borrows from Christoph Sigwart, a second-rate nineteenth-century German logician—only added to the confusion. Once again, the relevant footnote is omitted from the English-language translation, *PTL*, but see Kelsen, *RR 2*, § 16 (77–8, at n.), and see Christoph Sigwart, *Logic*, trans. (from the 2nd German edn., 1888) by Helen Dendy, vol. 1 (London: Swan Sonnenschein, 1895), 17, at n. 1.

[32] See my essay 'An Antinomy in Kelsen's Pure Theory of Law' (1990), in this volume, ch. 14.

that we have been able to bring out how Kelsen's views on the necessary consistency of law stem from his Kantian doctrine of the normativity of legal science, a doctrine which I believe Kelsen was right eventually to reject. His analogy between the 'chaos of sensual perceptions' and the products of the activities of legislative organs[33] is extremely weak, as is his analogy[34] between laws of nature—a product of the observation and description of certain regularities by the natural sciences—and positive laws, created by human actions.[35]

Thus deprived of its original theoretical framework, moreover, the thesis that law is necessarily consistent is clearly to be rejected. The idea, which at one point Kelsen explicitly endorses,[36] that if there were contradictions between legal norms then the corresponding legal propositions would be contradictory, too, is an extravagant one. Consistent descriptions can surely be given of inconsistent states of affairs.

3. The Principle of Prohibition and Kelsen's Completeness Thesis

Kelsen's having granted, as he does from 1960 onwards, that *Rechtssätze* are descriptions of legal norms—having granted, in other words, the distinction between norms and norm-propositions[37]—we are now in a position to assess Kelsen's equally unwarranted views on the completeness of law.

The thesis that all legal systems are necessarily complete is one that Kelsen firmly holds throughout his works, even after 1960. He bases this idea on the putative principle that everything that is not legally prohibited is legally permitted. We may refer to this, for short, as the 'principle of prohibition'. Let us examine Kelsen's argument.

'Genuine gaps', Kelsen writes in 1934, 'do not exist.'

A genuine gap would mean that a legal dispute could not be settled in accordance with prevailing norms because the statute—as one says—lacks a provision addressing the case, and therefore cannot be applied. Every legal dispute consists in one party making a claim against another party, and the decision granting or rejecting the claim depends on whether or not the statute—that is, a valid norm to be applied in the concrete case—establishes the claimed legal obligation. Since there is no third possibility, a decision can always be made, and, indeed, can always be made on the basis of the statute, that is, by applying the statute. Even a decision rejecting the claim is made by appeal to the prevailing legal system. By imposing obligations on human beings to behave in particular ways, the legal system guarantees them liberty outside those obligations.[38]

[33] See passage quoted at n. 16, this chapter.

[34] See, for example, Kelsen, *LT*, § 11(b) (at 24–5).

[35] For detailed criticism, see my essay 'Kant y la filosofía del derecho contemporánea', in Alchourrón and Bulygin, *ALD*, 371–82.

[36] See Kelsen, *RR 2*, § 16 (at 76–7), *PTL*, at 74.

[37] This terminology was introduced by von Wright, *NA*, at 106. Since then it has been widely adopted in the literature.

[38] Kelsen, *LT*, § 40 (84).

There are similar passages, for example, in *General Theory of Law and State*,[39] in the second edition of the *Reine Rechtslehre*,[40] and even in the posthumously published *Allgemeine Theorie der Normen*.[41] Here is Kelsen in 1960:

A positive legal order can always be applied by a court to a concrete case, even when the legal order does not contain, according to the court's view, a general norm positively regulating the behaviour of the defendant or accused… For in this case his behaviour is regulated negatively, that is, legally not prohibited, and in this sense permitted.[42]

The popular idea that law has gaps is, according to Kelsen, merely a 'fiction' concocted by jurists and judges—and also by legislators—in order not to apply norms that they regard as unjust.

The intention obviously is that the judge has to assume the role of legislator if there is no general legal norm stipulating the obligation of the defendant asserted by the plaintiff and if the judge considers the lack of such a norm unsatisfactory, unjust, inequitable. The condition under which the judge is authorized to decide a given dispute as legislator is not—as the theory of gaps pretends—the fact that the application of the actually valid law is logically impossible, but the fact that the application of the actually valid law is—according to the opinion of the judge—legally-politically inadequate.[43]

It is relatively easy, however—now that we are equipped with the distinction between norms and norm-propositions—to prove that the principle of prohibition cannot fulfil the function that Kelsen expects it to fulfil, namely, to render all legal systems as necessarily complete.

Kelsen argues that law prohibits some actions; by virtue of the principle of prohibition, then, all other actions are therefore permitted. The conclusion is that all actions are attributed a normative status—either prohibited or permitted—by any given legal system, whatever its content. There is therefore no conduct that the law does not regulate.

The argument is fallacious. Let us consider what the terms 'prohibited' and 'permitted' mean in this context. An action φ is prohibited by a given set of norms—call this set 'α'—if α contains a norm prohibiting φ, but to say that an action or state of affairs φ is permitted may mean one of two different things. It may mean that there is in α a norm permitting φ, that is, that φ is positively (or 'strongly') permitted. Alternatively, it may mean that there is in α no norm prohibiting φ, that is, that φ is negatively (or 'weakly') permitted. We can thus distinguish between two concepts of permission as they may occur *in a norm-proposition*. These two *descriptive* concepts are both relative to a given action or state of affairs φ and to a given set of norms or system α. By contrast, the concept of permission as found *in norms* is a genuinely *prescriptive* concept, used to permit or to authorize some given action under certain circumstances and not relative to a system.

39 See Kelsen, *GTLS*, at 146–9.

40 See Kelsen, *RR 2*, § 35(g) (at 251–5), *PTL*, at 245–50.

41 See Kelsen, *GTN*, at 131, 227.

42 Kelsen, *RR 2*, § 35(g) (251–2), *PTL*, 246–7.

43 Kelsen, *GTLS*, 147–8.

With this in mind, we can now turn our attention to Kelsen's principle of prohibition—'everything that is not legally prohibited is legally permitted'. It can be understood in either of two ways, either as a norm—as a *positive* norm, for Kelsen recognizes no other kind—or as a normative proposition. If conceived of as a positive norm, however, then the principle of prohibition must be contingent rather than necessary. It will exist only if and when it has been either issued by a legal authority or created by custom. Therefore, it cannot *necessarily* belong to all possible normative systems. If, on the other hand, the principle of prohibition is conceived of as a normative proposition, then, as we saw, we need to establish whether in it the term 'permitted' occurs in its negative, weak sense or, rather, in its positive, strong sense. If it is used in the negative sense, then 'permitted' means 'not prohibited'. Consequently, what the principle says is that *what is not prohibited is not prohibited,* which is analytically true but completely trivial, as well as perfectly compatible with the existence of non-regulated actions (that is, 'gaps' in the law). If, on the other hand, 'permitted' is taken in its strong sense, then the principle says that *what is not prohibited is positively permitted.* This is surely false. From the mere absence of a prohibition we cannot infer the existence of a positive permissory norm. Whether or not such a positive permission exists in some given system is a purely contingent matter. (The principle of prohibition holds true only in one very special case: when the system happens to contain a general closure rule permitting all actions not prohibited by the system. The *nullum crimen sine lege* principle, which is characteristic of modern criminal law, would be an example of such a rule, but, again, whether or not any such rule exists is a contingent matter.)[44]

Now Kelsen seems in his early works to have adopted the *strong* reading of the principle of prohibition, that is, he used 'permitted' in the sense of 'positively permitted'. In the first edition of the *Reine Rechtslehre*, for example, he states that

> [b]y imposing obligations on human beings to behave in particular ways, the legal system guarantees them liberty outside those obligations... The legal system embraces not only the principle that one is obligated to behave in a certain way (in so far as behaving in the opposite way is set as condition for the specific consequence of an unlawful act), but also the principle that where one is not obligated to do or to forbear from doing, there one is free. It is this negative norm that is applied in a decision rejecting a claim directed to behaviour not established as obligatory.[45]

This presupposes the truth of the principle of prohibition in its strong version, but, as we saw, in its strong version the principle is false. At a later stage, in the second edition of the *Reine Rechtslehre*, Kelsen seems to change his approach. He no longer claims that every legal system contains a norm permitting all actions

[44] For a more complete development of these arguments, see Alchourrón and Bulygin, *NS*, at ch. 7, and, on the general theme of gaps in the law, see also the exchanges collected in Fernando Atria, Eugenio Bulygin, José Juan Moreso, Pablo E. Navarro, Jorge L. Rodríguez, and Juan Ruiz Manero, *Lagunas en el derecho: una controversia sobre el derecho y la función judicial* (Madrid: Marcial Pons, 2005).

[45] Kelsen, *LT*, § 40 (84–5).

that are not prohibited; he now seems to adopt the *weak* version of the principle.[46] As we saw, however, this version is perfectly compatible with the existence of 'gaps' in the law.

In short: qua norm, the principle of prohibition is contingent, qua norm-proposition, it is either vacuous or false. In no case can it support Kelsen's thesis that legal systems are necessarily complete.

4. Are the Consistency and Completeness Theses Really that Strange?

Oddly enough, many important legal philosophers have endorsed versions of the completeness thesis, as well as, in some cases, the consistency thesis. This includes not only such legal positivists as Kelsen and Joseph Raz, but also an anti-positivist author such as Ronald Dworkin. The common problem with their views is that they do not always clearly distinguish between norms and norm-propositions—a distinction that lies, as we have seen, at the core of both issues. Not for nothing did Georg Henrik von Wright once remark, alluding to this distinction: 'It has taken me nearly thirty years to see its full significance. And not all logicians and philosophers have seen it even now.'[47]

A. Raz and the silence of the law

Raz's case is particularly interesting. In his well-known paper 'Legal Reasons, Sources, and Gaps',[48] Raz defends the principle of prohibition by means of *exactly* the same argument as Kelsen's, simply using different terminology, which gives the impression of novelty. Instead of norms, Raz speaks of 'reasons for action'. He also employs several rather unusual and cumbersome formulae,[49] but I think we can dispense with these and translate his arguments into plain English.

Raz distinguishes between two types of legal gap. The first type is due to the indeterminacy of the law; it stems either from the vagueness of the relevant concepts ('where the law speaks with an uncertain voice') or from unresolved conflicts between reasons for action ('where [the law] speaks with many voices').[50] Such gaps, according to Raz, are unavoidable. The second type stems from the silence of the law, and Raz emphatically denies that such gaps can exist. This means that

[46] See e.g. Kelsen, *RR 2*, § 6(b) (at 42–5), see also § 35(g) (at 248–9), *PTL*, at 42–4, see also at 243–4.

[47] Georg Henrik von Wright, 'Value, Norm and Action in My Philosophical Writings', in *Actions, Norms, Values. Discussions with Georg Henrik von Wright*, ed. Georg Meggle and Andreas Wojcik (Berlin: de Gruyter, 1999), 11–33, at 20.

[48] Raz, 'Legal Reasons, Sources, and Gaps', in Raz, *AL*, 53–77.

[49] The formula '$LR_c x,\varphi$' means the same as 'legally (or according to law), there is a conclusive reason for x to φ', where x is a person and φ an action. '$LPer_c\, x,-\varphi$' means 'legally, there is a conclusive permission for x not to φ'. See Raz, *AL*, at 71.

[50] Raz, *AL*, 77.

Raz accepts, at least in this restricted form, the completeness thesis as we have discussed it so far.

It is Raz's argument against the possibility of legal gaps of this second kind—gaps stemming from the silence of the law—that can be shown to be precisely the same as Kelsen's.

Raz's proof of the impossibility of legal gaps of the second kind is relatively simple. His starting point is that such gaps can exist only if it is simultaneously possible that (a) it is not the case that, legally, there is conclusive reason for *x* to φ; and (b) it is not the case that, legally, there is a conclusive permission for *x* not to φ.[51] A 'conclusive permission' to φ is defined as the absence of a reason to omit φ-ing.[52] Thus, a gap of the second kind can exist only if it can be simultaneously *not* the case that, legally, there is a conclusive reason for φ-ing, *and* that, legally, there is no conclusive reason for φ-ing. But to say that *it is not the case that, legally, there is a reason to* φ is the same, according to Raz, as saying that, *legally, there is no reason to* φ. It follows that a gap of the second kind is possible only when the two following statements are both true. 'Legally, there is no reason for *x* to φ' and 'It is not the case that, legally, there is no reason for *x* to φ'. This is a contradiction; one statement affirms and the other denies that, legally, there is no reason for *x* to φ. Hence the condition can never be satisfied, and therefore there can be no gaps of the second kind. Moreover, Raz claims, the statement 'it is not the case that, legally, there is a conclusive reason for *x* to φ' is logically equivalent to 'legally, there is a conclusive permission for *x* not to φ'. This, he writes, is 'the familiar closure rule that whatever is not legally prohibited is legally permitted and vice versa'.[53] His conclusion:

> Contrary to much popular imagining, there are no gaps when the law is silent. In such cases closure rules, which are analytic truths rather than positive legal rules, come into operation and prevent the occurrence of gaps.[54]

It can easily be shown, however, that Raz is wrong. Gaps of this kind are perfectly possible.[55]

Raz's 'familiar closure rule that whatever is not legally prohibited is legally permitted' is what I have called in the previous section the 'principle of prohibition'. In Raz—as in the second-period Kelsen—it is the *weak* version of this principle that is at issue, not the strong version. For here 'permitted' means only 'not prohibited'. It means only that there is no reason not to φ. Raz's 'conclusive permission', in other words, is the mere absence of a prohibition—it is a negative or 'weak' permission. Indeed, a 'conclusive permission' is defined as the absence of a reason for omitting to do an action, and the mere absence of a reason is not a reason. Raz grants this when he writes that '[i]ntuitively, the negation of a legal reason is nothing more than the absence of a legal reason', and that although '[e]xplicit

[51] Raz, *AL*, 76. [52] Raz, *AL*, 64. [53] Raz, *AL*, 76. [54] Raz, *AL*, 77.

[55] In what follows I sketch some arguments first presented in my essays 'El silencio del derecho', *Análisis Filosófico*, 22 (2002), 103–14, and 'The Silence of the Law' (2002), in this volume, ch. 18.

permissions are always source-based, conclusive permissions never are'.[56] If conclusive permissions have no sources, then they are not reasons, not *legal* reasons at any rate. Raz's conclusive permissions are weak permissions, which do not regulate actions. It is hard to fathom what is 'conclusive' about them.

Therefore, Raz's argument against gaps owing to the silence of the law is exactly the same as Kelsen's; it is based on the weak version of the principle of prohibition, and, as we have already seen, the weak version of the principle of prohibition merely states that what is not prohibited is not prohibited. This is a rather trivial tautology. It tells us just as much about legal gaps as the sentence 'it is false that it is raining if and only if it is not raining' tells us about the weather. That his closure rule amounts to a tautology is something that Raz explicitly acknowledges in the passage just quoted; he calls it an 'analytic truth'. It is far from clear, however, how analytic truths can prevent the law from having gaps.

Indeed, rather than showing that the law cannot have gaps of that second kind, Raz is *defining* such gaps out of existence. For according to him, as we saw, a gap due to the silence of the law is *possible* only if the statements are simultaneously true that (a) legally, there is no reason for x to φ, and that (b) it is not the case that, legally, there is no reason for x to φ'.[57] However, *precisely* because this is a contradiction, the very condition postulated by Raz for the existence of gaps can by definition never be met. This seems to be a case of what Hart once called a 'definitional stop'.[58] It is hardly surprising that Raz claims that such gaps cannot exist, but that would be too easy a way of getting rid of them.

Raz's core mistake lies, I think, in his characterization of these second-type gaps. On the one hand, he writes:

> A legal system is legally complete if there is a complete answer to all the legal questions over which the courts have jurisdiction. It contains a legal gap if some legal questions subject to jurisdiction have no complete answer.[59]

A 'complete answer is provided', he says, 'by pointing to a decision which the law requires'.[60] So far one could agree, but soon thereafter Raz adds that regarding the question of 'whether or not a person ought (conclusively) to perform a certain action [φ], there are two possible complete answers'—(1) that the law conclusively requires the performance of φ and (2) that the law conclusively permits the omission of φ.[61] Now, (1) means that there is a norm requiring the performance of φ, and (2) means that there is no norm requiring the performance of φ. In other words, differently from what Raz suggests, the two answers are not independent—(2) is

[56] Raz, 'Legal Reasons, Sources, and Gaps', in Raz, *AL*, 67. Also, 'x has explicit permission to φ' is defined as 'there is a fact with some force to cancel reasons for not φ-ing', see Raz, *AL*, at 64.

[57] Raz, *AL*, 75–6: 'Gaps of the second kind can exist only if it is possible that $(-LR_c x, \varphi)$ & $(-LPer_c x, -\varphi)$.'

[58] H. L. A Hart, 'Prolegomenon to the Principles of Punishment', in Hart, *Punishment and Responsibility. Essays in the Philosophy of Law* (Oxford: Clarendon Press, 1959), 1–27, at 6.

[59] Raz, 'Legal Reasons, Sources, and Gaps', in Raz, *AL*, 70.

[60] Raz, *AL*, 71. [61] Raz, *AL*, 71.

but the negation of (1), and, thus, if (1) is true, (2) is false, and vice versa.[62] Hence the disjunction of (1) and (2) is analytic, and the conjunction of the respective negations is a contradiction.[63] It follows that there is always a complete answer for every legal question and that all systems are complete—although of course something is seriously wrong if one supposes that it can be proven by purely logical means that all legal systems are complete.

The problem lies in (2)—that is, in the second answer—and in Raz's notion of a 'conclusive permission'. In fact, a conclusive permission to omit φ-ing, as Raz defines it, is *not* a complete answer if by a complete answer one understands a proposition stating that the action at stake is legally regulated in some way. The mere fact that an action is not prohibited does not imply that it is legally regulated; it is legally regulated if the law *positively*, that is, strongly permits it. Note also that even though, in the essay I have been discussing, Raz maintains that analytic closure rules can eliminate legal gaps by regulating (by weakly permitting) those cases that are not explicitly regulated by the law, he affirms elsewhere—in an essay included in the same book—that '[a] normative system does not... regulate behaviour which is merely weakly permitted by it. An act is weakly permitted if the system contains no norm prohibiting it. It is strongly permitted if the system contains a norm permitting it.'[64] This is a contradiction, not in the law, but in Raz.

Contrary to Raz's opinion, in summary, gaps stemming from the silence of the law are perfectly possible and, as a matter of fact, occur rather frequently in legal practice. The problem of the completeness of law is a contingent, empirical question depending on the content of each legal system.

B. Dworkin, 'right' answers and true answers

Surprisingly, Kelsen's and Raz's views on the completeness of law bear a striking resemblance to some consequences of Dworkin's idea of law as an interpretive concept.[65] If, as Dworkin maintains, interpretation consists in showing the law in its best moral light, then it seems to follow that the law must be complete and consistent, that, as Dworkin would have it, there is always one right answer to every legal problem.

[62] For the possibility of working with von Wright's T-Logics, in which there are propositions which are neither true nor false (a possibility that Raz grants *expressis verbis*), see José Juan Moreso, Pablo E. Navarro, and Maria Cristina Redondo, 'Legal Gaps and Conclusive Reasons', *Theoria*, 68 (2002), 52–66, and 'Sobre la lógica de las lagunas en el derecho', *Crítica*, 33 (2001), 47–73.

[63] This is precisely how Raz defines his second-type gaps: '"(–$LR_c x$, φ) & (–$LPer_c x$,–φ)" is true', Raz, 'Legal Reasons, Sources, and Gaps', in Raz, *AL*, 71.

[64] Raz, 'The Institutional Nature of Law', in Raz, *AL*, 103–21, at 117, n. 4. Compare Raz, *PRN*, at 150: 'A normative system regulates all the acts regulated by its norms. This means that a normative system regulates all the acts permitted by norms of the system which grant exclusionary permissions. But a system does not regulate acts which are merely weakly permitted by it, that is, acts permitted merely because of the absence of a norm requiring their omission.'

[65] See Ronald Dworkin, *Law's Empire* (Cambridge, Mass.: Harvard University Press, 1986), at chs. 2 and 11.

What, exactly, does 'right answer' mean?[66] We can say that a legal system provides answers to legal questions. The form of a typical legal question is 'is action φ obligatory (prohibited, permissible) in circumstance *q* according to legal system *L*?' Now, answers to such questions are of two kinds: *positive* and *negative* answers. An example of a positive answer would be 'according to *L*, φ is obligatory (prohibited, permissible) in circumstance *q*'. I call this a 'positive' answer, for if the answer is true, the law *determines* the normative status of φ in *q*. An answer can also be negative, which is the case if the law *does not determine* the status of φ. Negative answers, in turn, are themselves of two (sub)kinds. If there is a normative gap in *L* regarding φ in *q*, the answer is that φ is *not regulated* by *L*. In other words, φ is neither prohibited, nor obligatory, nor permissible. If, on the other hand, the system is inconsistent, the answer is also negative in the sense that it does not *univocally* determine the deontic status of φ; for example, 'φ is obligatory and prohibited' (or 'φ is prohibited, but not-φ is permissible').[67]

Let me introduce another distinction, that between two different (though related) issues. One is whether there can be true statements about the law; this we can call the issue of legal 'objectivity'. A legal system is objective in so far as it provides a *true* answer to a legal question. The answer can be either positive or negative, which is something that turns on the content of each system. In other words, an incomplete or contradictory system is just as 'objective' as a complete and consistent one. The second issue is whether the deontic status of any given action φ is legally determinate; this is the 'determinacy' issue. These two issues are obviously independent. That some legal system *L* does *not* determine the normative status of some action φ certainly does not mean that there is no *true* answer to the question 'is action φ obligatory (prohibited, permissible) according to legal system *L*?' On the contrary, one of the two possible negative answers will be true, that 'neither φ nor its negation is obligatory *or* permissible according to *L*', or that 'φ is both obligatory and permissible according to *L*'.

In contemporary debates, authors refer to '*right* answers' rather than to *true* ones. The difference, I suspect, is the product of some confusion between *describing* and *evaluating* the law. A 'right' answer is not merely a true answer. It is a satisfactory or good answer, and in order for an answer to a legal question to be a good one, it must, it seems, inform us of the obligations and rights that we have according to the law. *Negative* answers such as 'the legal system *L* says nothing about this situation', even if true, would not count as 'good' answers to legal questions, at least in the sense in which the phrase is commonly used. Moreover, the 'objectivity' of law is often defined in terms of whether or not there are *right* answers to legal questions. This confuses the two issues that I have distinguished in the previous paragraph. It may be objectively true that the law is incomplete or inconsistent

[66] In what follows I take up some lines of argument first presented in my essay 'The Objectivity of the Law' (2004), in this volume, ch. 19.

[67] Strictly speaking, it is only in the former case—that is, the case of a normative gap—that the status of φ can be said to be *un*determined. In the latter case—the case of inconsistency—φ is rather *over*determined. But the practical outcome is similar in both cases; the law does not univocally determine the status of φ.

and, therefore, that it does not (not at all, or not univocally) determine the normative status of some given action. In such cases there may be no 'right' answer, but there certainly is a *true* answer to the corresponding question about the legal status of that action.

The motivation behind the conception of legal objectivity in terms of *right* rather than *true* answers is probably that negative answers to legal questions cannot be used to justify judicial decisions. If the legal system contains a gap or a contradiction, then it does not determine a positive answer and the judge will not be able to justify his decision by appealing to the norms of that system. Here we face the following alternative. Either we must accept that our legal systems may actually be defective and thus that there may be cases in which judges are unable to justify their decisions on the grounds of *legal* norms (in which case they will have to make use of other, non-legal criteria), or we can simply deny—as Dworkin does—that the system can be defective in such a way. In the latter case, however, in order to ensure that the law is complete and coherent, we would have to inject moral principles into the law and suppose that such principles will remedy all defects, doing away with all gaps and contradictions. Quite apart from its other flaws, then, Dworkin's conception unwarrantedly assumes that a system containing both legal and moral rules would be complete and consistent.[68]

5. Conclusion

Comparing the ideas of these three outstanding philosophers concerning the completeness and the consistency of law yields the following.

Kelsen always maintained that there can be no gaps in the law, and so all legal systems are necessarily complete. Over a long period of time he also maintained that legal systems are necessarily consistent. He came, however, to abandon the latter claim; it was rooted in that Kantian aspect (mentioned earlier, in section 3) that, although present in much of his work, is nevertheless incompatible with the other, positivist aspect, which is also a trademark of the Pure Theory of Law and which became more and more dominant in the course of his many active years.[69]

[68] Others have expressed this doubt. Thus John Mackie thinks (owing to his meta-ethical views) that resorting to moral norms would amount to 'automatically inject[ing]... subjectivity into statements about what the law is', given that judgments about what is 'morally best' have an 'irreducibly subjective element'; see John Mackie, 'The Third Theory of Law', *Philosophy & Public Affairs*, 7 (1977/8), 3–16, at 9, repr. *Ronald Dworkin & Contemporary Jurisprudence*, ed. Marshall Cohen (London: Duckworth, 1984), 161–70, at 165. See also Brian Leiter, who remarks that '[i]f... one thinks that adjudication is "objective", in the sense that there are objectively right answers to legal disputes, then it might seem a bad idea to make right answers in law depend on moral considerations as Dworkin does', in 'Objectivity, Morality, and Adjudication', in *Objectivity in Law and Morals*, ed. Brian Leiter (Cambridge: Cambridge University Press, 2001), 66–98, at 66–7, and Russ Schafer-Landau, who has convincingly argued that it is by no means clear that ethical theory can be construed as the project of developing 'a coherent set of rules from which one can infer all determinate moral verdicts', Russ Schafer-Landau, 'Moral Rules', *Ethics*, 107 (1996/7), 584–611, at 584.

[69] See text at n. 2, this chapter.

Kelsen's evolution, in fact, should also have led him to abandon the completeness thesis. He was on the right path, but did not take the last step. In the end, this is the only charge that can be made against Kelsen. And, taking into account the fact that he was already in his 80s by the time his 'late' period began, the omission is quite understandable.

Raz grants the possibility of inconsistency, but he emphatically denies the possibility of legal gaps stemming from the silence of the law. His position is considerably more questionable. Although Raz accepts both the distinction between norm and norm-proposition and the distinction between strong and weak permission, he treats the principle of prohibition ('all that is not legally prohibited is legally permitted') as an analytic truth (with 'permitted' meaning simply 'not prohibited'). This is clearly insufficient for doing away with gaps. What Raz calls the 'familiar closure rule'[70] does not in fact close the system. A closure rule must provide a solution to cases that are not regulated (that is, to *normative* gaps), and this is something that no trivial tautology can achieve.[71] Thus the charge that can be made against Raz is that he fails to follow through on the implications of his own premisses.

Dworkin's case is different. He regards law as necessarily complete and consistent, but this tenet is a direct consequence of his conception of law. For Dworkin there is no sharp distinction to be drawn between law as it is and law as it ought to be. Moreover, law as it ought to be determines (at least partially) the law as it is. Whereas, however, the idea of a complete and consistent legal order is acceptable as a rational *ideal*, it is certainly wrong as a description of what happens in actual legal systems.[72] To use Raz's metaphor, then, we can say that for Dworkin the law is never silent and it always speaks with a single voice. The law's voice is always there. One must only look for it, albeit with Herculean energy.

The outcome of our discussion, then, is that Kelsen, Raz, and Dworkin all endorse some version of the thesis that the law is necessarily complete, even if they do so for different reasons. That the greatest philosophers sometimes make mistakes is nothing new. That these three very different, prominent legal philosophers happen to have made the same mistake is, however, rather curious.

[70] See text at n. 3, this chapter.

[71] For a detailed analysis of the concept of closure and of closure rules, see Alchourrón and Bulygin, *NS*, at ch. 7.

[72] In addition, there is no room in Dworkin's theory for the distinction between norms and normative propositions. His 'propositions of law' are neither norms nor normative propositions proper, for they are normative *and* descriptive at the same time. See, for example, Ronald Dworkin, 'How Law is Like Literature', in Dworkin, *A Matter of Principle* (Cambridge, Mass.: Harvard University Press, 1985), 146–66. For criticism of this aspect of Dworkin's theory see my essay 'Norms, Normative Propositions, and Legal Statements' (1982), in this volume, ch. 11.

Appendix I

My View of the Philosophy of Law (2009)*

Eugenio Bulygin

I. My Philosophical Development

Two persons had a decisive influence on my philosophical development: Ambrosio Gioja and Carlos E. Alchourrón. Gioja, who held the chair in the philosophy of law at the University of Buenos Aires, was an exceptional teacher. One day, while I was still a student, I entered by chance a classroom where I encountered a professor explaining Husserl's phenomenology to a group of students, using the piece of chalk in his hand not to write but as emphasis for his many vivid gestures. His explanation of *noesis* and *noema* so fascinated me that I was immediately addicted, not to Husserl's philosophy, but to Gioja's way of teaching. Instead of offering solemn expositions larded with citations, here was a professor who philosophized in the classroom. In addition to Kant and Husserl, Gioja taught Hans Kelsen's Pure Theory of Law, and this turned out to be my gateway to the philosophy of law. While my enthusiasm for Husserl dissipated very quickly, Kelsen's theory has remained a permanent bedrock for me. Even today I believe that a good Kelsenian education is fundamental for all who want to take up legal philosophy.

Alchourrón, who was my contemporary and became over time a most beloved friend, introduced me to analytic philosophy and to logic. He was the person most responsible for the change in the philosophical climate in the Institute for Legal Philosophy directed by Gioja. Kant and Husserl were replaced by the works of Wittgenstein, Carnap, Quine, and Tarski. The imprint of these authors on those who followed after them—Alf Ross, H. L. A. Hart, and Georg Henrik von Wright—is found in all of my writings. I took from Kelsen his thematics: the structure of the legal order and of the norms that make it up, as well as his legal positivism and his scepticism on the question of values, scepticism strongly reinforced by Ross, Hart, and above all von Wright. Thus, analytic philosophy, logic, and the Pure Theory of Law were the pillars of my philosophical development.

* [*Editors' note*: Eugenio Bulygin's paper, first published as 'Mi visión de la filosofía del derecho', in *DOXA*, 32 (2009), 85–90, was translated for the present volume by Bonnie Litschewski Paulson and Michael Sherberg.]

2. Analytic Philosophy and Logic

At the heart of my conception of the philosophy of law, then, are analytic philosophy and logic, owing largely to the influence of two great logicians and philosophers, von Wright and Alchourrón. These two had a profound impact on my philosophical activity and on my life. They were both close friends of mine, whose absence deprives me of many important things. I miss our philosophical discussions, our reciprocal criticism, stimulus, and support. Von Wright's work was a model of conceptual analysis for me. Alchourrón and I worked together for 40 years, and I should say here that a substantial majority of the ideas contained in the books and articles that we wrote together stemmed from Carlos.

I could ask the question that I have been asked many times: Why logic? Why not focus more on legal reality? The answer to these questions is very simple. Philosophy in general and the philosophy of law in particular are not concerned with reality, which is the concern of other sciences, among them legal science. Philosophy focuses on the necessary aspects of reality, whether these be called ideas, categories, concepts, or a priori syntheses. This implies adherence to the notion that philosophy is, in essence, conceptual analysis. In my opinion, the principal task of legal philosophy is analysing the structure of law and its component parts, primarily legal norms, as well as general legal concepts. This is the understanding of the great philosophers of law, from Plato, St Thomas, and Suárez, to Hobbes, Kant, and Bentham, and on to Kelsen and Hart. It is true that the earlier philosophers did not use the tools of logic in their analyses, but this is because logic in its present form developed very late, toward the end of the nineteenth century and in the twentieth century, with the pioneering efforts of Boole, Russell, and above all Frege. Interest in modern logic on the part of philosophers of law is owing largely to the work of von Wright, who, although not a jurist, exercised a profound influence on the philosophy of law, most especially in the Latin countries, primarily in Argentina, in Spain, and in Italy. The importance of logic for the law consists not simply in using ever so many logical formulae. I am reminded of something the distinguished Argentine-Spanish criminal law scholar and philosopher of law, Sebastian Soler, said to me once: Logic is, like springs in an easy chair, indispensable, but it need not be seen. This is what Alchourrón and I tried to do in *Normative Systems*, where we confined logical formulae to the appendix, which hardly anyone ever reads but which in this case does contain the whole text of the book in summary form, in a few (or maybe not so few) formulae.

The attacks against using logic in the law usually come from jurists whose knowledge of logic is sketchy at best. This does not worry me. Lately, however, questions have been raised by some logicians, and this does seem to me more worrisome. I am confident, nevertheless, that we are dealing more with misunderstanding than with a true discrepancy of views.

3. Legal Positivism

I continue to be a strong partisan of legal positivism, which consists basically of the distinction between describing the positive law and evaluating it as just or unjust. This has several implications. In the first place, the sharp distinction between description and evaluation implies, in turn, recognizing that the word 'law' should not be used as a term of praise (which many authors do), since the law, as the product of human activity, can be good or bad, just or unjust. In the second place, there is the implication that something like natural law does not exist. As Mario Bunge once said, the expression itself seems very much to be a contradiction in terms, since the law is fundamentally artificial and has nothing natural about it. If one considers that an unjust norm cannot be a legal norm (according to Gustav Radbruch's well-known formula), then all of law is just and therefore impossible to criticize as unjust. Criticizing the law, however, is an extremely important part of the business of jurists. In order to be able to evaluate and to criticize the law, one must know the law, since knowledge of an object is logically prior to its evaluation. All of the most eminent legal positivists have understood this, from Bentham and Austin to Kelsen and Hart. Arguing that an unjust law is not law is tantamount in the end to nothing more than a change in name. Rather than calling unjust norms 'law', we give them another label, but the change in name neither changes anything else nor eliminates the injustice.

It is true that, at present, legal positivism appears to be on the defensive. Not only its adversaries think so, but many positivists do, too. Ricardo Guibourg, for example, argued just recently that 'positivism lost the game when the legislator, who is its prominent spokesman, sided with natural law'. Riccardo Guastini says that 'natural law advances throughout the whole world, and positivism is in total retreat'. Not long ago, Manuel Atienza and Juan Ruiz Manero published an article with the suggestive title, 'Abandon Positivism'.

These are all significant thinkers whose work I admire and who are, moreover, dear friends of mine. Nevertheless, I do not share their pessimism. Even though it may be true that the number of philosophers of law who declare themselves to be positivists has recently diminished and that the number who claim diverse orientations to natural law has increased, this does not seem alarming to me. What has happened is that the term 'positivist' has taken on a certain pejorative tint that is new. Philosophers of law like Kelsen, Hart, and Bobbio had no trouble proclaiming themselves to be positivists and doing so with pride. Today, things have changed. Many positivists prefer the use of attenuating qualifiers, speaking, say, of 'exclusive' or 'inclusive' positivism, and the like.

That the ideas of legislators and their constituents reflect natural law does not seem to me to be anything new. Previously, God was invoked to support the divine right of kings or as the source of all reason and justice. Today, the appeal is to liberty and human rights. I fail to see, however, just how these more or less respectable ideas can influence the philosophy of law. Consequently, despite the exhortations of my friends Manolo and Juan, I am not thinking of abandoning positivism.

4. Legal Science

Following Aristotle, I understand science to be a set of true and systematically ordered statements that transmit knowledge to us about a determinate portion of the universe. Legal science is no exception. It is a set of true statements about this complex phenomenon we call 'law', that is, its function is fundamentally descriptive. I agree with Max Weber, Kelsen, and Hart on this. Without a doubt, the law is based on values, but it seems to me possible to describe these without evaluating them. Indeed, I am inclined to think that 'non-evaluative science' is a pleonasm and 'evaluative science' comes very close to being a contradiction in terms.

Of course, not everything that jurists, judges, and lawyers do can be qualified as science. To the extent, however, that they describe the law and refrain from evaluating it, their activity is scientific. Lawyers and above all judges also perform political functions. For judges, this is usually when the law does not contain a univocal answer to a legal problem. There may be more than one answer and these are incompatible (antinomies or normative contradictions), or the law may contain no answer at all (normative gaps). It may be, too, that the solution offered by the law is vaguely formulated, leaving in doubt whether the individual case before the judge is or is not within the ambit of the application of a general norm (penumbral cases or gaps in recognition).

The most interesting situation arises when the law gives a clear and univocal solution that the judge considers to be extremely unjust or mistaken. This happens when the judge's values do not coincide with those of the legislator, either because some circumstance that the judge considers relevant has not been taken into account by the general norm (axiological gaps), or because there is a direct conflict between the values of the judge and those reflected in the legislator's norm. In such cases, judges commonly resort to various strategies to avoid applying the general norm that is in principle applicable and to apply instead another norm, perhaps one created by the very judge applying it. Because judges are obligated to justify their decisions by appeal to prevailing law, they try to obscure the fact that it is on the basis of values that they are departing from the law. Sometimes they try to justify their decision by appeal to the constitution, declaring a law unconstitutional. Sometimes they declare a case unresolved because a normative gap exists, when in reality there is indeed a solution, but it is, in their opinion, unjust. At other times, judges resort to the theory of defeasibility.

In all of these cases, judges participate in creating law, understood as general norms, whose creation is in principle incumbent on the legislator. This phenomenon is called judicial discretion by Hart. Discretion, however, does not mean arbitrariness; the judge applies his values (moral or otherwise) and normally takes great care in justifying his departure from the law.

Some important authors distinguish between two perspectives, that of the observer and that of the participant. Consequently, they speak of two concepts of law. I do not agree with this overly sharp distinction. I believe that both the legal dogmatist who describes the law (the typical observer) and the judge (the participant *par excellence* in the 'game' of law) employ the same concept of law. A judge, whose function is to resolve a case by applying prevailing law, must determine what solution is provided by legal norms, and this activity is comparable to that of the legal scientist. If the judge finds a clear and univocal solution, he ought to make use of it. If he does not find such a solution, however, he must still resolve the case, and here the path of descriptive legal science parts company with the function of the judge. The judge must offer a solution, and if this is not found in the prevailing legal norms, or if the solution provided is, by the judge's criteria, extremely unjust, then he must modify the law. Herein lies the political activity of the judge. What the judge modifies in such cases is not the concept of law but the norms he applies, using the unchanged concept of law.

5. Axiological Scepticism

One could say that my conception of the philosophy of law and my adherence to legal positivism rest on my axiological scepticism. This in turn is based on the idea that moral, political, and aesthetic judgments depend largely on emotions, feelings, and tastes, and therefore they are not subject to rational control. To the extent that such judgments depend on emotional factors, they are not susceptible to being true or false. This in no way implies that they are unimportant. There are people who sacrifice their lives for their political, moral, or religious ideals, but the importance of these ideals is one thing, their truth, quite another. Despite my axiological scepticism, I do hold firm political, moral, aesthetic, and culinary convictions. I do not, however, believe in the truth of such judgments. This does not stop me from considering Mozart more valuable than a tango or from preferring the Chartres cathedral to the Victor Emmanuel monument, the moral stature of Gandhi to that of George W. Bush, a democracy (even if defective) to a dictatorship, and a good red wine to Coca Cola. Still, I do not believe that these are true.

Consequently, I shall continue to indulge in my heresies, to go on appreciating art, criticizing political evils, respecting human rights, and relishing culinary delicacies.

Appendix II

An (Auto)biographical Sketch (2014)*

Written with Bonnie Litschewski Paulson

Eugenio Bulygin was born on 25 July 1931, in the Ukrainian Republic, in Kharkov, one of the largest cities in the Soviet Union at the time. His family had belonged for generations to the intelligentsia; his father Victor was an engineer, his mother Maria, a secondary-school teacher of German and French. She and her mother, Vera Kandyba, taught reading and writing to young Eugenio from an early age, inculcating in him, among other things, an abiding love of poetry. An only child, Eugenio did so well at home intellectually that his parents did not enroll him in public school until he was nine. During these early years, Bulygin writes, his three best friends were 'older and much stronger', which did not stop them 'from playing together and from quarelling'.

These early years were, however, darkened by Stalin's reign of terror, especially 1937–8, which snared the younger brother of Eugenio's grandmother in its tentacles. Professor Lev Kandyba, a renowned bacteriologist, was arrested and disappeared, only to be 'pardoned' 30 years later, under Krushchev, in an official letter that also confirmed the professor's death in the 'gulag archipelago'.

When Eugenio was ten, the German army occupied Kharkov, and the ensuing hunger and deprivation, combined with the desperate cold of the winter of 1941–2, forced the family to seek refuge in a village 500 kilometres west of Kharkov. Eugenio found life in the countryside 'rather pleasant…no schools and I spent my days reading, playing, and bathing in the river'.

Things changed after the battle of Stalingrad. When the front lines came dangerously close, the entire Bulygin household—Eugenio, his grandmother Vera, his mother Maria, his father Victor, as well as his uncle Nicholas with his wife and 12-year-old son, and a maid—all decamped for Paris with six horses and three cars. They were stopped by German police near the Polish border and sent to Germany, landing eventually (September 1943) in a labour camp near Linz, Austria.

Because Eugenio was just 12, he did not have to work and could spend his time reading the Russian classics and even Shakespeare's historical dramas, playing chess with his cousin, and studying mathematics under the tutelage of his uncle

* [*Editors' note*: Eugenio Bulygin and Bonnie Litschewski Paulson have written this sketch as an appendix to the present volume. It has not appeared previously in any form.]

Nicholas. Eugenio was taught mathematics so well that he never had to study it in school later, neither in Austria nor, as a teenager, in Argentina.

In May of 1945, the War over, the family moved from the labour camp into the city of Linz, where Eugenio, in 1946, was finally enrolled in school again, and where German became his second language. Bulygin says of these years in Linz that he was 'quite happy', that he had lots of friends and some 'very good teachers' to whom he is still grateful, and that he 'started to play chess rather intensely'.

By 1949, Eugenio's parents had decided to emigrate, under UN auspices, to Argentina. 'A country that produces wine,' said Eugenio's father, 'must be a nice place to live.' Linz was divided by the Danube River between the American and Soviet zones, and not only did the Bulygin family worry about living in such close proximity to the Soviet army, they also, understandably, had no interest in returning to Kharkov, in the Soviet Union. And so they all travelled, including Eugenio's beloved grandmother, on a big US Navy ship to Buenos Aires.

Here, Spanish became Bulygin's third language, which he acquired in less than a year, owing at least in part to his solid background in French. Later on, he also learned English and Italian.

Upon his arrival in Buenos Aires, Bulygin worked first in a factory and then in an office, but his mother insisted that he go to school. His studies in Austria were not recognized, and so he began at the beginning, passing a rigidly scheduled series of examinations covering primary school and, year by year, secondary school. In March of 1953, he finished, having covered five years of secondary school in two and a half years.

Two young Estonian men, also 'displaced persons', took these examinations at the same time as Bulygin. Raul Sargava, a 'brilliant personality', and Leopoldo Niilus, a devotee of Spanish classical literature, became Bulygin's great friends, and the three of them decided together to study law. Bulygin also decided, on the day he matriculated at the University of Buenos Aires, 'not to play chess any more... it took too much time.'

The decision to study law did not come easily, but Bulygin's primary interests—literature, philosophy, mathematics—seemed 'impractical' to him, except as fields to be taught, an enterprise disdained at the time by Bulygin. Today, however, he reports 'still teaching with great pleasure'. Having heeded Jacob Burckhardt's dictum on the importance of studying a 'dogmatic' science, Bulygin harbours no regrets over his choice of the law.

From 1953 to 1958, Bulygin studied at the Law School of the University of Buenos Aires. There he was fascinated, from the beginning, by the head of the Institute for Legal Philosophy, Ambrosio Gioja. According to Bulygin, Professor Gioja 'was a phenomenologist and a great admirer of Husserl'. An extraordinary teacher as well, a 'true Socratic philosopher', Gioja introduced Bulygin early in his studies to the work of Hans Kelsen. In 1956, Bulygin met another student, Carlos E. Alchourrón, in Gioja's Institute. Alchourrón had a strong background in logic and analytic philosophy, and his discussions with Gioja played a major role in the genesis and development of analytical legal philosophy in Argentina. Bulygin and Alchourrón quickly became fast friends and uncommonly close collaborators, working together until Alchourrón's death in 1996. Their most important books are *Normative Systems* (1971), translated into Spanish, German, Italian, and Russian, and *Análisis lógico y derecho* (2001).

In 1959, Bulygin was appointed lecturer at the Law School and, in 1960, assistant professor. He earned a PhD in 1963 and, that same year, was awarded a fellowship from the Humboldt Foundation, enabling him to conduct research in Germany in 1963–4. His sponsors were Ulrich Klug in Cologne and Hans Welzel in Bonn. Ernesto Garzón Valdés, Bulygin's brother-in-law, was serving then as the cultural attaché in the Argentine embassy in Bonn, and he and Bulygin became the closest of friends, reading philosophy together and working on translations into Spanish.

Bulygin spent almost two years in Oxford, beginning in 1968, with a fellowship from the British Council for Cultural Relations. His supervisor was the incomparable H. L. A. Hart, with whom Bulygin enjoyed many lengthy and fruitful discussions. Georg Henrik von Wright, Peter Strawson, Arthur Prior, and John Mackie became good, lifelong friends of Bulygin's, and his acquaintances in Oxford included Elizabeth Anscombe, Peter Geach, Alfred Ayer, Isaiah Berlin, and Anthony Kenny.

Bulygin and his friends shared not only affection, but also intellectual interests. Bulygin was impressed by Strawson's book on Kant and took part in Prior's seminar on logic. There Prior expressed great enthusiasm for Alchourròn's paper on the logic of norms and normative propositions, a paper that was, according to Bulygin, the 'logical skeleton' of Alchourrón and Bulygin's book, *Normative Systems*. Mackie was enormously helpful in the actual writing of the book and, during a later visit of Bulygin's to Oxford, interceded with Hart on behalf of Bulygin's gifted student, Carlos Nino. Bulygin had been invited to dinner by Hart and noticed Hart's reticence when asked about Nino's dissertaton thesis. Hearing this from Bulygin, Mackie asked Hart for a copy of the thesis, read it, and then wrote a letter to Hart showing that Hart's objection was based on an incorrect interpretation. Hart accepted the arguments, and Nino's dissertation was approved. Bulygin adds, '[t]his was really surprising and shows what kind of persons Mackie and Hart were. I do not think that such generosity is shown very frequently in academic circles.'

Bulygin's special connection to von Wright began in 1953, when Bulygin attended Professor Carlos Cossio's seminar on von Wright's paper 'Deontic Logic'. Later on, Bulygin and Alchourrón were overwhelmed by von Wright's book, *Norm and Action*, work that was exactly what they had been looking for. Von Wright's very successful lectures in Argentina, in 1968, offered Bulygin, Alchourrón, and Garzón Valdés the chance to accompany him around the clock, in particular in La Plata, Córdoba, and Santa Catalina. Their strong personal relationship continued in Oxford and throughout the decades thereafter, lasting until von Wright's death in 2003.

Upon his return to Argentina from Oxford, Bulygin was appointed professor for the philosophy of law at the University of Buenos Aires (1970), becoming dean of the Law School after the fall of the military junta in 1984 and emeritus professor in 1997, a title that allows him to continue to teach. Also in 1970, he was appointed professor at the University of La Plata, a post he held until 1980. From 1986 to 2001, Bulygin served as a judge on the Argentine Court of Appeals in civil matters.

From 1972 to this day, Bulygin has lectured at innumerable universities in Europe and the Americas, and he has been a guest professor at universities in Mexico, Spain, Italy, Germany, Finland, Israel, Venezuela, and Chile.

Bulygin's professional life is replete with high honours. In addition to the fellowships mentioned above, from the Humboldt Foundation and the British Council, Bulygin was awarded a fellowship from the Guggenheim Foundation in 1975, the Konex Prize in 1986, and the Humboldt Prize for Foreign Scholars in 1996. He holds honorary doctorates from the National University of the South (Argentina), the University of Alicante and Pompeu Fabra University (Spain), and the University of the Republic (Uruguay).

Bulygin was elected to the executive committee of the International Association for Philosophy of Law and Social Philosophy (IVR) in 1987 and served as the Association's president from 1999 to 2003. He has been its honorary president since 2007.

Bulygin's publications include 17 books and 146 papers, written in Spanish, English, German, Italian, French, and Russian. In addition to the two books already mentioned, written in collaboration with Alchourrón, there is a third book considered to be among Bulygin's most important, namely, *El positivismo jurídico* (2006), translated into Italian.

Eugenio Bulygin's beautiful wife of many decades, Elvira, is an accomplished artist, not a philosopher. Bulygin notes, however, that her 'good sense' in reading and correcting his papers has given rise to 'practical advice' to him, 'to change or to suppress some phrases (especially when I become aggressive, which happens sometimes).' As for his children and grandchildren, Bulygin attests to their 'mere presence [as] always very stimulating'.

Bulygin's main philosophical interests are (normative) logic, logical structures of legal concepts, and analytic philosophy, but these are not, of course, his only interests. He likes dogs and horses, he says, as well as 'architecture, literature (especially Russian), chess, and, above all, the company of friends and nice ladies.'

Index

Editors' note: Proper names ('Hart', 'Kelsen', and the like, as well as book titles) are recorded in the index only if they appear in the text or preface. Not recorded in the index are proper names appearing in the footnotes, or the name 'Alchourrón', which occurs with great frequency in the text, or the names of the editors appearing in the preface. Where a term in the index captures the theme of an entire chapter or of an entire section within a chapter, the corresponding page numbers appear in italics.

The manufacturer's authorised representative in the EU for product safety is Oxford University Press España S.A. of el Parque Empresarial San Fernando de Henares, Avenida de Castilla, 2 – 28830 Madrid (www.oup.es/en or product.safety@oup.com). OUP España S.A. also acts as importer into Spain of products made by the manufacturer.

www.ingramcontent.com/pod-product-compliance
Lightning Source LLC
LaVergne TN
LVHW011906200926
848484LV00002B/543

9780198729365